A Scientific Search for Religious Truth

Phil Mundt, PhD

A Scientific Search for Religious Truth
Published by Bridgeway Books
2100 Kramer Lane, Suite 300
Austin, Texas 78758

For more information about our books, please write to us, call 512.478.2028, or visit our website at www.bookpros.com.

Library of Congress Control Number: 2006930497

ISBN-10: 1-933538-61-9
ISBN-13: 978-1-933538-61-7

Printed in Colombia.

CONTENTS

ACKNOWLEDGMENTS

First mention must go to my wife of fifty-five years, Lorraine, for her patient forbearance during the four years dedicated to this project. She helped throughout with proofreading and helpful suggestions. We probably lost 1000 hours of "togetherness"— the only upside was that she had extra time to knit fifty baby blankets for Seton Hospital and could participate in some extra sessions with the Lago Vista bridge community.

Our minister, Gary Olsen, at Rolling Hills church was very helpful in providing much reference material. He also took time out of his busy schedule (he is working for his D.Min. degree) and gave thoughtful and constructive suggestions on how to improve the text and avoid some mistakes. Also, it should be clear that any errors or controversial comments are mine only.

Dr. Doak Worley, leader of our adult Bible studies, made available at least fifteen useful books, reviewed my chapters concerning religion, and added helpful commentary.

Dr. Wes Gardner, an old friend and fellow geologist, reviewed the entire book including all of the "Science Annex." He also provided the key reference material and helped a great deal on the Mormon chapter.

Dr. Gernot Schmidt, a citizen and resident of Germany, reviewed the section on global warming in order to provide a European perspective. Gernot is one of the smartest geologists I have ever known.

Erdem Serim, an old friend from Turkey and an erstwhile Muslim, reviewed the chapter on Islam. Erdem and his wife Bilge have become U.S. citizens and live in California.

Dan Dworsky is an old friend from high school and after his football days established a very successful architectural business in Los Angeles. He reviewed early versions of the chapter on Judaism, although he says he is not active in Jewish religious activities.

Another who continually fed me new information was Bruce Vernier, an engineer with an advanced degree from Caltech. Ben Howle and Jim Meserole both read almost all the text and gave much appreciated continuing support. Other active supporters were John Magee, Jim Peck, Lisa Blaucher, and both my brothers, John and Paul.

My sister, Kay Hilde and her Billings friends were especially supportive and furnished many thoughtful comments and suggestions. That group included Darlene Hoklin, Dr. Bob Hagstrom, Willis and Ethel Jones, Millie Fry, Hilda Nolte, and Alice Layman. Kay's daughter Mary Jo Starkey (my niece) of the Victory Church in Missouri also sent a key publication and she and her minister husband both added useful advice.

Other encouragement was given by John H. Marburger III (Director, President's Office of Science and Technology Policy) and published authors Michael A. Corey (*The God Hypothesis*, Rowman &Littlefield) and Jim Jordan (*Something that Lasts*, WinePress Publishing).

Mike and Kay Carr took time from their busy professional schedule running "namestormers" to list some possible titles for the book, and these were winnowed down to the final selection.

Drew Stephens of Computer Troubleshooters helped to cure various computer problems and my son Alan gave computer support at several critical times. Grandsons Philip and Steven Mundt are also computer-skilled and made quick work of indexing the list of pre-selected words.

The team at BookPros in Austin provided their publishing expertise, and I was especially impressed by the cover illustration they created and their editing skills. My editor had a healthy interest in the subject matter and helped enormously with her thoughtful comments and suggestions.

1

INTRODUCTION

This investigation, conducted over a time-span of about four years, had two broad objectives. The first was to try to resolve some of the main misunderstandings between science and religion. The second was to answer some life-long questions concerning religion, and search for religious truth; this was for the purpose of personal fulfillment and perhaps, salvation.

As the research unfolded it became more challenging, hope for success became stronger, and some worthwhile ideas developed. Therefore I decided to publish the material in language intended to be interesting and intelligible to the ordinary reader. I believe millions of people have concerns and questions just like mine.

I consider myself to be a scientist and therefore need to ask why and how, to deal with facts, and in fact search for the truth. Some scientists have tried to keep science and religion entirely separate but this approach is evasive, indeed ridiculous, if a Supreme Being was responsible for creating the universe, all of its physical laws, and life on Earth. If a God exists then he must have been involved in such things as time and space, creation of matter and life, mankind, and man's soul and spirit. The God Question certainly has a yes or no answer—no maybe or anything in between.

In my attempt to reconcile science and religion, I first compiled chapters summarizing mainstream knowledge of the universe, geologic time, Earth history, life forms, extinctions, DNA, evolution, genes, and the history of mankind. The intent here was to create a brief but accurate account of pertinent scientific knowledge, an absolutely necessary step in order to establish a solid scientific basis before trying to understand how religion might be involved. Peer review was sought throughout the project to avoid making outright mistakes and to attain the most balanced and reasonable conclusions.

The chapters on science have been placed in the "Science Annex" in the second part of the book. The intent is that the reader can refer to the science chapters to the extent desired. Where appropriate, instead of footnotes, reference is made to certain pages of the Annex.

My information was gathered from literature (including the Bible), individuals, and the Internet. It was, necessarily, abbreviated and not exhaustive—after all, a huge number of dedicated scholars have spent lifetimes studying pieces of the same puzzle. Throughout, Google was of great help in fixing dates and rounding out information but discretion was imperative; I found that opinions freely offered at no cost are frequently worth the cost, i.e.,—nothing.

As a scientist, my credentials include a PhD from Stanford in Geology, election to Sigma Tau and Sigma Xi, and over the years I was named to eight different *Who's Who* categories. During the thirty-four years I worked for Mobil, I was Manager of Geology/Geochemistry Research for five years and a successful Exploration Manager for eleven years. Also included were contributions to professional activities and technical publications. My background in physics and chemistry was only adequate, but my professional career will speak for itself and I expect my peers would say I was a pretty fair geologist.

Geology is a fine background for a project such as this; it involves nature, time, early life, logic, and analysis, plus work and travel in much of the world. A good geologist is optimistic and conducts an intense search for the secrets of Mother Nature. It is essential to obtain accurate geologic facts, often at great expense (and the information is never enough) when faced with the responsibility for developing a plan and expending tens of millions of dollars in an exploration project.

I had the benefit of a childhood influenced by good religious exposure. Since our marriage in 1951, my wife Lorraine and I have been members of various Protestant congregations and have attended church on a fairly regular basis. We have some very good Jewish friends and since college days have always admired our Catholic friends for their lifestyle and strong faith. In addition, during my working years we lived in four different Muslim countries for twelve years. The latter gave us exposure to another religion, new friends, and an appreciation of the fact that Muslims are just as honest, kind, friendly and interested in their children's welfare as anyone else.

An added advantage came from the fact that while we were in Turkey, we were able to visit at least eleven of the places Saint Paul walked some 1900 years ago. In Indonesia we saw for the first time how competent and industrious the Chinese people are, and were impressed with how they rebuilt Singapore into one of the finest cities in the world once they were able to operate under a free and open political system.

After completing the science chapters it was possible to develop a working hypothesis, described in the chapter called "RESPECT SCIENCE – HONOR GOD." To me, the most logical conclusion was that God created the universe 13.7 billion years ago and created the first life on Earth about 3.8 billion years ago. DNA was key to the main steps in evolution, culminating in *Homo sapiens* about 195,000 to 150,000 years ago. The infusion of man's soul may have been contemporaneous with man's evolving brain.

Concerning evolution, Darwin's theory was a good beginning but some serious improvements are needed as it cannot explain the beginning of life or the Cambrian explosion, and species changes seem to be abrupt rather than gradual. Also, Darwinian evolution, or "survival of the fittest" does not explain such factors as altruism, compassion, generosity, cooperation, aesthetics and love—positive virtues important to man's soul and spirit.

To a surprising degree, it seems once physical laws and order were established, God has maintained a hands-off approach. This is seen in the many weird species reaching dead-ends in evolution, and in the widespread pain and suffering of mankind. The most logical explanation is that God has given mankind an orderly and beautiful world subject to his laws, but that man is free to make, and is responsible for, his own mistakes. In other words, a kind of tough love Other people can easily interpret these facts differently and I'll admit, this is a good example of seeing "…through a glass, darkly…" as Saint Paul told the Corinthians.

Having a belief in God as the foundation, the next step was to try to determine if there is a preferred path to seek salvation, in other words, to find the one true religion if such a thing exists. In trying to answer this question I used the same logical approach as with the science, i.e., assemble the facts in an orderly way and see where they lead. The main Judeo-Christian religions were emphasized, together with the history and theology of Islam. All three sprang from Abraham and the Semitic race, are monotheistic and developed (and competed with each other) in the same general geographic area. Together they are the professed faiths of 64 percent of the Earth's religious population.

A careful analysis of how the Old Testament was written led to the suggestion that the first eleven chapters of Genesis require a "scientific paraphrase" in order to conform to solid scientific knowledge. This would help address the problems with (1) six days of creation, (2) Adam, Eve and original sin, (3) Noah's story, (4) the unrealistic ages for Methuselah and others, (5) introduction of life on Earth and evolution, and (6) mankind and his soul.

An understanding of this kind could benefit millions of people. Those who are scientifically inclined would be more accepting of religion, and it would help move fundamentalists into the mainstream. Then we could all be on the same page and begin to talk about the real issues rather than argue about a few symbolic or metaphorical words.

Each of the three religions has made terrible mistakes, ranging from the crucifixion of Jesus to the Inquisition to suicide bombers—all beyond comprehension. The Hindus had their caste system, and Buddhists claim transmigration. All these religions have their own beliefs and have important differences, so they can't all be right. Is one religion better than others, or do many roads lead to the same place?

An account of Jesus' life begins with a miraculous birth, miracles that he performed during his ministry and the miracle of his Resurrection. Many people find this hard to swallow but thousands were witnesses to the miraculous events, were absolutely convinced that they happened, and were willing to die for those beliefs. The Resurrection of Jesus was the fourth main point of evidence for the existence of God—an act of God could be the only explanation for such a miracle. The resurrection of God's Son is an overwhelming argument that Christianity was the new chosen religion, building on Judaism.

The twenty-seven books of the New Testament were written between fifteen and sixty-five years after the death of Jesus, by individuals who were either direct witnesses or received the information from direct witnesses. Hence, after an active ministry lasting a little over two years, Jesus was able to inspire the founding of a Christian religion that has ministered to billions of people and which today has 2 billion members, one-third of the world's population.

Knowing Jesus better now than before starting this project, I realize he was not politically correct about social or religious matters. His ideas were provocative, challenging, and frequently surprising. He could display anger, was tolerant with social outcasts (tax collectors), religious outcasts (Samaritans), sinners (prostitutes and adulterers), and thought that love and concern for the weak, sick, and poor were far more important than observing religious laws pertaining to food, cleanliness and the Sabbath. Therefore, if he were here today I wouldn't be at all dismayed to hear him say that love, and living in obedience to the one God (by whatever name) should be the goal of mankind, and lead to peace on Earth and personal salvation.

Working on this project for four years has served to move me toward Catholicism. Some of the reasons include the following: the Catholic Church has served billions of people over the centuries; the Church has fought communism and held firmly to its basic principles in the face of pressures supporting political correctness and relativism; our personal Catholic friends serve as good examples of an admirable faith and lifestyle; the Church has shown a willingness to change, especially since Vatican II. A new tolerance for other religions is important, and as a scientist I especially appreciate Catholicism's moves toward respectful consideration of mainstream scientific thinking, including astronomy, the Big Bang and evolution. Past mistakes, such as the early stifling of science and then the Inquisition, were deeply troubling, as has been the most recent foot-dragging in dealing strongly with pedophile priests.

Another result of this project is to gain a better appreciation of the Jewish culture and legacy. The same can be said for Islam with the caveat that people of that faith desperately need their own "Vatican II."

To make the book more readable, footnotes have been avoided. Further explanations are cross-referenced with appropriate page numbers, especially in reference to the "Science Annex." In the text, the most important conclusions or statements have been italicized. God is referred to as if male, and "mankind" is used throughout. I hope everyone will understand this is only a matter of convenience and doesn't represent any chauvinistic attitude. [In a few places, personal notes, comments or observations are considered useful to explain a setting or situation, and these are identified by brackets. As this was a personal search for religious truth, comments are made in the first person.]

To answer my questions, it became necessary to develop a summary of the universe and selected elements of science, plus the history of mankind and the main religions. This made it possible to propose a logical reconciliation of science and religion; the "scientific paraphrase" of Genesis 1–11 may help to reduce adversarial opinion. The project was certainly more ambitious than first envisioned, but it was totally engrossing and one of the most fascinating subjects I have ever researched.

Some have said that such a structured, intellectual approach to faith is impossible, but I would argue otherwise. I cannot claim an epiphany, but without doubt I am closer to my goal today than when I started four years ago.

2

PITFALLS OF SCIENCE AND RELIGION

In this world of complex uncertainty, it is recognized that science and religion are fundamentally similar in that they both seek the truth and both have faith in their principles. Scientists have faith in a vast array of factual knowledge such as the speed of light, electromagnetics, mathematics, etc. In religion, faith is at the heart of belief in something that cannot be proven (or disproven) by scientific methods.

The very definition of science is "a search for the truth" and as John reported (8:32), Jesus said "the truth shall make you free". Also, Paul advised the Thessalonians to "Prove all things" (I Th. 5:21).

Science is based foremost on observations or evidence which can be measured and described. It is concerned with understanding and describing the natural world. New findings are subject to peer review through a process of reporting at meetings and in scientific journals. Extensive testing follows, including the need for reproducibility in the laboratory. A characteristic of the scientific method is the openness to challenge. Every new postulate or theory must be tested repeatedly, preferably by different investigators using different methods. Over time, a fact may come to be recognized as a physical law whereas a theory is always provisional in the sense that it is only a hypothesis, or tentative explanation, until it can be proven.

Especially since World War II a torrent of new scientific information has been developed, in large part because of sophisticated new equipment including the computer. In the physical sciences, geologists have gained a good understanding of plate tectonics including related mountain building, earthquakes and volcanoes. With the advent of the Hubble telescope we are just beginning to observe the awesome extent of the cosmos and the formation of other galaxies and solar systems.

The rules of classical mechanics (Newton's Laws) have been found to hold for those cases where velocities are much smaller than the speed of light and distances greatly exceed atomic scales. Yet another domain exists, best described by Einstein's theories and Planck's equations of quantum mechanics, which describe the behavior of sub-atomic particles.

Charles Darwin's *Origin of Species*, published in 1859, has had a profound influence on scientific thought at the time and ever since. In 1953 a new world opened when James D. Watson and Francis Crick discovered the famous spiraling double helix structure of DNA, the substance that transmits hereditary information. In 1966 the genetic code was cracked, showing how DNA gives the directions for making proteins, and in 2000 the Human Genome Project was completed—an international effort to map all human genes. Biotechnology, gene therapy, cloning, stem cells, etc. are all part of a whole new field with great promise and some moral questions.

Scientists can provide mankind with powerful insights into the physical world and tools to improve our life on this planet. They must do this with honesty and integrity and provide our political decision-makers with accurate, unbiased information about good and not junk science. Writers of excellent, scientifically responsible articles for public consumption provide a valuable service but need to avoid serving the various shrill advocacy groups. One disturbing trend is that several of the scientific journals have become engaged in both scientific and political advocacy. Their reputations for careful and unbiased science reporting and peer review are bound to suffer. I always look forward to the fine science articles and wonderful illustrations in *Scientific American* but resent the three opinion (editorial) pages which always have a point of view and lead me to suspect their choice of articles may be politicized as well.

Carl Sagan did a fine job in popularizing science with his TV science series *Cosmos* seen in sixty countries by 400 million people. His 1980 book of the same name was a wonderful contribution. He quite correctly bemoaned the abysmal state of science knowledge in the U.S. and argued the need for an improved education approach. He positively beamed when describing the joy of scientific discovery, saying, "science invariably elicits a sense of reverence and awe." Unfortunately, he not only revealed new mysteries of the cosmos but also took on the role of high priest in telling us how we should live. At times he also seemed to take positions that were politically correct and/or unnecessarily supportive of some activist groups. Gratuitously, he stated (p. 331 of *Cosmos*) that a belief in God tended to accompany slavery, killing, torture and mutilation of enemies, promoting the inferiority of women, and physically punishing infants.

[When I was manager of Mobil's Geology and Geochemistry Research facility I came to understand scientists better. Many of them were much smarter than me and some had strong international reputations in their respective specialties. So I respected them all, but of course recognized that some were stronger than others. I concluded that what drove them was a desire to make worthwhile contributions, to publish, and to gain prestige among their peers and management. Certainly nothing wrong with that, but their needs also suggest some potential temptations.

MISUSING SCIENCE

This problem is of great concern to me because of the danger it presents. When controversial and complex scientific matters are reported by the media, the public may be unable to interpret what is right or wrong. In a republic such as ours, intelligent decisions can be made only by an accurately informed electorate and if people believe lies or misrepresentations, terrible mistakes can result. In his 2004 book *State of Fear*, Michael Crichton warned of politicizing science and recounted how eugenics, politically correct and widely supported during the first part of the 20th century, eventually led to Nazi perversions and the Holocaust.]

Sometimes bad science originates, probably infrequently, from scientists who either misinterpret their data or fudge results to get a desired result. An example of an apparently honest mistake got worldwide attention in 1989. Two reputable chemists in Utah reported that they had induced cold fusion of deuterium nuclei and thereby generated energy (heat). The results were announced with great fanfare and breathlessly reported by some of the media. It took some years for independent researchers to refute the main claim, but some uncertainty still persists as experimental results are sometimes puzzling.

"Salting" of mining properties is an old trick. If the promoter can involve a reputable geologist he can sometimes get away with grand theft. The Bre-X case is a recent example; investors lost $5 billion and the geologist ended up "accidentally" falling from a helicopter to his death in the Borneo jungle.

Environmental extremists have emerged as some of the worst offenders in taking selected bits of science and developing scare tactics to influence public opinion (and raise funds to further their own purposes). The Endangered Species Act of 1973 has been used abusively in a number of cases. A recent example is the spotted owl controversy in the northwest, where logging of old growth trees was halted for the last ten years, in order to encourage nesting. It turns out that the population of spotted owls has continued to plummet—because of barred owls taking over. In brief, an industry was destroyed (130,000 lost jobs, and more than 900 sawmills) on the basis of faulty science. Irresponsible elements of the entertainment and communications media often help the environmentalists by embellishing and reporting unfounded speculations, pseudoscience and lies. And worst of all are politicians who slant or twist the facts to support their preconceived ideas and then compound the error by trying to pass bad legislation.

An especially egregious case was the great Alar scare of 1989. Alar was developed in the 1960s to prevent the pre-harvest rotting of apples; its active ingredient is daminozide, a hormone-like chemical. In 1968 the FDA approved Alar for commercial use after conducting two years of normal tests. But in the 1970s a Dr. Bela Toth reported that high doses of Alar caused tumors in mice. In 1985 the EPA required tests of UDMH, a breakdown product of Alar. These tests utilized unrealistically high doses of UDMH on mice (equivalent to drinking daily, for life, 19,000 quarts of juice from Alar-treated apples). Eighty percent of the mice died—not from cancer but rather from the toxic effects of the huge doses of UDMH.

Then in 1989 the National Resources Defense Council (NRDC) compiled a report by two of their activists (never peer reviewed) and engaged a PR firm to disseminate the results that claimed Alar was "the most potent cancer-causing agent in our food supply." At that point, irresponsible elements of the mass media took over. The CBS program *60 Minutes* was aired showing skull and crossbones superimposed on an apple and Ed Bradley asserted daminozide (which he mis-termed a pesticide) was the worst carcinogen in our food. Phil Donahue on his talk show, and film star Meryl Streep on TV both damned Alar. Mass hysteria ensued and apple markets were ruined overnight; the industry lost about $400 million. Through all this the radical environmentalist group NRDC prospered, taking in hundreds of thousands of cash contributions.

Since then, expert health authorities have blasted the false alarms about Alar. The British government concluded there "was no risk to health," the United Nations dismissed carcinogen concerns, the journal *Science* rejected the concerns as well, the American Medical Association (AMA) stated "Alar does not pose a risk," former Surgeon General Dr. C. Everett Koop said "Alar never did pose a health hazard," Dr Adamson of the National Cancer Institute said the risk of cancer from eating Alar-treated apples was "nonexistent," the FDA has described Ed Bradley's *60 Minutes* claims as "total baloney" and on and on.

A particularly reprehensible form of abuse has developed in the last few years due to the actions of personal injury lawyers; by distorting scientific data, they have induced certain groups of people to support class-action litigation. An example is that of the 850,000 asbestos-related lawsuits that have cost $54 billion and bankrupted seventy companies. U.S. District Court Judge Janis Jack has concluded that plaintiff lawyers, litigation doctors, and mass screening companies have participated in a scheme to manufacture fraudulent diagnoses for use in lawsuits by the asbestos bar. She blamed the handful of doctors whose countless "diagnoses were driven by neither health nor justice; they were manufactured for money." She sent 10,000 cases back to state courts and more than half were quickly dismissed. The scandal is massive enough to rank with the Teapot Dome, Enron and WorldCom frauds.

Concerning current affairs and civic responsibility, many scientists are torn between the extremes of no involvement at all and too much, which inevitably leads to the destructive process of politicization of science. The Royal Library of Alexandria (283 B.C.– A.D. 365) housed an impressive group of the world's best scientists who made some outstanding discoveries, but the ordinary man in the street was told nothing and did not benefit. At the other extreme, scientists who lose their objectivity may shade the truth in order to support a public cause. Stephen Schneider, at Stanford, recognized the dilemma and admitted that "we have to offer up scary scenarios, make simplified, dramatic statements, and make little mention of any doubts we might have." Why do we have to?

Recently, California voters approved Proposition 71 authorizing the state to spend $3 billon for stem cell research. Proposition 71 has been criticized for lacking clear ethical guidelines but evidently started a feeding-frenzy for grant money. The Oversight Committee has argued that members of the peer-review group should be from outside the state in order to discourage the opportunists who are "coming out of the woodwork."

Irving Weissman, who conducts cutting-edge cancer research at Stanford, says "I've never seen so many people, even at my own university, who now tell me that they are stem cell biologists. It's sick."

In 2005 another scandal concerned Korean researcher Woo Suk Hwang and his stem cell research. Hwang and his team announced they created eleven stem cell lines using the SCNT technique (p. 423) to clone early-stage embryos. Remarkably, each stem cell line genetically matched its skin cell donor. Veterinarian Hwang gained worldwide fame and in December, *Scientific American* named him as "Research Leader of the Year." It was later found that Dr. Hwang fabricated his data and his reputation was destroyed. Also damaged was Dr. Gerald Schatten at the University of Pittsburgh who wrote the key research paper and was listed as the senior author. Schatten was not accused of participating in the falsified experiments but rather of poor judgment in allowing his name to be used. Later, the editors of *Scientific American* retracted their honoring of Hwang.

For the last 15,000 years the earth's inhabitants have been enjoying interglacial warming. In fact, the logical claim could be made that because of this warming, mankind has been able to create a cultural and scientific explosion, achieving 99 percent of all human progress.

Environmentalists, on the other hand, predict adverse effects due to global warming caused by mankind and his greenhouse gases. Unfortunately, "noise" from activists, environmentalists, politicians, and the media has tended to distort reporting of the science which has turned out to be faulty and incomplete (p. 365–374). Under the Kyoto Protocol, thirty-eight industrialized nations were required to cut greenhouse gas emissions (mostly CO_2). But by the time of the 2005 conference in Montreal it was becoming clear that Kyoto was failing. Of the thirty-eight, only Britain and Germany had complied and then only because of one-time events in those two countries.

All these examples of the faulty use of science certainly do not refer to the vast majority of scientists. The enormous advances in technology and scientific discoveries during the last century or so are truly exciting, and I have tried to describe the essence of some of them in the SCIENCE ANNEX. Like Sagan, I love the physical sciences but expect to get my share of criticism from scientists who may be upset, for various reasons.

ERRORS IN RELIGION

The bulk of my work on religion deals with the Jewish, Christian and Muslim faiths. I have made this choice because these three make up about 64 percent of the total recognized religions in the world. Even more importantly, their influence is felt throughout the world, affecting the actions of individuals and nations. Islam, with 1.3 billion members, is the fastest growing of the three, about 1.6 times faster than Christianity.

All three originate from a common ancestor, Abraham. His descendents can be traced directly to the principals of the three faiths, who all lived in the same small part of the world. They cooperated to some extent but usually competed, sometimes violently, and even today have competing claims to some parts of the biblical world, especially in Palestine. Some of the main mistakes of the three were truly earth shaking and are discussed in more detail in following chapters.

In analyzing how the books of the Old Testament were written, it seems likely that the most accurate part of the text was the portion beginning with II Samuel; they were the first events recorded in real time by a court biographer instead of relying on memories passed on orally. The stories about Adam and Eve, Noah, and intervening generations are more doubtful because the Redactor (Ezra?) was writing about things that had happened at least thirty-three hundred years earlier (p. 95–100).

The first eleven chapters of Genesis flatly contradict some solid science and I have suggested that this imbroglio be corrected with a "scientific paraphrase" of the offending verses. This step could be helpful to millions of people and is more fully explained on page 100.

Christianity grew directly out of Judaism and the New Testament frequently refers to prophets and other personalities in the Old Testament. Throughout the Old Testament, prophets predicted the coming of a Messiah, a strong leader and perhaps military conqueror who would lead the Hebrews to better days. When Jesus appeared, many hoped he was the one, especially to free the Hebrews from Roman rule.

The chief priests and Sadducees decided he was not the Messiah and because he was causing some difficulties, conspired to have Jesus crucified. This may have been the biggest mistake in world history and is an example of the terrible damage that can be inflicted upon a permissive populace because of bad leadership. If the Jewish leaders had recognized Jesus as the Messiah, a single, merged Judeo-Christian religion could have been in place when the Roman Empire adopted Christianity less than 300 years later (p. 107).

With the Resurrection of Jesus, his followers were absolutely convinced that they had witnessed the greatest miracle of all time. Almost overnight they changed from wimps to brave martyrs and were ready to die for their beliefs. This was the beginning of the Christian church, which had some of its finest hours in the first few centuries. When the Roman Empire embraced Christianity in the fourth century, a huge number of people were added to the early Catholic Church which gained enormous new power. Its influence spread throughout the civilized world, mostly in a positive way but also with some bad mistakes.

In the seventh century, Islam (p. 169–199) arose to challenge the Christians and Jews. Muhammad was a prophet for his God, Allah, and compared in importance to the earlier prophets Abraham, Moses and Jesus. Muhammad was primarily a religious leader and responsible for much of the Koran, but he was also a politician and military leader (much like Samuel in the Old Testament). Utilizing these skills, he was able to unite all the Arab tribes and create a culture with common interests and brotherhood based on the new religion, Islam. After his death in A.D. 632, his lieutenants led the fervently inspired tribesmen on an incredible series of military conquests. This acquisition of territory and competition between cultures began a long-running conflict with Jews and Christians which continues to this day.

In reading about the life of Muhammad and his new theology, one is struck by the similarity of some of his basic tenets to those of Jesus. Both preached belief in one God, who was the God of Abraham and Moses. Both stressed concern for the weak and poor, mercy and benevolence. Both appealed to fairness, dignity, and social justice for the underclass, challenging the moral and social structure of the ruling class with its system of privilege.

Arabs are the descendents of Shem, the oldest son of Noah, hence the term "Semite." Their more direct ancestor was Ishmael, the son of Abraham and Hagar (p. 75–76). It is surprising that Judaism and Islam are related in so many ways, especially in view of their intense hatred in the Middle East today. Racially, the two sprang from the same Semitic tribes that settled in the area at least 100,000 years ago during the migrations of *Homo sapiens* out of East Africa. Both religions are monotheistic, believe in an afterlife, and claim Abraham as their founding father some 4500 years ago. Both are male-oriented, follow the religious practice of circumcision and observe somewhat similar dietary requirements. At times during the Middle Ages, Jews and Muslims had a respectful if not friendly relationship, especially in such places as Spain and North Africa. Today's bitterness in Palestine stems largely from land disputes and the behavior of extremists on both sides.

Territorial claims, a demand for access to religious sites, and some other miscalculations led to the Crusades, beginning in 1095 (p. 205–229) These wars went on for about 200 years and have caused an uneasy relationship between the Christian and Muslim worlds.

In part growing out of the Crusades, the Catholic Church became embroiled in the Inquisition (p. 229–243), one of the worst mistakes ever made by organized religion. The first stages of the Inquisition began in 1163 and continued for over 600 years. A large number of people were tortured and killed, all in the name of religion; Cornwell reported "hundreds of thousands" were killed. Even Galileo was ensnared, and in 1633 he was forced to recant his scientific belief, something that enraged scientists at that time and since.

The mistakes of these three religions had lingering effects. The Jews made their worst mistake 2000 years ago when they failed to recognize Jesus as the Messiah. The crucifixion was a grossly excessive punishment and the recriminations are still with us to some extent. The Catholic Church took the first (Albigensian) steps of the Inquisition in 1163 and the last victim was hanged in 1826.

Continuing abuses of the Inquisition and sale of indulgences led to the Protestant Reformation in 1517, and indirectly the French Revolution. These two events were critically important steps in damaging the influence of the Church. Finally, in 1962 the Catholic Church undertook the serious corrective changes of Vatican II which have had very positive results.

During the first four decades of the twentieth century, the pseudo-science of eugenics had the support of presidents, Supreme Court justices, politicians and liberal Protestant and Jewish clergy. The human race was to be improved by limiting the reproductive rights of those deemed unfit, in other words "the menace of the feebleminded." In 1907, Indiana passed a state law to "prevent procreation of confirmed criminals, idiots, imbeciles, and rapists" and in 1927 the U.S. Supreme Court ruled eight to one that Virginia's compulsory sterilization law was constitutional. During the U.S. experience, thirty states had sterilization laws and 60,000 U.S. citizens were victimized. The experiment ended in Europe with the Holocaust, when Nazis decided who should live and who should die.

The Jesus Seminar (p. 159–161) was organized in 1985, ostensibly to learn the truth about the historical Jesus and to see if words in the Bible could be "retained as an article of faith" in today's scientific age. Results of this project have been very distressing to a great number of people and are flatly rejected by most Catholics and Protestants. The failure was almost preordained by the composition of the participants, and poorly considered attestation requirements that eliminated 82 percent of the Gospel sayings attributed to Jesus. Some elements of the Seminar—voting with colored beads, and the reporting of results—were almost juvenile, but some of the anti-religious elements of the print media reported on it with glee.

The third religion, Islam, is facing a defining challenge as we speak. Basically, Islam is a fine religion but gets a bad press in the Western world. It seems Islam's most vivid characteristic right now seems to be that of terrorism, highlighted by suicide bombers, even though the terrorists are a tiny minority. But the danger is enormous. If the moderate elements of Islam fail to take control, terrorism could careen out of control leading to a confrontation with the rest of the world. Instead of encouraging terrorism and suicide, the imams need to convince young Muslims that education and opportunity are possible. The world cries out for a tolerant, enlightened and engaged form of Islam, just as the Catholics addressed many of their problems with Vatican II.

3

RESPECT SCIENCE—
HONOR GOD

It seemed logical to me that if there is a God, nature and science should reflect His works. To address this subject intelligently, the first step was to make an orderly summary of today's mainstream scientific facts and interpretations. This framework of scientific findings and knowledge was aimed at trying to answer the question "What is the evidence, if any, that God created the universe and life?"

The scientific material is compiled in the section called "Science Annex" beginning on page 358(?) and is intended for the reader to refer to as desired. The different chapters were chosen as a logical way to approach the problem, using the chronological sequence of geologic time. Thus, the first chapter is about the Universe, followed by Solar System, Earth, Life Forms/Evolution, DNA/Genetics, and Mankind. Age-dates are very important, of course, and those presented are considered to be quite reliable.

[To be honest, as the work began I was not hopeful for new insights. But as the subject matter was developed I began to see that conventional theories could not explain some of the science. In fact, it became increasingly clear that there must be a Great Designer involved, rather than calling upon random chance to explain the many complexities. I developed a working hypothesis that the major events below were initiated by God.]

CHRONOLOGY OF MAJOR EVENTS

- Creation of universe (Big Bang), 13.7 billion years ago (ba)

- Milky Way formed, 10 ba

- Formation of Solar system and Earth, 4.5 ba

- First life on Earth, creation of RNA/DNA, 3.8 ba

- Cambrian explosion, 530 million years ago (ma)

- Hominids/chimpanzees diverged, 5–6 ma

- First Homo species evolved 2.6 ma

- Homo sapiens sapiens evolved 195,000 to 150,000 years ago

- Mankind gained speech, an improved brain, and a soul and spirit 100,000 to 10,000 years ago

If God created the universe, an obvious question is: What did He do during the 9 billion years between creation of the universe (13.7 ba) and formation of our Earth (4.5 ba)? During this time most of the galaxies were formed including suns, planets and moons. As Newtonian laws of physics and chemistry came into play on the Earth, it is logical to expect the same on other planets. If scientists did not create the laws of physics, who did?

God's possible role in science has inspired a good deal of thoughtful introspection by many scientists, especially in considering (1) the creation of the universe, and (2) the introduction of life on Earth. These same two subjects have prompted many prominent scientists to express their sense of awe and wonder, and their thoughts about God. Archaeology, evolution and ontogeny can hint at the time of the infusion of man's soul and spirit.

BIG BANG

At present, the majority of scientists favor the Big Bang theory to explain the creation of the universe (p. 309–316). As now understood, this theory posits that 13.7 billion years ago a "singularity" of infinite density and temperature created matter and energy in an ineffable explosion, trillions of degrees in temperature. This was also the beginning of space and time itself. During this inflationary flash, elementary particles, with Planck dimensions, began to form quarks, and the incipient universe expanded in size at a rate many times the speed of light. Physicists calculate that it took about 380,000 years before the density of the quark-gluon plasma decreased to the point that light could escape.

From the initial phase of infinitely dense radioactive plasma, when matter first appeared as sub-atomic particles, quarks combined to form hydrogen, then helium. Further accreting helium nuclei formed lithium and beryllium whereas carbon and all heavier elements up to uranium came from supernova explosions. All 114 of the known elements have an orderly interrelationship, according to atomic number in the Periodic Table. This table, of fundamental importance, was established in 1869 by Mendeleev, working with the sixty-five elements known at that time.

The first star may have formed after 400 million years, and the first galaxy after one billion years. The 100 billion galaxies sometimes occur as globular clusters, each containing 100,000 to several million stars. All the stars in each galaxy orbit their own black hole (once every 250 million years, in the case of our Solar System in the Milky Way galaxy). Galaxies are moving away from each other and the universe is expanding with the most distant galaxies moving faster. Stars moving away are shifted toward the red part of the visible spectrum, or "red shifted." This optical effect is analogous to the Doppler shift, an acoustic effect. Hubble was able to use this red shift to measure the rate of expansion of the universe and this rate is called the Hubble constant.

Our Milky Way spiral galaxy was formed about 10 billion years ago and includes about 400 billion stars. Our star (Sol) is an unremarkable yellow dwarf located halfway out on one of the four spiral arms, about 25,000 light years from the center of the galaxy. Sol and its nine planets formed about 4.5 billion years ago. All the planets (except Pluto) are aligned along a thin disc, orbit the sun in the same direction, and, except for Venus, rotate in the same counter-clockwise direction.

Instead of chaos, which would be expected as the result of an "ineffable explosion" it seems that the universe is expanding in an orderly way. All the stars and planets are characterized by spin and rotation in circular or elliptical orbits. Each galaxy seems to have its own black hole with enormous gravitational pull, which controls the movement of all its entrained stars. Gravity of the black hole is so strong light cannot escape, and the only way to deduce that the black hole exists is to observe its effect on nearby objects. With its immense gravitational pull, a black hole sucks in dust, gas and entire stars if they get too close. Captured material may spiral into the black hole at near the speed of light, giving off intense radiation, including X-rays, as it is heated to millions of degrees.

There seem to be at least three kinds of black holes: (1) stellar-mass type, equal to three to fifteen solar masses, caused by the supernova explosions of dying, super giant stars, (2) medium-size black holes, each with a mass of several thousand suns, and (3) super massive black holes that have as much matter as several billion suns. Two black holes have been found in at least one highly active galaxy and they are expected to merge eventually with repercussions throughout the universe. Professor Karl Gebhardt at the University of Texas has recently made the observation that each black hole—no matter its size—appears to contain almost precisely one-half of one percent as much mass as that making up all the stars that surrounds it.

Perhaps the current greatest unsolved mystery to the community of astrophysicists is the problem of "dark matter." Because the visible (baryonic) matter is affected in unaccountable ways, most astronomers believe that large quantities of some unidentified material are present in the universe. The concept of dark energy has been introduced to explain the accelerating expansion of the universe. It seems clear that the inter-related phenomena of black holes, black matter and black energy are of fundamental importance but cannot yet be measured or even observed directly.

Consider again what the Big Bang scenario requires. First, a point in physics/mathematics terms concerning time-space, where matter is infinitely dense, i.e., a singularity. Then for some reason this point source, also with infinitely strong gravitational strength, flies apart in an ineffable explosion "too great or extreme to be expressed or described in words." Matter explodes at a rate many times the speed of light.

It is a delicious irony* that it was a Catholic abbé and astronomer, Georges LeMaître, who first hypothesized that the universe began with the explosion of a "primordial atom" of infinite density. (*For years, the Catholic Inquisition has been condemned for its treatment of the scientist Galileo. So there is some recompense in that it was a Catholic abbé who first suggested the concept of an infinitely dense point source—now called a singularity—as the origin of an expanding universe, and thereby introduced Big Bang technology).

LeMaître, a Belgian, made his startling proposal in 1927. He also asserted that the universe must be expanding, and predicted that there should be some form of background radiation in the universe left over from the initial explosion of the primordial atom. LeMaître was deeply convinced that a Creator was responsible and talked frequently to his friend Albert Einstein about it. In making his prediction, LeMaître had been influenced by the general theory of relativity, proposed by Einstein about ten years earlier. Einstein had shown that the universe had a beginning, the instant when space-time began. LeMaître realized that this beginning was the creation event, the apparent moment when the universe was created out of nothing (creation *ex nihilio*).

LeMaître's first description of a singularity proved to be prescient. In 1929, Edwin Hubble discovered that galaxies were moving apart at high speed, and in 1963 Arno Penzias and Robert Wilson found apparently uniform, cosmic microwave background (CMB) radiation. In 1992 the COBE satellite reconfirmed the background radiation and strongly indicated that the universe was created about 15 billion years ago. George Smoot, the Lawrence team leader said "It's like looking at God." Frederick Burnham, a science-historian said, "These findings, now available, make the idea that God created the universe a more respectable hypothesis today than at any time in the last 100 years." The NASA team leader John Mather told the Washington Post he saw a parallel between the scientific and biblical versions of creation, and astrophysicist Robert Jastrow averred that "the astronomical evidence leads to a biblical view of the origin of the world."

About the same time that Sir Fred Hoyle first used the term "Big Bang" in the 1950s, he converted from atheism to a belief that a "purposeful intelligence" was present in the universe. LeMaître's friend Albert Einstein often talked about God, saying "Everyone who is seriously interested in the pursuit of science becomes convinced that a spirit is manifest in the laws of the universe—a spirit vastly superior to that of man." Astronomer Allan Sandage declared the Big Bang could be understood only as a "miracle" and Nobel laureate Charles Townes said physical phenomena "seem to reflect intelligence at work." The brilliant physicist Stephan Hawking—who sits in the Newton chair at Cambridge—talked about the "mind of God."

The reason for the explosion of the original singularity, or black hole, remains a mystery. And it takes metaphysical explanations to describe the original conditions and subsequent processes. The Big Bang theory requires accepting impossible conditions that cannot be described, and the initiation of processes that cannot be explained except by metaphysics. Everything in the universe was created out of nothing and in that first microsecond, all subsequent physical laws and constants were determined. Physicists cannot explain how the Big Bang was initiated, but some outside power—like God—must be one possible explanation.

To those of us on Earth, the laws of physics and chemistry have been revealed, for the most part, in the last few hundred years. This is a blink of the eye in geologic terms, and leads to wondering if the same laws apply to life on other planets. At least 150 other planets are known to exist, orbiting other suns. Sagan estimated there could be as many as a million other civilizations in the Milky Way. This claim led to the project SETI (Search for Extraterrestrial Intelligence), utilizing the impressive array of twenty-seven radio telescopes near Socorro, NM. So far, no radio signals showing intelligence have been identified from space.

On Earth, conditions favorable for life combine, perhaps uniquely so. In benefiting mankind, this condition was termed the "anthropic principle" by Cambridge physicist Brandon Carter in 1974. The favorable conditions include the following (after Ward and Brownlee).

- Correct distance from the sun
- Stable orbit of other planets
- Correct tilt of Earth's axis
- Limited number of asteroid impacts
- A protective magnetosphere
- Oceans in right proportions
- Sufficient carbon
- Plate tectonics

Roger Penrose, a famous Oxford mathematician, also calculated the precision needed to fine-tune the universe for life at the moment of the Big Bang. His analysis showed a likelihood of less than one chance in 10^{123} (10 with 123 zeroes after it) that such a universe could be formed by random events. Among other factors, Sir Penrose considered the cosmological constant, the mass of the neutron, the strong nuclear force, the weak nuclear force, the gravitational constant, the electromagnetic force, and the decay rate of the proton (from Kevin Miller).

DNA

Deoxyribonucleic acid was isolated in 1869 and as early as 1892 it was speculated that DNA might be able to convey hereditary information. Its crucial characteristic is that it can replicate itself over thousands of generations, faithfully passing along its genetic information in the process. Rarely, just like a computer glitch, a random mutation will occur. Mutations in

DNA occur in a number of ways. Cosmic rays, gamma waves, X-rays, ultraviolet radiation and radioactive decay are constantly bombarding life forms. Parental age or sex can have an influence and enzymes that protect or repair DNA can break down. Sometimes the mistake has a favorable effect, allowing the mutant DNA to out-replicate its competitors and so come to dominate. This process of favoring mutations with superior fitness acts like a ratchet, locking in the advantageous errors and eliminating the less fit. The process was called natural selection by Darwin in 1859 and was the basis for his theory of evolution (p. 383).

In 1953, James Watson and Francis Crick deduced that DNA had a double helix structure after seeing the pattern of X-rays diffracted through wet DNA crystals. Their famous right-handed double helix model of DNA shows it to be parallel strands of sugar-phosphate "rails" connected by "rungs" of simple molecules called bases. The four letters used, A, C, G, and T are shorthand for the bases adenine, cytosine, guanine, and thymine. C always pairs with G and A with T to form a full rung. The sequence of bases along a section of DNA is a molecular message describing the order of amino acids needed to form a protein. A base sequence of C-C-A followed by C-A-G is a message saying that to form a particular protein, an amino acid called proline is to be followed by one called glutamine. The sixty-four possible combinations of the four letters give instructions for the twenty amino acids, plus signals to start and stop protein synthesis. A DNA molecule includes, on average, several thousand genes with one gene every 40,000 bases, and a given section of the DNA molecule comprises a gene (p. 403–404).

The awesome complexity of DNA might be appreciated by looking at the structure of a human cell. The human body has about 100 trillion cells, including 100 billion brain cells. About 200 cells would fit into the period at the end of this sentence. Each cell nucleus contains its own set of twenty-three pairs of chromosomes, one from each parent. Each of the chromosomes has a protein core with a DNA molecule wound tightly around it. Each molecule has 100 million turns and 100 billion atoms. Fully extended, the DNA strands in a single cell would stretch up to six feet—if the entire DNA in the human body were placed end to end it would reach 12 million miles. In just one human cell the DNA stores an amount of information equal to 1000 books, each with 500 pages. As a cell divides, 3 billion letters of code must be copied accurately; actually, the error rate is about one mistake in every 10 million bases.

Within the cell, but outside the nucleus, thousands of scattered ribosomes busily produce tens of thousands of different proteins. The ribosomes get their instructions from single-stranded RNA molecules, reading the message like a laser scanning a bar code. The RNA, in turn, gets its message from the DNA which specifies the sequence of amino acids linked together to produce the desired protein. A new technology called RNA Interference is being developed to stifle bad genes by selectively cutting off information passed to the ribosomes.

A recent paper by Freeland and Hurst explains the sophistication of the genetic code and how it has evolved. The underlying premise of Darwinian natural selection remains the same; a small change in the DNA of a single gene (a mutation) can be beneficial. However, the genetic code has evolved and the number of amino acids involved in protein growth has increased. Some of the amino acids have six codons (units of genetic code) whereas others have only one or two. Furthermore, standard codons can mean different things to different organisms. They found that existing genetic codes of natural organisms have developed redundancy in order to resist damaging errors and outperformed all but one in a million of the possible alternatives. Their conclusion was (1) that the genetic code has evolved to speed-up evolution, (2) that small rather than extreme mutations were statistically more likely to be beneficial, and (3) that organisms with codes that best coped with change were more likely to survive.

The human genome includes about 20–25,000 genes, not much different than many other organisms. But mankind's DNA is about 98 percent "junk," i.e., not involved in genetic coding. Included in the junk, however, are bits of DNA called transposons, which serve to activate or silence genes in an important epigenetic process. Other parts of the junk eventually may prove to have unique advantages to humans.

Francis Collins believes that God "who created the universe, chose the remarkable mechanism of evolution to create plants and animals." Collins is director of the Human Genome Institute and an avowed evangelist. When completion of the Human Genome Project was celebrated at the White House in the spring 2000, Collins said "it is humbling to me and awe-inspiring to realize that we have caught the first glimpse of our own instruction book, previously known only to God." He added "I am unaware of any irreconcilable conflict between scientific knowledge about evolution and the idea of a creator God."

In the human body several hundred thousand types of protein, perhaps a million are involved, and each requires the assembly of thousands of amino acids in a precise sequence. Dr. Stephen Myer calculated that one functioning protein had one chance in 10^{125} power of forming randomly in nature and that there was "no realistic possibility that the 100 proteins necessary for the operating of a simple cell could have come together randomly and begun functioning."

Amino acids, the chemical building blocks of life, have been identified in meteorites and possibly in the dense interstellar clouds where solar systems form. Various research groups have synthesized amino acids in a mix of water, methanol, ammonia, carbon dioxide, etc., in lab environments similar to conditions in space. And of course, the Miller-Urey experiment in 1953 made some tar-like organic material that contained constituents of proteins and nucleic acids. But the noted chemist and evolutionist Dr. Robert Shapiro pointed out that such a mixture of chemicals, even when "enriched in a few amino acids, no more resembles a bacterium than a small pile of real and nonsense words, each written on an individual scrap of paper resembles the complete works of Shakespeare."

Nucleic acids (DNA and RNA) have been compared to computer software in that they store the code that gives directions for amino acids to form proteins. Proteins, in turn, have been called the hardware or building blocks of cells and enzymes (chemical catalysts). As the nucleotides, amino acids and proteins are interdependent and work together; it seems clear that they must have evolved together, in tandem.

In any case, it seems impossible that life processes could ever begin, anywhere, by a chance, random linking of the requisite nucleic acids with amino acids/proteins. When Francis Crick calculated the possibility of the spontaneous origin of a prescribed protein sequence of 200 common amino acids his result was one chance out of 10^{260}. That in itself is a larger number than all the atoms in the universe.

Considering these odds, the creation of life should be considered a scientific (and religious) miracle. Evidently this fact helped influence Sir Fred Hoyle to convert from atheism. When Francis Collins helped discover the faulty gene responsible for cystic fibrosis, he expressed a "sense of awe at uncovering something that God knew."

The confluence of life, together with the nucleotide/protein partnership, would seem to qualify as a miracle, that is "a highly improbable or extraordinary event not explicable by natural or scientific laws and considered divine." It is beyond belief that DNA could link by chance with a random formation of the requisite amino acids to create life. When Fred Hoyle converted from atheism, he said, "the probability of life originating at random is so utterly miniscule as to make the random concept absurd." In more colorful language, he also said that the chance for the spontaneous assembly of life is like a whirlwind sweeping through a junkyard and producing a fully functional Boeing 747.

In the last fifty years, DNA has become a household word and its uses are widely recognized in the fields of genetic disorders, agricultural biotechnology, forensics, cloning and more recently, "systems biology." It is, of course, fundamental to understanding how evolution works, and has also been very helpful in tracing migration patterns of the human race (p. 432–34).

DNA is one of God's most valuable gifts, at the heart of life and entirely compatible with, indeed controlling, evolution. Creationists have unnecessarily suffered a good deal of heartburn by fighting the concept of evolution.

INTELLIGENT DESIGN

The book of the same name, by William Dembski, has provoked a good deal of discussion in the worlds of science, religion, and academia. He is a senior fellow at the Discovery Institute and has defined intelligent design as the process of creating a complex and specified effect by an intelligent being. As an illustration, a long sequence of random letters is complex but not specified. If the letters were organized into a Shakespearean play, they would be both specified and complex. Degrees of complexity could be described further by the improbability of an organism forming by random chance. Biochemist Michael Behe says that the "irreducible complexity" of all interacting components at the molecular level defines intelligent design. Neither of these authors doubts that evolution has occurred—the only claim they make is that the process was designed, rather than beginning by random happenstance.

Intelligent design, as applied to evolution, is the crux of the matter. Our present state of knowledge indicates that life on this planet started some 3.8 billion years ago in the form of simple bacteria, and has evolved into increasingly complex organisms with mankind as the most advanced form. As life began, the genetic control by RNA/DNA and the synthesis of proteins were intimately involved as interdependent factors. Dembski and many other scientists argue that this was the ultimate product of specified complexity—or intelligent design. Skeptics argue with equal passion that all this happened by chance, either on Earth or elsewhere in the universe. They claim that chaos and complexity theory have established the possibility that self-organizing order can appear spontaneously in the interactions of a developing system. Richard Dawkins and Francis Crick, both avowed atheists, have remarked that the design of organisms is only apparent, not real.

Perhaps the order-from-chaos argument could explain some simple inorganic compounds, but hardly the simultaneous appearance of the complex and interdependent trio of DNA, the ordering of amino acids to form proteins, and life. As Dembski argues (his p. 113) an undirected mutation-selection mechanism cannot explain the origin of life, multi-cellular life, the origin of sex, the Cambrian explosion, the development of irreducibly complex molecular structures, and the lack of transitional forms in the fossil record.

It seems to me that with the present state of knowledge, evolution as a scientific theory (including its problems) needs to be taught in public schools. Also, the arguments for intelligent design are reasonable enough to warrant that it be examined as a possible explanation for initiating and/or controlling the process of evolution. Recently, President Bush has taken exactly the same position. It is interesting that the John Templeton Foundation "vigorously disagrees with the intelligent design position" but at the same time argues that university campuses are "precisely the place where important debates…should be aired."

Most people would agree that this is a scientific matter and most certainly should not be ruled on by judges or legislatures. To me, the arguments in preceding paragraphs against random chance first need to be answered. And as argued in the chapter FINAL THOUGHTS (p. 274), this subject could lead to the recognition that God and science are not only compatible but substantively related.

EVOLUTION

Many researchers have estimated the age of the genetic code at 3.8 billion years, to coincide with the earth's first bacterial life. This may have been where life began, including the two crucial factors of metabolism and reproduction. Denton has described the complexity of a single-celled bacterium:

"Although the tiniest bacterial cells are incredibly small, weighing less than 10^{-12} grams, each is in effect a veritable micro-miniaturized factory containing thousands of exquisitely designed pieces of intricate molecular machinery, made up altogether of 100,000 million atoms, far more complicated than any machine built by man and absolutely without parallel in the non-living world....The recently revealed world of molecular machinery, of coding systems, of informational molecules, of catalytic devices and feedback control, is in its design and complexity quite unique to living systems."

When Darwin proposed his theory of evolution in 1859 the idea attracted considerable interest. His explanation of new species rising from incremental improvements due to adaptation of random favorable mutations, seemed logical and fit observations fairly well. Geologists could better understand the fossils found in rocks with ages over a range of at least 500 million years. Biologists also loved the idea and their cataloguing of species took on new interest and directions.

But the theory of evolution caused immediate consternation among many religious leaders who could see a huge discrepancy with the time and years as laid out in the Bible. Darwin's process of natural selection required hundreds to thousands of years (more accurately generations), much more time than allowed by Bishop Ussher's 4004 B.C. date of creation. Ussher's calculation was widely accepted at the time but since then, solid evidence has shown that he was far off the mark.

A heated controversy broke out and has continued to this day with able and passionate proponents on both sides. Darwin himself went through some difficult introspection, motivated to a large extent by his relationship with his wife Emma, whom he loved dearly. Emma was a devout Christian and they agonized over their irreconcilable religious differences during their many years of marriage.

As a youth, Darwin believed the Bible to be the word of God and he very nearly became a clergyman. However, during his time on the *Beagle*, 1831–36, Darwin began to question the literal truth of the Bible. Also contributing to his slow disenchantment with Christianity was his concern about the extent of the misery in the world. But he still seemed to believe in God, commenting in 1860 about the "impossibility of conceiving this immense and wonderful universe, including man with his capacity of looking far backwards and far into futurity, as the result of blind chance or necessity." In 1873 he said he had never been an atheist but might be considered an agnostic. In 1879 he commented again on the immense amount of suffering in the world but said "the impossibility of conceiving of this grand and wondrous universe, with our conscious selves, arose through chance, seems to me to be the chief argument for the existence of God."

With its ability to pass on genetic instructions and preserve advantageous mutations, DNA was the key factor in controlling the evolution of species. Evolution, controlled by DNA, has ultimately resulted in five (or fifty, according to ornithologist Ernst Mayr) billion speciation events. Seemingly a large number, this would average only 1.3 (or thirteen) new species each year but in this case averages are quite misleading. Because of mass extinctions and the rapid recovery from extinctions, plus such things as the Cambrian explosion, we know that the evolution of organisms is characterized by abrupt changes. As the tree of life expanded many species died out; in fact 99 percent of the total became extinct. Additionally, many strange and weird species developed only to die out after an average survival span of 4 million years. One very logical question that agnostics ask is why didn't God just create the final versions of the different species, in perfect form, instead of by trial and error, and why all the dead ends?

Sir Francis Crick, co-discoverer of the DNA molecule, is one of the prominent scientists who believe simple, early life forms originated in outer space and then reached Earth. This idea is called "directed panspermia" but clearly it does nothing to help explain the origin of life. It only compounds the problem by, first, requiring an explanation of how life could begin in the harsh and unlikely environment of outer space, and then adding the requirement of explaining how life could survive the transfer to Earth.

The oldest fossils found on Earth are curious cushion-shaped mounds called stromatolites, 3.5 billion years old. The stromatolites, in Western Australia, are formed by primitive bacteria that deposit layered mats of mineral grains. These bacteria are single-celled microorganisms lacking a nucleus. They reproduce simply by dividing and are not in the same evolutionary line as the living fossil microbe *Methanococcus jannaschii*, which survives in an extremely harsh physical environment. *M. jannaschii* has 1682 genes in its DNA and seems to be locked into its original evolutionary niche (p. 484). By analogy, the microbe can be traced back to an ancestral Eucarya (cell with a nucleus) having only two million base pairs of DNA, perhaps as early as 3 billion years ago, that led to plants, animals, and eventually, man.

To this time, authenticated examples of DNA date back only about 70,000 years for animals and 400,000 years for plants. It is believed that radioactivity will destroy any DNA older than 500,000 to one million years. Hence, DNA reported from 1.8 million year-old hominids is considered questionable, and ribosomal RNA (rRNA) sequenced from bacteria in 425 million-year-old salt crystals is very controversial.

By 2 billion years ago, according to Sagan, sex helped to speed up the process of evolution. Before then, new species could arise only from random mutations, an agonizingly slow process. But sex allowed two organisms to exchange great batches of their genetic code, speeding up evolution dramatically. Species that found sex uninteresting soon became extinct. The successful ones took up the new habit enthusiastically.

By about 600 million years ago, a few primitive bilateral microbes, and soft-bodied but large (to a few feet) Ediacaran animals left their enigmatic traces on the sea floor. But beginning 530 million years ago and continuing for ten million years, the "Cambrian explosion" (p. 382–383) created the most astonishing episode in the fossil record. Millions of fossils representing at least thirty new phyla of advanced animal forms were found in the Burgess shale of British Columbia. Trilobites were the most numerous and their 15,000 species dominated marine animal life for the next 300 million years. Paleontologists recognized the explosion as enormously important but the cause is still obscure; certainly the introduction of hard parts that could be preserved as fossils has to be part of the explanation.

During the 500 million years following the Cambrian Period (from Cambria, the medieval Latin name for Wales, where Cambrian rocks are well exposed and first described), animals and plants evolved much as Darwin explained. It is estimated that a total of five billion species developed, with 3 to 100 million living at this time. Over 99 percent of all species have become extinct, mostly because they failed to adjust to changing conditions, usually climatic. During this same time many weird creatures developed, evidently to fill some niche in the environment (p. 429-32). Strange plants and animals evolved and then faded out after reaching a dead end. Some land animals even returned to the sea (p. 435-42). The evidence leads a reasonable observer to wonder about the apparent inefficiency of the process and absence of a master plan.

[A reasonable argument could be made that the genetic system was jiggered a few times to develop sea life 600 million years ago (ma), fish 450 ma, seed plants and fruit trees 210 ma, fowl 150 ma, cattle 60 ma, whales 53 ma, etc. (more or less the order of life specified in Genesis).]

It has also been noted that evolution seems to follow an episodic, stepwise pattern, called "punctuated equilibria" by paleontologist Stephen Jay Gould. This phenomenon, if real, might be explained by various environmental influences such as changes in climate or sea level, asteroid impacts, wobble in the Earth's axis of rotation, magnetic reversals, etc.

The preponderance of evidence points to a date of five to six million years ago for the divergence of hominids (man-like creatures) from the chimpanzee line. The idea of a chimp relationship offends some people but as early as 1950, Pope Pius XII in his encyclical *Humani Generis*, stated that evolution of the human body was an acceptable doctrine so long as divine infusion of human souls was recognized also. Nearly fifty years later, Pope John Paul II, in his document "Truth Cannot Contradict Truth" stated that accumulated evidence showed that evolution could no longer be doubted by people of intellect and goodwill. In his words, an "ontological discontinuity" during primate evolution led to humankind.

Fossils of some of the first humans were found at Olduvai Gorge by the Leakeys in 1959. *Homo habilis* was dated at 2.6 million years and other finds showed that ancestors of mankind seem to have evolved along the Rift Valley in East Africa. *Homo erectus* was the first to migrate out of Africa and in a second attempt eventually evolved to *H. sapiens neanderthalensis*, who became extinct in Europe about 30,000 years ago.

H. sapiens sapiens evolved about 195,000 to 150,000 years ago (ya), in East Africa. They comprised the third migration out of Africa about 100,000 ya. About the same time or a little later, speech developed, together with the astounding design of the human brain. With 500 trillion connections, it is the "most complicated arrangement of matter known to man."

About 40,000 ya, Cro-Magnon man brought a new level of culture to ancient Europe in the form of advanced tools and artistic skills. These new skills, together with a rapid growth in population, led different authors to call it the "Great Leap Forward." Especially impressive is the fact that it occurred during a period of severe climatic conditions in the middle of the last glacial phase (Würm in Europe, Wisconsin in North America) of the Pleistocene Ice Age. The rapidly changing climates certainly affected the migration patterns, if not the survival of mankind, and one suspects evolutionary effects were involved.

But if there was a cultural explosion it came with the end of the last glaciation, and beginning of interglacial warming. Worldwide warming (about 16°F to this time) began about 15,000 ya. During this time, several important civilizations rose and flourished. Writing was developed, all the major religions were revealed, and technology opened amazing vistas. In fact, a strong argument could be made that perhaps 99 percent of mankind's progress (and failings) have come about in the current interglacial warming, beginning about 15,000 years ago.

MAN'S BRAIN

Science in general seems to be making advances at an ever-increasing pace and Barbour (1997, p. 277) has made a similar observation about the acceleration of the evolution of mankind. He says, "...the pace of biological evolution has increased as higher levels of complexity are achieved. Our genes represent the cumulative legacy of a long history of interaction of organisms and environments, stretching back to the dawn of life. The past is built into the present, and it shapes the future, providing the starting point for further evolutionary change but not determining it. Human nature is not static or complete, and there is no reason to think that we are the end of the line." Where mankind is concerned, evolutionary complexity derives mostly from brain development.

People have called the three-pound human brain "marvelous and mysterious" and have said it is "the most complex and orderly arrangement of matter in the universe." The brain operates at teraflop speed (trillions of floating point operations per second) and has been likened to a supercomputer. The human brain includes about 100 billion specialized nerve cells called neurons. Each neuron has an axon that transmits information, across a gap or synapse, to a target cell called a dendrite that may have thousands of connections. The information, in the form of an electrical signal, is converted to a chemical message (modulated up to 100 times) across the synapse, then back to an electrical pulse. Thus there are about 500 trillion connections in the human brain. Compared to a computer, the human brain is much more powerful, millions of times more energy-efficient, and far more compact.

Intelligence can be roughly correlated with brain size. The chapter MANKIND shows that the human brain has increased in size from 600 cc to 1350 cc over a period of 2.6 million years (p. 434). More protein (meat) in the diet is believed to be the main reason for this increase. Recent support for this comes from Dr. Stedman, at the University of Pennsylvania, who found a genetic change in jaw muscles of early man, leading to smaller jaw structure, along with the changing diet, beginning about 2.4 million ya.

Some of the animals appearing during the Cambrian explosion 530 million ya may have had the first, tiny brains, employed mostly for seeking food and avoiding predators. But even the most primitive bacteria, 3.8 billion ya, probably could react instinctively, in sync with a myriad of other individuals. Hence, the bacteria could be considered "sentient" or capable of being aware of their environment.

More importantly, bacteria had the earliest nucleic acid, able to pass on genetic information to succeeding generations. Early, primitive microbes had only a few hundred or so genes, whereas the genome of modern man has about 20–25,000. A given gene from an early ancestor can show up in a modern descendant as an exact copy, just as a molecule of water today is the same as a water molecule 3 billion years ago.

As different organisms developed during the process of evolution, an interesting phenomenon appeared. Whereas bacteria had no "junk" DNA, modern man's DNA is about 98 percent junk, that is, non-coding for genes. Ridley calls this "selfish DNA" because it is only good for replicating itself, serving no useful purpose in building protein. The most common of-fender, called LINE-1, makes up nearly 15 percent of the human genome. As mentioned earlier, scientists are beginning to find that some of the junk has epigenetic properties that affect health, growth and brain development. A great deal of good research is being done to understand how different parts of the brain control perception, memory, thought, emotions, reason-ing, etc. In short, overall behavior. Good work is also being done concern-ing therapeutic measures and implants. Genetic differences in people with behavioral problems are another area of intense interest. To date, and in general, it appears that about half the difference between individuals is genetic, and the other half is due to epigenetic or environmental factors.

Because the brain and the body are part of the same system, outside factors such as stress, or even the possibility of stress, can turn on a gene that controls the hormone cortisol. Cortisol alters the configuration of the brain, interferes with the immune system, changes the sensitivity of ears, nose and eyes, and affects various bodily functions. On the other hand, a smile can trigger activity in the "happiness center" of the brain, and a happy thought can cause a smile.

A study of 17,000 civil servants in England found that heart disease could be correlated more closely with their levels of stress than with obesity, smoking or high blood pressure. Genes were found that influence personal-ity, intelligence, learning and memory. Characteristics that were inheritable seemed to affect such things as crime, divorce, obesity and trouble-mak-ing. Ridley stated that "genes do influence behavior" and concluded with the statement that each person has "a whole human nature, flexibly preor-dained in our chromosomes and idiosyncratic to each of us. Everybody has a unique and different, endogenous nature. A self."

Classic Darwinian evolution called for survival and reproduction as the main goal of any species. Ever since the genetic purpose of DNA was recognized, modern scientists such as Dawkins (1995, p. 105) word it a little differently, "the true utility function of life, that which is being maximized in the natural world, is DNA survival" and (p. 19) "Darwinism is now seen to be the survival of the survivors at the level of pure, digital code." The founder of sociobiology, Edward O. Wilson, said "The organism is only DNA's way of making more DNA."

Matt Ridley has written a number of fascinating books about genes. His narratives are cleverly done and he does an admirable job of passing on huge amounts of good information in an interesting, readable style. In his 1999 book *Genome* he uses man's twenty-three chromosomes as the inspiration for each chapter, describing numerous examples of how genes control certain diseases and influence certain human behavior.

Ridley concluded his book *Genome* with the carefully worded statement that each person has "a whole human nature" and a unique and different "self." This pretty well defines "soul" and perhaps he planned to discuss that subject in follow-up books. But in *Genome* the word soul does not appear. I noticed that Dawkins did the same thing in his *River Out of Eden*. He wound up that book with a summary of ten thresholds of replication, nicely following mankind's progress. He showed brain development being followed by human awareness, then speech, and next cooperative technology that he called Threshold 8. When he mentioned human culture and selfish genes it looked like a good chance to discuss the meaning of soul. But he did not mention the word and one could conclude that these two atheists could not bring themselves to say the word because it could have religious implications.

SOUL

From my Oxford dictionary the definition of soul involves the following: individual—a person's moral or emotional nature or sense of identity—essence—emotional or intellectual energy or intensity—spiritual or immaterial part of a human being. In other words, the soul of an individual comprises the intellect, mind and will, together with the senses which control emotions. The soul is the site of a person's personality and self-awareness. With free will, an individual may choose to be lazy or energetic, responsible or irresponsible, honest or dishonest, etc. Humans are the only life form to have a soul, and Dr. Robert Schuller argues that the human brain is "hard-wired" to the soul, leading to religious faith.

Thoughts and behavior certainly define the moral character of an individual. Components of a person's character are included in the following alphabetical list of positive attributes, or virtues—many people would put love first in the order of importance. The second list is of personal vices or sins, which lead to evil.

List 1. Virtues: aesthetic, altruistic, care-giving, charitable, chaste, civil, compassionate, conscientious, constructive, cooperative, ethical, fair, <u>faithful</u>, forgiving, friendly, generous, <u>gentle</u>, <u>good</u>, happy, helpful, honest, hopeful, humble, <u>joyful</u>, just, kind, <u>longsuffering</u>, loving, meek, merciful, moral, open-minded, optimistic, patient, <u>peaceful</u>, pure, quiet, reasonable, reliable, repentant, respectful, <u>righteous</u>, sacrificial, sharing, supportive, sympathetic, temperate, thoughtful, tolerant, trustful, truthful, wise. (Underlined virtues are called "fruit of the Spirit" in Gal. 5:22, Eph.5:9 and 1 Pet 3:4).

List 2. Vices: adulterous, angry, arrogant, <u>avaricious</u>, blasphemous, blood-thirsty, contemptuous, corrupt, covetous, cruel, dishonest, disorderly, dogmatic, drunken, egoistic, <u>envious</u>, gloomy, <u>gluttonous</u>, greedy, hateful, hostile, idolatrous, insulting, intimidating, intolerant, jealous, lawless, licentious, <u>lustful</u>, lying, murderous, oppressive, over-bearing, pessimistic, prejudiced, <u>proud</u>, ruthless, selfish, self-righteous, <u>slothful</u>, stubborn, superior, vain, vindictive, violent, wicked, <u>wrathful</u> (the underlined vices are called the seven capital sins).

A third list, below, includes certain human behavior that could lead to virtue or sin, depending on the intent of the individual. For example, a Hitler could show flashes of courage, and knowledge, together with responsibility for social order—but consumed with anger, arrogance, cruelty, dogmatism, enmity, envy, hate, intolerance, jealousy, prejudice, self-righteousness and vindictiveness—brings on the Holocaust.

List 3. Depending on intent then, the following characteristics can be supportive of either virtue or vice: active, contemplative, courageous, creative, heroic, learned, obedient, obsessive, perceptive, self-aware, self-controlled, skillful, strong, and willful.

DeChardin believed that the introduction of evil was a certainty in the process of evolution over time. He called it a statistically inevitable by-product of the creation of man and his "endless stream of transgressions." Original sin, then, would consist of a pattern of behavior rather than a single act, and be controlled by the "negative forces" or what I would interpret to mean some of the vices in list 2 above.

Some of the preceding paragraphs showed that behavior can sometimes be related to genetic effects and that remedial effort could be helpful. This tempts one to ask the obvious question: is there such a thing as "good" or "bad" DNA influencing behavior, and even more interesting, could some properties of junk or selfish DNA be helpful? When Matt Ridley made his irreverent remark about a "soul gene" he might have been more perceptive than he realized.

Knowledge about the evolution of the soul and related genetic influences are obvious goals to be pursued by biologists, archaeologists and theologians. In 2003, James Watson, co-discoverer of the double helix, had the same thing in mind when he suggested that a young, beginning researcher might be well advised to work on the relationship between genes and human behavior. From that advice, it is not too hard to think in terms of components of the soul and how they are stored and manipulated in certain genes in the brain. This might involve some mysterious and yet-to-be discovered form of energy flitting through the axons, synapses and dendrites in the human brain.

Although Moore's Law concerns doubling of processor speed every eighteen months, the current generation of genome data shows an eight-fold increase in an eighteen-month time frame. Leading this effort is Virginia Tech's VBI or Virginia Bioinformatics Institute where the technology is concerned with the evolutionary genetics of organisms and the genetic basis of human, animal, and plant diseases.

Understanding that genes can affect human behavior, the *sine qua non* of the soul, an obvious question is; when did the negative forces of list 2 infect the human genome? And did the virtues of list 1 appear at the same time? DeChardin hinted at the idea that virtues may have come later to man as he "attained a sort of fullness of his consciousness and responsibility."

Pope Pius XII stated that the divine infusion of souls was the critical factor in human evolution. The initial appearance of virtue and vice—components of the soul—could have come at several possible points in the history of mankind. The earliest (archaeological) time could have been (1) 2.6 million years ago with the advent of *Homo habilis*, but certainly not what Paul had in mind in 1 Corinthians 15:45 when he said "....The first man Adam was made a living soul" (2) 100,000 years ago, as *Homo sapiens sapiens* migrated out of Africa and developed the power of speech at about the same time (3) 40,000–75,000 years ago as evidenced by the advanced tools and artistic skills of early Cro-Magnon man, and his burial habits suggesting preparation for an afterlife (4) 15,000 years ago at the beginning of the most recent interglacial warming and the widespread migration of different tribes and races (5) 10–11,000 years ago, which saw multiple advances including organized farming, writing, and the earliest civilizations. Or has been suggested, perhaps the soul evolved as mankind evolved.

Schroeder (p.108-110) believed "Adam may have been the first hominid with a divinely created human soul" the *neshama*, or free will; this would have been about 3754 B.C., calculated from generations in the Old Testament. He argued that God imbued Adam with the first human soul, instantaneously, at the age of twenty (when Jewish men become divinely responsible for their actions). He also firmly stated that animals have no souls—and neither did Neanderthal or Cro-Magnon man.

Uncertainty also exists about the question of just when an individual develops a soul. [In my informal survey, respondents agreed that a soul is the "spiritual principle in man," animates every human body, and is immortal (survives death). But when asked if the soul was imbued (1) at conception (2) at birth or (3) at another time, the same people split evenly on these questions.]

Dr. David Barash, a professor of psychology at the University of Washington has made some pertinent ontogenic observations. He pointed out that during the time of gestation, a human fetus gradually develops a brain and then a mind, when the "brain cells aggregate and start whispering electrochemically to each other, whereupon a mind gradually coalesces" sometime before birth. The soul "presumably pops into existence at some point" after the mind is operative.

All of the main religions have considered the human soul as the center of an individual's mind, will and character. They all agree that life is a continual struggle between the virtues and vice evidenced in everyone's behavior and/or thoughts. Even agnostics and atheists seem to be uncertain and Barna Research (November 11, 2003) reports that half of them think that every person has a soul, that there is a life after death, and that heaven and hell exist. Each religion represents a compilation of time-tested wisdom concerned with the salvation or deliverance of the soul. Most religions, but not all, teach how to save souls by obeying a wise, eternal, sole Creator of the universe. The guidelines for proper behavior are provided by a set of moral values, usually reinforced by specified rituals.

Islam espouses a firm faith in, and worship of, one God (Allah), by devout believers whose mission is to build a just and benevolent social order. Through a lifetime of daily effort, correct choices, and purity of heart, faith in Allah can lead to salvation. Suffering during life is only a trial of each human soul; with good deeds, avoidance of evil and trust in Allah, the individual soul passes into the next world. The souls of worthy believers will eventually enjoy eternal Paradise but those of sinners will experience eternal hellfire.

Jewish, Christian and Muslim doctrine each holds that choices made during one's life will determine their afterlife—either belonging with God in some comfortable situation or being removed from God and in a very unhappy status. The Buddhist and Hindu traditions consider that all suffering is deserved, and that the soul reappears in a cycle of rebirths (is reincarnated) in appropriate human or animal forms according to previous behavior. Aristotle had a somewhat similar idea in that upon death, the soul of an individual returned to a "collective force."

In the Old Testament the soul or "animating principle" is mentioned in 395 verses, according to the folks at Blue Letter Bible. The Jewish scriptures often referred to men as "souls" comprising the intellect, individuality, personality and behavior. The covenant between God and his "chosen people" was a central theme of Judaism. Writers of the Old Testament chapters were mainly concerned with describing and shaping Israel's faith and practices, i.e., the character of the Jewish community. A central belief was a God of power and justice who would punish wrongdoers. Mankind was made in God's image and considered as a unique species in having a soul. According to Schroeder, Adam was the first man to have a soul, and Catholic theology holds that the creation of Adam's soul was an actual historical event.

The "Spirit of God" and "Spirit of the Lord" are frequently used in the Old Testament to describe God's influence on the human soul. Jews were continually admonished to follow God's laws and conform to the covenant in order to have eternal life rather than death. This idea of God's spirit being actively involved in development of the human soul is touched on 469 times in the Jewish scriptures. Death of the soul could result from deliberately breaking the commandments, or the covenants, that deal with such factors as idol worship, circumcision, preparation of food, eating pork, breaking the Sabbath, breaking a vow, etc. Sin through ignorance could be assuaged through a penance or offering. A key functional role of Judaism (as in most other religions) was in establishing and preserving a social order based on moral values.

In the New Testament, and especially by Paul, much emphasis is given to recognizing the Spirit, or God's influence on the soul. In Hebrews 4:12, the word of God "divides asunder the soul and spirit"; in Galatians 3:14 "...that we might receive the promise of the Spirit through faith." Facing death, Jesus cried "…Father, into thy hands I commend my spirit…" (Lk 23:46), and Stephen did the same when he was stoned "…Lord Jesus, receive my spirit." (Acts 7:59). The premise here is that one's Spirit, if accepted by God, leads to "eternal life." This term for personal salvation is used fifty times in the New Testament.

The Jesuit paleontologist Teilhard de Chardin believed that evolution of the human soul is not directed according to a pre-existing plan. Rather, he argued that it is destined to reach the "Omega point" a yet-to-be-achieved final stage, representing communion with God, where science and religious spirit coincide.

The Catholic catechism states that (1) every spiritual soul is created immediately by God (not by the parents) (2) is immortal (3) does not perish upon death (4) will be reunited with the body at the final Resurrection. To a scientist, the mechanics of all this is hard to understand—unless put into more familiar terms.

Reuniting a soul with a dead body needs some form of quantum physics, where all quanta are retrievable. This would require reassembling a body atom by atom, but would be relatively simple compared to retrieving information from a black hole. Mind-boggling quantum possibilities include "spooky" behavior, properly called "entanglement," wherein remote particles act in unison though physically widely apart. This property of quantum physics, known for seventy years, confounded Einstein.

To deal with the spiritual soul, the Church has cleverly devised the concept of a holding place (Purgatory) where souls reside until the time of the Last Judgment, when properly spiritual souls will be reunited with their respective resurrected bodies.

Islam has similar theology wherein souls return to their physical bodies for the Day of Judgment. Pious individuals with a history of only good deeds will go directly to Paradise to enjoy eternal blessings beyond imagination. Evil-doers go directly to hellfire for eternity, or until their sins have been purged. Most people will go to hellfire for a period of time, until redemption, which can be accelerated by the intercession of the prophets and their successors.

Seeking togetherness with one's own kind seems to be a trait strongly developed during the evolution of all organisms. In its earliest forms, masses of bacteria and blooms of algae probably acted instinctively in reacting to stimuli and seeking favorable environments. Later, schools of fish, flocks of birds, herds of antelope and troops of chimpanzees sought food and protection as a group, and some of the higher mammals began to display affection between mates. This eventually was followed by mankind's families, clans, tribes, nations and empires.

Religion holds societies together and is the major force in fostering morality, altruism and social stability. Adopting a particular religious faith often means joining a community of believers and a social group. This can lead to a sense of comfort and protection as a member of a group but in a negative sense may encourage exclusivity.

Some of the most contented groups of people can be observed in religious events such as Jewish Bar Mitzvahs or the mass prayers of Muslims. In my own case, singing some old favorite hymns in a congregational setting provides a feeling of peace and satisfaction. Our little congregation (497 members, including children) currently holds about 1500 services, classes, meetings and social events per year. This probably is representative of other churches and shows the desire of people with similar interests to meet together for constructive purposes.

LIKELY CHALLENGES TO MANKIND

Under this heading, the purpose is not to discuss the perennial but mostly localized problems of war, terrorism, earthquakes, floods, drought, etc. Rather, an attempt will be made to put in perspective three of the threats to mankind that could have worldwide effects, including massive extinctions. Each of these three is certain to occur at some time in the future. The three threats are: climate changes, asteroid impacts, and magnetic reversals.

Several mass extinctions have occurred when abrupt calamities wiped out many species simultaneously. In these disasters, an average of 38–58 percent of the living genera was destroyed. For example, two hundred fifty million years ago in the Permian, 80 percent of all genera and 96 percent of all species were lost, and 65 million years ago the K-T event eliminated 80 percent of all plants and animals. Both these disasters were exacerbated by great volcanic eruptions that affected worldwide climate.

Climate Change

Long before Mark Twain commented on it, mankind was concerned about the weather, and for good reason. The last glacial phase of the Ice Age no doubt caused great physical difficulty for early *Homo sapiens* and affected worldwide migration patterns. During the past 10,000 years, several civilizations were overcome by long-term drought conditions.

A new polar ice cap formed during worldwide cooling that began 2.5 million years ago, culminating in the Pleistocene Ice Age 1.6 million years ago. During the Pleistocene, enormous glaciers, up to two miles thick, covered much of the polar portions of the northern and southern hemispheres. Thirty three percent of the total land area of the world was covered with ice (versus ten percent now). So much water was locked up as ice that ocean levels were 400–450 feet lower than today (p. 364).

During the Ice Age, at least fifteen glacial cycles have occurred, on average every 100,000 years. The cold, glacial periods in these cycles average 80,000 years in length, and the warm or interglacial periods average 20,000 years. This 100,000-year cycle can logically be related to changes in the earth's orbit relative to the sun; the ellipticity of the orbit has a periodicity of about 100,000 years.

Presently, we are some 15,000 years into the most recent interglacial period which, statistically, should last another 5000 years. Overall warming in the last 15,000 years is about 16°F. The latest warming is comparable to the warming in previous interglacials, as is the change in sea level. Furthermore, previous interglacials have seen increases in CO_2 comparable to the increase we see today. In fact, in the last nine glacial cycles of the Pleistocene, the atmospheric CO_2 content during the interglacials was about double that during the glaciations. Another sobering fact is that CO_2 increases lagged temperature increases by 400–600 years and did not cause them. Some scientists have explained this relationship as entirely natural, i.e., lowered solubility of CO_2 in warmer ocean water. If the statistical averages hold, we could see a further warming of about 3°F in the next 5000 years.and then a return to glacial conditions (19°F colder).

But according to many environmentalists, academics and others, global warming caused by the greenhouse effect of man-made CO_2 is the main danger to be feared in the near future. They point to the increase from 290 ppm to 360 ppm CO_2 in the atmosphere during the last 200 years (Industrial Age). Although only 3 percent of atmospheric CO_2 is due to man-made emissions, some drastic actions have been proposed, e.g. the Kyoto approach. This would have enormous economic costs but the decrease in atmospheric CO_2 would be trivial. In the face of intense pressure, President Bush has resisted Kyoto as ineffective and unfair; instead, he has promoted technological changes helped by market-place economics.

In summary, the earth is presently enjoying "global warming" as the natural result of interglacial warming that began about 15,000 years ago. If the natural cycles continue, as they have more than ten times in the past million years, we should reach the peak of the warming in a few hundred years and then return to the next glacial stage. Another 3°F of warming could be expected which in general will have beneficial effects for mankind.

For example, during the last 15,000 years, in the current interglacial warming, it could be argued that *H. sapiens* has made 99 percent of all the cultural and technological progress during our total history of 150,000 years.

Asteroid Impacts. Although such impacts on Earth are rare in geologic terms, they have occurred in the past and will happen again in the future. Over 150 impact craters are known on the earth's surface and numerous craters are recorded in rocks from earlier geologic time.

Asteroids orbit the sun in a broad band called the Asteroid or Main Belt that exists between Mars and Jupiter. The Asteroid Belt includes millions of rocky bodies having rounded but odd shapes, and over a million of them are larger than a kilometer in size. They are composed of rock, iron, and ice, and are believed to be leftover fragments from the formation of the solar system. They each rotate and take three to six years to orbit the sun. Circular or elliptical orbits have been calculated for 7000 of the larger asteroids. Some asteroids move as a group that can include up to 1000 individual rock bodies.

Some asteroids stray into and others orbit within the inner solar system, crossing the path of Earth. In early 2001, NASA scientists reported there were 500 to 1000 asteroids larger than a kilometer in diameter in the "immediate neighborhood" of Earth. Even more disturbing is the knowledge that many others are as yet undetected; in 1989 a surprise asteroid came within 414,000 miles of Earth and in 1994, also undetected, XL1 passed within 65,000 miles. In 2004 an asteroid named 2004 MN4 was discovered which will miss Earth by only 15,000 to 25,000 miles on April 13, 2029. The rock body is only 1000 feet wide, but would have an impact equivalent to 10,000 megatons of dynamite, more than all the combined nuclear weapons in the world.

Even relatively small asteroids such as 2004 MN4 could cause massive damage to life forms, including mankind. If an asteroid this size collided with Earth it could destroy an area the size of Texas, or cause catastrophic tsunamis in the ocean. An impacting asteroid only four miles in diameter would mean long-term climate change and mass extinction of species. NASA has recognized the danger and in 1996 launched the NEAR-Shoemaker spacecraft to begin surveillance of asteroids that might approach

Earth's orbit. The NEAR craft enjoyed great success in 2001 when it landed on the Eros asteroid, 196 million miles away. Eros is some eight miles wide and twenty-one miles long.

Sixty-five million years ago, an asteroid about the size of Eros struck the earth offshore, near the Yucatan Peninsula, forming a 120-mile crater on the seafloor. As the asteroid entered the earth's atmosphere, part of the rock body broke off and hit near Manson, Iowa but the main part impacted in Mexico. The magnitude of the fireball explosion was 100 million megatons, (about 7 billion Hiroshima-sized atomic bombs). Huge tsunami waves up to a mile high traveled around the globe seven times. All life, including microbes, within 300 miles of the impact was instantly incinerated. Fires erupted as far away as Texas and Central America, and half the forests in the world were burned. Earthquakes were triggered around the globe. In addition, the shock waves triggered another huge flow of lava from the Deccan Traps in proto-India. Most of the damage to life forms resulted from a virtual blackout of the sun, due to the amount of smoke, soot, ash, dust, and debris that filled the air. Photosynthesis ceased and worldwide temperatures fell drastically, disrupting the food chains of most species. This lasted for nine months and resulted in the mass extinction of plants and animals including the dinosaurs and ammonites. Altogether, 80 percent of all plants and animals became extinct. This event ended the Cretaceous Period and Mesozoic Era.

Statistically, the chance of an asteroid impact is very small and no cause for alarm. NASA's NEAR-Shoemaker spacecraft is a good first step and additional surveillance may be expected to give adequate warning of a threatening asteroid. The reality, however, is that no defense exists at present, despite Hollywood imagination.

Magnetic Reversal
Earth acts as a huge magnet and has a magnetic field that makes compasses point north. Other than helping in navigation the magnetosphere surrounding the earth serves to help protect life forms from the effects of the sun. The Outer Van Allen belt extends 31,000 miles into space and intercepts lethal high-energy particles (ultraviolet and X-rays) from the sun. The solar wind, traveling at one million miles per hour, impacts and distorts the magnetosphere, compacting it on the sun-side of the earth. Some of the charged particles from the sun are channeled toward the north and south magnetic poles where they collide violently with gas atoms giving off spectacular light displays (e.g. Northern Lights).

The sun is a mighty engine and a typical solar flare flings into space lethal high-energy particles, releasing the energy equivalent of a billion hydrogen bombs. Normally, the magnetosphere and atmosphere of Earth are enough to deflect and neutralize the dangerous rays. But if the magnetosphere were to be disrupted in some way, the effects on life could be devastating.

Sooner or later the magnetosphere is bound to be disrupted by a reversal of the earth's magnetic field. This phenomenon has occurred hundreds of times in the past 500 million years. For some reason, internal currents in the earth have flipped the magnetic field—North Pole for South Pole and south for north—on average every 500,000 years. The most recent reversal was 780,000 years ago, so our odds become worse every year (p. 357–358).

We can only speculate about what the harmful results of a magnetic reversal might be. Certainly migrating birds might be confused but the real, harmful effects would result from the unimpeded high-energy rays of the solar wind. It would be logical to expect genetic effects but there seems to be no obvious correlation of the past extinction of major species with magnetic reversals. Even the time it would take for a reversal is uncertain. Some scientists have estimated it might take 1200 years; others make an equally valid guess that it might happen overnight.

In the upper part of Earth's atmosphere—the stratosphere—thirty miles high, ozone is not abundant but serves to filter out lower-energy ultraviolet radiation. Ozone or O_3 is a form of oxygen in which each molecule has three atoms instead of two. At ground level it is component of smog, and a nuisance. But in the stratosphere it is beneficial, in fact critically so. When an ultraviolet ray strikes an O_3 molecule, the latter is broken into O_2, atomic oxygen or O, and heat. The O soon recombines with O_2 to reform O_3. This process of controlling ultraviolet radiation is called ozone photodissociation and recombination.

Beneficial ozone's deadly enemy is chlorofluorocarbon, or CFC, developed in the early 1930s as a refrigerant. One pound of CFC can destroy 70,000 pounds of atmospheric ozone. A CFC molecule is 10,000 more times effective than CO_2 as a greenhouse gas agent—and the CFC can persist for one hundred years—so the recent outlawing of the use of CFC was quite timely.

GOD'S ATTRIBUTES

This summary has served to demonstrate how God has revealed his role in science, especially in terms of the Big Bang and creation of life. But also, it seems he is a hands-off God, content to provide physical laws to control creation and evolution but not inclined to shield mankind from natural disasters (as examples above) nor manmade mistakes. According to science, then, God

- Is all-powerful, with incomprehensible wisdom and vision
- Created the universe in a way suggestive of the Big Bang
- Established physical law and order in the universe
- Introduced life forms and evolution on Earth using the mechanism of DNA
- Guided evolution of Homo sapiens sapiens 195,000 to 150,000 years ago
- Imbued mankind with speech, a superior brain, a soul, and a spirit
- To a surprising degree, exhibited a hands-off approach during the process of evolution, and man's misfortunes.

The "hands off" statement may be disconcerting to many people but it seems to be demonstrated over and over. For example, once DNA had been created, evolution proceeded in a very inefficient way with many strange and weird species leading to dead ends and extinction—less than one percent of the total number of species has survived. Mass extinctions wiped out whole populations with only a few genera surviving.

In historical times, mankind has suffered equally, facing decimation by natural disasters such as earthquakes, floods, volcanoes, pestilence and famine. Self-inflicted pain and suffering have occurred during war and smaller scale fighting, which seem to be never-ending. Up to 25 percent of all men were killed in wars during early-recorded time, and more recently, weapons of mass destruction have killed millions, including non-combatants. For political purposes, evil men have inflicted torture, starvation, imprisonment and death. In the face of such things as the Holocaust, some people (including Einstein) have turned away from religion, saying in anguish, "there can be no God." The carnage continues; 1.6 million people met violent death in 2000, and this may be an average annual total.

The most logical explanation is that God has given mankind an orderly and beautiful world, subject to physical law and order. The evolution of man has been crowned with an incredibly complex brain and the infusion of a soul and spirit. Part of the package is that man is free to make, and is responsible for, his own mistakes. In other words, a kind of "tough love."

4

SCIENTISTS AND GOD

The previous chapter concluded that God's control was most evident in three situations:

- Creation of the universe in a way suggestive of the Big Bang.
- Introduction of life and evolution on an anthropic Earth, using the mechanism of DNA.
- The infusion of man's soul and spirit

Some writers have tried to disparage the first two points as a "God of the Gaps" explanation, i.e., subjects of temporary scientific ignorance that eventually will become known...but, I wonder. It seems unlikely that there will ever be scientific proof that purely natural, random processes are responsible for either point because neither event can be duplicated or tested through controlled experiments in the laboratory. Hence, in scientific terms, both propositions, assuming natural processes, are only theories and cannot be proven to be factual. Furthermore, it is precisely in consideration of these two phenomena that many prominent scientists have commented on their sense of awe and wonder, and their thoughts about God.

CREATION OF THE UNIVERSE

First, consider the Big Bang theory. Cosmologists invoke this idea to explain that space and time began, and the universe originates from the explosion of an infinitely dense singularity or black hole about 13.7 billion years ago. Hawking says "the actual point of creation lies outside the scope of presently known laws of physics." Physicists are able to create particles of matter by concentrating energy using large accelerators, but that raises the question of the source of the original energy.

It seems clear that at the instant of the Big Bang, a perfectly calibrated and orderly set of natural laws and constants came into being. The fundamental rules of nature were incredibly fine-tuned and are almost certainly applicable throughout our galaxy, if not the universe. These laws of physics and chemistry are vitally important to all forms of life, and seem to have been designed to make Earth suitable for mankind to evolve and thrive. This argument is called the "anthropic principle" and was proposed by Cambridge physicist Brandon Carter in 1974.

Albert Einstein (1879–1955) was uniquely qualified to comment on the nature of the universe. In a 1952 letter to Maurice Solovine he said "...one should expect a chaotic world... (but there is)...an order...of a high degree which one...has no right to expect. That is the 'miracle' which grows increasingly persuasive with the increasing development of our knowledge." Other quotations from Einstein include "If something is in me which can be called religious then it is the unbounded admiration for the structure of the world as far as our science can reveal it." Also, "It is hard to sneak a look at God's cards. But that he would choose to play dice with the world...is something that I cannot believe for a single moment," "The Lord is subtle, but malicious he is not," and "Religion without science is blind. Science without religion is lame." Although Einstein in his later years admitted "the presence of a superior reasoning power" he never did accept the reality of a personal God. Einstein was also active politically, first as an antiwar advocate and later, because of Hitler, became a strong Zionist.

Stephen W. Hawking (1942 –?) is considered the most brilliant theoretical physicist since Einstein. His book *A Brief History of Time* has sold over 5.5 million copies, a record number in the history of science writing. The book sold so well because he made it readable to the average person, despite the esoteric subject matter involving black holes, boundary conditions and quantum mechanics. His achievements are astounding, when the facts of his personal life are considered. His mother was a member of the Communist party in England in the 1930s and he carried that baggage for the rest of his life. In 1963 he was diagnosed with ALS (Lou Gehrig's disease) and given only two years to live (that was forty-three years ago). About the same time he met his future wife, Jane Wilde, and it is widely acknowledged that she gave him the inspiration and desire to live that had much to do with his success. She was a strong Christian and influenced his writing. Hawking mentions God throughout his book; on page 127 "It would be very difficult to explain why the universe should have begun in just this way, except as the act of a God who intended to create beings like us." In his conclusion he asks why the universe exists and believes that when that question can be answered, the ultimate triumph of human reason will be to "know the mind of God."

Sir Isaac Newton (1642–1727) was the preeminent scientist of his time. His *Principia Mathematica* was published in 1687 and was surely the most influential book ever written on physics. In it he described how bodies move in space and time, and a law of gravity that explained the motions of the sun, moon and planets. He provided the complicated mathematics needed to analyze these motions; he also developed calculus, a branch of mathematics widely used in modern physics. *Principia* was so complex that when it was added to Benjamin Franklin's library in 1731, it was said that only one person in America had the scientific background to comprehend it. Newton himself wrote "This most beautiful system of sun, planets and comets could only proceed from the counsel and dominion of an intelligent and powerful Being." Newton saw God as a "power" he called a "dominion" and said our knowledge of God was only through his works or "by His most wise and excellent contrivance of things." Newton was not a pleasant person and during his career got into several bitter disagreements with other leading scientists and mathematicians.

Other scientists of Newton's time also expressed their belief in God. Galileo Galilei (1564– 1642) said "I do not feel obliged to believe that the same God who has endowed us with sense, reason and intellect has intended us to forgo their use." Johannes Kepler (1571–1630) said "I give myself over to my rapture. I tremble; my blood leaps. God has waited 6000 years for a looker-on to His work." Robert Boyle (1627–1691) said science is "the disclosure of the admirable workmanship which God displayed in the universe." Sir William Hershel (1738–1822) said "All human discoveries seem to be made only for the purpose of confirming more and more the truths contained in the Sacred Scriptures."

Corey (his p. 73–107) has compiled some of the "just right" parameters of nature that seem to have interacted cooperatively to favor an anthropic Earth. Because many of these factors were so precise and accurate, rather than being "coincidences" Corey is convinced that God put them in place. Some of these are summarized, as follows.

1. The initial distribution of matter in the universe had the correct "roughness" to allow galaxies to form.

2. The amount of matter created by the Big Bang allowed galaxies and solar systems to coalesce but kept expansion in balance.

3. Gribbin and Rees commented on the incredible precision of the Hubble expansion rate: "The most accurately measured number in all of physics, and suggests a fine-tuning of the universe, to set up conditions suitable for the emergence of stars, galaxies, and life, of exquisite precision..."

4. The energy density (ρ), also called the cosmological constant, is remarkably favorable. The universe is expanding at just the right velocity to prevent it collapsing back upon itself. This value at Planck time had to be precise to less than one part in 10 to the 60th power.

5. Organic life is based on the element carbon, believed to originate in red giant stars. The amazing process of carbon formation begins with the fusion of two helium nuclei to form a highly unstable beryllium isotope Be8. Because this isotope resonates favorably with a single helium nucleus, a carbon nucleus in its radioactive state is then formed, which decays into normal carbon.

6. The creative interaction of these and other factors led Sir Fred Hoyle to observe "Some supercalculating intellect must have designed the properties of the carbon atom, otherwise the chances of my finding such an atom through the blind forces of nature would be utterly miniscule." Before this, Hoyle had been a firmly entrenched atheist but eventually the facts became "so overwhelming as to put the theistic hypothesis virtually beyond question."

Earlier, Ross (1993, p. 111–114) had listed twenty-five parameters for the universe that required narrowly defined ranges for any kind of life to exist, and on p. 129–132 listed thirty additional life-supporting parameters required in our solar system.

LIFE AND EVOLUTION

The second proposition concerns the beginning of life, evolution and how DNA was involved. In the preceding chapter, DNA was shown to be a double-stranded nucleic acid that has the ability to store and pass on hereditary information. The sequence of bases along a section of DNA is a molecular message describing the order of amino acids needed to form a protein. The sixty-four possible combinations of the four bases (shorthand letters A, C, G, T) give instructions for certain of the twenty amino acids to be assembled in a precise order to form a specific protein (p. 403). In the human body up to a million types of proteins are involved.

A DNA sequence is recognized as a gene when it is able to pass on the code to form a protein. It is interesting that only 2 percent of the DNA in human chromosomes is involved in gene coding and the rest has been called "junk DNA." But it is also true that the human genome, with perhaps 20–25,000 genes and 98 percent junk DNA, is the most complex organism of all. A mouse genome, on the other hand, has 70,000 to 100,000 genes, half of which may be non-coding and a bacteria genome may have no junk at all.

Recent work by Gibbs and others is beginning to reveal a new world of hidden genes in the junk that can encode proteins. These RNA-only genes tend to be short and difficult to identify but may be important in differentiating between individuals and species. Epigenetic information seems to affect health and growth aspects, and micro-RNA may be involved in size, shape and possibly brain development. Work in Ronald R. Breaker's lab at Yale suggests that "RNA switches" may have influenced the formation of chemical precursors before DNA and proteins existed. "This implies that they were probably present in the last common ancestor," Breaker says.

Another complication is the characteristic Gould called "punctuated equilibria." This idea was developed to explain why fossil organisms did not seem to follow the smooth curve of incremental change predicted by Darwin's theory. Gould's model said that a species remains in equilibrium for a long time, then changes rapidly in response to some environmental stress. These stresses could be due to climate change, an asteroid impact, changes in sea level, volcanic eruptions, a magnetic reversal, a wobble in the earth's axis of rotation, etc.

In the previous chapter it was shown that many respected scientists have calculated that the odds are enormous against the random chance that nucleotides and proteins could combine and begin life. Because of that, intelligent design—implicitly by God—has to be recognized as a possibility. Evolution on Earth began with the first organisms, bacteria, about 3.8 billion years ago. From that beginning, the tree of life expanded to perhaps 5 billion species, with up to 100 million living at this time. Other than introducing the original species of bacteria, it is logical to consider this same intelligence might further have tweaked the process, especially for the Cambrian explosion, the divergence of hominids 5–6 million years ago and for *Homo sapiens* 195,000 to 150,000 years ago.

WHY SCIENTISTS HAVE DOUBTS

Surveys taken over a period of 100 years show that a fairly consistent 40 percent of all scientists have religious beliefs. Some of those in the negative camp flatly disbelieve and evidently would need some kind of direct proof to change their minds. Others who are less adamant, and some who may consider themselves agnostic, seem to have a questioning if not negative attitude, mostly for three reasons. (1) They flatly reject illogical dogma, based on erroneous interpretations, (2) they are offended by the inappropriate claims and actions of some past and present religious leaders, and (3) they, like millions of people throughout history, wonder why God allows the evil and suffering in the world to continue.

The first reason hinges importantly on the literal interpretation of the Bible, a position held by a diminishing minority in the Judeo-Christian community. Scientists, especially, simply cannot accept the idea of creation in six days of twenty-four hours each. Other numbers, such as the longevity of biblical figures, people killed, tribal members, days in the desert, etc. are impossible. The early Christian church erred badly in trying to make science conform to scriptures, and the treatment of Galileo by the Inquisition is a more recent example especially resented by scientists.

Scientists (me included) take a dim view—in fact can be outraged—when hard science is challenged. For example, some of the young-earth creationists have attempted to discredit or debunk radioactive age dating of rocks. Isotopes of uranium, rubidium, potassium and carbon, with their respective daughter pairs are very effective in determining the age of rocks (or organic material in the case of carbon); the science is well established and thoroughly tested.

Another outlandish claim is that the Grand Canyon was carved out about 6000 years ago in the space of a few months during Noah's flood (p. 97-99). Geologic facts developed by professional geologists show that it has taken about 6 million years for the Colorado River to sculpt the Grand

Canyon. The river cuts through 5000 feet of Paleozoic sedimentary rocks that overlie basement rocks that are one-half to one billion years old.

Close to home, dinosaur tracks were found in 113 million-year-old Glen Rose limestone of the Early Cretaceous age, in rocks from the bed of the Paluxy River in Texas. The tracks were made by the herbivore *Pleurocoelus* and the fearsome predator *Acrocanthosaurus*, which may have been stalking the former. (Sometime after the dinosaur tracks were found, it was claimed that other impressions or markings in the same rocks were made by early man. Responsible experts have examined the evidence and determined that the impressions/markings were naturally formed solution and/or erosion depressions in the limestone; they definitely were not made by humans.)

A few religious people act in ways that are self righteous, dogmatic, stubborn, superior, vindictive, self-satisfied, intolerant, etc. The occasional despicable personal behavior of a few religious leaders is always damaging, and adversaries of religion are always ready to make the most of it.

Many religious writers have struggled to explain how human pain and suffering can apparently be ignored by a compassionate God. It caused doubt for both Darwin and Einstein, who could not understand how an all-powerful and compassionate God could seemingly ignore evil and human suffering. Millions of other people, including myself, have wondered about this.

War, pestilence, famine, and all kinds of natural disasters have been with us throughout human history. Unfortunately, death, fear and suffering, on an impersonal basis, are a natural part of life. But as Cambridge's Polkinghorne points out, moral evil arises from the willful choices of men. During the terror of the Soviet Gulag and Nazi Holocaust, evil men selected those to be exterminated on the basis of class or race. And during the Inquisition, religious leaders themselves tortured and killed an uncounted number of victims, ostensibly for the crimes of witchcraft or because they had the wrong religious beliefs. Mankind today faces a new kind of evil and suffering in the form of suicide bombers and terrorists who are only too willing to carry out the mass killing of innocent civilians if they can get their hands on the weapons to do so.

The traditional biblical explanation for original sin described Adam and Eve in the Garden of Eden, where everything was perfect. God told them to enjoy all the delights of the garden but not to eat the fruit of the tree of knowledge. Tempted by a snake, Eve convinced Adam they should eat the fruit anyway. In his anger, God expelled them from Paradise and at that point all human travails commenced, including loss of innocence, evil and death. Adam was blamed for original sin and sentenced to a life of physical labor. Eve's part in the fall condemned all women thereafter to pain at childbirth and subservience to man.

Augustine (A.D. 354–430) was the most influential in describing the Christian position that Adam's original sin led to all evil and suffering. God allowed Adam the freedom to make a choice, and he chose to do wrong. This explains why moral evil exists; humans without free will would have the character of sheep. Others have argued that suffering leads to hope and moral growth; when others suffer it elicits sympathy and compassion. Moral courage arises to meet danger, fear and struggle. The world is a place of "soul-making" and a "furnace of affliction." Colson said, "without free will, we would not be capable of moral responsibility, creativity, obedience, loyalty or heroism. The only way God could create beings that are fully human was to take the risk that they would use their freedom to choose evil."

To those Jews in Auschwitz, or those nuns in the Gulag punishment cells, however, these kinds of arguments would be thin gruel indeed to feed their hopeless desperation. Christians often treat pain and suffering as an unanswerable problem. They conclude there is no rational solution to the puzzle of God's seemingly unconcerned detachment. Barbour (1997, p. 301) says it is "a mystery that we do not understand but that we should accept in faith and submission to God."

Muslims are concerned about the same questions and acknowledge that life is full of suffering, starting as early as childbirth. They believe a person who experiences a life full of suffering may enjoy a blissful and everlasting life in the next world. Many who embrace sinful pleasures in the material world may go through a grievous torment in the life to come. Mankind is seen as the most recent stage of evolution, and Allah has "shown him the way, (giving him full freedom of choice) whether he be grateful or ungrateful" (Holy Koran 76:2–4).

Abuse of this freedom, especially in causing suffering, pain and death to others, will incur God's (Allah's) punishment in the life to come. "Humans remain responsible to God and not God to humans." Islam says that all pain, grief and fear in life are actually tests and trials from God. If a person meets the test successfully through patience, prayer, in living a good life and trust in God, the end result will be boundless joy and happiness. One of the most important obligations taught by Islam is to establish a just society.

Pierre Teilhard de Chardin (1881–1955), who was a scientist before he was a priest, clearly stated that the evidence of science must be respected. Therefore, the evolution of man must be considered which led to some interesting takes on the concept of original sin. He recognized that mankind traces back to an early *Homo sapiens* (in East Africa) and that no individual can be labeled as "Adam" and be held responsible for all of mankind's sins. Also, no place can be identified as Eden though from what I have seen, a locale in East Africa would be much more likely than Iraq. Without an Adam and Eden there could be no "Fall" tied to a person, place or time.

As explained in the chapter on mankind, anthropologists have used mitochondrial DNA (mtDNA) to trace our beginnings back about 7500 generations to a "mitochondrial Eve" who lived in East Africa about 150,000 years ago. The DNA patterns define ten original lineages on the male side and eighteen on the female side. Some prehistoric Adam was the last common ancestor but he never knew mitochondrial Eve (p. 435–437).

De Chardin pointed out that the "world" of the early church could only mean Earth and not the universe. Specifically, biblical scripture would not apply to possible other civilizations in the universe. With his typical "opaque imagery" he also defined original sin as the inevitable chance of evil (negative force) which accompanies the evolution of all life. Optimistically, he could see the evolution of man moving in a positive direction, and that the "second Adam" was represented by the Crucifixion and Resurrection. He warned that the greatest future problem might be apostasy, or the loss of religious belief.

Mankind's conceit leads some to look upon *Homo sapiens sapiens* as the final step in evolution-but further reflection leads others to believe that the unattainable goal of perfection is man imbued with a Christ-like soul and an inspired spirit (de Chardin's "Omega Point").

DEISM

This is the belief that God created a world that follows the classical laws of physics and chemistry and then, like an absentee landlord, left it to run on its own. This idea has appealed to many scientists as it provided for the creation by a superior entity who then ignored all pain and suffering in the world. Deists often describe a God who created the universe, "wound it up like a clock" and then went away. Hawking (p.140) used some of the same language "...people have come to believe that God allows the universe to evolve according to a set of laws and does not intervene in the universe to break these laws. However, it would still be up to God to wind up the clockwork and choose how to start it off."

The term Deism refers to a belief in one God (Deus) as opposed to belief in many gods (polytheism) or no god (atheism). It considers that God exists, on purely rational grounds, because he created everything in the universe. Deists disagree with atheists who claim there is no God but neither do Deists rely upon any revealed religion such as described in the Bible or Koran. Deism is not associated with any established religion and has no priesthood, hierarchy of authority or network of places of worship. They believe God did not choose Jews or Christians as recipients of any special revelation or gifts. Deists think the Bible is an historical document containing important truth but is not inerrant or divinely inspired.

As early as 1624, Deists listed their five guiding principles as:

- belief in the existence of a single supreme God
- humanity's duty to revere God
- linkage of worship with practical morality
- repentance and rejection of sin will earn God's forgivenes
- good works will be rewarded both in life and after death

Early Deism appealed to many scientists, philosophers and politicians. Deism was a significant influence among our founding fathers including George Washington, Thomas Jefferson, Benjamin Franklin, James Madison, Thomas Paine, John Quincy Adams and Ethan Allen. Some of these men had a major role in writing the religious freedom clause of our Bill of Rights that confirmed the right of individuals to practice different religions, but that there would be no designated state religion.

Washington, Jefferson and Franklin were sometimes considered Deists, and God-fearing, but did not maintain membership in an organized church. However, during the difficult days of the drawing-up of a constitution in 1787, Franklin moved to start each day's session with a prayer, saying the delegates needed heavenly aid and "that God governs in the affairs of man." Ratification of the Constitution by the states was assured when Virginia signed in early summer 1788. This followed an impassioned plea by Franklin which included "I have so much faith in the general government of the world by Providence that I can hardly conceive a transaction of such momentous importance to the welfare of millions now existing, and to exist in the posterity of a great nation, should be suffered to pass without being in some degree influenced, guided, and governed by that omnipotent, omnipresent, and beneficent Ruler."

Early French Deists of the Enlightenment included Rousseau and Voltaire. Later, traditional religion was pictured as the enemy of reason, and attacks on the institutional Church became increasingly bitter and vehement. Anticlericalism led to militant atheism, eventually erupting violently in the French Revolution. This culminated in the Terror, led by Robespierre and the Committee of Public Safety, with at least 1200 people losing their heads under the guillotine.

Despite the excesses of the French experience, Deists often led the campaign for social and political reform. They advocated universal suffrage, factory reform, public health, prison reform, temperance, and the abolition of slavery.

At the end of the day, the God of Deism proved to be too nebulous to inspire religious commitment. People want a more personal relationship with God, seen statistically in the fact that 85 percent of the world population of over six billion people identify with such religions. An active religious life requires that people are personally involved and that God is continually at work within the process. It might be a reasonable concept to think of a Deistic God at the time of the Big Bang and for the next nine billion years, who then became more involved when he introduced life on an anthropic Earth.

AGNOSTICS AND ATHEISTS

In the first part of this chapter, an attempt was made to explain some of the reasons scientists have doubts about God. One reason has to do with the unsatisfactory actions of some past and present religious leaders, plus the conflict with scientific facts if the Bible is construed literally. Some religion can be just as counterproductive as the junk science described in earlier chapters. A second reason is the difficulty of reconciling a compassionate God with the pain and suffering in the world. These are just two explanations; individual scientists no doubt could list several more.

Defenders of the faith could turn the tables and also ask scientists for plausible answers to some difficult questions. First and foremost is the matter of creation. Scientists credit the Big Bang with creating the universe 13.7 billion years ago but cannot explain why a singularity of infinite density (and gravity) would ever fly apart in the mother of all explosions.

Logically, black holes should explode in the same way, but no examples exist. Genesis answered this question thousands of years ago with "In the beginning God created the heaven and the earth."

Most scientists believe in some form of Darwinian evolution, as do many theologians, but several problems remain. For example, religious scientists such as Schroeder, Hoyle, Behe, Dembski, Collins, Davies, Ross, Corey, and others have argued that life did not begin by random chance. They cite the complexity of DNA, proteins and life, all appearing interactively at the same time in the history of the earth.

Furthermore, evolution did not proceed smoothly by incremental change due to natural selection of advantageous mutations. The head skeptic, Michael Shermer, argues that the absence of transitional fossils is not important. He says that we "know evolution happened" because of the "convergence of evidence" from diverse fields. Not very scientific, and the main problem still remains. Was it by chance, or by divine guidance?

The first one-celled life on Earth rapidly came into being as soon as water was present 3.8 billion years ago. Somehow, clusters of molecules were transformed into living cells containing RNA, the precursor to DNA. Life for the next 3.2 billion years then showed very little more complexity beyond the one-celled organisms until the Cambrian explosion 530 million years ago. At that point, a sudden burst of advanced forms appeared almost simultaneously around the world, with body parts represented in the thirty-four extant animal phyla.

Evolution is often described as survival of the fittest in that the biggest, strongest, fastest, best, smartest, etc. have a slight advantage in survival and reproduction. If this stress on total selfishness is the controlling factor in evolution then why do things such as altruism, compassion, cooperation, generosity and love appear? Martin Hoffman at NYU has shown that babies "have rudimentary empathy in place, right from birth" (Wingert and Brant, 2005).

Some sociobiologists have offered some pretty weak explanations: love and altruism are cover-ups for self-interest, in anticipation of a payback; genuine charity does not exist and we are nice to others so they will be nice to us; only cynical expediency prevents some individuals from maiming and murdering their own. Even sadder are some scientists who think life is meaningless, pointless and without purpose.

Even in ant and bee colonies, individuals override their selfish genes to demonstrate cooperative behavior of benefit to the group but harmful to the individual. [During floods on our lake I have observed imported fire ants (*Solenopsis invicta*—an especially nasty little critter) form themselves into balls of thousands of living ants several inches in diameter that float in the water, thereby keeping alive the ones on top, but tough on those on the bottom. (Admittedly, this is more likely a case of instinct rather than a reasoned response.)]

Carried a step further, why did mankind evolve to the stage of possessing a soul, and beyond that, spirit? Neither of these would help in the matter of survival or reproduction. And finally, why do homosexuals keep appearing, in about the same percentages, as they have for thousands of years? They do not reproduce themselves, and could not claim to be the fittest (p. 80-82).

Polls show that 70–80 percent of American people "believe in a personal God" but only 40 percent of scientists do. Of the scientific group, Einstein and Hawking made frequent references to God but many others seem to have a deep reluctance to use the "G" word. Hence we have a long list of evasive and sometimes derogatory words such as supercalculating intellect, purposeful creator, cosmic intelligence, super intellect, intelligent power, creator, intelligent designer, super spook, higher power, natural theologian, supernatural agency, cosmic spirit of order and harmony, supreme being, benevolent designer, cosmic designer, and "an imaginary superhero in the sky who loves us." The same people define religion as: myth-making activity, supernaturalism, fine-tuning of the universe, cosmic creationists, and "a medieval Christian invention."

A large and growing number of people have been called "nones" for their response to the question in surveys "what is your religion, if any?" This group numbers nearly 30 million in the U.S., almost double in the last ten years. Characteristically, a member of the group tends to be younger, single, and male. Education levels are the same as the rest of the population. Politically, 17 percent are Republicans, 30 percent are Democrats, 43 percent are independents, and 10 percent are uncategorized. Many of them are quite spiritual and believe in God. A common position is rejection of organized religion. Some of them see religion as "death insurance" and they are not willing to pay the premiums. They do not belong to any group with similar feelings, but recently an effort to organize has started under the name "Brights," mostly as an Internet constituency.

Paul Kurtz has spent a good part of his life in promoting the concept of "secular humanism," defined by my Oxford dictionary as "the belief that humanity is capable of morality and self-fulfillment without belief in God." I believe that Kurtz would not argue with this, but in his own literature he has expanded considerably.

In support of his beliefs Kurtz has been a very effective advocate, beginning with founding the publisher Prometheus Books in 1969, then helping get the *Skeptical Inquirer* off the ground in 1976. In the same year The Committee for the Scientific Investigation of Claims of the Paranormal (CSICOP) was founded, and later, U.S. and international "Centers for Inquiry" were established.

The movement espouses learning, hope, optimism, truth, tolerance, love, compassion, altruism, integrity, and responsibility, the right to privacy and enjoying life here and now. Their goals are to understand the universe and to work toward the noblest and best possible human beings. Methods include the use of compromise and negotiation, the skeptical analysis of untested claims to knowledge, and the use of reason and science for understanding of the universe.

Kurtz takes pains to point out that secular humanism is not antireligious, but simply nonreligious. He also argues that the word atheism means the lack of belief in God-not the active denial of God's existence. Clearly, Kurtz would agree that his secular humanism is atheistic but in their mounds of literature they avoid the word, perhaps because they know it has such a negative connotation.

No one could argue with the stated standards, goals and methods listed above, but in practice the secular humanists speak quite differently. Kurtz seems to take some pride in reporting that adults in the U.S. claiming no religious affiliation have increased from 8 percent to 14 percent in the last decade; he also seems to wish the number was higher, like the 26 percent in Canada and over 50 percent in Europe.

In the special September/October 2001 expanded issue of the *Skeptical Inquirer*, a series of eleven articles were purported to represent a discussion of issues involving science and religion. However, the issue contained no—zero—representation by anyone with credentials on the religious side. Instead, the articles were filled with a series of insulting and provocative statements, viz., "I suggest that we rename the 'departments of religion' in academia and call them 'departments of supernaturalism'" (Pandian, p. 28–33); and "sanctimonious nitwits are calling for a return to morals based on superstition" (Clarke, p. 61–63).

[Neil deGrasse Tyson is a famous and honored astrophysicist but I have to take exception to his statement (Tyson, p. 24–27), "I have yet to see a successful prediction about the physical world that was inferred or extrapolated from the content of any religious document." The following paragraph describes an actual situation in the physical world described in the Bible, which led to a discovery of enormous economic value.

In Daniel 3:20, Nebuchadnezzar "commanded the most mighty men that were in his army to bind Shadrach, Mesach, and Abednego and to cast them into the burning fiery furnace." It so happens that the fiery furnace is an actual place in northern Iraq called Baba Gurgur. The "furnace" is a pit of fire continually fueled by natural gas and oil leaking up through the soil from an underlying hydrocarbon reservoir 1500 feet deep. Geologists read the Bible, recognized the significance of the surface indications, and picked a drilling site half a mile away. The Kirkuk oil field was discovered in 1927 and production began in 1934. Kirkuk turns out to be one of the largest oil fields in the world, has already produced billions of dollars worth of oil, and is still going strong.]

Atheists continue to make unnecessarily incendiary statements such as Richard Dawkins "a case can be made that faith is one of the world's great evils, comparable to the smallpox virus but harder to eradicate (*The Humanist* 57, January/February 1997). [Some of his other public statements are even more outrageous.] Other leading scientists have said "there are no signs of a benevolence that might have shown the hand of a designer" and "there is almost certainly no purposeful creator and certainly no benevolent God." Bertrand Russell once said "I am as firmly convinced that religions do harm as I am that they are untrue." (The poor man also said that the world was "purposeless" and "void of meaning" which to him led to a "firm foundation of unyielding despair.")

In the special issue of the *Skeptical Inquirer* mentioned above, some of the writers made sneering remarks about the efforts of the Templeton Foundation to promote cooperation between science and religion. Pandian called it "dangerous" and the previous quotations show how some scientists regard religion with contempt. Contrast this with John Templeton's comments concerning tolerance and humility. To him the latter approach requires, and/or is

- the opposite of ego, pride, self-righteousness, and certainty,
- recognition that mandkind is an infinitesimal speck of nature,
- the gateway to understanding, progress and knowledge,
- a duty to be open minded,
- the need to be humble toward science,

- the willingness to see truth in other religions, and
- admitting that other theologies contain valuable insights into God that our own may lack.

Blaise Pascal (1623–62) was a French contemporary of Descartes. Pascal showed a precocious talent for mathematics and science but at the age of twenty-seven turned to religion as his main interest. He is best known for an argument he made for believing in God which has come to be called "Pascal's Wager." His seemingly simple proposition, for almost the first time in history, used probability and decision theory, and the concept of infinity. Without getting into the mathematical details, his wager is best understood in the decision matrix below. Note that a bet on God can have one very favorable result and one that is neutral, whereas a bet against God can lead to nothing but misery at worst, or an indeterminate result at best. Pascal argued that "it is foolish to be an atheist" and that a wise person should bet on God. Of course many people would point out that a bet on God is an insufficient initiation fee; faith and proper behavior are also minimum requirements.

	GOD EXISTS	*GOD DOES NOT EXIST*
WAGER FOR GOD	PARADISE	NO GAIN—NO LOSS
WAGER AGAINST GOD	ETERNAL MISERY	NO GAIN—NO LOSS

Pascal said there is a yes or no answer to the God question but that it is incomprehensible. Despite that, he chose to follow his faith and showed what he thought was the best way to direct one's efforts.

[Just for amusement, I drew up the following table for agnostics and atheists; if they cared, it could not be too comforting to them because they lose on all counts.]

Calphalon

KITCHEN OUTLET

North I-35
Round Rock, TX 78664-2415
(512) 819-0151

8 INCH SANTOKU KNIFE 0108320010870824   1
ORIGINAL PRICE   49.99
PROMO PRICE   24.16
REGULAR PRICE

SUBTOTAL $24.15
8.25% TAX   1.99
TOTAL $26.14
VISA CHECKCARD $26.14
###############6574
PURCHASE
ENTERED
APPROVED
AUTH# 130931
INVOICE #   1696
08-20-2006 09:08AM
REFERENCE #2   00000014

30 DAY RETURN POLICY
Merchandise must be returned in
original condition for a return
without a receipt, an in-store
credit will be given at the
item's current selling price.
All clearance item sales are
final. We regret that we cannot
accept returns on merchandise
purchased through other
retailers. Thank you for shopping
at the Calphalon Kitchen Outlet.

9981030116351295X

08-28-06 02:08PM   Store No. 1696 R60

	GOD EXISTS	**GOD DOES NOT EXIST**
AGNOSTICS	PARADISE LOST	NO GAIN—NO LOSS
ATHEISTS	ETERNAL MISERY	NO GAIN—NO LOSS

WORLD RELIGIONS

Some 33,800 religious denominations are known in the world, according to demographers David Barrett and Todd Johnson. Their *World Christian Encyclopedia* shows that 2 billion Christians in all 238 countries constitute 33 percent of the world's population. Islam, with 1.3 billion members is represented in 204 countries and Baha'i, with only 6 million members is present in 218 countries. The world's atheists and agnostics number 918 million, but appear (in the pie chart below) as slightly fewer than the Adherents. Judaism with 14 million members makes up about 10 percent of the "Other" category.

The major religions of the world are shown by percentages. Barrett and Johnson (2001) report that Islam is growing at the rate of 2.13 percent whereas Christianity is growing at 1.36 percent. Other surveys show that Muslims score highest in daily observance of their faith, followed by South Korean and born-again Christians. Israeli Jews and European Christians are among those who practice their religion the least. Almost all groups rate the importance of education and family time above religious involvement and rate politics in very low categories. Almost all agree with the idea that a more religious society is good for a country.

The first religion may have been represented in the elaborate burial practices of Neanderthal and Cro-Magnon humans 100,000 to 50,000 years ago. These early modern humans buried their dead, laying out the bodies with flowers, tools and other artifacts. Concepts and emotions about death may be one of the first indications of religious concepts. The idea that gods prescribed moral rules and controlled people's afterlife may be one of the first indications of religious concepts. The idea that gods prescribed moral rules and controlled people's afterlife may have followed.

Major Religions of the World Ranked by Number of Adherents

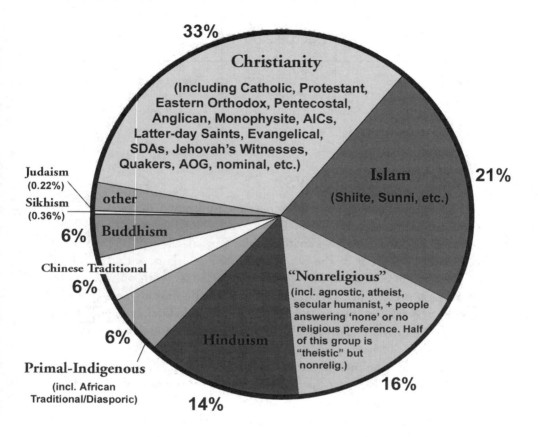

By permission, www.adherents.com

1. Christianity 2 billion
2. Islam 1.3 billion
3. Hinduism 900 million
4. Nonreligious 850 million
5. Buddhism 360 million
6. Chinese traditional 225 million
7. Primal-indigenous 150 million
8. Other 140 million

Pascal Boyer believed that religion was a likely outcome given that these early humans preferred to live in clans or groups, and communicate with others leading to increasingly complex mental processes.

Religions provide meaning and purpose to life, and encourage ethical attitudes and behavior. This in turn serves to fill psychological needs and leads to a better way to live. A characteristic of all the main religions is to seek a better or richer experience. Personal and group involvement is required to effect the changes and progress needed in the struggle for salvation.

The salvation or deliverance of the soul is considered to be the main purpose of most religions. Usually this is understood to mean obeying a wise and eternal Creator of the universe, and requires appropriate behavior while living. Consideration for others is part of the package as peace can come only through improved human relations.

As Huston Smith says, "…respect prepares the way for a higher power, love-the only power that can quench the flames of fear, suspicion, and prejudice, and provide the means by which the people of this small but precious Earth can become one to one another." Different religions have many common features for example, "every religion has some version of the Golden Rule." Having said this, however, Smith goes on to note that differences may cause difficulties that cannot be overcome.

This seems to me to be one of the biggest problems facing all who earnestly seek the true path to salvation—is there one and only one correct religion—or can there be more than one way?

Following 9/11, at a national interfaith service including clerics for Jews, Christians, Moslems, Buddhists and Hindus, Oprah Winfrey declared that all people pray to the same God. In another setting, President George Bush has said of Muslims and Christians "I believe we worship the same God."

Early Judaism claimed God's covenant with Israel and the idea of a chosen people, but did not restrict salvation to Jews. Islam went through a period of conquest and conversion by the sword but modern scholars quote Sura 10, verse 47 of the Koran, "To every people was sent an apostle to teach them in their own language, in their own country, making things clear" Early Christians were quite intolerant of differing interpretations and required the effort toward salvation to go through the Church. These views led to the crusades and other religious wars, the Inquisition, subversion of science, persecution of Jews and the rationalization of colonialism and slavery.

Beginning in 1962, Vatican II took important steps in moving away from these earlier mistakes. The new approach noted that salvation was also possible for Jews, Muslims, Protestants and those who, through no fault of their own, do not know Christ or the Church.

At the present time, certain Protestant groups, especially Fundamentalists, take positions quite similar to the Church prior to Galileo. The movement is not quite one hundred years old and is founded on a strict and literal interpretation of the Bible. Fundamentalists believe the Bible is authoritative and sufficient, revealing the inspired, infallible and inerrant word of God. This leads to problems with some parts of Genesis, which even most Jews consider to be symbolic rather than literally true. This matter will be discussed in the next chapter.

Kenneth Richard Samples and others have pointed out that the various religions have fundamental and irreconcilable differences, including the nature of God and salvation. In Judaism and Islam, God is singular but most Christians hold to the concept of the Trinity. Christian redemption requires a personal relationship with God whereas Hinduism affirms a cycle of rebirths of the soul, possibly leading to higher positions of stature. Jews, Christians and Muslims all interpret the identity of Jesus differently, meaning all three positions cannot be true (though they all could be false).

John Hick, on the other hand, holds that there is a common object of devotion in all religions and that "God has many names." He thinks that Christianity has influenced Hinduism in encouraging a greater concern for social justice. Buddhism has no gods or higher powers but teaches a reverence and appreciation for nature—the here and now, rather than future salvation. Christianity has seen greater material progress and social change, but also more warfare and imperialism.

Hick says we can be loyal to our own tradition and revere Christ as the path to salvation, without saying there is no salvation other than in Christ. "Christ is God's revelation, but not the only one."

Hinduism says that God takes countless manifestations and that "truth is one, paths are many." This hesitancy to claim certainty may be a prudent approach, as certainty is fairly rare, even in science. As reported by Wakefield, astronomer Sir Martin Rees has even more profoundly expressed the same thing "…even something as basic as an atom is quite difficult to understand. This alone should induce skepticism about any dogma or claim to…insight into any profound aspect of our existence."

The first two years of my work was to summarize the essence of relevant science. I believed this was necessary in order to understand the interface between science and religion. I then used the same analytic approach in developing the chapters on religion. Facts and mainstream thinking about the three great religions flowing from Abraham were compiled, starting with Judaism and the Old Testament. Although Judaism is practiced by only a tiny fraction of the people in the world, it provided the beginnings for both Christianity and Islam. Together, these three comprise 64 percent of all religious people in the world.

To ascertain the truth and validity of each, I gave a good deal of attention to their origins. That is, how each religion was developed and reported—by whom, how and when. This questioning was intended to be a net positive, by pinpointing the unlikely and affirming the most reasonable. The purpose was to strengthen certain aspects of religion and hopefully, encourage those whose faith is temporarily on hold because they are turned off by some of the obvious inadequacies and claims made. The stress was on overall understanding, rather than a study of scriptures, and each chapter addressed some of the greatest failures of each of the religions.

CALENDARS

Creation stories, religious holidays and dogma are always tied to certain dates or years, a fact that required the development of calendars. Therefore, it should not be surprising to find that priests and other religious personages have had a great deal to do with the matter. All calendars are made up of days, weeks, months and years.

The Sumerians of Mesopotamia were probably the first people to develop a calendar. It was based on the phases of the moon, using twelve lunar months as a year. To calibrate with annual seasons they inserted an extra month every four years. The new year began at the time of the vernal equinox (about March 20), when the sun appears to cross the equator in favor of the northern hemisphere. The day began and ended at sunset.

The ancient Egyptians created their own calendar about the same time, over 5000 years ago, possibly with help from the Sumerian model. It also was based on the seasons which in the case of Egypt meant the beginning of the annual flood stage of the Nile River. Temple priests soon realized that the brightest star, Sirius was useful because it first became visible about the same time as the annual flood and was much more precise in defining the exact time of the trip of the earth around the sun. (Also, it has been claimed that Sirius revealed the entrance to the tomb of Akhenaton, believed to be the first monotheistic pharaoh.)

The first day of the new year was determined by the first new moon after the reappearance of Sirius every summer. The priests of the Old Kingdom also realized that the use of lunar months resulted in "short" years of twelve moons or "long" years of thirteen moons. Therefore in about 1000 B.C. they introduced a standard calendar of twelve months of thirty days each. This gave a year of 360 days with five extra days needed at the end of every year. By missing the true length of the solar year by one-quarter day the error accumulated over time to the extent of one year in 1460 years. Augustus solved the problem with the "leap year" in 30 B.C.

In China, years were originally grouped in cycles of sixty but these cycles became uncertain when the lengths of some early emperors' reigns were used instead. The first beginnings of a Chinese calendar can be traced back to about the fourteenth century B.C., but a legend exists that Emperor Huang Di introduced one in 2637 B.C. The current version was designed by Adam Schall (1591–1666) and is based on solar and lunar observations. A special Chinese calendar is used to determine the dates of various holidays including Chinese New Year, the main holiday for a quarter of the world's population. For civil purposes, however, the Chinese government uses the Gregorian calendar.

Ancient Israelites developed a calendar that began with the date of creation calculated by early priests to be 5,765 years ago, by summing up the generations since Adam. The first six days of creation, plus day of rest, also established the week, even though many Jews acknowledge that the "days" of creation are not necessarily twenty-four-hour days. Days of the week are numbered but the seventh day is called the Sabbath, which begins at sunset on Friday and ends with sunset on Saturday.

The Jewish calendar is primarily lunar, with each month beginning with the new moon. The problem is that a solar year has about 12.4 lunar months. This required adding seven extra twenty-nine-day months in each nineteen-year cycle. The first month of the Jewish calendar is in the spring to coincide with Passover, but the New Year begins with the seventh month. The Jewish calendar is the official calendar of Israel and Judaism. Jews in general do not use the terms B.C. and A.D., as they do not recognize Christ as the Lord. Instead, they use the terms B.C.E. (before the Common Era) or C.E. (Common Era).

Numa, the second king of Rome, established a calendar of twelve months having either twenty-nine or thirty-one days. This served for some 650 years until Julius Caesar introduced the Julian calendar and gave his month of July thirty-one days, stealing a day from February. Augustus Caesar also gave his month thirty-one days by taking a day from February. Every four years during leap year a day was given back, as required to adjust to the fact that the earth orbits the sun every 365.2422 days.

The artificial term of 365.25 days was only slightly different than the actual but after some centuries became a problem. Hence, in 1582, Pope Gregory XIII instituted the Gregorian calendar, widely used ever since. This involved the rule that the end of every century would be a leap year only if it was divisible by 400. For example, 2000 would be a leap year whereas 1700, 1800 and 1900 would not be. The net effect was to make the average length of a year 365.2425 days, in error by only 3 days in 10,000 years. When adopted, the adjustment required dropping ten days out of October and moved New Years to January 1.

Muslim time begins in A.D. 622, the year the prophet Mohammed traveled to Medina from Mecca to establish the first Islamic community. The trip is known as the Hegira, which in Arabic means to break away from or abandon one's tribe. The Islamic calendar year of 1383 C.E. thus corresponds with 2005 C.E. in Gregorian time. The Islamic calendar is based on lunar months and has thirty-year cycles with nineteen years of 354 days and eleven years of 355 days. The months alternate between twenty-nine and thirty days, and holy times like Ramadan shift every year. For normal business records, all Islamic countries except Saudi Arabia use the Gregorian calendar because of its accuracy and wide acceptance.

PERSECUTION

Historically, Christianity evolved from Judaism, Buddhism from Hinduism and the Baha'i faith from Islam. However, its Islamic roots have not saved Baha'i from savage persecution in Iran for the past 30 years.

But the most persecuted of all are Christians, 70 million of whom have been killed since the time of Christ. More than half of those occurred in the twentieth century under godless communism. In the thirteenth and fourteenth centuries, Genghis Khan and Tamerlane killed over 12 million Nestorian Christians in central Asia. Percentage-wise, the Jews have suffered the most with 9 million killed, 6 million in the Holocaust alone. A group called Muslims Against Terrorism (MAT) has compiled a list of more than 32 million Muslims killed or displaced during the past fourteen hundred years. Of these, more than 11 million were killed by the Communists in the twentieth century, 8 million were killed or displaced by the Czars of Russia and 5 million have been killed or displaced in Palestine since 1948. Crusaders killed a half million Muslims according to MAT, a relatively small number compared to all the negative emotions stemming from that infamous episode.

5

JUDAISM— OLD TESTAMENT

A proper beginning to this chapter first requires a look at the Jewish people. Theirs is a remarkable story indeed, from their beginnings nearly 3800 years ago to their position in the world today. Though totaling only about 14 million people, less than one-fourth of one percent of the world's population, they have a hugely disproportionate influence in current events.

Much of their strength stems from their achievements in science, finance, medicine, literature, art, music, academia and the media. By combining financial power with political skills, they have achieved a considerable degree of influence in the U.S., though making up less than two percent of the population. Since being formed in 1948, the state of Israel, with only 6.8 million people, has faced off the entire Arab world and currently has the Middle East tied up in knots.

[My appreciation for Jewish people and their abilities began in high school, where Dan Dworsky was one of my best friends. Dan was a football hero but what I admired most was in terms of personal behavior and culture. He was always studious, quiet, soft-spoken, courteous, friendly and polite, plus had musical skills on the piano and saxophone. We double-dated to the senior prom and have stayed in touch ever since he left for the University of Michigan and I went to Northwestern. Later, in California, my wife and I had several good Jewish friends and again were impressed by their basic decency, plus warm and hearty cooperation involving social events and community projects.]

In the year 2000, authors Elvira and Mehai Nadin published a compilation of 279 responses they got from their query to well over 2000 Jews asking each individual to explain what their Jewishness meant to them. In large part the question was directed at professionals, including many Europeans, so results may not be representative of the Jewish population in general. Also, responses to the survey were probably somewhat idealistic in emphasizing only the best points—there was little or no criticism of individuals or the Jewish community. Nevertheless, the results are helpful in pointing out those things most important to Jews, and the following paragraph extracts the words and phrases that represent the most common ideas.

"Being Jewish has influenced all that I am and do...Judaism encourages a freedom of expression and questioning...we have been persecuted for centuries...energy for action...a Jew cannot remain indifferent to human suffering...respecting those who have departed...My values are the ones based on the Torah: the six hundred thirteen mitzvoth...being a chosen people, to be a light, an example, to the other nations...oppose discrimination in any form...responsibility...deal humanely, honestly, and generously with others...traditions, learning, creativity...behavior reflects on the entire community...loyalty to the country that gave them the chance...Israel and Zionism are the most important...love of peace...shalom...care for others...I want to make a difference...I am not Orthodox...I am an atheist and attend services...the desirability of peaceful, harmonious, tolerant, cooperative human behavior...solidarity in time of trouble...nonviolence...knowledge and education...Jews are born singers and dancers...a source of positive energy and a determination to achieve...blessed with an extra helping of intelligence...a tendency to work hard and achieve maximum potential...we have one common, Jewish soul...a strong affinity with Jews worldwide...must do what is right, correct, ethical...we have a direct connection to God...love to argue...a certain sense of destiny...the joy of being part of a unique ethnic culture and reveling in its history and humor, its language and literature, its music and moods, its festivals and foods...traditional values...the Jewish religion and the Jewish people belong to each other...a source of pride in the spiritual, intellectual and artistic achievements of Jews throughout our history...celebrate life, which is now, not the potential rewards of a hereafter...value of education...try to lead an honest, decent life...you will experience prejudice, so you'd better be much better than everybody else... rule of law and simple justice... close family ties, the value of education, the concept of justice, freedom of expression...the privilege and the burden of belonging to the oldest literate, moral, and religious heritage, unbroken in its continuity…Jewish existence plays a role in the fate of humanity…pass on the Jewish traditions to my children: the holidays, lighting candles…not religious…history and culture…learning Torah and Talmud…a sense of humor…music and art…devotion to Israel…the family is the nucleus of Jewish life…our holidays and life celebrations—circumcision, bar mitzvah, bat mitzvah, marriage—all these bind us and guide us and enrich our lives…intellectual inquiry, learning and wisdom…no conflict between science and religion…ask questions…care for the sick…I like being Jewish…one family, friends, cousins, responsible to and for each other."

And finally, "As a Jew, not only do I believe that Jews are God's chosen people, but I believe that Judaism presents the only way that one can be true to God."

Out of this whole book, the only negative comment (and that somewhat facetiously) was "there is a kind of loud New York Jew that I can't stand."

Jews have been in control of their "promised land" only four times since Abraham, only 1,027 years of 3,784, that is, 27 percent of the total. During much of their absence from Israel, Jews were dispersed (the Diaspora) around the world, frequently suffering persecution and violence. Reasons for the persecution range from "being different" to outright anti-Semitism. No doubt the idea of being a "chosen people" or that Palestine is the "promised land" does not endear the Jews to the rest of the world. After all, the Old Testament in which the "chosen people" and "promised land" passages appeared was written by the Jews themselves, so some people might suspect self-serving motives.

JEWISH HISTORY

Key events are listed, according to the Old Testament for the most part. Dates are in Gregorian time whereas the Jewish calendar begins 5764 years ago with Creation as described in Genesis. Years are shown as B.C. and A.D. but Jews use B.C.E as they do not believe in the divinity of Christ.

Abraham (known then as Abram) grew up in Ur, a city in Mesopotamia, during the reign of Hammurabi. At the time, the Babylonian empire was at its peak after taking over from the Sumerian/Akkadians about 1950 B.C. Sumerians developed the first writing about 3800 B.C. and later the Akkadians established one of the world's greatest cultures. During his reign in 1795–1750 B.C., Hammurabi wrote his famous code of laws, in cuneiform script.

JEWISH HISTORY TIMELINES

3760 B.C.	Creation, Adam and Eve (Genesis 1)
Ten generations	
2949	Noah's flood
Ten generations	
1780	Abraham
Isaac and Ishmael	
Jacob, twelve sons	
1600	Joseph, Egypt, enslavement
1280	Moses, Exodus
1240	Joshua
1150–1050	Judges
1050–1005	Samuel and Saul
1005–965	David
965–922	Solomon—first temple
860–800	Elijah, Elisha
742–700	Isaiah I
722	Fall of Israel to Assyrians
715–687	Hezekiah
649–617	Josiah
625–587	Jeremiah (Baruch)
587	Fall of Jerusalem to Babylonians
540	Daniel
538	Jews return to Judah—second temple
457	Ezra comes from Babylon to Judah with Torah
332	Alexander takes Judea
285	Septuagint (Greek translation of Old Testament)
167	Maccabees—Hasmonian dynasty
63	Romans capture Jerusalem
8 B.C	Christ born

33 A.D.	Christ crucified
70	Second temple destroyed, Diaspora
500s	Talmud
1948	State of Israel

Abram was the son of a prosperous craftsman. Although writing had been developed in the same area, literacy was a rare thing in those days, limited to the priest class and some of the rulers and the wealthy. But Abram was intelligent and no doubt capable of keeping records. Even more important, he was inquisitive and curious and questioned the rationale for the idolatrous religion of the time. He was able to convince his father, Terah to start a new life so they left Ur and moved to Haran, now in southern Turkey. At age seventy-five, Abram left Haran, leaving his father there who lived another sixty years. (It is interesting that at Haran in 53 B.C., Parthian archers handed Roman legions under Crassus their worst defeat ever, killing 20,000 and capturing 10,000).

Abram and Sarai, his wife, traveled south as far as Egypt because of drought in Canaan. Eventually they returned to Canaan, and "Abram was very rich in cattle, in silver, and in gold" (Gen 13:2). As Sarai was barren it was decided that Abram should father a child by Sarai's Egyptian maid Hagar. When Hagar conceived, Sarai was jealous but the angel of the Lord told Hagar that her son should be called Ishmael and that her seed would be multiplied "exceedingly" (Gen 16:10, 11).

According to Genesis 17, when Abram was ninety-nine years old, God confronted him directly and made the defining covenant with him, including the following:

- Abram henceforth was to be faithful to the Almighty God;

- Abram's name would be changed to Abraham;

- Abraham would become the "father of many nations;"

- The everlasting covenant would be between God and Abraham's seed after him;

- All the land of Canaan would be given to Abraham and his seed;

- Abraham and all males should be circumcised immediately, and all male babies thereafter when they were eight days old;

- Abraham's wife Sarai should be renamed Sarah and she would have a son to be named Isaac, even though she was ninety years old; and

- God's covenant would be with Isaac, but Ishmael would be fruitful and would lead a great nation.

After Isaac was born, severe famines at times forced Abraham and Isaac to leave Canaan, but they always returned when things got better. At God's command, Isaac's son Jacob had his name changed to Israel and his twelve sons began the twelve tribes of the Hebrews. The sons and tribes were Reuben, Simeon, Levi, Judah, Issachar, Zebulun, Dan, Joseph, Benjamin, Naphtali, Gad and Asher.

Jacob's favorite son Joseph was sold into slavery in Egypt by his eleven jealous brothers but soon proved his value and fidelity to the pharaoh. Joseph therefore was put in positions of responsibility, becoming viceroy of Egypt. When famine came during Jacob's old age, the entire clan (seventy people) left Canaan, eventually winding up in the delta area of Egypt and "got possessions there and were fruitful and multiplied greatly" (Gen 47:27). They also brought their early form of the Hebrew language with them, retained during their stay in Egypt.

The Hebrews prospered and multiplied so successfully they became a potential danger to the new Egyptian ruler. So forced labor was imposed; biblical chronology and other documents detailed that 200 years of slavery for the Hebrews followed, although 400 years had been threatened (Gen 15:13). As the Israelite population continued to grow, it was decreed that all male Hebrew babies would be drowned at birth. This led to an Israelite baby being put in a basket that was floated down the Nile, rescued by the Pharaoh's daughter, and named Moses. This story is very similar to one 1000 years earlier concerning Sargon, the legendary leader of the Akkadians: "My mother was a temple priestess (temple prostitute)...she bore me in secret, and put me in a basket of rushes, sealing the lid with pitch...put the basket into the river...the basket floated downstream to Akki."

Because of Pharaoh's daughter, Moses gained the privileges enjoyed by the priesthood. This meant a good education including history, mathematics, poetry, philosophy, astronomy, Egyptian hieroglyphics and Babylonian script. Moses was the great-grandson of Levi, son of Jacob, and was well aware of his Hebrew ancestry. This led to his killing an Egyptian overseer who mistreated an Israelite slave. Fearing the Pharaoh's anger, Moses fled to the desert where he married, raised a family and stayed for forty years.

Moses began his role as founder of the Jewish faith when he had a startling interview with God at a burning bush. His instructions were to go back to Egypt and free the Israelites, then lead them to the land promised to Abraham. From this encounter came the name for God "Yahweh" derived from the verb "to be" and translated as "He who is." Also he gained the help of his older brother Aaron, who was a better public speaker, whereas Moses was handicapped with a stutter.

Back in Egypt, Moses urged Pharaoh (believed to be Ramses II) to free the Hebrews, and emphasized his arguments and power through a sequence of plagues—rivers of blood, frogs, lice, flies, cattle disease, boils, hail, locusts, dust storms and finally, the death of first-born babies. Hebrew babies were spared when lamb's blood was smeared on the doors of every Hebrew home, so Yahweh would "pass over" that house while exacting retribution from all the others. With this, Pharaoh caved in and let the Jews go free. A possible contributing factor, never mentioned, is that at the same time (1280 B.C.?), Egypt was engaged in a disastrous war with the Hittite empire.

In their flight the Hebrews took their flocks and herds, silver and gold, plus food and clothing. According to Exodus 12:37, the emigration included 600,000 men of military age, plus older men, women and children. This would have meant a vast horde of two to three million people, but Kamm suggests a more likely size as six or seven thousand in all. He derives this number from assuming only descendants of Israel's clan of seventy; also, in Exodus 1:15 the entire Hebrew community had only two midwives just one generation earlier. In any event, in the history of all mankind this was the fourth migration out of Africa.

When the fleeing Hebrews were pursued by a fickle but angry Pharaoh, they were able to escape through a marshy area called the Sea of Reeds, when a fortuitous wind drove back the water. The pilgrims passed on dry ground but the wind died and the water rushed back, engulfing and destroying Pharaoh's chariots as they entered the same area. To the Hebrews, this episode signified their emergence as a people and, even more important, the revelation of God's supreme power and intent to deliver his people.

After only a few days, the complaints began, about the discomfort, lack of food and water, poor leadership, etc. Continual grouching like this tested Moses' patience, and at one point Aaron and Miriam, his elder siblings, even started a whispering campaign against him.

After about three months, the Hebrews had reached a mountain called Sinai. The location is uncertain but Kamm thinks the most likely place is Jebel Musa (Arabic for Mount Moses), about 7400 feet high, near the southern tip of the Sinai Peninsula. It was here that Moses passed on God's words to the Hebrews, as instructed: "Ye have seen what I did unto the Egyptians, and how I bare you on eagles' wings, and brought you unto myself. Now therefore, if ye will obey my voice indeed, and keep my covenant, then ye shall be a peculiar treasure unto me above all people" (Exodus 19:4, 5).

Next, after forty days and nights on the mountain in communion with God, Moses returned to the Hebrew camp with two stone tablets depicting the Ten Commandments "written with the finger of God" on both sides of the tablets. What Moses found was a campful of people singing and dancing around a golden calf that had been molded by Aaron as an object of worship. Moses was outraged and threw down the tablets, breaking them, and then burned the calf in the fire. He then had the Levites take their swords and slay 3000 men to make an example.

God threatened to exterminate the whole lot for their unfaithfulness, but Moses argued in defense of the people and God relented. So two new tablets were reinscribed, either by God (Exodus 34:1) or by Moses, as dictated by God (Exodus 34:27). The first four commandments express the people's duty to God and the other six are rules about their behavior toward each other. The Commandments are listed in Exodus 20 and again in Deuteronomy, Chapter 5. Punishments for breaking them are summarized in general by the "eye for eye, tooth for tooth" verses in Exodus 21:23–25 but also in much detail, especially in Leviticus and Numbers. Some uncertainty exists as to what language was used on the tablets but it seems likely that Moses might have been familiar with Phoenician alphabetic cuneiform script by that time.

In Exodus 25:10–22, God gave Moses elaborate and detailed instructions for building an Ark of the Covenant to carry the tablets of the Ten Commandments. The ark had specific dimensions and was made of special wood overlaid with pure gold, inside and out. Also to be included were two cherubim of beaten gold, and a mercy seat, again of pure gold. Once the ark reached Jerusalem it was to be kept in the Temple permanently—a reasonable assumption because the ark described above would have weighed ten tons. The ark accompanying Moses was a portable chest containing the tablets, and the Levites were designated as the priests responsible for carrying it. They were no longer one of the twelve tribes so in order to maintain the magic dozen, the tribe of Joseph was replaced by two tribes, named for his sons Manasseh and Ephraim.

The encampment next moved to the border of Canaan where twelve scouts (one from each tribe) infiltrated the opposition. After forty days they returned to report that the Canaanites, Amorites, Hittites, etc. were too strong to be overcome. The reaction by the Israelites was to wail and bemoan their fate, blame their leaders and talk about returning to Egypt. God, in his anger, threatened the people with pestilence and disinheritance. Moses was able to dissuade God from this course of action but not from the sentence that all those older than twenty years (except for Caleb and Joshua) would never see Canaan. Instead they would wander in the wilderness for the full forty years.

As a digression at this point, the (over)use (157 times) of the number forty in the Bible has always puzzled me. For example, soldiers and armies seem frequently to be listed as forty thousand, viz. in Numbers the tribes of Reuben, Gad, Ephraim, and Asher; in Joshua 4:13 and Judges 5:8; 40,000 horsemen in 2 Samuel 10:18; 40,000 soldiers in 1 Chronicles 12:36 and 19:18. Forty years is cited as the age when Isaac and Esau were married; the main divisions of Moses' life; Israel's wandering in the wilderness; Israel free and enslaved in Judges 3:11 and 13:1; the years Eli judged Israel 1 Sam 4:18; the reigns of David and Solomon; the desolation of Egypt in Ezekiel 29:11. It rained for forty days and nights during the Flood in Genesis; Jacob's death was honored for forty days; Moses twice lived on the mountain for forty days and nights; spies were in Canaan for forty days; Moses pleaded with God for forty days and nights in Deuteronomy 9:25; Philistines confronted for forty days in 1 Samuel 17:16; forty days also were cited for Elijah's trip to Horeb and Jonah's warning to Nineveh.

New Testament authors may have been influenced because they talked about Christ's stay in the wilderness for forty days and nights in Matthew 4:2 and after his passion, being with the Apostles for forty days, Acts 1:3.

Another basic question exists. According to both Exodus 4:28 and Deuteronomy 9:9, Moses did not drink water during the forty days he was on the mountain. Experts say people can survive for three weeks or more without food, but for only a few days without water. So it could be possible that the literal use of "forty" in this case is doubtful and together with the other examples, suggests that sometimes the number forty, as it appears in the Bible, may have only some symbolic meaning, not a literal one.

To one Jewish author, this emphasis on "forty" refers to the belief that "a man of forty attains understanding" and another says that a reign of forty years for a judge or king meant that "a lifetime of work had been accomplished. Dundes explained that forty is the traditional ritual number of the Middle East, signifying "a lot of."

In the last part of Exodus, together with Leviticus, Numbers and Deuteronomy, a good deal of attention was given to laws and penalties plus a census of the tribes, the order of march and the various encampments. But the bulk of the text concerned religious matters such as the duties of the priests, the Ark of the Covenant, the tabernacle and altar, offerings and sacrifices, collections and tithes, dietary rules, holidays and feasts, and conditions concerning the Levites, named as the main religious order. Altogether, the total number of covenants was 613, including the Ten Commandments. Almost all the laws concerned with non-religious matters have antecedents with Sumerians, Akkadians and Babylonians 500–1000 years earlier.

Capital punishment was the price for a long list of crimes, most numerous of which were transgressions against God. For example, death was required for cursing God (Lev. 24:16 and 23) for sacrifice to another God (Ex. 21:20) for working on the Sabbath (Num. 15:36 and Ex. 35:2) for serving another God (Deut. 17:5) for urging others to serve another God (Deut. 13:9) for disobeying a priest's judgment (Deut. 17:12) and for being a false prophet (Deut. 13:5). Death was also the penalty for smiting and killing a man (Ex. 21:12 and Lev. 24:21) for killing your mother or father (Ex. 21:15) for cursing your mother or father (Ex. 21:17 and Lev. 20:9) for bestiality (Ex. 21:19 and Lev. 20:15) for being a witch (Ex.22:18 and Lev. 20:27) for adultery (Lev. 20:10) for sex with your mother-in-law (Lev. 20:14) and for homosexual sex (Lev. 20:13).

Breaking a covenant was a very serious crime and Leviticus 26 spelled out the things that would befall such a sinner: terror, consumption and ague, sterility, sorrow and losing to his enemies. After that, seven times more punishment, loss of power, crop failure, then seven times more punishment, loss of power, crop failure, then seven times plagues, wild beasts, pestilence, captivity, then seven times more punishment including starvation leading to eating his sons and daughters, destruction of his cities, and total desolation.

In Leviticus 18:22, homosexual sex was called an abomination and death as punishment was called for in Lev 20:13. Incest, homosexuality and bestiality were placed together in Lev. 18, each calling for the punishment of death, because they violate order and the purpose of creation. Death was to be by stoning, although no actual instances are cited in the Old Testament. Another possibility was the *kareth* or divine curse of extinction for the individual and progeny, a penalty which medieval rabbinic scholars such as Maimonides and Nahmanides associated with the afterlife.

Today, not many people would agree with a death decree but many do consider homosexual sex as a sin and believe perpetrators should be encouraged to change their behavior. Of course the homosexual community disagrees and has become quite vociferous in campaigning for "gay rights" and "gay pride." They have effectively used the anti-discrimination clause of the civil rights movement to make their argument, and are now making an effort to redefine marriage so as to include same-sex marriage.

Homosexuality seems to have affected a certain minority of humans, probably from the beginning, and homosexual behavior has been observed in at least 450 other animal species as well. Obviously, this aberration does not follow the rules of Darwinian evolution because homosexuals do not reproduce at normal rates and as a result, they should tend to die out. Therefore, it could be argued that homosexuality is not a genetically caused characteristic found in DNA. Homosexuals keep appearing as a constant small but significant percentage—estimates range from 2 to 8 percent of the population—and include some very famous names in history.

It seems the jury is still out, however, concerning the role of genetics and whether or not homosexuals are "born that way." Studies of identical twins have given results that are puzzling. In one case, nearly half of the twins studied did not have the same sexual preference; if homosexuality were inherited, identical twins should be either straight or gay. But in another study of 114 gay men, Dr. Dean Hamer, with the National Cancer Institute, reported that "their brothers, maternal uncles and maternal male cousins were more likely to be homosexual than would be expected among the general male population. In some cases, gay relatives could be traced back for three generations. Thirty-three of forty pairs of gay brothers had co-inherited genetic markers in the region called Xq28 on the sex-linked X chromosome that men inherit only from their mothers (Thompson, 2003).

One interesting line of research involves serotonin, one of the neurotransmitters that carry messages between nerve cells. Abnormal levels of this chemical in humans causes everything from depression to violent behavior. In experiments with lab animals, low levels of serotonin caused an increased sex drive and homosexual behavior. With fruit flies, the effect was to cause a frenzied gay orgy by the male flies.

A related study concerns the hypothalamus, a part of the brain believed to regulate sexual behavior. Dr. Howard Moltz, of the University of Chicago, reported results of positron emission tomography to monitor the neurochemical function of the hypothalamus. He found a significantly greater level of activity in eight straight men compared to eight gay men.

Begley (2004) has described a study of baby rats by Professor Michael Meaney at McGill University that found changes in DNA can be caused by the mother's behavior. Positive rearing-licking, grooming, care and attention-reduces the number of stress hormones in the hippocampus region of the brain. Positive behavior by the mothers tends to reduce the molecules that silence the stress-receptor gene, in other words, alter the chemistry of the gene. "Altering genes by adding or removing silencing molecules is part of a new field called epigenetics."

At present, homosexual orientation seems to be too complex to be described by any simple model. If epigenetically related, it is probably part of a complex relationship between brain chemistry, other genes, and the environment, especially during adolescence (nature *and* nurture).

Deuteronomy served to review the covenants and laws, plus the punishments for breaking them, all designed to maintain the moral life of the tribes. By far the most important concept was that of the free choice of the Israelites to recognize divine authority and embrace a relationship with God. As they were about to enter the Promised Land, Moses reminded the assembled tribes "...the Lord promised that you would be his people and that he would be your God. He first made this promise to your ancestors Abraham, Isaac and Jacob...this same promise ...isn't just for you; it is also for your descendents" (Deut. 29:13–15). Also in Deut. 30:15 (Holy Bible, Contemporary English Version) "Today I am giving you a choice. You can choose life and success or death and disaster." Possession of the Promised Land was given but could also be taken away if Israel did not keep the covenants and maintain unqualified loyalty to God.

Moses never entered the new land but was buried nearby in an unmarked grave. Joshua, as his designated successor, led the Hebrew fighting forces across the Jordan River in about 1240 B.C. Yet the earliest Hebrew records of this event were not made until at least 300 years later. Confirmation of the 1240 date is in the annals of Pharaoh Merneptah, about 1220 B.C. He used the word "Israel" for the first time, outside the Old Testament, and listed the people Joshua defeated.

Keeping in mind the 300-year delay in writing up oral reports, the story of Joshua's exploits is open to considerable interpretation. It seems that Joshua led the soldiers of the Reuben, Gad and half of the Manasseh tribes to conquer the land, and the other tribes followed as settlers. The biblical account began with the conquest of Jericho and

Ai. This causes historians some problems, however, as both places were only piles of ruins at the time of Joshua. Following that, Joshua's forces killed the five allied kings and then obliterated all their cities (except Jerusalem) and all their inhabitants. Joshua conquered the Amorites, Canaanites, Hittites, Hivites, Jebusites, and Perizzites and thirty-one kings in all.

When cities were destroyed, men, women and children, plus all the livestock, were killed by the sword. This bloodbath was appalling and has caused considerable consternation to those who try to understand the role of God. The biblical point of view is that human sin is to blame and that God required the conquest (1) because of promises to Israel, and (2) because of the wickedness of Canaan. Part of the latter involved Canaanite worship of Baal, which included graven images, the sacrificial burning of children, and temple prostitution.

In Joshua, Chapters 13–17, some of the conquered lands were allotted to five of the individual tribes. All the assembled tribes then built a tabernacle at Shiloh and installed the Ark of the Covenant. At the same time, further assignments of lands were made to the remaining seven tribes (Chapters 18–22). As the priest class, the Levites got no lands but were awarded forty-eight cities instead.

Although lands were promised to Hebrews, each tribe had to fight the inhabitants for their allotted areas. Complete subjugation did not occur for nearly 300 years, in the time of David. (It is interesting that at the same time Joshua was fighting in Canaan, the Trojan War was underway about 750 miles away.)

The Book of Judges describes a very unsettled period after Joshua's death, when Israel had no strong leader. The tribes were trying to consolidate their gains and many of the indigenous people remained, together with their pagan religion. Baal and the other Canaanite gods had wide appeal; much was promised with few demands, allowing people to behave as they pleased. The result was a recurring series of at least six reversals when the Hebrews fell into the hands of their oppressors. This was explained as God's punishment for evil behavior. After the Hebrews repented and vowed to change their ways, a leader emerged to save them. In three instances, the ensuing period of peace lasted for forty years!

Archaeological evidence shows that the time 1200–1025 B.C. was one of the most disturbed periods in Israel's history, with cities destroyed and rebuilt up to four times. Compiling the people killed, as listed in Judges, gives 275,000; adding a reasonable estimate for "the very great slaughter" in an additional twenty-two cities, one can arrive at a total 400,000 people killed. Some of the Israeli heroes and heroines during this time were Ehud, Deborah, Barak, Jael (Heber's wife, who killed Sisera with her tent peg), Gideon, and Jephthah. Shamgar and Samson were especially hard on the Philistines; Shamgar killed 600 with an ox goad and Samson killed 1000 with the jawbone of an ass. Over 40,000 from the tribe of Benjamin were listed as killed by opposing Hebrew armies before both sides regained their senses.

At about the same time Joshua was crossing the Jordan River, Philistines were moving into the coastal areas of Palestine. The Philistines came from Crete by way of Cypress and were joined by others from Greece and refugees of the Trojan wars. Once there, they adopted the religious beliefs and practices of the Canaanites. The Philistines had the ability to smelt iron, giving them a big advantage in tools and weaponry and apparent invincibility against the Hebrew tribal levies. Obviously, the two nations were competing for much of the same land and this friction continued for over 200 years.

The showdown between the two armies came in about 1050 B.C. After an initial loss, the Israelites brought the Ark from Shiloh, hoping it would energize their troops. But the gambit failed; 30,000 Hebrews were killed in the battle of Ebenezer, and the Philistines captured the Ark. At that point, their troubles began.

When they brought the Ark to Ashdod they put it next to the statue of their god Dagon. By the next morning Dagon had fallen over and when it was put upright it fell again, in pieces. When the people of Ashdod were then afflicted with hemorrhoids, they sent the Ark to four other cities, each of which also came down with a massive case of hemorrhoids. The Ark next went to the city of Bethshemite, accompanied by a peace offering from the Philistines to the God of Israel. The offering included five gold molds of hemorrhoids and five gold mice, for each place the Ark had been set down. In spite of that, when the unfortunate people looked inside the Ark, 50,070 men were struck dead. The Ark then wound up at a town called Kirjathjearim, where it remained for twenty years (1 Sam 7:2).

Evidently the Philistines overran Shiloh, but their depredations were stopped by an exceptional man named Samuel, recognized as a prophet but also a full-fledged religious leader, judge, politician and military genius. The critical battle at Mizpeh was decided when a killer hailstorm struck the Philistine army which was then driven from the field by the Hebrews. Israel recovered all its captured cities and Samuel remained in power for the rest of his life.

When Samuel was an old man, the elders of Israel approached him and demanded that he name a king because they needed a military leader and wanted to be like other nations. Samuel argued against the idea and pointed out the problems, but the elders persisted. Samuel finally bowed to popular pressure and, at a meeting of all the tribes, selected a king by lot. Saul was chosen and in 1 Sam 10:24 Samuel said, "See ye him whom the Lord hath chosen, that there is none like him among all the people? And all the people shouted, and said "God save the king."

It turned out that Saul was a poor choice. During his short reign (maybe only two years), he was constantly at war with the Philistines and later had a disastrous falling-out with Samuel. Saul's personal behavior exacerbated the problem and he had symptoms which today would be called manic-depressive. Saul and three of his sons were all killed at the devastating defeat at Mount Gilboa and their bodies impaled by the Philistines on a city wall.

During much of this time, Samuel was busy scheming to replace Saul with the young hero David, eighth son of Jesse, from Bethlehem. David had a private army of dissidents and at times they served as mercenaries for the Philistines. David scrupulously avoided direct conflict with Saul, even though Saul recognized the danger and tried to capture David and destroy him. When David was supported by the priests at Shiloh, Saul had them all killed (except for one, Abiathar, who escaped). David was also a clever politician and shared some of the booty from his raids with elders of his tribe of Judah and other supporters; later this led to David being anointed as king of the House of Judah. David's credentials were good; he was a member of the royal house through his first marriage, was divinely designated, was a hero in battle and was skilled politically.

Standing in the way of complete power, however, was Ishbosheth, Saul's fourth son, who was supported by Saul's general, Abner. The disagreement involved members of the two tribes of Benjamin and Judah and was resolved in a very messy way. After twelve young men from each tribe killed each other simultaneously, Abner defected to David. This came about because Ishbosheth rashly criticized Abner for taking over one of Saul's former concubines. Part of the defection agreement involved returning

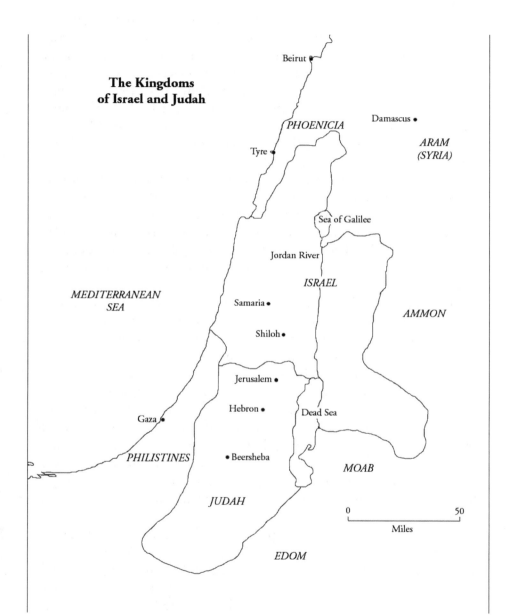

The Kingdoms
of Israel and Judah

Beirut •

PHOENICIA

Damascus •

ARAM
(SYRIA)

Tyre •

Sea of Galilee

Jordan River

ISRAEL

MEDITERRANEAN
SEA

Samaria •

Shiloh •

AMMON

Jerusalem •

Hebron •

Dead Sea

Gaza •

PHILISTINES

• Beersheba

MOAB

JUDAH

0   50
Miles

EDOM

David's former wife Michal (Saul's daughter) to him. All this double-dealing and bloodshed cleared the way for David to become undisputed king of the Hebrews. He turned out to be a very effective leader and surrounded himself with exceptionally able administrators. He reigned for thirty-three years, and provided security and justice as never before. He raised a professional army of part-time conscripts, led by career officers and with this force he beat back the Philistines and expanded the Empire from Egypt to Syria, with an outpost as far as Damascus. David ruled the surviving Canaanite city-states although they kept their religion and culture. One of his most important moves was to capture Jerusalem, with Joab leading the way into the city by a surprise attack through the rock tunnel under the eastern wall and up a 150-foot near-vertical shaft (now known as Warren's Shaft).

The "City of David" was then made the administrative and religious center of the kingdom. This was a key factor in uniting the tribes because it put the capital in a central geographic position between the northern and southern groups. David retrieved the Ark of the Covenant and triumphantly brought it to Jerusalem where according to tradition, it was installed in a portable tabernacle. He also needed a supportive priesthood for religious legitimacy. His imaginative solution was to have two chief priests, thereby recognizing theological and geographic realities. Zadok, from Hebron, was an Aaronid priest and Abiathar, the survivor from Shiloh, represented the Moses tradition.

David intended to consolidate the nation; faith and a permanent temple were part of his plan. Toward that end he began assembling building materials for his son Solomon to use after his death. David was loved as no other man in Israel's history in spite of the fact that he had some serious failings. One example was his seduction of Bathsheba, the wife of his faithful soldier, Uriah the Hittite. He then compounded the crime by directing that Uriah be exposed to certain death in battle. While in Hebron, David had six sons by six different wives, and eleven more while in Jerusalem.

Of great significance is the fact that events during David's reign were recorded in real time by a court biographer. Hence II Samuel and I Kings are probably the first parts of the Old Testament that reflect contemporaneous events. David was a major figure in the Hebrew bible, close to Moses in significance. The dynasty of ruling families that he established during the period 1005 to 587 B.C. was one of the longest lasting in all of history.

Solomon, David's son, ruled from about 961 to 922 B.C. He was famous for having wisdom but the Hebrew word also means "skill" which is equally applicable. He was a good businessman, a great builder and had a taste for luxuries and women. Early in his reign the kingdom of Israel reached its maximum size in Bible history, taking in new territories east of Jordan and extending to the northeast as far as the Euphrates River.

He had a full-time force of 12,000 chariots with stalls for 40,000 horses stationed at strategic chariot towns. Garrison towns and cavalry towns were also established, all requiring a road network. Slaves for this work came from the people who had inhabited Canaan. In addition, Solomon resorted to a forced-labor levy on all Israel. This included 30,000 men who rotated for work in Lebanon. In addition he had 80,000 quarriers plus 70,000 other workers in the hills (1 Kings 5:13–15).

Solomon held a royal monopoly on foreign trade and gained great wealth as a merchant prince. Trade with Arabia utilized camel caravans, and through his alliance with the king of Tyre he got timber to build ten merchant ships. The timber was transported on 8000 camels to a seaport at the north end of the Red Sea.

Solomon's signature achievement was the seven-year project to build a temple to house the Ark of the Covenant. Phoenician craftsmen created splendid carvings of various woods, many of which were overlaid with fitted gold. The building itself measured twenty by sixty cubits and was thirty cubits high. The temple was dedicated in 950 B.C. at a ceremony lasting fourteen days, when 22,000 oxen and 120,000 sheep were sacrificed (1 Kings 8:63–66).

His palace was even larger and took thirteen years to build. It included his residence, a hall of judgment, courtyards, and a palace for his principal wife. No doubt additional housing was required for his 700 royal wives and 300 concubines. Solomon had acquired all his queens by marrying every available daughter of various rulers, thereby cementing friendly relationships helpful to his trading empire. By indulging their religious beliefs, even building shrines for his foreign wives, he antagonized many of his own people.

Solomon was a randy ruler. When the Queen of Sheba visited, they exchanged gifts and perhaps more; the 1955 state constitution of Ethiopia states that the royal line of kings traces to Solomon on the paternal side.

Solomon was most famous for his wisdom, and was the moving force behind the writing of the book of Proverbs, if not the author himself. It is said that he composed 3000 proverbs and 1005 songs (1 Kings 4:32). Ecclesiastes and the Song of Solomon are two other biblical books attributed to him, together with a general flowering of literary endeavor. The latter may be due mostly to the fact that Hebrew writing had just been developed; both David and Solomon encouraged priests and scribes to begin writing their observations and comments to establish a record of religious history. This was the literary beginning of the Old Testament and it began just as Solomon's empire began to splinter into two separate, northern and southern kingdoms-Israel and Judah-and the term "Jew" first came into use.

The earliest written language began in Mesopotamia about 9000 years ago, in the form of "counting tokens" when it became necessary to make records of property and grain supplies in an agrarian economy. By 4100 B.C., the tokens became symbols or pictographs representing items, ideas, organisms, etc. Eventually the pictographs were standardized and about 3400 B.C. became Sumerian cuneiform script, recorded by impressions in clay made by a wedge-shaped stylus. Individual characters represented words or syllables, not letters, and this form of cuneiform was used by the Akkadians, Babylonians and Assyrians. It was in widespread use throughout the Middle East, even replacing hieroglyphics in Egypt as the official diplomatic script.

It seems that by about 1500 B.C. the Phoenicians were the first to improve cuneiform syllabics into a quasi-alphabetic script of twenty-two characters. Their inscriptions read from right to left with no space between words which had no vowels, only consonants. The evolution of the Phoenician alphabet is considered to be the forerunner of all the Semitic, (Canaanite, Hebrew and Arabic) Greek, Roman, and in fact all the European and Asiatic alphabets. It was so important because it radically simplified all writing.

The Phoenician alphabet was used to write most of the ancient Hebrew language of the Old Testament. Moses no doubt learned Babylonian syllabic cuneiform writing while in Egypt. But tablets from about 1400 B.C. show that Phoenician (or Hebrew) alphabetic script was in use by that time so it is likely that the Commandments were inscribed in that way. There is no archaeological evidence of written Hebrew before 1400 B.C. however, and no existing original documents from the time of the monarchy. The earliest biblical script was written by Shiloh priests about 922 B.C., augmented and revised extensively during the next 465 years, and finalized by Ezra in 457. Hebrew has remained the Jewish language of religion, learning and literature ever since.

Spoken Hebrew began to die out, especially after the Greek conquest in 332 B.C. and was replaced by Aramaic well before and during the time of Jesus. When the state of Israel was established in A.D. 1948, Hebrew was designated as the official language and is spoken today by most of the 5.4

million Jews of that country. Modern Hebrew writing is similar to the Old Phoenician in that it has twenty-two letters, all consonants, and is written right to left. By approximately A.D. 600, symbols for the vowels were introduced; called nikkud or "points," they are a system of dots and dashes which function as vowels and affect pronunciation.

WRITING THE OLD TESTAMENT

This section deals with one of the most controversial questions in this section, that is, should the Old Testament be accepted as literally true and every word taken as direct from God? This would mean that God dictated the thoughts or guided the hand of each of the writers of the various chapters. Fundamentalist Christians, especially, are of this school and thereby dismiss logic, and evidence. They also oppose some solid science, going so far as to say the science is wrong.

[I believe they are mistaken and that science (emanating from God) and religion must be compatible. I think there is a way to do this, and will try to develop the argument in the following pages.]

An important part of this argument is in understanding how the Old Testament was written, who was involved, timing of events, and the reliability of historical material. According to Genesis 1, a six-day series of events in the Old Testament described Creation, beginning 5764 years ago. After a gap of 1980 years, Hebrew history then began with Abraham in about 1780 B.C. This history, from 1780 through the end of Solomon's reign in 922 B.C., has been summarized in the text above.

As noted, all Hebrew history prior to 922 B.C. was passed on as oral history or "orally transmitted tradition." Other words such as folklore, myth and legend have been used, but these terms are somewhat disparaging and suggest a fictional status. Certainly Abraham and all that followed had a factual basis, although reporting may not have been perfectly accurate and interpretations may have been influenced by human factors.

Numerous errors and discrepancies have been noted in Old Testament scriptures, and biblical scholars have devoted an enormous amount of research toward understanding the problem. The consensus opinion of these scholars is that various Jewish priests and prophets, in different settings, interpreted the oral traditions and source documents in slightly different ways, emphasizing different points-of-view.

The authors are believed to be priests, or groups of priests, and have been labeled E or Elohim (for God), J or Jehovah (Yahweh), P or Priests,

D or Deuteronomist, and R or Redactor. E and J were believed to be active for the 200-year period before the fall of Israel to the Assyrians in 722 B.C. They are considered to be responsible for writing the first four books of the Old Testament. Traditionally, Moses was thought to be the author of the first five books, hence Pentateuch (or Torah, meaning "law"). But subsequent historians found that many things mentioned in the Torah did not occur until long after Moses died. Also, Deuteronomy was strikingly different in its language from the first four books, so a different author (D) was required.

The net result was that the first four books result from the input of two, three or even four sources, identifiable by differences in style, language and interests. Two versions of the creation story differed, and even contradicted each other. The first (E) version referred to God as Elohim thirty-five times, whereas the second (J) version used the term Yahweh eleven times. The first version never uses Yahweh and the second version never says Elohim. Genesis 1, according to the E source, had plants created first, next animals, and finally man and woman. Genesis 2, by the J author, gave the order as man, plants, animals and then woman.

In the same way, the flood story had two versions, in this case a complex mixture of J and P (Friedman, 1989, p. 54–59). According to him, in the J version Noah loaded seven pairs (male and female) of all clean beasts (meaning suitable for sacrifice) and birds, plus two pairs of unclean beasts, whereas the P version had two pairs of each. In J, it rained for forty days and nights, but in P the waters were strong for 150 days. In J, a dove was sent out after forty days, and the ark landed after fifty-seven days; in P a raven was sent after forty days, but the ark landed on Ararat after 194 days (Jewish calendar). In J, they disembarked from the ark after fifty-seven days, but in P, after 421 days.

The author of E came from Israel and the author of J from Judah. Then E was found to be two sources rather than one, and the priestly source P had input as well. Each of them wrote versions favorable to their own viewpoints, E favoring Israel and J favoring Judah. Non-Levite priest(s) most likely were the P source and included matters of concern to them, namely laws about priests, rituals, sacrifice, dates, numbers and measurements. The P priests made sure Aaron was included as an important player in the scriptures and looked out for the rights of priests, that is, a 10 percent share of all sacrifices and that only Aaronite priests would comprise the priestly family.

Friedman points out many differences between E and J writings, but also many similarities. He concluded that both were written before the fall of Israel, E from 922 to 722 B.C. and J from 848 to 722 B.C. With the Assyrian conquest in 722, ten Hebrew tribes were exiled and lost to history. This may have prompted the migration of some E authors to Judah where the tribes of Benjamin and Judah were living (the term Jew also appeared then, for the first time). Recombining the two E and J versions into one then became a practical matter, after 200 years of separation.

King Hezekiah ruled Judah from about 715 to 687 B.C. He carried out the centralization of religion at the Temple in Jerusalem, enhancing the status of priests. He managed to protect Jerusalem from the massive attack of Assyria's king Sennacherib, but each side described quite different results. II Kings 19:35 reported that the siege ended when 185,000 Assyrians were killed by the angel of the Lord. But the Assyrian record of the same battle said over 200,000 people were taken captive, together with many animals, and a tribute was exacted from Hezekiah, including his daughters, harem and singers plus gold, silver and other valuables.

When Hezekiah's grandson, King Amon, was assassinated, Amon's son Josiah became king of Judah-at the age of eight. When he was forty he was killed by the Egyptians and three of his sons became king in turn, with indifferent results. A fourth son, Hezekiah, was enthroned as a Babylonian vassal, but after eleven years had the poor judgment to rebel against Nebuchadnezzar. The Babylonian army conquered Jerusalem and thousands of Judeans were exiled to Babylon. Thus King David's family rule of over 400 years ended, and in 587 B.C., Nebuchadnezzar returned because of another insult and burned Jerusalem. The Temple was destroyed and the Ark was lost for all time. The population went as captives to Babylon, or fled as refugees to Egypt.

During the reigns of Hezekiah and Josiah, hope and vision were furnished by the prophets Isaiah, Jeremiah and Ezekiel. The books of Isaiah, Micah, and Hosea were probably written during this time, and Deuteronomy, a "book of the Torah" was found in the Temple by the priest Hilkiah in 622 (II Chronicles 34:15).

The P scriptures were produced after 722 and before 609 B.C., and were probably the product of Aaronid priests. They carefully made the distinction between themselves and the Shiloh priests who were not descendants of Aaron and hence not qualified as legitimate priests. P extolled the merits of King Hezekiah, even adding eighty favorable verses in II Chronicles; the king, in return, gave the priests strong support. The P version rated

Solomon and Hezekiah as the best kings—the two who did the most for the Aaronid priests.

Deuteronomy for many years was thought to be a summary by Moses of the first four books, shortly before his death. But there were too many discrepancies and scholars recognized that Deuteronomy was more closely related to the next six books—Joshua, Judges, 1 and 2 Samuel and 1 and 2 Kings. The seven books told a continuous story of the history from Deuteronomy through the destruction of Judah. Several authors may have contributed, but the finished product was the work of one person, since known as the Deuteronomistic historian. He lived during the reign of King Josiah and finished his narrative with that king; a later writer added enough text to include the fall of Judah in 587 B.C. It is believed that a Shiloh priest (or priests) was the Deuteronomist and that the prophet Jeremiah was closely involved. The two books had some passages that were almost identical, and Jeremiah was the only prophet to refer to Shiloh (four times). The scribe Baruch was another possibility—he wrote documents for Jeremiah—so he may have been a collaborator.

The Hebrews survived amazingly well in captivity. The literature of the exile includes Psalm 137 and the book of Lamentations, the entire book of Ezekiel and the last parts of both Jeremiah and Isaiah. In 538 B.C., some good luck came their way. Cyrus the Great of Persia conquered the Babylonians and allowed the Jews to return to Judah. According to Jeremiah, 4600 people were deported to Babylon but II Kings said it was 11,600. Only fifty years later, 42,360 returned, according to Ezra 2:64.

Twenty years after they returned, the Hebrews completed building the second Temple and it was dedicated on Passover, 516 B.C. Ezra, in a delayed return from Babylon, arrived in Jerusalem fifty-eight years later. He carried with him two important documents, one the "torah of Moses" and the second a letter of authorization from the Persian emperor giving Ezra religious control in Judah. Ezra shared authority with Nehemiah who was the governor, also appointed by the emperor. Their enforcement powers included fines, imprisonment and the death penalty.

The torah in Ezra's hands included material from J, E, D and P, in other words the full Torah as we know it. The person who arranged and reassembled the four sources into the books of the Bible is known as the Redactor. The evidence suggests that the Redactor was an Aaronid priest during the time of the second Temple, was a lawgiver, a scribe, and had access to all the documents. Ezra was all of these things and had broad powers, so it is logical to identify him as the Redactor.

In merging the texts, the Redactor had to deal with the paradox of God's justice versus mercy and compassion. He based much of his work on the P version which never mentioned a merciful and gracious God, as J, E, and D did seventy times. P stressed divine justice and the legal principle of "an eye for an eye and a tooth for a tooth." But the Redactor skillfully showed the deity to act more compassionately than that. He gave weight to the other view of divine mercy, and portrayed God as a parent who could be loving and faithful, but sometimes angry. Another thing he did was to integrate the Book of Generations (the begats) into Genesis. He did this by placing the ten appropriate generations between Adam and Noah, and another ten generations between Noah and Abraham. This gave some atrocious results, which will be discussed below.

The Redactor (actually an editor) and his earlier sources both shaped and added to the oral tradition they put into written form. In their first eleven chapters of Genesis they described events that they dated as beginning over 3300 years before Ezra. These eleven chapters have caused more heartburn and disbelief than all the rest of the Bible put together. The problems concern the six days of creation, Adam and Eve, the Fall, the Flood, the longevity of people's lives and hence question the literal truth of this part of the scriptures.

Concerning the creation events, Ezra's description closely followed the outline established in other ancient cultures. The chart on the next page demonstrates the astronomical bodies, geological divisions and organic life as described in Chapters 11-16. These things are listed in order, according to their appearance during the first six biblical days and the actual times are shown as determined from extensive scientific work.

CREATION

DAY	GENESIS	ACTUAL YEARS AGO
1	heaven	13.7 billion (Big Bang)
	earth	4.5 -do-
	waters	3.5 -do-
	light	13.4 -do- (light overcomes gravity)
	darkness	13.7 -do-
2	firmament (heavens)	10 -do- (milky way galaxy)
3	dry land	4.5 -do-

	seas	3.5 -do-
	grass	40 million
	herbs/seed	210 -do-
	fruit trees	210 -do-
4	firmament	10 billion
	day and night	4.5 -do- (rotating earth)
	sun, moon	4.5 -do-
	stars	13.5 -do-
5	sealife	530 million (Cambrian explosion)
	winged fowl	150 -do-
	whales	53 -do-
6	cattle	40 -do-
	creeping things	400 -do- (amphibians)
	beast of earth	220 -do- (mammals)
	man and woman	150 thousand (*Homo sapiens*)

For more than three thousand years, biblical scholars have agonized over the meaning of a day, as used above. In Psalms 90:4, King David was one of the first when he said "a thousand years in thy sight are but as yesterday." Almost all the early church fathers thought the creation days were longer than twenty-four hours, and Augustine said "What kind of days these were it is extremely or perhaps impossible for us to conceive." Hebrew scholars say the word "yom" can mean day or age, so they say Genesis days mean "very long periods of time" or "vast, unspecified periods of time."

But in Chapter 1, each day's work is closed with the statement "and the evening and the morning were the (numbered) day" so it is hard to escape the idea of a twenty-four-hour day. This has led millions of people to believe that the universe is less than 10,000 years old, and no less a person than Pat Robertson said the creation event took place about 7000 years ago, based on Bible arithmetic. By counting biblical generations, Bishop Ussher in 1658 calculated that the six days of creation began the night of October 23, 4004 B.C. and his number was widely accepted for many years. Protestant fundamentalists are especially adamant about their belief in six twenty-four-hour days for creation and the literal reading of Genesis, even more so than do Jews about their own scripture.

Dr. Gerald Schroeder, a MIT-trained physicist, has studied the Book of Genesis in the original Hebrew for the last thirty years. He has made a valiant effort to explain how the six days of creation were measured in cosmologic terms, whereas the days since Adam are the twenty-four-hour days we understand. Schroeder's scholarship is impressive. He noted that 800 years ago, Nachmanides had the insight to discern from the Torah's phrasing that time was created on Day One, and that before the universe there was nothing. Many years later, in his Laws of Relativity, Einstein explained in more elegant terms that there was a creation of time, space, and matter.

Schroeder argued that the Big Bang began on Day One with creation of the universe, about 15 billion years ago. After 380,000 years, light was able to escape from the intense gravity of the singularity, stars and galaxies began to form. Since then, expansion of the universe has stretched space billions of light years. This has the effect of attenuating the wavelengths of radiation, and the ratio to the emitted wavelength is defined as the red shift, z. Since the time of the Big Bang (less .00001 seconds), radiation has been stretched a million million times, resulting in a red shift, z, of 10^{12}. Because of this, the cosmic clock reads one minute, while Earth time is a million million minutes. Six days on Earth would therefore be 15 billion years of space-time! Schroeder goes on to equate the start of Day One to 15 ¾ billion years (before Adam), Day Two to 7 ¾ billion years, Day Three to 3 ¾ billion years, Day Four to 1 ¾ billion years, Day Five to 750 million years, and Day Six to 250 million years.

Schroeder has written a whole series of books on this, and related subjects, and is a popular lecturer in the field. As might be expected, many scientists have disagreed with him although their arguments seem to be less of substance and more of the nit-picking variety. For example, Peter B. Weichman agrees that Schroeder's science is generally sound when he talks about "a universal clock tuned to the cosmic radiation at the moment when matter formed." This approach makes use of the Cosmic Background Radiation (CBR)—a microwave relict from the Big Ban-discovered by Penzias and Wilson in 1963. The average wavelength of this radiation, when shortened 4 trillion times to the instant of the Big Bang, converts 15 billion years of cosmic time to six days of Earth time. Actually, Schroeder used "quark confinement" about ten microseconds after the Big Bang, as the moment when protons, neutrons, and electrons (matter) began to form. Weichman's main complaint seems to be that Schroeder used 2 as the divisor for the length of each succeeding cosmic day, rather than the natural logarithm of 2.718287. Mark Perakh agrees that the red shift effect can be used to estimate the time of the Big Bang, but that the rate of deceleration of time cannot be known. Victor J. Stenger's complaint seems mainly to be the use of "quark confinement" as the beginning of time, rather than the moment called "decoupling" when light first escaped the extreme density of the singularity, about 300,000 years after the Big Bang. Stenger's argument that dividing each succeeding cosmic day by 2 is "a completely arbitrary, unjustified procedure" has merit, but he can't seem to resist the impulse to use personal invective in discussing Schroeder's work.

My own view is that Schroeder has made a valuable contribution in introducing billions of years of time into the creation question. Understanding his use of cosmic time, or "God time," i.e., 15 billion years to equal the first six days of Bible time, certainly requires cognitive effort. Everything before Adam would be on a different time scale than the time after. And the matter of Adam's time is not all that certain either!

Concerning Adam and Eve, in an earlier chapter it was pointed out that the scientist/priest de Chardin insisted that scientific evidence must be respected. All the evidence points to East Africa as the birthplace of *Homo sapiens*. Using mitochondrial DNA (mtDNA), anthropologists can trace our beginnings back about 7500 generations to a "mitochondrial Eve" who lived there about 150,000 years ago.

At the time of the biblical Adam, 3754 B.C., the scriptures describe Adam and Eve as the only people living but in fact there may have been 10 million people worldwide. This value is derived by a simple-minded graphing of Olson's (2002, p. 101) population numbers on five-cycle log paper. All of his numbers define a fairly smooth curve, except for the 250 million people he estimates at the year 0 B.C./A.D. We know that by 3754 B.C., mankind had settled on all the continents (except Antarctica) and the first people reached the Americas by about 12,000 B.C. Human civilization, based on organized farming, was known in the Fertile Crescent as early as 8500 B.C. Hence, portraying Adam and Eve as the first two humans in 3754 B.C. seems to be seriously in error.

Schroeder has introduced another controversy by claiming that Adam was the first man to have a soul, the *neshama*, or free will. He recognized that other hominids, including Neanderthals and Cro-Magnon man, existed before Adam, but like animals they had no soul. Schroeder, Jewish himself, implied that Adam was Jewish, or at least the progenitor of the Jewish ethnic group.

According to the Old Testament, Noah's flood occurred in the year 2949 B.C. It has been said that there were over 200 flood stories in that part of the world, the most famous of which was the epic of Gilgamesh, the great king who lived in Sumer about 2700 B.C. As described, Noah's flood was very similar to the king's narrative. In both, a man was instructed to build a big ark and load it with species of all living things so life could be preserved. When the flood came, the man and his family floated for days while all other life on Earth was drowned. The main difference in the two stories is that one of the floods was ordered by multiple angry gods, whereas Noah's was precipitated by the one God, Elohim (or Yaweh) of the Hebrews.

Several parts of the Genesis story cannot be factually correct, i.e., literally true. The flood was described as being worldwide. But in my work on six continents as a professional geologist, I found no evidence of a worldwide flood in the last few thousand years, and I believe 99 percent of all geologists would agree with that. The most extensive sedimentary rock units in the geologic record are of Cretaceous age, 65 to 142 million years old, and they occur on only a small fraction of the earth's surface.

A simple material balance calculation illustrates another serious error. In Gen. 8:4 and 5, after 194 days the ark landed on Mt. Ararat, and then after 265 days other mountain tops began to appear as the water started to recede. This implies the ark grounded near the top of Ararat, which has an elevation of 16,946 feet. Now, if all the ice in Antarctica melted, it would raise sea level only 200 feet, and the ice on Greenland would add another 20 feet. (Melting the ice in the Arctic Ocean would make no difference as the ice there is floating). Simply put, not enough water exists on the earth to submerge Ararat. More than 16,000 feet of water would be needed, worldwide, on top of the present oceans which average only 12,450 feet deep. Even more challenging, wherever did that 16,000 feet of water ever go?

Another problem involves loading the ark with two (or seven) each, of all the beasts and fowl. At present 72,000 animal species have been identified, together with 140,000 plant species. Reducing that to a more reasonable total would still leave 4500 mammal and 9500 bird species.

In reality, all the flood stories may have stemmed from an actual event 5100 years before Ezra. Drs. William Ryan and Walter Pitman, senior scientists at Lamont-Doherty Observatory at Columbia University have described some startling results of scientific work they have done in the area of the Black Sea, using the most modern geophysical technology. They found that floodwaters from the Mediterranean Sea poured into the Black Sea about 5600 B.C. as a result of melting ice during the present interglacial warming. At the time, the Black Sea was a fresh water lake, 350 feet lower than the Mediterranean. When the water broke through the restriction in the Dardanelles, the flow was 200 times the volume of water over Niagara

Falls (a fall of 158 feet). The raging water roared at fifty miles per hour for 300 days, terrifying all living things in the region. As the Black Sea filled up with salt water, the ensuing flood drowned and/or displaced thousands of people. Survivors fled to surrounding countries, and the flood story became history (and oral tradition). Actually, the Ryan-Pitman description is supported to some extent in the P version, viz. "the waters grew strong on the earth a hundred and fifty days" (Gen, 7:24) and "the fountains of the deep…were shut…" (Gen. 8:2).

Another result of the erroneous creation and flood dates was that in adding up generations, it became necessary to assign unreasonable life spans to the people. (Remember, Ezra put ten generations between Adam and Noah, and ten generations between Noah and Abraham). Because of this, prior to Noah the Bible indicates the mean life span was 900 years and the average was 840. Women first gave birth at the average age of 115; Sarah was ninety years old when Isaac was born, and Abraham was ninety-nine. Adam lived 930 years after he ate the forbidden fruit, and Methuselah lived to be 969. Some authors have claimed that these long lives were due to healthier conditions at the time, but this is totally at odds with long-term trends. Life expectancies in the U.S. have more than doubled, to seventy-seven years in 2001, from thirty-seven years in 1840. The same trends are worldwide and are explained by better sanitation, better medical attention, better diets, improved conditions in the workplace, and lower birth rates.

Clearly, it seems the Creation, Adam and Eve, and Flood stories cannot be literally true as written. Much of the problem no doubt stems from the fact that Ezra and other authors were writing about things 2500 to 3300 years earlier. They tried to assign dates and names, all based on oral traditions, and perhaps with a few scraps of original written material. Even Jews recognize that this part of the Old Testament used poetic license, similes, and metaphors to tell the story. The well-known Jewish law professor at Harvard, Alan Dershowitz, says that reading Genesis "does not, of course, require a literal fundamentalist approach." Pope John Paul II recognized a symbolic or figurative meaning for some of the scripture and said "Fundamentalism…places undue stress upon the inerrancy of certain details in the biblical texts, especially in what concerns historical events or supposedly scientific truth…Fundamentalism likewise tends to adopt very narrow points of view. It accepts the literal reality of an ancient, out-of-date cosmology, simply because it is found expressed in the Bible…"

[*I suggest one positive step could be taken, however, to make the first eleven chapters of Genesis conform to scientific knowledge. That would be to develop a formal amplification or "scientific paraphrase" of the questionable verses. This could benefit millions of people. It would help move many scientifically knowledgeable people toward accepting religion, and at the other end of the spectrum would help move fundamentalists into the mainstream. Writing could be done simply, by a few appropriately selected theologians and scientists. Some of the key phrases might read:*

"In the beginning, God created the universe, 13.7 billion years ago."

"God introduced organic life into Earth 3.8 billion years ago, using DNA to control evolution of the species."

"Mankind evolved as a new species, Homo sapiens, about 195 to 150 thousand years ago, and was imbued with a soul _____ thousand years ago" (to be filled in by people with more experience and background).

From what Pius XII said in his encyclical "Humani Generis" of August 12, 1950, I think he might not disagree with this. In paragraph thirty-eight, concerning the same part of Genesis, he implied that the language was not to be taken literally but gave a "popular description of the origin of the human race" in "metaphorical language adapted to the mentality of a people but little cultured." And in paragraph thirty-six he said "…the Catholic faith obliges us to hold that souls are immediately created by God." Even further, in 2005 the Catholic Church explained that the first eleven chapters of Genesis did not conform to "full scientific accuracy or complete historical precision."]

THE COMING OF JESUS

Of the thirty-nine books of the Old Testament, nearly half (seventeen) bear the names of prophets. These religious figures were unlike any others in the ancient world and they have been called "spokesmen of God." They used such sayings as "Hear the word of the Lord" and "So said the Lord." If a false prophet should use the Lord's name to advocate an action falsely, that person could be put to death (Deut 13:5 and 18:20).

The essence of the prophetic messages was to restate what Moses and Abraham had said before them, to teach sinners how to repent and to warn against idolatry. Spiritual awareness was required and Jeremiah especially had a difficult time dealing with the claims of false prophets. He was accused of being one himself, a dangerous label in those days and punishable by death.

Many of the prophets are quoted in the New Testament and many predictions were made about the coming of a Messiah who would save Israel. Jews saw this to mean a benefactor for Israel, whereas Christians took it to mean Jesus Christ. To non-believers, some of these Old Testament predictions have to be eerily prescient, and to the faithful, nothing less than divine revelations. Some examples follow:

- My God, my God, why hast thou forsaken me? Ps. 22:1.

- …the assembly of the wicked have enclosed me: they pierced my hands and my feet. Ps. 22:16.

- They part my garments among them, and cast lots for my vesture. Ps. 22:18.

- False witnesses did rise up; they laid to my charge things that I knew not. Ps. 35:11.

- Yea, mine own familiar friend, in whom I trusted, which did eat of my bread, hath lifted up his heel against me. Ps. 41:9.

- …in my thirst they gave me vinegar to drink. Ps.69:21.

- The Lord said unto my Lord, Sit thou at my right hand…Ps. 110:1

- …and your sons and your daughters shall prophesy…Joel 2:28

- …I will cause the sun to go down at noon, and I will darken the earth in the clear day. Amos 8:9.

- Therefore the Lord himself shall give you a sign; behold, a virgin shall conceive, and bear a son, and shall call his name Immanuel. Isa. 7:14.

- For unto us a child is born, unto us a son is given: and the government shall be upon his shoulder: and his name shall be called Wonderful, Counsellor, The mighty God, The everlasting Father, The Prince of Peace. Isa. 9:6.

- And in that day there shall be a root of Jesse, which shall stand for an ensign of the people; to it shall the Gentiles seek: and his rest shall be glorious. Isa. 11:10.

- Behold my servant, whom I uphold; mine elect, in whom my soul delighteth; I have put my spirit upon him: he shall bring forth judgment to the Gentiles. Isa. 42:1.

- But he was wounded for our transgressions, he was bruised for our inequities: the chastisement of our peace is upon him; and with his stripes we are healed. Isa. 53:5.

- But thou, Bethlehem...though thou be little among the thousands of Judah, yet out of thee shall he come forth unto me that is to be ruler in Israel...Mic. 5:2.

- And this man shall be the peace... Mic. 5:5.

- And the remnant of Jacob shall be among the Gentiles...as a lion... Mic. 5:8.

- ...behold, thy King cometh unto thee: he is just, and having salvation; lowly, and riding upon and ass, and upon a colt the foal of an ass. Zech. 9:9.

- ...So they weighed for my price thirty pieces of silver. Zech. 11:12

It has been claimed that Jesus fulfilled over 300 prophecies in the Old Testament scriptures. Jesus said as much in Luke 24:44 "And he said unto them, these are the words which I spake unto you, while I was yet with you, that all things must be fulfilled, which were written in the law of Moses, and in the prophets, and in the psalms, concerning me."

Only 125 years after Ezra, Palestine was conquered by Alexander the Great and the city of Alexandria in Egypt was founded as a great cultural center, anchored by the famous library which eventually housed 500,000 papyrus scrolls. The Greek influence in Judea became so strong that Jews lost the use of the Hebrew language. In about 250 B.C., this led to translating into Greek the Hebrew Pentateuch (first five books of the Bible). This translation was done by Jewish scholars in Alexandria and became known as the Septuagint (meaning seventy, from the number of men making up the translation team). The rest of the Hebrew Bible was translated into Greek during the next 100 years and Jewish elders established a final Hebrew version in A.D. 90.

After Alexander died in 323 B.C., factions of his army competed for control of the area and Ptolemy won out in 301 B.C. The Ptolemies kept control for the next 100 years, but just as granted by Alexander, the Jews were allowed to keep their own religion and traditions, including their own high priest. In 198 B.C., the Seleucid Antiochus III of Syria captured Judea, with the support of rich, Hellenized Jews. The Greek influence in literature, science, arts, architecture and government was welcome, but the successor Antiochus IV made some disastrous mistakes when he mixed into religious matters. His first misstep was to sell the position of high priest to the highest bidder (not even of the priestly class), who then helped steal some of the treasures from the Temple. When this caused a riot his answer was brutal repression; when he defiled the Temple with the sacrifice of a pig, it led to war which began in 167 B.C.

The revolution against the Seleucids was headed by the Hasmonaean family. The third son, Judas, known as Maccabee (The Hammer), was leader of the army and a military genius. He employed guerrilla warfare and defeated superior numbers of regular troops with his fighters who were actually fighting the first war in history on the issue of religious freedom. Also, they were fighting for their families and freedom, whereas their opponents were mostly mercenaries. After five battles the Maccabees took Jerusalem and the Temple was rededicated on December 14, 164 B.C. A popular legend is that the candles burned for eight days, with a supply of oil for only one day. This event is celebrated annually as Hanukkah (meaning dedication) over a period of eight days. Each day, one more candle is lit and small gifts are exchanged. The holiday is also known as the Festival of Lights, the Feast of Dedication, Feast of the Maccabees and coincides, in time of year, with the Christian holiday of Christmas.

Armed conflict between Judea and Syria continued, however, with the youngest Maccabee brother, Jonathan, in charge of both the military and diplomatic reins of government. When Jonathan was murdered, his older brother Simon took over and he was able to eliminate Syrian rule by 141 B.C. Simon was considered the first of the Hasmonaean rulers but he was assassinated by his son-in-law Ptolemy in 134 B.C., meaning that all five Maccabee brothers died violently.

The Hasmonaean dynasty was involved in governmental and religious affairs for the next seventy years. Hyrcanus and Alexander were strong leaders who pursued bloody militant expansionist policies. Hyrcanus employed foreign mercenaries in his conquests and when he took over Idumaea he imposed Judaism on the population and forcibly circumcised the males. Alexander conquered additional territories until Judean control matched the size of the kingdom in the time of David and Solomon. Alexander was also the high priest and began having trouble with the Pharisees, a religious group organized at about the same time as the Sadducees. At one religious event he was insulted and pelted with lemons; his response was to massacre 6000 people. This led to six years of civil war, after which Alexander regained control and had his bloodthirsty vengeance. According to

Kamm (p. 155) "As he feasted with his concubines, eight hundred of his opponents were publicly crucified, and then, while they were still alive, the throats of their wives and children were cut before their eyes."

Protracted wrangling between the different factions continued, and appeals were even made to the Roman general Pompey for support. Devout Jews wanted an end to the Hasmonaean royal dynasty and a return to rule by priests. Eventually Pompey invaded Judea and took Jerusalem. At the same time, Hyrcanus II, the high priest, was appointed ethnarch (a ruler subservient to another authority) and Antipater was made procurator (administrator) of Judea. Antipater appointed a son Herod (to become Herod the Great) as governor of Galilee. Thus Judean independence came to an end in 63 B.C.

The program of economic and military expansion by the Hasmonaean rulers was supported by the Sadducees, a sect of wealthy Jewish aristocrats who embraced Greek culture. Consequently the Sadducees had a good deal of influence and most of the priests in the Temple were Sadducees. When Herod became king in 37 B.C., the Sadducees held the high priesthood, and the majority of seats on the Sanhedrin (the final authority on Jewish law).

The Pharisees came primarily from middle-class families and had tremendous influence with the common people. They stressed the importance of study of the Torah in order to achieve holiness. Pharisees differed from the Sadducees in that they believed in a Resurrection, whereas the Sadducees did not. Herod was on fairly good terms with the Pharisees as they had given him some support and, as a party, did not get involved in politics.

In contrast, he came down hard on the Sadducees, executing forty-five of their Sanhedrin members when he became king because they had supported his rival. In addition, he confiscated their property to pay off a political debt. He also made the Sanhedrin a court for religious matters only, with no power over secular matters. As he was only half-Jewish, Herod knew he could not be high priest as well as king, so he began appointing high priests at his own discretion.

The Temple in Jerusalem was noted for the awesome solemnity of its worship, its ritual, sacrifice, burning incense and singing by the choir. All this was enhanced by the appearance of the high priest, dressed in a magnificent full-length embroidered violet robe embellished with jewels and gemstones. Two lambs were sacrificed every day, and four on the Sabbath. The Temple was also the state treasury and moneychangers exchanged foreign coins for the shekels required for offerings. A staff of 20,000 was required to take care of the business of the Temple. Levites filled these positions and also served as assistants to the twenty-four teams of priests who rotated weekly.

Another group, called the Essenes, was a monastic sect that lived in remote places and rejected the authority of the Temple at Jerusalem. Their writings include the Dead Sea Scrolls at Qumran. The scrolls referred to events as early as 175 B.C., but the community was also active during the time of Jesus and later. The scrolls were made of sheep and goatskins and written largely in Hebrew but also Greek and Aramaic. They have been invaluable in confirming all the books of the Old Testament, except Esther, and parts of the Apocrypha. One of the finds was a leather scroll twenty-three feet long, containing the complete text of the Book of Isaiah. It was written in Hebrew, and has been dated at 100 B.C. The Essenes waited for a royal messiah from the line of David and in some ways were similar to early Christians in that they were "poor in spirit" and considered themselves to be members of the New Covenant.

The priest class in Jerusalem was well aware of the prophetic claims that a Messiah was to appear in order to save Israel. When Jesus began his ministry, and performed miracles, healing and other good deeds, the hierarchy of priests investigated the reports and evidently came to the conclusion that this was not the Messiah they were looking for. They were hoping for someone to lead against Roman rule but instead, Jesus' interests were not of this world-excepting love and compassion for the unfortunate. Then as Jesus' fame spread and he began to attract a following, they decided that he would have to be destroyed.

Their animosity seemed to be based on three things: 1) He questioned the behavior of the priest class, asked embarrassing questions, and took a new look at some of the Jewish traditions. People began to believe he was Christ (Greek translation of the Hebrew word Messiah, or "anointed") and prophet. 2) He disrupted Temple routine, especially when he routed the moneychangers; this put into question the authority of the chief priests and Sanhedrin, not to mention their economic interests. 3) The chief priests served as a sort of liaison between the Roman authority and the people. The priests were expected to keep the Jewish populace in line and peaceful and this may be what Caiaphas had in mind when he said "…it is expedient for you that one man may die for the people, and that the whole nation not perish" (John 11:50). It is more likely, however, that what Caiaphas really had in mind was his own status and perquisites when he talked about saving the nation.

Joseph Caiaphas was the son-in-law of the famous Annas, high priest from A.D. 6 to 15. Caiaphas was high priest from A.D. 18 to 36 and also served as president of the Sanhedrin. High priests were normally drawn from the aristocracy of the Sadducees and were appointed by Rome, so politics and bribery came into play.

Scriptures mention the Pharisees most frequently in the persecution of Jesus, but there seem to have been two schools, that of Hillel and that of Shammai. The latter group was rigid and unforgiving and Jesus took them to task as self-righteous hypocrites. In any event, there is no doubt that Caiaphas took an active role in organizing the vindictive and murderous campaign against Jesus.

Healing on the Sabbath was considered work and hence forbidden by Jewish law. In the eyes of the priests, this seems to have been one of the worst crimes that Jesus committed. "Then the Pharisees went out, and held a council against him, how they might destroy him" (Mt. 12:14). "And the Pharisees went forth, and straightway took counsel with the Herodians against him, how they might destroy him" (Mk 3:6). "And therefore did the Jews persecute Jesus, and sought to slay him, because he had done these things on the Sabbath day" (Jn 5:16).

Because he said he was the son of God, Jesus was accused of the serious crime of blasphemy, punishable by death in Jewish law. "Therefore the Jews sought the more to kill him, because he not only had broken the Sabbath, but said also that God was his Father, making himself equal with God" (Jn 5:18). "Jesus said unto them, Verily, verily, I say unto you, Before Abraham was, I am. Then they took up stones to cast at him..." (Jn 9:58, 59). "I and my Father are one. Then the Jews took up stones again to stone him" (Jn 10:30, 31).

The priests increasingly saw Jesus as a threat to their own status because the people were impressed by his miracles. "And many of the people believed on him, and said, When Christ cometh, will he do more miracles than these which this man has done?" (Jn 7:31). After Jesus raised Lazarus from the dead "Then gathered the chief priests and the Pharisees a council, and said, What do we? for this man doeth many miracles. If we let him thus alone, all men will believe on him: and the Romans shall come and take away both our place and nation" (Jn 11:47, 48). After this, in order to stifle widespread interest in the Lazarus miracle "...the chief priests consulted that they might put Lazarus also to death" (Jn 12:10).

In culmination of these events, the chief priests and Sanhedrin, headed by Caiaphas, conspired to incite a mob and successfully pressured the Romans to crucify Jesus. Certainly Jesus threatened no harm to the Roman Empire, and the Caiaphas crowd was inconvenienced only to the extent that someone questioned their methods and wanted them to change their ways.

This sorry event was probably one of the biggest mistakes in world history. It was made by a few leaders consumed with hate and able to manipulate others into following. It is the premier example of the damage that bad leadership can inflict upon a permissive population.

Consider how different the world would be if the Jewish leadership had recognized Jesus as their Messiah. Christianity and Judaism could have merged, conforming to the reforms espoused by both Jesus and Hillel. Less than 300 years after the crucifixion of Jesus, Christianity was adopted by the Roman Empire and came to be the dominant religion in the world.

[Shortly before Jesus' ministry, Hillel was the spiritual head of Israel, the head of the Sanhedrin, and the highest authority among the Pharisees. He was compared with Ezra, and was known as a saint and sage who practiced the virtues of morality in his private and public life. His reputation for meekness and mildness, and strong backing of the Golden Rule undoubtedly influenced Jesus. Hillel's grandson Gamaliel was a contemporary and sympathizer of Jesus and may have been one of Paul's teachers. After the fall of Jerusalem, the teachings of Hillel gradually seemed to gain preference, stressing a more humane, flexible approach. Concern for the poor mirrored Hillel's admonition that the basis of the Torah was to "love thy neighbor as thyself." Today, Hillel's name is used by many Jewish religious and benevolent organizations.]

Not long after Jesus was crucified, festering animosity between the Jews and Greeks eventually involved the Romans, who were required to put down several riots. In A.D. 66 a revolt broke out and soon turned into a full-fledged war when Jewish troops ambushed a Roman military column. In retaliation, the Romans, with three full legions plus auxiliaries, a total force of about 50,000, advanced through Galilee by early spring in A.D. 70 when they began the siege of Jerusalem. By that time the besieging force reached 80,000 men, under General Titus (later Emperor). The Jews fought valiantly but, of a population of 600,000, well over 100,000 people died in battle or by starvation. In August, A.D. 70, Jerusalem and the Temple fell, and were utterly leveled except for a small part of a retaining wall. This wall helped support the temple mount built by Herod in 20 B.C., and is now known as the Western Wall, or the "Wailing Wall." Hence, Jesus' words shortly before his death largely were fulfilled "there shall not be left one stone on another" (Mk 13:1 and Lk 21:6).

Masada, a tough, hilltop fortification in the desert, held out until A.D. 74 and all 960 defenders died, many by suicide as the end approached. The destruction of the Second Temple meant the end of the Sadducees, and the Essenes also disappeared at the same time. The Jewish people lost the symbolic center of their religious life and all national aspirations. Jews claim the meaning of "chosen people" is that they were chosen to preserve the word of God. Abraham was to be the "father of many nations" and Isaiah said God's servant would judge the Gentiles. But the Diaspora prevented the Jews from actualizing these prophecies and instead it was Paul and the Apostles who did it, leading a small minority of Jews in the name of Christianity ("Go ye therefore, and teach all nations).

Although dispersed throughout the world during the Diaspora, Jews tended to stay close-knit and faithful to their religion. Local communities stuck together and synagogues took the place of the Temple. Olson has shown some very interesting genetic results that seem to reflect the Jewish culture. When Jews returned to Palestine after 1800 years, their genes were different than when they left, but not to the extent of other groups that intermarry more. Of the 13 to 14 million Jews in the world today, about 10 million or three-quarters are Ashkenazim who settled in central and Eastern Europe. They are taller and lighter-skinned than other Jews due to intermarriage, but at the rate of less than one percent of Jewish women in each generation.

The Jewish word for priest is *kohanim*, from which the surnames such as Cohn, Cohen and Kahn are derived. In Exodus, God decreed that Aaron, Moses' older brother, and all his descendants would be the high priests. Since men pass their Y-chromosomes on to their sons, all of Aaron's descendants should have his Y chromosome. When checked, Jews who were non-priests had a wide assortment of Y-chromosome markers, whereas in the priest group, about 50 percent had the particular marker, called the Cohen Modal Haplotype, proving a common ancestor.

An interesting case involves the Lemba tribe of black Africans in southern Africa. The Lemba traditions say their ancestors came by boat, were Jewish and introduced circumcision and certain food taboos. When tested in 1997, their Y-chromosomes showed that two-thirds of the population had a Middle Eastern origin. Furthermore, they were the Cohen Modal Haplotype-the marker for the Jewish priesthood. Evidently the priests contributed more than just their religious beliefs.

In this summary of the Jewish people and their religion, their ability to survive stands out as the most astonishing thing. They overcame slavery in Egypt and at least six national defeats during the days of Judges in unsettled Canaan. After that they experienced exile, first in Assyria and then in Babylon, following the fall of Jerusalem. After returning from Babylon they ruled their own country for only 206 years, until Alexander the Great took over. His rule led to a strong Greek influence and the very loss of the Hebrew language. The Maccabee/Hasmonaean dynasty provided a respite of 104 years but then the Romans conquered and demolished Jerusalem, scattering the Jews worldwide.

One has to be amazed by the ability of the Jews to retain their ethnic coherence during the 1878 years of the Diaspora, including the Holocaust when at least half their population was exterminated. Their hopes of returning to Palestine (Zionism) got a significant boost when the Balfour Declaration was signed in 1917, during some dark days of World War I. Basically, this was a British statement of support for a Jewish homeland in Palestine. In typical British fashion, the benefits for England were the main concern, rather than any high-minded thoughts about helping the Jews. For example, Britain thought the move would influence Jewish interests in America to help get the U.S. into the war, as well as keep Russia in the war by way of the large number of Jewish Bolsheviks involved in the Russian revolution. Prime Minister Lloyd George had already decided to abrogate the 1916 secret Syke-Picot agreement with France and take over Palestine by force. Chaim Weizmann did much skillful negotiating for the Zionist cause, including manipulation of the British media. The final letter to Lord Rothschild, dated November 2, 1917, declared Britain's "sympathy with Jewish Zionist aspirations."

Against all odds, the modern state of Israel emerged in 1948, formed by tenacious Jewish patriots who utilized all their military, economic and political skills. In leading up to 1948, Jews at times used terrorist methods of their own (most prominent were the Stern Gang and Irgun, who killed British diplomats and police; Yitzak Shamir was the most famous member of the Stern Gang and Menachem Begin was a member of both groups).

Israel's War of Independence began even before May 14, 1948, when the United Nations created the state of Israel. But that date signaled the assault of five Arab armies, with 720,000 troops, from the neighboring countries. Simultaneous attacks from the north, east, and south were repulsed by the Israeli army of 140,000, almost the entire military-age population. By the time the Israel-Syria armistice agreement was signed July 20, 1949, the Arabs had lost 8000 and the Israelis 6000. In 1949 Israel initiated the formation of a Swiss-style reserve force, based on a small standing officer corps, universal conscription, and an extensive pool of well-trained reservists that could be mobilized quickly.

In 1965 and 1966, Gamal Nasser in Egypt and Hafez Assad in Syria began stepping up their rhetoric and hostile actions against Israel. In May, 1967, Nasser closed the Straits of Tiran (entrance to Gulf of Aqaba) to all ships headed to Eilat, effectively cutting off Israel's oil supply. By early June, Iraq had joined the military alliance with Egypt, Syria and Jordan, and Israel was facing 250,000 troops, 2000 tanks and 700 aircraft.

On the morning of June 5, 1967 Israel struck first and in a surprise attack destroyed Egypt's air force on the ground. Israel's army then proceeded to defeat enemy forces in the Sinai, at the Golan Heights and in East Jerusalem. At the end of the six-day war, Israel controlled the Sinai, Gaza Strip, the Golan Heights and a reunited Jerusalem. Jordan, drawn into the war because of mixed signals, lost the West Bank, by far the most important prize.

Throughout much of 1972 and 1973 Egyptian President Anwar Sadat threatened war unless Israel withdrew from the 1967 territorial gains, as specified in UN Resolution 242. On October 6, 1973, Egypt and Syria made a surprise attack on Israel. The day was Yom Kippur, the holiest day of the year for Jews. Along the Suez Canal, 80,000 Egyptian troops faced 500 Israelis, and at the Golan Heights, 1100 Syrian tanks faced 157. At least nine Arab states, plus four other nations from outside the area, actively supported the Arabs. Initially the Israeli forces were thrown back but after a few days they gained the advantage and struck deep into Egypt and Syria. Israel was in position to destroy the Egyptian Third Army west of the Suez Canal when the UN called for a cease-fire, which became effective October 25, 1973. Israel lost a total of 2688 soldiers killed, and considered the war a diplomatic and military failure.

Since 1948, harsh repression of the Palestinians has caused worldwide revulsion, but needs to be weighed against the right of Israel to protect its people from terrorism. Since 1949, the U.S. has given financial assistance to Israel totaling about $100 billion, two-thirds of which has been in the form of military grants. In addition, various Jewish organizations have contributed another $11 billion.

Politically, the U.S. has been a steady, long-term supporter of Israel. Since 1972, the U.S. has vetoed thirty-five UN resolutions that were unfavorable to Israel, and in many cases the U.S. did this as the sole supporter.

Israel has ignored several UN resolutions it does not like, including 242, 181, 338 and especially 194, which calls for the right of return of Palestinian refugees.

Another worrisome matter is the atomic arsenal Israel is believed to possess. Israel denies it has atomic weapons but knowledgeable sources say it may have 100–200 nuclear bombs, deliverable by guided missiles. The facts about this situation are murky indeed; how was it accomplished, and what are the numbers and kinds of weapons involved? The Nuclear Nonproliferation Treaty (NPT) has been ratified by 189 nations, including the five major nuclear states. Israel refuses to allow any inspections, putting it in the same class as North Korea, which is thought to have atomic weapons capability.

There are about 6 million Jews in North America today. Their religious grouping is 18 percent Conservative, 16 percent Reform and 10 percent Orthodox. More than half are unaffiliated, but all Jews seem to retain a strong degree of loyalty to their ethnic culture.

6

CHRISTIANITY—
NEW TESTAMENT

The New Testament is primarily concerned with Christ, his ministry, his crucifixion and resurrection, and the creation of his church. The four gospels, plus the epistles of Paul, set forth God's purpose to form a new community of Christians, transcending all distinctions of race or nationality. Jews such as Jesus, Philip, Stephen, Paul and others were the initial champions of a plan for a universal fellowship which was expected to include Jews. As it turned out, within a few decades the Christian community was almost entirely made up of Gentiles and today, two billion people or one-third of the world population, are Christians.

Jesus and his disciples worshipped in the temple in Jerusalem and Jesus himself spoke there, and in various synagogues. They considered the Jewish Torah as part of their bible, although at that time in history the Greek translation, the Septuagint, was commonly used and the spoken language was Aramaic. The earliest Christians were Jews, as was Jesus himself, and considered the Old Testament to be the foundation of the New. As Jesus said, according to Matthew 5:17, "Do not think that I have come to abolish the Law or the prophets. I have not come to abolish them, but to fulfill them."

The teaching of Jesus was often in line with many of the prophets of the Old Testament, especially Isaiah, Jeremiah, Hosea and Amos, and sometimes the Essene sect. But Jesus refused to identify with any political group, be it Jewish, Roman or Greek. He especially rejected the idea of being a Messiah to rescue or restore the kingdom of Israel. He strongly criticized the priest class (Sadducees and Pharisees) for their hypocrisy, love of wealth and power, and neglect of the poor and weak.

The Old Testament has been called the rule of law, the New Testament, the rule of love. The concept of "an eye for an eye" contrasts with "turn the other cheek" though in practice, the usual approach seems to have been "hate your enemy when he deserves it." The Old Testament is built around the idea of God's covenant with Israel, and the New Testament is about Jesus and the church. Many Christians recognize that the Old Testament contains some erroneous history, doctrine they do not believe, and morality that cannot be practiced. Hence, the Bible makes more sense as a record of man's response to God's presence and influence rather than as an inerrant or literal historical account.

The literature of the Bible describes the human condition of ordinary people and occurrences of contemporary life. It is an accurate portrayal of human nature in which people can readily identify with the struggles, temptations, deceptions, achievements and failures described. God is depicted as demanding and jealous, but also as long-suffering, loving and compassionate. This image of God mirrors in some respects mankind's evolutionary progress from selfishness to the first glimmer of altruism. Man's advance often seems snail-like in absolute terms but actually has been fairly rapid, helped and encouraged by the guidance of such people as Jesus.

Throughout the Bible, God's influence on evolution of the human soul is recognized. The Old Testament repeatedly refers to the "Spirit of God" and "Spirit of the Lord" for example "...take not thy holy spirit from me" (Ps. 51:11). Later, Isaiah seemingly predicted, with breath-taking precision, the coming of Jesus (7:14, 9:6, 11:10, 42:1 and 53:5); in the 42:1 passage God even said "...I have put my spirit upon him...." In the New Testament, careful attention was given to the concept of the Holy Spirit or Holy Ghost, and the Doctrine of the Trinity was developed.

MINISTRY OF JESUS

It is reasonable to assume that his mother, Mary, explained to Jesus the unusual nature of his birth. That, plus early education and reading of the scriptures, provided Jesus an early understanding of who he was. It was an unusually perceptive youth who met with the priests in Jerusalem and held mature discussions at the age of twelve. It is believed that Jesus had four brothers and two sisters (stepsiblings?), but details of his childhood are almost completely lacking. In any event, he was about thirty-five years old when he began his active ministry, which may have lasted only a little more than two years, beginning in Galilee.

Even before his baptism by John the Baptist, Jesus began to receive attention throughout the region because of his powers of healing, considered miraculous by many. This fact is attested by the words of Luke. When John's emissaries queried Jesus, he responded (Lk 7:22): "tell John what things ye have seen and heard; how the blind see, the lame walk, the lepers are cleansed, the deaf hear, the dead are raised, to the poor the gospel is preached."

John the Baptist lived in the wilderness wore crude garb and ate locusts and wild honey. He called upon men to be baptized by water to show their penitence, but prophesied one would follow who would baptize with the Holy Ghost. When Jesus asked to be baptized, John said "Behold the Lamb of God, which taketh away the sin of the world" (Jn 1:29). After the baptism of Jesus, John saw the Spirit descending from the heavens like a dove, and testified that "this is the Son of God" (Jn 1:33, 34). Matthew and Mark both added that a voice from heaven also said this is "my beloved Son, in whom I am well pleased."

The contemporary Jewish historian Josephus confirmed that John the Baptist was a good man who urged the Jews to strive for perfection, and walk humbly with God. As many people flocked to him for baptism, John attracted attention, including that of the ruler Herod Antipas, son of Herod the Great. Antipas lusted after his brother's wife, Herodias, and eventually married her. John the Baptist denounced this marriage as being against Jewish law and thereby enraged Herodias. When his new daughter-in-law Salome danced entrancingly for Herod, he promised her anything she wanted. What she wanted was the head of John the Baptist, and Herod complied.

Jesus' healing power gained a great deal of favorable comment and attention, and attracted a crowd of followers from whom he selected twelve disciples. Miraculous cures and events were described in all four of the gospels, and at least thirty-three specific instances were described. A few of the well-known cures included the centurion's servant, Peter's mother-in-law, devils transferred from madmen into a herd of swine, the man with palsy brought on a bed, the two blind men at Jericho, the dumb man possessed of a devil, and the lunatic son. Three cases of reviving the dead were described, including that of Lazarus. Other familiar miracles included turning water into wine, walking on water, calming the storm, the loaves and fishes, and the transfiguration of Jesus when he met Moses and Elijah on a high mountain.

It is interesting that miracles, such as summarized above, seem to be almost a characteristic of the ministry and life of Jesus. As a fundamental, other religions have rejected the concept or possibility of miracles. The Old Testament may have described some unbelievable and impossible situations, but they were never considered miracles. Dembski pointed out that in China, Confucius did not accept miracles. Buddha was also opposed to the idea, and Muhammad rejected all miracles other than the Koran.

As early as Cicero (106–43 B.C.), scientists argued that nature required proof and logic, and he said "...we therefore draw this conclusion: what was incapable of happening never happened, and what was capable of happening is not a miracle." My Oxford dictionary defines a miracle as a highly improbable or extraordinary event, development, or accomplishment; also a surprising or amazing event that cannot be explained by natural or scientific laws and is considered to be divine.

A logical argument could be made that reporting may have been biased and/or faulty. However, a large number of people were witnesses to Jesus' miracles and even the chief priests and Pharisees admitted to "many miracles" (Jn 11:47). My own conclusion is that many of these things apparently happened but cannot be explained, hence by definition they were miracles of the divine variety.

[As an aside, and by way of comparison, in the scientific world we know certain inexplicable things occur, or have happened, but are not considered scientific facts because proof does not exist and processes cannot be repeated in the laboratory. Two examples are (1) a singularity or black hole, and (2) the sudden appearance of as many as thirty new, advanced animal phyla almost simultaneously during the Cambrian explosion. Scientists cannot explain why virtually all the major animal body forms (phyla) showed up, almost instantaneously in geologic terms, and no new phyla have evolved since.]

It is clear that the power of Jesus to perform miraculous cures got the attention of John the Baptist, priests and Pharisees, the general populace, and even king Herod. It also may have been the main factor in explaining why people were literally willing to drop whatever work they were doing to follow Jesus. By doing so, they committed themselves to a full-time effort, with no pay, with poor and sometimes dangerous living conditions, a cause that must have been uncertain and not even fully understood.

Apparently, the first two disciples were fishermen, one named Simon Peter and the other his brother, named Andrew. Both were from Galilee and followers of John the Baptist. When Jesus said "follow me and I will make you fishers of men" they left their nets and followed him. Walking a little further they came upon two other brothers, also fishermen, James and John, mending their nets in a ship with their father Zebedee. When Jesus called them, they immediately left their father and ship and followed. This version (Mt. 4:18–22) is somewhat different than that of Luke 5:8–11, in which Simon Peter, James and John were partners. They were all astonished when they netted an enormous catch of fish after following the directions of Jesus, and became his original followers. These three were some of those closest to Jesus.

Simon Peter was married, a warm-hearted and impulsive man. When Jesus tested the disciples, he was recognized by Peter as the Son of God. At that, Jesus blessed him and stated that Peter was the rock upon which he would build his church. At the time of the crucifixion, Peter faltered in fear but afterward became a strong and steady leader of the Church.

John was believed to be the disciple whom "Jesus loved." Before he died, Jesus entrusted John to look after his mother. John was one of the three main leaders of the Church in Jerusalem.

Philip was from the same town as Peter and Andrew. The gospel of Philip was one of the Coptic texts found at Nag Hammadi in 1945 (more about this later). Philip's friend was Bartholomew (aka Nathanael) and after the crucifixion they traveled together in Asia.

Matthew (aka Levi) was a tax collector, a despised occupation then and now. When Jesus called him, he followed, and later they had dinner together. When the Pharisees complained, Jesus said he would expend his efforts in redeeming sinners and outcasts, rather than spending unneeded time with the righteous.

Thomas Didymus was another disciple who sometimes voiced his uncertainty while Jesus lived, and John called him "doubting Thomas" when he asked to see Jesus' nail and spear wounds. The gospel of Thomas was also found at Nag Hammadi and some scholars believe it should be accepted as an authentic fifth gospel, of equal stature to the synoptics and John.

Two other disciples were James, son of Judas the Galilean, and Thaddaeus, (name used instead of Judas, son of James). Another was Simon the Zealot, that is, a patriot who opposed Roman rule. And finally, Judas Iscariot, the only disciple from Judea, and the traitor who ultimately betrayed Jesus. According to Mt. 27:5 he committed suicide by hanging, but in Acts 1:18 he fell in the field he bought with the thirty pieces of silver, burst open, and "all his bowels gushed out."

In sum, Jesus recruited a total of twelve disciples, a number chosen purposefully to conform to the original twelve tribes of Israel. His disciples were mostly members of the middle class, and most were illiterate as were the vast majority of people at that time. There were no priests included, and evidently some potential volunteers were turned down because they were not sufficiently motivated or free to devote their full time and support. Jesus made his selections as carefully as possible from willing and able Jewish laymen of Galilee, but of course made a mistake when it came to Judas.

Almost immediately, Jesus began a training program, instructing the disciples in the meaning and purposes of his ministry. As the group walked from place to place in Galilee, Jesus continued to demonstrate his concern for the poor and neglected, and at times his ability to effect miraculous cures of the disabled. He preached in various synagogues, especially at Capernaum, and on a daily basis talked to the disciples, frequently using parables.

About one-third of Jesus' teachings were in the form of parables and even the controversial Jesus Seminar recognized the validity and accuracy of many of those recorded in the Gospels. Each parable was designed to make a point, and required the listener to compare his interpretation to events or the situation in his own life. All required thought, but some of the parables were more straightforward than others, and the meaning of some is still being debated. Jesus used simple examples, situations familiar to people at that time, to illustrate the proper behavior for those who wanted to be in God's new kingdom. The synoptic gospels (from the same perspective) of Matthew, Mark, and Luke record a total of forty-two parables, but John reports none. Some of the best known are the prodigal son, the Good Samaritan, the pearl of great price, the good shepherd, the hidden treasure, and the lost sheep.

Another part of his teaching for the disciples was in the form of pithy words of wisdom such as the Golden Rule, the Beatitudes, and how to pray. The Golden Rule appears in most religions. Its earliest expression may have been about 3000 B.C. in the first forms of Hinduism. It was present in ancient Egyptian, then in the Torah and later in Buddhism, Confucianism, and Islam. No doubt, Jesus was familiar with Leviticus 19:18 "thou shalt love thy neighbour as thyself," re-emphasized by Rabbi Hillel the Elder only a generation before Jesus.

In Mt. 5:1–12, known as the Beatitudes, from the Sermon on the Mount, Jesus summarized the actions and attitudes, the hope-sustaining promises, and the blessings and rewards of those who followed God's wishes.

- Blessed are the poor in spirit: for theirs is the kingdom of heaven.

- Blessed are they that mourn: for they shall be comforted.

- Blessed are the meek: for they shall inherit the earth.

- Blessed are they which do hunger and thirst after righteousness: for they shall be filled.

- Blessed are the merciful: for they shall obtain mercy.

- Blessed are the pure in heart: for they shall see God.

- Blessed are the peacemakers: for they shall be called the children of God.

- Blessed are they which are persecuted for righteousness' sake: for theirs is the kingdom of heaven.

- Blessed are ye, when men shall revile you, and persecute you, and shall say all manner of evil against you falsely, for my sake. Rejoice, and be exceeding glad: for great is your reward in heaven.

Jesus also instructed the disciples to try to follow and to repeat his message which he further elaborated in a series of "wise sayings" (aphorisms). The disciples were handicapped by almost a total lack of written records, hence limited in their ability to accurately pass on all they heard. After the crucifixion their testimony was mostly verbal, to different audiences and other third parties. Keeping this deficiency in mind, the following list of sayings by Jesus has been selected from Matthew, in chronologic order:

- …Man shall not live by bread alone… 4:4.

- …your Father knoweth what things ye have need of, before ye ask Him. 6:8.

- For where your treasure is, there will your heart be also. 6:21.

- No man can serve two masters…Ye cannot serve God and mammon. 6:24.

- Consider the lilies of the field, how they grow; they toil not, neither do they spin: and yet I say unto you, That even Solomon in all his glory was not arrayed like one of these. 6:28–9.

- Judge not, that ye be not judged. 7:1.

- ...neither cast ye your pearls before swine...7:6.

- Ask, and it shall be given you; seek, and ye shall find; knock, and it shall be opened unto you. 7:7.

- ...by their fruits ye shall know them. 7:20.

- Why are ye fearful, O ye of little faith? 8:26.

- Heal the sick, raise the dead, cleanse the lepers, drive out demons. Freely ye have received, freely give. 10:8.

- Come unto me, all ye that labor and are heavy laden and I will give you rest. 11:28.

- He that is not with me is against me...12:30.

- ...blessed are your eyes, for they see: and your ears, for they hear 13:16.

- A prophet is not without honor, save in his own country, and in his own house. 13:57.

- ...if the blind lead the blind...15:14.

- For what is a man profited, if he shall gain the whole world, and lose his own soul? 16:26.

- For where two or three are gathered together in my name, there am I in the midst of them. 18:20.

- ...it is easier for a camel to go through the eye of a needle, than for a rich man to enter into the kingdom of God. 19:24.

- For many are called, but few are chosen. 20:16.

- Render therefore unto Caesar the things which are Caesar's; and unto God the things that are God's. 22:21.

- Thou shalt love the Lord thy God with all thy heart, and with all thy soul, and with all thy mind. This is the first and great commandment. And the second is like unto it, Thou shalt love thy neighbor as thyself. On these two commandments hang all the law and the prophets. 22:37–40.

- When the Son of Man shall come in his glory…he shall separate them one from another, as…sheep from the goats. 25:31-2.

- …as ye have done it unto one of the least of these my brethren, ye have done it unto me. 25:40.

- …the spirit indeed is willing, but the flesh is weak. 26:41.

- …for all they that take the sword shall perish with the sword 26:52.

- Go ye therefore, and teach all nations, baptizing them in the name of the Father, and of the Son, and of the Holy Ghost. 28:19.

The Gospels of Mark, Luke and John added the following:

- …if a house be divided against itself, that house cannot stand. Mk 3:25.

- What therefore God hath joined together, let not man put asunder. Mk 10:9.

- Suffer the little children to come unto me, and forbid them not: for of such is the kingdom of God. Mk 10:14.

- But many that are first shall be last; and the last first. Mk 10:31.

- … condemn not, and ye shall not be condemned; forgive and ye shall be forgiven: give, and it shall be given unto you…Lk 6:37–8.

- And he said to the woman, Thy faith hath saved thee; go in peace. Lk 7:50.

- But even the very hairs of your head are numbered. Lk 12:7.

- For unto whomsoever much is given, of him shall be much required. Lk 12:48.

- Except a man be born again, he cannot see the kingdom of God. Jn 3:3.

- God so loved the world, that he gave his only begotten Son, that whosoever believeth in him should not perish, but have everlasting life. Jn 3:16.

- God is a Spirit: and they that worship him must worship him in spirit and in truth. Jn 4:24.

- He that believeth on me hath everlasting life. Jn 6:47.

- He that is without sin among you, let him first cast a stone at her Jn 8:7.

- And ye shall know the truth, and the truth shall make you free. Jn 8:32.

- ...I am the way, the truth, and the life: no man cometh unto the Father, but by me. Jn 14:6.

- ...Thomas, because thou hast seen me, thou hast believed: blessed are they that have not seen, and yet have believed. Jn 20:29.

The transfiguration episode was witnessed by Peter, James, and John and described in the three synoptic gospels. According to them, apparently at night, Jesus met with the apparitions of Moses and Elijah on a high mountain. While he was praying, his face shown as the sun and his raiment became white as snow. Then, a bright cloud appeared above from which a voice said "This is my beloved Son, in whom I am well pleased; hear ye him." Deffinbaugh has explained that this was the one occasion when "the veil of His humanity was momentarily lifted and His divine splendor and glory burst forth."

Primarily, the transfiguration was for the purpose of demonstrating to the three disciples the divine confirmation of Jesus' status. The three were sleepy and confused but no doubt the event they witnessed was a mind-boggling experience. Through it, they began to understand that the purpose of the Messiah was not to break the bonds with Rome; eventually they finally realized his true purpose was to redeem men from sin by dying on the cross. Peter made some silly comments on the mountain, while stressed-out, but years later, when he comprehended fully, he described the event more appropriately in II Peter 1:16–18 "For we...were eyewitnesses of his majesty. For he received from God the Father, honor and glory, when there came such a voice...this is my beloved Son, in whom I am well pleased. And this voice which came from the heaven we heard, when we were with Him in the holy mount."

In addition to the disciples, a number of women were strong supporters of Jesus and closely associated with his ministry. First, of course was his mother, Mary, who sometimes traveled with Jesus and according to Matthew was at the cross when Jesus was crucified. Traditionally, in the last years of her life she lived in Ephesus and was looked after by John, the beloved disciple.

Mary Magdalene was the most important woman disciple and a cloud of literature has been written about her, much of it false. What seems most likely is that she was from Magdala, on the west shore of Lake Galilee, hence the surname. She was first mentioned in Luke 8:2, 3, together with Joanna and Susanna and many others, as "certain women...which ministered unto him of their substance." Magdalene was described as "out of whom went seven devils," but never as a prostitute. She was next mentioned in all the Gospels as standing at the foot of the cross and then as the first witness of the Resurrection. The Gnostic Gospel of Mary adds evidence of her importance to early Christianity.

Some of the most novel claims about her are that she wrote the Gospel of John; that she, Lazarus and others went to southern France and converted the whole of Provence; that she was linked to the Holy Grail and the Knights Templar. Dan Brown's astonishing novel, *The Da Vinci Code*, is a recent best-seller that enlarges on the latter story, adding that Jesus and Mary Magdalene were married and had children (see p.306).

Joanna was the second woman, of the three named by Luke, who found Jesus' tomb empty and reported this to the apostles. She was the wife of Chuza, who was a steward of Herod Antipas.

Martha of Bethany, together with her sister Mary and brother Lazarus, were mentioned prominently in Luke and John. It was this Mary who bathed Jesus' feet with an expensive ointment, and dried them with her hair (Jn.11:2 and 12:3).

After the last supper, Jesus personally washed and dried the feet of each disciple, as an example of humble love. [I can especially appreciate this gesture because I have frequently seen poor Kurdish women, in southeast Turkey carrying huge loads of kindling on their backs as they trudged along a dusty, rocky road, with simple sandals or barefoot. In fact, when they came to sharp rocks they would take off the sandals to avoid wear—on the sandals.].

Another Mary was the wife of Zebedee and the mother of the disciples James and John. Matthew and Mark both described how this "other Mary" and Mary Magdalene witnessed Jesus' body being put into the sepulcher and then being gone on the third day.

The love and loyalty exhibited by the male and female disciples attested to Jesus' concern for them, and for the crowds of people. His parables and wise sayings, his concern for the weak and poor, plus miraculous cures of the sick, were the essence of Jesus' ministry which had the goal of convincing people to have faith in God.

Thomas Jefferson once said that he found in the words of Jesus *"the most sublime and benevolent code of morals which have ever been offered to man." My own observation is that Jesus was the most perfect man to ever live.*

THE CRUCIFIXION

Numerous passages in the Gospels attest to the fact that Jesus was on a collision course with the "scribes, Pharisees, and chief priests" almost from the beginning. Initially, John the Baptist called them a "generation of vipers" and that Jesus would soon baptize them with fire and the Holy Ghost. As Jesus conducted his ministry, some of his miraculous cures took place on the Sabbath, which "work" drew the attention and condemnation of the Pharisees. Jesus pointed out that his accusers would care for their own animals on the Sabbath, yet charged him with breaking the law by taking care of sick and crippled people. In two instances, the Jews wanted to kill him for curing someone on the Sabbath (Mt 12:14 and Jn 5:5–18) and for blasphemy in another case when he said he was the Son of God (Jn 8:37–59). In three other instances, plans to kill Jesus were discussed by Caiaphas, chief priests, Pharisees and scribes, in different groupings.

A brief explanation of these people may help explain the interplay of the forces involved in the crucifixion of Jesus. The scribes were a literate, learned profession who maintained the Law of the Torah, and often answered questions over interpretation of the sacred books. Because the scribes maintained records of the Law, they had an affinity with the Pharisees who venerated the Law.

The Pharisees wanted to educate everyone in Israel through a study of the Torah. They came primarily from middle-class families and became a significant force in Jewish affairs because of their influence with the common people. Many Pharisees were in the lower ranks of priests. In the synoptic Gospels, Jesus accused the Pharisees of being wicked, hypocrites, self-righteous, serpents and vipers, ready to kill prophets and wise men, and notorious for seeking titles, praise, and luxury for themselves. (For good measure, Luke added lawyers to the list—maybe the first case of antagonism between doctors and trial lawyers).

As will be shown later, Pharisees were not the main instigators of crucifying Jesus. Jesus ate dinner with Pharisees, and Paul himself was a Pharisee and proud of it. Another one, Nicodemus, asked Jesus how to become born-again, and the early church included a large number of Pharisees. In terms of Jewishness, eventually the Hillel school won out and this form of Pharisaic Judaism survived the catastrophe of A.D. 70 and came to be practiced by Jews throughout the world.

The Sadducees were generally wealthy members of the Jewish upper class who embraced Hellenism. Most of the chief priests in the Temple were Sadducees who also held the majority of seats on the Sanhedrin. The high priest was appointed by Herod; bribery was involved so the high priest regularly came from a small group of wealthy Sadducean families. During Herod's reign, the position of high priest was changed an average of every four years. At the time of Jesus, Caiaphas, as high priest, was also the official head of the Sanhedrin and consequently responsible for conducting Jesus' trial before seventy Jewish elders. From the Gospels, McKenzie (1982) has compiled the following list of the times people were identified as being involved in the death of Jesus: chief priests fifty-eight times, scribes twelve, Jews ten, and Pharisees two.

Before his crucifixion, Jesus told the disciples what was going to happen. In Mark 10:33–34 he said "Behold, we go up to Jerusalem; and the Son of man shall be delivered unto the chief priests, and unto the scribes; and they shall condemn him to death, and shall deliver him to the Gentiles: and they shall mock him, and shall scourge him, and shall spit upon him, and shall kill him: and the third day he shall rise again."

Jesus also emphasized that all this had been prophesized in the Jewish scriptures. According to Luke 18:3, "…all things that are written by the prophets concerning the Son of man shall be accomplished." He was, of course, referring to the words in the previous chapter, especially from Psalms, Isaiah and Zechariah.

Jesus spent much of his last week in Bethany, a village just outside Jerusalem. He stayed at the home of Simon the leper; while there he ate with Lazarus, who he had raised from the dead. Two sisters of Lazarus were there, Martha who cooked, and Mary who bathed Jesus' feet with expensive ointment and used her own long hair as a towel. Many people came to see Lazarus, further inflaming the Pharisees to the point they considered having Lazarus killed because of the adulation given to Jesus, the miracleworker. (Jn 12:1–11 and Mt 26:6–13).

Jesus went to Jerusalem by way of the Mount of Olives; from there the city below was a beautiful sight and the temple complex was the most magnificent of all. The temple itself was of light marble, with decorations of pure gold. The east-facing façade was 150 feet high and the breadth was the same. The Tabernacle was in the center and the whole set of buildings was surrounded by a huge wall with four corner turrets almost 120 feet high.

As foretold, Jesus rode on an ass and was met by a multitude of people who carpeted his way with palm branches and articles of clothing, shouting "Hosanna in the highest." When Jesus reached the Temple he further antagonized the priests by chasing out the moneychangers and those who sold animals for sacrifice. When he went back to Bethany, Caiaphas and the chief priests made final plans to apprehend Jesus, try him, and have him executed, all before the Sabbath of Passover.

The last twelve hours of Jesus' life commenced at 3:00 A.M. on the Friday before Passover. Jesus and eleven of the disciples were gathered in the Garden of Gethsemane on the Mount of Olives when Judas came, leading "a great multitude with swords and staves, from the chief priests and the scribes and the elders" (Mk 14:43). With little resistance, Jesus was taken into custody and delivered to Annas, Caiaphas' father-in-law, where Peter three times denied knowing Jesus. From there, he was brought before Caiaphas and the Sanhedrin, perhaps seventy people in all, although it must have been about dawn. After a short "trial" Caiaphas pronounced the death penalty on the charge of blasphemy, because Jesus said he was the Son of God. It is clear that it was the temple hierarchy—Caiaphas, the chief priests, and Sanhedrin—who were the sole perpetrators, certainly not the ordinary Jew (many of whom had demonstrated their respect and adulation a few days before, and during most of the previous weeks and months).

At that time, Pontius Pilate was the Roman procurator of Judea and existing law required that he had to confirm the death sentence. So early in the morning, the Jewish leaders, together with a "mob" (probably the Temple police) took Jesus to a hearing before Pilate. Pilate said he could "find no fault in this man" (Lk 23:4) and sent him to Herod when it was disclosed that Jesus was from Galilee, which was in Herod's jurisdiction. The result of this was that neither Herod nor Pilate found Jesus "worthy of death" (Lk 23:6–15).

But the mob persisted, screaming "crucify him, crucify him." Pilate may have been persuaded when the Jews said Jesus had claimed to be king (Jn 19:12). This would be treasonous to Caesar, and could threaten Pilate himself for neglect of duty in acquitting a rebel. Pilate at the time was in poor standing with Rome, so he caved in and permitted the crucifixion, presumably on the basis of sedition, a civil crime.

With that, the Roman execution squad took over. Romans were experts at performing this horrible punishment, called by Cicero "the most cruel and frightful means of execution" and by Josephus "the most pitiable of all forms of death" (Keller, p. 387). The process began with "scourging" which always preceded crucifixion. In this stage of the torture, the person was stripped naked and flogged with metal or bone-tipped thongs that shredded flesh into bloody strips. In his *The Passion of the Christ* Mel Gibson tried to create an accurate portrayal of this historical event. This required showing the raw violence inflicted upon Jesus, and the suffering and agony he experienced. The seemingly endless scourging scene was the most difficult to watch of the whole movie, even more shocking than the nails of the crucifixion itself.

After the scourging, the Roman soldiers continued their abuse by spitting on him, further blows, mocking, putting a crown of thorns upon his head, and at some point cast lots for his coat. The Roman detail, headed by a centurion, took Jesus to nearby Golgotha, the place of execution, also called "the place of a skull." By that time Jesus was too weak to carry his own cross, so they forced Simon, from Cyrene (in Libya) to carry the cross. Mark 15:23 says wine laced with myrrh was offered to Jesus at this time, a form of anesthetic to numb his pain, but he refused it. When the nails were driven into Jesus' feet and hands, Mark says it was the third hour, or about 9:00 A.M.

During his six hours on the cross, Jesus spoke seven times:

- "Father forgive them; for they know not what they do." Lk 23:34.
- To the thief who believed, "Verily I say unto thee, Today shalt thou be with me in paradise." Lk 23:43.
- To Mary, his mother, "Woman, behold thy son!" And to John, "Behold thy mother!" Jn 19:26, 27.
- Near the end, "My God, my God, why hast thou forsaken me?" Mt 27:46.
- "I thirst" Jn 19:28.
- "Father into thy hands I commend my spirit." Lk 23:46.
- After the vinegar, "It is finished." Jn 19:30.

It was not unusual for victims of crucifixion to stay alive on the cross for two days or even longer. Jesus was not a robust, physically strong person, however, and he had been badly abused by scourging, so by all accounts he died at about the ninth hour, or 3:00 P.M. It is known that some of the chief priests observed all this because they complained about the sign

Pilate put on the cross: "THIS IS JESUS THE KING OF THE JEWS" (This wording is different in each of the four Gospels). They also mocked him and, later, requested that Jesus and the two thieves crucified with him be killed by "crurifragium" in order that their bodies could be taken down from the cross before 6:00 P.M., when the Sabbath day began. The crurifragium meant breaking the victim's legs below the knee so he could not rest his weight on the footrest attached to the vertical beam. The two thieves were dispatched in this way, which means they died rather quickly of heart failure. When the soldiers came to Jesus they saw he was already dead, but to make sure thrust a spear into his side which drew a flow of blood and water. As it ended, the centurion said either "this was a righteous man" or "this man was the Son of God."

According to John 19:25 and 26, Mary Magdalene, John, Mary the mother of Jesus, and Mary's sister all stood by the cross. All the other disciples seem to have been too fearful, and nowhere in sight.

All four Gospels describe how Joseph of Arimathaea, a member of the Sanhedrin and supporter of Jesus, approached Pilate to request that he be allowed to take the body and prepare it for burial. After the centurion confirmed that Jesus was dead, Pilate agreed to the request. Nicodemus, another Sanhedrin member, brought a hundred pounds of myrrh and aloes, used with fine linen to wrap the body. The body was then placed in a nearby sepulcher, originally intended for Joseph's own burial. The burial chamber was newly excavated out of rock, and never used before. The final step was to roll a large rock into place to seal the sepulcher. Some of the women witnessed the burial process and Matthew 27:62–66 describes how the chief priests asked Pilate to seal the stone and set a watch of soldiers to make sure the disciples did not steal the body.

THE RESURRECTION

Early in the morning following the Sabbath, some of the women went to the sepulcher where they found the rock had been rolled away and the body of Jesus was gone. Matthew named the women as Mary Magdalene and the other Mary; Mark named Mary Magdalene and Mary the mother of James and Salome; Luke named Mary Magdalene, Mary the mother of James, Joanna, and other women; and John named only Mary Magdalene. Matthew and Mark both described one angel as being present, whereas Luke and John had two angels; all were in white and/or brightly illuminated. Matthew was the only Gospel to describe soldiers guarding the tomb, and in 28:11–15 told how the chief priests gave a bribe to the soldiers to lie about the disciples stealing the body while they slept.

Each of the synoptic Gospels had the angels telling the women to go and tell the disciples that Jesus was risen and no longer in the tomb, but in Mark they were too frightened to do so. According to John, Mary Magdalene of her own accord ran to tell Peter and John and they both ran back to the sepulcher. John got there first and looking inside, saw the linen wrapping. Peter was right behind and went into the tomb and he too saw the empty wrappings; those from the head were in a separate place. John 20:8 and 9 seems rather strange in saying (about John, when he came inside the tomb) "…he saw, and believed. For as yet they knew not the scripture that he must rise again from the dead." Strange, because in Mark 10, Jesus had told the disciples, in detail, what was going to happen, including rising from the dead on the third day.

The resurrected Jesus soon appeared to his followers in a number of places, five alone on that first Easter Sunday. Apparently the first to see him was Mary Magdalene, just outside the tomb. She first thought it was the gardener, but when he said "Mary" she realized who it was and said "Master." In John 20:17 "Jesus saith unto her, Touch me not; for I am not yet ascended to my Father: but go to my brethren, and say unto them, I ascend unto my Father, and your Father; and to my God, and your God."

This account conflicts somewhat with that of Matthew 28:9 which tells of Mary Magdalene and the other Mary meeting the risen Jesus as they were leaving the tomb. This verse says the women worshipped him, but also "held him by the feet."

Later that same day, Cleopas, one of the followers and another, while walking to Emmaus, were joined by a stranger. They proceeded to tell him of the sad events of the crucifixion, and how the women had found Jesus' tomb empty that same morning. The stranger called them fools for not remembering that the prophets had said Christ would suffer the things they described. Later, while they ate together, "…he took bread, and blessed it, and brake, and gave it to them" (Lk 24:30). With that, they recognized him as Jesus, and he disappeared.

The same night, when the two returned to Jerusalem they joined the eleven disciples (except Thomas), and others, telling them of their experience. They announced that "The Lord is risen," and that he had appeared to Simon (no details given). As they were speaking, Jesus appeared in the flesh, ate with them, and invited them to inspect his wounds. He again reminded them of the prophetic scriptures, saying "And that repentance and

remission of sins should be preached in his name among all nations...."
He then led them to Bethany, where he left them and was "carried up into
heaven" (Lk 24:51). When the group returned to Jerusalem it was with
great joy, and they were evidently beginning to believe and understand the
full import of what had happened.

The group later told Thomas about seeing Jesus, but he said he would
not believe it until he had physical proof. Eight days later, Jesus appeared
again and invited Thomas to check his wounds. Thomas acknowledged
"My Lord and my God" and Jesus pointed out that others were blessed
because they were able to believe without having the opportunity of a personal inspection (Jn 20:29).

The risen Jesus showed himself again to seven disciples while they were
fishing at the Sea of Tiberius (Galilee). John 21 told that the group included
Simon Peter, Thomas Didymus, Nathanael of Cana, the sons of Zebedee
(James and John), and two others. Jesus gave them advice, and they caught
huge netfuls of fish in a reprise of an incident almost exactly like that
described earlier in Luke 5:4–7. In this chapter, John said it was the third
time that the risen Jesus had shown himself to the disciples, and speaking
of himself, said "This is the disciple which testifieth of these things, and
wrote these things: and we know that his testimony is true" (Jn 21:24).

Matthew 28:16–19 tells how the risen Jesus joined the eleven disciples
at a designated mountain in Galilee and told them to "teach all nations."
This was quite similar to the Easter episode in Jerusalem (Lk 24:33–36).

Paul described how the risen Jesus was seen by more than 500 brethren
at once, and most were still living (1 Corinthians 15:6). After that, the
risen Jesus was seen by James, then by all the apostles, and finally, by Paul
himself (1 Cor 9:1, 15:7, 8, and Gal 1:15, 16).

*It seems clear that these appearances of the risen Jesus, over a forty-day
period after his death, absolutely convinced the disciples that his resurrection
was real, and this became the central teaching of the Apostles and focal point
of the Christian faith. The crucifixion demoralized the frightened disciples but
the resurrection gave them renewed faith and conviction. At great personal
risk, their leaders took bold and principled stands against the chief priests, and
hundreds of people became willing to die for their belief in the new covenant
"I am the resurrection and the life: he that believeth in me, though he were
dead, yet shall he live: And whosoever liveth and believeth in me shall never
die" (John 11:25, 26). The Resurrection is unique to the Christian faith—no
other religion has such a tenet. The miracle of the resurrection of God's son is an
overwhelming argument for Christianity as the one true religion.*

Peter quickly became the leader of the new group of disciples and followers in Jerusalem. In a group of about 120 people, he organized the choosing, by lots, of a new disciple to replace the traitor Judas.

On Pentecost, the seventh Sunday after Passover, the 120 plus a multitude of others witnessed people from "every nation" speaking about the works of God in their own languages ("tongues"). They were amazed, and perplexed, but Peter rose and reminded them that according to the prophet Joel, God had said "I will pour out of my Spirit upon all flesh: and your sons and daughters shall prophesy, and your young men shall see visions…and it shall come to pass, that whosoever shall call on the name of the Lord shall be delivered" (Joel 2: 28–32). Peter then said that Israel had crucified Jesus, a man chosen by God, as shown "by miracles and wonders and signs." But God had raised up Jesus, making him Lord and Christ. They asked, "what shall we do?" And Peter said "Repent and be baptized every one of you in the name of Jesus Christ for the remission of sins, and ye shall receive the gift of the Holy Ghost" On that day, 3000 were baptized (Acts 2:1–41).

As Peter's faith grew, so did his resolve and he even gained the ability to perform miracles. Acts 3:2–8 describes a man who had been lame since birth and had to be carried being cured when Peter said "In the name of Jesus Christ of Nazareth rise up and walk…he leaping up stood, and walked, and entered with them into the temple, walking, and leaping, and praising God." Following that, Peter and John talked to crowds of up to 5000 people, telling of the lame man's faith and the resurrection of Jesus. Eventually they were seized, jailed overnight, and then taken to a court hearing before scribes, rulers, elders and chief priests, including Annas and Caiaphas. In this intimidating setting, Peter, who only fifty days earlier, had denied, three times, knowing Jesus, stood up and said, regarding the lame man, "Be it known unto you all, and all the people of Israel, that by the name of Jesus Christ of Nazareth, whom ye crucified, whom God raised from the dead, even by him doth this man stand here before you whole" (Acts 4:10). When the priests ordered them to not speak further of Jesus, they answered "…we cannot but speak the things which we have seen and heard" (Acts 4:20). The council was nonplussed, recognized that a "notable miracle" had occurred, and after admonishing Peter and John let them go, finding no reason to punish them.

Not long after this, Stephen, a converted Jew who had a strong belief that Jesus was the Messiah, defended himself in a similar setting, against the chief priests and Sanhedrin. He was accused of blasphemy because he had predicted the destruction of the temple and Jerusalem. In a long oration, he reviewed the history of the Israelites and pointed out that theirs had been a long series of sin and rebellion against God's grace. He said God had no need of a man-made building, that they had disobeyed God's law and rejected God's prophets. As for the coming Messiah, he described "…the coming of the Just One; of whom ye have been now the betrayers and murderers" (Acts 7:52). With a "gnashing of teeth" they ordered that Stephen be stoned to death, a verdict he accepted with equanimity and even forgiveness for his executioners. In order to throw harder, and be more lethal, the stone-throwers took off their cloaks and threw them at the feet of an enthusiastic supporter named Saul.

THE FIRST CENTURY

To discuss this subject, it is necessary to deal with some calendar dates. The true origin of "B.C." may have been Roman, meaning "Before Caesar." Christians soon changed this to mean "Before Christ" and defined "A.D." as Anno Domini, or year of the Lord, i.e., years after the birth of Jesus. But the Christian calendar, devised by the sixth century A.D. Byzantine monk Dionysius Exiguus, was found to be erroneous in that Jesus was actually born no later than 4 B.C.

Wade Cox has recounted an apparently accurate and well-reasoned analysis that considered Greek translations, scriptures, Roman history, writings of Shurer, etc. This work reached the following conclusions, all compatible with events described in Matthew, Luke, and Acts:

- The first general census was ordered by Augustus and carried out by Quirinius in 8 B.C. (or possibly 12 B.C.).

- Herod's death was in the period between March 28 and April 10, 4 B.C., just after an eclipse of the moon on March 13, referred to by Josephus.

- The most probably date for Jesus' birth was 8 B.C., the last full census before Herod's death, making Jesus thirty-five years old at the time of his baptism (in his thirties, not thirty).

- John the Baptist was imprisoned at Passover of A.D. 28 so Jesus had to be baptized in the period from October 27 to Passover of A.D. 28.

- Christ's ministry lasted a little over two years, until Passover of A.D. 30.

- He died in the afternoon of 14 Nisan, or Friday, 7 April.

In a little over two years' time, Jesus was able to introduce a new faith that has profoundly influenced people around the world. Employing mostly peaceful-but provocative-words and deeds, he was able to challenge people to strive for better human behavior, and belief in God. His success vastly exceeded that of any of the great conquerors such as Alexander, Caesar, Attila, Genghis Khan, etc.

The Resurrection is unique to the Christian faith-no other religion has such a tenet central to its beliefs and faith. It is clear that the disciples of Jesus were absolutely convinced that his resurrection was miraculous and real; they changed from a group of frightened men to strong, principled adherents. To keep, and promote their convictions, they were willing to undergo horrendous punishments and death, and thousands of other people did the same.

After Christ, Stephen was the first in a long list of Christian martyrs who unflinchingly went to their deaths because of their intense belief in Jesus Christ and the new religion. Of the twelve disciples, only John died a natural death; by church tradition, all the rest were killed in various ways. Six of the deaths were by crucifixion, used only by the Romans, but Paul was beheaded, the "advantage" of being a Roman citizen. It seems fairly clear that most of the deaths, at the hands of the Romans, were not because of Christian beliefs, but mainly because of general "Jewish problems." The Romans first saw Jesus as "King of the Jews" and until Nero, did not distinguish between the two religions.

By the time of Trajan (A.D. 98–116), it is estimated that there were about 10,000 Christians. This grew to 217,000 at the time of Tertullian (A.D. 225), and 34 million by A.D. 350, after the Roman Empire became Christian. At the beginning, and especially after A.D. 70 when Jerusalem fell, many Jewish individuals were quite willing to consider Jesus the promised Messiah, and today there are an estimated 70,000 to 80,000 Messianic Jews worldwide. But the chief priests and hierarchy of the temple were bitter opponents, and the Talmud of ca A.D. 200–500 was harshly critical.

From the first days and even now, others have argued that the Resurrection required a divine miracle; therefore Christianity is based on a false claim. Some are almost irrational, going so far as to argue that Jesus never existed! A short summary of the arguments may be helpful.

One was the "swoon theory" that is, the crucifixion did not kill Jesus and he was still alive when placed in the tomb. Another is the "hallucination theory" that the disciples were so emotionally distraught that they only imagined what they saw. The "imposition theory" argues that the disciples stole the body of Jesus from the tomb, and then proclaimed that he arisen. Another is the "conspiracy theory" that it was all a giant hoax in which the apostles, Paul, and other writers of the New Testament copied each others' works and made up the whole account. All these ideas have been thoroughly discredited by a long list of scholars who have written learned treatises concerning the Resurrection. A very incomplete list, in alphabetical order includes William F. Albright, Paul Althaus, Thomas Arnold, E.M. Blaiklok, F.F. Bruce, George Currie, Lord Darling, Michael Green, Simon Greenleaf, Lord Lyttleton, Paul Maier, Josh McDowell, Clark Pinnock, William Ramsay, A.N. Sherwin-White, David F. Strauss (a skeptic), Gilbert West, Brooke F. Westcott, and Edwin M. Yamauchi. The statement given by Dr. Greenleaf, Professor of Law at Harvard, is especially compelling.

Beginning with a personal belief that the Resurrection was a myth and a hoax, his research convinced him otherwise. In his 1874 book, *An Examination of the Testimony of the Four Evangelists by the Rules of Evidence Administered in the Courts of Justice* he concluded that according to the legal evidence, the resurrection of Jesus Christ was the best-supported religious event in all of history.

In 1982 the late Gordon Stein said it was "quite unlikely that Jesus ever existed." In addition, concerning Josh McDowell's book *Evidence that Demands a Verdict*, Stein was downright vituperative, using language such as dishonest, ignorant, liar, purposely misleads, and "McDowell is a fool." (I have noticed that some atheists and skeptics tend to use extreme, personal, and denigrating language in discussing religious authors). Stein questioned the validity of certain historical documents that mentioned Jesus; some of these are discussed below.

Flavius Josephus (A.D. 37–101) was a famous Jewish historian who was an eyewitness to Christianity. For centuries, his works were the most widely read except for the Bible. He came from a distinguished family and was widely known in leading circles. At the age of twenty-seven he went to Rome where he gained influence with the emperor. When the Jewish revolt broke out in 66, he returned to Jerusalem and was chosen by the Sanhedrin to be commander-in-chief in Galilee. When his army was defeated by the Romans in 67, he ingratiated himself with the winning general Vespasian, who became emperor in 69.

Back in Rome, he remained in favor with the rulers and was free to pursue his historical writings in elegant Greek. His second book, the *Jewish Antiquities*, written in about A.D. 94, contained twenty volumes, of which

XII–XX covered the time of Christ and the foundation of Christianity. Josephus mentioned Herod the Great in Vol. 15–17 and John the Baptist in Vol. 18. In Vol. 20 he referred to James, the brother of Jesus, and Ananias the high priest of Acts 23:2. His most famous passage (known as the *Testimonium Flavianum*) is from Vol. 18, Chapter 5, paragraph two.

"Now about this time there lived Jesus a wise man, if one ought to call him a man, for he was a doer of wonderful works, a teacher of such men as receive the truth with pleasure. He won over many Jews and Greeks. He was the Messiah. When Pilate, upon hearing him accused by men of the highest standing among us, had condemned him to be crucified, those who in the first place had come to love him did not forsake him. For he appeared to them alive again on the third day, as the holy prophets had predicted these and many other wonderful things about him. And the tribe of the Christians, so called after him, continues to the present day."

This version, and the other three I have read, all vary somewhat in the wording. Furthermore, there seems to be a general agreement that the passage has been tampered with and embellished by early Christians, although the core statement is authentic.

According to Suetonius, in A.D. 49, the emperor Claudius "…drove the Jews out of Rome who were rioting because of Chrestus." This spelling has caused some argument but the usage seems to refer to Christ rather than some other Jew. It demonstrates that a Christian community was established in Rome, only nineteen years after the Crucifixion. Confirmation is found in Acts 18:2 when Paul came to Corinth in A.D. 52. "And found a certain Jew named Aquila, born in Pontus, lately come from Italy, with his wife Priscilla; (because that Claudius had commanded all Jews to depart from Rome)."

About A.D. 117, Cornelius Tacitus wrote his Annals, which in Vol. XV, Chapter 44 includes "Nero looked around for a scapegoat, and inflicted the most fiendish tortures on a group of persons already hated by the people for their crimes. This was the sect known as Christians. Their founder, one Christus, had been put to death by the procurator Pontius Pilate in the reign of Tiberius." Nero was also responsible for the beheading of Paul in 66 and the crucifixion (upside down) of Peter in 68.

As previously mentioned, when the disciples were convinced that Jesus had arisen from the dead, an amazing transformation changed them from a band of wimps to strong, bold proponents. Equally amazing was the epiphany of Saul on the road to Damascus. After witnessing and encouraging the stoning of Stephen to death, Saul's next step was to get from the high priest a list of Jesus' followers in Damascus, men and women, with the intent of arresting them and bringing them back to Jerusalem for punishment.

Near Damascus, a blinding light suddenly struck him to the ground, and a voice said "Saul, Saul, why are you so cruel to me?" and when asked, the Lord said "I am Jesus." In Damascus, still blinded after three days, Saul regained his sight when a follower of Jesus was instructed to go to Saul, saying "Saul, the Lord Jesus has sent me. He is the same one who appeared to you along the road. He wants you to be able to see and to be filled with the Holy Spirit." (Acts 9:3–5 and 7–17). After he was baptized, Saul regained his strength and went to Jewish meeting places where for three years he preached powerfully that Jesus was the Messiah and the Son of God. In Damascus, some of the Jews tried to kill him, just as they did in Jerusalem when he returned there.

When the disciples were convinced that Saul had become a strong and dedicated convert, for his own safety they sent him to Tarsus (his hometown). Sometime later he was joined there by Barnabas and the two of them then went to nearby Antioch [Syrian then, now in Turkey], where the new church was thriving and converting the Gentiles. (This translates a Greek word that means "people who speak Greek" but also means "people who are not Jews.") It was also at Antioch that Jesus' followers were first called Christians. After preaching there for one full year, Saul and Barnabas plus a helper, John (whose other name was Mark), began their first missionary journey. The first stop was the island of Cyprus, where Saul changed his name to Paul, after temporarily blinding (with words only) an advisor who gave bad advice to the governor. From there, the three went to Perga, in southern Turkey (where John left them), and thence to Pisidian Antioch in Anatolia, near the present-day Turkish village of Yalvach, about 150 miles southwest of modern Ankara.

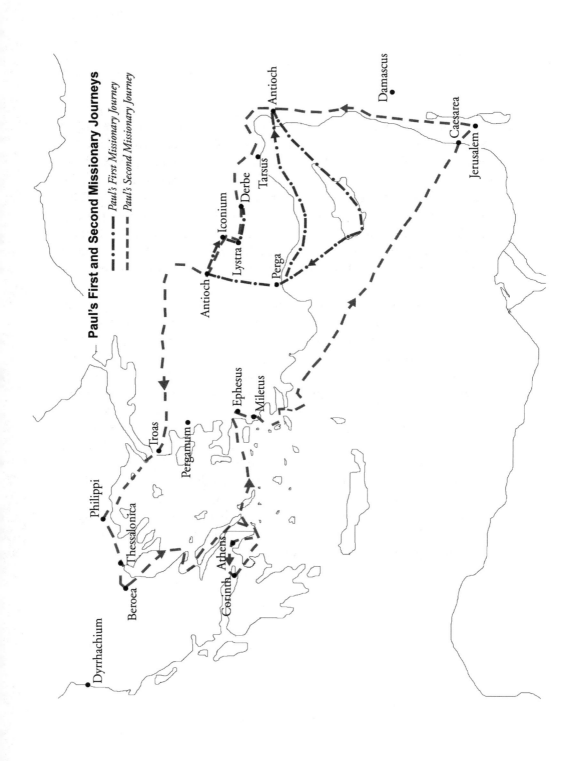

Paul's First and Second Missionary Journeys

— — — *Paul's First Missionary Journey*

– · – · – *Paul's Second Missionary Journey*

Dyrrhachium

Philippi

Thessalonica

Beroea

Athens

Corinth

Troas

Pergamum

Ephesus

Miletus

Antioch

Iconium

Lystra

Derbe

Tarsus

Perga

Antioch

Damascus

Caesarea

Jerusalem

THE FIRST CENTURY TIMELINES

8 B.C.	Birth of Jesus
A.D. 28–30	Jesus' ministry
30	Crucifixion
32	Stephen stoned to death in Jerusalem
34	Conversion of Paul on road to Damascus
37	Flavius Josephus born
43	James (son of Zebedee) beheaded in Israel
48	Paul's first missionary journey
46–48	James (son of Judas the Galilean) crucified in Persia
49	Claudius expels Jews from Rome
50	Paul's second missionary journey
52	Paul in Corinth
45–60	"Q" written
50–60	Gospel of Mark written
50–63	Ten epistles to churches and individuals written by Paul
55–63	Gospels of Matthew, Luke written
60	Matthew (Levi) killed by a spear in Ethiopia
60	Paul under house arrest in Rome
62	James, brother of Jesus, killed
64	Acts written by Luke
66	Paul beheaded by Nero in Rome
66–70	Jewish War
68	Simon Peter crucified by Nero in Rome
70	Jerusalem, second temple destroyed
70–80	Jude written
72	Thaddeus (Judas, son of James) crucified in Turkey
74	Simon (the Zealot) crucified in Britain
94	Josephus' Antiquities written
90–95	Letter to Hebrews written, perhaps by Timothy
90–100	Gospel of John, John's three letters written
90–95	Revelation written
100	John dies at age 100

When the Jews of Pisidian Antioch rejected the message of Jesus, Paul said the Jews were given their chance but failed to see the truth, hence "... we turn to the Gentiles" (Acts 13:46), thereby opening the door of Christianity to the world. After more trouble from the Jews, Paul and Barnabas "shook off the dust of their feet" and went to Iconium (Konya), about eighty miles to the southeast. They were well received by the Gentiles, but the Jews threatened stoning so they next went to Lystra, about twenty-five miles to the south. At that place, Paul cured a man crippled from birth, and the people thought Paul and Barnabas were Greek gods. Jews from the first two towns stoned Paul and left him for dead but he soon revived. Next the two went to Derbe, a short distance away, then returned to the previous three towns, appointing leaders for each church and encouraging followers to remain faithful. (Later, Paul's letter to the Galatians was written to these churches). They then returned to Perga and sailed back to Antioch and headquarters. [While we were in Turkey, we had the opportunity to visit Tarsus, Perga, Konya, the Cilician Gates and Antioch—though at the time not fully appreciating all aspects of their religious significance.]

Paul and Barnabas stayed in Antioch for a "long time" (three years?), after which they went to Jerusalem to argue with the Pharisees over the need for Gentiles to be circumcised in order to be saved. Paul made the point that this was a burden Gentiles did not need, so long as they followed the rules about eating meat and abstained from fornication. The two then returned to Antioch and prepared for the second missionary journey. Barnabas and John Mark went to Cyprus while Paul chose Silas to go with him to Galatia and Greece.

Back in Derbe and Lystra they met Timothy who became a companion after being circumcised (because his mother was Jewish). More people were converted and the churches were strengthened, as they traveled from town to town. Eventually they reached Troy, sailed to Macedonia and came to Philippi where they established the first Christian church in Europe. It was there, also, where Paul and Silas were whipped and asked to leave the city, so they went to Thessalonica. Many conversions were made there but some of the Jews again caused an uproar so they moved on to Berea. The same thing happened there; many conversions were made until Jews from Thessalonica arrived and forced them to leave. In Athens, Paul's sermons about Jesus and the resurrection resulted in a command performance at the Areopagus, where leading citizens and the highest government council met daily. Before a distinguished audience, Paul made the points that (1) the God who made the world and everything in it did not need human shrines (2) all people and nations are God's offspring (3) all people should repent because their righteousness will be judged by Jesus Christ, who God raised from the dead.

The most reasonable calculations show that Paul arrived in Corinth in A.D. 52 where he stayed for one and a half years and probably wrote the first of his ten epistles to various churches and individuals. Acts 18:19 say he next traveled to Ephesus but 18:21–23 are confusing because they describe a side-trip to Caesarea, Jerusalem, Antioch, Galatia and Phrygia before again showing up in Ephesus in 19:1 (by land, cross-country?). At that time, Ephesus was the grandest city in Asia Minor and had a population of over 200,000, with elaborate temples, libraries and a 24,000-seat stadium, beautiful homes with muraled walls, marble streets, plumbing and a sewage system, hot and cold baths, etc.

In any event, Paul spoke in the synagogue there for three months, making little progress with the Jews. The next two years, at the hall of Tyrannus, were better in that "all they which dwelt in Asia heard the word of the Lord Jesus, both Jews and Greeks" (Acts 19:10). In addition, Paul performed "special miracles" wherein sickness and evil spirits in third parties were vanquished by handkerchiefs and aprons he touched. Near the end of his three-year stay in Ephesus, Paul's campaign against idols stirred up the silversmiths whose livelihood depended on making idols for the goddess Diana. So they rioted, crying out "Great is Diana of the Ephesians." After that, Paul returned to Macedonia and Greece for three months. From Philippi he sailed to Troy and from there to Miletus, just south of Ephesus. Calling the Ephesian elders to Miletus, he said his goodbyes at that place and sailed back to Jerusalem. [While in Turkey, we were fortunate to be able to visit several of these places, including Troy, Ephesus, Miletus, Pergamum, Corinth, and Athens. Paul's travels no doubt took advantage of the wonderful road system built by the Romans and still in good shape today, after 2,000 years. The picture on the following page, taken in 1960, was on one of the Roman roads in southwest Turkey].

After only a few days in Jerusalem, Paul was seized by some of the temple Jews who began to beat him; fortunately he was rescued by the Romans. The Romans became deferential when they learned he was a Roman citizen, and the Jews at least were willing to give him a hearing when they learned he was a Pharisee and rabbi. In testifying before the chief priests and their council, he averred his belief in resurrection of the dead and soon the Pharisees and Sadducees were arguing with each other over that question. The Romans took Paul away for his own safety, at which point forty Jews banded together, swearing they would neither eat nor drink until they had killed him.

Learning of this, the Roman commander sent Paul, protected by 270 troops, to Felix, the governor at Caesarea. Felix found no fault in Paul's actions but held him for two years until Festus arrived as the new governor. At a hearing before Festus, Paul, as a Roman citizen, requested a trial before the Emperor in Rome. A few days later, King Agrippa, who was visiting Festus, heard Paul's first-hand account. He said Paul could have been set free if he had not asked to be tried by the Roman Emperor. Hence, before long Paul was on a ship with other prisoners, on the way to Rome. A captain in charge of the prisoners was lenient with Paul and protected him when they were shipwrecked on the island of Malta. They reached Rome in A.D. 60 and Paul was allowed to live in a house by himself and have visitors, while under house arrest.

Paul wrote four of his epistles while a prisoner in Rome. This arrangement continued for two years and normally it would have been assumed that Paul would be freed. After all, three different Roman authorities had said as much. However, Paul had the misfortune to fall under the purview of Nero, Emperor from A.D. 54 to 68.

Nero had directed the murder of his own mother, Agrippina, who was also ruthless and murderous, and whose brother was the madman Caligula. Later, Nero arranged for the staged suicide of his wife, Octavia, an innocent, blameless lady so that he could marry Poppaea. When the great fire of Rome broke out in July, 64, Nero was not in the city but sought a scapegoat to blame. Poppaea, his mistress at the time, deflected his anger toward the Christians, a small part of the Jewish population which included 40,000 people and fourteen synagogues. This was the first instance where the Romans distinguished between Christians and Jews. As previously cited, Tacitus described the "fiendish tortures" inflicted upon the Christians, including soaking them with tar and burning them as human torches. Paul was included in the list of victims but, as a Roman citizen, had the privilege of execution by beheading.

After Jesus himself, Paul is often considered the most important person in the establishment of Christianity. Over 40 percent of the New Testament concerns Paul and/or the fourteen letters written by himself or in his name. His amazing conversion took place only four years after the Crucifixion, stemming directly from a personal encounter with Jesus. As he told the Galatians (1:15, 16), God "was kind and had decided to show me his Son, so that I would announce his message to the Gentiles." And in 1 Corinthians 9:1 "have I not seen Jesus Christ our Lord?"

After his change from being a hater of Christians to a convinced believer, Paul promoted Christianity with courageous, implacable fervor for thirty-two years. He traveled thousands of miles (often walking), proselytizing thousands of new converts, establishing new churches, and then lending his advice and support to the different congregations in maintaining the faith. He was whipped, stoned and left for dead, imprisoned, threatened with immanent death by Jewish partisans in at least six cities and finally beheaded by Nero.

Paul's activities were described mostly in Acts, and he personally wrote at least ten epistles to give further advice and support to some of the churches and individuals with whom he had been associated. Typically, Paul exhorted individuals to serve one another for the common good, citing examples of teaching, diligence, compassion, generosity, wisdom, knowledge, healing, cheerfulness, and especially faith (faith was mentioned 187 times in his epistles).

Another thing he stressed was the Spirit of God, or spirit of man (S/ spirit), mentioned 140 times in his letters. As a former Jewish rabbi, Paul saw Christianity as in continuity with the covenant of the Old Testament, and a succession to the people of God, as Jews and Gentiles together. From his Jewish heritage, he called the recipients of his letters "saints" meaning God's "holy people." All, of course, were first-generation believers or converts who had experienced the Holy Spirit, or the personal presence of God, coming into their lives. Salvation meant entering the family of the people of God by experiencing the Spirit, including concern for each other, and living and worshiping together.

Paul felt that, next in importance to Christ, the Spirit was fundamental to understanding the gospel. Believers enjoyed the "fruit of the Spirit" as a continuing reality and their righteousness was a result of empowerment by the Spirit. For Paul, the Spirit was a key to Christian life, and guaranteed the future bodily resurrection of "spiritual bodies." As summarized by Fee (1996, p. 52) "The death and resurrection of Christ and the gift of the Spirit mean both death to the old and a radical, newly constituted life in the present."

In the Old Testament the "Spirit of God" and "Spirit of the Lord" were frequently cited as positive influences in shaping man's soul. But in the early Catholic Church a distinction was made between soul and spirit so that the whole man has three parts: body, soul and spirit. Saint Paul used three Greek words for these parts. *Soma* was the word for body, meaning the entire body including the brain. *Psyche* was the word for soul, including will, intellect, mind, emotions, character and personality. And *Pneuma* was the Greek word for spirit.

Over time, the Catholic concept of the soul has come to mean the "spiritual principle in man" the innermost aspect of man, and the "temple of the Spirit." "Every spiritual soul is created immediately by God," not by parents. Souls are immortal, and reunited with the body at the time of the final Resurrection. The "Spirit signifies that from creation man is ordered to a supernatural end and that his soul can be raised....to communion with God." Man is made of a unity of body and soul, a union of spirit and body forms a single nature and a human body is animated by a spiritual soul.

This led to the concept of the Trinity or *trinitas*, first used by Tertullian, as early as A.D. 200. The idea of God, the Son and Holy Spirit in three persons, as the Godhead, has been one of the most controversial and misunderstood of all canons of the Christian church. The words are in the Apostle's Creed and the Holy Spirit was part of the *filoque* clause defining the Trinity at the First Ecumenical Council in Nicaea in 325. The Trinity dogma was restated at the ecumenical councils in 381, 431, 451, and 553. Final wording came 1274 years after the first attempt.

The Trinity concept views God as a unity of three persons, the Father, Son, and Holy Spirit (or Holy Ghost). The Father is considered to be the one creative and sovereign God of Hebrew scriptures. Jesus was affirmed as the Son of God—"the Word made flesh." The third element was the Holy Spirit, important to believers as God's presence in their midst. Other names for the Holy Spirit or Holy Ghost are comforter, Light of Christ, Paraclete and Spirit of Truth. Some good examples are: "Go ye therefore, and teach all nations, baptizing them in the name of the Father, and of the Son, and of the Holy Ghost" (Mt 28:19); "But the Comforter, which is the Holy Ghost, whom the Father will send in my name, he shall teach you all things...." (Jn 14:26); "The grace of the Lord, Jesus Christ, and the love of God, and the communion of the Holy Ghost, be with you all" (II Corinthians, 13:14); "For there are three that bear record in heaven, the Father, the Word, and the Holy Ghost: and these three are one" (I Jn 5:7).

My copy of the Catholic Catechism shows that a great deal of attention has been given to the matter, in fact it is the fourth most-extensively documented of all subjects. Probably stemming from Catholic influences, in our Protestant church we sing "praise Father, Son, and Holy Ghost," "God in three persons, Blessed Trinity" "Glory be to the Father and to the Son and to the Holy Ghost" and confirm that we believe in the Holy Spirit of the Apostle's Creed, and in "the divine presence" in the Affirmation of Faith.

The Holy Spirit in Paul's letters is discussed in Gordon Fee's *God's Empowering Presence*, a massive tome of some 915 pages smothered by 700 pages of explanation, or exegesis. Happily, two years later, in 1996, Fee wrote *Paul, the Spirit, and the People of God*, a "reader-friendly" distillation of the earlier book.

Many people (myself included) find it difficult to understand the concept of a third person of the trinity. Fee words this concern nicely "We believe in God the Father, Almighty, Maker of heaven and earth; and we believe in Jesus Christ his Son; but we are not so sure about the Holy Spirit." Fee also explains the basis of Paul's theology, and why the idea of the Spirit was so important to Paul.

That Paul understood the Spirit as a person is implied in a number of his letters, especially 1 Corinthians 2:11. "...God's Spirit is the only one who knows what is in God's mind," and Romans 8:27 "All of our thoughts are known to God. He can understand what is in the mind of Spirit..." (CEV). On the other hand, in a number of Paul's letters the usage of the word Spirit could just as likely mean (as in the Old Testament) the presence, power, or influence of God. A good example is 1 Corinthians 6:11 "...ye are justified...by the Spirit of our God" (KJV)."

Fee points out that there are problems with translating the word "person" from the Greek word hypostasis, or Latin persona. Neither the Greek nor the Roman includes all the meaning we attach to the word. [So for me, the third person of the trinity will mean God's power or presence, not a person, and I can be comfortable with that]

The rest of the New Testament is comprised mainly of the four Gospels. The first three (synoptic) Gospels likely were written in the period A.D. 50-60 whereas John's writings were in the period 90–100. All four describe events for only a short time after the death of Jesus, so only Acts helps much in unraveling the time frame. The reasoning goes something like this: Acts was finished while Paul was a prisoner in Rome, before his death in A.D. 66, because his death is not mentioned. Acts is considered to be the second part of the Gospel written by Luke, who in turn got some 50 percent of his material from the writings of Mark. Matthew took about 90 percent of his material from Mark. Both Luke and Matthew also took material from "Q." Hence, Mark was written first; Matthew and Luke followed and were approximately contemporaneous. Working backward from Paul's death in A.D. 66, the time frame for writing the synoptic Gospels would have Matthew and Luke in the years 59–66, and Mark 50–58. This means that the synoptics plus Acts were all written twenty to thirty-six years after the Crucifixion, largely from the oral testimony of eyewitnesses to the events.

[This analysis is based upon the assumption that Acts was written prior to the death of Paul. The result is that the Gospels of Mark, Luke and Matthew could have been written anywhere from twelve to thirty-six years earlier than calculated by Howard C. Kee, for whom I have great respect. However, it seems to me that Kee bases his argument too strongly on equating the burned city in Mt 22:7 to Jerusalem destroyed in A.D. 70. A solution to this conundrum would be the assumption that Acts was written before Luke. That would allow dating Mark as 68–70 and Luke and Matthew in the range 85–100, as given by Kee.]

"Q" refers to an unidentified and hypothetical, but useful source document called Quelle or "source" in German. The Q material comprises about 200 verses in Luke and Matthew, mostly sayings of Jesus, where Mark has nothing comparable. Luke seems to preserve the order of Q better, according to some scholars (but how would we know?). The recently discovered Gospel of Thomas provides some support for the Q concept. Loader has compiled a list of subjects for which he thinks Q has been an important source, including: John the Baptist, divorce, tithing, conflict with the Pharisees, hope for the future, and the inclusion of Gentiles. [Note: Recently some scholars have questioned the logic and need for a Q document: they point out that no such document has been found, nor was such a document mentioned by the earliest writers.]

The Gospel of Mark is attributed to John Mark, a companion of Paul, and Barnabas, who was related to Mark's mother, a rich Christian widow in Jerusalem. Mark accompanied them on their first journey as far as Perga, and went with Barnabas on the second missionary trip; he also accompanied Paul in later travels. Many of Mark's words had to be based on the recollections of Jesus' disciples, and especially Peter, because the two were frequently together. For example, when Peter escaped from Herod's prison, he went to the house of Mark's mother. Peter is mentioned seventeen times in Mark's Gospel, and in I Peter 5:13, Mark is called "my son." Mark's Gospel was written in grammatically poor Greek, and began with the matter of John the Baptist with no reference to the birth or childhood of Jesus. Other than that, his account covered some of the miracles, stories and parables, the disciples, the last days and events concerning the crucifixion and resurrection. His words were copied to some extent by Matthew and Luke (Luke called him a minister), in their Gospels.

The Gospel of Matthew is considered to be written by Matthew, or Levi, the tax collector (if early) or by an unknown author (if Kee is correct about a later date). Mark called Levi an agent for receiving customs, and Matthew used those same words (Mt 9:9). Matthew used the term publican (Mt 10:3), but did not call himself Levi. Some have argued that Matthew was originally written in Hebrew but Kee has shown that it was "clearly written first in Greek" in the Antioch area, where Greek-speaking Jewish Christians were prevalent.

In part, Matthew was aimed at the Jews, to show that Jesus was their Messianic King and fulfilled the Old Testament prophecies. The early oral version of the Matthew Gospel may have formed an important part of the sermons that Paul preached in his missionary journeys.

The Matthew gospel has long been considered the most important and hence is listed first in order in the Bible. It may be the most skillfully written of all the gospels, and the best transition from the Old to the New Testament. Its words are the most familiar and it is only in this Gospel that Jesus called Peter the rock on which his church will be built. Although supportive of Jewish law and morality, Matthew felt Christianity was the divine fulfillment of the law and Jewish prophecy. As a convert from Judaism, he was troubled by the Jews' refusal to embrace the new theology. Matthew was also quite critical of Jewish leaders whom he called hypocrites. In Mt 28:13–15 was the only apostle to accuse the chief priests of suborning perjury by the Roman soldiers to say Jesus' disciples stole his body away while they slept. Some records show that Matthew was killed in A.D. 60 with a spear while in Ethiopia.

The Gospel of Luke was written by Luke, a physician and traveling companion of Paul. Paul called him "beloved physician" (Colossians 4:14) and Ireneus, more than 100 years later, recognized Luke as one of Paul's companions. During his final imprisonment in Rome, Paul wrote plaintively, after Demas, Crescens, and Titus had left him "Only Luke is with me" (2 Timothy 4:10–11). Luke took some of his material from Q and Mark, and his is considered one of the three synoptic Gospels. The people who comprised the Jesus Seminar rated Luke as the most accurate in reporting the actual words of Jesus.

Luke and Matthew were the only two Gospels to cover the birth of Jesus, agreeing on the Virgin Mary, and descent from the house of David. Surprisingly though, they did not agree (or, rather, confirm each other) on the tax-census, manger, shepherds, angels, Magi, star of the east, Herod and the flight to Egypt. Matthew had Mary and Joseph coming from Bethlehem and Luke had them coming from Nazareth.

Luke is considered to be the best written of the Gospels, giving the fullest account of the birth of Jesus and his early life. It stresses Jesus' concern for women, the poor, sick, outcasts and sinners. It was the last of the synoptic Gospels to be written, and most scholars believe that Luke also wrote Acts as a follow-on. Acts does not report Paul's death so it may have been written as early as A.D. 66, meaning the Luke Gospel could have been written in the period 55–65, some thirty to forty years earlier than calculated by Kee. The synoptic Gospels are in the form of an historical narrative, in contrast to the spiritual approach of John's Gospel.

John was one of the most important and trusted of the disciples; he was present at the Transfiguration, stood at the foot of the cross with Mary, and, after the Crucifixion, was with Peter when he raised the lame man at the Beautiful Temple. Second-century Christians attributed the Gospel of John (son of Zebedee) to this "disciple whom Jesus loved" and who was entrusted to care for Mother Mary. The assumption was made that a certain John the Elder, who lived in Ephesus in the early second century, was one and the same. Irenaeus formulated this theory about A.D. 180, but Kee strongly questions the timing that would be required. Referring to the John Gospel, the Jesus Seminar suggested that "In the judgment of many scholars, it was produced by a "school" of disciples, probably in Syria." [On the other hand, an impartial observer might suggest that the John Gospel was written by an individual—and self-serving at that, as shown by use of the term for himself, the "disciple whom Jesus loved." This term appeared five times in John, but in none of the synoptic Gospels.]

With John at the foot of the cross with Jesus' mother, named as her son, and charged to take care of her, there is no doubt that Mary was closer to John than anyone else. Therefore it is puzzling that his Gospel did not add anything to the nativity story, and mentioned Mary only twice; the first time in turning water into wine, and the second at the cross. Again, this might be confirmation that, as Kee suggests, the Gospel of John was actually written by an unknown author, or authors, one or two generations after the Crucifixion.

The Gospel of John differs from the other three in several ways. It is dated as much as forty years later, about A.D. 90–100. No parables were included and the language was more abstract, dealing more with Jesus' relationship with his Father. John introduced many of the more striking appellations for Jesus such as the Word, the Lamb of God, the bread of life, the light of the world, the good shepherd and the resurrection and the life. In the discussion of soul and spirit, in an earlier chapter, it was shown that John spoke eloquently on that subject. John 3:16 is one of the Bible verses most important to Christians: "For God so loved the world that he gave his only begotten Son, that whosoever believeth in him should not perish, but have everlasting life." [Additionally, 3:3 explains the goal desired by millions of people—and one of my personal goals in writing this book, "Except a man be born again, he cannot see the kingdom of God."]

The Book of Revelation (in Greek, apokalypsis) to John is believed to be authored by yet another, "John the seer," either as an exile or a prisoner on the small island of Patmos, about thirty miles off the coast at Miletus. Revelation was written at about the time, A.D. 90–95, and was occasioned by Domitian's persecution of the rapidly spreading

Christian movement. The Book is full of imagery and visions similar to Jewish apocalyptic writings in Daniel and Ezekiel, and coded so as to be unintelligible to Roman officials.

Revelation described evil forces that would hurt Christians, that the evil forces would be vanquished by God, and that faithful people would enjoy wonderful rewards. In his first vision, John was told to deliver seven letters of instruction to the churches of western Asia Minor (Turkey). In another vision, on God's throne Jesus removed seals from a scroll upon which was written the divinely predetermined course of history. The first four seals released the four horsemen, i.e., war, famine, pestilence and death, the fifth the martyr's pleas, the sixth all kinds of natural disasters, and the seventh made way for seven trumpet-sounding angels—who in turn led to another series of seven visions.

EARLY CHURCH AND BIBLE

This discussion covers the critical time from about A.D. 100 to 363, when the Council of Laodicea named all the books of the New Testament except Revelation. During these years early Christians struggled to establish a Christian community, church, and canon, often in the face of severe opposition from the Roman authorities. The new Christian theology considered Christ the son of God and that salvation must be through him; as Jesus said, "no man cometh to the Father except through me" (Jn 14:6).

The new church leaders called Jesus the Messiah, or Christos (in Greek, "the anointed one")—a long-awaited deliverer keenly desired by the Jews. But Jesus himself saw his role as a suffering servant rather than a political leader or ruler. Hence, most potential Jewish converts turned away from Jesus and the Christians came to be comprised almost entirely of Gentiles. Questions arise as to how an obscure messianic group of Jewish dissidents, at the edges of the Roman Empire, was able to form the dominant religion in the Western world. Certainly the Resurrection was a central tenet. When over 310 men and women (listed in the *Bibliotheca Hagiographica Latina*) martyrs were willing to die for their belief, the world took notice. As Colson reported (p 214) "they attained such towering strength of soul that not one uttered a cry or groan." The message of compassion that Jesus delivered had great appeal, and the role of women became more important. In contrast to the Greco-Roman world, women enjoyed a much higher status under Christianity, including prohibition of the infanticide of female babies. Of course the main impetus came when Emperor Constantine made Christianity the official religion of the Roman Empire. By the time of Laodicea, Christians numbered 34 million and accounted for more than half of the empire's population (Sheler, 2001).

As the new religion struggled to get its act together, a new generation of men (and women) took up leadership positions in various scattered locations. They were called elders, deacons, bishops, or "Apostolic Fathers," and had not known the apostles personally but were very knowledgeable. Their writings and arguments served to winnow out the wide range of opinions, move the church toward a more centralized, moderate and broadly acceptable theology, and determine the makeup of the Christian canon. The names mentioned in the following chronologic summary are intended to show the range of opinions, but their arguments are severely limited in scope; in some cases, entire books have been reduced to a few sentences.

In about A.D. 96, Clement, a prominent Christian leader in Rome, rebuked some of those in Corinth for divisiveness in choosing their leaders. He reminded them of the admonitions of Jesus and Paul, and urged them to honor the established order.

Ignatius, the second Bishop of Syrian Antioch, added to this message in the seven letters he wrote to different churches as he traveled, under armed guard, to his execution in Rome. Ignatius urged the churches to maintain their faith in Christ, using language from the Gospels plus Paul-like, self-deprecating phrases. When he reached Rome in 110, he was martyred by Emperor Trajan.

Papias was the bishop of Hierapolis in Phrygia (southern Turkey) who had heard John preach, and avidly sought to interview those second-generation Christians who professed to have known Andrew, Peter, Philip, Thomas, James and Matthew. He reported that Mark wrote down Peter's words and evidently he listened to an account from the daughters of Philip about the Crucifixion and the Resurrection. In about 130 he wrote five books concerning "Sayings of the Lord" but only small fragments have survived to this day.

Among the early martyrs, Justin Martyr is one of the best known and his name has come to define those who were willing to die for their beliefs. He was born of pagan Greek parents near modern Nablus, in Samaria, about A.D. 100 and suffered martyrdom in Rome about 165. He had a good education in philosophy, history, mathematics, astronomy, speech and music at Ephesus and Alexandria. He first came under the influence of a Stoic, then a Pythagorean and later a Platonist. While at Ephesus, he was impressed by the steadfast Christians and in his writings explained that the moral beauty and truth of Christianity were the strongest influences in his conversion. He became a Christian in about 130, and then a strong advocate of the faith in extensive writings, debates and in his schools of Christian philosophy at Ephesus and Rome. After the Cynic philosopher Crescens was defeated in debate, it is possible that the spiteful Crescens denounced Martyr to the Roman authorities.

When tried before Rusticus, the Roman prefect, Martyr refused to sacrifice to pagan idols as the law required. Threatened with death, Martyr said "That is our desire, to be tortured for our Lord, Jesus Christ, and so to be saved..." Martyr and six of his students, including one woman, were then beheaded, at the "customary place."

Apollonius must have known of Justin Martyr, and died under very similar circumstances. Little is known about him except that he was from Alexandria, he was a philosopher, a pious follower of Christ and a courageous man. Brought before the Senate Tribunal in Rome, he was advised to abjure, and that "Sacrifices should be made to the gods and to the statue of the emperor Commodus." Apollonius flatly refused and was beheaded in 185.

The most serious challenge to emerging Christian orthodoxy in the second century came from a movement known as Gnosticism. Gnostics taught that a special wisdom and secret spiritual knowledge (gnosis) was the way to salvation, and thereby implicitly limited the number of people who were fortunate enough to be saved. Following Plato's dualistic philosophy, they saw the goodness of spirit competing with the evil of matter. They believed that Jesus was a spirit who only seemed human, and this idea led to various Gnostic persuasions such as Marcionism, Arianism, and Nestorism.

Marcion was born about A.D. 85 in Sinop on the Black Sea, and became a wealthy marine merchant. In 135–40, he traveled to Rome and presented the church there with 200,000 sesterces which bought him a certain amount of esteem and attention. With that prestige, he developed his theory of two Gods the characteristically despotic and cruel creator God of Law in the Old Testament, the Demiurge, and the Supreme God or God of Love revealed in the person of Jesus Christ. Marcion claimed that Paul was the only true Apostle, who portrayed Jewish law as irrelevant to salvation, and that Luke was the only reliable Gospel. By his early effort to gather Christian writings into a cogent whole, Marcion gave impetus to formation of an orthodox canon for the Catholic Church. However, his personal ideas were emphatically rejected, his money was returned to him, and he was excommunicated in 144.

Valentinus studied religious philosophy in Alexandria and was in Rome at the same time as Marcion. After twenty-five years of Gnostic teaching, he left in 160 when he was denied the position of bishop of Rome. Some historians claim he was the author of the Pistis Sophia, Greek for "Faith Wisdom" supposedly taught by Christ after his Resurrection.

Polycarp (69–155) was bishop of Smyrna (Izmir, Turkey), and be-friended Ignatius when the latter made a stopover on his trip to death in Rome. Polycarp was also a friend of Papias, and talked to many of those who had seen Christ. Irenaeus described how Polycarp had exclaimed, when confronted by Marcion "Aye, I recognize the first-born of Satan." When Polycarp refused to renounce Christ, he was brought to the stadium to be killed by wild beasts. When it got too late for that, it was decided to burn him alive and the crowd helped gather fuel, the Jews being especially helpful. The bones of the martyr were gathered later by the Christians, and interred in a suitable place.

Irenaeus (ca.130–202) was born in Smyrna and, as a boy, listened to the sermons of Polycarp, the great bishop and martyr. As a young man, Ire-naeus was a priest in Lyons, France and in 177 became bishop there when his predecessor was martyred. Because of his prolific writings he became known as "father of the church" and was perhaps first in speaking of a uni-versal or "catholic" church. He strongly opposed Gnosticism and his most important treatise was the Refutation of Heresies, or the detection and overthrow of false knowledge. His main arguments were as follows:

- Individual churches in Corinth, Ephesus, Antioch, etc. comprised the over-all, universal Church.

- The Hebrew Scriptures provided an understanding of one God among a single people, but Christianity preached the truth to all nations.

- Faith was grounded in the Gospels, and expressed in the sacraments of baptism and the Eucharist.

- Loyalty to the one Church was to be assured through the authority of a carefully selected hierarchy of bishops, priests, and deacons.

Clement of Alexandria may have been born in Athens, and died ca. 215. He was well traveled, a prolific writer, and long-time teacher. He was familiar with the various Gnostic approaches but considered the only authoritative Christian scripture to be the four Gospels, Acts and the epistles of Paul (including Hebrews), plus 1 Peter, 1 John and the Revelation.

Tertullian of Carthage (ca. 160–225) was the son of a centurion, trained as a lawyer in Rome, and became a Christian by 197. He wrote against the Gnostic Marcion but his work was denigrated as being anti-intellectual; this seems strange as he wrote eloquently in both Greek and Latin, and created 982 new words in his work. His extensive writings on a large number of subjects were always based on authoritative references (thirty in the case of his *Apology*). The subject matter included such things as first use of the Latin word *trinitas* to explain the Trinity concept, the use of Aristotelian logic in support of the Resurrection, and reproaching the Roman authorities for their harsh repression of Christians. In the latter case, Colson (his p. 299) recalled how Tertullian remonstrated with the Romans "Your cruelty… does not profit you…we grow in number…We have filled…cities, islands, forts, towns, assembly halls, even military camps, tribes, town councils, the palace, senate and forum. We have left you nothing but the temples." As early as 200, Tertullian had assembled the main elements of what would become the Apostle's Creed, in 542.

Origen of Alexandria (ca. 185–254) lived during turbulent times for the church. He was considered one of the greatest of all Christian theologians. When he was only eighteen years old he was appointed to replace Clement as head of the catechetical school in Alexandria. Persecution by Caracalla in 215 forced him to move to Caesarea in Palestine, where he preached successfully as a layman. This breach of ordination caused his petulant bishop to recall him to Alexandria and in 230 the same bishop had him excommunicated from the church there, for the same cause. With that, Origen moved back to Caesarea where he opened a new school, preached, and continued his extensive literary work. In 250 Decius had him imprisoned, tortured and condemned to burn at the stake. Because Decius died, this punishment was not carried out but the mistreatment may have contributed to Origen's death at Tyre in 254.

In his travels, Origen visited many of the first congregations and gained insights helpful to his writings that addressed some of the big questions of the early church. His extensive output was soundly based; it is said that he commented on almost all the books of the Bible, not once but three times. His most important treatise was *On First Principles*, wherein he described the Trinity as a hierarchy, grading downward from the Father, to Christ the Son, to the Holy Spirit. His concept of the human soul was that mankind's misuse—of his freedom to make choices—required an individual to strive for salvation through moral improvement and that redeemed souls would define "spiritual bodies. He saw salvation as a reunion of all souls in God, rather than as the saved rejoicing in heaven while the damned suffered in hell.

Origen not only refuted Gnosticism but offered an alternative Christian system that was more acceptable and rigorous. He accepted as authentic the four Gospels plus Acts, fourteen epistles of Paul, 1 Peter, 1 John, Jude and Revelation. Origen mentioned the Epistle to the Hebrews more than 200 times in his writings, but toward the end of his life admitted that someone else may have written it, perhaps Luke or Clement of Rome. Disputed books included James, 2 Peter, and 2 and 3 John. Thomas was among the gospels he considered to be heretical. Almost 100 years later, Eusebius came to almost the same conclusions including that about Thomas. The *Didache* or "Teaching of the Twelve Apostles" was a supplementary document by others that did not make its way into the canon.

Concerning Thomas, this Gospel is attributed to Didymus Judas Thomas, an apostle who was especially revered in the Syrian church; it was only in that area that he was known as Judas Thomas. His Gospel consists of 114 sayings and parables, most of which are attributed to Jesus. Thomas, like Q, is a sayings gospel with no narrative framework; that is, no account of Jesus' birth, trial, death or resurrection. One analysis of the verses in Thomas show fifty-four similar sayings in Matthew, thirteen in Mark, forty-four in Luke, nineteen in John, and thirty-one nowhere else in the New Testament.

The Jesus Seminar suggested that Thomas may be the first written Gospel, even earlier than Q, or perhaps about A.D. 55. However, other scholars, who seem more reliable to me, agree that to a large extent, Thomas mainly followed the synoptic Gospels and therefore postdated them. Early Greek fragments of Thomas (P. Oxy. 1) are dated at A.D. 200 or younger, and Hippolytus was the first to refer to it by name in about 222. Also, it seems that some of the verses in Thomas reflect and originated from the Gnostic worldview of the second through fourth centuries. As Thomas reportedly traveled to India, some believe his writings show a Buddhist and/or Hindu influence. [A puzzling thing to me is that nowhere in the Thomas gospel is there any mention of Thomas inspecting Jesus' wounds; does this serve to discredit Jn. 20:26–29, Thomas, or neither?]

The Thomas Gospel was only a small part of the fifty-two titles, on 1100 pages, found in December 1945 near Nag Hammadi, 300 miles south of Cairo. The ancient papyrus manuscripts were bound in twelve (or thirteen) leather codices, sealed in an urn, and buried near the east bluff of the Nile valley. The texts were Coptic translations from the original Greek, and were copied about A.D. 367 by monks at the Saint Pachomius monastery. The age of the original Greek documents is somewhat uncertain, but the Gospel of Philip has been dated at about A.D. 70, the Gospel of Truth by Valentine at about 150, and Thomas, either ca. 55—or 200. Other important texts found there included the Sophia of Jesus Christ, the Apocryphon of John, the Gospel of Peter, the Gospel to the Egyptians, the Secret Book of James, the Apocalypses of Paul, and Peter, and the letter of Peter to Philip. As explained by Elaine Pagels, these mostly Gnostic writings were considered heretical, hence banned by the church authorities at the time. Fortunately, some monks who were concerned about preserving historical documents took it upon themselves to hide the material in a buried urn.

Elaine Pagels is an unusually resourceful person who has made some valuable contributions. [With satisfaction, I also note her Stanford connections.] She completed her academic work with a strong record and, in order to read ancient Christian texts, gained a working command of Latin, Greek, Coptic, Hebrew, French, Italian and German. Her four books have been concerned with the development of Christianity in the first few centuries; especially enjoying wide acclaim have been her 1979 *Gnostic Gospels*, and 2003 *Beyond Belief: the Secret Gospel of Thomas*.

The *Gnostic Gospels* gave details of the great discovery at Nag Hammadi, and a summary of some of the texts which were considered Gnostic teachings and hence, heretical, by orthodox Christians. Pagels seemed to consider Gnosticism as an appealing, sophisticated approach that had some support in parts of the New Testament scriptures, and posed a real threat to the early church. She concluded, however, that the orthodox bishops took appropriate steps when they rejected the Gnostic movement and said "I believe that we owe the survival of the Christian tradition to the organizational and theological structure that the emerging church developed."

Beyond Belief is concerned with the Gospel of Thomas, called the fifth Gospel by some scholars. Pagels showed that Thomas emphasized each person's search for God, having direct access to him in accordance with the Book of Genesis where everyone was created in the image and likeness of God. This was in contrast to John, who said the only way was through Jesus or God in human form. She told *Time* that her exposure to Thomas "was like opening a window, allowing more room for openness, for possibilities." In her discussion of Gnostic beliefs she also reviewed the attainment of personal enlightenment through non-orthodox approaches, mystical spirituality, and a better appreciation of the feminine experience. In view of the latter, it is not surprising that 114, the last verse of Thomas, was not quoted: "Simon Peter said to them: Let Mary Magdalene depart from among us, for women are not worthy of the life. Jesus says: Behold, I shall look after her so that I make her male, in order that she herself shall become a living spirit like you males. For every female who becomes male shall enter the Sovereignty of the Heavens."

The friction with Peter was confirmed in *The Gospel According to Mary Magdalene*, believed to have been written in Greek sometime in the second century (Karen King). The fragmentary Gospel includes only eight pages of the original eighteen, preserved in a fifth century Coptic codex, named Papyrus Berolinensis 8502. In Mary 5:5–11, Peter acknowledged that Jesus loved her more than any other person and asked what words the Savior had said to her that the other disciples did not know. Four pages of her response are missing, but what remains is intellectually impressive, speaking of the soul in apocalyptic terms in the same style as Revelation. In 9:3 and 4, Peter questioned whether Jesus would so speak to a mere woman and in 9:5 "Then Mary wept and said to Peter, My brother Peter, what do you think? Do you think that I have thought this up myself in my heart, or that I am lying about the Savior?" Matthew then admonished Peter as being hot tempered, that Mary should be respected, and that (important to the Gnostics) the Savior loved Mary more than the others. Her actions served to strengthen the wavering disciples and demonstrated the ability of women; this fact was also emphasized in Elaine Pagels' work.

It is interesting to me that Ms. Pagels is an active participant in her (Episcopalian) church; she must be an exceptionally valuable contributor to discussions of the considerable amount of controversy in the first few centuries, when the canon was being formulated.

By 250, Irenaeus' main arguments were fairly well encapsulated in church dogma, and became even more solidified with the arrival of Constantine. Outside of the one church there could be no salvation, and other viewpoints were rejected as heresy. With the new backing of the Roman Empire, the penalty for heresy became a serious matter indeed.

Constantine (ca. 274–337) was a capable military commander, the son of a Roman emperor, and a shrewd politician. Through various strategies and battles he defeated his three main rivals for the throne, but his most important victory was at a crossing over the Tiber River at a place called Milvian Bridge. On October 28, 312, he crushed the army of Maxentius who lost his life there. Prior to the battle, a vision of a cross in the sky with its shaft made from a sword and the words "In Hoc Signo Vinces" (In this sign, conquer) had assured Constantine of victory. Fighting against five to one odds, but with the cross on their shields, his army prevailed.

He was quick to show his gratitude. Early in 313 he and Licinius issued the famous Edict of Milan which granted religious freedom to all. As the "imprisoned Christians were released from the prisons and mines, and were received by their brethren in the Faith with acclamations of joy; the churches were again filled, and those who had fallen away sought forgiveness." In 314, Constantine gave Miltiades, the thirty-second pope, a palace as papal residence, then in 321 decreed Sunday as the official Roman/Christian day of rest. In 330 he dedicated Saint Peter's Basilica over the traditional burial site of Saint Peter on Vatican Hill in Rome. From the beginning, Constantine granted privileges to the church because it took care of the poor, and bishops' courts sometimes had jurisdiction over civil courts. He established asylums for "exposed" children, or orphans, prohibited the abduction of girls, and protected women by making divorce more difficult. He established rules protecting the rights of slaves and encouraged their emancipation.

Constantinople (formerly Byzantium) became the seat of the Roman Empire in 331 and shortly before his death, Constantine was baptized there by Eusebius. One of the most momentous actions by Constantine was to convene the Council of Nicaea in 325. This was the first ecumenical council, called for the purpose of confronting the problem of Arianism.

Arius (ca. 250–336), as a priest in Alexandria, taught that Jesus was not quite human and not quite divine, nor equal or eternal with the Father. Beginning in 319, Arianism grew to be one of the most widespread and divisive heresies in the history of Christianity. In 321, nearly 100 Egyptian and Libyan bishops accused Arius of heresy, excommunicated him, and caused him to flee to Palestine. While there he was befriended by Eusebius, whose close ties to Constantine proved to be very helpful.

Eusebius (ca. 260–341) was called the "father of church history" and in Metzger he is referenced more often than any other author. In his position as bishop of Caesara he developed a close relationship with Emperor Constantine. As a sign of this trust, in 332 Constantine charged Eusebius with the responsibility of preparing fifty copies of the scriptures by expert scribes, for use by the growing number of Christian churches. These magnificent, elaborately bound volumes were delivered in a timely manner and one copy may have survived, as the codex Sinaiticus (found by Mrs. Lewis and Mrs. Gibson in 1892). Of interest is the New Testament portion, organized as directed by Eusebius and similar to the recommendations of Irenaeus, Clement and Origen.

When Constantine convened the Council of Nicaea in 325, it was a command performance for the 300 bishops assembled from the main churches. The Arian heresy and schism were tearing the church apart and threatening to weaken Constantine's grip on the empire so he provided the bishops with transportation, protection by the army, housing, meals and use of his own palace near present-day Iznik, about seventy miles southeast of Constantinople. To his credit, he allowed the bishops full freedom of discussion and accepted their vote, even though it went against his personal preference. All the bishops except two signed the Nicene Creed, which has survived to this day in slightly amended form. Other actions involved fixing the date of Easter, and establishing the rank and jurisdiction of the Alexandrian church.

When Arius appeared at Nicaea, the "confession of faith" he presented was torn to pieces. The bishops then issued an anathema (formal denunciation) and he was exiled to Illyricum (southeast Europe). In 328 Eusebius persuaded Constantine to issue letters of indulgence ordering the bishop in Alexandria to readmit Arius to the church there, and that was followed by a similar order to the bishop of Constantinople. Arius died before the latter was acted on, and Arianism was outlawed by Theodosias I in 379. But the Vandals and Visigoths carried Arianism into Europe and Spain, and it lasted until the mid-sixth century.

Athanasius (297–373) was present at Nicaea as an assistant to the bishop of Alexandria, a position he had earned by his treatise affirming that Jesus was both God and Man. He continued this argument against Arianism for the rest of his life and was recognized as the "father of orthodoxy." He became bishop of Alexandria in 328 but for the next thirty-eight years he fought a continuing battle against Arianism and unfriendly emperors. He was expelled from Alexandria at least five times, and when recalled, each time he was met with a joyous welcome by the citizens. In 367, in his thirty-ninth Festal Epistle, he formalized in writing the conclusions made at Laodicea four years earlier. These deliberations served to finalize selection of the twenty-seven books of the New Testament, accepted as the canon for Christian theology at that time and ever since.

While Jesus was on Earth he promised his disciples that he would send the Holy Spirit to guide them. Thus, John 14:26 says "…the Holy Ghost, whom the Father will send in my name, he shall teach you all things, and bring all things to your remembrance, whatsoever I have said unto you." In 1 Corinthians 14:37, Paul assured them that "…the things that I write unto you are the commandments of the Lord" and in II Timothy 3:16 said "All scripture is given by inspiration of God…"

By 500 B.C. papyrus sheets were being joined together to make rolls averaging thirty feet in length, with writing usually on one side. Much of the Old Testament was written on animal skins. By about 200 B.C. parchment, a predecessor to vellum, was developed and was used as late as A.D. 800. In the first century A.D. the papyrus rolls began to be replaced by a new format called a codex, that is, papyrus sheets bound together at one edge in the form of a book.

The twenty-seven books of the New Testament were written during a period of about fifty years, and within fifteen to sixty-five years after the death of Jesus. Some 4000 handwritten manuscripts, in Greek, have been discovered to date and subjected to critical analysis like no other book.

Some small fragments of the Matthew Gospel were found at Luxor in 1901 and are known as Magdalen Papyrus 64, as they are kept at the Magdalen College library in Oxford. Recently, Peter Thiede, a German scholar, has claimed the fragments were as old as A.D. 70–100. His work was comprehensive but controversial, reflecting the current intense competition among scholars.

In 1930 Mr. Chester Beatty made his first acquisition of an extremely valuable collection of papyrus manuscripts from an antiquities dealer in Egypt. The material came from Fayum, a few miles south of Cairo, and eventually consisted of eighty-six nearly perfect pages out of a total of 104. Most of Paul's epistles, as well as Hebrews, made up the package. They have become known as P 46 (Papyrus 46) housed in part at Dublin, in the Chester Beatty Collection, and partially at the University of Michigan. Scholar Y.K. Kim has dated these texts at about A.D. 100. Other parts of the Beatty collection are P 45, which includes two pages of Matthew, seven of Luke, two of John and thirteen of Acts; also P 47 that comprises about one-half of the Book of Revelation.

Papyrus 52 is a small fragment of the John gospel, discovered in Egypt in 1920. It has been dated at A.D. 100–125, and is kept in the John Rylands University library in Manchester, England.

A massive effort at Oxyrhynchus, Egypt, about 125 miles south of Cairo, has recovered 5000 fragments of Greek texts on papyrus. Among them are three pieces of the Thomas gospel, including twenty of the 114 verses, making possible a careful comparison with the complete Coptic text at Nag Hammadi, 200 miles to the south. The Oxyrhynchus fragments have been dated at 130–250 A.D; Rufinus has described the city at the time as a thriving Christian center, with "ten thousand monks and twenty thousand virgins."

Two of the oldest copies of the entire Bible are the Codex Vaticanus, in Greek, on vellum, in uncial (all capital letters) script, and the other is the Codex Sinaiticus, described earlier. Both are believed to date from the first half of the fourth century.

JESUS SEMINAR

The Jesus Seminar was organized to learn the truth about the historical Jesus and the words attributed to him. As stated, the goal was to probe the relation between faith and history "behind the Christian façade of the Christ." The question to be answered was "whether the worldview reflected in the Bible can be carried forward into the scientific age and retained as an article of faith." [This question is, of course, some of the subject matter of my own work, so I studied the Seminar results with a great deal of interest. Too, the Seminar scholars covered almost exactly the same time in history as I have, in the last fifteen pages, specifically pp. 144–159.]

The Jesus Seminar was first convened in 1985 by Robert Funk under the auspices of the Westar Institute. At its peak, the research involved about 200 "Fellows" from mostly Protestant denominations. These critical scholars worked from ancient texts in the original language, i.e., Hebrew, Aramaic, Greek, Coptic, Latin, etc. They met twice a year to debate technical papers, then voted on the authenticity of Jesus' words. Voting was done with colored beads, red for Jesus "surely said this," pink for "he probably said that," gray for "he probably didn't say that," and black for "he definitely didn't say it." By scoring this way they wound up with four ranges of probability: .75 and up, .5 to .75, .25 to .5 and under .25.

[In their explanation of the project, the Seminar leaders stressed their high level of scholarship and the importance of science in today's world. I was disappointed in the way they handled both. First, the group of Fellows was selected to represent only one part of the spectrum of scholarly opinion, certainly not a "consensus of modern scholars" and with few Catholics or Europeans. Conservatives were mostly excluded so only the left-most fringe of opinion was represented. Alternative opinions, an important advantage of peer review, were thereby eliminated. Fundamentalist views should have been considered (even though I also tend to disagree with some of them, especially concerning Chapters 1–11 of Genesis). Even without the desirable, broad range of views, I was surprised at the primitive method used to vote and derive percentages. A Monte Carlo simulation would have worked better and provided results in a more accurate, scientific, and flexible form of probability distributions.]

Study material included 1500 versions of 500 items, presumably including copies of critical Greek texts P 46, P 47, Magdalen Papyrus 64, Codex Vaticanus, etc. The Seminar concluded that the Mark Gospel preceded Luke and Matthew, and contributed to them. Q and Thomas were thought to be the oldest of all and, hence, given precedence. A saying common to Mark, Matthew and Luke was considered to be only one source and required further attestation in Q or Thomas. The result was that the hypothetical Q, and latecomer Thomas, both sayings-only gospels, were given precedence over Matthew, Mark, Luke and John. The attestation requirement was much more severe than for any other historical document, and if applied across the board would wipe out much of our record of history.

Another argument is that Jesus' disciples remembered his ideas, as expressed in sayings and parables, and not his exact words. These were then retold to the third-party authors of the Gospels and "bear the imprint of orality: short, provocative, memorable, oft-repeated phrases, sentences, and stories." In the synoptic gospels, Jesus spoke in short, pithy one-liners, couplets, aphorisms and parables. His speech was distinctive and often "cut against the social and religious grain." In John, such language did not appear at all, and John had Jesus speaking in lengthy discourses or monologues.

Therefore, according to the Seminar, the Gospel of John did not have a single authentic saying of Jesus, and Mark had only one. The overall conclusion was that only 18 percent of the Gospel sayings attributed to Jesus were actually spoken by him. The other 82 percent, then, were "imaginative creations" added to the text by unscrupulous early Christians trying to develop a canon with a predetermined agenda.

The Jesus Seminar has been widely publicized and negative results were eagerly reported by some factions of the press. Thus we see *Time*, January 10, 1994 breathlessly reporting "While Jesus may have been a carpenter…he did not preach salvation from sin…he probably never delivered the Sermon on the Mount…he never cured any diseases. As for the other miracles? No loaves and fishes, no water into wine, no raising of Lazarus. And certainly no resurrection."

[I wonder if this gleeful, and destructive, use by the media was an intended product of the Seminar? And if so, do members of the Seminar still attend church? Without the Gospel of John, and very little of the synoptic Gospels, what kind of Christianity do they believe in? Critics point out that the eyewitness testimony of people actually there at the time of Jesus, and willing to die for their beliefs, effectively has been replaced by the choices of presumptuous Fellows.

My conclusion is that members of the Jesus Seminar have performed much like a new, liberal "priest class"—exhibiting moral and intellectual condescension, and contempt for different opinions, "coming especially from those who lack academic credentials." If 82 percent of Jesus' sayings never happened, whatever did he say to warrant the horrible punishment of crucifixion? That act, and the following Resurrection, may be the most powerful events in all of history. Eyewitnesses, people who were there, were absolutely convinced that it happened.]

One of the most profound events in world history was when Emperor Constantine led the Roman Empire to embrace Christianity. The new imperial religion was soon backed by Roman power and organized with Roman efficiency. The church dioceses, each headed by a bishop, were made to correspond to the imperial provinces, all increasingly dominated by the idea of "one God, one emperor, one empire, one church and one faith."

Constantine had a tolerant policy for all religions but after his death in 337, his sons were much more fanatical, and Constantius threatened the death penalty for pagan superstition and sacrifice. Christianity began to influence all political thought, art and culture and other religions were forcibly suppressed. In 380, Theodosius the Great declared Christianity the official state religion, and made heresy a crime against the state. Christians could be punished, as well, if their views were deemed inappropriate.

Constantinople was the main center for this new movement and the site of the Second Ecumenical Council in 381. At this council, the concept of the Trinity was reaffirmed in more detail, as well as the birth of Jesus to a virgin. These two basic elements of church dogma were restated at the third ecumenical council at Ephesus in 431, the fourth at Chalcedon in 451 and the fifth at Constantinople in 553. At the Lateran Council in 649 the virgin birth was again defined and as recently as 1854, Pope Pius IX proclaimed the Immaculate Conception.

Christians believe that the prophet Isaiah was predicting the birth of Jesus when he said "…Behold, a virgin shall conceive, and bear a son, and shall call his name Immanuel" (Isa. 7:14). Matthew referred to this same verse in Mt 1:22 when he said "Now all this was done, that it might be fulfilled which was spoken of the Lord by the prophet."

From other sources, it seems that Mary was born to Ann and Joachim in 23 B.C., and betrothed to Joseph in 11 B.C., at the age of twelve and a half (normal at that time). That would make Mary fifteen and a half when Jesus was born. Tying dates to Luke 2:2, stating Jesus was born "while Quirinius was governor of Syria," gives the most likely birth year as 8 B.C. (see p. 131).

Concerning the virgin birth, Luke had Mary saying "…How shall this be, seeing I know not a man? And the angel Gabriel answered and said unto her, the Holy Ghost shall come upon thee…therefore also that holy thing which shall be born of thee shall be called the Son of God" (Lk 1:34–35). An angel explained the situation to Joseph, saying "…thou son of David, fear not to take unto thee Mary thy wife: for that which is conceived in her is of the Holy Ghost" (Mt 1:20). Mary evidently passed this information to Luke and Matthew either directly or through intermediaries. It is puzzling to me that John made no mention of it, even though he was closer to Mary than any of the others. The Church explains that Mary and Joseph handled this potentially divisive situation (even dangerous under Jewish law), as a reason to mutually devote their efforts toward supporting the Divine Child.

There is a considerable body of literature that attempts to explain the virgin birth (actually should be virgin conception). The strongest case seems to be that Mary confided to someone who recorded the event in Aramaic, which was then translated into Greek, and then utilized by Luke. A clinical look at the matter raises interesting questions.

Cloning, and the harvesting of egg cells, is done routinely today by skilled people in modern research laboratories. In 1999 about 170,000 babies were born in the U.S. as the result of in vitro procedures where embryos are created in a dish and then implanted in women. This procedure is certainly no miracle, and to take it one more step, the pregnancy of a virgin need not be a miracle if the embryo is provided for implantation.

The real question about Mary's conception is then, who provided the X, Y, and other chromosomes? If God furnished them all, then in terms of today's technology, Mary would be considered a surrogate mother for the implanted embryo. If Mary's own X chromosome was involved, then the miracle would be the Y chromosome furnished by God. Further to this matter, it seems clear that in the scenario above, God acted to (a) implant a viable embryo, or (b) furnished the male, (including the Y) chromosomes. Mary, in either case, was the virgin mother of Jesus. To be able to analyze the DNA of the cells that grew to be the baby Jesus would be nothing less than mind-blowing.

To further muddy the waters, another possibility could be that God divinely infused the soul of Jesus while he was still a fetus. This would be a neat solution to the matter of virgin conception, which, let us face it, has some practical and historical problems. The divine infusion of Jesus' soul would accomplish the same ends and would obviate a rather questionable claim.

For her act of faith, Mary was considered to be born free of sin, and remained free for her entire life. The Church held that Mary remained a virgin all her life. Jesus' brothers and sisters mentioned in the scriptures are explained as cousins or as the children of Joseph from an earlier marriage. At the Third Ecumenical Council of Ephesus in 431, Mary was decreed the Mother of God. Veneration, a Catholic form of worship one step below adoration, was assigned to Mary in 787 at the Ecumenical Council of Nicaea.

When the emperor Theodosius died in 395, the Roman Empire was divided into a Western empire centered in Rome, and an Eastern or Byzantine Empire with capital in Constantinople. The Eastern Catholic Church had the larger population and was stronger economically, culturally, and militarily. Byzantium led spiritually, with centers of learning and monasteries, and held all the ecumenical councils, called under the auspices of the emperor. The Eastern Church was also was more tolerant toward Gnosticism and other heresies.

The Church in Rome was strongly supported by Aurelius Augustine (354–430) the bishop for thirty-five years of Hippo, in Algeria. For Augustine, Rome was the center of the empire, and Latin became the official language of the Western Church and remained so for over 1500 years, until Vatican II. Siricius, the thirty-eighth bishop of Rome (384–99), was the first to call himself "pope" and during these years, Augustine's councils reconfirmed the twenty-seven books of the New Testament.

Following Romans 5:12–19, one of Augustine's main arguments was the concept of original sin, stemming from the fall of Adam in Genesis. He explained that because of the sex act, original sin was transmitted at birth and every infant required baptism to escape eternal death. He also believed in predestination and following Paul, stressed salvation through faith. Augustine became the main theologian of the Western Church, and is honored as one of its four doctors. His influence was exceeded only by Saint Paul.

Augustine argued that science should be subservient to faith, and implied that science was unimportant, if not dangerous. This helped lead the Church to adamantly insist that all astronomical bodies, including the sun, revolved around the earth, as taught by Aristotle (384–22 b.c.). This irrational approach impacted many sciences, and caused astronomical observations to cease for 1100 years, until Copernicus and Galileo. St. Augustine died in 430, shortly before the Vandals sacked Hippo, his home.

HYPATIA

The story of Hypatia is directly tied to the famous library at Alexandria. She was a well-known scholar and philosopher, widely admired for her virtue, wisdom, and oratorical skills.

In the year 415, bishop Cyril of Alexandria incited a mob of Christians to attack the Jewish quarter—in excess of 200,000 people—and drove a large number of Jews out of the city. In this pogrom, property was looted, synagogues were sacked, and people were killed. As a result, Orestes, the prefect of Alexandria, ordered Cyril to compensate the victims but this stirred up more trouble. Some stone-throwing monks hit Orestes with a rock, whereupon he had the offending monk arrested, tried and executed. That really inflamed the mob which turned on Hypatia because she was a friend of Orestes.

When they caught her on the street, they took her to a nearby church, stripped her naked and then tore her body to pieces with (a) broken pottery or tile or (b) oyster shells They then dragged her mangled body through the streets and burned her remains. At the time of her death she was believed to be sixty years old, neither a Christian or Jew but highly esteemed for her academic achievements—in fact one of the most famous women in the world. Her status, and details of her murder, brought great disgrace upon the Alexandrian church, and Cyril.

Her relationship with the great library stems from fact that Theon, her father, who was also highly educated, was believed to be the "last member of the Library of Alexandria. Ptolemy II founded the Royal Library in 283 B.C. Located in the Royal quarter, it had a museum, gardens, a zoo, shrines and lecture areas. The Serapeum was an adjunct structure housing a small part of the library and also served as a temple. Over 100 scholars lived in the complex full time to do research, write, lecture, translate and copy documents. Over 500,000 documents from around the world were stored there. Many books were borrowed from other countries and copied; the copies were then returned to the lending owners and the originals kept in the Alexandrian library. Complaints about this practice got nowhere.

Original discoveries were made in mathematics (Eratosthenes, Euclid, Pappas), astronomy (Hipparchus, Aristarchus), geometry (Eratosthenes), mechanics (Archimedes, Hero), and medicine (Herophilus, Eristratos, Galen). Callimachus was the most famous librarian, creating for the first time a subject catalog for efficiently filing 120,000 scrolls. [Twenty-two hundred years later, two Stanford students developed Google using data from the Digital Library Initiative. This search engine, launched in late 1998, was designed to organize, for retrieval, the entire Internet's 500 billion web pages (and growing). Google was an advance over Yahoo! ("Yet Another Hierarchical Officious Oracle"), developed earlier by two other Stanford students.]

Destruction of the library at Alexandria was a huge loss to mankind, but strangely, very little is known about how or when it happened. Most accounts say it was burned (a) by Julius Caesar in 48 B.C., (b) by Caliph Umar in A.D. 640, or (c) at the time of Hypatias's death. The Serapeum may have been destroyed in 391 when Theodosius ordered the elimination of all pagan temples. [Another possibility, at least for ruining the scrolls and documents in the main library, may have been by tsunami waves on A.D. July 21, 365. A sub-sea earthquake caused the huge tsunami (p. 358) that carried ships and debris two miles inland and killed 50,000 Alexandrians. This timing would fit well with Hypatia's father serving as "a last member" of the library.]

DECLINE OF ROME

A few years after Hypatia's death, Cyril, by then archbishop of Alexandria, clashed in an all-out battle with archbishop Nestorius of Constantinople. Emperor Theodosius II had named Nestorius to the post in 428, but the latter made the mistake of arguing against the concept of Mary as the Mother of God. Similar to Arianism 100 years earlier, Nestorius argued that Jesus Christ had two natures, one human and the other divine. Cyril bitterly opposed this and used his political skills to defeat Nestorius. In 431 he convened a council at Ephesus and arranged to have his supporters arrive early. They promptly excommunicated Nestorius for heresy before his delegates got there. At the Ephesus council, orthodox Catholic doctrine was reaffirmed, pronouncing Jesus true God and true man, inseparably joined in one person. Nestorius fought back ineffectually, was deposed, and even exiled from Antioch, his hometown. He went to Arabia and Egypt and the Nestorian movement eventually spread to Syria, Armenia, Ethiopia, China and India.

Pope Leo I (440–61) was called "the Great" because of his effective leadership in establishing the primacy of the pope's authority over the whole church, independent of and even superior to the emperor. Leo vigorously fought several heresies, especially that of the Manichaeans. He was mainly responsible for dissuading Attila the Hun from attacking Rome in 452, and when the Vandals sacked Rome in 455, he was able to protect the citizens to some extent.

The Huns emerged from Central Asia in 372 and burst upon the various tribes in Eastern Europe. The Chinese had already built the Great Wall of China to protect themselves from the horde, and for good reason. From birth, the Huns endured cold, hunger and thirst. They were incredibly hardy and superb horsemen. They employed skilled cavalry tactics to route their opponents, routinely killing the men and abducting the women for sexual slavery. According to Colvin, the Huns did not cook their food but ate raw meat that they prepared by riding with it between their thighs and the flanks of their horses. One disturbing habit was to slit the noses of children before raping them, then to cut off chunks of flesh, for eating, from the legs of the still-living child.

First to be wiped out were the Alans, a Nordic tribe that ceased to exist. Ostrogoths in the Ukraine were next, with survivors streaming to the west. Visigoths in the region of Bulgaria put up a futile resistance and then withdrew to Roman territory across the Danube, while the Huns occupied Rumania. In about 400, pressure from the Huns caused an East Germanic tribe called the Vandals to move westward, vacating their lands in Poland, Germany, Hungary and Rumania. After defeating the Franks in Gaul, the Vandals plundered their way west and south, crossing into Spain in 409. From there, they moved to North Africa, taking Carthage in 439, and eventually became a naval power.

By 432 the Huns occupied a large part of eastern and central Europe and were collecting an annual tribute from Rome. Attila became king in 433 and soon gained his sobriquet "the scourge of God" as he consolidated his position with barbaric ferocity. Attila was short, slant-eyed and swarthy, with a reputation for cruelty and terror. In 451 his army, with some Ostrogoth mercenaries, began moving west with the intent of finishing off the rest of Europe. This army sacked many of the main cities in northern Gaul, but a united Roman and Visigoth force caught up with the Huns at Orléans just as they were entering the starving town after a five-week siege. Attila ordered a retreat toward Troyes in central France, and in a daylong battle the Huns were defeated and retreated once again. Gathered for a last stand at Châlons-sur-Marne, the Huns were defeated for the final time by a joint force of Romans, Visigoths, Franks and Burgundians, led by Aetius and Theodoric.

Attila met with Leo soon after this, and then returned all the way to Hungary. It is said that in 453 he suffered a fatal stroke (or nosebleed) caused by over-exertion on one of his many wedding nights, when he married a blond German princess. After Attila's death, the Huns never recovered, but the face of Europe had been changed for all time.

During their eighty years of terrorizing Europe, the Huns served to push the Germanic and other European tribes closer to the Romans. As a result, the Goths and others became Arian Christians and took control of Europe; Imperial Rome had seen its last victory. Instead of the Huns, Rome was overrun by the Visigoths under Alaric in 410 and by the Vandals in 455. The Vandals plundered the city for two weeks, departing with countless valuables including the Empress and her two daughters.

Romulus Augustulus was forced to resign as the last emperor of the Roman Empire in 476 (he was only fourteen years old). With the collapse of the Roman Empire, the Catholic Church began a period of turmoil and division; in fact, the next 500 years were called the Dark Ages. Irish monks, led by St. Patrick, played a key role in establishing monasteries and preserved much of the world's literature, art and music. By copying and preserving the Bible, Greek and Roman classics, and every other book they could obtain, they "saved civilization Several thousand monasteries were established in Europe, and the Catholic Church established the order of Benedictines to work with historical documents. Just as Plato's Academy in Athens was closing, about 529, Benedict and his monks were building the monastery and town at Monte Cassino. For many centuries the Church, through the Benedictines, shaped the culture, religion and morality of the primitive Germanic and French tribes.

With the decline in the West (meaning Europe), the eastern empire became politically superior to Rome. Byzantium became the main center of Christianity and emperor Justinian (527–565) fully established the state church and completed building Hagia Sophia (Holy Wisdom) in 537. This was the most magnificent Christian church in the world, measuring 260 x 270 feet, with the 110-foot (diameter) dome rising 210 feet above the floor. The church had a permanent staff of 550 people and was in operation for over 900 years. When Sultan Mehmet seized the city in 1453, the church was converted into a Moslem mosque. In 1935, Turkish president Kemal Ataturk had it made into a museum.

Gregory I, pope from 590 to 604, was the last of the Latin Fathers of the Western church. At the time he took over the papacy, the West was crumbling before the advances of the new barbaric kingdoms of Europe. As the Roman Empire was no longer a factor, Gregory took on the temporal powers and responsibility for the welfare of the people, and successfully negotiated a truce with the invading Lombards. In addition to the civic affairs, Gregory completed a monumental work on the Book of Job, created a form of musical worship called the Gregorian Chant, and was active in liturgical reform. A mission he sent to England resulted in the conversion of that country to Catholicism. In this regard, the historian Edward Gibbon remarked that Caesar required six legions to conquer Britain whereas Gregory needed only forty monks. He was also considered to be the cofounder of the Benedictine Order and after his death in 604 was canonized by popular acclaim. After Leo, he was the only other pope to be called the "Great." Gregory laid the foundation for a church-state in the West, to be dominated by the Catholic Church for the next eleven centuries.

Only six years after the death of Gregory the Great, a new prophet in Arabia received the first of many messages from the archangel Gabriel. The prophet's name was Muhammad, and the revelations led to founding an important new religion, Islam.

7

ISLAM

[This religion has been of keen interest to me for a long time. During my work overseas, we lived in four different Muslim countries for a total of twelve years. Each country was quite different and the people's practice of Islam was different, also.

For example, Turkey was a secular republic, with a prime minister and president, (both sentenced to death in a 1960 coup d'etat, two years after we got there). Kemal Ataturk was widely admired as the first president, in 1923, and he had taken some harsh steps to get religion out of government. We found the most conservative Muslims were in the villages, and the Kurds in southeastern Turkey added a different aspect to politics. During our five years in Turkey we came to have a number of Muslim friends, and found they were good, generous, honest, hardworking people who were concerned about their children, just like anyone else.

Our company had a policy of sending promising young Turkish engineers and geologists to stateside universities for advanced degrees. Several of these people, including women, had fine careers in the industry, and some later became U.S.citizens. One of the most outstanding men in this group was Erdem Serim; he became very successful, remained a Muslim, and has helped me in this project. He provided one of my main references, the book by Dr. Farah, and was one of my reviewers for this chapter.

In our two years in Libya, we found a somewhat more strict form of Islam and we were fortunate to be there during the reign of King Idris. This led to a more relaxed environment for expats, as contrasted to that under the regime of Muammar Kaddafi who overthrew the king. Two years in

Nigeria exposed us to more good people who struggled under tough living conditions. A fairly strict form of Islam was practiced by Hausa tribes in the north part of the country, but they seemed to get along fairly well with the Christian Ibo tribes from the south. Muslim, military dictators governed the country and treated the Christians fairly well, considering that the latter had been defeated in the Biafran war only a few years before.

In Indonesia, about 90 percent of the population (220 million) was Muslim, but with a strong Buddhist and Hindu influence. Of the four countries, the Indonesians were the happiest group of people, with a comfortable style of living in a beautiful and lush setting. We made many friends there, and I enjoyed working with their highly qualified technical people, both in the industry, and in PERTAMINA, the government company.]

MUHAMMAD

Muslims think that Muhammad was a messenger or prophet, and as such, was a calm, sensible, truthful, judicious, and humble person who recorded and passed on the revelations of God. In full, his name was Abū al-Qāsim Muhammad ibn 'Abd Allāh ibn 'Abd al-Muttalib ibn Hāshim, but thankfully, the single name is used. Muhammad was born about A.D. 570-71, in Mecca, into the Banu Hashim clan of the Quraysh tribe. Orphaned before the age of six, he was adopted by his grandfather, and after his grandfather died, by his uncle Abu-Tālib. The uncle's son Ali, Muhammad's cousin, many years later married Muhammad's daughter Fātimah.

The uncle was a trader and on one trip to Syria, Muhammad was put in charge of some goods belonging to a rich widow, Khadijah. She was so impressed by Muhammad that she offered marriage. The year was about 595; she was forty years old and fifteen years senior to Muhammad. They were married for about twenty-four years before she died in 619. During that time she bore him two sons who died young and four daughters. Muhammad did not remarry until several years after Khadijah's death.

Arabia, at that time, just as today, was sparsely settled because of the difficult climate which created a dry, barren landscape. The term "Arab" derives from the root word for "nomad" or people that wandered from place to place, seeking pasture for their flocks of sheep and goats. [In Turkey we saw many of these people, with their black tents, especially in the southeastern part of the country.] The few scattered tribes were believed, by oral tradition, to be descendents of Shem, the oldest son of Noah—hence the term "Semite." Today, Arabic is spoken by nearly 250 million people.

Villages and towns were clustered at those places where a source of water allowed a limited form of farming to develop. Trading via camel caravans was an important part of the overall economy, and Mecca grew to be a key town on the trade route. The Quraysh tribe was the dominant power in Mecca and they grew to have trade connections from Syria to Abyssinia. Muhammad was a member of an important family of the Quraysh tribe.

Traders in Mecca welcomed the inviolate security provided by the "Black Stone" believed to be a meteorite, kept within the Kaaba, a cubic structure named for the Arabic word for cube. The surrounding area was declared harām (violence forbidden), and the Quraysh tribe kept enlarging the safe area in order to attract more visitors. For the same reason, the idols of other tribes were displayed around the Kaaba.

Tradition says that in about A.D. 610, it was decided to rebuild the Kaaba at the site of Abraham's original construction. After completing extensive work, four factions argued bitterly over who would have the honor of moving the precious Black Stone back into the sanctuary. To avoid bloodshed, some wise person suggested that they follow the advice of the next person to walk through the gate. Muhammad was that person, and his ingenious solution was for a member of each of the four tribes to lift a corner of his cloak, where the Black Stone was placed.

The common wisdom is that, at the age of forty, in the year 610, Muhammad received his first revelation one night during the month of Ramadan. He had secluded himself in a cave on Mt. Hirā and the message from God was brought by the archangel (high-ranking angel) Gabriel (Jibril) who told him "You are the Messenger of God." Khadijah and her Christian cousin Waraqa reassured him that he was not possessed by the *jinn* ("spirits"). Waraqa, who was literate, helped Muhammad understand that he had been chosen to pass on these messages to other Arabs, and that they were similar to those sent by God to earlier Jewish and Christian prophets. Many years earlier, Muhammad had met the Christian monk Bahira, who predicted Muhammad's future greatness. Nestorians were also active in the area, so the Christian theology was known to some extent. The Jewish influence was even stronger, as many Jews had fled from the Roman conquests of A.D. 70 and 132. They had several settlements in Arabia and in the important city of Yathrib (Medina) about half the population were Jewish.

It was astonishing to me to learn of the references made to Jewish and Christian scriptures by Muhammad and Islam. God's message to Muhammad was believed to be delivered by the angel Gabriel. Some 1060 years earlier, Gabriel had prophesized and explained visions to Daniel. Then, 500 years after that, Luke told how Gabriel had explained that the virgin birth of Jesus was to occur. Bloom and Blair (2002, p. 44) have listed some of the biblical events and people named in Islamic writing. Their list comprises most of the following: the six days of creation, Adam and Eve, Noah, Lot, Moses, Aaron, Abraham and his first-born son Ishmael, Isaac, Jacob, Ezra, Zechariah, John the Baptist, Joseph, Mary and Jesus. Ishmael, the son of Abraham and Hagar, got special attention as the direct ancestor of the Muslims. It seems clear that Muhammad was knowledgeable about Ishmael's history, as described in Genesis, viz. his Egyptian wife (21:8–21), Abraham's death (25:9), his twelve sons (25:12–16), and his daughter, as one of Esau's wives (28:9 and 36:3).

Muhammad believed that Moses and Jesus were the most important of God's messengers for the Old and New Testaments. Muslims hold that Muhammad was a prophet of God, just as Abraham, Moses and Jesus. But unlike the Christian view of Jesus, Muhammad was not considered divine. "At first, and by his own admission, Muhammad had no intention of founding a new religion. He merely wanted his fellow Arabs to worship one God, the only God, as worshiped by their neighbors, the Christians and Jews" (Farah p. 62). Muslims call Jews and Christians "People of the Book" and "Believers, Jews, Sabeans, and Christians— whoever believes in God and the Last Day and does what is right—shall have nothing to fear or to regret."

As Muhammad received the messages from Gabriel he had scribes record them, and his companions memorized some of them. This soon led him to begin preaching his belief in one God, social justice, mercy, benevolence and compassion for the weak, sick and poor. The new religion was called Islam (submission, or surrender to the will of God, or Allah) and followers were called Muslims (those who have surrendered). After three years of rather low-key preaching, only thirty individuals were converted, mostly from the lower classes.

But as his message of equality began to take hold, the Quaraysh ruling tribe in Mecca recognized the danger to their privileged position. They first tried to bribe him, and then turned to threats and persecution. As the physical danger grew, over 100 of his followers left Mecca to take refuge in the Christian kingdom of Abyssinia (Ethiopia), and later his Hāshemite relatives were forcibly moved outside the city.

When his wife and uncle died, he began a year of grief, and one night envisioned the Night Journey, an intense supernatural experience. In this vision, Muhammad saw himself astride a winged animal called Buruq, on a mystical flight from the Kaaba to Jerusalem where he landed at the site of the former Temple of the Jews. Once there, he was introduced to Abraham, Moses and Jesus, who prayed with him. From a rock at the site, he saw himself rising to the limits of the knowable heavens, and a divine radiance descending upon him (remarkably similar to the transfiguration episode of Jesus). Along the way, the unity of the prophetic revelations was reaffirmed to him, and Moses advised that five daily prayers should be required by Muslims (three required by Jews).

About the same time, he prudently decided that he should leave Mecca, and accepted the invitation of a delegation from Yathrib to move there. (They believed Muhammad could resolve a bitter intertribal feud that was rupturing the social fabric of the city). About 100 families escaped to Yathrib, 280 miles to the north of Mecca, in the year A.D. 622. This emigration became known as the "Hegira" (Hijrah). After his death, the city was known as "Madīnat al-Rasūl" (city of the messenger), or Medina. The first year of the Muslim calendar was 622, so that 1383 C.E. (after Hegira) is equivalent to A.D. 2005 on the Gregorian calendar.

Up to this point, Muhammad's message was similar in many ways with that told by Jesus nearly 600 years earlier. That is, belief in one God, knowing about many of the personages in the Old Testament, serving as a messenger for God, and belief in social justice, mercy, benevolence and equitable treatment. One result of the Hegira was that Muhammad became more involved with political and military matters. Perhaps he realized he had to change his tactics, because his previous approach, while in Mecca, failed to gain many supporters.

At any rate, Muhammad was able to unite the community, including the Jews, who made up nearly half the population. His skill at restoring order earned widespread respect and recognition of his power and authority. In 623 he personally led three unsuccessful razzias (raids) against Meccan caravans and another failed in 624, even with 315 men.

In early 624 an army from Mecca was defeated at Badr and Muhammad became recognized as a successful prophet, administrator, and military commander (like Samuel, 1700 years earlier). Prior to this battle, Muhammad promised his fighters that martyrs would earn direct entry into Paradise. He described their reward, which would include luxurious surroundings, cool beauty, and cups of the purest wine, served in the company of eternal virgin lovers, "dark-eyed houris, chaste as hidden pearls." After the battle of Badr, Muhammad ordered that Muslims henceforth should pray toward Mecca, rather than Jerusalem. He also married Hafsah, the widow of one of the Muslims killed in the battle. This marriage, five years after his first wife died, was one of a series in which Muhammad seemed to show concern for the widows of those who had been killed, or other women in difficult circumstances.

Not long after this he married his third wife A'ishah, the daughter of his most trusted companion, Abu Bakr. She was his only virgin wife, the other ten being mostly old widows, and none beautiful. Only Khadijah was wealthy, and the four daughters he had with her were his only children to reach adulthood.

The next year his army of 700 was defeated by 3000 from Mecca, led by Abu Sufyan, at the battle of Uhud. Again, after that battle he married Umm Salamah, whose husband had died from his wounds. Medina was not damaged but some of the Jews came under pressure because they had turned against Muhammad, in violation of the agreement made when the community was formed. Because of that, he banished the Jewish Banū al-Nadir tribe, allowing them to leave Medina with what they could carry.

In 627, Mecca attacked again with 10,000 men led by Abu Sufyan. Mecca was turned back at the Battle of the Trench, but they had been supported by the Jewish tribe Qurayzah, in violation of their oath. After the battle, at a trial conducted by an ally of Muhammad, all the fighting men (700–800) of the Qurayzah were condemned to death, and the women and children were sold as slaves. Muhammad took one of the widows, Rayhana bint Amr, as another wife.

In 628 Muhammad led a large group of men to Mecca for the annual pilgrimage, and soon after married Umm Habibah, a daughter of Sufyan and the widow of a Muslim man. In the same year he led Muslim forces in a campaign against the Jewish agricultural center at Khaybar. After several battles there he took control of the area and forced the Jews to share half their crops with him. He also took the widow Safiya as his second Jewish wife. Treatment of the Jews at Khaybar was the beginning of the practice of *dhimmi*, one element of which was the payment of a tax, in lieu of a forced conversion to Islam. In addition, *dhimmi* was highly discriminatory in placing a long list of restrictions on the non-Muslims. When Umar conquered Christian Syria in 636, he formalized the law, making Christians and Jews protected, but second-class citizens, a practice that governed relations for several centuries. In Israel today, Palestinians are treated in a somewhat similar way.

During the pilgrimage in 629, Muhammad was reconciled with an uncle in Mecca and married Maymunah, the uncle's sister-in-law. In 629 he also married Zaynab, the widow of Zayd who had been his Christian slave until Muhammad adopted him.

In 630 he marched with 10,000 men to the gates of Mecca, where a more-friendly Abu Sufyan and other leaders met him and formally submitted. A general amnesty was declared and the Muslims entered Mecca peacefully. The inhabitants were treated with mercy and Muhammad gained the allegiance of most of the Meccans. In the Kaaba he personally destroyed 360 idols with his staff and the Kaaba became the principal shrine of Islam. When two more tribes were subdued but treated with magnanimity, they subsequently turned to Islam with ardent zeal.

Muhammad had quickly become, militarily, the strongest man in Arabia as various tribes sought alliances with him and adopted Islam. His greatest razzia occurred at the end of 630 when he led 30,000 men on a one-month journey to Syria, as a preliminary to later invasion.

In 632 he made his last pilgrimage to Mecca. Nine days before his death in June, it is believed that he received his last revelation, claimed by some to be "This day I have perfected your religion for you, completed my favor upon you, and have chosen for you Islam as your religion." He died on June 8, 632, at the age of sixty three.

THE KORAN—QUR'AN

The Koran is considered to be the collective revelations, to Mohammad, of God's literal words. In contrast to the Old and New Testaments of the Jews and Christians, the Koran (meaning 'recitation' or the body of 'readings') was written almost contemporaneously with the revelations of Gabriel. As Muhammad received the messages he had them recorded by scribes as he could not read or write himself. He also taught the verses to his companions, many of whom memorized the different surahs (chapters) of the Koran. Over a period of two decades, the 114 surahs were received and recorded in a unique "lyrical flow of poetic rhymed prose."

Zayd ibn Thabit ibn al-Dahak played a key role in compiling the Koran. His work was similar to that of Ezra, Redactor of the Old Testament. However, Zayd was actually present and in daily communication with Muhammad whereas, in some cases, Ezra tried to explain events that had occurred as long ago as 3300 years in the past.

Zayd, from the Bani al-Najjar tribe, was only twelve years old when he met Muhammad for the first time. Zayd wanted to join the Muslim army, preparing for the battle of Badr. He was rejected as too young, but got the prophet's attention when he recited seventeen surahs from memory. Two years later he again tried to join the army before the battle of Uhud. Instead, Muhammad recognized that Zayd had value as a scholar, and because he could read and write was named as the Chief Scribe of the Koran. Muhammad also told Zayd to learn Hebrew and Syriac (an eastern dialect of Aramaic) so that by the time he was in his early twenties, Zayd was familiar with the Jewish and Christian scriptures, and enabled Muhammad to communicate with those groups in their own language.

When Muhammad received a new revelation, it is reported he said: "Call Zayd for me and let him bring the board, the ink pot and the scapula bone." Zayd is also reputed to have witnessed a meeting of the prophet with Gabriel during the last Ramadan, when "Jibril came to me and ordered me to place this ayah in this place in this surah." When Muhammad died, all the surahs (chapters and verses) were in written form, but the Koran was not yet assembled in one master text.

One of the most important things Abu Bakr did during his short reign (632–634) was to assign Zayd the project of compiling the Koran in book form. Zayd had impeccable credentials but was only twenty-two years old, so he assumed the responsibility with some trepidation. A "law of witness" methodology was used to assure the best possible accuracy. This rule required all the twenty to sixty different scribes (or more) who had any copies of written material (recited by Muhammad) to submit the verses, attested by two witnesses, for examination. Verses had been written on parchment, palm leaves, smooth stones, or whatever was at hand, and those accepted were compiled along with those in Zayd's own records. Zayd's efforts produced the first assembled copy of the Koran but the format of this version is not known. On his deathbed, Abu Bakr bequeathed the codex to his successor Umar, who later turned it over to Hafsa, his daughter, and widow of Muhammad.

The Koran is not arranged chronologically. The first chapter is the opening prayer. All other 113 chapters are in order of length, that is, chapter two is the longest and chapter 114 is the shortest. Each one is named by one word taken from each chapter. Originally, Arabic was to be the sole language of the Koran, beginning with the language used by the archangel Gabriel and so written. It was held that proper understanding could only be possible from the Arabic, and for centuries the faithful recited verses of the Koran in Arabic regardless of their native language. That meant that only nineteen percent of users fully understood the words they repeated. Today, unauthorized translations have been made in forty-three different languages.

The essence of teachings in the Koran is simple and direct: God, or Allah, is the sole, all-powerful Creator. He is compassionate and merciful, and humanity must submit completely to his divine will. Allah had been revealed to Abraham previously but the Jews and Christians had erred in their interpretations, necessitating that Muhammad be dispatched to correct the mistakes. God is depicted as the creator (in six days), omniscient, sovereign, and omnipotent. God breathes a soul into each new life, and has guardian angels (*jinn*) keep a record of each person, to be tallied on the day of reckoning. Analogous to commandments are the injunctions (1) Worship no other God, (2) Honor your parents, (3) Respect the rights of others, (4) Be generous, (5) Do not kill except when justifiable, (6) Do not commit adultery, (7) Be fair and honest, (8) Protect orphans, (9) Be pure of heart, (10) Be humble and unpretentious.

Allah has allowed individuals to have freedom of choice, upon which they will be judged. The righteous will do good works and obey the word of God, while the wicked will perform evil deeds. At death the body returns to the earth while the soul goes into an out-of-world state of unconsciousness. At the Day of Judgment, the body will leave the earth to rejoin the soul. After a period of protracted waiting, all mankind, *jinn*, and animals will be judged. People may hope for intercession by their prophets, but Paradise or Hell will be the final destination for everyone.

All Muslims have five duties, termed the Five Pillars of Islam. First (Shahāda) is the profession of faith, in Arabic "There is no god but God and Muhammad is His messenger" and the name of God may be invoked at least twenty times per day. The second requirement (Salāh) is prayer five times a day—at dawn, noon, midafternoon, sunset, and nightfall. A muezzin calls the faithful to prayer in a unique singing chant—in these days usually a recording played from a minaret. On Fridays, all male Muslims attend the noon prayer together in a mosque and listen to a sermon, in Arabic. Women may also attend, but are segregated. The third rule is to fast (Sawm)—abstain from food and drink (plus sex and smoking)—between sunrise and sunset during the month of Ramadan. Months are calculated on a lunar cycle meaning that each year, Ramadan moves ahead eleven days. The end of Ramadan is marked by a popular feast called Id al-Fitr. The fourth rule (Zakāt) is to give alms to the poor, which may be a tithe, in different forms. Fifth is to go on a pilgrimage to Mecca at least once in a lifetime, health and finances permitting. This pilgrimage is called the Hajj, and those who do it are called Hajji. Two million pilgrims visit Mecca every year, where the Kaaba is at the center of activities. At the end of the hajj, Muslims (worldwide) celebrate the feast of Eid-al-Adha [In Turkey, it is called Būyūk Bayram.]

Additional sayings and deeds of Muhammad have been amassed as non-canonical texts. These eyewitness accounts of the Prophet are called Hadith (if utterances), and Sunnah (observed actions). Together with the Koran, Muhammad's convictions have influenced the hearts and minds of hundreds of millions of Muslims during the last thirteen centuries. Islamic law, called the Sharī'ah, is derived from the Koran and Hadith with no distinction between the religious and temporal. The legal system was pre-determined during the lifetime of the Prophet, with precedents from that time guiding jurists in later years. When confronted with a new problem, jurists will first seek guidance from the Koran, then decisions made by Muhammad himself, then the common law of Medina, and lastly, personal judgment based on equity.

Under *dhimma*, Jews and Christians living in Muslim lands have usually been accepted and tolerated, and their social and religious status was respected. They were allowed to carry on their private businesses and enjoyed formal safety in keeping with ancient Arab hospitality. With much more freedom, at least 300 million Muslims now live in China, Southeast Asia, India, and Europe. In the U.S. there are about three to four million (possibly as many as seven million) Muslims, who enjoy complete freedom of religion, and unparalled economic opportunities.

The concept of jihād has two meanings, the first and main one being the need of the individual to strive constantly for inner purity and to live according to the requirements of the faith. Stephen Schwartz has made a thoughtful argument concerning the two forms of jihād, an important part of his *Two Faces of Islam*. In his view, the first form of jihād was represented by Sufism, derived from the word for wool (suf) or the rough clothing worn by the self-denying seekers of truth. This somewhat mystical approach stressed goodwill, tolerance and pluralism, preached the principle of divine love and spiritual union, and protested the corruption of wealth, and conflict between creeds. The premier example of Sufism in action was Cordoban Spain, where tolerant Islam allowed Jews and Christians to participate in outstanding cultural, architectural, scientific and economic advances.

The second form of jihād involves the militant approach and is of major concern in the world today. While the Koran itself does not require a militaristic form of jihād, the Hadith defines "active struggle" as a "holy war." The incentive for jihād, especially in earlier days, was for booty and plunder in raids or war. Militant jihād had early beginnings in the fundamentalist movement among Arabs. The backward, anti-scientific, totalitarian and militaristic tendency of fundamentalists was exemplified in the assassination of almost all the early caliphs, and hatred of Sufism and Shi'as. Islam's own inquisition came in 833 and bloodthirsty tyrants have appeared with regularity.

Of growing importance, and the form of most concern now, is that of organized terrorism, ostensibly in the defense of Islam. This promises adherents immediate entry into eternal bliss as a reward for being killed in righteous battle, and some of the more extreme imāms include suicide bombers in this category. In the mid-eighteenth century the worst elements of Islam culminated in the Wahhabi cult (more about that later).

THE CALIPHATES

The Muslim leader following Muhammad was his father-in-law and most trusted friend, Abu Bakr. Abu Bakr was named the first caliph (from khalifa meaning "successor") but only served for two years, dying of natural causes in 634. As mentioned above, his greatest accomplishment was to see that the first written Koran was compiled by Zayr.

Umar was the second caliph and under his leadership (634–644), Islam began to spread like wildfire in what Muslims call the "First Great Jihad." In 636 the armies of Persia were defeated and that wealthy and ancient society traded Zoroastrianism for Islam. Syria and Egypt followed, both of which were Roman Christian. Syria at that time included Lebanon, Israel, Palestine and Jordan, a rich and powerful province. When Umar entered Jerusalem in 638, the Christian Patriarch of the city met him and they prayed together at the Jewish Temple Mount (original site of Solomon's Temple). Sixty years later the Dome of the Rock was built nearby to house the stone where Muhammad is reputed to have tethered his mount Buraq at the time of his Night Journey. This was also supposed to be the place where Abraham went to sacrifice his son Isaac (or Ishmael, according to the Muslims).

By 654, Islamic control had expanded into Persia, India, Russia, China, Asia Minor, Syria and North Africa. Disputations arose among the Muslims in the new lands concerning the true content of the Koran, so the third caliph, Uthman, decided that an authoritative, universal version should be prepared. Zayd was called on again and with the help of three associates, made the final redaction and the required copies. Twenty-four years after Muhammad's death, the caliph pronounced that the Uthman Codex was the official version of the Koran. Some skeptics believe Zayd may have allowed some alterations and "extras" to slip into the final version, just as Ezra may have done with the Old Testament. Though Shiites and Sunnis have bitter differences, both groups accept the Uthmani Koran as the authorized canon. Over time, many *fatwa* have been issued confirming the official authenticity of the Uthman version. The *fatwa*, or religious-legal opinion, is declared by an imām who may also declare jihād.

Uthman was murdered in 656 and succeeded by Ali, the Prophet's nephew and son-in-law, married to Fatima. After being elected the fourth caliph, Ali was himself assassinated after five years in office. Supporters of Ali were known as Shiites, from Shia ("party" or "faction"). They argued that the head person should be a direct descendent of Muhammad through his daughter Fatima and her husband Ali. The caliph should also be a divinely guided, infallible religious teacher, or imām. Ali's son, Hasan became the next imām but managed to disqualify himself by marrying ninety times and having 300-400 concubines.

Hasan's brother Husayn was next in the Shi'a line but in 680, while on the way to Damascus to claim the Muslim leadership, he and his family were massacred by Umayyids at Najaf, near Karbala. Husayn's severed head was displayed in Damascus. Ever since that time, October 10 has been commemorated as Ashura (the tenth) and is the most important date on the Shiite calendar. Najaf is the site of Ali's tomb and the world's largest Muslim cemetery. The murders of Ali and Husayn caused the great schism between the Shiites and Sunnis that persists even today.

The Shi'a succession after that became more complicated. The fifth imām may have been Zayd, Ali's younger son, and Shiites holding this view were known as Fivers. The Seveners became prominent in North Africa and Egypt as the Fatimid dynasty, and in Iran as the Assassins. The forty-ninth direct descendent of Ali is called the Aga Khan, and is the Shiite leader in India and central Asia. The twelfth imām inspired the Twelvers in 940, who have persisted until the present time and comprise the large majority in Iran. The highest leader of the Shiites in Iran is called the ayatollah (Khomeini, leader of the 1979 takeover from the Shah).

After the murder of Ali, the Umayyads moved the Islamic capital from Medina to Damascus. The first Umayyad caliph was Mu'āwiyah (661–680) and with him the position became more like a kingship and lost much of its spiritual orientation. The Umayyids ruled during the first great wave of Muslim conquests that lasted until the mid-eighth century. They were the first in a sequence of temporal rulers that continued for over 1240 years (terminated by Ataturk).

The Dome of the Rock was completed in 691, under the Umayyad caliph Abd al-Malik. The north coast of Africa as far west as Morocco came under Muslim control, and Spain was invaded in 711. The narrow neck of water separating Africa and Europe became known as the Strait of Gibraltar, after the large rock on the Spanish side named for the Umayyad general Jebel ul-Tarik. Within twenty years, most of Spain had been subdued and the Muslims then pushed across the Pyrenees into southern France.

In the French campaign the Arabian commander Abdur Rahman led a "countless multitude" of Syrian, Moor, Saracen, Persian, Greek, Tartar and Copt forces that brought their wives and children with them. Their attacks in battle consisted mostly of poorly coordinated charges of light cavalry. Loot and booty were part of their objective, but territorial gains were also desired. To this day, the memory of Muslim atrocity and devastation remains in that part of France.

The Muslim forces reached as far as Lyons on the Rhone, Vosges, Burgundy, and Bordeaux—in short, more than half of France. The opposing force of Franks, Goths and Gascons was led by an outstanding general, Charles Martel (the Hammer), the illegitimate son of Pepin II. The armies clashed at Tours in 732, and after six days of sparring, the final battle was won by the Europeans. When the Muslim commander was killed, his troops fled the field and with their families, returned to Spain.

At about this same time, at the other end of Christian lands, Constantinople was under attack by a large Muslim force. Fortunately, the Byzantines were led by an exceptional general, Leo the Isaurian, who had been crowned as Emperor Leo III (717–741). The Muslims were under the overall control of Caliph Omar who had an army of some 200,000 men and a navy of 2500 ships. To begin the campaign in 717, Muslim general Muslemah, with perhaps 80,000 men, crossed the Hellespont (Dardanelles) and marched about 180 miles north to Constantinople. When his attack on the city failed, a blockade was established on land with a system of trenches. A fleet of some 1800 ships, carrying 80,000 soldiers and commanded by Admiral Suleiman, moved to cut off supplies to the city from the Black Sea. When this fleet had some difficulty in maneuvering in the Bosporus, Leo lowered the huge chain across the mouth of the Golden Horn, and his oared galleys sallied out of their harbor.

Leo's ships, maybe 200 in all, carried about 300 men each and were armed with bow tubes throwing the terrifying "Greek fire." Greek fire burned a mixture of sulfur, naphtha, and quicklime that could be thrown a few tens of feet by the pressure of water cannon. The attack was effective and deadly. The blockade by sea was broken and the supply line from the Black Sea was kept open. On land, the Muslim soldiers remained in their trenches all winter, suffering from cold, disease and starvation, which led to cannibalism. Thousands of troops died in that disastrous winter.

In the spring, an Egyptian fleet moved through the Bosporus into the Black Sea but was soon destroyed by Greek fire, in another sea battle. Leo then sent an army against a Muslim force on the Asiatic side of the Bosporus and won again. After thirteen months of warfare, the Muslim land forces returned to their home base with only 30,000 survivors of an original 200,000. As for the Muslim navy, out of 2500 ships, only five returned to their homeports. This success by the Christians helped insure the security of Constantinople for the next 735 years.

A significant change in Muslim philosophy took place after the Abbasids forcibly overthrew the Umayyads in 749. The Abbasids moved the center of the Islamic world to Baghdad from Damascus. Once they gained power, the Abbasads before long became Sunnis, who now comprise the vast majority (90 percent) of the 1.3 billion Muslims in the world. Their origin was in the eighth century by "people of tradition and unity" (ahl al-sunna wa'l jamaa) or simply Sunnis. They accepted the caliphs as political successors but not as spiritual leaders. They developed a long list of Traditions, second only to the Koran. In the ninth century these oral sources of wisdom were compiled into a multi-volume set of books. The most important book after the Koran was a collection of Traditions called the Sahih ('true' or 'valid').

According to Schwartz, the Abbasads "established the first great Islamic culture" with a university where all the great works on mathematics, medicine, chemistry, and philosophy were translated into Arabic. In the west, when the Muslims retreated back to Spain, a 760-year period called the golden age of Muslim rule began; it lasted until 1492. Cordoba, Granada and Seville were transformed into beautiful cities. Cordoba especially, fostered art and culture and became the "Ornament of the World" rivaling Baghdad and Constantinople. By their skillful engineering of water resources and irrigation, the Arabs made Spain green and introduced orange and other fruit orchards, sugar and rice.

From the Muslim viewpoint, although Jews and Christians were living under the restrictions of *dhimmi*, they enjoyed "a beautiful cultural dialogue" with their Muslim occupiers who were guided by the tenets of Sufism. The Spanish experience may be the best example in world history where "religious tolerance led to cultural and economic success." The three religions put emphasis on their similarities and common interests rather than on differences. Teams of rabbis, priests and Muslim scholars worked together on the translation of great texts, just as was being done in Baghdad. Both Sūfis and Christians shared the conception of God as love, and that mankind was created in God's own image. A natural bridge between the two faiths was provided by the same moral discipline, stressing repentance, abstinence, poverty, patience, and trust in God.

Kabbalah, or Jewish spirituality, was influenced by Sufism as seen in the works of the son of Maimonides, a great Judeo-Arabic jurist (1135–1204). Medieval Kabbalah was discussed by Isaac the Blind (1160–1236) and Leon Moses was considered to be the author, or redactor of the Zohar in 1250, accepted by all cabalists. At times the Kabbalah is considered to be the oral equivalent of the written Torah. It consists of a large body of speculation on creation, the origin and fate of the soul, and an individual's role in restoring nature to its original perfect condition. The golden age was terminated by the Spanish Inquisition that began shortly before 1492, when all Jews and Muslims were ordered out of Spain, Grenada being the last Moorish stronghold.

In 1034 Seljuk Turks moved west out of central Asia bent on plunder, destruction, and the seizure of new lands. Muslims called them "Turkomans" and they adopted Sunnite Islam. In 1055, the Abbassad caliphate in Baghdad (also Sunni) asked for their help and the Seljuk leader Tuğrul was made sultan when he entered Baghdad. Tuğrul's nephew, Alp-Arslan took over in 1063 and defeated Byzantine armies at Aleppo and in Armenia. In 1071 the Byzantine Emperor Romanus IV left Constantinople to stop the Seljuks. He had an army of about 100,000, about half of which were foreign mercenaries, including Normans, Franks, Slavs and Turks.

They met at a place called Manzikert, about twenty-five miles north of Lake Van in far eastern Turkey, 750 miles from Constantinople. He split his forces, and with others' treachery plus his own poor battlefield tactics Romanus was soundly defeated and captured by the Seljuks. Arslan treated him with respect and peace terms were fair. On the return trip to Constantinople, Romanus fell into the hands of a turncoat and was badly mistreated. He died in the summer of 1072 after being blinded. This was considered to be the worst defeat in Byzantine history, and opened up all of Asia Minor (Turkey) to control by the Seljuk Turks.

The Seljuks ruled Turkey for over two centuries from their capital in Konya. Their enlightened approach led to one of the richest and most inventive periods in Turkish history. In 1096, the First Crusade arrived in western Anatolia on the way to Jerusalem. The Crusaders and Seljuks fought a number of times and at one point a third of Anatolia was taken back by the Christians. But the Crusaders passed on through Turkey and there was little net effect for either side. In the Second Crusade in 1147, several battles were fought in southwest Turkey and the Christians failed mainly because of the Seljuks.

Between crusades, an exceptionally capable ruler, Kiliç Arslan II, was leader of the Seljuks and ended Byzantine rule in Anatolian Turkey. This came about when he won a decisive victory in November of 1176 at the pass of Myriocephalum, just south of Sultan Dağ, ninety miles west of Konya. Thereafter, trade and the economy flourished, construction grew and madrasahs (seminaries for theology) were opened, similar to those elsewhere in the Islamic world. During the Third Crusade, Arslan II allowed the German emperor Frederick Barbarossa free passage across southwest Turkey. However, Frederick drowned in the Gök River near Silifke in June, 1190, and the German contingent went no further.

In 1258, the Seljuk dynasty ended abruptly when the Mongol hordes, led by Hulagu Khan, a grandson of the great Genghis Khan, obliterated Baghdad after forty days of killing. Genghis and his successors created the largest land empire in world history, with half the population of the world, four times the size of that of Alexander the Great. Genghis Khan's style of warfare was bloodthirsty and barbaric, characterized by total destruction. In China, he may have been responsible for 40 million deaths, and at Nishapur (Iran) killed 1.7 million people in one hour.

A cluster of Y chromosome variants in one-twelfth, or 16 million, of the men in an area of the Mongol empire points to about the time of Genghis Khan. He had only four known sons but his male relatives may have been more prolific. For example, his son Tushi had forty sons and his grandson Kublai Khan added thirty virgins to his harem every year.

The Ghazi brotherhood of religious fighters (mujahidin) was among the refugees from the Mongol advance. The Ghazi leader was a Turkish sultan named Oşman I (Othman), hence the name Ottoman. Oşman Gazi's son and successor was Orhan whose forces overthrew Seljuk remnants in 1307. In 1326 they captured Bursa, which became the capitol of the Ottomans who were also ardent Sunnis. It was about this time, not long after the end of the Crusades, that Orhan formed the Janissary Corps. This was an elite military unit, using captured and recruited Christian boys between the ages of fourteen and eighteen. After military training with strict physical and moral discipline, they had the reputation of being "the most feared soldiers in the world."

Several Anatolian conquests came rapidly, and the first on the European side was Gelibolu (Gallipoli) in 1354. In 1362, Orhan's son Murad I captured Edirne (Adrianople), 110 miles west of Constantinople. From Edirne, Murad carried wars of conquest into the Balkans, capturing territory in Macedonia, Albania, Bulgaria, and Serbia.

In 1389 the Serbs and Christians fought to a draw at the "Field of the Blackbirds" near Kosovo. The Byzantine army was led by Lazar, king of Serbia, who had 100,000 troops made up of Serbs, Hungarians, Moldavians, and others. Sultan Murad was killed in his tent by a Serbian noble, and Lazar was taken prisoner and executed. Serbs honor Lazar for his heroic effort in rallying the defense at Kosovo, and the Ottoman advance was slowed further while they were distracted by Tamerlane's conquests in Anatolia.

The name "Timur the Lame" was altered to Tamerlane by Europeans. Tamerlane (1336–1405) was born near Samarkand in Uzbekistan; he was partially lamed on his left side by an accident in his youth. He was skilled at riding and fighting, and clever, scheming, and ruthless in achieving his goals. By the age of thirty-four he had created a huge military force built around cavalry armed with bows and swords, leading spare mounts carrying supplies for long campaigns. He falsely claimed Genghis Khan was an ancestor, and set out to emulate the great Khan. Tamerlane eventually gained control of lands from the Mediterranean to China, and from India to Russia.

Barbarism and atrocities characterized his style of warfare. In his wake, he left behind massive destruction and as memorials to his victories, huge pyramids of the skulls of his victims. When his army overran Delhi in 1398, he was proud to have penetrated India further than either Alexander the Great or Genghis Khan, and 100,000 captured Indian soldiers were put to the sword. At Isfahan in Persia his troops massacred 70,000 to 100,000 people. In Damascus 20,000 residents were killed. In several campaigns in Persia, Syria, Mesopotamia, Armenia and Georgia, Tamerlane and the Khans together killed over twelve million Armenian and Nestorian Christians.

In 1402, Tamerlane fought a great battle with Ottoman forces near Ankara in central Turkey. The Ottoman sultan, Bayezid I, was captured and his army was routed. It may have been during this same campaign that Sivas, about 150 miles northeast of Ankara, was destroyed, its inhabitants enslaved, and 4000 Armenian cavalrymen buried alive. At this same time, Tamerlane sent a message to the Hospitaller Knights in Smyrna (Izmir) demanding that they convert to Islam. When they refused, thinking their city was impregnable, Tamerlane soon convinced them otherwise. When he conquered the city, he annihilated the entire population including women and children. As a monument to his success, he left the usual pyramid of human heads, adding to his lifetime record for the most beheadings in human history. He died in 1405 at the age of sixty-nine, while on his way to China, presumably to pad his record of decapitations.

Back in the Balkans, Murad II, the great-grandchild of Murad I, invaded Serbia and in 1448 led the Ottomans to the second defeat of Christian forces at Kosovo.

In 1453, Mehmed II, the son of Murad II, conquered Constantinople after an artillery bombardment of fifty-four days. The city had been attacked twenty-eight times previously, over a period of several hundred years. The successful assault, on May 29, was the eighth attempt by the Muslims. The Ottoman Turks had 80,000 troops and much equipment, whereas the defenders were reduced to about 7000 men. The final attack was led by 12,000 Janissaries and once inside the walls, the end came quickly. Several thousand civilians seeking refuge in the St. Sophia church were raped and massacred, and the emperor Constantine XI was beheaded. Mehmed ordered Hagia Sophia to be changed to a Muslim mosque but the Orthodox Patriarch has remained in Constantinople as a guest resident ever since.

Although the fall of Constantinople was viewed with shock and dismay throughout Europe, the population of the city increased seven times in the next thirty years. It became a city of Turks, Greeks and Armenians and a strong influx of Jews fleeing from Spain. Despite the *dhimma* in place, many intellectuals and experts in arts, science and medicine were attracted to the city and it became quite cosmopolitan.

During this same time Mehmed continued his territorial gains which included much of Greece, Serbia, Bosnia, and Crimea. He occupied the heel of Italy but was turned back at Belgrade. In 1480 he failed as well at

Rhodes, which was defended by the Knights of St. John, also called the Hospitallers. Because he had vanquished the Byzantine emperor, Mehmed made claims to all the lands formerly under the influence of Constantinople, including Syria, Palestine and Egypt.

In 1529, Suleiman I took over Hungary but was turned back at Vienna three years later. The 1532 defeat at Vienna, only forty years after the Muslims were expelled from Spain, coincided with the beginning of the Reformation in Europe, and early riches coming from the New World. It marked the peak of Islamic influence in Europe and the beginning of a long decline in Ottoman fortunes around the world.

In 1565, the Muslims attacked the Hospitallers for the second time, on their new base in Malta. The Roman emperor Charles V had given Malta to the Knights when they left Rhodes in 1522, the annual rent being one Maltese falcon. The Muslim force of 40,000 men was under the command of Admiral Dragut, a successful veteran often called "The Drawn Sword of Islam." For most of his life, Dragut had been a Barbary pirate and privateer, plundering Mediterranean towns along the African and European coasts, and capturing thousands of Christians he sold into slavery. The Hospitallers were badly outnumbered but fought valiantly under the firm direction of their Grand Master Valette. During the siege of about four months, Dragut was mortally wounded when struck in the head by rock fragments, splintered by a cannon ball. When Christian reinforcements appeared, the Muslims withdrew.

One more decisive sea battle was fought at Lepanto, at the entrance to the Gulf of Corinth, west of Athens. The Ottomans' 230 galleys were opposed by the Grand Fleet, a joint force of Spanish and Venetian galleys. Altogether, 160,000 men were involved. The Christian fleet had vastly superior firepower—1815 guns to 750—and on October 7, 1571, destroyed or captured 200 of the Ottoman galleys and 30,000 men. One of the casualties at Lepanto, or soon thereafter, was Miquel de Cervantes, who suffered a maimed right hand. He later wrote *Don Quixote*.

Kara Mustapha led 180,000 troops in a second attack against Vienna in 1683. Opposing him was the tough Polish veteran, King Jan Sobieska. His army consisted of 30,000 of his own proven infantry plus 40,000 other German, Austrian, French, Scottish, Irish and Spanish troops. On September 10, the Christians routed the Ottomans with several crushing cavalry attacks, backed by infantry. The Turks lost 10,000 men plus their entire baggage train and vast quantities of other booty. After that, they never returned to Vienna.

Before 1200, Islam had spread as far east as Indonesia and the southern Philippines. Aceh, the northernmost part of Sumatra, was always the most devout Sunni Muslim area whereas Java was less so and retained a good deal of the Hindu/Buddhist influence. The island of Bali never was under Islamic control. The Portuguese arrived in about 1511 and tried to monopolize the spice trade, spices being worth their weight in gold in Europe at that time. When the Dutch took over in 1595 with the East India Company, the Christianizing effort became stronger, but Indonesia remained about 85–90 percent Muslim, as it is today.

WAHHABISM AND OTHER INFLUENCES

In 1703, Muhammad Ibn Abd al-Wahhab was born in the Najd region, an extremely dry, forbidding part of Arabia 420 miles east of Medina. By 1737 he was advocating a drastic change from traditional Islam and a liquidation of the Ottoman caliphate. He denounced all Muslims who did not agree with him, saying they should be killed, their wives and daughters violated, and their possessions confiscated. Sufis, and especially Shi'as, should be exterminated. He worked to downgrade the status of Muhammad, condemning celebrations of the prophet's birthday and those hajjis who visited Muhammad's tomb in Medina. It seems clear that Wahhab considered himself equal to the Prophet or maybe even superior. He hated traditional praise for Muhammad because he thought it was similar to the Christian worship of Jesus. He went even further and ordered that the graves of Muslim saints be dug up and scattered. He tried to burn all books, except the Qur'ān which he felt would suffice alone. He also despised music, and that part of Muhammad's personality which showed compassion and mercy.

In 1744 he took shelter in a village that later would become Riyadh, the capital of Saudi Arabia. He linked up with the Sa'ud family, the local rulers, and by 1788 the Wahhab-Sa'ud alliance controlled most of the Arabian Peninsula. They attacked the Shi'a holy city of Karbala in 1801, destroyed the tomb of Husayn, and slaughtered thousands of the citizens. Soon after, Mecca fell to the Wahhabis who covered the Kaaba and forbade the entry of a band of Ottoman pilgrims. They then demonstrated their cruelty at the surrender of Ta'if, about twenty-five miles east of Mecca. They "killed every woman, man, and child they saw, slashing with their swords even babies in cradles. The streets were filled with blood." Thus, over 200 years of Islamic militant fundamentalism began, leading to suppression of modern advances and eventually the terrorism of 9/11.

Ali Pasha was the Ottoman governor and founder of modern Egypt, who in 1811 undertook to end the Wahhabi-Sa'ud terror. Mecca and Medina were freed, and two of the worst terrorists were paraded through the streets of Constantinople before being executed. Numerous *fatwas* and some eighty books were written condemning the Wahhabi approach and the movement was silenced for a time but not terminated. The Janissaries were suppressed in 1826 and the Ottoman weakness and decadence was becoming apparent. Turkey was called the "sick man of Europe" and the Ottoman Empire was beginning to totter. For their part, the British lent their support to the Wahhabis, thinking they could hasten the Turkish collapse and the loss of Ottoman territories. Finally, in 1901, the waiting Wahhabi-Sa'ud conspirators saw their chance. Abdul Aziz Ibn Sa'ud, then twenty-one years old, killed the ruler of Riyadh and took control of the city.

As early as 1910 Ibn Sa'ud began having Wahhabi preachers stir up the tribes for a jihād against the Turks. When World War I started in 1914, Turkey made the fatal mistake of joining the German and Austro-Hungarian side. By the end of the war all would be destroyed—the Ottoman and Austro-Hungarian empires plus the Russian tsardom.

T.E. Lawrence was an idealistic dreamer who gained fame as "Lawrence of Arabia" while serving as a British liaison officer to the Arabs. He showed the Arabs how to blow up Turkish trains and joined a successful surprise attack on the port of Aqaba. Living with Arabs in the Hejaz region of western Arabia, Lawrence promised Hussein of Mecca that if the Hashemites cooperated with the British, they would rule the Hejaz as their own kingdom after the war. Lawrence did not know that the Sykes-Picot secret talks of 1916 had already carved up the Middle East into zones of influence for the benefit of France and Great Britain.

The situation was muddled further by the "Balfour Declaration" of 1917 in which the British Foreign Secretary pledged that England favored "the establishment in Palestine of a national home for the Jewish people and will use their best endeavors to facilitate the achievement of that object, it being clearly understood that nothing will be done which may prejudice the religious and civil rights of existing non-Jewish communities in Palestine. Over the years, Jews have used the Balfour Agreement as a legal claim on the West Bank, but have ignored the stated principle of "the consent of the governed."

In 1919, Great Britain imposed the Anglo-Persian Agreement on Iran. Lord Curzon, Britain's Foreign Secretary, explained his country's policy relative to Iran but applicable in any number of places, that is, (1) to protect the future safety of the empire, (2) prevent misrule, intrigue, financial and political disorder (by local, independent governments) and (3) maintain access to the oil fields.

At the Treaty of Sèvres in 1920, the self-serving French and British seized pieces of the Ottoman Empire through the ruse of "mandates" established by the League of Nations. Arab nationalists had boldly named Hussein's son Faisal as the king of Syria, but the French quickly dethroned him and drove him into exile. France took control of both Syria and Lebanon under the mandate, while creating the Republic of Lebanon out of a former Ottoman vilayet.

Faisal, who prior to his coronation had not set foot in the country he was to rule, was given rule over the mandate of Mesopotamia in 1921 as a consolation prize. The area was renamed Iraq and included the three vilayets (provinces) of Kurdish Mosul in the north, Shiite Basra in the south and Sunni Baghdad in the middle (all three hated each other). On July 14, 1958 the entire Iraqi royal family was killed in a coup, and military rule began for the next forty-four years.

The Balfour Agreement was ratified by the League of Nations in 1922 and was embodied in the mandate giving Great Britain control of Palestine. Palestine was then divided in two, and Faisal's brother Abdullah was named ruler of Transjordan, east of the Jordan River. The Hashemite Hussein was named king of the Hejaz, but in 1925, Ibn Sa'ud seized the Hejaz from Hussein and called the entire area Saudi Arabia. Another provision called for a homeland for the Kurds to be carved out of Turkey, but Ataturk later blocked the scheme.

Even before Sèvres, European oil companies in 1914 had formed the Iraq Petroleum Company (IPC) that maintained a monopoly position within part of the Middle East, including Turkey, Iraq, and Syria. The French called it "the beginning of a long-term plan for the world control and distribution of oil." After intense pressure from Esso, Americans were finally allowed in 1928 to take a 23.75 percent share, divided between Esso and Mobil. Hence, BP, Shell, CFP, and Esso-Mobil each had 23.75 percent shares, with the remaining 5 percent share going to Calouste Gulbenkian (Mr. 5 percent) who became one of the richest men in the world. Within the redline area the companies formed a joint operation, with no competition as individual companies.

Kemal Ataturk became Turkey's first president in 1923. He embarked on a vigorous campaign to westernize the nation in a number of ways. He ended the caliphate system that had existed for 1291 years; gave women the right to vote; introduced the Latin alphabet (abolished Arabic); closed religious schools; introduced the civil code, based on Swiss law; dropped Islam as the state religion; moved the capital to Ankara. In 1930, the city of Constantinople was officially renamed Istanbul. Not long before Ataturk took office, 1.5 million Armenians had been killed by the Turks in the first systematic genocide of the twentieth century.

In 1932 the Kingdom of Saudi Arabia was formed under King Abdul Aziz Bin Abdul Ibn Sa'ud, and gained independence from Britain. Though they were still allies, the Wahhabis condemned Ibn Sa'ud for allowing such innovations as telephones and automobiles.

Another swashbuckling, and not altogether admirable, character in the mix was Harry St. John Philby. He was a former British colonial official in India but was sent to Iraq early in WW I because of his command of Arabic. He did some work with the legendary Miss Gertrude Bell, an influential advisor at the highest levels (she helped draw the final boundaries of the new nation of Iraq). St. John Philby was a master of intrigue and scheming—his son was Kim Philby, who in the 1940s was exposed as an infamous traitor and Russian spy. After WW I, the elder Philby insinuated himself into a powerful long-term position in the court of Ibn Sa'ud and even became a Wahhabi Muslim. Somehow, Philby was on the payroll of Standard Oil of California (SOCAL) at the same time that SOCAL was negotiating with King Sa'ud for a sixty-year concession in Saudi Arabia (not part of the redline deal).

In 1933 the agreement was signed and Texaco became a co-partner in 1936. In 1938 the new partnership made their first oil strike in Saudi Arabia. On February 14, 1945, after the Yalta Conference, President Franklin D. Roosevelt met King Ibn Sa'ud on the heavy cruiser Quincy in the Suez Canal. In exchange for secure, long-term oil supplies, the U.S. agreed to protect the Kingdom militarily, and one concrete step was to construct the air base at Dhahran in 1946. The world's largest oil field was found at Ghawar in 1948, and in the same year ARAMCO (Arabian American Oil Company) took in two more partners, Esso and Socony-Vacuum; Socony had a 10 percent share and the others 30 percent each. After years of persistent negotiating, Mobil (former Socony) was able to increase its share to 15 percent but in the following year, 1980, Saudi Arabia bought out 100 percent of the ARAMCO partnership.

In 1935 a fiery Syrian cleric named al-Qassam was killed by British troops in Palestine. Years later, al-Qassam became an inspirational force behind the Islamic Jihad group and Hamas, which called for jihad against British, French and Zionist forces in the Middle East.

England reneged on the Balfour Agreement in 1939 and a British "white paper" called for separate, independent Jewish and Arab states in Palestine. Both sides rejected the plan and the Jewish terrorist paramilitary group Irgun began operations against the British.

In 1941, Britain moved boldly to quell a rebellion in Iraq, and occupied Syria and Lebanon. Also in 1941, British and Russian troops invaded Iran and put Reza Pahlavi in place as Shah—for the next thirty-eight years, as it turned out.

By 1943, France helped work out a power-sharing plan for Lebanon whereby the president would be a Christian, the prime minister would be a Sunni Muslim, and the speaker of the parliament would be a Shiite Muslim. This arrangement worked for some thirty years, but by the 1970s Beirut had become a witch's brew of conflicting and intransigent interests including the PLO, Phalangists, Hezbollah, Druzes, Christians, Sunnis, and Shiites. The outside influences of Syria and Israel complicated the problem, and eventually led to the 1975 civil war. By 1981, fifty-three private armies existed, and the fifteen-year war had devastated the city, previously recognized as the most gorgeous place in the Middle East, called the "Paris of the East."

The Arab League was formed in 1945 for the purpose of protecting Palestine. Included were the nations of Egypt, Syria, Lebanon, Transjordan, Iraq, Saudi Arabia and Yemen. Also in the same year, Transjordan was renamed Jordan, with Abdullah as king. The Kingdom had been formed as a mandate twenty-four years earlier, and the British had trained an excellent police force, called the Arab Legion, which served with distinction in WW II.

In 1946, the Ba'ath ("Renaissance") Party was formally established in Syria, growing from early organizational efforts in the 1930s. By combining Socialism and Islam, it sought Arab unity in order to "restore a glorious Arab and Muslim past." By 1963 the Ba'athists grew strong enough to seize power in both Syria and Iraq.

In 1947 the United Nations voted to partition Palestine into Arab and Jewish states, with Jerusalem as a neutral, international area. The U.N. plan was rejected by the Arabs because they were to be given only 48 percent of the land, whereas they were presently using 94 percent of the land, and comprised 69 percent of the population.

The state of Israel was created by the United Nations on May 14, 1948. Beginning on May 15, Israel forcibly expelled close to 800,000 Palestinian residents from their homes. Five hundred thirty-one villages were destroyed, and houses were blown up or bulldozed so that today, "all that remains is a scattering of stones and rubble across a forgotten landscape." All these people became homeless refugees and according to the UN there now are more than 3 million Palestinian refugees, many living hopelessly in squalid refugee camps.

[The impact of that event on those people struck me forcefully on the first day of the six-day war in June, 1967. At the time we were living in Tripoli, Libya, and all the locals were getting their news from Radio Cairo. On that morning, after the Israelis had destroyed the Egyptian air force on the ground and it looked as if the Arabs would lose, one of our little Palestinian secretaries was heartbroken and started to leave the building, crying bitterly. I brought her back and tried to console her, but what do you say to someone who has lost her home, all of her possessions, and been forced to leave her country?]

Israel's War of Independence also began in mid-May, 1948 when five Arab armies invaded from the neighboring countries of Egypt, Iraq, Syria, Lebanon, and Jordan. Simultaneous attacks came from the north, east and south, but coordination must have been poor because, incredibly, the Israelis were able to fight and win. The combined forces of the Arabs added up to about 720,000 versus 140,000 for the Israelis who mobilized their entire military age population. Total combat deaths were about 8000 Arabs and 6000 Jews. Israel grew even stronger during the war and ended with more territory than at the beginning.

One explanation for Israel's amazing success must be their tenacious and absolute will to survive. They knew they must succeed or die, and that there was no alternative to victory. About 3500 volunteers came from around the world, adding their skills and boosting morale. Too, at that time, the entire world had a good deal of sympathy for the Israeli cause, partly in recognition of what the Jews had suffered in the Holocaust during WW II. In 1967 and 1973 Israel fought two more wars against the combined forces of neighboring Arab countries. Against seemingly overwhelming odds, Israel won both times and not only preserved its very existence but destroyed its enemy and acquired additional territory.

There is no doubt that the U.S. has given unstinting support to the state of Israel ever since it came into being in 1948, concerned that Israel succeed as a democracy. There has been no animosity toward any Arab state, except as a threat to Israel's existence or U.S. security. A perception exists that U.S. economic support has been totally one-sided, but the facts say otherwise. For example, during the period 1949–2004, total cumulative U.S. military and economic assistance to Israel amounted to $100 billion. During the same period of time, the total U.S. assistance to the Arab states of Egypt, Jordan, and the Palestinians, added up to $70 billion.

Over the last sixty years, worldwide sympathy for the Jews has gradually diminished, due in part to distaste for the way they have treated the Palestinians, millions of whom now live in fifty-one refugee camps in Jordan, Lebanon, Syria and the West Bank. For the Palestinians in these refugee camps, generational hopelessness and hatred has festered. The one million Arabs who remain in Israel often seem to be treated with contempt, as second-class citizens, and an Arab life seems to be less valuable than that of an Israeli. Jews, on the other hand, certainly have a right to defend themselves against the attacks of terrorists. (When Israel recently left Gaza, 472,000 people in 8 camps were freed).

Terrorism is not new to the Middle East. During the Crusades, one sect was known as the Assassins, operating in northern Persia. They were nominal Muslims but became skilled at killing anyone, as ordered. Their weapon of choice was the dagger, and they were fearless when high on hashish. Their headquarters featured beautiful gardens where real, live black-eyed hūris were on display and promised to an Assassin if he died while on assignment. With that incentive, and hyped with drugs, the Assassins spread terror everywhere until the Mongol horde defeated them in 1256. Mamluks (ex-slave warriors) finished the job in 1272 when they destroyed the Assassin's last Syrian stronghold ruled by a leader known to the Crusaders as the "Old man of the Mountain."

The Muslim Brotherhood was formed in Egypt in 1928, as an Islamic approach to politics. Members reject Western influences, and state their belief in Allah, Muhammad, the Koran, and jihād as a way to power. They have branches in seventy countries and have fomented Islamic revolution in Algeria, Sudan and Syria but most of their efforts have been involved with Egypt. They were responsible for the creation of Hamas and "virtually all of today's jihad terrorist groups" including al-Qaeda. In the 1950's, Nasser forcibly put them down, reinstated them, then crushed them again. They were involved in the assassination of Anwar Sadat in 1981 after he made peace with Israel in 1979.

The Palestine Liberation Organization (PLO) was founded in 1964 as an umbrella group aimed at the establishment of an independent state of Palestine. In 1969, Yasser Arafat became chairman of the Executive Committee and held that position for twenty-six years until elected President of the Palestinian Authority (PA) in 1996. The latter was established as a part of the Oslo accords to govern the Gaza Strip and the bulk of the West Bank. The PA has observer status in the UN and maintains a quasi-military force of 40,000 to 80,000 men, but has only limited effectiveness.

In 1967, Hamas had its beginnings in the Gaza Strip as an arm of the Muslim Brotherhood. Through the 1970s and 1980s its main effort was concerned with social and community projects in the West Bank and Gaza, and was even supported by Israel in those endeavors. In 1987, however, the movement was taken over by a militant faction and the term Hamas first appeared, meaning "zeal" or "courage." Beginning with attacks on Israeli military targets, and punishment of collaborators, it has developed into one of the most extreme terrorist groups, and Israeli civilians are now considered "military targets" (because many are reservists). Hamas rejects peaceful solutions, uses suicide bombers, and wants to eliminate the state of Israel and replace it with an Islamic state. In January 2006, Hamas swept Palestinian parliamentary elections, adding another complication to the mix.

The Palestine Islamic Jihad (PIJ) was formed in 1979, splitting off from the Muslim Brotherhood they considered too moderate. The PIJ is committed to the destruction of Israel and creation of an Islamic Palestinian state. They have had contact with Iranian Revolutionary Guards and get funding from Iran. The Sunni PIJ has cooperated with Hamas in terrorist attacks in Israel, including numerous suicide and car bombings.

Hezbollah (the Party of God) is a Lebanese organization of radical Shiites, formed in 1982 when Israel invaded Lebanon. It has close links to Syria and Iran, and sprang from Shiite strongholds in the Bekaa Valley, southern Lebanon, and parts of Beirut. Its core consists of several thousand militants who have conducted nearly 200 attacks including the truck bombing of the U.S. Marine barracks in 1983 (killed 241), the 1985 hijacking of TWA flight 847, and several kidnappings of Americans in the 1980s. Additionally, they have planned ship attacks in the Malacca Straits, and killed 124 Jews in two raids in Argentina.

Of all the terrorist groups, al-Qa'ida (The Base, i.e., camps in Afghanistan) is by far the most dangerous. It was established in 1988 by Osama bin Laden just before the Russians withdrew from Afghanistan. Bin Laden had helped finance, recruit and train Sunni militants to fight the Russians, sometimes with the help of the CIA and use of Stinger missiles, deadly against Soviet helicopters. When the fighting stopped, bin Laden returned to his home in Saudi Arabia as a war hero. When the Gulf War broke out in 1991, U.S. forces stepped in to protect Kuwait and Saudi Arabia. This enraged Osama so beginning around 1992, he led al-Qa'ida in a new direction, to drive the U.S. out of the Gulf. Before long, his horizons had expanded to oppose Muslim governments, which he viewed as corrupt. The larger goal, then, was to drive Western influence out of all Muslim countries, especially Saudi Arabia. He preached that Muslims had the duty to kill U.S. citizens, civilian or military, and their allies everywhere.

Al-Qa'ida became international, with a worldwide presence. Existing Islamic terror groups were sought out, and their senior leaders filled in al-Qa'ida leadership positions. Al-Qa'ida probably has several thousand members and is allied with at least twenty-four Sunni and other terrorist groups, including Islamic Jihad, Hamas and Hezbollah. Cells exist in at least forty countries, including sleeper cells in the U.S. It is known that they have an interest in acquiring nuclear and chemical weapons of mass destruction.

Their most atrocious attack so far was that on September 11, 2001, when al-Qa'ida crashed two hijacked jetliners into the twin towers of the New York Trade Center, one into the Pentagon, and another in a field in Pennsylvania. Altogether, 2749 people were killed that day. Other attacks—both those carried out and those thwarted—include: in 1993, eighteen U.S. servicemen killed in Somalia when two helicopters were shot down; in 1994, a plan, fortunately disrupted, to assassinate Pope John Paul II in Manila; in 1995, plans were disrupted to kill President Clinton in the Philippines, and the midair bombing of twelve trans-Pacific flights, in 1996, a truck bomb at Khobar Towers in Riyadh killed nineteen and wounded hundreds; in 1998, bombings of U.S. embassies in Nairobi and Dar es Salaam killed 301 and injured 5,000; in1999, a plan was disrupted to bomb L.A. airport, and kill Israeli and U.S. tourists in Jordon; in 2000, seventeen sailors killed, thirty-nine injured when the USS Cole was bombed in Aden, Yemen; in 2001, an attempted shoe bombing of Paris–Miami flight failed; in2002, the bombing of a Mombasa hotel killed fifteen and injured forty, and a nightclub bombing in Bali killed about 180 while the bombing of a synagogue in Tunisia killed nineteen and injured twenty-two; in 2003 the bombing of three expatriate apartments in Riyadh killed twenty and injured 139, the bombing of a Jewish center in Casa Blanca killed forty-one and injured 101, the bombing of a hotel in Jakarta killed seventeen and injured 137, the bombing a housing complex in Riyadh killed seventeen and wounded 100, the bombing of two synagogues in Istanbul killed twenty-three and injured 200, and the bombing of the British consulate and the HSBC bank in Istanbul killed twenty-seven and injured 455.

Terrorism by Islamic extremists is of great concern to the whole world. The terrorists seem to have a blind, unreasoning hatred for their opponents, i.e., all who disagree with them. They despise Western culture and religion, as well as traditional Islam if it departs even slightly from Wahhabi fundamentalism. Especially for the last ten years, the terrorists have sought out "soft" targets—civilians—defenseless men, women and children. Car bombs have become the primary murder weapons for this incomprehensible form of terrorism, and the families of suicide bombers are paid in cash. If terrorists like this had access to weapons of mass destruction, there is no doubt that such weapons would be used against innocent civilians, rather than military targets.

Islamic terrorists in general seem to follow Wahhabi rules of behavior.

Saudi Arabia has had a long-standing relationship with Wahhabi ideology, going back over 200 years to their first collaboration in pressing militant fundamentalism. More recently, there have been several intermarriages of the al-Wahhab and Ibn Sa'ud families. One of the beneficiaries was an illiterate Yemeni laborer for ARAMCO, named Muhammad bin Laden, who became known as the personal construction boss for the royal family. His seventeenth son was named Osama, destined to become the infamous mass murderer Osama bin Laden; his acts were so outrageous that he lost his Saudi citizenship in 1994.

The Saudi royal family, because of its oil wealth, has had an enormous influence in the world for the last 50–60 years. Ibn Sa'ud had twenty-two wives and hundreds of concubines, and a total of forty-four male offspring. His favorite wife was Hussah Sudair and all five kings, since the death of Ibn Sa'ud in 1953, have been one of her sons, the "Sudairi Seven." By the end of the twentieth century there were 4000 princes, each receiving an annual allowance of $500,000 plus favored treatment in business and government. The "Saudi oil princes" became a symbol for ostentation and waste with their fleets of private jets, yachts and limousines, palaces, pampered wives and spoiled children. Not surprisingly, the rest of the Arab world came to despise the oil princes and their show of wealth, all based on Saudi oil reserves amounting to a quarter of the world total.

The Bedouin societies in Saudi and the other Gulf states have been rapidly replaced by an increasingly restless population of young people (more than half under the age of twenty-five). Frustrated young men have flooded into the cities and, with an unemployment rate of 25 percent, become susceptible to the exhortations of troublemakers. To placate their young population of 20 million people, the Saudi regime undertook two broad programs, one economic, the other religious. The economic approach was designed to develop a new middle class, including managers, administrators, executives, doctors and other professionals. New hospitals and schools, together with a booming construction business, have helped in this effort. New industries of particular interest include desalination plants, which convert seawater to drinkable water which is then sometimes pumped hundreds of miles inland. The Kingdom leads the world in this effort. In addition, wheat farming now provides the world's sixth largest export volume, and intensive dairy farming plus beef production has been developed. Fish and shrimp farms have been successful also.

The religious approach is more problematical. Building on the long-term embrace of Wahhabism by the Saudis, a rigid, puritanical form of fundamental Islam has been promoted. Wahhabi clerics administer floggings and amputations according to the Shariah-type law. Shi'a Islam is condemned as sinful and heretical and is even called a Jewish conspiracy. State funding for madrasas (religious schools) has resulted in instilling the harsh Wahhabi brand of Sunnism in tens of thousands of fanatical Muslims, ripe for advanced training by the likes of bin Laden. Rabid clerics assure the fanatics that they are Muslim heroes, engaged in a holy war. In looking at the long-time efforts of the Wahhabi-Sa'ud partnership in Saudi Arabia, it is not surprising to see that of the fifteen Saudis involved in the 9/11 suicide bombing, twelve came from the Ta'if area where Wahhabi activism has a long and deplorable history.

There has been a tardy but clear recognition of the need to undo this Saudi bargain with the Wahhabi devil. Expulsion of Osama bin Laden in 1991 was the first step, and initially Osama muted his criticism of the royal family in order to maintain his Saudi connections. More recently, however, government offices and institutions have come under attack from the terrorists, and many observers believe the Kingdom has reached a turning point. Prince Bandar, Saudi ambassador to Washington, has said "This is a defining moment in Saudi political life." The eighty-one-year-old Abdullah became king in 2005, has a reputation for reform, and has been the main force behind a heavy crackdown on al-Qa'ida militants.

The first few whiffs of freedom throughout the Middle East have given new hope to the young people who are well aware of what is happening elsewhere in the world. Outbursts of democracy in Afghanistan, Iraq, Cairo and even Riyadh do not go unnoticed and the 2005 joyous demonstration in Beirut indicated the hope that resides there. The counter-demonstration on March 8, the next day, orchestrated by the Hezbollah, featured people waving pictures of Syria's president Assad. Support for Syria's presence in Lebanon cannot be very wide or deep and one wonders if this Shia show of strength is similar to that in Iran, where the future promised by the Mullahs does not appeal to the young people there.

The struggle for Islam's soul pits a small, militant minority of Muslim terrorists, such as al-Qa'ida, Taliban, and Wahhabi extremists, against a mostly quiet majority of moderate Muslims who simply wish to live their lives in peace and progress. Professor Akbar S. Ahmed in his *Islam Under Siege* has shown how a tiny minority of fanatical extremists, masquerading as faithful Muslims, has tried to transform a good and peaceful faith into a religion of terror. Somehow, the imams have been able to brainwash terrorists to ignore two basic concepts of Islam, (1) that prohibits suicide, and (2) that condemns any killing of innocent people, especially women and children. On March 11, 2005 (one-year anniversary of Spanish train bombings) Muslim clerics, representing one million, mostly Sunni Muslims in Spain, issued the first *fatwa* (scholarly opinion) condemning Osama bin Laden for his terrorist actions. Hopefully, this Islamic edict by responsible Muslims will encourage a similar response by others.

UCLA law professor Khaled Abou El Fadl is controversial, but says the soul of Islam is at risk, and in his view the schism is as profound as the sixteenth century Protestant Reformation that split Christian Europe. Mr. Wahid, former president of Indonesia, points out that a coordinated global campaign is needed to counter the formidable strengths of the worldwide terrorist movement.

At times, it seems Islam has been taken over by the small, poisonous element characterized by suicide bombers. The daily abattoir scenes in Iraq of Muslims slaughtering other Muslim men, women and children are abhorrent to all civilized people. By some twisted logic, these suicide bombers have become convinced that they are martyrs on their way to Paradise because they have died in war.

The millions of moderate Muslims need to take over their own religion; certainly genuine change must come from within, not from outside their society. Just as the Catholics made timely, necessary and profound changes with Vatican II, so does the Muslim hierarchy need to reform itself and put in place a form of enlightened, tolerant and engaged Islam for today's world. As Europe becomes more Islamic, as it seems certain will happen, people there will be especially concerned to see what form of Islam takes precedence.

8

DIFFICULT TIMES FOR
THE CHURCH

The rivalry between Rome and Constantinople began in the early centuries, becoming even stronger when Constantine established his capitol in the East. The different languages and cultures—Latin in the west and Greek in the east—were important factors in misunderstanding and disagreements. As Rome fell under the influence of Germanic and Frankish tribes during the Dark Ages, Constantinople took on a sense of superiority and smugness, often looking on Rome as barbarous, corrupt and dissolute.

Rome, on the other hand, saw the Greeks as arrogant, devious and deceitful. Constantinople always suffered conflict and intrigue inside its walls. Eunuchs schemed, various factions struggled for control, and some rulers met terrible deaths. One such was the emperor Leo V who, on Christmas Day, 820, was beheaded in the magnificent St. Sophia church. His body was thrown into a privy and his sons were castrated.

For several hundred years, the Eastern Church was unhappy over real and perceived slights by Rome. When Pepin, the son of Charles Martel, was anointed king by Pope Boniface, it initiated the concept of "by the grace of God," i.e., the pope. The East was also unhappy when Pope Leo III crowned Pepin's son, King Charles (742–814) of the Franks, as Emperor Charlemagne on Christmas Day 800, and gave Charlemagne the title of Caesar. Prior to that, the title had been reserved for the emperor of Byzantium.

Charlemagne fought costly wars to achieve a Holy Roman Empire; in Saxony, forced conversions resulted in killing nearly one-fourth of the population. Charlemagne maintained a close relationship with the papacy and required that the official liturgy be celebrated uniformly in Latin, exacerbating the long-smoldering alienation with the Eastern Church. Other irritants during the same time were various church forgeries including the "Donation of Constantine" and "Pseudo-Isidorean Decretals" although they were not totally revealed until the Reformation.

During the next century, Byzantium enjoyed a golden age of the empire. Basil II (976–1025) helped bring the Balkans and greater part of the Holy Land under Byzantine rule. But in his old age, his willful daughter Zoë, who was nothing more than a high-classed prostitute, entered into an arranged marriage with a worthless noble. She then adopted her lover Michael as her son, murdered her husband, and installed her lover as Michael IV. However, he lasted only four months before being blinded and deposed. Next, she married an old lover who refused to give up his current mistress. So the new emperor was seen, at affairs of state, seated between his two whores.

Leading up to the Great Schism, the personal behavior of some of the Western popes was no better. A good example, described below, is the case of Pope Sergius, whose bastard son became pope.

In 896, Pope Stephen VII convened a solemn trial—the "Synod Horrenda"—of the corpse of Pope Formosus who had died eight months earlier. Formosus had made the mistake of crowning, as emperor, one of Charlemagne's illegitimate descendents. Stephen wanted to render the crowning illegal so the corpse was propped up, in priestly garb, while Pope Stephen raged at the decayed body. Legal counsel provided to defend the corpse wisely kept silent. When the deceased was found guilty, the corpse was stripped and the three fingers of benediction on the right hand were hacked off. The body was then dragged through the street by a howling mob which later threw it into the Tiber River. Not long after that, Stephen was seized and strangled. Cardinal Sergius, present during the Synod Horrenda affair, was nominated by his faction as pope.

There were other claimants, however, and Sergius was chased out of the city. Four others were named pope for a few weeks (or only a few days) before they were killed, all in the period of one year. In a little over six years, seven popes and one anti-pope appeared and then disappeared. After seven years' exile, Cardinal Sergius returned to Rome, backed by the forces of a feudal lord. After the reigning pope and his supporters were killed, Sergius became Pope Sergius III (904–911).

During this same time an unusual woman, Theodora I, held the reins of power in Rome. She was the wife of a senator but the period 900–924 was known as the "monarchy of Theodora." Her daughter Marozia was later known as the "Senatrix of Rome" but even more importantly, was the teenage mistress of Pope Sergius. Theodora, meanwhile, found a new lover, John, a young cleric who she soon made bishop of nearby Ravenna. To keep his services close at hand, she brought him to Rome and had him named pope. Bishop John thereby became Pope John X in 914. He lasted until 928 when he was thrown into a dungeon and soon died, evidently to make way for Marozia's bastard son John, by Pope Sergius. Bastard John became Pope John XI in 931 at about age twenty.

One of Pope John XI's first duties was to marry his mother Marozia to Hugh of Provence, the half-brother of her husband Guy who she tired of and discarded. After the wedding in 932, a drunken Hugh made the mistake of insulting Alberic, another of Marozia's sons, by her first husband, and half-brother to John the pope. Alberic rallied a Roman mob and Hugh fled for his life. When he took over as ruler of Rome, Alberic had his mother imprisoned for life, but otherwise conducted his reign in good order for twenty years. It was agreed that when he died, his supreme temporal power would be turned over to his son Octavian, who was only sixteen years old at the time.

A year later the pope died, so the final part of the bargain with Alberic was concluded and Octavian was elected Pope John XII (955–964). He was a callow youth and the corrupting influence of absolute combined power of prince and pope was more than he could handle. It brought out all the worst of his character and he soon proved to be a coward, bully, greedy exploiter of the weak, and a gambler. His sexual appetite was insatiable and he was specifically charged with turning the Lateran religious center into a brothel. As pope, when threatened by invasion and rebellion in 960, he asked Saxony emperor Otto I (912–973) for help.

Otto was a truly great king who had reenacted Charlemagne's coronation in Aachen when, in 936, the German crown was put on his head in the same beautiful circular church. At the time of this ceremony, Otto received the Frank's great sword, the scepter and the priceless Sacred Lance used by the Roman soldier Longinus to pierce Jesus on the cross. But Otto's fame was mainly due to defeating the Hun horde at Augsburg on August 10, 955. German soldiers died by the tens of thousands but the Hun dead were uncountable, and they did not threaten Europe for many years after that.

Enjoying towering prestige in Europe, Otto soon took care of the military matter in Italy and entered Rome on February 2, 961, to be crowned by John XII as emperor of the Holy Roman Empire. Otto was about fifty years old and a first-rate statesman, with top-notch advisors. John XII was in his early twenties and seemingly totally lacking in sound judgment. As soon as Otto left Rome, John got busy trying to form new alliances in order to undo the agreement with Otto. Eventually Otto lost his patience and called for a synod of the Roman Church to review John's transgressions.

The assembled cardinals, bishops and archbishops gave their testimony which was carefully recorded. The charges included ordaining a deacon in a stable, being paid for ordaining bishops, blinding his spiritual father Benedict, castrating a sub-deacon (thereby causing his death), and sexual intercourse with Ranier's widow, with Stephana, (his father's concubine), with the widow Anna, and with his own niece. In 964 John was formally deposed by the synod and Leo VIII was named the new pope. John XII met his end when he reportedly was caught in adultery with another man's wife and was so severely beaten that he died three days later.

A series of unremarkable popes ruled for the next 130 years. Notably, Count Gregory of Tusculum, through his wealth and military backing, coerced the election of one of his sons to the papacy. When that son died, the crown passed to his brother, and when that brother died, Gregory's grandson was "elected" to the position. The grandson was fourteen years old when he became Benedict IX in 1032. Only six months later, a planned assassination failed. After five years Sylvester, another claimant to the papacy appeared. Sylvester ruled for three months but fled when Benedict came back with an armed escort. Benedict then agreed to sell the papacy to his godfather Gratiano for 1500 pounds of gold. Gratiano became Gregory VI in 1045, but the crime of simony on such a scale raised questions as to its actual consequences so for a time, Benedict, Sylvester, and Gregory were all claiming to be pope. In 1046, Emperor Henry III settled the matter when he installed Clement II in their place.

Celibacy of priests had been encouraged by Tertullian (160–225), Eusebius (260–341), Pope Siricius (384–399), and most emphatically by Pope Leo the Great (440–461). The last married pope was Adrian II (867–872). So personal behavior, including the sexual outrages of Sergius, John XII and others, gave leaders of the Eastern Church good reason to deeply resent subservience to the Roman hierarchy.

EASTERN ORTHODOX CHURCH

The final split with Rome came in 1054 and came to be recognized as the Great Schism. Direct blame can be assigned to the obnoxious Cardinal Humbert of Silva Candida, a tough enforcer of absolutist Papal rule. Humbert persuaded Pope Leo IX to excommunicate, without a hearing, Bishop Photius of Constantinople, who was venerated in the East as a saint. After the split, Eastern-Rite Catholics continued to be faithful to the pope, but the other Eastern churches were termed by Rome to be schismatic or heretical. Since 1054, several attempts at reconciliation have failed to heal the break between the Eastern and Western churches.

The Orthodox Eastern Church is a community of Christian churches, especially in Eastern Europe and the Middle East. The Second Nicene Council of 787 was the last of the seven church councils accepted as authoritative by both the Roman Catholic and Eastern Orthodox churches. Both Churches agreed upon the veneration of the Virgin Mary, and considered as heretical the Nestorian, Jacobite, Coptic and Armenian faiths.

The main disagreement, however, was over the position, authority and claims to infallibility of the pope. The Eastern Church holds that only the church, as a spiritual body guided by the Holy Spirit, is infallible. Roman Catholics, on the other hand, believe the pope is infallible when he speaks ex cathedra (from his official position). Since 1870, it has been held that an ecumenical council is also infallible when ratified by the pope.

Another, more esoteric disagreement arose from the *filioque* clause, added to the Nicene Creed in an expanded version by the Roman Church. The Council of Nicea in 325 and the Council of Constantinople in 381 both accepted the words "and we believe in the Holy Spirit" (proceeding from the Father). The *filioque* added the words "and the Son" to the statement that "the Holy Spirit...who proceeds from the Father." The Eastern Church argued about the words, but also the fact that they had not been consulted.

Disgust with the immorality of some of the Roman popes has already been mentioned but real, physical damage to Constantinople and the Eastern Church came during the Fourth Crusade. The city was sacked and vandalized by the crusaders and Rome has never been forgiven. In 1409 the Council of Pisa was supposed to end the Great Schism by deposing two rival popes and electing a replacement. In 1414–18 the Council of Constance "officially" ended the Great Schism by replacing the papal monarchy with a conciliar government, but the reconciliation failed. Jan Hus, a respected theologian and defender of Wycliffe (first English translation of Bible), went to the council to propose his reforms. The emperor personally guaranteed Hus' safety but no matter, in 1415 he was seized and burned at the stake for heresy.

Another disagreement between the two Churches has to do with the date of Easter. When Pope Gregory XIII devised a new calendar in the sixteenth century, he did so without consulting the Eastern leaders. The Orthodox Church maintains that Easter should fall on the Sunday after the first full moon after the vernal equinox and never before the Jewish Passover.

There may be 250 million members of the Orthodox churches today. It is sometimes called the Greek rite because the original language was Greek, but the liturgy has been adapted to many other languages. Originally the four patriarchates included Constantinople, Antioch, Alexandria and Jerusalem, but the last three faded in importance. This arrangement has evolved to churches self-governed by a synod, comprised of a board of bishops and laymen. The Orthodox communion now consists of sixteen independent churches, seven of which are national churches. The Russian Orthodox Church is eight times as large as all the others put together. The Russian Church was first under Constantinople, but a new patriarchate in Moscow was set up under the czar in 1589. In 1721 Peter the Great established a synod which he controlled through the lay leader. Beginning in 1917 the Communists killed or imprisoned many priests and bishops and much church land and property was confiscated. Mikhail Gorbachev reversed this treatment and by 2004 the Russian church had regained its full ownership of churches and other land.

THE CRUSADES

Religious crosscurrents were in play leading up to the crusades. In 1066, only twelve years after the Great Schism, the Norman duke William prevailed over the English king Harold at Hastings. Prior to the battle, Pope Alexander II (1061–1073) blessed William's cause and at the same time excommunicated the English. Some historians think that affected the attitude of the participants, and outcome of the battle. In 1071, the Seljuk Turks had defeated a large Byzantine army at Manzikert, in eastern Turkey.

Before Pope Alexander was even in his grave, Gregory VII (1073–1085) had himself made pope by the College of Cardinals. Gregory was hard and tough, with passionate convictions. He declared that the pope was the sole ruler of the church, superior to all rulers and emperors, inerrant—in short, with unlimited power. When the German king Henry IV challenged this new authority, Gregory shocked the world by excommunicating the king, suspending all the bishops who supported the king, and releasing all the king's subjects from their allegiances. In abject defeat, King Henry begged for forgiveness. During the bitterly cold winter, a barefoot Henry, dressed as a penitent, stood with his young wife and two-year-old son in front of the pope's hillside castle. At the end of three days, Gregory relented, and reinstated Henry as king.

Gregory was one of the first to agitate for a great campaign in the East to fight the Muslims and at the same time establish Rome's control over Byzantium. After defeating the Turks, conquest of the Holy Land could follow, and the latter was one of Gregory's main objectives. Gregory believed in the need for papal control to establish the "right" brand of Christianity. Gregory took the fifth century theory of Augustine, arguing that Christian leaders could fight a just war, and enlarged on the idea, claiming that the Church had a legitimate right to use force to spread Christianity.

Although Gregory never realized his dream, Pope Urban II (1088–1099) during the next few years was able to strengthen the moral and political authority of the papacy. Therefore, the time was right and he was in a position to act when Alexius I Comnenus of Constantinople sent an envoy to Rome in 1095, asking to enroll 500 Flemish knights in the Byzantine army. Urban's response was nothing less than to rally the entire Western Christian world in a crusade to regain control of lands which had been conquered by the Muslims.

He called for a great church council at Clermont, France and on November 27, 1095 preached one of the most effective speeches in human history. Urban argued that the Seljuk Turks were molesting Christian pilgrims and defiling the Christian shrines in the Holy Land. He pointed out that the Holy Land had great wealth and promise, and that participants in a crusade campaign would be given relief from all penances, and the expiation of all sins. By appealing to their highest selfless motives, plus self-interest and greed, Urban stirred the crowd of thousands to respond with passionate enthusiasm, shouting "Deus le volt!" (God wills it)—which later became the battle cry of the crusaders.

His words led to undertaking eight major crusades over a period of nearly 200 years, the deaths of at least a million people, and an enduring resentment by the Muslim world for almost a thousand years. Urban made freeing of the Holy Land the main goal; help for the Eastern Church was secondary. In addition to the eight crusades, which began as armed pilgrimages, several lesser wars were sanctioned against enemies of the faith. Among other results, interaction with the more advanced Byzantine and Islamic civilizations proved to be important in expanding the cultural horizons of Western Europe.

August 15, 1096, was set as the departure date for the armies of the First Crusade which was shaping up as the most ambitious military operation since the days of the Roman Empire. Approximately 40,000 fighting men marched east, and of that number, experienced knights comprised only a minority. Up to 150,000 people in all may have donned the cross, including rich and poor, saints and sinners, women and elderly. A crusade army was actually a core of soldiers with an accompanying mob of clergy, servants and followers. The leaders found it impossible to control the people once the 2000-mile march began.

The main body departed on schedule, but thousands left early (and were wiped out). Peter the Hermit was especially convincing and gathered an unprepared mob of thousands, including women and children. They formed the "People's Crusade" and left in April 1096. After crossing the Bosporus in August, they got as far as Nicaea before they were slaughtered in two different engagements with the Turks. Because he was back in Constantinople at the time, Peter the Hermit was virtually the only survivor of his army of innocents.

Another mob also left early but took a different route. This one, led by Count Emicho of Leiningen, marched down the Rhine, plundering and killing Jews in cities such as Wűrms, Mainz, Trier and Cologne. When Count Emicho reached Hungary, his army was crushed and eliminated.

Four armies of fighting men comprised the main body of the First Crusade. These were led by Godfrey of Bouillon, Hugh of Vermandois and brother of the king of France, Bohemond of Taranto, and Raymond, Count of Toulouse. Godfrey made a considerable financial sacrifice to raise money for his army, and Raymond divested himself of all his properties which were greater than most kings, including the king of France. Bohemond was the poorest of the four, and the most eager for personal gain.

Godfrey and his troops reached Constantinople by December, 1096. Although Emperor Alexius expressed pleasure at the help given by the thousands of Christian soldiers, mobilized to fight the enemies of Byzantium, he was somewhat apprehensive. He had some fear that he might be trading a Muslim enemy for a Christian one. Just as with Hugh earlier, in exchange for transportation across the Bosporus, Alexius required Godfrey to take two oaths—one of loyalty, the other that any captured lands would be returned to the emperor. Godfrey resisted strongly but eventually gave in. When Bohemond arrived he also agreed to the oath but Raymond was of sterner stuff. He finally agreed to a lesser, rather meaningless oath and was transported across the Bosporus where the other three armies were waiting.

The first objective was Nicaea. After the crusaders had established their siege lines, the Turkish sultan, Kiliç Arslan was decisively defeated when he appeared with his army. As he fled the scene, he left his wife, family and treasury behind. The crusaders then got a taste of Byzantine politics. In the dead of night the Turkish garrison turned over control of the city to Alexius and his troops. In the morning Alexius thanked the crusaders for their assistance, sending them on their way.

From Nicaea, the crusaders made their way to Antioch, arriving in October, 1097. The march took four months, in brutal summer heat, with little water, across dry and desolate Anatolia. Meanwhile, two cousins of Bohemond had split off from the main force to seek their own fortunes in the Christian, Armenian part of Asia Minor. The two were Baldwin of Boulogne (Godfrey's brother) and Tancred. They were welcomed in Edessa (now Urfa, Turkey, about 150 miles east of Antioch) and a coup soon put Baldwin in power there. Edessa was the capitol of the area, which became the first of the crusader states.

Antioch (now Antakya, Turkey) was one of the world's great cities and had been one of the original four patriarchs; the population was mainly Greek and Armenian Christians. When the crusaders arrived, Turkish defenders were in control of the massive fortifications. Its long and high walls were bolstered by 400 towers. For the 40,000 crusaders outside the walls of Antioch, the winter of 1097–1098 was very difficult. Starvation and disease forced the army to eat their own horses and dogs, and there were some cases of cannibalism. Desertions soared, and one band of deserters met Alexius on his way to reinforce the crusaders. They convinced Alexius and his army that the situation at Antioch was hopeless and all went back to Constantinople.

During the winter, Bohemond managed to subvert and eventually bribe a captain of the guard to betray the defenders. On the night of June 3, 1098, the traitor let Behemond and his men open the Antioch city gates for the whole army to pour through. The city was captured in only a few hours, and only the citadel held out. A Muslim relief force arrived from the east shortly thereafter and surrounded the city. Fortunately, they had been delayed for three weeks at Edessa so they did not get to Antioch while the crusaders were in a vulnerable position outside the walls.

Once inside the city, the crusaders were still in dire straits and faced with starvation. Morale was low, fear and despair wracked the army, and desertions increased. In that setting, a certain Peter Bartholomew had a vision of where to find the Holy Lance, used to pierce the side of Jesus at the time of his crucifixion. Peter led Raymond and a procession of clerics into the St. Peter cathedral and showed them where to dig. After some hours of digging with no success, Peter jumped in the hole himself and soon found the worn lance head after digging with his bare hands. The discovery of the Holy Lance was almost miraculous in its timing and served to uplift the spirits of the entire army. Later, Raymond mounted the lance head on a spear shaft and carried it into battle to inspire his troops.

Some cynics have questioned the fortuitous event. There seems to be good reason for their doubts. Even today, four "certified original" Holy Lances exist in various museums. Gaius Cassius Longinus was the first owner of the spear, but subsequently various reports say it has belonged to Constantine, Attila the Hun, King Alaric of the Visigoths, King Theodoric of the Ostrogoths, Charles Martel, Charlemagne, Otto I, German king Henry IV, Frederick Barbarossa, and even Hitler, who was fascinated by the spear's role in Richard Wagner's opera *Parsifal*.

In any event, Bohemond (because Raymond was sick) led the newly energized crusaders outside the city walls and quickly routed the Turkish forces. With dissention in their ranks, the Turks had lost interest in fighting and they scattered.

But the crusaders also had their disagreements and their armies delayed the march to Jerusalem until cooler weather. Raymond insisted that Bohemond and his troops were needed, but Bohemond wanted to stay behind and be the ruler of Antioch. The matter was finally resolved by making Raymond commander in chief, and the army started south on January 13, 1099. Beirut, Sidon, Tyre, Acre and Haifa were willing to help with supplies, if left alone, so they were no problem. On June 6 the little town of Bethlehem welcomed the crusaders as liberators.

The first attempt against the high walls of Jerusalem was easily repelled. The crusaders then began construction of two huge wheeled assault towers that could be brought up against the walls. Another vision was seen by a priest, Peter Desiderius, who divined that if the army would fast, do penance, and lead a procession around the city, Jerusalem would fall nine days later. This resulted in the amazing sight, on July 8, of the barefoot crusade army, singing prayers and carrying the Holy Lance, walking around the walls of Jerusalem. A few days later the assault towers were wheeled up against the walls and the attack began. Soldiers on Godfrey's tower were successful in breaching the wall and they then opened a city gate to a flood of crusaders. All Christians had been expelled from the city previously, so remaining civilians were put to the sword, including men, women and children. The massacre took place on July 15, 1099.

Although the crusader's first armies did not make a pretty sight, and at times allowed rape, plunder and slaughter, their achievements were unmatched by any of the crusades that followed during the next 200 years. The primary objective, Jerusalem was freed and Godfrey was named Protector of the Holy Sepulcher. Additionally, the port of Jaffa was secured as an entry point for supplies coming from Genoa, Venice and Pisa. Raymond was disgusted that he wasn't given the recognition he deserved, but less than a month after taking Jerusalem he returned to the battle of Ascalon, were he was a key part of the Christian force that surprised and wiped out a threatening Egyptian force.

Godfrey served as Protector for only a year. When Godfrey died, Baldwin was summoned to Jerusalem to replace him. While on the way from Edessa, Baldwin found it necessary to divert to and secure Antioch which had been left defenseless when Bohemond was captured by the enemy. Baldwin I (1100–1118) was crowned as the first king of Jerusalem on Christmas day, 1100.

The enormity of the success of the First Crusade was more fully recognized in 1100-1101 when disaster struck several European armies of late-comers who wanted to share in the glory. Making some foolish tactical blunders, they were wiped out in Asia Minor before they could even reach Antioch. A factor in their defeat was that the Turks began to realize the scope of the crusades, and revised their battlefield tactics to counter those of the enemy.

In the aftermath of the victory at Jerusalem, further complications arose. At one point, a freed Bohemond and his troops were engaged in war against the Byzantines and suffered humiliating defeat. Raymond sought to conquer the port of Tripoli for himself but died before the long siege was successful. When Tripoli finally surrendered in 1109, Raymond's son Bertrand was given control of the new County of Tripoli, holding it as a fief from King Baldwin. In less than ten years, Baldwin had succeeded in conquering the entire Palestinian coast and all of its cities except Tyre and Ascalon. He led an unsuccessful invasion of Egypt but fell sick and died in 1118. And a Christian army was crushed by the Turks at Aleppo in 1119, on a battlefield called the "Field of Blood."

In 1118, the Knights Templar was the first to form a military order. A group of nine French knights took vows of poverty, chastity and obedience, swearing to protect the Christians who came from Joffa, and those going on pilgrimage to the River Jordan. Baldwin II accepted their services and assigned them quarters in the Temple of Solomon, hence their name "pauvres chevaliers du temple" (Poor Knights of the Temple). Having renounced all pleasures of life, they faced death with no fear; they were the first to attack and the last to retreat. They wore a distinctive white habit with a large red cross.

Recruits flocked to their ranks, seeking to be a part of a group famous for their religious fervor and martial skill. The order had four ranks: the knights, equipped as heavy cavalry; the serjeants, who formed the light cavalry; farmers, who were the infrastructure; and the chaplains, who ministered to spiritual needs.

Some of their famous castles were: Safed, built in 1140; Karak of the desert, built in 1143; and Castle Pilgrim, built in 1217. Popes exempted them from all taxation, or any other authority except that of the pope. Gifts from wealthy benefactors, together with their humble lifestyle, led to the accumulation of considerable wealth. In Europe the Templars possessed 9000 estates and found need to develop an efficient banking system. Temples in Paris and London became solid banking centers where wealthy individuals kept their valuables. In Paris the royal treasury was kept in the Temple (which later led to disaster).

Another active military order was the Knights of the Hospital of St. John, or the Hospitallers. John the Baptist was their patron saint and Belvoir castle was their stronghold. First starting in 1113 as a religious order with a hospital dedicated to the care of sick pilgrims, they before long created a military arm which eventually overshadowed the care of the poor and sick. They were given control of a fortress in 1136, and later the Krak des Chevaliers, the greatest Christian outpost in the entire area. Initially the Templars and Hospitallers provided stability to a situation where crusaders came and went, with no overall control, but eventually the two orders became competitors. The Hospitallers won out in 1307, when all Templars in Europe were arrested and their wealth was confiscated (p. 232–233).

In 1145, Pope Eugenius III (114–553) called for a second crusade. Edessa had fallen and there had been no major crusading effort for nearly fifty years. The pope listed the standard benefits to each crusader, and Ber-

nard of Clairvaux tirelessly preached a "new chivalry" as a means of redemption. He argued convincingly to large crowds that God was giving a
chance for glory and salvation to those who took up the cross. The armies
of King Conrad III (1138–52) of Germany and King Louis VII (1137–80)
of France made up most of the manpower.

The crusade was delayed by two minor diversions, the first of which
was to convert the pagan Wends, living in the east part of Germany. The
Wendish Crusade was sanctioned by the Church to impose conversion or
death. Another, larger effort was directed toward the Muslims in Spain.
One result of this campaign was to plunder the Muslim-held city of Lisbon, after a three-month siege.

Conrad and his German armies got to Constantinople first, in Septem-
ber 1147, but did not wait for the French and pressed on toward Antioch.
They did not get far, however and were virtually destroyed by the Turks at
Dorylaeum (now Eskişehir), less than 200 miles from Constantinople.
King Louis joined Conrad and the remnants of his army, about a month
later, and they decided to march along the Aegean coast, rather than across
Anatolia. When they finally reached Adalia (now Antalya), they decided
the land route was too risky so the leaders all boarded ships to sail the remainder of the way to Antioch. The armies were instructed to continue the
march, but were continually attacked by the Turks so that a greatly reduced
force reached Antioch.

In June 1148, Conrad, Louis, and a number of the Christian leaders in
Palestine met at Acre to determine a strategy of attack. A large number of
reinforcements had joined them so a powerful force was available. Edessa,
the original target, was not even considered. The most logical place would
have been Aleppo, where their greatest enemy, Nur ed-Din was based, and
where he had only recently ordered the massacre of all Christians in the
city. Instead, the leaders chose to attack nearby Damascus, which actually
was allied with Jerusalem at the time. This blunder was exacerbated by a
stupidly conducted attack, with the result that it failed, an ally became an
enemy, and the Second Crusade ended as an overall disaster.

Baldwin III (1143–63), king of Jerusalem, captured heavily fortified
Ascalon, with much booty, in 1153. Baldwin died ten years later, and his
brother Amalric was named the new king. Amalric skillfully took advantage
of dissension among the Muslim forces in Egypt, and marched into Alexandria, a one-time, important patriarchal city. He negotiated with the Fatamid
caliphate to the point that Egypt almost became a Christian protectorate.

About this same time, the legend of Prester John was widely discussed in Europe and the Holy Land. In reports, he called himself the Christian Priest-King of India and Ethiopia, that he was vastly rich and powerful, and was going to rescue the Crusader kingdoms. In 1165 a cleverly forged letter was delivered to the emperor of Byzantium, allegedly from Prester John, making extravagant claims as to his intentions. Later, Pope Alexander III sent a letter to Prester John (never delivered) and Bishop de Vitry of Acre added to the rumors with an Arabic prophecy of a conqueror from the east. It took several centuries for Europeans to admit that the Prester John legend was a hoax.

Salah ed-Din Yusuf, or Saladin (1137–93) was a Kurd, born in Tikrit (also the birthplace of Saddam Hussein). During the Egyptian campaigns he was at the side of his uncle, a general who was later made vizier of Egypt. When the general died, Saladin was made vizier and he immediately began to put Egypt back in order, demonstrating that he was a gifted and effective leader. In 1171 he deposed the Fatamid (Shi'ite) ruler and replaced him with a Sunni Abbasid. In all, Saladin was successful in turning back three different invasions of Egypt led by Amalric. When Nur ed-Din died in 1174, Saladin quickly occupied Damascus and two years later married Nur ed-Din's widow (this marrying of a bereaved widow was very similar to what Muhammed did several times, 550 years earlier). Saladin was named overlord of both Syria and Egypt, uniting the Muslim kingdoms.

In a further move to consolidate Islamic forces, in 1180 Saladin made an alliance with Seljuk Sultan Kiliç Arslan II, and three years later they captured Aleppo. In 1185 he allied with Mosul, and also made a four-year truce with the Franks. At the same time he signed a treaty of friendship with the Byzantines. Saladin was deeply religious, and supported building new mosques, convents, and libraries. He was considered to be an outstanding administrator, diplomat, statesman and general—in short, the greatest Muslim leader of his time.

When Amalric died, he was succeeded by his thirteen-year-old son, Baldwin IV (1174–85). Baldwin was a leper and lived to be only twenty-six. Because of the disease, his arms and legs deteriorated and he eventually went blind. Incense was burned around him to mask the smell of his decaying body. Raymond III of Tripoli was the first regent and served capably, working to assure a successor to Baldwin, keep close ties to Europe and Byzantium, and maintain mutually respectful working relationships with Saladin and the Muslims.

Baldwin's recently widowed sister Sibylla became infatuated with the newly arrived Guy of Lusignan, who was disgraced and penniless but nevertheless appealing to Sibylla because of his bold, brash and daring persona. So she married him and Guy gained considerable power, including the regency. When Baldwin finally died, his child nephew Baldwin V became king, but died after only one year under suspicious circumstances. Sibylla was in line to be named queen of Jerusalem, but because her husband Guy was so widely disliked she was required to divorce him before being crowned. According to the agreement, however, she was allowed to pick her next husband; after her own coronation she put the crown on his (Guy's) head with her own hands.

Another troublesome character was Reynald of Châtillon who was the root cause of disaster for the crusaders. Violent, headstrong, reckless and foolhardy, he provoked the wrath of almost all the crusaders including King Guy. From his castle at Kerak des Chevaliers, Reynald often led his men in raids on passing tradesmen, but made the mistake of plundering one of Saladin's large caravans that not only was carrying expensive goods on the important trade route from Syria to Egypt, but also included Saladin's sister. Guy ordered Reynald to make restitution to Saladin, but typically, Reynald ignored the order. The result was a furious Saladin leading an army of united Muslims who soon destroyed the crusaders at the Horns of Hattin.

Madden estimates the crusaders assembled a large army, about 20,000 men, including 1200 heavily armored knights. The Muslims had about 30,000 men, almost half of whom were light cavalry. The Christian forces were just east of Acre, led by King Guy with the able assistance and advice of Raymond. The Muslims were at Tiberias where they had captured the city, but Raymond's wife was besieged in the citadel, in the same town. Guy's strategy, proven successful in previous battles, was to wait out the Muslims, knowing the latter could not hold their positions for long. Even Raymond counseled holding tight despite the situation his wife faced. A barren, waterless plain separated the two armies, and crossing it would be perilous in the summer heat.

But that night the king was visited surreptitiously by Gerald, the Grand Master of the Templars, and the treacherous Reynald, who convinced Guy that Raymond was not to be trusted. So the next morning, the indecisive King Guy countermanded the previous day's decision, and ordered the army to march toward Tiberias, about twenty miles away. Saladin was delighted to learn the crusaders were on the march, and moved to set a trap at an extinct volcano where two projections were known as the Horns of Hattin, just west of the Sea of Galilee. The thirsty and exhausted Crusader army camped that night near a dry well. They were further tormented by brush fires that the Muslims set, and a rain of arrows through the night.

On July 4, 1187 the Muslim troops were drawn up in a crescent, the wings forward, so the crusaders were effectively encircled as they tried to move forward. Seventy pack camels brought the Muslims a plentiful supply of arrows which flew as "thick as locusts." Frankish horsemen fought with great courage, inflicting heavy loss on repeated charges of the Muslim light cavalry. But the Christian infantry, desperate for water, broke and ran for the lake. As they fled downhill, they were systematically killed, wounded or captured. Knights lay on the ground, exhausted and beaten. Raymond and a small group with him were the only ones to escape. Gerald, Reynald, the king and other nobles were all captured. They were treated well, except for Reynald who was beheaded, perhaps by Saladin's own hand. In addition, about 200 Templars and Hospitallers were beheaded. Thousands of foot soldiers were sold on the slave market.

The Horns of Hattin was the greatest defeat in the history of the crusades. The cities of Acre, Ascalon and Jerusalem all capitulated so that two years later, only Tripoli, Antioch and Tyre remained in Christian hands. Tyre was saved only at the last instant when Conrad of Montferrat arrived to repudiate the surrender that had been agreed to. When Saladin entered Jerusalem he reclaimed the al-Aqsa mosque which had been used by the Templars. The Church of the Holy Sepulcher was not touched but many of the other churches were pillaged. He allowed all Christians who could afford to purchase their freedom to leave Jerusalem unmolested. Many who could not afford the cost were sold into slavery.

The "greatest defeat" seems to be the end result of the strongest Muslim leader appearing on the scene at the same time that one of the weakest Crusader leaders was in power. The leper king Baldwin IV was no match for Saladin. Baldwin ruled through regents, the first being Raymond, who was wise and helpful. The second regent Guy was not so wise, however, and at the critical moment was swayed by bad advice, and as king made a disastrous and costly mistake.

As an aside, it is tempting to wonder if the origin of the Catholic rosary, from "rosarium" (rose garden), might stem from Islamic prayer beads. Pope Pius V decreed that St. Dominic (1170–231) was the official inventor of the rosary, and Saladin came to power at exactly the same time. But it seems that both Muslims and early Christians used prayer beads long before that, most likely adopting the tradition from Buddhists, who got it from the Hindu faith, perhaps as early as the eighth century B.C. The Buddhists used 108 beads, the Muslims ninety-nine, and a full Catholic rosary has 150. In all four faiths, the beads are used to count prayers or devotions. In southeast Europe, "worry beads," with 33 beads on a strand, are likely inspired from Islamic prayer beads but need to be repeated three times. [Indelible in my memory of Turkey is the scene of men in black baggy pants, working a string of worry beads behind their backs while walking down the road.]

It is said that when Pope Urban III heard of the Crusader defeat at Hattin, and the loss of Jerusalem, he died of a broken heart. Though pope for less than two months, Gregory VIII, within nine days of Urban's death, issued a call for the Third Crusade. His crusading bull imposed a seven-year truce throughout Europe so that all efforts would be devoted to the Crusade. Even if they could not fight, all Europeans should support the Crusade, spiritually and through the "Saladin Tithe" or general tax.

From the beginning, the Third Crusade was supported by the highest echelons of kings and nobles. King William II of Sicily was the first to mobilize, and he was followed by Henry II of England, Philip II of France, and Frederick Barbarossa of Germany. It marked the height of the crusading movement and was the largest military venture of the middle Ages.

When Barbarossa took up the cross, he was seventy years old but alert and vigorous. Because he had previous crusading experience, he planned mass troop movements skillfully and his envoys arranged for safe passage through Anatolia. Initially, Emperor Isaac II of Constantinople hampered his passage somewhat, but submitted to superior strength and gave him provisions and transport across the Hellespont. In Asia Minor, Kiliç Arslan II had to be reminded that safe passage had been promised. A sharp military engagement sent the Turks scattering and Barbarossa was soon on his way, unimpeded. But on April 25, 1190, Barbarossa was drowned as he tried to cross the Gök River on horseback, near the coast. Without his strong leadership, the German army dissolved, and only a few of his troops went on to Palestine.

Henry II and Philip II were consumed with acrimony making no progress toward their crusading pledges, when Henry died and Richard I the Lionheart (1189–99) became king. Richard was well educated, intelligent, decisive, tall, blond, and physically imposing. At age thirty-two he was a brilliant general, bold in action, and fearless, but obsessed with the safety of his troops. This quality of course endeared him to his men and they gave him their strong loyalty. Richard sold off many of his properties to add funds to the Saladin Tithe, so his war chest was quite healthy. Whatever successes could be claimed by the Third Crusade in the next three years were almost all due to the wise and skillful actions of Richard the Lionheart.

Philip II was only twenty-five, small, sickly and cynical—lacking in charisma and not at all like Richard. Before they left, the two agreed to evenly split their share of all conquests and plunder of the Crusade. Philip left by ship from Genoa and Richard left from Sicily. While there, waiting for his ships, Richard had trouble with Tancred who had seized the Sicilian throne. Richard eventually had to capture Messina to get Tancred's attention. Tancred agreed to repay the dowry that Richard's sister had brought to the wedding with William II, now deceased. Philip then demanded half the city of Messina, half the dowry, and that Richard make financial restitution for breaking his engagement to Philip's sister.

When Richard's ships got to Cyprus, he found that some of them had been wrecked in a storm and then looted by the local Byzantine ruler, Isaac Comnenus. When he was captured, Isaac asked to not be put in irons, so Richard used silver ones. Cyprus turned out to be a valuable supply base, and remained so for the next four centuries.

When Richard got to the Holy Land he found that Philip had joined Guy and Conrad in the siege of Acre. The siege was going nowhere, and Guy and Conrad seemed to be more concerned about who should be the king of Jerusalem, which would be in name only as Saladin had actual control of the city. The assault on Acre became more intense with Richard's help and on July 12, 1191 the garrison asked for terms of surrender. The agreement called for Saladin to pay 200,000 dinars, release all of his Christian hostages and return the True Cross, captured at Hattin (possibly a fragment, by that time). In return, the Muslim defenders would be freed.

When Saladin did not make payment of the first installment on schedule, Richard was beside himself with rage. He had 2700 men of the Muslim garrison marched outside the gates of the city and executed before the eyes of Saladin and his army. Saladin, in return, killed about 1000 Christian hostages.

During the siege of Acre, pious Germans formed another order called the Teutonic Knights. It was very similar to the Hospitallers, that is, originally dedicated to caring for the sick but militarized later. It became a potent force in the crusades and was awarded substantial real estate in Palestine and Germany.

Before Philip returned to France, he and Richard judged the claims made by Guy and Conrad on the crown of Jerusalem. They decided that Guy would remain king as long as he lived, and that after his death the crown would pass to Conrad. After Philip left, Conrad went back to Tyre to sulk, and Richard took overall control of all the Christian forces. On September 7, Saladin and Richard faced off in the only battle they ever fought as direct opponents. Richard won decisively and Saladin never again risked battle with Richard.

In 1192 Richard's armies made two advances toward Jerusalem but backed off both times when the leaders, including the Templars and Hospitallers, decided the risks were too great. For the sake of unity, Conrad was named king of Jerusalem and Guy was given Cyprus in consolation. Conrad's reign lasted only a short time, as two Assassins murdered him in the street. They had a grudge against Conrad, and Saladin had offered their leader, the Old Man of the Mountain, a large reward for killing either Conrad or Richard.

Richard fell ill and became increasingly concerned about reports from home that his domains were being carved up by his brother John, and Philip. Before he left in October, he concluded a three-year agreement with Saladin which safeguarded the Christian territories along the coast, and gave Christians freedom to visit all the holy sites including those in Jerusalem. The Third Crusade was considered a success, except for reclaiming Jerusalem, and when Saladin died in March 1193, the Christian presence became even more secure.

Pope Innocent III (1198–1216) was only thirty-seven when he became pope. Though young he was "keenly intelligent and politically astute." He was extremely busy and his actions helped establish the character of the Catholic Church for the next 750 years. One of his main goals was to reclaim Jerusalem in a new crusade, but in reality, during his time as pope his main victims were other Christians. The Fourth Crusade, in 1201–1204, culminated in the sack of Constantinople, and the Albigensian Crusade of 1209–1229 resulted in the deaths of thousands of people in southern France.

The Fourth Crusade was supported by a group of nobles, and their strategy was to attack Jerusalem by way of Egypt. Ships would be needed so arrangements were made with the Venetians for a fleet of 500 large vessels, sufficient to transport 33,500 men and horses for 4500 knights. The cost was 85,000 marks, plus half the booty. However, only 11,000 troops showed up at Venice, and only half the promised payment could be raised. To be absolved of the remaining payment, the crusaders agreed to help the Venetians regain control of the rebellious city of Zara, on the Dalmatian coast. In this regard, the papal legate advised the Crusaders to do whatever was necessary to keep the army intact. Hence, a letter from Innocent III forbidding attack on Zara was ignored. The city surrendered in less than a week and was plundered of everything of value. When the crusaders asked the pope for forgiveness, he gave them absolution, but formally excommunicated the Venetians.

About this time, envoys arrived from Alexius Angelus, the young prince of Byzantium, with an intriguing proposition. He explained how his brother Alexius III (1195–1203) had blinded and deposed their father, Emperor Isaac II (1185–1195). Angelus had managed to escape, however, and asked the crusaders to return him to Constantinople where the people would welcome him. In return, he would pay the crusaders 200,000 silver marks, join the Crusade with 10,000 men, and return the Greek Church to papal control. The proposal was tempting and the timing was perfect, so the leaders of the Crusade agreed to the plan although the rank and file was opposed. Innocent III wrote a strong letter forbidding the diversion to Constantinople, but again, it was ignored and the Crusade went to Byzantium.

Alexius III had a garrison three times the size of the crusader army, and citizens of the impregnable city jeered Angelus when he appeared. Nevertheless, when the first crusader attack made a small advance, and a fire destroyed part of the city, Alexius panicked and fled, taking as much money as he could carry. Soon after, Angelus was crowned Alexius IV (1203–04). After paying half the money he promised, he made a few token payments for the rest but that was too much for the citizens of the city, and a mob at the Hagia Sophia church forcibly crowned a young nobleman they controlled. When he heard the news, Alexius IV was frightened and made the fatal decision to put his trust in Mourtzophlus, an aide who had been faithful up to that point. Mourtzophlus quickly put Alexius IV in jail, then had him strangled and had himself crowned Alexius V, a position he held for a little over two months.

The leaders of the Fourth Crusade did not accept Mourtzophlus as a legitimate ruler. Instead, they condemned him as a murderer and believed that the citizens had aided and abetted the crime. Therefore, they concluded that an attack on Constantinople was a legitimate function of the Crusade. This contradicted the commands of Pope Innocent III, but the vast majority of crusaders never knew this.

On April 12, 1204, the crusaders attacked the city, making very little progress. However, one group of about seventy men managed to make a small opening in the wall, and one lone priest scattered the Greek troops inside when he ran at them with raised sword. Once inside, the small band of men was able to open the city gates and the entire army of crusaders swarmed inside. One day later, the city surrendered and the citizens lined the streets to welcome a new emperor.

Instead of a brotherhood of Christians, however, the victors became a mob, greedy for everything of value in Constantinople. Hagia Sophia was stripped of all valuables; the altar was smashed for the precious gems and metals. In other churches icons were broken up for their silver and gems, and all other precious furnishings were stolen. The sack of the city was one of the most shameful in history and witnesses have said that Saladin would have been less harmful than were the crusaders. Innocent III was filled with shame and wrote "For they who are supposed to serve Christ rather than themselves, who should have used their swords against the infidel, have bathed those swords in the blood of Christians. They have not spared religion, nor age, nor sex, and have committed adultery and fornication in public, exposing matrons and even nuns to the filthiness of their troops."

However, faced with a *fait accompli*, the pope absolved the crusaders and emphasized the value of again uniting the two churches. For the Byzantines, a state in exile was formed in Nicaea and in 1261 the offices of the Byzantine Empire were moved back to Constantinople. But the lost glories were never regained, and the deep sense of anger and betrayal remains to some extent, even today.

The Fourth Crusade did much more harm than good and was a great disappointment to both the pope and the crusader states. The crusaders stayed in Constantinople for one year and then took their plunder and went home.

The Children's Crusade of 1215 was based on the conviction that God would see that the poor, innocent and righteous could succeed where armies had failed. In addition to children, women and the elderly joined the naïve and bizarre movement. In two huge groups, the throngs of people made their way to the southern coast of Europe, expecting the sea to withdraw and allow them to walk to the Holy Land. People along the way gave the "People's Crusade" food, money, gifts, and called them heroes. When the sea did not open, people melted away or tried to go to other ports. Many died and girls frequently ended up in brothels. Some of the participants who reached Marseilles were offered free transportation to Palestine. Instead, the ships went to Alexandria and the unsuspecting passengers were sold on the Egyptian slave market. Other pilgrims went back home to ridicule, and the Crusade ended ignominiously.

Innocent III apparently had little to do with the Children's Crusade, but actively supported other crusades in the Baltic, in Spain, and even in southern Italy. His immediate concern, however, was fighting the Albigensian or Cathar heresy in the Languedoc area of southern France. Catharism held that life is a battleground between good and evil, where the spiritual world is the zone of goodness and the material world is inherently evil. All living creatures, therefore should strive to become free from the bonds of matter. An individual could become a "Perfect" when he underwent the *consolamentum* which was both a baptism and an ordination. Once in that state, a Perfect pursued a sinless life, refrained from sex, and practiced great austerity including rigorous fasting and eating neither meat nor eggs. Most did not undergo the *consolamentum* until they were quite old.

These beliefs were tied to their accepting Christ as God, but not as man. They believed that resurrection of the body was a cruelly misleading concept and the idea of Purgatory was a fiction. These ideas were directly opposed to Catholic dogma, and the Cathars thought the pope and bishops were active agents of Satan. Cathars were found in every social class and were well represented among the nobility. Templars were friendly supporters, as both groups held Gnostic views about the exalted position of Magdalene in the first century. The Cathars were especially strong after 1194, when Count Raymond VI of Toulouse came into power, 100 years after his ancestor had been one of the leaders in the First Crusade.

Three other religious groups were active at the time and played important roles. The Waldensian movement began in about 1170, originated by Waldo, a rich merchant of Lyons who renounced his wealth to live a life of poverty and evangelical effort. He had the Gospels and other books of the Bible translated into common language, and taught the Gospel widely. He encouraged his listeners, including women, to preach the message which, simply, was an early form of lay ministry. Their activist form of Christianity followed totally orthodox theology, except that they had contempt for ecclesiastical power and argued that they were not subject to the pope or any prelates of the Roman Church. The Waldensians have been considered as forerunners, by 350 years, of the Protestant Reformation.

The second group was formed by Francis of Assisi, born in 1182. He renounced all material possessions and devoted himself to caring for the sick and poor. It is said he cared for lepers, fed them, bathed their sores and embraced them. In 1210 the pope authorized forming the Order of Friars Minor, commonly called the Franciscans. Francis told his associates they would have no money, and no property individually or collectively, and that their mission was to preach to the poor. They were to teach by example, "using words if necessary." Within 100 years, the Franciscans had split into two groups, one of which was allowed to hold some property in common. This branch was offended by the other "Spiritual Franciscans" and in 1318, several of the latter were burned at the stake.

In 1219 Francis joined the crusaders in Egypt. His idea was to end the Crusade by converting the Muslim sultan to Christianity. When he went to the sultan's tent, the Muslims thought he was an envoy sent to negotiate peace. Instead, when Francis started talking about the errors of Islam, the Muslim attendants wanted to kill him but the sultan restrained them. No conversion was made, and Francis was sent back to the crusader camp. Saint Francis is a great favorite of Catholics and the city of San Francisco was named for him.

Similarities between the Waldensians and Franciscans were quite striking. Both lived in voluntary poverty, traveled widely, and preached the gospel. Both denounced the Cathar doctrine and also were critical of the Roman Church for failure to fully follow the ideals of scripture. They differed in their obedience to papal authority, so that the Franciscans got papal approval whereas the Waldensians did not. In 1215 the Waldensians were excommunicated from the Roman Catholic Church and they soon became targets for the Inquisition.

Another order, known as Dominicans, was confirmed by the pope in 1216. The order was founded by the Spaniard Dominic who was born in 1170. Early in life he was recognized for his love of learning, charity, and intense religious beliefs, and was ordained at the age of 25. He lived as he preached, a life of humble poverty. Thomas Aquinas (1225–1274) was another famous Dominican who faithfully supported Augustine's doctrines, including his scorn for women. Aquinas was conflicted with some of Aristotle's concepts but papal supremacy was central to his beliefs and he stated "to be subject to the Roman pope is necessary for salvation."

The chief aim of the Dominican Order of black-robed priests was to spread the word of the gospel. Dominic himself was credited with the miracle of raising a child from the dead, and he established at least three homes for nuns. The rules he wrote for one of them included strict penance, contemplation and restriction to their quarters, with the spinning of wool as their daily occupation. There is no evidence that Dominic supported the harsh measures used to put down the heresy of the Cathars and Waldensians, although Aquinas firmly supported the Inquisition. The Dominicans, together with the Franciscans, were the main Orders used to conduct the formal interrogations of the Inquisition.

Because Raymond VI of Toulouse was not inclined to put down the Cathar heresy in Languedoc, Innocent III had him excommunicated. After the pope's legate to Raymond was killed, in 1208, Innocent declared a major Crusade against Raymond and the Cathars. Innocent spoke of "exterminating" the Cathars who he said were "worse than the very Saracens." He offered all the indulgences of a normal crusade and required only forty days military service from an individual. Most enticing was the right to take over the lands and property of the heretics, so in short order a 30,000-man crusader army was formed, mostly of men from northern France. Raymond quickly scrambled to gain his absolution (and protect his lands), and rode with the crusading army. Their first target was the fortified city of Béziers, in the heart of the Cathar country.

When the city was overrun, all inhabitants were slaughtered, Cathars and Catholics alike, women, invalids, babies and priests. The papal legate, Arnald-Amalric bragged that nearly 20,000 people were put to death, and when he was told that many good Catholics were among those massacred reportedly said, "Kill them all, God will recognize his own." Carcassonne fell next. Although the people were allowed to leave unharmed, their possessions were plundered by the crusaders. Raymond left the Crusade at that point and returned to Toulouse.

Simon of Montfort was named the leader of the Albigensian Crusade. The Church had already agreed that all conquered lands would be assigned to him so he was hungry for new lands and thirsty for blood. In 1213 his army killed King Peter of Aragon and 17,000 of his men at the battle of Muret. Peter was a hero, recently returned from fighting Muslims in Spain. After 12,000 people were killed at St. Nazaire, and 10,000 at Toulouse, Raymond VII signed the Peace of Paris in 1229 that effectively ceded Languedoc to France.

Innocent called the Fourth Lateran Council in 1215, one of the most important ever held and a fitting climax to his career. Two thousand bishops and other important clergy attended and confirmed the seventy-one well-prepared decrees. Most importantly, the Council confirmed the supremacy of papal political power. Innocent had already established his dominance in confrontations with King John of England and King Philip of France. In an argument over appointing the Archbishop of Canterbury, Innocent had the king excommunicated and declared the throne of England vacant. John gave in and was re-named as king at the permission of the pope. Philip likewise gave way when he was ordered to take back his queen, whom he had tried to discard for another woman. It was also established that payment of church tithes held precedence over payment of governmental taxes.

Other important issues were adopting the Confession of Faith, and accepting the concept of transubstantiation during the Eucharist. Another decree concerned heretics and their punishment, including excommunication and legal penalties. Already in effect under the declared crusade, lands and properties of heretics were subject to seizure by Catholics, and death by the sword or burning was frequently the ultimate penalty. Four of the decrees were aimed at Jews, requiring them to wear an identifying badge, and restricting their activities and places to live. The seventy-first decree called for the Fifth Crusade of 1218–1221.

Innocent III was one of the most talented popes; he died in 1216, apparently at the highest point of his career. After all, he had prevailed in personal confrontations with the kings of England and France. The Fourth Crusade had gained control of Constantinople, and the Western and Eastern Churches were together again. The Albigensian Crusade against heresy was headed toward a successful conclusion, and another crusade to regain Jerusalem was about to commence. The papacy appeared to be at the peak of its power, and important religious concepts and statements had just been adapted.

In the long term, however, many of his "accomplishments" laid the foundation for future problems. The sack of Constantinople was never forgiven and a wedge was driven between the two churches. Innocent had won in confrontations with two kings, but could not control the crusaders. He ordered them not to attack either Zara or Constantinople, but forgave them, when they disobeyed his orders. The Children's Crusade was an unmitigated but predictable disaster, and thousands of innocent people died. No doubt Innocent could have stopped, or at least given helpful guidance to this crusade, but seemed to have a "hands-off" approach.

The campaign against heresy was largely an effort to enforce absolute papal supremacy and to eliminate all opposing views. Innocent approved of the bloody massacres of the Cathars, and personally declared that anyone who conflicted with Church dogma "must be burned without pity." Burning at the stake was also supported by Emperor Frederick II of Germany, and this was the usual form of execution used during the Inquisition, both of which grew out of the Albigensian Crusade.

In decrees 67–70 of the 1215 Council, Jews were subjected to restrictions, very similar to those Hitler imposed on them in the 1930s.

In summary, the actions of Innocent III, one of the most brilliant of all popes, had the following long-term effects:

- Exacerbated the split between the Eastern and Western Churches
- Initiated the first steps toward imposing the Inquisition
- Antagonized governments, contributing eventually to such things as the Church of England, the separation from Rome, and the French revolution
- Formalized persecution of Jews, that lasted for over 700 years

CRUSADES— INQUISITION TIMELINES

1095	Urban II—preached a Christian Crusade
1096–1099	First Crusade—captured Antioch and Jerusalem
1118	Knights Templar military order
1147–1148	Second Crusade—confused disaster
1187	Horns of Hattin—Saladin led greatest victory of Muslims
1190–1192	Third Crusade—Barbarossa, Richard the Lionheart
1201–1204	Fourth Crusade—sack of Constantinople
1209–1229	Albigensian Crusade—squelched Cathar movement in Southern France
1215	Children's Crusade—total disaster
1215	Innocent III called Fourth Lateran Council—declared supremacy of pope, religious rituals, punishment of heretics, repression of Jews, called for Fifth Crusade
1218–1221	Fifth Crusade—disastrous invasion of Egypt
1228–1229	Sixth Crusade—successful diplomacy by Frederick II
1231	Medieval Inquisition
1248–1254	Seventh (French) Crusade—Louis IX led Egyptian disaster
1258–60	Mongols severely set back Muslim world
1270	Eighth Crusade—Louis IX died in Tunisia
1291	Acre fell, end of Crusader States
1307	Knights Templar destroyed by Inquisition

1431	Joan of Arc burned at stake
1478	Spanish inquisition
1542	Roman inquisition
1633	Galileo convicted
1741	Benedict XIV gave imprimatur to works of Galileo
1822	Pope gave same official sanction to works of Copernicus
1826	Last victim of Inquisition hanged

The Fifth Crusade to the Holy Land was one of Innocent's most carefully planned enterprises, and was to be fully managed by the church. Preachers were dispatched throughout Europe to fire up the enthusiasm of the faithful. The pope promised to pay 30,000 pounds of silver and a five percent tax was imposed on all clergy for the first three years. In addition to the usual indulgences for the crusaders, non-combatants could earn a share of the benefits by paying to outfit and supply a crusader. Once underway, the actual operations were characterized by a series of blunders, misdirection, and interminable waiting for Emperor Frederick II to perform as he repeatedly promised.

The assembly at Italian ports was to begin in June 1217. Austrian forces left in August, and Hungarians soon after. After landing at Acre they were joined by smaller armies from Antioch and Cyprus. In the absence of Frederick, they decided to undertake an Egyptian campaign with general agreement that this was the best way to succeed at Jerusalem. In May 1218, the crusader fleet arrived at Damietta, a fortified city on one of the main distributaries of the Nile River. The Muslim defenders were completely surprised, and a long siege commenced.

The crusader army lacked leadership and was marked by the constant arrival of new troops, and the departure of others. When the papal legate, cardinal Pelagius of Albano arrived in September, he became the de facto leader because of his strong personality. He was imperious and brash, but shared Innocent's view that the church should be in charge of the Crusade. It did not take long for him to make an incomprehensible mistake.

The Muslim commander al-Kamil had his own internal command problems and fearing the arrival of Frederick's forces, made a generous offer. If the crusaders would leave Egypt immediately, he would turn over the entire kingdom of Jerusalem and grant a thirty-year truce to the Christians. In addition, he would pay an annual fee of 15,000 bezants for leasing two forts in the Transjordan. In other words, he would give up all of Saladin's conquests in the Holy Land in exchange for lifting the siege of Damietta. The Templars and Hospitallers opposed the deal, and Pelagius turned it down.

In November 1219 Damietta was taken amid the stench from 50,000 bodies, all dead from disease. All through 1220 the army did nothing, and in May 1221 Fredericks's first troops arrived under the command of Duke Louis, a respected Bavarian baron. In July, Sultan al-Kamil repeated his enticing offer but Pelagius made his second mistake and turned it down again. A large part of the crusader army then marched south toward the sultan's defensive position, at Mansurah. Pelagius blundered again and positioned his troops in a place were they were soon surrounded, and supplies cut off. When they tried to escape, al-Kamil opened sluice gates and flooded their route. Pelagius had to sue for peace and this time the terms were not so pleasant. To live, they would have to leave Egypt. An eight-year truce would be offered but al-Kamil also promised that the True Cross would be returned.

Hence, what could have been a wonderful success turned into a humiliating failure. And the True Cross was never returned—apparently al-Kamil did not have it.

As for Frederick II, he finally arrived at Acre in September 1228, ten years after he was expected. The ten years was full of delays, false starts, broken promises, recruiting problems, deaths of old wives and marriages with new ones, births, contested claims, illness and even excommunication. Frederick immediately told al-Kamil that he was ready to accept the sultan's earlier offer. When al-Kamil stalled, Frederick made a show of force at Jaffa, which brought the sultan back to the bargaining table. An unprecedented agreement emerged. The crusaders would be given Jerusalem, Bethlehem and Nazareth plus an access route to the coast. Jerusalem would become an open city, and Muslim residents would retain their own justice system and religious freedom. A ten-year truce, to 1239, would be in effect. Many of the local powers, including the Templars and Hospitallers, opposed the deal, in part because Frederick was under excommunication. When Frederick entered the Church of the Holy Sepulcher for his coronation many of the usual dignitaries boycotted the ceremony, and he ended up putting the crown on his own head.

With no bloodshed, Frederick had succeeded in winning back Jerusalem. If Pelagius had accepted the same thing eleven years earlier it would have been regarded as a stupendous victory. Instead, Frederick's accomplishment was accepted only grudgingly, and when his entourage left Acre early on the morning of May 1, 1229 the inhabitants showered them with garbage.

In 1239, Frederick's truce expired and the Muslims immediately took back Jerusalem. The city changed hands again when an alliance was made with Egypt but in 1244 a final devastating campaign wiped out all Christian holdings except for the few port cities on the Mediterranean coast.

Back in France, King Louis IX (1226–70) observed all this with dismay, as his most cherished goal in life was the Christian control of Jerusalem. Louis had the resources of his kingdom to support a new, totally French Crusade and Pope Innocent IV supported him wholeheartedly. Louis was a revered and moral leader with integrity and concern for justice. As a crusader-king, he inspired his troops with his courage, caution and concern for his men. Louis saw to it that the Seventh Crusade was well funded and carefully planned. A huge stockpile of provisions was put in place on Cyprus, to support operations anywhere in the eastern Mediterranean.

Just as so many before him, Louis felt that a campaign in Egypt was the best strategy, and the first step toward regaining Jerusalem. Hence, the crusader fleet arrived at Damietta on June 4, 1249. After a brief, initial encounter with the Muslim defenders, the city was abandoned and the crusaders marched in unimpeded. When reinforcements arrived in November, the Crusaders marched south to Mansurah, their nemesis once before. And through a series of tactical errors they were defeated again and had to ask for terms of surrender. The result of this was that Damietta was to be freed, the Christians were to evacuate Egypt and a ransom of 800,000 bezants was to be paid. As security, Louis would have to remain in Egypt until half the money was paid.

Before all the terms were carried out, the Mamluks (slave troops) rebelled and killed the sultan. The ransom was paid to the Mamluks and Louis was released, but contrary to the agreement, thousands of the captured Christian soldiers were still held prisoner. Louis refused to leave the Levant until his men were released so he went to Acre with the remnants of his army, about 1000 troops. In Acre, he was greeted by an adoring crowd that knew of his fame and glory, and saw him as full of Christian virtue. During the next five years he was able to win the release of his imprisoned people and helped strengthen the defenses of the crusader cities along the coast. In April, 1254, he returned to France, almost six years after leaving.

The Mongols (p. 184) under Hulagu Khan disrupted Muslim control in the Middle East during this time, and may have helped the crusaders to some extent. While he was still in Palestine, Louis IX was in contact with the Great Khan and the suggestion was made that the Khan convert to Christianity. In reply, France was told to surrender and send an annual tribute—obviously, the two sides were talking past each other and nothing happened. In 1260, the Mamluk troops under General Baybars defeated the Mongols, and in the next few years took several of the Christian positions. Baybars was a ruthless leader and slaughtered all the populations at Safad, Jaffa and Antioch. The greatest single massacre of the entire crusades took place at the latter city, which had survived for 170 years.

Louis IX watched all of this with great anguish and in 1267 took up the cross one more time, even though he was in his fifties and becoming frail. He talked of regaining Jerusalem, and got the support of King James I and King Henry III. As usual, he made fine arrangements for supplies and shipping. Leaving from Genoa in 1270, Louis surprised everyone by making Tunis his objective. Once there, their camp was on the site of ancient Carthage. During the summer heat, sickness swept through the camp and Louis himself died on August 25. His brother Charles arrived a few days later and took command. Charles negotiated an agreement with the emir of Tunis, winning a large payment for himself; in return, the crusaders departed. Louis was sainted twenty-seven years later, but it must have been for good intentions rather than actual results.

In Palestine, Baybars was followed by Kalavun, who was just as ruthless and as determined to drive out the Christians. After taking Latakia and Tripoli, his forces besieged Acre which fell with great slaughter in May 1291. Tyre, Sidon and Beirut soon followed, together with the last two Templar castles. Acre, Tyre and Tripoli became empty ghost towns, and the crusader states were eliminated after almost two centuries. The island of Cyprus was all that remained in Christian hands as the crusades wound down. Henceforth, crusading no longer involved armed pilgrimages but became wars, mostly in Europe against other Christians.

THE INQUISITION

[This is a very difficult subject to describe with confidence because of so much misinformation, from different sources. On one hand, 600 years of the inquisitional process was soft-pedaled, explained away, or even excused, to the extent possible. At the other extreme, outlandish and extreme accusations were made of the most fiendish tortures and number of executions. Hence, depending on the source, the total number of victims has been estimated at anywhere from six thousand up to 68 million! My goal was to try to be as factual as possible, using the best-documented information. The sources I relied on most, included *The Catholic Encyclopedia*, Wikipedia, Dennis McCallum, Bernard Hamilton, Thomas Madden, E.R. Chamberlin, John Cornwell, Hans Küng, and Tim Dowley, *et al.*]

Some authors have divided the history of the Inquisition into three stages called the Medieval Inquisition, initiated by Pope Gregory IX in 1231; the Spanish Inquisition, authorized by Pope Sixtus IV in 1478; and the Roman Inquisition, initiated by Paul III in 1542. Other authors include the Albigensian Crusade, which had a different organization but similar objectives and results. Some also include the German witchcraft episode. The *Malleus Maleficarum* was aimed at punishing witchcraft and sorcery, and any opposition was labeled heretical, hence, a very dangerous position to take.

The Inquisition began as a follow-on to the Albigensian Crusade which had the primary purpose of combating Catharism. Inquisitors were commissioned by the pope to investigate cases of heresy in their area. The crime of heresy was defined as a deliberate, obstinate denial of Catholic orthodoxy, and was considered a sin and a crime, punishable by law. Therefore, as excommunication was not a very effective deterrent, it became necessary to use coercion against religious dissenters.

The inquisitors were usually Dominicans because they had a history of fighting heresy, were educated, skilled in debate, and accustomed to travel, with no personal gain. As the Inquisition grew, it began to seek out persons believed to be heretics, and added witches and other sacrilegious people to the list of those investigated. Beginning in 1252, inquisitors were authorized to use torture to force individuals to disclose information that would help in obtaining either a conversion or a conviction. Bloodshed, mutilation and death were not allowed, so a favorite form of torture was the rack. Another torture was known as the *strappado*. This involved suspending the accused with a rope tied to his (or her) hands bound behind his back. This resulted in dislocating the person's joints in both arms which was not only excruciatingly painful, but crippling as well. Weights to the legs were sometimes used, to dislocate leg joints also.

The usual investigative procedure in a new town was to gather the people together and invite them to step forward and admit their own guilt in exchange for a light punishment, usually "penances." But they would also need to inform on other heretics, which they could do anonymously. In this way, a list of suspects was developed, and the trials could begin.

The trial of an individual was conducted in secret, and his accusers were not named although the defendant was invited to name those who had a "mortal hatred" against him. This step was meant to reveal local grudges and could boomerang against the secret accuser. The defendant was not told the charges but was invited to confess. Testimony could be taken from blood relatives plus criminals, convicted heretics, and those who had been excommunicated. Sentences could not be appealed, and defendants could be kept in prison for years while the inquisitors sought new information. A defendant could have a lawyer, but the lawyer could lose his license if a conviction was obtained—*voila*, lawyers for the defense were very rare.

Penances were required to gain absolution for grave or mortal sins which if not forgiven, could lead to damnation. The penance could be severe, and was often public. Typically, it could call for a difficult pilgrimage, or sometimes flogging. The pope could grant an indulgence, or pardon from a penance, and did so for those who joined Louis IX's Crusade. A penance that was not completed at the time of death would have to be completed in Purgatory.

For the heretic who had confessed and repented, the punishment was life imprisonment. For those who did not repent, the penalty was death by burning at the stake. In some cases, where the accused had died prematurely, the remains were exhumed and then burned, and in one instance an old, crippled woman was carried out of the city and burned in her bed. In all cases of life imprisonment or death, the property of the accused was confiscated, meaning that the victim's family suffered as well. All executions were carried out by secular authorities. Apparently the advice given by Frederick II in 1224 may have guided the penalty phase; he recommended that heretics be burnt, but if spared they should have their tongues cut out.

The Medieval Inquisition was used primarily in southern France and northern Italy. England and Bohemia were mostly untouched, along with most of northern Europe. By 1321 the last Cathar in France had been burned. Including those in the Albigensian Crusade, the total number of Cathars killed must have been well over 100,000. Whereas the crusade usually killed with the sword, the Inquisition killed with fire. Hamilton has listed some of the mass burnings as follows: 183 people at Mont-Aimé in 1239, 215 at Carcassonne in 1244, eighty at Agen in 1249, and 174 at Sirmione in 1276. Cornwell stated that the "inquisitions in their entirety killed hundreds of thousands of dissident Catholics, heretics and alleged witches." The last victim was hanged in 1826, over 600 years after the beginning of the Albigensian Crusade.

In general, medieval inquisitors were despised and excessively zealous inquisitors attracted many mortal enemies. Peter Martyr was assassinated, Robert the Bulgar was imprisoned, and Conrad of Marburg was murdered—"his bigotry was ardent to the pitch of insanity." Bernard Gui spent most of his career as an inquisitor and, in the class, was well regarded. He tracked down the last Cathar to be burned, and could easily have been the inspiration for Victor Hugo's character "Javert" some 500 years later.

One of history's most abominable injustices occurred on Friday, October 13, 1307, when secret orders were sent throughout France to arrest all the Knights Templar. The military Order of Templars had been blessed by the pope nearly 200 years earlier as an unselfish, monastic group of knights, dedicated to protecting crusaders in the Holy Land. Since that time, they had accumulated considerable wealth in Europe and for their own needs had formed a banking system. These Templar banks were so strong and reliable that they were also used by kings and nobility to protect their wealth. The French king's huge debt to the Paris temple was a factor in the arrests—in fact Philip IV's goal was to erase his debt, in the process getting his hands on the Templar's wealth.

"Philip the Fair" (1285–1344) was the grandson of Louis IX and got his sobriquet from his appearance—he was tall and handsome, with blond hair and blue eyes. It certainly was not a reflection of his moralistic tendencies. He had an insatiable thirst for money, and used the power of the throne to carry out large-scale theft. Early in his reign he had arrested Italian bankers and confiscated their wealth. In 1306 he seized the wealth and property of all Jews in France, and then had them expelled from the country. As the Templars were protected by papal decree, Philip had to attack them through the offices of the Inquisition.

He did this through the weak Pope Clement V (1305–1314). Clement was a former French bishop, who set up papal headquarters in Avignon in southern France. Philip pressured Clement to charge the Templars with sodomy, heresy and black magic. Confessions to these trumped-up charges were obtained through the use of torture. When they had a chance to publicly testify in their own defense, over 500 Templars volunteered to do so. All fifty-four who were heard were convicted of being relapsed heretics because they retracted their confessions that had been made under torture. No matter, they were all burned at the stake. In 1312 the Templar Order was formally dissolved and all its property was given to the Order of Hospitallers, the Templar's main competitors. In 1314 the Grand Master, Molay, and another leader retracted their confessions made under torture, but before the judges could rule, Philip IV had them burnt alive. While suffering, Molay was heard to condemn Philip and Clement, and in fact both died within a year.

Before he died, however, Philip saw the cancellation of all his debts to the Paris temple, and extracted 310,000 livres tournois (approximately 170,000 pounds sterling) from the Hospitallers as an expense fee. The destruction of the Templar brotherhood, in order to seize their wealth, was the worst example of the corruption of the Inquisitional procedure.

As Dan Brown's 2003 *The Da Vinci Code* indicated, the Templar organization produced some extremely competent individuals whose descendents became members of important organizations that exist today. In Portugal they became Knights of Christ, Vasco da Gama was a member of the Knights, and the father-in-law of Christopher Columbus was a Grand Master.

Of all the surviving organizations with a lineage traceable back to the Knights Templar, the most important may be the Freemasons. A large number of Templars fled to Scotland where they were given haven by King Robert the Bruce. Evidently, many of the Templars became involved in the Freemason organization. In order to avoid persecution and indeed the threat of death, they began a tradition of secret meetings and handshakes. There were over 500 Templar properties in Scotland by the end of the sixteenth century, and in 1717 the first Masonic Grand Lodge was founded in England. They may have been influenced by the Rosicrucians, with their "Rosy Cross." The Rosicrucians were another secretive order at the time, moral and religious reformers, scientifically inclined, with a mystic or Gnostic orientation. Beethoven, Newton and da Vinci were members.

Freemasonry is now a worldwide fraternal organization with no central authority but belief in a Supreme Being, truth, tolerance, fraternity, equality and support for civil authority are basic principles. Individual masons may advance through three stages to Master Mason, and the Scottish Rite allows for thirty-two degrees.

The Freemasons have had a significant influence on American politics. Except for one, all the signers of the Declaration of Independence were Freemasons. George Washington was a Grand Master, and fifteen other presidents were Freemasons, including Monroe, Jackson, Lincoln, McKinley, both Roosevelts, Truman, both Johnsons, and Ford. The founder of the Mormon religion, Joseph Smith, was a Freemason, and the first five presidents of the Mormon Church were as well. Many Mormon rituals and symbols are similar to those used in Masonic practices. Masonic influence is also seen in the original architecture of Washington D.C., and even on the one dollar bill, i.e., the all-seeing eye and the pyramid.

Pope Clement XII first opposed the Freemasons in 1738, and the Catholic Church continues this opposition today. The Free Methodist and Southern Baptist churches also prohibit their members from joining the Freemasons.

The "Illuminati" is another secret society but had minimal Freemason connections. It was formed in 1776 by a Bavarian professor, Adam Weishaupt. He developed a plan for abolition of organized religion and a worldwide nation to be controlled by a supreme council of wise, enlightened individuals (Illuminati). The Freemason connection is that, for a time, Weishaupt and some of his minions infiltrated Masonic temples and adapted some of their methods of secrecy. A cult of conspiracy theory has developed that claims all kinds of dire events have been orchestrated by the Illuminati, beginning with the French Revolution. The Freemasons have been included, to a limited extent, but conspiracy to foment revolution is certainly diametrically opposed to their basic beliefs.

Between 1961 and 1984, a Frenchman, Pierre Plantard, described the mysterious Priory of Sion as an offshoot of the Order of Sion, formed during the crusades with the Knights Templar as a military and financial front. The Priory was portrayed as a Goddess mystery religion, originating with Jesus and his wife, Mary Magdalene. Their daughter was a progenitor of the royal French Merovingian dynasty which—surprise—led to Plantard as the true modern French king. Along the way, the Priory had a long list of alleged illustrious Grand Masters, including Leonardo da Vinci, Robert Boyle, Sir Isaac Newton, Victor Hugo and Claude Debussy. All this was found to be an elaborate hoax, which Plantard admitted, under oath, to have been totally fabricated. Dan Brown's *The Da Vinci Code* encouraged a provocative new interest in the idea, but the opposing facts seem quite clear.

William of Ockham (1290–1349) was a Franciscan at Oxford who challenged conventional wisdom about some church matters. He was critical of the papacy and rejected papal authority in secular affairs. He stressed the importance of natural science and developed the principle of "Ockham's razor" which held that proof of a theory was more likely correct if it used fewer, rather than more, assumptions. Some modern-day scientists love to quote "Occam's or "Ockham's razor," but do not seem to remember that William had a strong, positive theology and believed that "God was known by faith alone."

After Clement V died in 1314, his successors maintained the papal headquarters at Avignon, and in fact built a magnificent court within a walled city. The pope remained in Avignon for seventy years, and this period has been called the Babylonian captivity of the Papacy, equating it to Jerusalem 1900 years earlier. While in Avignon, 82 percent of the newly named cardinals were French, and in 1381 the split became more serious. Two competing popes, each with his own retinue of cardinals and other church officials, established two headquarters, one in Rome and one in Avignon. Some unyielding cardinals were tortured to death and there were political effects as well. Italy, England, Hungary and Scandinavia supported the Roman pope, whereas France, Spain and Scotland were in the Avignon camp. In 1409 a council met in Pisa to resolve the matter, but it wound up with three popes instead of two. The Council of Constance finally named a single pope, Martin V, in 1417.

This was also the time of the Hundred Years War (1337–1453) between France and England. In addition to the wars, a great epidemic of bubonic plague, called the Black Death, killed about one-third of the European population in the years 1347–50. The Catholic Church had to deal with another serious matter, that of John Wycliffe (1329–1384) and his new bible. Wycliffe was a leading philosopher at Oxford University who criticized the church for protecting corrupt clergymen, and argued that people did not need a priest to mediate for them with God. Toward the end of his life, he translated the Latin, Catholic Vulgate Bible into English (called the Wycliffe Bible) making the bible available to everyone in their own language, an important first step toward Lutheranism in the following centuries.

The fourteenth century ended with a humiliating defeat of Western chivalry by the Turks. Charles VI of France enthusiastically supported a Crusade to rescue King Sigismund of Hungary, and urged French and German noblemen to join with their troops. An impressive army was assembled and met the Turks, under Sultan Bayazid, at Necropolis, Bulgaria in 1396. A rash frontal assault by the knights of Western Europe failed, and they were totally crushed by the more skillfully handled Turkish troops. Most of the crusaders were killed or captured; about 3000 of them were stripped naked, paraded before Bayazid and then decapitated.

One of the most famous victims of the Inquisition was Joan of Arc (1412–1431). She became involved, in the most unlikely circumstances, while fighting on the French side against the English during the Hundred Years War. As the simple daughter of a poor peasant farmer, she never learned to read or write but was very pious and compassionate for the needy. At the age of thirteen and a half she became conscious of "voices" talking to her, and by May 1428 the voices were insisting that she offer her military help to the king of France. After much opposition, she finally saw the king on March 8, 1429. To test her, he had disguised himself but she recognized him without hesitation. After further testing, she finally led troops at Orleans, dressed as always like a man. The siege was lifted on May 8, and as she had predicted three months earlier, Charles VII was crowned in Reims in July.

After further fighting, Joan fell into the hands of the English in May, 1430. They were determined to have her killed and used the tools of the French Inquisition to get this done, as that part of France was under English control. The unscrupulous Pierre Cauchon charged her with witchcraft and heresy, and she courageously faced her judges alone, without legal help or support. While being held in prison, for a time she was kept in an iron cage and chained by the neck, hands, and feet. Her conviction was partly based on the fact that she persisted in wearing men's attire, and she was burned at the stake on May 30, 1431. Twenty-five years later, under Pope Calixtus III, her trial was ruled to be illegal and her sentence was reversed. In 1909, Pope Pius X issued the decree making her a saint of the Catholic Church, a unique honor of all those burned by the Inquisition.

For a period of thirty-two years, beginning in 1471, a series of three corrupt, hypocritical, licentious and vindictive popes did great damage to the Church. By their actions they created many critics, contempt for the office of pope, and hastened the coming of the Protestant Reformation.

Sixtus IV (1471–1484) ordained thirty-four cardinals, and of those, six were his own nephews, hence the word "nepotism." Sixtus drew on the papal treasury to support in comfort his own family—a brother, three sisters, and fourteen nephews and nieces (though two of the "nephews" may have been his own sons). The six nephew/cardinals were sexually profligate, had mistresses, and fathered several illegitimate children. Pietro, one of the nephews, was made cardinal at the age of twenty-six but lived such a dissolute life that he died of his vices when only twenty-eight years old. Sixtus appointed one young man to be cardinal at the age of sixteen, and one of the cardinals he appointed became his successor. Other than nepotism, Sixtus was indirectly involved in a plot to control the city of Florence, in which one dé Medici was assassinated at Mass, and another brother was wounded. On the positive side, Sixtus sponsored the building of the Sistine Chapel.

Giovanni Battista Cibò became Innocent VIII (1484–1492), following

Sixtus. To win the papacy he bought the votes of the cardinals with signed promises—all of which he repudiated after becoming pope. As a youth, Cibò fathered two illegitimate children, and in later life sired eight boys and eight girls. Wags said he could be called the Father of Rome. He also made arrangements for his illegitimate children to have lavish weddings in the Vatican. Like Sixtus, he practiced nepotism, making one nephew (who later became Leo X) a cardinal at the age of thirteen. To raise money for his depleted treasury he began to create new official positions, and sold them to the highest bidder. He may have been one of the most vindictive popes of all time. A proposed Crusade against the Turks got nowhere, but one against the Waldensians was supported by plenary indulgences. He took severe measures against witches in Germany and listed the principles of prosecution used later to draw up the infamous *Malleus Maleficarum*. He was a strong supporter of the Spanish Inquisition and in 1487 appointed Tomás de Torquemada as the grand inquisitor of Spain. Shortly before he died, Innocent was pleased to see successful completion of the *reconquista*, when Granada, the last Muslim possession in Spain, was retaken.

Callixtus III named his Spanish nephew, Rodrigo Borgia, a cardinal at the age of twenty-six, in the year 1457.

A year later, Rodrigo was appointed vice-chancellor of the church, and in addition to being a cardinal soon became an archbishop, a bishop and an abbot of different localities. This generated a high personal income and it was said he was wealthier than all other cardinals put together, save one. To minister to the different places in his name, he assigned vice-priests, hence the word "vicar." Borgia served in the Curia under five different popes, acquired much administrative experience, and displayed good judgment in performing his duties. He wrote well, was astute and energetic, and an eloquent speaker, able to charm men as well as women. He was a patron of the arts and enjoyed the rediscovery of the classical world during the Renaissance; Michelangelo, Botticelli, Leonardo da Vinci, and Machiavelli were no strangers to his court.

Soon after he became cardinal, he began a long-time affair with a married woman, Vannozza dé Catanei. During the next twenty years she bore him four children and had three husbands, who furnished their names as cover. Borgia devoted a great deal of attention and material wealth to all his children, but Cesare and Lucrezia were his favorites. When Vannozza was in her mid-forties, Rodrigo left her and placed six-year-old Lucrezia in the care of his cousin, Madonna Adriana.

As it happened, the cousin had a son who was married in Rodrigo's palace to the beautiful, sixteen-year-old Giulia Farnese. Giulia's situation as a new wife was quickly changed to being the new mistress of Cardinal Borgia. Giulias's husband disappeared, but her brother was made a cardinal as soon as Borgia made pope, and others of her family enjoyed the largesse as well. Rodrigo had at least nine children, two of whom were born while he was pope.

When Innocent III died in 1492, the twenty-three existing cardinals were secluded for the purpose of selecting a new pope. After four days, Borgia had bought the votes of the required fourteen cardinals. The most obdurate was Ascanio Sforza, a very wealthy rival, with the support of important families. Sforza bargained hard, and won the position of vice-chancellor as well as four mule-loads of bullion (gold or silver). The College of Cardinals went through the motions of voting, "praying to the Holy Ghost for guidance" to the annoyance of Sforza. Thus Rodrigo Borgia became Pope Alexander VI on August 11, 1492, just two months before Columbus landed in the New World. Together with two of his children, Cesare and Lucrezia, he was to leave an astonishing record as one of the most corrupt popes in history.

An extravagant coronation ceremony was conducted, and the triumphal arches proclaimed "Rome was great under Caesar, but far greater under Alexander. The first was only a mortal man, the second is a God." It soon became apparent that the new pope lusted after power and wealth, the better to advance the position of his many children and other relatives. One of Pope Alexander's first official acts was to make his son Cesare a cardinal, at the age of eighteen. (Sixtus IV had obliged earlier when Cesare was four years old, granting a dispensation for "being born of a cardinal and a married woman"). Instead of faith and religion, greed, ambition, and sexual perversion were the characteristics of the new administration.

In June, 1493, thirteen-year-old Lucrezia was married at the Vatican. Legally, it was her third marriage, as two previous marriage contracts had been signed with Spanish noblemen. But as the pope's daughter, her value increased dramatically so the two previous contracts were cancelled and Giovanni Sforza became the new husband. Giovanni was suitable because he was a kin of Ascanio, one of the most powerful men in Italy.

When the French invaded Italy in 1494, the Dominican monk, Girolamo Savonarola reformed Florence and instigated the "burning of the vanities" when the townspeople made a bonfire fifteen stories tall of cosmetics, paintings, books, etc. He denounced Pope Alexander and his court as corrupt. For this, in 1498, Savonarola was excommunicated, tortured, and then hanged and burned at the stake in exactly the same place as the bonfire. His deeply religious persona and opposition to the papacy were an example to the early Protestants, who soon followed.

That same year, Lucrezia plotted to marry the son of the king of Naples, in a scheme to acquire the throne. Her husband Giovanni stood in the way of the plan and refused to agree to a divorce. So a commission was established and conveniently declared that Giovanni was impotent, Lucrezia was still a virgin, and therefore her marriage was null and void. That cleared the way for her next marriage to the king's son, who was the duke of Bisceglie.

When the daughter of the king of Naples refused to marry Cesare, King Louis XII of France, for an appropriate bribe, furnished a substitute bride and the dukedom of Valentinois. Cesare was twenty-two years old, and after four months never saw his pregnant wife again. In 1500, Cesare returned to Rome in triumph, and in short order got rid of Lucrezia's second husband who had lost his value as an entrée to the kingdom of Naples. When assassins failed to kill the husband on the street, but left him badly wounded, Cesare finished the job by strangling the bedridden young man himself. Soon after this episode, in order to raise money, Alexander VI named nine new cardinals, each of whom paid handsomely for the position. In all, 120,000 to 130,000 ducats were collected.

In late 1501, the infamous "Banquet of Chestnuts" orgy was staged in Alexander's private quarters, with Cesare and Lucrezia both present. After the meal, chestnuts were scattered on the floor, and by candlelight, fifty of the city's prize prostitutes were challenged to pick them up without using their hands. On their hands and knees, the nude prostitutes began collecting the chestnuts, but were then seized by male servants (or guests) and the whole scene became a contest to see which man could copulate with the most whores. At the end of the contest, the pope handed out awards to the winners.

A few months later, Lucrezia, at the age of twenty-two, married her third husband. Understandably, Alfonso d'Este was hesitant about joining the ill-fated list of husbands but hefty bribes persuaded him. Alexander postponed the beginning of Lent so that wedding festivities were not subdued by restrictions on food or other activities. Not long before her wedding, Lucrezia performed as a kind of deputy-pope while her father was gone from Rome. It was also about this same time that another Borgia was born to one of the mistresses. Some records suggested Alexander was the father but others pointed to Cesare.

Before he died, Alexander initiated the first censorship of printed books. The *Index* of the Catholic Church was to be used for over four hundred and fifty years. Alexander died of fever in 1503. As he was dying, Cesare's men forced their way in his quarters and seized all available treasure. The pope's body was badly contorted so his remains had to be pounded into the coffin. Though widely despised by the people, his energetic efforts for his children were acknowledged and Machiavelli approvingly noted that Alexander had skillfully out-maneuvered all opponents, using his ability to "divide and rule."

The Spanish Inquisition was organized somewhat differently than in Italy and France, and probably has a worse reputation. In 1478, Sixtus IV gave permission for Queen Isabella of Castile to institute the Inquisition there, and the same permit was given in 1481 to her husband Ferdinand IV of Aragon. The *Suprema*, or High Council, was set up to direct the work and the Dominican friar Tomás de Torquemada was made inquisitor-general. He remained the leader of the Spanish Inquisition for fifteen years and was responsible for the execution of thousands of victims. By 1538 there were nineteen courts, and three more were added in Mexico, Lima and Cartagena. This centralized authority, directed by the crown, became very efficient at prosecution, torture and executions. At first, Muslim and Jewish converts to Christianity were the main targets, suspected of secretly practicing their old religions. Küng reported that under Torquemada, about 9000 heretics and Jews were burned at the stake, also known as *auto-da-fé* (act of faith).

The Inquisition was also called the Holy Office, because the church considered its work so praiseworthy. It persisted in Spain for more than 350 years and was finally terminated in 1834. Winchester reported that after the 1755 Lisbon earthquake, which killed 60,000 people, "priests roved around the ruins, selecting those they believed guilty of heresy and…had them hanged on the spot." Jean Antoine Llorente, secretary to the Spanish Inquisition for 1790–92 said: "The horrid conduct of this Holy Office weakened the power and diminished the population of Spain by arresting the progress of arts, sciences, industry, and commerce, and by compelling multitudes of families to abandon the kingdom; by instigating the expulsion of the Jews and the Moors, and by immolating on its flaming shambles more than 300,000 victims" (R.W. Thompson, 1876.)

The Inquisition also became involved in the trial of sorcerers or witches. Theologians had determined that witchcraft involved a pact with the devil, hence apostasy of the Christian faith and therefore heresy. One could be branded a heretic simply by questioning the existence of witches, and often the mere accusation was enough to send some poor soul to the stake. Nearly all of the accused were women and/or outcasts—i.e., old, ugly, midwives, Jews, gypsies, poets or others who appeared to be suspicious. Innocent VIII had listed some principles to follow in convicting witches, and this was formalized in 1486 by Kramer and Sprenger. They published *The Malleus Malefucarum* (The Witch Hammer), one of the most infamous books ever written. It served as a guidebook specifying how to identify, prosecute, torture, and kill witches.

Some authors estimate the death toll for witches was 600,000 to 9,000,000, but others say it was more like 60,000. Historian William T. Walsh reported 30,000 went to the stake in England, and 100,000 in Germany. Significantly, the latter two death lists were the result of Protestant atrocities, as were the more recent Salem witch trials in New England.

The last Roman phase of the Inquisition was initiated by Pope Paul III in 1542 as part of the Catholic response to Luther's Protestant Reformation (p.247-249). In the same year, the first *Index of Prohibited Books* was published by the Catholic Church, expanding on the initial steps of Alexander VI, forty years earlier. Within a few years, three-quarters of all books published in Europe were being censored. The Spanish model for the Inquisition was used, and the Council of Trent in 1545 formalized the counter-reformation.

There was no attempt made toward compromise or serious reconciliation and the Inquisition became more concerned with Protestant apostasy. The fundamental doctrines of the Catholic Church were established for the next 400 years, and the important claim of papal infallibility was defined at the First Vatican Council in 1870. Trent was designed to defeat the Reformation, by diplomacy where possible, but by military force if needed.

Galileo Galilei (1564–1642), was a famous Italian scientist whose life and work have been of great importance and controversy, mainly for two reasons. First, Galileo made many scientific discoveries and was largely responsible for development of the scientific method. Secondly, his problems with the Inquisition have come to epitomize the potential for conflict between science and religion.

His early contributions were in mechanics where he described the law of inertia and developed a mathematical formula to define the uniform rate of acceleration due to gravity. His genius was in making careful quantitative measurements in controlled experiments, now a fundamental feature of scientific research. Most of his fame came from his work in the field of astronomy, and construction of a vastly superior telescope. This allowed him to make a whole series of major discoveries in the heavens, beginning in 1610.

The telescope also helped him to reaffirm the heliocentric (sun as the center) theory, described by the Polish astronomer Nicholas Copernicus (1473–1543). Earlier support for this idea had come from the Dane Tycho Brahe, who had all the planets except Earth orbiting around the sun. Tycho's German assistant, Johannes Kepler discovered that planets moved around the sun in elliptical orbits rather than perfect circles, but surprisingly, Galileo did not fully appreciate the significance of this until later. Kepler (1571–1630), who was a Lutheran, struggled under the economic impact of the Thirty Years War and also had to devote considerable effort (eventually successful) to get his mother released, without torture, when she was arrested as a witch.

Galileo's problems with the Inquisition were mainly based on differences over Church dogma, made more sensitive by the Protestant Reformation. Misunderstandings with key church personnel, and turf-battles between the Jesuits and Dominicans were all exacerbated by Galileo's offensive and belligerent personality, totally tone-deaf to the politics of the time.

The official position of the Church for over 1100 years, since Augustine, was that the sun orbited the earth. This geocentric theory was based on arguments by two Greeks, the philosopher Aristotle and the astronomer Ptolemy. Augustine and Thomas Aquinas later gave church approbation. Hence, long-standing church doctrine was challenged when Galileo began strong public support for the heliocentric ideas of Copernicus' 1543 book *On the Revolution of the Celestial Spheres*. At the Council of Trent in 1546, the Catholic Church had declared itself the only authority to interpret the Holy Scripture, in contrast to the Protestant view that individuals could form their own interpretations.

In 1616, cardinals of the Inquisition met to decide the merits of the Galileo matter. Not surprisingly, the investigation found that "the proposition of a stationary Sun is foolish and absurd" and "the doctrine attributed to Copernicus...cannot be defended or held." "Not surprisingly" because only sixteen years earlier Giordano Bruno had been burned at the stake for his support of the heliocentric theory. Also, he had the temerity to say that Holy Scripture was written to teach morals but not to teach astronomy. As a result of the 1616 decision, the book by Copernicus was added to the *Index* until it had been "corrected." Another result was that

Cardinal Bellarmine furnished Galileo with a written letter stating he could continue to discuss the merits of the Copernican theory but was not allowed to support or teach it as truth. Bellarmine had also presided over the Bruno investigation.

Galileo may have made a misjudgment when his friend Maffeo Barberini was elected Pope Urban VIII. The Pope treated Galileo as a good friend until Galileo foolishly published a satirical work *Dialogue Concerning the Two Chief Systems of the World—Ptolemaic and Copernican* in 1632. One of the protagonists was named Simplicio, made to look like a simple-minded dolt and claimed by some to represent the pope, who became very upset. The *Dialogue* was put on the *Index* and Galileo was called before the Inquisition in 1633. A questionable, unsigned document from the 1616 hearing was produced which helped convict Galileo. After a forced recantation, Galileo was sentenced to lifelong imprisonment, in reality a house arrest.

The after-effects of this matter continue to this day. The actor Richard Griffiths has said "By stifling the truth, which was there for anyone to see, the Church destroyed its credibility with science." Many scientists see it as "the suppression of truth in the name of religion" (Brooke and Cantor, p. 106).

In 1741, Benedict XIV belatedly instructed the Inquisition to grant an *imprimatur* (official sanction) to the complete works of Galileo. And in 1822, the *Dialogue* was removed from the Index and an *imprimatur* was given to cover Copernicanism as physical fact, not a hypothesis. In 1992, as the result of a formal investigation of the Galileo affair, Pope John Paul II admitted the Church had erroneously tried to make facts of science conform to theological doctrine, whereas there were actually "two realms of knowledge." Slow to be sure, but in the last eighty years or so the Catholic Church has taken the lead, among religious factions, in embracing astronomy (including the Big Bang) and recognizing the reality of evolution. Sadly, a few Protestant elements today seem to be more closely tied to the times of Galileo, and denigrate solid science because it does not conform to their interpretations of scripture.

9

AFTERMATH OF THE PROTESTANT REFORMATION

Certainly the hypocritical immorality and corruption of some of the Renaissance popes, plus excesses of the Inquisition, were important factors leading to the Reformation. However, it was the sale of indulgences, to shorten one's stay in Purgatory, that was the direct incentive for Luther to post his ninety-five theses in 1517. The following paragraphs explain how this situation developed.

Pope Julius II (1503–13) was the next important pope after the despicable Alexander VI. Julius was a humorless but honest man who harshly enforced law and order. During his reign of over nine years, he stamped out simony, took back the Papal States, completed the Sistine Chapel, and insisted on a careful approach to Church expenditures. The result was that he faithfully passed on a treasury of some 750,000 ducats to his successor. This was fortunate, as Leo X proved to be more of a spendthrift than Julius was frugal.

Cardinal Giovanni dé Medici was elected Pope Leo X (1513–21) on March 9, 1513. Giovanni was the son of Lorenzo the Magnificent, a powerful man in Florence. The House of Medici was one of the most important clans in Italy, and over a period of 200 years provided kings, queens, several dukes and other noblemen, plus two popes. Lorenzo saw to it that his "shrewd" son Giovanni had every advantage. At the age of eight, he was made an abbot of a small abbey and three years later was named to the same post at Monte Cassino. He was made cardinal at the age of fourteen, one of the youngest cardinals ever. Lorenzo advised him to stay in the background and be observant and respectful among the other cardinals, because of his youth. This he did, until he became pope at the age of thirty-seven.

His coronation took place in a tent in front of the dilapidated façade, all that remained of the 1000-year-old St. Peter's. The procession to the Lateran palace was even more lavish than Borgia's, and no expense was spared. Groups of dignitaries marched, including cardinals and their retinue, Roman and Florentine nobles, soldiers, clergy, bureaucrats of the curia, Swiss guards and two chamberlains kept busy throwing gold and silver coins to the crowd. Leo rode a white stallion and no doubt was in some pain due to his ulcerated hemorrhoids. The inauguration spectacle and the following celebration cost Leo 100,000 ducats, a sizable part of the treasure Julius had left him.

Leo was corpulent, and not a handsome man, but was quite likeable and lived in high style, keeping everyone in good spirits as he spent money freely in the pursuit of happiness. He would have agreed with the saying "it's good to be pope." He loved the classics, liked to be surrounded by interesting people and artists, including Michelangelo and Raphael, and one of his favorites was Pietro Aretino, famous for his pornographic stories. At the time, there were 7000 registered prostitutes in Rome, out of a population of 50,000. Instead of mistresses, Leo seemed to prefer courtesans.

A good deal of time and effort was spent on a hopeless plan for a Crusade against the Turks under Sultan Selim I. Leo got the youthful new king of France, Francis I (1515–21) to put the resources of his kingdom squarely behind the Crusade. With new enthusiasm, Leo then contacted Henry VIII of England, Maximilian I of Germany, Charles I of Spain and the Netherlands, and Manuel I of Portugal. They were urged to take up the cross but all had doubts about France. When the Turks took Syria and Egypt, the matter became more urgent and a plan was drawn up for two great armies that would operate separately but in cooperation. A complex, three-year campaign was proposed by Maximilian, with the objective of driving the Turks out of Anatolia and Syria. Leo proclaimed a five-year European truce in 1518, as a necessary step to the forthcoming Crusade. This pleased everyone but in 1519 Maximilian died, Charles became Emperor Charles V, and Francis dropped out of the alliance. Pope Leo began to realize that he had much more serious problems, right at home.

These problems had started in 1517 when group of cardinals, headed by Cardinal Riario, conspired to have Leo poisoned. The poison was to be administered in the ointment used to treat Leo's rectal ulcer. The plan failed when his usual physician was gone and Leo refused to be treated so intimately by a strange doctor. One of the conspirators talked too much and was lured back to Rome with the promise of safe-conduct, guaranteed by the Spanish ambassador. He was immediately clapped into prison, and under torture implicated a number of other cardinals. Leo dismissed the safe-conduct with the comment "faith need not be kept to a prisoner." Five conspirators were identified, but only one suffered death by red-hot irons and hanging.

Faced with a group of cardinals whose loyalty was suspect, Leo's masterstroke was to confirm thirty-one new cardinals simultaneously, thereby gaining a faithful majority of the Sacred College. He also raised more than half a million ducats by charging each new cardinal for the appointment. The money was badly needed, to augment that being raised to help his nephew Lorenzo, the new duke of Urbino. Machiavelli wrote a handbook of ruthless politics called *The Prince*, and dedicated it to Lorenzo. Unfortunately Lorenzo died before he could take full advantage of the book's guidance which urged a politics of cynical deceit to achieve the axiom "better to be feared than loved."

There was never enough money to pay for Leo's extravagances, including mercenary forces, exquisite trinkets and artwork, and the papal bureaucracy numbering 700 people. Income was mostly from the Papal States, the vinegar, salt and alum monopolies, and fees, benefices, and sale of over 2000 offices in the curia. Taxes were levied on brothels, and additional money came from sales of dispensations, annulments, pardons, and "expectations" and "preferences" for appointed positions. Leo determined that the income from the sale of indulgences would be used to pay for the construction of the basilica of St. Peter's.

Four hundred years earlier, Urban II had granted indulgences and full remission of sin to those who went on Crusade. Later, cash contributions to the crusades earned the same act of grace. Leo took the next step by offering an indulgence for a cash contribution to the Turkish Crusade, together with the St. Peter project. The doctrine on indulgences was quite complex. Basically, it held that after sin was absolved by the sacrament of penance, further punishment in Purgatory could be reduced or eliminated through indulgences. For example, viewing certain rare relics, plus payment of necessary fees, could earn a person a 1,443 year indulgence.

A Dominican monk named Johann Tetzel was put in charge of the money-raising campaign. The new technology of the printing press provided an unending supply of indulgence slips, sold to buy future credits or immediate escape from Purgatory. Individual contrition was of small matter, and a saying quickly became popular: "As soon as the coffer rings the soul from out the fire springs." When Dr. Martin Luther understood what was happening, he was outraged and what he did about it changed the world.

Luther (1483–1546) was thirty-four years old at the time. He was a professor at Wittenberg University, having earned a doctorate in theology there in 1512. Earlier, he had entered the Augustine monastic order in 1506, and was ordained a priest a year later. In 1510 he had visited Rome and was appalled by the inappropriate behavior of the popes and other high-level church figures. The sale of indulgences was the final straw, and on October 31, 1517, he nailed his ninety-five theses to the wooden door of the Castle Church in Wittenberg. These points were aimed at challenging the legitimacy of selling indulgences, and he was inviting anyone to engage in debate over the matter. The theses were written in Latin but were soon translated into German and read throughout the country. Luther's choice of the Castle Church was no accident—the standard remission of Purgatory time was calculated to be 1,902,202 years and 270 days for viewing relics of the church, plus paying the fees.

In summarizing the ninety-five theses, some of the most important points Luther made were as follows

- Only God can remit guilt, and indulgences can only forgive penalties imposed by the church.

- Forgiveness cannot be bought, and only follows from true contrition.

- Charity or works of mercy are far superior to buying pardons.

- Letters of pardon are a vain hope for salvation.

- Preaching the Gospel is 100 times more important than pardons.

- Charity and truth are much more important than pardons, which cannot take away the guilt of even venal sins.

- It is blasphemy to compare the Papal arms with the Cross.

- Money only encourages avarice, and it is madness to think it can release a soul from Purgatory.

- Why doesn't the pope release souls from Purgatory for the sake of holy charity and pay for the basilica with his own money?

Luther's argument was that salvation was by faith in Christ's work alone, and he wanted to reform the Catholic Church. But all it did was to get him in serious trouble with the Church hierarchy. He was summoned to Rome but was wise enough to refuse, well aware of previous victims (notably Jan Hus burned in 1415) who trusted in promises of safe passage. In 1520, Luther publicly burned a papal bull condemning his views. In 1521, he was formally excommunicated and all his works were banned. Threatened with arrest, he took refuge at Wartburg castle. While there, he translated the New Testament into German and began a translation of the whole Bible, completed in 1534. In 1525 he married Katharina von Bora, a former nun, and they had six children. He died at the age of sixty-three in 1546, after Trent but before the beginning of the great religious wars.

When Luther translated the Old Testament it was from the Septuagint, that is, the Greek translation of Hebrew scripture for Jews who no longer spoke Hebrew. Luther labeled some books such as Tobit and Maccabees as "Apocrypha" which is why the Old Testaments of the Catholics and Protestants are different. Gutenberg's printing press, invented in 1455, made it possible to quickly give the new Bible wide distribution and, in fact, the Bible was the first complete book published. With his translations of the Bible, Luther united the Germans culturally, centuries before they were joined politically.

Some reformers were more radical than Luther and urged immediate action. The Peasant's War of 1525 was one result, bitterly opposed by Luther. The enormous destruction of farms and livestock led to 100,000 fatalities, and was a precursor to the religious wars later in the century. Huldreich Zwingli of Zurich was the first of the Reformed theologians and had been greatly impressed by the great Augustinian writer, Desiderius Erasmus of Rotterdam. Zwingli had some intractable differences with Luther, arguing for the spiritual presence of Christ at the Eucharist. Zwingli had considerable influence on certain Protestant denominations but had a militaristic bent and was killed in battle against a Catholic army in 1529.

Luther's principled stand against the pope and emperor got the rapt attention of Europe, and he further elucidated his views in book after book during the following years. In 1529, at the Diet of Speyer, some of the German princes rose in protest when Emperor Charles V tried to squelch Luther's activities. Thus, the name "Protestant" was originated.

Lutheran

In 1530, Luther approved the Augsburg Confession, drawn up by Melanchthon and this is considered the beginning of Lutheranism. Most important was the idea of salvation by faith alone, or "justification by faith only." The value of good works was denied as a condition of justification but good works were seen, rather, as the evidence of justification. Every Christian was encouraged to read and interpret the Bible in his own way (free interpretation). The sacraments of baptism and penance were retained and similar to the Catholic belief, the body and blood of Jesus were present at Holy Communion. Rejected were the authority of the pope, Purgatory, indulgences, and invocation of saints. The Book of Concord was finalized in 1577 and comprised a compilation of the basic concepts important to the Lutheran faith.

Luther wrote several church hymns and virtually sustained the reformation single-handed. Later, Johann Sebastian Bach (1685–1750) composed over 300 pieces of religious music for the Lutherans, including the *B Minor Mass* and *St. Matthew Passion*. Other German composers did much of their work for their churches. Included was the *Messiah* of Handel (1685–1759), *Mass in D:Missa Solemnis* of Beethoven (1770–1827), *Elijah* of Mendelssohn (1809–47), and the *Creation* of the Austrian, Haydn (1732–1809).

The new religious freedom, plus the power of the printing press, helped encourage a number of scholars to undertake new translations of the Bible. William Tyndale is considered to be the father of the English Bible. He translated from the original Hebrew and Greek (the latter known as the "received text") rather than from the Latin, which itself was a translation. Tyndale completed translation of the New Testament in 1525, but the Catholic Church fought a determined battle to keep it from being available to the public. In 1534 Tyndale was imprisoned, and in 1536 was strangled and burned at the stake. His friend Miles Coverdale published a translation in 1535 that used much to Tyndale's work. A flurry of other translations and revisions followed, culminating in the King James Bible in 1611. About fifty of the best Hebrew and Greek scholars completed the project in seven years. The King James Version, written in classic English, has been the first choice for nearly 400 years, although the New International Version is now more popular. In 1546, at the Council of Trent, the Catholic Church reaffirmed the Latin Vulgate Bible, which was then translated into English in 1609. Today there are about seventy-five recognized English translations of the Bible.

In addition to work on the Bible, the newfound freedom in religion and science led to a virtual avalanche of scientific discoveries and important advances in literature, philosophy and government. Names of some of the key people (in chronologic order through the seventeenth century) include Henry VIII, Nostradamus, Queen Elizabeth I, William Shakespeare, Kepler and Galileo (previously mentioned), Francis Bacon, William Harvey, René Descartes, Oliver Cromwell, Rembrandt, Antony Van Leeuwenhoek, John Locke, Isaac Newton, Peter the Great and Voltaire.

Unfortunately, dispute over the real truth also resulted in a torrent of violence and wars of religion between Catholics and Protestants. In France there were eight civil wars against the Huguenots (Calvinist Protestants), with 3000 of them killed in the St. Bartholomew's Night massacre in Paris in 1572. The war between Spain and the Netherlands lasted more than eighty years. One event in the latter conflict was the destruction of the Spanish Armada in 1588. Of the 141 ships in the Spanish fleet, bad weather destroyed most that escaped the British navy. The bloody Thirty Years War (1618–48) began as a conflict between Calvinists and Catholics. It was fought mostly in Germany but involved Danish, Swedish and French forces as well. Of the fifty significant battles, Magdeburg in 1631 was the most atrocious, when 22,000 Protestant civilians and defenders were massacred. At the end of the war, the Peace of Westphalia demarcated religious boundaries that have remained, for the most part, for more than 350 years.

From this beginning, three main traditions evolved: the Lutheran in Germany and Scandinavia; the Calvinist and Zwinglian in Switzerland, France, Holland and Scotland; and the Anglican in England. All three refused to acknowledge the authority of the pope, and rejected the need for intercession by the virgin, or interpretation of scripture solely by the Church hierarchy. The Lutherans became the largest Protestant church in the world with 76 million members, according to the 2001 *World Christian Encyclopedia* of Barrett and Johnson. U.S. membership is 8.35 million, concentrated in the upper Midwest.

Baptist

In Zurich, "Anabaptists" developed contemporaneously with Zwingli. They were strong pacifists but otherwise had very similar beliefs. Their name meant "re-baptism" by immersion of older children or adults in other words, a "born again" process. They believed in a complete separation of church and state, and resisted military service. Anabaptist subgroups that immigrated to America, such as the Mennonites, Huttites and Amish, became conscientious objectors and stayed out of the mainstream. The first congregation of "Particular" Baptists in England met in 1612, and gradually adopted full Baptist views. They too, believed in separation of church and state and the full immersion, or born-again form of baptism. Baptists form the largest Protestant group in the U.S. with 36.4 million members concentrated in the Old South, and 48 million worldwide.

The Frenchman John Calvin led the formation of a puritanical form of non-Lutheran Protestantism, headquartered in Geneva. He believed in justification by faith alone, and the predestination of some individuals to heaven and others to hell. After several years of struggle, Calvin became the virtual religious and political dictator of Geneva in 1541. He enforced a strict regime of diligent work habits and righteous living, with no drinking, dancing, gambling or singing. He was intolerant toward heretics and witches, and retained the use of inquisition, torture and death by burning at the stake. His most famous victim was Michael Servetus, a Spanish physician and theologian. Servetus was burned because he did not believe in the doctrine of the Trinity. Calvin's strict form of Protestantism was mirrored by the Huguenots in France, Presbyterians in Scotland, and Puritans in England (Calvinist views were despised by Thomas Jefferson).

Anglican

King Henry VIII (1509–47) initiated a huge change in world history in 1534 when he led England into a separation from Rome, and formed the Church of England. Henry had been born a Catholic and was praised by Pope Leo X for writing a book against Luther. Even though he was excommunicated, Henry remained a Catholic all of his life, and the Anglican religion has been called "Catholic Light" or the middle way between Catholics and Protestants.

In large part, the lurid story of Henry's six wives and several mistresses revolves around his attempt to obtain a male heir in order to assure the continuation of the Tudor dynasty. Henry's first wife was Catherine of Aragon, the daughter of Queen Isabella and King Ferdinand of Spain. Catherine was betrothed to Henry's older brother Arthur when they were only two and three years old, and they were married when they were both fifteen. Less than six months after the wedding, Arthur died, so both royal families pushed for the marriage of Catherine and Henry. Catherine maintained that her first marriage had never been consummated, thereby making it feasible for the pope to grant a dispensation for the two to marry. On June 11, 1509, Henry became King Henry VIII and they were married nine weeks later.

In the next nine years Catherine had seven pregnancies, six of which involved miscarriages, stillborn babies or babies that lived only a short time. Finally, a daughter named Mary was born in 1516, who lived to be queen. During the ten years after 1518, Henry sired six bastards with four different mistresses. About 1526, when it was clear Catherine could no longer conceive, Henry began a surreptitious effort to get the pope to annul his marriage to her based on an obscure passage in Leviticus. When another mistress, Anne Boleyn, became pregnant, Henry must have felt a legitimate son was possible and his annulment campaign became more urgent. Cardinal Wolsey, who had a very distinguished and faithful record up to that point, was Henry's emissary to the See. However, Henry became irritated when Wolsey did not get results promptly enough, and dismissed him. Wolsey may have been fortunate to die before he went on trial.

Early in 1533, Henry and Anne Boleyn were married, and on May 23, the new Archbishop of Canterbury, Thomas Cranmer, officially proclaimed that the original marriage of Catherine and Henry was invalid. On June 1, Parliament had Anne Boleyn crowned as queen in a lavish ceremony, Catherine was demoted to "Dowager Princess" and her daughter Mary was deemed illegitimate and called "Lady" instead of "Princess."

The pope responded to these events by excommunicating Henry in July 1533. Urged by Thomas Cromwell, the new Chancellor of the Exchequer, Parliament reacted to this by passing a series of new laws in 1534. Sealing the break with Rome, these included the Act of Supremacy, the Act of Succession, the Ecclesiastical Appointments Act, the Treasons Act and the Statute in Restraint of Appeals. These laws served to affirm that the authority of Parliament and the King was superior to that of the Pope. All of the acts carried severe punishments, no matter who the perpetrator. Sir Thomas More, the previous Lord Chancellor, refused to acknowledge the religious authority of Parliament and was beheaded in 1535.

Anne Boleyn did her best to produce a male heir for Henry, but all her efforts failed. She "took to her chamber" three months after becoming queen but the long-anticipated baby born on September 7 was another girl, Elizabeth, destined to become queen. In the next two years, Anne became pregnant two more times but the babies were either miscarried or stillborn. With that, Anne's fate was sealed. Cromwell orchestrated a series of arrests of six men (including her own brother) and the queen herself, charged with adultery, incest and plotting to murder the king. All except one were found to be guilty and sentenced to the standard punishments, one of which was to be hanged, then cut down while still alive, and then disemboweled and quartered. Due to Henry's leniency, all six were merely beheaded.

Within days of Anne's execution, Henry married Jane Seymour, previously the queen's lady-in-waiting. Jane never had a coronation, but Edward, the son she had in 1537, became next in line for the crown. Henry's daughters, Mary and Elizabeth, were both declared illegitimate and therefore excluded by the Act of Succession. Jane died two weeks after giving birth but was the only one of Henry's six wives to be mourned by him, and she was the only one buried with him at Windsor Castle.

Suppression of Roman Catholics in northern England led to rebellion, and their leaders were executed in 1537. This also included the destruction of Catholic shrines and monasteries and Catholic property was transferred to the crown. Their representation in Parliament was also reduced and Thomas Cromwell was rewarded handsomely for effectuating these actions.

Because Prince Edward was a sickly child, Henry decided to marry again to assure himself of a male successor. Cromwell convinced him a foreign alliance could be helpful so a search began for a prospective bride in some of the other countries. Painters were assigned to paint likenesses of the leading candidates and on that basis, Anne of Cleves was chosen. The picture was too flattering, however, and Henry was quite disappointed when he saw her in person. The wedding went ahead in January 1540 but by mutual agreement was annulled in July. For his part in arranging the whole affair, Cromwell was convicted of treason and beheaded.

On the same day that Cromwell was beheaded, Henry married Kathryn Howard, lady to the queen, and the young cousin of Anne Boleyn. Henry by this time was forty-nine and his new bride was nineteen. She was vivacious and lifted the spirits of the aging king but she may have indiscreetly lifted her skirts, as well. Archbishop Cranmer brought evidence of Kathryn's dalliance with two different men and in December 1541 both were executed. The marriage was annulled, with no issue, and Kathryn was beheaded on February 13, 1542, about one and a half years after her wedding.

Henry's last wife was a wealthy widow, Katherine Parr, and they were married in July, 1543. She was a strong Protestant but smart enough not to be too vocal about it, as Henry remained a Catholic. She was solicitous about Henry's health and helped reconcile him with his two daughters. She also concerned herself with the education of Elizabeth and Edward, and got the best tutors for them. Henry died on January 28, 1547 and Katherine outlived him by about one and a half years.

Upon Henry's death, his son Edward VI became king (1547–53) at the age of nine. Edward was England's first Protestant ruler, but real authority was in the hands of a regency council that Henry had established in his will. Jane Seymour's older brother Edward was chosen as Lord Protector until overthrown and executed for treason by the Duke of Northumberland. Northumberland prevailed upon the sick, sixteen-year old Edward to make a will on his deathbed that named Lady Jane Grey, the Duke's daughter-in-law, as his successor.

Thus, Lady Jane was made Queen on July 10, 1553, only two weeks after her wedding. This had the effect of keeping the crown in the hands of Protestants but it also contravened the will of Henry. With this justification, Mary Tudor had reason to rally her troops, depose Lady Jane, her granddaughter, and then take the crown for herself. So after a reign of only nine days, Jane was imprisoned in the Tower of London and Northumberland was beheaded. On February 12, 1554 Lady Jane was also beheaded at the age of sixteen, together with her young husband. [Lady Jane could certainly be named a leading member of the "Life is not fair" club.]

Mary I (1553–58) became Queen at the age of thirty-seven. She was stubborn and courageous, but also bigoted and intolerant. She immediately began restoring Catholicism and the authority of the pope in England. Old heresy laws were revived and about 300 people were burned at the stake, including Thomas Cranmer, Archbishop of Canterbury and the giant of Anglican theology in England. Many people fled the country and "Bloody Mary" was widely hated. Mary and Philip II of Spain were married in 1554, but they had no children and she died in 1558.

No doubt Mary Tudor would have welcomed more help from a new order, the Society of Jesus, or Jesuits. By 1556, over 1500 Jesuits were diligently working in most European countries other than England. The order originated from the efforts of Ignatius of Loyola (1491–1556) a Spanish nobleman. After he was wounded he gave up the life of a soldier and organized a group of men wholly dedicated to serving the Church. The Jesuits became an elite group at the disposal of the pope, serving with absolute, unquestioning obedience. Their purpose was to fight the Protestant Reformation, strengthen the Church through education, and do missionary work overseas. Their schools became famous for the high-quality education they provided. Francis Xavier (1506–52) became the most-admired Jesuit missionary for his courageous service in the Far East.

When Queen Elizabeth I (1558–1603) took the throne, she began a long process of reinstating the Anglican Church and a moderate form of Protestantism. In addition to finding a balance between the Catholics and Calvinists, she faced the threat of civil war and the hostility of France and Spain (the Spanish Armada appeared on her watch). As Elizabeth did not marry, and had no heir, a succession crisis appeared likely.

According to Henry VIII's will, Lady Anne Stanley should have been named but James VI, King of the Scots, won out. James was to be the successor, according to his cousin Elizabeth, and just as importantly he had an army to back him up. James (1566–1625) was the son of the Catholic Mary, Queen of Scots, and Henry Stewart, Lord Darnley. In 1567, Darnley was killed and James' mother was forced to abdicate. After being imprisoned for nineteen years, she was beheaded in 1587.

James became king at the age of thirteen months, so Scotland was ruled by regency until he reached his majority. As King James VI (1567–1625), James ruled Scotland for fifty-eight years and as King James I (1603–1625) ruled England for twenty-two years. This dual position helped only slightly in bridging the gap of distrust and suspicion that separated the Scottish and English. He had only grudging acceptance in English society and never did have a very good relationship with Parliament. Guy Fawkes and four other (Jesuit?) conspirators were caught while attempting to blow up the House of Lords on November 5, 1605 the day James was scheduled to open the session. The miscreants were executed but the Gunpowder Plot stirred up a fresh wave of anti-Catholic sentiment in England. In trying to improve relationships with Spain, James acceded to their demands and allowed the execution of Sir Walter Raleigh. James was accused of homosexual relationships with several men but that charge seems doubtful in view of the nine children he had with his wife, Queen Anne, who he loved dearly.

James was sickly but loved hunting, was witty, well read, enjoyed learning and was fluent in Greek, Latin, and French, plus English and Scots. He was a Protestant and commissioned the compilation of the King James Bible, completed in 1611, and bitterly opposed by the Catholics. There is no doubt that the policies of both Elizabeth I and James I allowed several Protestant denominations to develop and prosper during their reigns. The first Protestant settlements in America were chartered under James. Jamestown, Virginia was founded in 1607 as an Anglican colony.

Puritans

The Puritans originated in 1570, led by T. Cartwright. They left the Church of England, hoping to reform or "purify" it of Catholic traits—hence their name. They were intensely concerned with a disciplined study of the Bible, preaching God's word of conviction and righteousness, good works, sound doctrine and reverent worship service. Daily work by individuals was encouraged and a belief in hard, honest work, thrift and sobriety became known as the Protestant work ethic.

The Puritans refused to follow the Anglican Act of Uniformity, i.e., wear the vestments, use the prayer book, kneel at Mass, the sign of the cross, etc. They followed the Calvinist or Presbyterian approach instead of Anglican/Episcopalian. Because of this, they suffered persecution ranging from prison to burning at the stake. The persecution drove many of them to leave England as Pilgrims, and one of these groups on the *Mayflower* landed at Plymouth Rock, Massachusetts in 1620. Nine years later, a group of Puritans established the Massachusetts Bay Colony.

Puritans in England favored local authority as opposed to the state-supported Anglican Church. They believed each congregation should be separate, independent and autonomous—a complete church in itself. This anti-establishment attitude tended to encourage openness to new ideas, including science. Science courses were included in the curricula of Puritan schools so it is not surprising that in the Royal Society, founded in 1660, seven out of ten members were Puritans. The Royal Society is the foremost organization of its kind, and serves as the British equivalent of the National Academy of Sciences. Some of its famous members include Robert Boyle, Charles Darwin, Sir Humphry Davy, Robert Hooke, Thomas Henry Huxley, Lord Kelvin, Sir Isaac Newton and Lord Rutherford.

With their strict religious beliefs, strong family ties, and work ethic, the Puritans became an important force in building the cultural framework of New England. But some people chafed under the strait-laced style of living and as early as 1636, Roger Williams left Massachusetts and established the colony of Rhode Island. In thanks to God, he named his settlement Providence and saw to it that settlers of all religious persuasions were welcome.

The Puritans also took considerable heat for contributing to the climate of suspicion and superstition that existed at the time of the Salem witch trials. During the 1600s, about 100 people were hanged as witches throughout New England. The hysteria culminated, and ended, in Salem in 1692. During that year, 185 people were arrested in the vicinity of Salem, fifty-four were put in prison, thirty-one were convicted and twenty-four died, nineteen by hanging. Two dogs were also executed as accomplices. The victims were mostly women, usually old and poor, but the suspects also included some wealthy widows and important people such as the two sons of a former governor, and Captain John Alden, the son of the legendary John and Priscilla, of Plymouth Colony. Increase Mather, the father of Cotton Mather, permanently ended the regrettable witchcraft episode with his sermon in which he famously said "It were better that ten suspected witches should escape, than that one innocent person should be condemned." Consider the contrast between these words of Mather with those of the Holy Office during the Inquisition: "better for a hundred innocent people to die than for one heretic to go free" (Peter De Rosa, *Vicars of Christ*, 163).

Congregational

This church was first formed by R. Brown in Holland in 1582 after leaving the Church of England. Early members in America founded Harvard University in 1636 and the American Congregational Church originated in 1648 when a group of Pilgrims and Puritans joined forces with their *Cambridge Platform* agreement. The U.S. combined membership today, for the Congregational/United Church of Christ is 1.9 million.

Presbyterian

In his younger days, John Knox (1505–72) was captured by the French and forced to serve as a galley slave. Back in Scotland, he led the reformation after working under Calvin in Geneva. His dissatisfaction with the Church of England led to a "Separatist" approach, basically Calvinistic but with not so much emphasis on the concept of predestination. Knox founded the Scotch Presbyterian Church in 1560 when he and five others drew up the Scottish Confession of Faith. Basic beliefs include the Trinity, the Nicene Creed, the Apostle's Creed, infant baptism, the Eucharist at certain times, election of presbyters, and simple and dignified services with a central sermon. The faith is called "Presbyterian" because elders, or presbyters, govern the activities of the church. Administrative aides are called deacons. The governing synod or presbytery is subject to the civil authorities. The Presbyterian Church was given full legal status after Queen Mary was deposed in 1567. Presbyterians from England settled in Maryland in 1683, and today there are 7.9 million Presbyterians in America, and 44 million in the world. One of the strongest churches is in South Korea, where there are more than 3 million members

Episcopalian

The American church was founded in 1620 by Samuel Seabury as part of the Anglican Communion. It was called Episcopal, for "bishop," because it was organized like the Church of England. It became independent from its English parent in 1789, but held the Archbishop of Canterbury in an honorary position. Presbyters or priests, deacons, and laypersons are subsidiary to the presiding bishop, but have an active voice in church affairs. Local congregations pick their own rectors, if approved by the bishop. Their biblical view of God is stated in the thirty-nine Articles of the Episcopal Faith: "There is but one living and true God, everlasting, without body parts, or passions; of infinite power, wisdom, and goodness; the Maker and Preserver of all things both visible and invisible."

Because the Episcopal Church was the state church of Virginia prior to the Revolutionary War, most of the early presidents were of that faith when they took office. Eleven presidents have been Episcopalians including Washington, Jefferson, Madison, Monroe, Tyler, Taylor, Pierce, Arthur, F.D. Roosevelt, Ford, and G.W. Bush. Washington, Jefferson, Madison, and Monroe also had strong Deist beliefs, as did Lincoln. Today there are 4.9 million Episcopalians in the U.S.

Quaker

An English shoemaker, George Fox, founded the "Society of Friends" in 1654. This unusual Protestant denomination became known as the "Quakers" because they shook and trembled "at the name of the Lord" in a meeting of "Friends." They felt a true believer was moved by the "indwelling Spirit and life of Christ." For this reason, the Spirit revealed the true meaning of the Scriptures, and all men were considered equal before this inner light. Women were very active in the movement and would often lead the meetings.

Because they did not believe in having clergymen, pulpits or songs, meetings were mostly silent, waiting for someone to be moved by the Spirit. If moved, the Friend would stand up and give the message, then the meeting would lapse back into silence. They rejected the concept of a Holy

Trinity, the paying of tithes to the state church, and most civil authorities and their laws. On top of that, they had their own distinctive style of clothing to purposely separate themselves from the worldly values of man. Being different and unusual made for an uneasy relationship with the governing authorities who had their own concerns.

At about this same time Oliver Cromwell (1599–1658) was ruling England as "Lord Protector" with most of the powers of a king (a title he was offered but rejected). Cromwell came to power first as a Member of Parliament (MP) in 1628, with strong Puritan convictions, then as a military leader. As one of the leaders of the Parliamentary forces, or "Roundheads," his first military action was in 1642. By the time of his last battle in 1646 he had been made Lieutenant General of Horse and was considered the greatest soldier in England. Even though he had no military training, his skill inspired his troops to great victories, using prayer for moral strength and singing hymns as they charged the enemy. After King Charles I was beheaded in 1649, Cromwell invaded Ireland where he crushed the Royalists and Irish Catholics. The infamous massacres at Drogheda and Wexford occurred during this campaign. In 1650–51, Cromwell was called upon to put down Charles II who was proclaimed King of Scots. During the eleven years of the Interregnum (between kings), a number of unsatisfactory Parliamentary governments were formed and then dissolved. Cromwell was "Lord Protector" from 1653 to 1658 when he died. The Restoration of the Stuart monarchy came soon thereafter, in 1660.

The first Quaker settlement in America was in New York in 1657. After the Restoration, the Quakers wisely became more moderate in their actions and public statements. With this new look, as seen by the Crown, William Penn won Letters of Patent to establish a Quaker colony in Pennsylvania in 1682. Although they have been noted for their pacifism, Nathaniel Greene was a Quaker (expelled for his militarism) who came to be the best American general (after Washington) in the Revolutionary War. His background was quite similar to that of Cromwell. He was very religious, first a politician, without any military background or training, but with the skill and judgment to organize his forces and win strategic victories. Two American presidents have been Quakers (Hoover and Nixon). Total membership is only about 180,000, but Quakers were actively involved in anti-slavery, women's rights, and civil rights movements, and have always been noted for their relief work in times of war or disasters.

Methodist

The movement began with a small group of students at Oxford, including Charles Wesley, who met regularly for the purpose of self-improvement through Bible study and keeping personal standards of proper behavior. Other students derisively gave them the nickname of "Methodists" because of their methodical approach to scriptures and Christian living. Their outreach activities included visits to poor, sick people, and prisoners.

Some years later, in 1738, Charles' brother, John Wesley, had a dynamic conversion when his heart was "strangely warmed" and he began a life of active evangelization. The Methodist Church was founded in England in 1744, by John and Charles Wesley. Like all Protestants, they rejected the authority of the pope but were also disappointed by failure of the Church of England to respond to the daily problems of the weak, poor, sick, and dispossessed. The Methodists became known as the "social conscience" of England, working to abolish slavery, protect women and children, improve worker's rights, and help establish schools, orphanages, hospitals, homes for old folks, and services for the homeless and unemployed.

Enthusiastic sermons are an earmark of the Methodists, together with congregational singing of hymns. Charles Wesley himself wrote 7000 hymns and poems. And John Wesley was an astonishing minister. He preached 42,000 sermons and traveled on horseback almost 300,000 miles. At the age of eighty-seven he preached three times a day, in different places. Despite this, John Wesley never ceased to be a priest of the Church of England, and died an Anglican.

Methodists follow the traditional belief in the Trinity, Baptism and Communion. They have a base in Calvinism but reject the idea of predestination, and believe that salvation is possible for every man and woman of true faith. Works and service are important, love of God and neighbor are linked; charitable work and alleviating suffering are to be encouraged. The goal is justice and freedom for all peoples in the world. The Methodist approach contributed to the successful results of the Protestant work ethic, and perhaps with a little more happy enjoyment than that of the Puritans. Methodists were early proponents of a free and democratic U.S. in the days leading up to the War of Independence,

After the Revolutionary War, the Church of England, in its petulance, cut off American members. This led to further estrangement and an American Methodist Church was chartered in 1784. Circuit riders traveled by horseback to preach the gospel and establish churches. The slavery issue led in 1845 to a split and northern and southern Methodist branches were not reunited until 1939. But the Church of England and the Methodist Church did not sign a covenant of cooperation until 2003. Today there are 29 million Methodists worldwide, and one of the strongest churches is in South Korea. There are 20 million Methodists in the U.S. the highest concentration being in states of the Midwest and Ohio Valley.

[Although I was raised as a Methodist, my older brother reminded me that we might not be alive except for the Lutherans. Our paternal grandfather was a Lutheran, and he was saved one day in 1881 because he had left home to work on their new church. When he returned home that night he found that his one-room shanty had been struck by lightning. The stovepipe was on the floor and soot covered everything. The gold on a picture frame was melted off and saws hanging on the wall were made so hard a file could not touch them after that. Grandfather said he would have been killed if he had been home. This all happened at his homestead near Grass Lake, SD, after living for two years in his first shelter, a sod hut.]

Unitarian

Unitarianism rejected the idea of a sacred Trinity in favor of a single God. The divinity of Christ and the Holy Spirit were thereby questioned and the movement was quite similar in many ways to Deism (p. 75-77?). The new teaching sprang from radical elements early in the life of the Reformation, and alarmed both Protestants and Catholics. Michael Servetus was an early martyr, burned at the stake by Calvin in 1553. The first Unitarian strongholds were in Eastern Europe but suffered periodic suppression and persecution. Theophilus Lindsay left the Church of England and opened the first Unitarian church in London in 1774. Dr. Joseph Priestley was a distinguished scholar, chemist and early Unitarian minister. Because of his support for the French Revolution, a mob in Birmingham trashed his house and he emigrated to the U.S. in 1794. The famous school of divinity at Harvard University was founded in 1816 and became the center of Unitarian thought. Ralph Waldo Emerson was a convert, but the most prestigious of all was Thomas Jefferson. Jefferson often attended Priestley's church when he was able, but never formally joined the Unitarians because there was no church in his vicinity. He so stated in a letter to Dr. Benjamin Waterhouse (January 8, 1825) "the population of my neighborhood is too slender...to maintain any one minister...I must therefore be contented to be a Unitarian by myself..."

Jefferson was also considered to be a Deist, and on paper was an Episcopalian vestryman, but his beliefs were Unitarian and exemplified in his

"Jefferson Bible." In it he tried to show that the moral and ethical structure established by Jesus was sound. As he wrote to William Canby (September 18, 1813) "Of all the systems of morality, ancient or modern, which have come under my observation, none appears to me so pure as that of Jesus." And in a letter to Rev. Jared Sparks "The religion of Jesus is founded in the Unity of God."

In personal correspondence with his contemporaries, Jefferson freely criticized certain themes in the Bible, and in his own "bible" omitted parts of the New Testament with which he disagreed. Some of his strongest negative feelings were expressed (privately) against the priest class; Calvinist and Presbyterian clergy; the concept of the Trinity and Paul's emphasis on the Holy Spirit; miracles concerning Christ's life and death; elitist attitudes that opposed equal rights and impartial justice for the common man; and coercion in support of religion (which he said had made "one half the world fools, and the other half hypocrites"). In his research he recognized that Jesus rarely talked about "Spirit" and never as if a third person was involved.

Unitarians argue that the concept of the Trinity does not appear in the Old Testament, where the "holy spirit" was understood to mean the power or presence of God. The Hebrew word for "spirit" (ruach) can refer to angels or evil spirits (Muslims called these same angels *jinn*). When Jesus, on the cross, said "Father into thy hands I commend my spirit" it is clear he was not referring to a third person. Unitarians conclude that Paul's fixation on a "Holy Spirit" as a third person of the Trinity is a man-made myth and as Jefferson noted, the cause of thousands of human deaths. They also note that Paul admonished "Wives should always put their husbands first" (Eph 5:24) and "Slaves, you must obey your earthly masters" (Eph 6:5)—passages pretty much discredited today.

These ideas, and distrust of organized religions, probably played an important role in Jefferson's unbending position on religious freedom. He strongly supported the Establishment Clause as part of James Madison's first amendment to the Constitution, stating that Congress should "make no law respecting an establishment of religion, or prohibiting the free exercise thereof." On the other hand, the Establishment Clause was written to prevent selection of a state religion, not to prevent national respect for and belief in a Creator. Jefferson's priorities were evident in his choice of his own epitaph which did not even mention his presidency but cited his authorship of the Declaration of Independence, the 1786 religious freedom statute for the state of Virginia, and creating the University of Virginia.

As a president, Jefferson was recognized as one of the most intelligent—a scholar, scientist, philosopher, and statesman. In the latter capacity he was responsible for the Louisiana Purchase and the follow-up expedition by Lewis and Clark. Atheists love to quote him because of his criticisms of conventional religions, but he was a Christian—on his own terms. Four other presidents were Unitarians, and he may have influenced both the Adams in that regard.

Literature of today's "Unitarian Universalists" seems to embrace a very diverse set of opinions on the existence of God, the origin of the universe and life, salvation, and the concept of an afterlife. Individuals may believe whatever they want, little direction is given, and the number of members in the movement is hard to pin down.

Church of Jesus Christ of Latter Day Saints (LDS)

[Members are commonly called "Mormons" because their Book of Mormon is an important addition to the Bible. This religion had a very unusual beginning and early history, but has overcome a number of obstacles and is quite successful today. Mormons we have known personally have been exceptionally good people, faithful to their beliefs, and exemplary citizens. Dr. Wes Gardner, an old friend and a Mormon, has helped with references and review of this section.]

Joseph Smith (1805–1844) as a young farm boy in western New York was concerned with the contradictions between Christian churches at the time. In the spring of 1820, he received a vision of God and his son Jesus who advised Smith to avoid any of the churches. In 1823, he was visited by the angel Maroni, the son of an ancient prophet named Mormon.

Mormon had abridged messages of ancient peoples of the Americas, and inscribed the messages on gold plates. In 1827, Maroni led Joseph Smith to a hill (a glacial esker) near Palmyra where Smith dug up the buried plates. Later in 1827, Smith began translating the words on the plates using an "Urim and Thummin" device, a special breastplate with attached lenses which functioned as spectacles. His wife, Emma, and Martin Harris served as the first scribes but the bulk of the writing was done by a schoolteacher, Oliver Cowdry. After two and a half years they had transcribed 275,000 words, and the Book of Mormon was complete. [To appreciate the magnitude of this accomplishment, consider that the New Testament contains only 181,253 words. Furthermore, the Book of Mormon appears to be a very scholarly piece of work. How could this be done by a person like Joseph Smith, whose formal education was quite limited?]

Several trusted witnesses were asked to examine the golden plates and sign statements that affirmed that fact. Later, Joseph announced that he had returned the plates to the angel who had first directed him, and Maroni took the plates away.

In 1830, after publishing the Book of Mormon, Joseph Smith founded the Church of Jesus Christ of Latter-day Saints (LDS), or Mormons. The *Book of Mormon* deals with the ancient inhabitants of the Americas, including the personal ministry of Jesus Christ. It describes how Jaredites, scattered from the Tower of Babel, settled on the east coast of Central America in 2250 B.C. They died out, but the lost tribes of Israelites came to America, by boat, in about 600 B.C. American Indians are descendents of the lost tribes. Jesus visited soon after his resurrection, but before his ascension.

In addition to the *Book of Mormon*, Joseph Smith wrote other revelations during the period 1823–1844 and these make up most of the "Doctrine and Covenants" of the Mormon Church. Other important Smith writings and extracts were first compiled in 1851 in *The Pearl of Great Price* which now includes the Books of Abraham and Moses. Together with the Bible, these comprise the four Mormon sacred books.

Joseph Smith was a charismatic, likeable personality, with a powerful presence. His church had strong early growth and by 1831 a successful Church was established in Kirtland, Ohio. However, because of their unusual beliefs, the LDS continually had trouble with their neighbors and Joseph was tarred and feathered by a mob in 1832. In 1838, the Mormons moved to Missouri where they were forced to flee, successively, settlements in Independence, Jackson county, Clay County and Far West. Later that year, the Missouri governor issued an "extermination order" that called for driving the Mormons out of the state. Three days after this order was issued, 200 armed men killed seventeen and wounded fifteen Mormon men and boys at Haun's Mill. This event, plus other forms of persecution, caused over 8000 Mormons to leave Missouri and cross the Mississippi into Illinois.

Meanwhile, Smith and five friends were imprisoned during the winter in Liberty, Missouri in a jail cell too constricted to stand upright, and the floor was cold, hard ground with a scattering of straw. After six months of this harsh imprisonment the group was helped to "escape" so authorities would not have to deal with the matters of illegality and lack of evidence. Smith and his friends then made their way to Quincy, Illinois where they were welcomed by the people there.

In time, the new Mormon city of Nauvoo was built thirty-five miles to the north, on the east bank of the Mississippi. The city prospered for five years and in 1845 had 11,000 residents, making it one of the largest cities in Illinois. During these years, some of the writings and translations of Joseph Smith were published which later, in 1851, were compiled into *The Pearl of Great Price*. But Joseph Smith and his brother, Hyrum, were killed by a mob while jailed in Carthage, Illinois. Smith was only thirty-eight when he died in 1844.

After 200 Mormon buildings were burned by hostile neighbors in 1845, LDS leaders decided another move was necessary. The goal was the Great Salt Lake valley, a place where they could settle permanently and practice their religion in peace. The first wagons left Nauvoo in February 1846, led by Brigham Young who succeeded Joseph Smith as leader of the Mormon Church. After struggling through Iowa mud, the wagons reached the vicinity of present-day Council Bluffs, and Omaha, on the other side of the Missouri River. Within two years, 30,000 Mormon pioneers reached or passed through the area and in the process, established eighty communities in southwest Iowa. They organized churches, schools, local governments, musical concerts and four newspapers.

From the Council Bluffs/Omaha area, the first caravan of 148 people left in the spring of 1847, and reached Salt Lake on July 24, almost four months later. The 1400-mile route was along the Platte and North Platte Rivers, past Casper, Wyoming and across the continental divide at South Pass. During the next twenty years, about 70,000 Mormons made the trip in covered wagons but also used handcarts quite extensively. Handcarts were pulled by men, not horses, and were fairly successful except for two groups caught in early winter storms. In summary, the Mormons conducted the best-organized mass migration in American history, and established thriving communities in an area many people considered to be worthless desert. July 24 is celebrated in Utah, in commemoration of the day in 1847 when the Mormon pioneers finally reached the Salt Lake valley.

It was also during this time that polygamy was practiced by some members of the Mormon Church. It was explained that, in those cases where a man's family was left in serious difficulty when he died, it became necessary for other, capable and responsible men, to take in the bereaved family as part of his own household. The practice was not renounced by the Church until 1890, twenty-eight years after President Lincoln had signed the Anti-Polygamy Act.

The "Thirteen Articles of Faith" were first listed by Joseph Smith in 1841. Some of the key statements can be summarized as follows:

- Belief in God, his son Jesus Christ, and in the Holy Ghost.
- Man will be punished for his own sins, not those of Adam.
- All mankind may be saved, because of Christ's sacrifice.
- Both the Bible and Book of Mormon are the word of God.
- The ten tribes of Israel will be restored, and Zion will be built on the American continent.
- Christ will reign personally on Earth.
- All men should have the right to worship God in their own way.
- All men are subject to their secular rulers and should obey the law.
- Belief in being honest, virtuous, benevolent, praiseworthy, chaste, and seeking after all good things.
- Because each president of the Mormon Church is considered to be a prophet, continuous revelation is possible. (An example of a recent revelation is elimination in 1978 of the last discrimination against African-Americans.)
- Abortion and homosexuality are wrong and homosexual marriage is opposed.
- Mormon ancestors may be saved by proxy ordinances such as baptism, confirmation, marriage, etc. The spirits of Mormon dead may accept or reject this procedure. Millions of ancestors have been saved in this way, and to expedite the process the world's largest computerized Geneaology Database has been established in Salt Lake City. It is available to everyone, at no charge.
- The family unit is emphasized as vital to the individual and society. One day of each week is set aside as "Family Home Evening" with various activities aimed at unifying the family. Youth are kept active in wholesome activities to become healthy, respectful and productive citizens. They are taught to love and revere their country, parents, teachers, Jesus and a loving Father in Heaven.
- Abstinence from alcohol, drugs, caffeine and tobacco is an admirable hallmark, often remarked upon by non-Mormons.

- The Mormon Tabernacle Choir in Salt Lake City, plus BYU (Brigham Young University) in Provo, UT are institutions of special pride to Mormons.

Mormons consider religious faith to be an important part of their life. Support is strong for the nearly 62,000 full-time missionaries, easily recognizable as pairs of clean-cut young men out in rain or shine, proclaiming their beliefs. When these missionaries knock on doors, making cold calls, they are generally rejected. Nevertheless, their dedication does not go unrewarded and the Mormon Church is one of the fastest-growing denominations. From the Internet, LDS FAQ's show worldwide membership in 2002 was over 11.7 million, including children. The 2001 totals included 5.2 million in the U.S., 2.5 million in South America and 1.5 million in Mexico and the general Caribbean area.

Pentecostal

As described in Acts 2, this movement originated on the seventh Sunday (Pentecost) after the Resurrection (Easter), when some astonishing things happened. The day started with a large gathering of some of the first Christians in a building in Jerusalem. Soon there was a display of unusual atmospheric activity including wind, thunder and lightning. A visit by the Holy Ghost inspired men to praise God in several different languages (other tongues). Then Peter reminded the crowd that the prophet Joel had foreseen that in the last days, sons, daughters, and servants would prophesy. Peter exhorted the large crowd to realize the significance of the Resurrection, saying "This Jesus hath God raised up, whereof we all are witnesses" (Acts 2:32). In response, about 3000 people were baptized that day. (p. 168?).

Fee has described the parts that tongues and prophesy played in Paul's first-century congregations. Speaking in tongues (glossolalia) was directed toward God. It was a Spirit-inspired utterance, unintelligible to both the speaker and other listeners. Hence, an interpreter was required to relay the message to the audience. In 1 Corinthians, Paul talked of "different kinds of tongues" and in 13:1 implied it was "the tongues of angels." Paul also made clear in Chapter 14 that he preferred prophesying to the Corinthian's obsession with speaking in tongues; prophesy was given in understandable language, whereas tongues needed to be interpreted (and sometimes the interpretation was questionable).

Prophesy was considered to be divinely inspired by the Spirit of God. It was done for the edification, encouragement and comfort of the assembled believers. Women were full participants in the worship in Paul's churches, and they shared in prophesying (a surprise, considering Paul's roots as a Jewish rabbi). After the first century, the Pentecostal approach had little theological attention until a revival in the late nineteenth century.

In recent years, the movement has gained enormous strength and has been called a "restructuring of Christianity." In the 1700-page, 2001 edition of the *World Christian Encyclopedia*, authors David B. Barrett and Todd M. Johnson estimate the Pentecostal/Charismatic religions encompass 524 million believers. This exceeds the total Protestant and Anglican churches combined, and is more than half the size of the Roman Catholic Church. Over 80 percent of Pentecostals are in third world countries, especially Africa, South America and Asia, and members tend to be poor, dispossessed, working-class, sometimes illiterate, and have many women leaders. The Pentecostal churches are "independent" with no formal ties to Catholic or Protestant organizations, and are growing at the rate of nineteen million members per year. The single largest church in the world is a Pentecostal church with 780,000 members, in South Korea.

Professor Elaine J. Lawless at the University of Missouri has written some very helpful material (available on the Internet) concerning the rise of Pentecostalism and its special language. She points out that the nineteenth century Holiness movement was born when some disenchanted Methodists felt the need for a return to sanctification or holiness. Following a Holiness camp meeting in 1867, other meetings stressed John Wesley's original admonition against alcohol, dancing, swearing, card-playing, theater-going, etc. Additional prohibitions, in time, came to include Coca Cola, chewing gum, cigarettes, ball games, rings, bracelets, earrings and neckties, i.e., all signs of "worldliness." Revival meetings would elicit the emotional fervor of earlier Methodist revivals where individuals would "shout, scream, speak in tongues, fall into trances, and even get the jerks."

In 1901, Charles F. Parham (1873–1929) at Bethel College in Topeka, led a group of students to the realization that the Book of Acts described speaking in tongues as evidence of the Holy Ghost. Acts 2:1–4 was especially cogent concerning the outpouring of the Holy Spirit upon 120 believers in the Upper Room, during Pentecost—hence, the name. The single most important factor was that speaking in tongues was proof of the possession of the Holy Ghost. The Pentecostals became "almost rabid in their assertion that glossolalia always accompanies an 'infilling of the Holy

Ghost." Initially, congregations were interracial but after 1924 split along racial lines. When the fervor of the "Pentecostal experience" was taken up by the black community, the somewhat negative press referred to them as "Holy Rollers." The closely related Charismatic movement began to flourish in the late 1950s. In 1998, the major white and black branches of the Pentecostal Church were reunified in a meeting known as the "Memphis Miracle." International Pentecostal leadership is largely in the U.S. but the overwhelming bulk of membership is in third-world countries, in about 11,000 different churches.

Pentecostal converts are expected to immediately and fully participate in church services including various uninhibited behaviors such as crying, singing, shouting, spiritual dancing, praying, and of course, speaking in tongues. Such behavior is believed to be supranormal and uncontrollable by the individual. Pentecostals call each other Brother and Sister and are saints, in contrast to sinners who are all those who are non-Pentecostals.

Sinners can become saints by first admitting their sins before the church congregation, then waiting (tarrying) at the altar, on bended knee, for the Holy Ghost to descend on them. This requires a trance-like state, including closed eyes, tears, raised arms, in fact, losing all inhibitions. Success is manifested by speaking in tongues, and may take minutes, hours, or years. Baptism is then possible, first with water, then with the Spirit. One ongoing duty is testifying verbally at church services; this means standing in the pew and giving an extemporaneous account of faith in God or receipt of God's goodness.

Pentecostals generally believe in God as three divine persons in one divine essence, the Bible as the infallible word of God, the virgin birth, the bodily Resurrection, the miracles and ascension of Jesus, and immersion baptism (only after the age of reason). The bread and wine of the Lord's Supper are only symbolic and the "wine" is non-alcoholic. Miracle healing is an "integral part of the Gospel." Pentecostals believes the end time of rapture is imminent, when Jesus returns to Earth to claim his saints, and all persons are held accountable for their lives and deeds.

Charismatics, faith-healing evangelists, schismatic offshoots and some wholly indigenous sects are all counted under the Pentecostal umbrella, although most of these groups do not adhere to the "tongues" requirement. The main denominations in the U.S. include the Church of God in Christ, Assemblies of God, Church of God, Pentecostal Assemblies of the World, and Four Square Gospel Church. In this group, some of the notable members include Gordon Fee, Oral Roberts, Pat Robertson, Jimmy Swaggart,

Jim Bakker, John Ashcroft, Al Sharpton, Jerry Lee Lewis, Dolly Parton, Elvis Presley and Denzel Washington.

Vatican I and II

Ecumenical councils of the Church have been held periodically, at different locations, to clarify religious doctrines. The forerunner was held in Jerusalem in about A.D. 49 (p. 138) and described in Acts 15. The First Vatican Council was the twentieth ecumenical; it was held in Rome in 1869–70, but was cut short by the Franco-Prussian War. As a result, Vatican I only had time to affirm the doctrine of papal infallibility. This doctrine holds that the pope, when he speaks *ex cathedra* (i.e., in his official position) on matters of faith and morals, is infallible. Definitive pronouncements of an ecumenical council are also held to be infallible when ratified by the pope.

Vatican I was, to some extent, a belated response to elements of the French Revolution, some seventy years prior. The French Revolution, over the period 1789–1799 was a turning point in European history and forced radical restructuring on the Roman Catholic Church. It marked the end of the *ancien régime*, the loss of power by the First Estate (the church) and the Second Estate (the nobility), and the assumption of governing power by the Third Estate (the citizenry).

Direct causes of the revolution included a resentment of royal, noble, and clerical privilege, unfair taxation, outdated feudalism, and a food shortage at the time. Important contributing factors were the Enlightenment and the American Revolution. Voltaire (1694–1778) was the preeminent leader of the Enlightenment and strongly promoted ideas of democracy, religious toleration, and intellectual freedom. His enemy Rousseau (1712–1778) had many of the same ideas but his extremism leaned more to socialism and communism.

With popular support, the "Third Estate" declared themselves the National Assembly on June 17, 1789. Their first act was to pass the Declaration of the Rights of Man, a statement of principles modeled after the American Declaration of Independence. On July 9 the assembly became the National Constituent Assembly and five days later the Bastille prison was seized, as a demonstration against the hated *ancien régime*. The governor of the prison, the mayor, and a few guards were killed, but only seven prisoners were freed—four forgers, two lunatics and a dangerous sex offender. On August 4, the National Assembly abolished feudalism and special privileges of the First and Second Estates. In 1790, legislation abolished the Church's right to levy certain taxes, and confiscated Church property. Up to that time, the Church had been the largest landowner in France. In following years, priests were killed and imprisoned throughout the country. Remaining clergy were made employees of the state, and were required to take an oath of loyalty to the constitution.

In 1792, war with Austria and Prussia was underway, in part supported by *émigrés* (fleeing nobles). King Louis XVI was accused of conspiracy with the enemies of France and paid the price, by execution on January 17, 1793. His queen, Marie Antoinette, was also beheaded in October of the same year. As the war went badly, and domestic affairs were unsettled, control was seized by the radical Jacobins who were supported by mob power. The Committee of Public Safety, led by Robespierre, unleashed the Reign of Terror (1793–94) and at least 1200 people met their deaths under the guillotine. An example of the terror was the May 8, 1794 execution of Lavoisier, one of the world's greatest chemists, and twenty-seven of his associates. They were tried, convicted and beheaded all on the same day. However, revulsion about excesses of the Committee led to violent reaction against it, and Robespierre himself was beheaded later in 1794 together with several of the other leaders.

In addition to Austria and Prussia, France was soon fighting against England and Italy. A young French officer, Napoleon Bonaparte (1769–1821) won some spectacular victories and returned to France as a hero. A *coup d'etat* led to his takeover of the government at the age of thirty, effectively ending the French Revolution. On land, Napoleon's armies were at first invincible but the British navy was superior, especially as led by Lord Horatio Nelson at the Battles of the Nile in 1798 and Trafalgar in 1805. Before becoming a megalomaniac and leading France into some military disasters, Napoleon introduced several worthwhile reforms. The Concordat of 1801 established a stable relationship with the Catholic Church that lasted for over 100 years. The Code Napoleon created the French civil code, which has endured until now and has been adapted by many other countries.

Following World War II, the Catholic Church was faced with new challenges driven by political, social, economic and scientific changes. Godless communism was on the rise and attendance at Mass was beginning to decline. Too, there was lingering resentment over Pius XII's relationship with Nazi Germany during the 1930s and 1940s. The Concordat of 1933 was signed before the true nature of Hitler's regime was known, but later the Holocaust was not condemned with the vigor it warranted.

The Second Vatican Council, or Vatican II, was called by Pope John XXIII in 1959, and held at the Vatican during the years 1962–65. It was the twenty-first ecumenical, and chaired by the pope. John XXIII wanted to "throw open the windows of the Church so that we can see out and the people can see in." At the opening session, 2540 men attended, including the appropriate Church officials plus representatives of eighty-six governments. Seventeen Orthodox and Protestant denominations sent observers and at the third session in 1964, eight religious and seven laywomen observers were invited. Pope Paul VI continued leading the meetings after John XXIII died in 1963. On December 8, 1965, the council was closed and sixteen documents were produced, introducing the most profound changes in the last 500 years of Church history.

Among the accomplishments, celebration of the Mass was permitted to be conducted in the local vernacular instead of Latin. This has led to increased participation by the laity. The Holy Office (the Inquisition) was severely criticized, in part by the young Joseph Ratzinger (now Benedict XVI, the 264th pope). A joint declaration by the Catholic and Orthodox Churches expressed regret for past actions that led to the Great Schism of 1054. To many people (myself included) the greatest advance was extending the olive branch to "those who have not yet received the Gospel" (Jews and Moslems) and to schismatics and heretics (Orthodox and Protestants). However, something does not add up—my 1995 copy of the Catholic catechism includes "Islam" and "Jewish" in the subject index, but the word "Protestant" does not appear.

Pope John Paul II (1978–2005) was the first Polish and non-Italian pope in almost 500 years and in his twenty-six years he transformed the papacy like few of his predecessors. His own life history gave him moral authority few world leaders could match. In an age of television and jet travel, his charisma gave him star power; praying at the Western Wall in 2000 was huge in repairing Catholic-Jewish relations. Millions of people appreciated his firm stand against godless communism and moral relativism. The Church moved quickly after his death to seek sainthood for him, a very rare honor (only six of the previous 152 popes during the last 1100 years have been named saints).

Canonization for John Paul would be in keeping with his own record; he himself canonized 484 saints and beatified 1337 individuals during his time as pope, more than all his predecessors combined in the last 400 years. John Paul streamlined the process, requiring fewer miracles and eliminated the challenge by the "Devil's Advocate." The required miracles almost always involve medical cures that are instantaneous, complete and permanent, without scientific explanation. The Vatican has established the Consulta Medica, a medical board of 100 Italian doctors who are asked to investigate the credibility of the cures. To advance to sainthood, another miracle must be performed after beatification. The generally accepted number of Catholic saints is about three thousand but there may be up to ten thousand if "beati", martyrs, Orthodox and early saints are included.

Today there are over 1 billion Catholics around the world, with 1.2 million priests, monks and nuns. Just in the U.S., total expenditures in all 19,200 parishes was $6.6 billion in 2000, not including the 230 Catholic colleges and universities, 8500 schools and 585 hospitals. On the other hand, weekly attendance at Mass has dropped from 79 percent in 1955 to 45 percent today. This trend may reflect some discontent. Instructions from the Vatican concerning birth control are regularly ignored, and Rome does not permit women to be priests even though 68 percent of American Catholics are in favor. There is also widespread disgust with the reluctant response to the problem of pedophile priests. Since 1950, 700 priests have been removed and dioceses around the country have spent at least $1.06 billion on settlements with victims, verdicts, legal fees, and other expenses. I am incredulous to read that gay priests may make up 30 to 50 percent of the priesthood; the Vatican plans a series of "visitations" early in 2006 to seminaries in the U.S. to determine the seriousness of the matter.

In Europe, church attendance has fallen even more drastically than in the U.S. For example, in France regular attendees have fallen to 12 percent, from 45 percent in 1965, and priest ordinations have plunged 90 percent. Catholic influence in Italy, Spain and Ireland has also declined, but the good news is that membership is growing in Africa, Latin America and Asia. As of 2000, 68 percent of all Roman Catholics lived on those continents, and Latin America alone had 50 percent of the total. One of the strongest of all is the Philippines, where 85 percent of the population of 80 million is Catholic.

10

FINAL THOUGHTS

Work on this book began four years ago as an effort to reconcile science and religion. I was reared as a Christian and consider myself a scientist by interest and profession. My natural instincts are to ask why, how, when, and where, and I had many doubts and questions about religion. It seemed to me that if there was a God, he must have been directly involved in the physical world, so that is where I began.

As I learned more about the creation of the universe and the beginning of life, I became convinced that God played the key role in both those events. Further understanding about the human soul added to this belief and the miraculous Resurrection of Jesus was the final convincing proof.

It is amazing to me that the famous cosmologist Allan Rex Sandage must have gone through a similar process of questioning, and gained the same insight, when he decided to become a Christian at the age of fifty. His trip was much more challenging than mine, however, as he was ethnically Jewish, a virtual atheist from childhood, and worked in a scientific environment where religion was viewed with suspicion. Sandage was a scientist at the Mount Wilson and Palomar observatories, worked as an understudy to Edwin Hubble, and was the recipient of many prestigious honors from international Astronomical societies (Strobel, 2004).

CREATION OF THE UNIVERSE

Georges LeMaître was the Belgian Catholic abbé who, in 1927, first suggested the concept of a "primordial atom" or an infinitely dense point source, as the origin of an expanding universe. This atom (now called a singularity), for some reason flew apart in an ineffable explosion "too great or extreme to be expressed or described in words." It formed all the stars (about 100 billion billion) in the universe in an event now called the Big Bang by most leading astrophysicists. Furthermore, LeMaître predicted that there should be some form of background radiation left over from the initial explosion. Hubble, in 1929, proved the claim of an expanding universe, and Penzias and Wilson in 1963 discovered the background microwave radiation.

No doubt, LeMaître was deeply convinced that a Creator was responsible and talked frequently to his friend Albert Einstein about it. About ten years earlier, Einstein had proposed his general theory of relativity, indicating that the universe had a beginning, when space-time began. LeMaître realized that this beginning was the creation event of Genesis, the apparent moment when the universe was created out of nothing (*creation ex nihilio*).

Scientists have developed elegant explanations for what has happened to matter after the Big Bang but are at a loss to explain the cause. And it takes metaphysical explanations to describe the original conditions and subsequent processes through which matter and energy were created out of nothing. Time began, and in that first microsecond, elementary particles began to form (quark confinement) and all physical laws and constants were determined. Physicists calculate that it took 380,000 years before the density of the "quark-gluon plasma" decreased to the point that light could escape. Another awesome thought is that the matter formed in the first micro-instant of creation was comprised of Planck-size particles (fermions with different "flavors" and bosons, together with their "anti-particles"). Creation of matter in the expanding universe began with quark confinement (in other words, from the smallest nanoparticles to the largest common measurement—light years). Sandage described the complexity of the Big Bang as a "miracle."

By different methods which confirm each other, scientists are able to assign a date to the Big Bang as about 13.7 billion years ago. Each of the billion galaxies seems to have its own black hole with enormous gravitational pull, which controls the movement of all its entrained stars. All the stars and planets are characterized by spin and rotation in circular or elliptical orbits. Simply put, the "ineffable explosion" has not created chaos, which would be expected, but an orderly and expanding universe.

Although Einstein never accepted the reality of a personal God, on many occasions he used such terms as "a superior reasoning power," "God," "The Lord," and the "miracle" of order in the universe. A typical statement of his was, "Everyone who is seriously interested in the pursuit of science becomes convinced that a spirit is manifest in the laws of the universe—a spirit vastly superior to that of man."

The amazing theoretical physicist Stephen Hawking mentioned God several times in his book *A Brief History of Time*. He said "the actual point of creation lies outside the scope of presently known laws of physics." It was also argued that quantum physics suggests that time becomes "fuzzy" as time approaches zero, and hence there was no definitive beginning of the universe. Hawking contended that the "no-boundary cosmology" removed the need for a Creator but was reproved by the Jesuit director of the Vatican Observatory, Father George Coyne, "Stephen, God is not a boundary condition."

Earlier scientists such as Nicolaus Copernicus (1473–1543) had expressed their belief in God, "this divine rather than human science"; Johannes Kepler (1571–1630) "...God has waited six thousand years for someone to understand his work"; Galileo Galilei (1564–1642) "...God who has endowed us with sense, reason and intellect..."; Robert Boyle (1627–1691) "...the admirable workmanship which God displayed in the universe"; Sir Isaac Newton (1642–1727) "This most beautiful system of sun, planets and comets could only proceed from the counsel and dominion of an intelligent and powerful Being"; Sir William Hershel (1738–1822) "...confirming more and more the truths contained in the Sacred Scriptures."

In the 1950s, about the same time that he coined the term Big Bang, Sir Fred Hoyle converted from atheism to belief in a "purposeful intelligence." Physicist Paul Davies said "...The impression of design is overwhelming" and astrophysicist Robert Jastrow said "the astronomical evidence leads to a biblical view of the origin of the world." Nobel laureate Charles Townes said physical phenomena "seem to reflect intelligence at work." NASA team leader John Mather saw a parallel between the scientific and biblical versions of creation and George Smoot, a Lawrence team leader said "It's like looking at God." The science-historian Frederick Burnham averred "These findings, now available, make the idea that God created the universe a more respectable hypothesis today than at any time in the last 100 years."

From all this it can be concluded that the universe was created about 13.7 billion years ago in a Big Bang event, the cause of which cannot be explained with certainty at this time, or perhaps ever. There must be an answer, perhaps beyond our comprehension, and many top scientists believe that there was control by some Supreme Power (God).

LIFE-EVOLUTION

The argument for a Supreme Power becomes even stronger and more understandable, in considering the beginning of life on Earth. In this case, the first primitive bacteria appeared about 3.8 billion years ago, relatively soon after the earth itself was formed about 4.5 billion years ago.

Harsh physical conditions existed at that time but it is possible to study modern descendants of those early, single-celled organisms. Genes from such primitive life forms commonly reappear as an exact copy in modern organisms with the same sequence of DNA, much as a molecule of water from 3 billion years ago is the same as one today. Some modern relatives of early microbes recently have been found in the vicinity of thermal vents called white smokers along deep-sea plate boundaries. Other than the 3,000 psi deep-sea pressure, these curious microbes exist in conditions similar to those on early Earth, with temperatures of 230ºF and little or no oxygen.

The specific microbe *Methanococcous jannaschii* has provided helpful insights. Carl Woese, Professor of Microbiology at the University of Illinois, had worked on such a class which he called archaea, so in the mid-1990s he and John Venter at TIGR collaborated to examine the DNA. They found that *M. jannaschii* had a circular chromosome with 1,682 genes and resembled plants and animals more closely than bacteria. By analogy, ancient relatives of *M. jannaschii* could be as old as 3 billion years, and were the first cells with a nucleus—the eukaryotes, the earliest ancestors of animals and mankind.

In 1974, physicist Brandon Carter proposed the "anthropic principle" i.e., that the laws of physics and chemistry seem to have been designed for the benefit of mankind on Earth. In 1993, physicist Hugh Ross in two lists named fifty-five parameters required for life in the universe and solar system. In 1999, Ward and Brownlee pointed out how several uniquely favorable conditions had combined for life on Earth. Michael Corey in 2001 also enumerated the precise requirements for life on Earth, including the observation by Gribben and Rees concerning the incredible and necessary precision of the Hubble expansion rate. Several other scientists have argued that extreme precision was required to fine-tune the universe in order for Carter's anthropic principle (conditions favorable for life on Earth) to prevail. Penrose has calculated the needed accuracy was one part in ten[123] (more zeroes than all the elementary particles in the universe).

In 1859, Charles Darwin proposed his theory of evolution in which the earliest, primitive organisms evolved into the complex plants and animals we see today. In this theory, environmental stress caused random changes or mutations in the genes of a given species. This "descent with modification" described the process of natural selection by successful species, which tended to dominate the gene pool of the surviving population. In the earliest life forms, new species could develop only from random mutations, an extremely slow process. But according to Sagan, about two billon years ago sex helped to speed up the process of evolution. Sex allowed two organisms to exchange great batches of their genetic code, instead of needing a mutation for each change.

Even at that time, Darwin was concerned that the required transitional forms were missing in the fossil record, and in his *Origin of Species*, he devoted an entire chapter to the subject. As the famous Harvard evolutionist Dr. Gaylord Simpson later observed, "...most new species, genera and families...appear in the record suddenly and not led up to by known, gradual, completely continuous transitional sequences." Colin Patterson at the British Museum of Natural History stated "The fossil record tells us almost nothing about the evolutionary origin of phyla and classes. Intermediate forms are non-existent, undiscovered, or not recognized." And Dr. Steven Stanley at Johns Hopkins has stated "The known fossil record fails to document a single example of phyletic (gradual) evolution accomplishing a major morphologic transition and hence offers no evidence that the gradualistic model can be valid." Because of this, the famous Harvard paleontologist Stephen Jay Gould found it necessary to propose the theory of "punctuated equilibria." This theory posits that a given species has long-term stability but that some sudden environmental stress can cause a rapid change to a new species.

Darwin's theory often required thousands of years between speciation events. It is estimated that over 5 billion species have developed on Earth during geologic time. Over 99 percent of these have become extinct, mostly because of changes to their environment, and the average species has persisted for about 4 million years.

Another puzzlement is the number of strange creatures that evolved and died out. These include the five-eyed *Opabinia* which cannot even be classified, *Pterygotus*, a scorpion some seven feet long, and *Helicoprion*, possibly some weird kind of shark's tooth—and there are thousands more. It appears that once life began, the initiating genius kept "hands-off" the evolutionary process for the most part.

The thousands of years of time required by Darwin's theory conflicted directly with theology of the day. After all, 200 years earlier, Bishop Ussher had calculated that the six days of creation began the night of October 23, 4004 B.C. This difference of opinion caused bitter arguments, at the time and ever since. The good bishop's number had been widely accepted, but was wrong—by a factor of over two million.

All life, and evolution, is controlled by DNA—deoxyribonucleic acid. Over 100 years ago, it was correctly proposed that DNA was able to transmit hereditary information. Furthermore, the DNA was able to replicate itself over thousands of generations and pass along the genetic information without error. A rare glitch could cause a random mutation and sometimes this mistake had favorable results, allowing the mutant DNA to out-replicate its competitors through natural selection.

In 1953 Crick and Watson described the double helix structure of DNA after seeing the pattern of X-rays diffracted through wet DNA crystals. They also determined that the parallel "rails" were connected by "rungs" of molecules called "bases." The sequence of bases described the order of amino acids required to form a particular protein. A section of the DNA molecule that can code for protein formation is called a gene and the average is one gene in every 40,000 bases. The human genome has about 20,000 to 25,000 genes, about the same number as many other organisms but with some important differences.

The human body has about 100 trillion cells, including 100 billion brain cells. About 200 cells would fit into the period at the end of this sentence. Each cell nucleus contains its own set of twenty-three pairs of chromosomes, one from each parent. Each of the chromosomes has a protein core with a DNA molecule wound tightly around it. Each molecule has 100 million turns and 100 billion atoms. The DNA in each cell stores 3 billion letters of code which must be transmitted accurately as the cell divides; actually, the error rate is about one mistake every 10 million bases.

To make the protein required for all living things, the DNA passes instructions for the assembly of amino acids in a precise sequence. Ribosomes, outside the nucleus, produce several hundred thousand kinds of protein, perhaps a million. Single-stranded RNA molecules pass along the instructions for this process in digital form from the DNA to the ribosomes.

Obviously, the nucleotides and interdependent amino acids/proteins must have evolved together—at the same time that their remarkable control of life began. It is beyond belief that life began with a chance or random linking of the exquisite complexity of DNA with the equally complex creation of proteins

Many prominent scientists have remarked on this. Dr. Stephen Meyer calculated that one functioning protein had one chance in 10^{125} (one with 125 zeroes after it) to form randomly in nature and that there was "no realistic possibility that the 100 proteins necessary for the operating of a simple cell could have come together randomly and begun functioning." Dr. Francis Crick said "...the spontaneous generation of a living organism is impossible." Sir Fred Hoyle calculated that the chance for a single bacterium to be spontaneously generated was one in $10^{40,000}$. It follows that spontaneous events certainly did not cause the simultaneous appearance of the complex and interdependent trio of DNA, the ordering of amino acids to form proteins, and life.

Mathematicians have devised a system of googols and factorials to deal with incomprehensible numbers such as in the preceding paragraph. A googol is defined as the number 10^{100} or 10 to the 100th power, or about seventy factorial (70!). Remember that the ratio of the universe (a few billion light years) to the thickness of a human hair is about 10 to the 30th power.

For nearly 150 years we have been told that classic Darwinian evolution called for survival and reproduction as the main goal of any species, the "survival of the fittest." Prominent sociobiologists word it another way as "DNA survival." If survival and reproduction are all that matters, then why are there such things as altruism, love, compassion and generosity, none of which can help the selfish gene? And what about music, art, literature, poetry, dance— and all the other enjoyable elements of culture? Sadly, some of these same experts think life itself is meaningless, pointless, and without purpose.

From all this it could be concluded that the Darwinian theory of evolution has some severe weaknesses, and at the very least needs some serious revisions. Darwin himself said, in his notes, that there would have to be another explanation for something his theory could not explain. The origin of life has not been explained (and perhaps never will be). Also, it seems that the Darwinian model of speciation may be applicable to only modest modifications or mutations within species, i.e., microevolution. [On the other hand, I am well aware of the tree of life, and personally believe in the overall concept of evolution—only that the Darwinian model needs some important improvements.]

Although anathema to some scientists, the idea of "intelligent design" to explain evolution has been gaining traction. The book of the same name, by William Dembski, has provoked a good deal of discussion in the worlds of science, religion, and academia. Dr. Dembski is a senior fellow at the Discovery Institute in Seattle, and has defined intelligent design as the process of creating a complex and specified effect by an intelligent source. As applied to evolution, this would mean that the process was designed, rather than that it happened by random happenstance. Dembski argues that an undirected, natural selection mechanism cannot explain the origin of life, multicellular life, the origin of sex, the Cambrian explosion, and the lack of transitional forms in the fossil record. The folks at the Discovery Institute do not specifically identify the intelligent designer as God, although that conclusion would be implicit to most people.

Darwin's theory called upon natural selection of random advantageous changes, leading to new species. Most scientists and many theologians believe that this theory is reasonably correct—the main unsettled question is to determine how life began. Numerous different scientists have calculated the outrageous odds against life beginning by spontaneous generation. Only the simplest inorganic compounds could have formed by random chance. In fact, after examining the various theories proposed by scientists to explain the first living cell, a logical conclusion would be that scientists do not "have the slightest idea of how life began."

With the present state of knowledge, valid arguments exist for the discussion in academia of both Darwinian evolution (with its problems), and intelligent design (with its problems). With further study more will be learned, and hopefully the truth of the matter will be determined. Scientists argue that intelligent design is a religious matter and not science. But what if it is true? Not too many scientists would rule out the possibility.

Even the head skeptic, Michael Shermer, gave God a 2 percent chance, using the Bayesian theorem proposed by Stephen Unwin in his book *The Probability of God*. (Unwin, by the way, with different assumptions, gave a 67 percent probability for God's existence).

When science cannot explain a physical event or situation, such as the Big Bang or the beginning of life, the scientific method calls for open-minded and comprehensive analysis of all available data in order to develop the most likely theories or postulates. Whether 2 percent or 67 percent, the idea of an Intelligent Designer has to be one possibility and may be the most reasonable of all, given the astronomical odds against random chance.

This is a situation that fairly cries out for the reasoning of Occam's Razor (also spelled Ockham's Razor). William of Ockham was an English Franciscan friar (died ca. 1349) who frequently used the argument so effectively that his name became associated with it.

Basically, Occam's Razor is the principle that the explanation of any phenomenon is most likely correct if it uses as few assumptions as possible. In other words, "keep it simple, Stupid." Validity of the principle has been demonstrated in statistics, philosophy, religion, science and the military (especially in hindsight after a disastrous campaign).

With the overwhelming odds against random chance as the explanation for creation of the universe, and beginning of life, Occam's Razor would say Intelligent Design is the most likely and reasonable explanation. *To repeat one more time, it is beyond logical belief that the universe had a spontaneous beginning or that life began with a chance linking of nucleotides and interdependent amino acids/proteins.*

Similar concerns have been echoed by a long list of top scientists, including Behe, Collins, Davies, Dembski, Gonzalez, Jastrow, Meyer, Moreland, O'Keefe, Polkinghorne, Sandage, Townes, Wells, etc. Strobel (2004) has neatly compiled the interviews he has had with a number of these scientists and has developed a well-reasoned "Case for a Creator."

SOUL-SPIRIT-BRAIN

Almost all religions (about 4.5 billion people) consider the human soul to be the private, inner center of an individual's mind, will, personality, character, and consciousness—his "self." With free will, an individual may choose to be good or evil, honest or dishonest, lazy or energetic, etc. They all agree that life is a continual struggle between the virtues and vice evidenced in everyone's behavior and/or thoughts.

Each religion represents a compilation of time-tested wisdom concerned with the salvation or deliverance of the soul. Most religions, but not all, teach how to save souls by obeying a wise, eternal, sole Creator of the universe. The guidelines for proper behavior are provided by a set of moral values, usually reinforced by specified rituals.

Islam espouses a firm faith in and worship of one God (Allah) by devout believers whose mission is to build a just and benevolent social order. Through a lifetime of daily effort, correct choices, and purity of heart, faith in Allah can lead to salvation. Suffering during life is only a trial of each human soul; with good deeds, avoidance of evil and trust in Allah, the individual soul passes, gratefully, into the next world.

Jewish, Christian and Muslim doctrine each hold that choices made during one's life will determine their afterlife—either belonging with God in some comfortable situation or being removed from God and in a very unhappy status. The Buddhist and Hindu traditions consider that all suffering is deserved, and that the soul reappears in a cycle of rebirths (is reincarnated) in appropriate human or animal forms according to previous behavior. Aristotle had a somewhat similar idea, in that upon death, the soul of an individual returned to a "collective force."

Atheists do not like the idea of a soul because it has religious implications. They think Darwinian evolution theory explains survival of the fittest and that the only purpose of any life form is to see that the DNA genetic code is preserved and passed on to following generations. At the opposite extreme are people like MIT-trained physicist Dr. Gerald Schroeder, who contends that God imbued Adam with the first human soul, instantaneously, at the age of twenty.

In the early Catholic Church a distinction was made between soul and spirit so that the whole person has three parts: body, soul and spirit. Saint Paul used three Greek words for these parts. *Soma* was the word for body, meaning the entire body, including the brain. *Psyche* was the word for soul, including will, intellect, mind, emotions, character and personality. *Pneuma* was the Greek word for spirit.

The Catholic catechism has given a great deal of attention to the matter. It states that (1) every spiritual soul is created immediately by God (not by the parents) (2) it is immortal (3) it does not perish upon death (4) it will be reunited with the body at the final Resurrection. Muslims also believe that on the Day of Judgment, the bodies of worthy believers will rejoin their respective souls and eventually enjoy eternal Paradise, but those of sinners will experience eternal hellfire. To a scientist, the mechanics of all this is confounding.

Reuniting a soul with a dead body needs some form of quantum mechanics, where all quanta are retrievable. This would require reassembling a body atom by atom—relatively easy compared to retrieving information from a black hole. To deal with the spiritual soul, the Church has cleverly conceieved the concept of a holding place (Purgatory) where souls reside until the time of the Last Judgment, when properly spiritual souls will be reunited with their respective resurrected bodies. Even the word "properly" has problems—what is the cutoff on a scale of 0 to 100, where Stalin might be a ten and Mother Teresa a ninety?

In the Old Testament the "Spirit of God" and "Spirit of the Lord" were frequently cited as positive influences in shaping man's soul. As a former Jewish rabbi, Paul saw Christianity as in continuity with the covenant of the Old Testament, and stressed the Spirit of God, or spirit of man (S/spirit). They were mentioned 140 times in his letters, second only to his stress on faith (mentioned 187 times). Paul felt that, next in importance to Christ, the Spirit was fundamental to understanding the gospel.

This led to the concept of the Trinity or trinitas, used first by Tertullian, as early as A.D. 200. The idea of the Father, the Son, and Holy Spirit in three persons has been one of the most controversial and misunderstood of all canons of the Christian church. Fee (1994 and 1996) has explained the problem exhaustively, including the uncertainty of translating the word "person" from the Greek or Latin. The Old Testament meaning of God's power or presence seems to me to be a good way to think of the third person of the Trinity.

Some behavioral problems in individuals have been related to genetic and epigenetic differences. Hence, it would seem that more knowledge about the evolution of the soul, and related genetic influences, are obvious goals to be pursued by biologists, archaeologists and theologians. In 2003, James Watson, co-discoverer of the double helix, had the same thing in mind when he suggested that a young, beginning researcher might be well advised to work on the relationship between genes and human behavior. From that advice, it is not too hard to think in terms of components of the soul, and how they are stored and manipulated in certain genes in the brain. This might involve some mysterious and yet to be discovered form of energy flitting through the axons, synapses and dendrites in the neurons of the human brain.

Dr. Robert Schuller feels that the marvelous human brain is "hardwired" to the soul. But Dr. Moreland has argued that the mind—or soul—functions at another level. The soul may reside in and be tied to the brain, but activity discernable in brain scans shows just that—activity, not the content. It may be that components of the soul are stored and manipulated in certain genes in the brain.

Ideas about the soul and spirit are what separate mankind from all other forms of life (although some atheists do not think mankind has a soul). Such concepts, are of course, the product of mankind's advanced brain, which is unique in the solar system and, so far as we know, in our

Milky Way galaxy.

The three-pound human brain has been called "the most complex and orderly arrangement of matter in the universe." The brain operates at tera-flop speed (trillions of floating point operations per second) and has been likened to a supercomputer. The human brain includes about 100 billion specialized nerve cells called neurons. Each neuron has an axon that trans-mits information across a gap or synapse to a target cell called a dendrite that may have thousands of connections. This information, in the form of an electrical signal, is converted to a chemical message (modulated up to 100 times) across the synapse, then back to an electrical pulse. Thus there are about 500 trillion connections in the human brain. Compared to a computer, the human brain is much more powerful, millions of times more energy-efficient, and far more compact.

During the nine months of gestation, neural cell division (mitosis) proceeds at a rapid pace and new brain cells are generated at the rate of 250,000 per minute. In this period of rapid growth, a complete cycle of cell development may take only 1½ hours. As the neural cells multiply, they migrate to apparently ordained destinations, in the correct cell layer, where they orient themselves and begin to make appropriate synaptic con-nections. By the end of the eighth week the spinal cord is present, cerebral cortex and hemispheres are differentiated, sex is determined, bone building has started and all the organ systems are established.

By about the twentieth week, the important process of synaptogenesis is well underway. This involves the vast assemblage of neurons and their axons connecting with dendrites through a myriad of connections called synapses. Each synapse is a point of contiguity (but not continuity) be-tween two neural elements. Synaptogenesis continues during pregnancy and there is good evidence that the unborn fetus has some awareness of its external environment, and will react to some stimuli.

At birth, the infant has 100 billion brain cells but most of the neurons are immature and need to be activated. For the brain to develop properly and reach its full potential, outside stimulation is required; in the case of infants, touch, holding, sound, smell and vision. Another important factor is that of myelination. Myelin is a fatty substance that serves as insulation around many of the axons. It allows conduction of nerve impulses at speeds ten to one hun-dred times faster. Fibers serving the primary functions of touch, smell, vision, hearing, etc. are myelinated soon after birth but those serving the higher cogni-tive processes are the latest to myelinate, perhaps in young adulthood.

By the age of eight months, given a secure, stimulating and loving environment, a normal infant will have sparked 500 trillion synaptic connections. By the age of two, an infant has developed 1000 trillion of these connections. At this time, the highest lifetime density of 15,000 synapses per neuron may have been reached. By the age of three, the root brain architecture is fairly well established, and the structure of the brain is almost complete. For the first twelve years of life the brain is at its most receptive, acting like a super-sponge in soaking up new information.

By the age of eighteen, trivial connections have been discarded and the total has been reduced to about 500 trillion. The resulting brain is less able to adapt but is stronger and more powerful. The remaining connections are more stable and give each person's brain a unique structure and chemical balance that determines mind, thought and emotions. It is this pattern—our soul—that influences who we are, and how we think and learn.

An attempt was made to determine the most likely time for the "divine infusion of the human soul" into the brain. Some people think it is at the instant of conception but that seems unreasonable when considering embryology. Physiologically, the earliest likely time during pregnancy would be about twenty weeks, when synaptogenesis begins in elements of the growing brain. This would be the time when the vast assemblage of neurons, axon, dendrites and the synaptic connections begin to organize. On the other hand, the process continues after birth (and with stimulation, into old age). Myelination and stimulation are important to the new infant, and progress is rapid during the years of childhood with the brain becoming mature at the age of about eighteen.

From all this, it seems possible that infusion of the human soul is more of a gradual, cumulative process, rather than instantaneous. The earliest stage may be at about twenty weeks after conception, with a spurt in the first two years of life, and complete maturity by the age of eighteen. It would not be too unreasonable to think of the soul in the same terms during the evolution of mankind. That is, a simple, primitive form during the first days of *Homo sapiens*, which then became more complex as man evolved.

THE RESURRECTION

The details of the Crucifixion and Resurrection of Jesus are recorded in the Gospels, which were written within fifteen to sixty years of those events. The authors were either first-person witnesses or wrote their accounts based on the recollections of people who had been witnesses themselves.

The Books of Matthew, Luke, Mark, and John are in reasonable accord about the events of the first Easter morning. With minor variations, they describe the stone rolled away, the linen wrapping, the angels, and—the empty sepulchre. The first women at the tomb that morning were Mary Magdalene, the other Mary (mother of James and Salome) and "other women." Peter and John both inspected the empty tomb.

The resurrected Jesus appeared to his followers in five different places that first day. Jesus later invited Thomas to inspect his wounds and appeared to many of his disciples for forty days after the crucifixion. Paul described how the risen Jesus was seen by more than 500 brethren at once (1 Cor 15:6).

It seems clear that these appearances of the risen Jesus, over a forty-day period after his death, absolutely convinced the disciples that his resurrection was real, and this became the central teaching of the Apostles and focal point of the Christian faith. The crucifixion demoralized the frightened disciples but the resurrection gave them renewed faith and conviction. They changed from a group of frightened wimps to strong, principled adherents. At personal risk, their leaders took bold and courageous stands against the chief priests, and hundreds of people became willing to die for their belief in the new covenant.

Stephen was the first in a long list of Christian martyrs who unflinchingly went to their deaths because of their intense belief in Jesus Christ and the new religion. Of the twelve disciples, only John died a natural death, all the rest were killed in various ways. Six of the deaths were by crucifixion, mainly used by the Romans. Paul was beheaded, the "advantage" of being a Roman citizen.

The epiphany of Saul (Paul) on the road to Damascus is an amazing story. A blinding light struck him to the ground, and a voice said "Saul, Saul, why are you so cruel to me?" and when asked, the Lord said "I am Jesus." In Damascus, still blinded after three days, Saul regained his sight when a follower of Jesus was instructed to go to Saul, saying "Saul, the Lord Jesus has sent me. He is the same one who appeared to you along the road. He wants you to be able to see and to be filled with the Holy Spirit" (Acts 9:3–5 and 7–17).

After his conversion, Paul became the foremost giant of the Christian movement. He told the Galatians (1:15, 16) God "was kind and had decided to show me his Son, so that I would announce his message to the Gentiles" and in 1 Corinthians 9:1 "have I not seen Jesus Christ our Lord?" Over 40 percent of the New Testament concerns Paul and/or his letters, written by himself or in his name. For thirty-two years he traveled thousands of miles, often walking, proselytizing new converts, establishing new churches, and supporting the different congregations. He was whipped, stoned and left for dead, imprisoned, threatened with death by Jewish partisans in at least six places, and finally, beheaded by Nero.

Justin Martyr was one of the early martyrs and his name has come to define those willing to die for their beliefs. He was executed in about 165 at the "customary place" near Rome, with six of his students, saying "That is our desire, to be tortured for our Lord, Jesus Christ, and so be saved..." In 155, Polycarp, the bishop of Smyrna (Izmir, Turkey) was burned alive in the stadium there when he refused to renounce Christ. Origen of Alexandria was condemned to burn at the stake in 250 but escaped death when his accuser died. In all, 310 men and women martyrs were listed by name in the *Bibliotheca Hagiographica Latina* and thousands more went unnamed.

To me, the reality of the Crucifixion was strongly demonstrated by the life-change it made in those who witnessed it, and by thousands of others who were willing to die for their beliefs.

To debunk the Resurrection, a lunatic fringe of atheists has argued that it was all a big hoax and some claimed Jesus did not even exist. Historians at the time prove otherwise. Suetonius (ca. 69–150) wrote that in A.D. 49 the emperor Claudius expelled all Jews from Rome because they were rioting over "Chrestus." That this was actually Christ was confirmed in Acts 18:2 when Paul came to Corinth in 52 and stayed with a Christian couple, namely "a certain Jew named Aquila, born in Pontus, lately came from Italy, with his wife Priscilla; (because Claudius had commanded all Jews to depart from Rome)."

Flavius Josephus was a famous Jewish historian who wrote the *Jewish Antiquities* in about 94. It included twenty volumes of which XII–XX covered the time of Christ. The most famous passage (known as the *Testimonium Flavianum*) described Jesus as the Messiah, Pilate's verdict of crucifixion, the Resurrection on the third day, and the persistent strength of Christianity.

Tertullion (ca.160–225) used Aristotelian logic to support the Resurrection and remonstrated with the Romans, "Your cruelty...does not profit you...we grow in number...We have filled...cities, islands, forts, towns, assembly halls, even military camps, tribes, town councils, the palace, senate and forum."

Many scholars (p. 133) have written treatises supporting the reality of the Resurrection. Dr. Simon Greenleaf, Professor of Law at Harvard, gave an especially compelling statement. He initially believed the Resurrection was a myth and hoax, but when he investigated all the evidence he concluded that the resurrection of Jesus Christ was the best-supported religious event in all of history. His 1874 book on the subject was entitled *An Examination of the Testimony of the Four Evangelists by the Rules of Evidence Administered in the Courts of Justice.*

A SCIENTIFIC PARAPHRASE

In my search for religious truth, I undertook what I thought was a logical and orderly analysis of the three main religions originating with Abraham. Members of the three, Judaism, Christianity, and Islam, comprise about 64 percent of all the religions in the world today. An important step in this process was to review the sources and writing of their religious texts, i.e., the Old Testament, the New Testament, and the Koran.

It is interesting that in terms of first-person witnesses, the Koran ranks first. According to Islam, the archangel Gabriel passed along Allah's words directly to Muhammad, who had the words written down by scribes almost in real time. The record shows that the words of Paul and the apostles in the New Testament, describing Jesus and his work, were written in the time frame fifteen to sixty years after the crucifixion. The information was furnished by eyewitnesses, or second-generation witnesses.

In the Old Testament, the most accurate material was written when court scribes first recorded events during the time of Samuel (about 1000 B.C.). The events concerning Abraham (about 1780 B.C.) may be fairly accurate, as reported in the Torah, and some of this same information was repeated later in the Koran. The real problem is with the years prior to Abraham, or the first eleven chapters of Genesis. Events during that time were orally transmitted between generations (oral tradition), as remembered by illiterate people. Sumerian cuneiform script, developed about 3400 B.C. may have played a role, but the earliest Hebrew biblical texts were written by Shiloh priests about 922 B.C. The final wording in the Old Testament was determined in about 457 B.C. by an editor or Redactor, possibly Ezra.

The Redactor relied upon text from other authors who were priests, or groups of priests. There may have been as many as six different groups of authors, and each emphasized different points-of-view. Hence, numerous discrepancies exist in the Old Testament, and most scholars think it is not the actual word of God but what men may have thought God desired.

Examples of some discrepancies are in Genesis 1:11–27, where the order of life is different than in Genesis 2:5–22. Also, in 7:2–3, seven pairs of animals and birds were loaded on Noah's ark whereas in 7:15 it was two pairs.

Noah's flood occurred in 2949 B.C. according to the Old Testament. It was very similar to the epic of Gilgamesh, the great king who lived in Sumer about 2700 B.C. In both stories, a man was instructed to build a large ark and load it with species of every living thing, so life could be preserved. When the flood came, the man, his family, and the other creatures floated for days, while all other life on Earth was drowned.

A real problem exists concerning the flood itself. Noah's flood was described as being worldwide, but 99 percent of professional geologists would say there is no physical evidence for such an event. Also, a simple material balance calculation shows a worldwide flood is impossible. According to Genesis, the ark grounded near the crest of Mt. Ararat, with an elevation of 16,946 feet, in eastern Turkey. If all the ice in Antarctica were to melt, it would raise sea level only 200 feet, and the ice on Greenland could add only 20 feet more. (Ice in the Arctic would make no difference, because it is floating.) Simply put, there is not enough water on the earth to submerge Ararat; more than 16,000 feet of water would be needed, worldwide, on top of the present oceans which average 12,450 feet deep. Even more challenging, wherever did that 16,000 feet of water go?

In reality, the flood stories may have stemmed from an actual Black Sea flood about 5600 B.C. Ryan and Pitman at Lamont-Doherty have described startling results, based on modern geophysics. They found that at that time, the Black Sea was a freshwater lake, 350 feet lower than the Mediterranean Sea. When the water broke through the restriction in the Dardanelles, the seawater, with 200 times the volume of Niagara Falls, roared at fifty miles per hour for 300 days, terrifying all living things in the region. As the Black Sea filled with salt water, people fled to surrounding countries, and the flood story became history in the form of oral tradition.

At the time of the biblical Adam, 3754 B.C., the scriptures describe Adam and Eve as the first living people. In fact, there may have been ten million people living, and on all the continents except Antarctica. Human civilization, based on organized farming, was known in the Fertile Crescent as early as 8500 B.C.

Chronologically, the Redactor placed the Noah flood story midway between Adam and Abraham and then put ten generations, the "begats," between Adam and Noah and another ten generations between Noah and Abraham. This necessitated assigning atrocious life spans to the people.

For example, before Noah, the mean life span had to be 900 years and the average was 840. Adam lived 930 years after he ate the forbidden fruit and Methuselah lived to be 969.

Even many Jews recognize that this part of the Old Testament used poetic license, similes and metaphors to tell the story. Dershowitz dismissed a "literal fundamentalist approach" and Pope Pius XII implied that the words should not be taken literally, as it was "metaphorical language adapted to the mentality of a people but little cultured." John Paul II also recognized a symbolic or figurative meaning. In 2005, the Catholic Church published a sixty-page training document called *Gift of Scripture* which explained that the first eleven chapters of Genesis were based on oral tradition that did not adhere to "full scientific accuracy or complete historical precision." As stated, "Both Augustine and Aquinas hold that the creation account in Genesis is not offered as a literal, scientific account."

Biblical scholars have agonized for 3000 years over the meaning of time, when considering the six days of creation. King David was one of the first to equate a thousand years to one day and Hebrew scholars say the Genesis days mean "very long periods of time" or "vast, unspecified periods of time." But in Chapter 1, each day's work is closed with the statement "and the evening and the morning were the (numbered) day," leading millions of people to believe in six 24-hour days for creation. Protestant fundamentalists are especially adamant about this belief and insist on a literal reading of Genesis. In this regard they think the Bible is inerrant, even more so than some Jews do about their own scripture.

The six-day argument may be comfortable, and avoids difficult questions. However, it conflicts with hard science and reason, and is a position almost identical to that which the Inquisition took in trying to stifle the science of Galileo, over 370 years ago.

Clearly, the six days of creation, Adam and Eve, and flood stories cannot be literally true, as written. Much of the problem no doubt stems from the fact that Ezra and other authors were trying to describe these events that had happened 2500 to 3300 years earlier (in reality, much earlier than that). They even tried to assign dates and names, based on oral traditions, and perhaps a few scraps of written material.

Expanding on the events listed below, a "scientific paraphrase" or formal amplification could be developed which would serve as a scientifically sound proxy for the first eleven chapters of Genesis. By accurately describing creation of the universe, life, evolution and mankind's progress, it could benefit millions of people and help move both fundamentalists and scientifically inclined agnostics, toward common ground. Some possible phrases might be that God—

- Created the universe, 13.7 billion years ago, perhaps in an event similar to the Big Bang;

- Devoted approximately 9 billion years to different parts of the universe;

- Introduced organic life into an anthropic Earth about 3.8 billion years ago, using DNA to guide evolution of the species;

- May have steered evolution at times with some critical input, but mostly kept "hands off";

- Influenced advent of the new species, *Homo sapiens sapiens*, about 195 to 150 thousand years ago; and

- Imbued mankind with a soul, _____ years ago (to be determined by people with more experience than me).

RELIGIOUS MISTAKES

All three of the Abraham-founded religions have made some terrible mistakes that have affected the lives of millions of people. Chronologically, the first was committed by the Jews when they crucified Jesus.

The priest class in Jerusalem was well aware of the prophetic claims, made throughout the Old Testament, that a Messiah would appear to save Israel. But they were confounded when the message Jesus preached was love and compassion for the unfortunate. As his fame spread, and he began to attract a following, he also antagonized the chief priests when he questioned their behavior, disrupted the Temple routine, and called into question the cozy relationship of the chief priests with the Roman authorities. Because of these things, Caiaphas and the priests conspired to incite a mob, and successfully pressured the Romans to crucify Jesus. Thus, a few vindictive leaders, consumed with hate, were able to manipulate others into supporting a frightful crime.

Think how different the world would be if the Jewish leadership had recognized Jesus as their Messiah. The reforms espoused by both Jesus and Hillel could have been merged in a joint effort. Less than 300 years later, Christianity was adopted by the Roman Empire and soon became the dominant religion in the world.

The Inquisition was the most abominable program ever carried out by the Catholic Church, and has repercussions to this day. It began as a Crusade against the Cathar heresy in southern France. The Cathars believed the material world was inherently evil, and accepted Christ as God but not as man. This deliberate, obstinate denial of Catholic orthodoxy, including rejection of the pope, was considered a sin and a crime, punishable under the law. The Albigensian Crusade of A.D. 1209–1229 enlisted a large army, mostly from northern France, enticed by the lure of land and properties seized from the Cathars. An estimated 100,000 Cathars were killed in this Crusade.

As the Inquisition grew, it began to seek out persons believed to be heretics, and added witches and other sacrilegious people. Dominicans were usually the inquisitors and beginning in 1252, torture was authorized. The usual procedure in a trial was to invite the defendant to confess, although he was not told the charges. Trials were conducted in secret, informers were anonymous, and testimony could be taken from blood relatives, criminals, convicted heretics and those who had been excommunicated. Sentences could not be appealed, defendants could be jailed for years while new information was sought, and a defense lawyer could lose his license if his client was convicted. For the heretic who confessed and repented, the punishment was life imprisonment. For those who did not repent, the penalty was death by burning at the stake. In all cases of life imprisonment or death, the property of the accused was confiscated, meaning the victim's family suffered as well.

The history of the Inquisition has been divided into the Albigensian phase, the Medieval Inquisition beginning in 1231, the Spanish Inquisition in 1478 headed by the outrageous Tomás de Torquemada, and the Roman Inquisition in 1542. Some also include the witchcraft episode, defined by the notorious *Malleus Maleficarum* which outlined how to apprehend, torture, prosecute and execute witches. Cornwell stated that the "inquisitions in their entirety killed hundreds of thousands of dissident Catholics, heretics and alleged witches." Even the famous Italian astronomer Galileo was caught up by the Inquisition in 1633 and forced to recant his belief in the heliocentric theory of Copernicus. Galileo was placed in house arrest, and scientists ever since have been enraged and have seen this as "the suppression of truth in the name of religion." The last victim of the Inquisition was hanged in 1826, over 600 years after the beginning of the Albigensian Crusade.

Partly because of some bad popes, but more specifically because of the sale of indulgences, Martin Luther posted his ninety-five theses in 1517. This soon led to the Protestant Reformation, Lutheranism, the Church of England, a whole list of Protestant denominations, and a related event, the French Revolution. These things were terribly damaging to the Catholic Church. Finally, in 1962 the Church undertook the serious corrective actions of Vatican II, which has had very positive results.

Some elements of the Judeo-Christian press today speak harshly of Islam, mostly because of terrorism carried out by a radical minority, and because of land disputes in Palestine. The vast majority of the 1.3 billion Muslims is comprised of decent, peaceful people, however, and cannot be blamed for the actions of a few. Abraham was the ancestral prophet for all three religions and therefore the three share much of the same history.

The Koran, and other Islamic writing, refers to the creation, Adam and Eve, Noah, Esau, Lot, Ishmael, Isaac, Jacob, Moses, Zechariah, Ezra, Joseph, Mary, John the Baptist, and Jesus. As Muhammad received God's messages through the archangel Gabriel, the theme was very similar to that of Jesus, 600 years earlier. That is, belief in one God, and the importance of mercy, social justice, benevolence, and compassion for the weak, sick and poor.

Muhammad was recognized as a successful prophet, administrator and military leader, much as Samuel was 1700 years earlier. Muhammad's first wife was a wealthy, older widow, with whom he had all his children, two sons who died young, and four daughters who survived. Five years after she died, he remarried and seemed to show compassion for the widows of slain soldiers, and others in difficulty. Of total eleven wives, only the first was rich and only one of the others was a virgin.

Muhammad had scribes record (he was illiterate) the messages from Gabriel as they were transmitted. His main scribe was Zayd, who completed the final, Uthman version of the Koran in A.D. 656, twenty-four years after Muhammad died. Zayd was the editor, much as Ezra was the likely Redactor for the Old Testament 1100 years earlier. In the Koran, God issues ten injunctions, very similar in content to the ten commandments of the Old Testament. All Muslims have five duties: to worship only Allah, to pray five times a day, to fast during the month of Ramadan, to give alms to the poor, and to become a pilgrim to Mecca at least once. And very similar to Catholic doctrine, worthy souls will rejoin their respective bodies on the Day of Judgment.

The first caliph (successor) after Muhammad was Abu Bakr, followed by Umar, Uthman, Ali and Husayn, all known as Shiites (or faction). A group of Sunnis murdered Hasayn near Karbala on October 10, 680, and took over power for the next 1,240 years. The Sunnis now make up 90 percent of all Muslims but Shiites still commemorate the date as Ashura (the tenth) and the great schism between the Shiites and Sunnis persists to this day.

Beginning in 1096, for a period of almost 200 years, Christians and Muslims clashed over the Holy Lands in a series of eight major Crusades. The bloody battles resulted in a great loss of life and bitter memories which still persist. The most gifted and effective leader on either side was Saladin, a Kurd from Tikrit. Saladin led the Muslim forces at the Horns of Hattin in 1187. This was the worst defeat for the Christians in the entire Crusades and was due in part to the ineffectual leadership of the leper king Baldwin IV, who made bad choices in his appointments.

During the first part of the Crusades, the Seljuk Turks were an important force opposing the Crusaders but the Mongol, Hulagu Khan abruptly ended the Seljuk dynasty in 1258 when he obliterated Baghdad. Ottoman Turks took over in 1307 and made considerable gains in southeast Europe, until a big defeat at the hands of Tamerlane in 1402. Between them, the Khans and Tamerlane killed an estimated 6 million Muslims, and 12 million Nestorian and Armenian Christians.

The Koran calls for jihād in terms of the individual striving constantly for inner purity and living according to the requirements of faith. The Hadith defines the militaristic form of jihād as an active struggle, or "holy war." This form of jihād originated with fundamentalists, whose backward, anti-scientific, and militaristic tendencies led to the assassination of almost all the early caliphs. In the mid-eighteenth century, the Wahhabi cult embraced this approach with enthusiasm.

By 1737, Abd al-Wahhab was pressing for a drastic change in Islam including downgrading Muhammad, destruction of the graves of Muslim saints, burning all books except the Koran, and exterminating all Shiites. He also despised music and Muhammad's belief in compassion and mercy. He soon linked up with the Sa'ud family and by 1788 the Wahhab-Sa'ud alliance controlled most of the Arabian Peninsula. In 1801 they attacked the Shi'a holy city of Karbala, then destroyed Husayn's tomb, closed the Kaaba at Mecca and killed every man, woman and child in Ta'if, twenty-five miles east of Mecca. Thus over 200 years of Wahhabi militant fundamentalism began, with close ties to the Saudi royal family. State funding for madrassas (religious schools) has helped support the harsh Wahhabi form of Sunnism, and Wahhabi clerics administer floggings and amputations, according to Shariah law. Of the fifteen Saudis involved in the 9/11 suicide bombing, twelve came from the Ta'if area which has a long history of Wahhabi activism. Pope Benedict XVI has called terrorism "the darkness of a new barbarism."

Recently there has been a tardy but well-advised effort to end the Saudi bargain with the Wahhabi devil. Also, on March 11, 2005, Muslim clerics in Spain, representing one million mostly Sunni Muslims, issued the first *fatwa* condemning Osama bin Laden and his Islamofascists. Hopefully, this Islamic edict by responsible Muslims will encourage a similar response by others.

Several terrorist groups sprang from the Egyptian Muslim Brotherhood, formed in 1928. These include Hamas, the Palestine Islamic Jihād (PIJ), Hezbollah, and al-Qa'ida, the most dangerous of all. Al-Qa'ida was established in 1988 by Osama bin Laden, just before the Russians withdrew from Afghanistan.

Al-Qa'ida has become an international terrorist group and probably has several thousand members. Cells exist in at least forty countries, including sleeper cells in the U.S. The terrorists have a blind, unreasoning hatred for Western culture and religion, and even traditional Islam if it departs even slightly from Wahhabi fundamentalism. Some rabid imams have been able to convince fanatics to undertake suicide bombing, even though it conflicts with two basic concepts of Islam that (1) prohibit suicide and (2) condemn killing of innocent people, especially women and children.

The vast majority of Muslims are moderates who simply want to live their lives in peace and progress. At times, it seems that Islam has been taken over by a small, vicious element, characterized by suicide bombers. The daily scenes in Iraq of terrorists killing other Muslim men, women and children are abhorrent to all civilized people. Moderate Muslims need to take over their own religion and throw out the Islamic radicals. Instead of teaching terrorism and suicide in the madrasas, the imams need to convince young Muslims that education and opportunity are in their future. Just as the Catholics made timely, necessary changes with Vatican II, so is there a need for a form of tolerant, enlightened, and engaged Islam for today's world.

THE CULTURE WAR

Paul Kurtz has been an effective advocate of an organized atheistic movement called "secular humanism" which claims that humanity is capable of morality and self-fulfillment without the need for a belief in God. His group has organized committees, international groups, a periodical and a publishing house, all aimed at furthering their secular beliefs. They claim to espouse tolerance, love and compassion in their goal to understand the universe and work toward developing the noblest and best possible human beings. They also argue that secular humanism is simply nonreligious, not antireligious, and that the word atheism means the lack of belief in God, not the active denial of God's existence.

These lofty claims are not borne out, however, when they discuss anything religious—their language unnecessarily becomes derogatory, insulting, provocative, sneering and incendiary. Considering tolerance and humility, their mean-spirited words are in stark contrast to the conciliatory remarks of John Templeton of the Templeton Foundation, which seeks to find common ground between science and religion (an effort the secularists call "dangerous"). In view of their admirable claims, one has to ask—where are the secularists' charitable organizations, hospitals, schools and colleges, youth camps, community outreach, donations of cash, food and clothing for refugees, volunteer help in shelters and food lines, etc?

Secularists are especially opposed to the moral absolutism of religion. Instead, they argue that right and wrong are relative and that there is no such thing as evil, or truth. The problem with moral relativism is that there is no firm underpinning for a safe, secure and orderly society. With no moral compass, a government must resort to fear and coercion. The Nazis and Communists knew this well, and Lenin relied on the conscience of bloody Bolsheviks and their "new democratic principles" as opposed to a conscience led by religion. Lenin further said his dictatorship would rely on "unlimited power, resting directly on force, not limited by anything." As Dostoyevsky said, "If there is no God, then everything is permissible."

Over 200 years ago, the French turned from religion and relied instead on a belief in the goodness of man as expressed in the "Enlightenment." They soon found that "Liberty, Equality, Fraternity" devolved into mob rule, the guillotine, and finally the despot Napoleon. Today, only 11 percent of the French people consider religion is important to them personally (compared to 59 percent in the U.S.). In the U.S., 40 percent of the people attend church at least once a week, whereas in Europe, the number is only 4 percent. As reported by the French Institute for Foreign Relations "Unless attitudes and behavior change dramatically, the Europeans face a slow but inexorable exit from history."

Western Europe's socialism and secularism are in strong contrast to

America's distinctive values—a Judeo-Christian society, free-market capitalism, and individual responsibility. Because of this, anti-Americanism is politically correct in Europe. Educated elites around the world, plus many of our own intellectual class, favor the Europeans, and condemn the U.S. position on the Kyoto Protocol, United Nations, International Court, and our attempts to obtain a fair and democratic resolution to problems in the Middle East.

Atheists love to selectively use the words of Thomas Jefferson because, as a Unitarian, he freely criticized and disagreed with some of the dogma of conventional religions. There was no doubt that Jefferson was a Christian. When he wrote the Declaration of Independence he said, "We hold these truths to be self-evident, that all men are created equal; that they are endowed by their *Creator* with certain unalienable rights; that among these are life, liberty and the pursuit of happiness." As president, he offered a national prayer which concluded "…all of which we ask through *Jesus Christ our Lord*" (my italics). As a strong defender of religious freedom, Jefferson was outspoken concerning support for the Establishment Clause of the first amendment, which says Congress should "make no law respecting an establishment of religion, or prohibiting the free exercise thereof." Atheists frequently quote the first part (which was aimed at thwarting a national religion, specifically the Church of England), but conveniently omit the far more important second part which provides the freedom for religion.

In an annual address, George Washington said in prayer "Let us unite, therefore, in imploring the Supreme Ruler of nations to spread his holy protection over these United States." And in his farewell address he wrote "Of all the disposition and habits which lead to political prosperity, Religion and morality are indispensable supports." John Adams declared "Our Constitution was made only for a moral and religious people" and as the Constitution was being written, Benjamin Franklin stood and said "God governs in the affairs of men."

"In God We Trust" is our national motto and on our currency. In 1954, Congress added "One nation, under God" to make the pledge of allegiance more reflective of the nation's character. Congress and state legislatures are opened with prayers to God. The Ten Commandments are depicted in several places in/on the building housing the Supreme Court. James Madison, known as the "father of our Constitution" said "We have staked the whole of all our political institutions upon the capacity of mankind for self-government, upon the capacity of each and all of us to govern ourselves, to control ourselves, to sustain ourselves according to the Ten

Commandments of God." These sentiments were adopted by our founders because they were religious men and women, believing in Judeo-Christian principles.

Islam has its own ten injunctions, very similar to the commandments, and all religions have comparable guidelines and especially emphasize the philosophy of the Golden Rule. Hence, it seems most reasonable to consider the Ten Commandments as an acknowledgment of God and representative of all religions, not any one in particular. That is how the founders viewed them, and in terms of the law are rules, not recommendations.

It seems clear that the secular approach to life in America has been marginalized; there is just not much interest. But another, more political attack has been more dangerous. This involves the conflict between Left and Right, or Liberals versus Conservatives. Although religion is only a part of the battle, the "religious Right" is blamed for a long list of problems as perceived by those who comprise the irreligious Left. This fight has been going on for seventy years, beginning with some of the same players as today. In the 1930s the ACLU supported the Communist party in the U.S. and today it is one of those taking the lead in attacking Christianity. The long-range strategy of the ACLU and its allies is to (1) denigrate American values and distort our history and heritage, (2) undermine all religion in the U.S., especially those naming God, Christianity and Christmas, and (3) put a liberal imprint on every social and political issue. Typically, they focus on America's mistakes rather than on our heroes and achievements, and try to dilute concepts of right or wrong through the fog of politically correct, relativistic choice.

In their drive to eliminate all Ten Commandment displays in public buildings, references to God, and to destroy our nation's undeniable religious heritage, the ACLU has even demanded that "God Bless America" signs be taken down because they say it is "a hurtful, divisive message." The judgments of the courts need to be refined and clarified in this regard so that recognition of religion in schools and in public is more in tune with the 92 percent of Americans who believe in God. Many school officials have been cowed by threats of litigation after unclear court decisions. Many colleges have ordered that American flags be taken down because they were "offensive," and individuals have been warned against patriotic stickers or red, white and blue ribbons. "On campus, you can burn an American flag but you can't wave one."

Although the ACLU can be relied upon to make the most extreme demands, their sympathizers on the left can be just as outrageous. The National Organization of Women (NOW) defends partial birth abortion even though most doctors say it is unnecessary and most people think it is outright murder. The North American Man Boy Love Association (NAMBLA) defends homosexual acts with children, Hollywood produces increasingly violent and obscene movies and music, and the courts have allowed pornography on the Internet. The Legal Services Corporation has managed to reward vice by getting drug addiction and alcoholism declared eligible for disability insurance.

The National Education Association (NEA) resists rewarding teachers on the basis of performance, and fights bitterly against letting children in failing inner-city public schools escape to better-performing voucher or private schools (even though the teachers send their own children there). One of the main problems is with discipline in the classroom, complicated by the threat of lawyers and litigation.

Incredibly, some elements of the liberal education establishment have fought bitterly against the use of phonics in teaching reading. They promoted the "whole language" approach with the result that by 1994, a heartbreaking 41 percent of fourth graders nationally could not read a simple children's book. California was tied for last place in the nation when prior to "whole language" it had been the best. When George Bush became governor of Texas in 1994, he found 23 percent of third graders could not read. He got a reading program passed, and the failure rate was cut to 2 percent. When Bush became president he was troubled by "the soft bigotry of low expectations" as applied to minorities. Nationally, an unbelievable 65 percent of black fourth graders were below the basic reading level and Bush initiated the No Child Left Behind Act. By emphasizing phonics, this Act will make sure that millions of children, especially blacks and Hispanics, will learn to read.

The Constitution has been eroded by judges finding new "rights" in what they call a "living document." Laws are subverted by shopping for ideologically sympathetic judges who will rule against the prevailing law. Jefferson warned of the judiciary becoming a possible "despotic branch" of government because it is not elected.

The liberal elite dominate in America's universities, professional associations, labor unions, the mainstream news media, foundations, and strive to do so in politics. In the 1960s, the "Destructive Generation" began their disruptive behavior on campus and by the 1970s, hard-core leftists took over the university faculties. Since then they have tried to see that only liberals are hired or gain tenure, and the nationwide ratio of liberal to conservative faculty is now 10:1. They proclaimed multiculturalism and asserted that all cultures are equal, something they know is not true.

Diversity of ideas is not allowed, even though it is one of the most important concepts in a university. Speech codes have been developed to ensure political correctness and to forbid the free speech of conservatives and Christians. On some campuses, conservative speakers are heckled, shouted down or even assaulted. Much of the intelligentsia has become like a new "priest class," secure in their tenure, indoctrinating impressionable students, and demanding obsequious agreement with their leftist dogma. Charles Townes (1964 Nobel laureate and recipient of 2005 Templeton award) has said "In the intellectual world, we shouldn't try to sell ideas, but we should be able to examine them freely." Years ago Voltaire said "Think for yourselves and let others enjoy the privilege to do so too."

Sadly, even the science of global warming has been politicized, tending to stifle the truth. No geologist would deny that interglacial warming as been going on for the last 15,000 years (during which time mankind has enjoyed 99 percent of all cultural and technological advances). The real problem is to quantify mankind's input to the warming and then allocate costs of corrective actions according to the related causes, feasibility, and commensurate with expected benefits. So far, governmental efforts have been mostly ineffective (CFCs excepted) whereas the influence of the marketplace has had impressive effects.

The religious right is part of a broad spectrum of Americans who believe strongly in values and plain virtues. Among these are honor, constancy, personal responsibility, self-reliance, and good citizenship. Vital institutions are families, churches, charitable organizations and voluntary associations. Education is essential country needs responsible, enlightened citizens to take responsibility. In this regard, the most important factor of all is the good family that motivates students to want to work and study hard. Our Declaration of Independence recognized our God-given right to liberty and freedom that was later defined in our Constitutional rule of law.

Lastly, the dignity of work, exemplified in the Protestant work ethic, meshed with economic capitalism to create jobs and wealth. Fueled by innovation, competition and rewards for success, American capitalism ignited a dynamo of job creation and opportunity, and has become the envy of the world. The private sector, blessed with free-market forces, has maintained a vibrant, flexible and expanding economy. Pirates and thieves certainly exist in our capitalistic system, but laws and rules largely keep them under control. Liberals and socialists decry capitalism but the example of failed European socialism should be a warning. The European welfare states have suffered half the rate of U.S. job creation, staggering taxes to pay for lavish social benefits, and recently, civil unrest. Winston Churchill said it well, "Capitalism is the uneven distribution of wealth, but Socialism is the equal distribution of poverty."

PERSONAL COMMENTS

If there is strength in numbers, it seems to me that churches should take a hard look at ways to join forces. I speak from the experience of being a member in a church made up of four different denominations. In the early days of our little town, some of our wise founders decided individual churches were not viable and therefore it would make sense to join together in a community church. We call ourselves the Rolling Hills Community Church (RHCC), affiliated with the United Methodist Church (UMC), Presbyterian USA, United Church of Christ (UCC), and the Christian Church. The RHCC Constitution states, "The purpose of the Rolling Hills Community Church is to bind in love disciples of Jesus the Christ, so equipping them to: SERVE as our Lord's ministers of reconciliation, that their witness may REACH OUT beyond their fellowship UNITING human beings to each other and to God, making OPEN the fruits of the Spirit to all persons..."

It works and we currently have 497 members. One important factor is that our ministers each have had the wisdom to avoid political matters and have followed the example Jesus set, "render unto Caesar..." In terms of the sacraments, music, order of worship, and so on, we rotate every four months, in turn using those of the four churches. As a former member of both Methodist and Presbyterian congregations, I can never tell the difference. Ties to the four parent churches are mostly in terms of coordination and sharing of projects and facilities, including the periodic search for a new pastor. Recently, when we constructed a $1.5 million building to house church offices and a new activity center, the Presbyterian organization coordinated the capital fund drive and we obtained our financing from the Methodists.

I have often wondered what God thinks about the 33,000 Christian denominations that have been formed over the years. Human egos and minor differences can explain many of these, certainly nothing so important as to warrant what has occurred. Keeping in mind the key words listed above—*Serve, Reach Out, Uniting, Open*—it seems to me that a serious effort at reconciliation is overdue. We have shown that four, working together, are stronger than each one as a separate entity. So too, would be thousands working together, rather than separately. We have shown it can be done successfully on a small scale and logically could expand on that.

As a concurrent, logical step, it seems that the Orthodox and Roman Catholic churches should give reconciliation one more try. For almost one thousand years, ever since the Great Schism of 1054, the Eastern and Western churches have been at odds, sometimes violently so. The main point of contention has always been about the jurisdiction of the pope and papal infallibility. More minor differences concern the marriage of priests, the date of Easter, and autonomous leadership of the sixteen Orthodox churches.

Pope John Paul II met with Orthodox leaders several times, trying to build closer ties, and in 2001 apologized for "sins of action and omission" by Catholics against Orthodox. Pope Benedict XVI has followed up on this and already declared a "fundamental commitment" to heal the divide.

If that could be done, perhaps Protestants could consider rejoining the mother church, in keeping with Christ's final prayer "…that they may be one, even as we are one" (John 17:22). For both the Orthodox and Protestant communions, the pope is the big problem, partly because of all the abuses by such bad popes as Sergius III, John XII, Alexander VI (Rodrigo Borgia), Leo X, and others.

It is certain that the first pope, Saint Peter, set an example that few, if any, popes have equaled. During the last 1100 years, only six popes have been named as saints; when you stop to think about it, with their mantle of infallibility, all popes should be saints. John Paul II has been proposed for canonization and the honor seems to be well deserved.

In any event, the pope question is the main problem separating the Protestant and Orthodox churches from Roman Catholics. But to people of good will, with a little innovative thinking, perhaps the pope question could be finessed (although it may take a double or triple finesse). The potential advantages of such a rapprochement are so huge that both sides should put their best minds to work to see if they could make it happen.

A good example of what is possible is that of the 760-year "golden age" in Spain when Muslim, Christian and Jewish groups worked together on matters of common interest. They shared the same moral discipline of modesty, patience, repentance and trust in God. Although the Christians and Jews were under *dhimmi*, the Muslim form of Sufism provided religious tolerance, allowing "a beautiful dialogue" that led to cultural and economic achievements.

Not surprisingly, my four years of work on this project has influenced me in several ways. First of all, it was one of the most fascinating things I have ever done and I found myself looking forward to the time at the computer when I wrote up results of my research. I developed a newfound open-mindedness, tolerance, and respect for other religions. In studying different religions it became apparent that each has good points and embraces some version of the Golden Rule. I came to admire what the Jews have done, and I realize that that I have moved toward Catholicism. This attitude came despite some lifelong prejudices and knowledge that the Catholic Church has done some heinous things. Our Catholic friends have been a positive influence and I especially appreciate Vatican II, the Church's apologies for past mistakes, and moves toward embracing mainstream scientific thinking.

To me, Christianity seems to be the overwhelming and convincing choice, largely because of the Resurrection which is God's most astonishing miracle of all history. On the other hand, I believe that Oprah Winfrey and George Bush had it right. Oprah said all people pray to the same God and Bush said "I believe we worship the same God." I also think that Jesus would say the same thing. I cannot believe he would condemn 1.3 billion Muslims as being evil and beyond redemption.

Instead, I picture him working respectfully and modestly with them, quietly emphasizing the similarities and things in common. It is likely he would point out how all three Abrahamaic religions consider as most important the matter of worshipping one God and stressing love, compassion and concern for our fellow man. One goal of course would be to help Islam recognize terrorism as a product of the devil and evil *jinn*, and encourage Muslims to realize the promise of their better angels. It also seems likely that Jesus would emphatically declare that the murder of innocents by suicide bombers is a reprehensible crime. In no way can it be considered a way to martyrdom, and those who encourage such acts are equally guilty in the eyes of God.

CONCLUSIONS

The amazing conversion of the famous astronomer Allan Sandage was described earlier in this chapter. My own thought processes must mirror those Sandage followed in making his profound decision. First of all came the conviction that God exists; this conviction stemmed from recognizing the miracles of the Big Bang, the beginning of life on Earth, and the infusion of mankind's soul and Spirit. Understanding the purpose of Jesus' life and the reality of his Resurrection must have inspired Sandage's conversion.

A large amount of new subject matter was analyzed in order to gain an adequate understanding of the subject and to "get it right." Almost from the beginning of the research it was clear that many of the critical scientific factors and religious matters could not be called proven facts—both disciplines deal with uncertainties. With this in mind I believe that the structured approach lent discipline to the project and the conclusions that have been made are reasonable and valid.

The most important conclusion made was that an intelligent control was responsible for the sequence of events that have formed our world. First was the miraculous creation of the universe in the Big Bang event. Ten billion years later, life was introduced on an anthropic Earth. Numerous scientists have shown the astronomical odds against random chance being an explanation for the creation of the universe and the beginning of life. The most direct, simple explanation, with the fewest assumptions (Occam's Razor) would name God as the answer.

As life began, DNA was key to guiding evolution, and modern man appeared about 150,000 years ago. Man was given a soul and Spirit but sinful humans continued to make a series of errors and mistakes. Hence, God arranged for Jesus, his Son, to demonstrate a new direction and message of hope for salvation. Proof of the Father-Son relationship was provided when Jesus was resurrected, as promised, some thirty-five to forty hours after his death on the cross.

In analyzing how the Old Testament was written, it became clear that the first eleven chapters of Genesis needed a better explanation and I have suggested the idea of a "scientific paraphrase." Since that thought (about three years ago) the Catholic Church has made a similar statement to the effect that those chapters of Genesis are historically and scientifically incorrect. This understanding should be welcome to many people who have had heartburn over that part of the Bible which describes creation being accomplished in six 24-hour days.

This action by the Catholic Church has served to strengthen my appreciation of its support of science, more so than any other Christian denomination, or any other religion. Catholics eventually realized how badly they had erred in squelching Galileo, 400 years ago, and have taken positive steps to correct that mistake. Their recent embrace of science was encouraged by the Belgian priest Georges LeMaître who introduced the concept of the Big Bang in 1927, and the priest/scientist Teilhard de Chardin who for years argued that scientific facts must be respected. The Church has established the Vatican Observatory, a respected astronomical facility under the brilliant twenty-five-year leadership of Father George Coyne. Both Popes Pius XII and John Paul II have stated that the theory of evolution cannot be denied, so long as the divine infusion of the human soul is recognized.

In considering the human soul and Spirit there is an obvious need for more good scientific research as it seems certain that components of the soul must reside in certain genes of the brain. A mysterious form of energy may be involved with genetic and epigenetic effects on human behavior. How mankind's soul has evolved, and the process of "infusion," cry out for answers; for example, does an individual's soul "pop into existence" or more closely follow ontology of the human brain?

One personal result of this project is a more positive outlook toward the Church, and I would like to see efforts made toward some kind of rapprochement of all Christians including Catholic, Orthodox, and Protestant churches. Strength in numbers and combined talents are needed to overcome all the evil and negativity in the world today. Too, Christians with a coordinated approach and speaking with one voice could be much more effective in dealing with a Muslim community, assuming that the moderate voices of Islam can prevail in their own critical struggle.

SCIENCE ANNEX

11

UNIVERSE

For some fifty years, the standard cosmology theory, favored by a majority of scientists, has been called the inflationary "Big Bang." This theory involves the ineffable explosion of a "singularity" having infinite density and temperature. The singularity concept (not word) was suggested by Georges LeMaître in 1927. The term Big Bang was coined by the world-renowned astronomer Sir Fred Hoyle in the 1950s, reluctantly, because he favored a different origin for the universe.

Such an explosion, 13.7 billion years ago, was also the beginning of space and time itself. Quantum theory suggests that in the sequence of events, after only 10^{-43} second (Planck time), the four forces of nature—strong nuclear, weak nuclear, electromagnetic, and gravity—were combined in a single "super force." According to S.S. Scott "Elementary particles known as quarks begin to bond in trios forming photons, positrons and neutrinos along with their antiparticles. Minuscule numbers of protons and neutrons existed at this stage, 1 for every billion photons, electrons or neutrinos." During this inflationary instant of creation, physicists think a "quark-gluon plasma" existed; the mother of all matter.

The incipient universe expanded in size at a rate many times the speed of light. Heavy hydrogen (deuterium) began to form whose nuclei combined in pairs to form helium nuclei. After three minutes, the temperature had dropped to one billion degrees and 25 percent of the universe was comprised of helium.

After 380,000 years, temperatures had dropped to 10,000°K and helium atoms began to bond to form lithium. The density of the singularity was also reduced to the point where microwave light could escape. As the bonding of energy and radiation ceased, all the matter that ever will be, began to form. In these more stable systems of stars and galaxies, more complex elements such as carbon began to appear and the laws of physics and chemistry described by Newton and Mendeleev took over.

Different researchers seem to agree that ordinary, (baryonic) matter with atomic structure, such as rock, water, air, life forms, *et al.* make up only 4 percent of the universe we know. The remainder is comprised of 23 percent cold dark (invisible) matter and 73 percent dark mass-energy. The cold dark matter is believed to be some undiscovered particle, not included in the Standard Model of elementary particles (discussed later). A likely candidate is the neutralino, a stable particle with zero charge, but quite different than the neutrino present in the Big Bang. The concept of dark energy is based on the accelerating expansion of the universe.

A star begins its life as a cloud of gas, mostly of hydrogen mixed with dust. Through millions of years, the cloud contracts as gravity pulls it together. As the collapsing cloud contracts, the gas at the center becomes extremely hot and, as the temperature reaches critical levels, nuclear fusion reaction begins. Hydrogen atoms at the core begin to form helium atoms, releasing great amounts of energy as they do. As nuclear fusion occurs, a helium nucleus is created from four hydrogen nuclei. This is the same reaction as when a hydrogen bomb explodes. As the released energy heats the surrounding gas, the gas begins to shine—and a star is born with the starlight mainly confined to near infrared, visible and ultraviolet wavelengths. Stars also are considered to be the source for heavier elements including carbon, iron, oxygen and silicon.

When dealing with time and distances of the cosmos, astrophysicists speak in terms of "light-years" or the distance light travels in one year. Light (and other electromagnetic radiation such as X-rays and radio waves) travels at the finite speed of 186,000 miles per second. Light from the sun takes 8.3 minutes to reach Earth; we thus see the sun as it was 8.3 light-minutes ago. The distance from the earth to the sun is 93 million miles and a light-year is 5.9 trillion miles. Light from a celestial body trillions of miles away began its journey years ago, so space telescopes see images from long ago. The diameter of the universe is a few billion light-years whereas the width of our solar system is about 20 trillion miles.

The largest stars are one thousand times as large as our sun, which is a medium-sized star. The nearest star (not counting the sun) is 25 trillion miles away. The first stars may have formed as early as 400 million years after the Big Bang. NASA's orbiting Swift satellite recently detected an exploding star 12.6 billion light years from Earth. The scientific realization that there are perhaps 100 billion billion stars scattered throughout the universe, collected in galaxies, is a fairly recent discovery.

Many stars were shining by one billion years ago and new stars are still forming in the clouds of gas and dust in the Milky Way and other galaxies. Star formation in the Milky Way is at the rate of about ten per year. Some common star terms are listed below.

Nebula (plural nebulae). A cloud of gas and dust in space, sometimes derived from gas thrown off by dying stars (or new stars). Slated to be the birthplace of new stars and classified according to whether they emit, reflect, or absorb light.

Neutron Star. After black holes, they have the most extreme properties of any body in the universe. Small, superdense, their atoms are compressed to neutrons. They have the strongest magnetic fields of all stars and enormous energies that flare gamma and X-radiation.

Pulsar. Thought to be rapidly spinning neutron stars that emit energy in regular pulses. First recognized in 1967.

Red Giant. A large, bright star, ten to 100 times the size of our sun, believed to be at the end stage of its life. As a star uses up its fuel, it expands and its surface cools (relatively), hence its red color.

Supergiant. A dying star whose diameter is up to 1000 times that of the sun. A large, bright star that has used up its hydrogen fuel, begun to expand and cool.

Supernova. An exploding supergiant, it is the explosive death of a star and attains the temporary brightness of 100 million suns or more. The most famous supernova in the Milky Way was observed in 1054 and produced a huge cloud of rapidly expanding gas called the Crab Nebula. The Crab Nebula has a spinning neutron star—a pulsar—at its center.

White Dwarf. A very dense, small, hot star in the last stage of life. After a red giant sheds its outer layers, the remaining core is hotter than the sun and extremely dense—a spoonful would weigh several tons. Our sun will likely meet its demise as a white dwarf in 5 to 7 billion years. About 10 percent of the stars in the Milky Way are white dwarfs. One of these, in the constellation Centaurus, has been identified as a diamond, 2500 miles in diameter.

Red Dwarf. Also known as M dwarfs, they have less than half the mass of the sun and are hundreds of times dimmer. By far the most abundant stars (about 400 billion) in the Milky Way galaxy, they outnumber our Sol-like sun more than ten to one.

Brown Dwarf. Less massive than a star but heavier than a planet. Twenty to forty times more massive than Jupiter but emits only one percent of the radiation of the smallest known star. Sometimes considered to be a failed star but may have its own planet(s) in tow. Brown dwarfs are difficult to detect.

In the late 1950s radio telescopes first detected some striking point sources, or "quasi-stellar radio sources"—quasars for short. Quasars have been found to be the most energetic objects in the universe, occur in the very bright center of distant galaxies, and seem to be related to the presence of a supermassive black hole (more than a billion solar masses). Quasars form early in the life of a galaxy and astronomers estimate there are at least 10 million in the visible universe.

Quasars are one example of active galactic nuclei (AGN) and in brilliance are similar to starbursts, in which stars form at an accelerated rate of up to 1000 suns per year. This is at least 100 times faster than stars form in our own galaxy. Starburst activity typically lasts about 10 million years and can be initiated by the proximity of another galaxy, which changes tidal forces on the interstellar clouds of gas. Both AGNs and starbursts are now believed to be closely related to the activity of the black hole controlling the entire galaxy.

A black hole, or singularity, is a region of incredible mass and hence such powerful gravity that not even light can escape. Because of this, black holes cannot be "seen" but their presence must be inferred from the effects on gas clouds swirling around the center. Calculations suggest the unseen mass to be the equivalent of up to several billion suns in the largest galaxies in order to keep the orbiting gas from flying away. Burning gas equivalent to 1 million suns may be swallowed by the black hole every year.

One likely scenario for the formation of a black hole is the progression from a super giant star as it runs out of nuclear fuel. When the hydrogen burns up, the star has a sudden and catastrophic collapse. The core turns into a neutron star and the remainder undergoes a powerful supernova explosion, leading to a gamma-ray burst (GRB). If the neutron star exceeds roughly twenty solar masses, it may become a black hole. These relationships help explain why black holes and GRBs are seemingly linked together.

A mysterious burst of gamma rays from an unidentified celestial source was first detected in 1967. GRBs, typically lasting twenty seconds, can be more than 10 million times brighter than an ordinary supernova and are "the most incredible astronomical events we know about." In addition to being the most energetic events ever recorded, GRBs can also be the most distant, nearly 12 billion light-years away. NASA launched the High Energy Transient Explorer or HETE in 2000 for the specific purpose of learning more about GRBs, at least one of which, on average, occurs every day, somewhere in the universe. As each of these natural fireballs slows down from near the speed of light, the gamma rays degrade to X-rays, then visible light and finally to radio waves. Researchers have hopes of creating tiny man-made black holes for further study when the Large Hadron Collider at CERN near Geneva begins operations in 2007.

The Hubble Space Telescope (HST) has served to open new vistas of the countless other galaxies that exist outside our own system. New scenes of spectacular sights become available almost daily, it seems, and literally every place HST has looked, it has found something fantastic. In recent years, astrophysicists/astronomers have been able to observe and identify a vast number of new galaxies and stars. The most distant images seen by HST appear as they were about 11 billion years ago. One surprise from HST is that there is a massive "black hole" in the center of every galaxy. [I highly recommend that people check out the "Astronomy picture of the day" (go to Google) which shows wonderful color images of space features, from the HST and other sources, with explanatory commentary by qualified scientists].

Some one billion years after the Big Bang, galaxies began to form, a total of about 100 billion altogether. These collections of stars, gas and dust speckle the universe and are not the isolated, static structures they were once thought to be. Rather, galaxies may collide, merge, and change shape as they cannibalize each other. Galaxies form at least several hundred thousand galaxy clusters (called nebulae by Hubble), each a compact blob containing anywhere from 100,000 to several million stars.

Before 1924 our own Milky Way galaxy was the only one known. The Milky Way is the galaxy that includes the sun, Earth, the other planets of our solar system—and all the stars that can be seen with the human eye. The Milky Way has about 150 globular clusters. Hundreds of "blue stars" have been discovered at the center of the clusters. These are young, hot stars formed in a recycling process of gases and dust released by explosions of older stars. From Earth, the Milky Way looks like a band of light formed by about 400 billion stars (other suns) spread across the night sky. Clouds of gas and dust tend to obscure portions of the band and smear out the light. Ancient Greeks saw the whitish band as milk spilling from the left breast of the seated Cassiopeia. Even the term galaxy is derived from the Greek word for milk.

From outside our galaxy, the Milky Way would look like a discus, altogether about 100,000 to 130,000 light-years in diameter, with a large bulge in the center. The Milky Way is 3000 to 10,000 light-years thick at the central bulge and tapers to about 2000 light-years at the ends. Stars, dust and gas fan out from the central bulge in four long, curving arms that form a spiral pattern. Older stars are concentrated in the central bulge whereas the outer spiral arms are characterized by glowing clouds of gas and dust where bright new stars are being formed. The Milky Way is a barred spiral galaxy, the "bar" being a long, luminous rectangle of stars.

Our solar system formed 4.5 billion years ago and is located in the Orion Arm of the Milky Way, about 26,000 light-years from the center. All stars and star clusters in the Milky Way orbit the center of the galaxy, completing one full, nearly circular orbit in about 230 million years. Almost all the stars in the system orbit like a pinwheel in the same direction. The rotation seems to be around a nucleus or center characterized by a powerful gravitational force. Sagittarius 'A' has been identified as the massive central black hole, 3.6 million times as heavy as our sun, and perhaps rotating rapidly.

A unified explanation is being sought to explain the large diversity of galaxies. Some of the common shapes they take include normal spirals, barred spirals, ellipticals, dwarfs and irregulars. Dark galaxies with no stars have been detected through feeble radio transmissions, seen only with radio-wave receivers. Some of these galaxies seem to be comprised of swirling clouds of hydrogen-rich gas having 100 million times the mass of the sun. It is anticipated that many more of these will be found.

In 1905, Einstein explained in his special theory of relativity that physical laws are the same to any observer, i.e., oriented in any direction and moving at any constant velocity. This means the speed of light appears the same to all observers, that a moving clock is slowed, that moving objects have a linear contraction, and that mass and energy have equivalence. In his famous equation, $E=mc^2$, where E stands for energy, m for mass, and c^2 for the speed of light squared, energy is proportional to mass. Then in 1917 he proposed his general theory of relativity which included the effects of gravity. General relativity is a classical theory (that is, nonquantum) and is more complicated than the special theory. Einstein showed that the force of gravity is represented by curved space-time in four dimensions. The theory implied that space-time began at the Big Bang singularity, i.e., the universe had a beginning (and possibly an end). One effect would be that the path of a ray of light is bent slightly by a large/heavy mass such as a galaxy or singularity. A good example of the phenomenon is seen in the image below, from the Hubble telescope.

"Gravity can bend light, allowing huge clusters of galaxies to act as telescopes. Almost all of the bright objects in this released Hubble Space Telescope image are galaxies in the cluster known as Abell 2218. The cluster is so massive and so compact that its gravity bends and focuses the light from galaxies that lie behind it. As a result, multiple images of these background galaxies are distorted into long faint arcs—a simple lensing effect...The cluster of galaxies Abell 2218 is itself about three billion light-years away in the northern constellation Draco."
(from Astronomy Picture of the Day).

Prematurely, in 1917 Einstein applied his new ideas to the structure of the universe. He claimed the universe was static and unchanging, and is homogeneous on a large scale. To explain why gravity would not collapse everything together, he introduced a new counterbalancing force called the cosmological constant. Some years later Einstein called the constant "my greatest mistake" but "black energy" as understood today has much the same effect as did Einstein's constant.

The profoundly important "redshift" effect was described by de Sitter in the late 1920s. This optical property is similar to the Doppler phenomenon, which is an acoustic effect. In Doppler shifting, the wavelength of something moving away from the observer is attenuated to a lower frequency. An example is a train whistle; when the train is coming toward you the pitch of the sound is higher and then lowers as the train moves away. The same effect occurs for all wavelengths including light, the result being that objects moving away are shifted toward the red part of the visible spectrum, or redshifted. The faster they move away, the more they are redshifted.

American astronomer Edwin Hubble utilized this phenomenon and in 1929 made the dramatic announcement that the universe is expanding. He had determined the velocities for forty-six extragalactic nebulae and accurate distances for twenty-four. The latter calculations were made by measuring the pulsating luminosity of Cepheid variable stars, then using the inverse square law for brightness to determine distance. This was enough to show a clear increase of velocity with distance, the famous Hubble velocity-distance law. This is known as the Hubble expansion and the rate of expansion is called the Hubble constant. Small wonder that the space telescope is named after this man. Another wonder is that Hubble in his youth very nearly became a professional boxer. Instead, he studied law before finding his true vocation in astronomy.

Recently, Amy Barger has described an approach called "cosmic stratigraphy" to reconstruct the sequence of galaxy and star formation since the Big Bang. This technique utilizes data from the Hubble Ultra Deep Field, the Chandra X-ray observatory and ground-based telescopes to obtain redshifts of galaxies. More distant and hence older galaxies are more redshifted; a redshift of one means the wavelength has been stretched 100 percent, or twice its original size. This would equate to about 6 billion years after the Big Bang. Some very bright, older galaxies formed more than one thousand suns every year, whereas in the Milky Way and other nearby spiral galaxies the rate of star formation is only a few per year. The older galaxies were more likely to be fewer, but larger and more energetic, with super massive black holes, compared to younger galaxies which are more numerous and dimmer.

Observable interstellar material is made up of about 90 percent hydrogen, 10 percent helium and everything else from lithium to uranium is about 0.1 percent—just a trace. Most astronomers believe that large quantities of some other, unidentified matter must be present in the universe because the visible (baryonic) matter is affected in unaccountable ways. Galaxies move about but do not escape because of gravitational pull from the rest of the system. Laws of physics show how much total mass should be present but the tally of what is actually observed falls far short of the calculation. Hence, about seventy years ago, the concept of "cold dark matter" was introduced and it may make up 23 percent of the total universe.

A likely candidate is the neutralino, with a hypothetical mass sufficient to make up the required mass of dark matter. Dispersed like a gas, the neutralino has zero charge but may react with the weak nuclear force. Researchers estimate that neutralinos may move at the rate of one billion particles/meter^2/second. Cline (2003) points out that neutralinos are not included in the Standard Model but are the lightest elementary particles that have characteristics of supersymmetry.

The concept of dark energy has been introduced to explain the accelerating expansion of the universe. But if dark matter and/or other material prove to be dense enough, then, in theory, all the matter in the universe could (in billions of years) coalesce back together again. The result would be an unimaginably dense and hot ball, or singularity, similar to the state the universe was in before the Big Bang. This possibility is sometimes called the "Big Crunch" by astronomers.

QUANTUM THEORY

Stephen Hawking holds Newton's chair at Cambridge and despite his terribly debilitating handicap of Lou Gehrig's disease is considered the most brilliant physicist since Einstein. His goal has been to develop a single, unified quantum theory, especially concerning singularities such as black holes where the red shift becomes infinite. In such cases, the effects of quantum mechanics become important and the general theory is less so. Where infinite density is involved, only quantum theory can deal with the factor of unpredictability in describing probability distributions of miniscule particles, called quanta, making up light or X-rays. He also shows how radiation is related to energy at a singularity (Hawking radiation), and utilizes a trick of mathematics called "imaginary time."

All physics except for gravity can be described by quantum laws. This may be one reason Einstein was not enthusiastic about the quantum rules that permitted chance and uncertainty to play a role in sub-atomic physics.

Although he was one of the first to work on the idea of a unified theory, Einstein was involved only peripherally during the quantum revolution of the 1920s and 1930s.

The Standard Model of particle physics was finalized during the period 1970–73. It is consistent with both quantum mechanics and special relativity but is an incomplete theory at this time because it does not describe gravitational force. The theory uses the strong, weak and electromagnetic forces as well as the fundamental particles that make up all matter. Today, the Standard Model is a well-tested theory applicable over a wide range of conditions.

To me, it is astonishing that the Quantum Theory was developed over 100 years ago by the German physicist Max Planck (1858–1947). In 1900 Planck proposed that radiant heat energy is emitted in units called quanta, limited to whole number multiples of hv ($E = hv$) where v is the frequency of light. The value of h, or Planck's constant, is 6.626×10^{-34} joules. Planck's constant is the basic parameter of quantum theory. Planck's length has come to mean a fundamental scale of about 10^{-35} meter, Planck time is 10^{-43} second, and Planck mass is 10^{-8} kilogram. These units are entirely theoretical and far beyond the range of the most powerful microscopes or high-energy colliders. To appreciate the numbers, consider that the thickness of a human hair is 10^{-30} of the distance across the observable universe.

In 1905 Einstein made the first scientific use of quantum mechanics when he recognized that light appearing as quanta explained the photoelectric effect. He also explained that Brownian motion was due to erratic movements of molecules. Together with his other publication on special relativity, they became known as the "Einstein trilogy."

Other giants of quantum mechanics are Niels Bohr (1885–1962) director of the Bohr Institute at the University of Copenhagen; Werner Heisenberg (1901–1976) who developed matrix mechanics and the uncertainty principle; Erwin Schrödinger (1887–1961) who produced the basic equation of quantum mechanics; Max Born (1882–1970) whose probability density concept described the cloud of probable locations for electrons in different states; Wolfgang Pauli (1900–1958) defined the exclusion principle to mean that no two electrons in an atom can share the same quantum state. Particles obeying the Pauli exclusion principle are fermions and all others are bosons; Paul Dirac (1902–1984) corrected Einstein's $E = mc^2$ formula and predicted that every particle possesses an antiparticle.

In the Standard Model, fermions are particles of matter and bosons are particles that transmit forces. All fermions have mass and all except neutrinos have positive or negative charges. Left-handed fermions in Generation 1 include electrons and positrons plus electron neutrinos, up quarks, down quarks and their three antiparticles. In Generation 2 the left-handed fermions include muons, muon neutrinos, charm quarks, strange quarks and their four antiparticles. In Generation 3 the left-handed fermions include tau leptons, tau neutrinos, top quarks, bottom quarks, and their four antiparticles. There are twelve different types or "flavors" of fermions. Quarks are fundamental particles of matter that form neutrons and protons; they have three "colors," a force between quarks that gets stronger with distance. This means quarks are always found in colorless combinations called hadrons, a condition known as quark confinement.

The bosons that mediate (or "carry") the forces are light photons (with zero mass), W and Z bosons, and eight species of gluons. Each set of mediating bosons are referred to as gauge bosons. Higgs bosons are predicted by the Standard Model, but as of 2006 had not been observed (nor have supersymmetric particles important to explaining dark matter).

Quantum bits or "qubits" are newer terms. Concerning the possibility of quantum computers, one with just 300 qubits could run more calculations in an instant than there are atoms in the universe. An essential step in quantum computing might be to harness the power of entanglement or "spooky behavior" of separated particles, which seem to dance in unison (Einstein deplored this phenomenon). Recently, physicists at Caltech entangled two groups of 100,000 atoms some ten feet apart.

String theory is considered a promising way to marry quantum mechanics with gravity. One of the basic ideas is that supersymmetry (SUSY) exists between fundamental particles (fermions and bosons). Further, the particles are actually one-dimensional, vibrating loops or strands, of Planck length, essentially a point. To be mathematically correct, a string would have to vibrate in ten dimensions, six of which are too small to have been detected so far. Strings always have their endpoints on sheets known as "branes" (from membranes, hence M-theory), adding one more dimension. This "theory of everything" can lead to a "simple" explanation for non-scientists as stated in the *New York Times* (Bryson, p. 167). "The ekpyrotic process begins far in the indefinite past with a pair of flat empty branes sitting parallel to each other in a warped five-dimensional space.... The two branes, which form the walls of the fifth dimension, could have popped out of nothingness as a quantum fluctuation."

Hard evidence for string theory is still lacking, however, leading one proponent, physicist Amanda Peet at the University of Toronto to remark that the theory is a "faith-based initiative." [She must have been reading II Corinthians 5:7 "But we live by faith, not by what we see."] The idea of a multiverse or different possible "pocket universes" with radically different physical properties is also difficult to grasp. Especially as the number of possible universes has been described in terms of googols (1 followed by 100 zeros).

It is also thought-provoking to realize how much is unknown about the universe in which we live. Higgs bosons have been mentioned but are a minor matter when compared to the major unknowns, namely dark matter and dark energy. Recall that 23 percent of the universe is comprised of cold dark matter and 73 percent is dark mass-energy. That leaves only 4 percent for the matter with atomic structure that we can actually detect directly.

SPACE EXPLORATION

When the Russians launched Sputnik in 1957 it set off an international race to explore space and develop hardware—missiles, et al.—for defensive and offensive purposes. Since that time a cumulative estimated few hundred billion dollars has been spent by different nations. Fortunately, in recent years more of the money has gone for scientific and commercial purposes as the Cold War wound down. Today, rockets are being launched into space from somewhere on Earth at the average rate of about one per week. There can be no doubt that this overall effort, though only loosely coordinated, is by far the most massive effort mankind, through their governments, has ever made to conduct pure scientific research. Furthermore, this effort will continue and probably grow; firm plans are in place for future hardware and space exploration. Some of the most important events are listed below but the list is certainly incomplete.

- 1957 Sputnik launched by Soviet Union.
- 1959 Russian Luna 3 reached the moon and sent back photographs of the far side of the moon.
- First American spy satellite.
- 1960 First American weather and navigation satellites launched.
- 1961 Soviet cosmonaut Gagarin became first man in space.
- 1962 John Glenn Jr. became first American to orbit Earth.

- Telstar, the first active communications satellite, was launched.
- U.S. space probe Mariner 2 passed within 22,000 miles of Venus.
- 1963 Syncom 2, first geosynchronous satellite.
- 1965 Mariner 4 passed within 7,500 miles of Mars.
- 1969 Apollo 11 landed on moon. American astronaut Neil Armstrong became first human being to stand on the moon. Four other lunar landings were made in the next three years.
- 1972 Pioneer 10 space probe was launched and in 1983 escaped from the solar system.
- Landsat 1 launched, covering Earth's entire surface in eighteen-day cycles.
- 1973 First Skylab mission.
- 1975 U.S./Soviet space cooperation began with the Apollo-Soyuz project.
- 1977 Voyager 1 and 2 spacecraft launched and eventually flew by Jurpiter, Saturn, Uranus, and Neptune. Called the most successful mission that NASA carried out; by 2002 spacecraft had traveled nearly 9 billion miles, almost to the limits of the solar system.
- 1980 VLA—Very Large Array—radio telescope began operations near Socorro, NM.
- 1981 Space shuttle Columbia launched.
- 1985 Construction of Keck telescope, the world's largest, began on Maui.
- 1986 Space shuttle Challenger exploded seventy-three seconds after launch.
- Russian Mir, the first permanently manned space station, launched.
- 1989 Spacecraft Galileo launched to study Jupiter and its moons. It was very successful, acquired extensive imagery, and crashed in September 2003.
- Cosmic Background Explorer (COBE) satellite launched to measure the diffused infrared and microwave radiation from the early universe, and elaborate upon the fundamental discovery by Penzias and Wilson in 1963.

- European Space Agency's Hipparcos satellite (named for 130 b.c. Greek astronomer Hipparchus of Nicea) began building a database of 2.5 million stars. The Sloan Digital Sky Survey (SDSS) later catalogued 200 million celestial objects, using a 2½-meter telescope at Apache Point, NM.

- 1990 Shuttle Discovery deployed the Hubble Space Telescope (HST) placing it in a 370-mile orbit. Four subsequent upgrades were made on HST giving it greatly improved capabilities.

- 1991 Compton Gamma Ray Observatory (CGRO) a 17 ton craft, carried instruments to detect gamma rays.

- 1995 SOHO (Solar and Heliospheric Observatory) launched to study complete eleven-year solar cycle. Positioned in orbit 1.5 million km sunward of planet Earth, in balance with gravitational influence of Earth and Sun.

- 1996 NEAR-Shoemaker spacecraft launched to begin surveillance of asteroids close to Earth.

- 1997 Cassini-Huygens joint NASA/ESA/ASI spacecraft launched from Cape Canaveral. Cost $3.3 billion and largest, heaviest, most complex spacecraft to date. U.S.-built Cassini orbiter reached Saturn, seven years later, after a trip of 900 million miles, then released European-built Huygens probe. After another 2.5 million miles, Huygens probe reached the surface of Saturn's moon Titan in January 2005. Titan's rugged surface seems to be sculpted by methane rain and running liquid methane, at -274°F, with erosional features much like on Earth which is sculpted by water.

- Pathfinder and Sojurner landed on Mars and performed scientific investigations.

- 1999 Endeavour crew began construction of International Space station.

- Chandra Observatory began assignment of detecting cosmic X-rays.

- Far Ultraviolet Spectroscopic Explorer (FUSE) launched.

- NASA lost Mars Climate Orbiter and Polar Lander.

- 2000 High Energy Transient Explorer (HETE) launched to study gamma-ray bursts.

- 2001 Mir space station plunged into Pacific Ocean after fifteen years in space

- NEAR spacecraft landed on the EROS asteroid after orbiting it for one year.

- NASA Wilkinson Microwave Anistrophy Probe (WMAP) launched to map in detail the CMB radiation of Penzias and Wilson detected by the COBE satellite twelve years earlier. WMAP showed the gross composition of the universe, that it was 13.7 billion years old, and that it will expand forever.

- 2003 Shuttle Columbia broke up over Texas, fifteen minutes before landing in Florida. Seven crew members lost.

- Space InfraRed Telescope Facility (SIRTF) launched to explore universe in infrared light—later renamed the Spitzer Space Telescope as the fourth and final leg of NASA's Great Observatories Program. (The other three are HST, Compton Gamma Ray, and Chandra X-ray Observatories).

- 2004 British Beagle 2 Mars lander failed.

- NASA's Spirit and Opportunity rovers began sending information from two different sites on opposite sides of Mars. Spirit landed in the Gusev Crater and Opportunity in tiny Eagle Crater. The latter found evidence of cross-bedded sedimentary rocks, signifying ancient running water.

- 2005 NASA launched the Deep Impact spacecraft, on a six-month mission to intercept the Tempel 1 comet, 268 million miles away. An 820-pound probe was positioned to impact the comet at a speed of 23,000 mph, with the purpose of helping to determine the composition of the comet.

- 2006 NASA spacecraft New Horizons launched on nine-year mission to fly by Pluto, 3.7 billion miles from the Sun and then on to a newly discovered planet (2003 UB313) some 10 billion miles from the Sun.

- NASA's Stardust mission returned dust particles to Earth in a sample-return canister after a journey of nearly 3 million miles. The spacecraft was launched in February 1999 to recover the particles from the tail of comet Wild 2. It is expected that the dust particles are representative of material present during the formation of the solar system, 4.5 billion years ago.

- NASA's Mars Reconnaissance Orbiter (MRO) entered an elliptical orbit around Mars on March 10, after a seven-month, 300 million mile trip. The two-ton orbiter will take another seven months to reach a near circular polar orbit 200 miles above the surface of the red planet. The $720-million mission will acquire ten times the data of all previous Mars probes put together. Information on the climate, geology, and especially the past and present presence of water, will all serve to prepare for future landers carrying humans.

12

SOLAR SYSTEM

Our Milky Way spiral galaxy formed about 10 billion years ago and includes about 400 billion stars, or suns, one of which is the center of our solar system. Our galaxy is moving at the rate of about 200 km/sec toward the Andromeda galaxy 2.3 million light years away.

The Milky Way is still forming and evolving. Over the past several billion years it has incorporated many smaller satellite galaxies. In addition, gas clouds are continually arriving from intergalactic space. These high-velocity clouds, or HVCs are comprised of mysterious clumps of hydrogen, up to 10 million times the mass of the sun and 10,000 light-years across.

The center of the Milky Way is obscured by a dense screen of dust and gas, heated to about 10 million degrees and impenetrable by ordinary telescopes. But recently, the Chandra X-ray observatory, launched in 1999, has been able to obtain images from more than a thousand sources. Analyzing the spectra of the X-rays determined that hundreds of white dwarf stars exist near the galactic center. Also present are neutron stars or black holes, both powerful sources of X-rays. The gravitational center of the Milky Way is a super massive black hole, possibly with a swarm of smaller black holes surrounding it. This Sagittarius A complex is three times the size of our solar system with a density of 3.6 million suns. It is the most active region of our galaxy, in "a constant roar of star formation and destruction."

Every star in the galaxy—including our sun, a G star—whirls around the center once every 250 million years. At this speed of 137 miles/sec, the sun, with the earth in tow, has completed about twenty circuits since our solar system was formed 4.6 billion years ago.

OUR SUN

Our sun is a yellow dwarf star called Sol, located about half way out on one of the galaxy's four spiral arms and about 25,000 light years from the center. The solar system formed when an enormous cloud of gas and dust collapsed upon itself, perhaps because a large, nearby star exploded as a supernova. The cloud was composed mostly of hydrogen and helium gas, left over from the Big Bang. The dust and other debris came from earlier generations of stars which exploded as they died. The latter also provided elements such as carbon, nitrogen and oxygen. Heavier elements such as lead and uranium are manufactured in supernova explosions.

The sun makes up 99.86 percent of the total mass of the Solar System. Everything else—the planets, moons and cosmic rubble—makes up only 0.14 percent, and two-thirds of that is in one planet, Jupiter. The sun has a diameter of 865,000 miles, 109 times that of Earth.

The sun is a ball of hot gas—actually plasma—made up of 71 percent hydrogen, 26 percent helium and at least seventy other elements. The density of the plasma at the core of the sun is twelve times that of solid lead and the temperature is 27,000,000°F or 15,000,000°C. Heat and light are generated by nuclear fusion as hydrogen nuclei are converted into helium nuclei, as in a hydrogen bomb. [Hans Bethe won a Nobel Prize in 1938 for his discovery of this process] Every second, 700 million tons of matter is converted into energy, like millions of hydrogen bombs all going off at once. In one second, the sun gives off more energy than all people have produced during their stay on Earth. Burning fuel at this rate, the sun has lost about 4 percent of its original supply of hydrogen in its 4.6 billion-year life to date. Yet Earth receives only a tiny fraction—two billionths—of the sun's total energy. The rest streams out into space.

Nuclear fusion reactions at the core of the sun release high-energy gamma rays, which are invisible to the human eye but eventually are changed into visible light near the surface of the sun. The sun's 340 mile-thick surface layer of hot gas, called the photosphere, is sometimes penetrated by seething magnetic activity which seems to be related to sunspots. It is now known that these are "cool spots" where the temperature is 3500°F cooler than the surrounding area. Sunspots usually occur in groups, up to 100 at a time and can be many times larger in area than the size of the earth. They may develop above the surface of the sun because the sun seems to rotate beneath them. Sunspot activity seems to influence our climatic conditions in that the earth gets colder when sunspot activity diminishes.

Above the photosphere is the 6000-mile chromosphere, which can be seen as a pink ring around the sun during a solar eclipse. Bright hot jets of burning gas, called solar flares, punctuate this 50,000°F layer. Above this is the sun's atmosphere, or corona, a 1,000,000-mile halo of 4,000,000°F gas surrounding the sun. Charged particles boiling outward from the corona form the solar wind, an electrified plasma that moves at about a million miles per hour. Activity on the sun, including sunspots and flares, seems to peak every eleven years or so and may be related to the solar magnetic field.

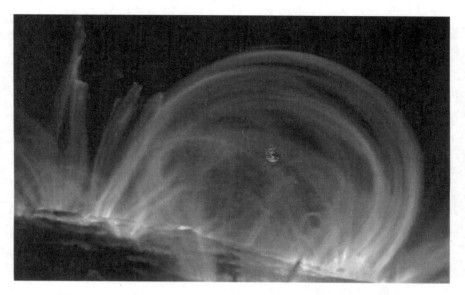

"Fountains of Fire. Giant fountains of fast-moving, multimillion-degree gas in the outermost atmosphere of the sun have revealed an important clue to a long-standing mystery— the location of the heating mechanism that makes the corona 300 times hotter than the sun's visible surface. Scientists discovered... immense coils of hot, electrified gas, known as coronal loops. These fiery, arching fountains now appear in unprecedented detail with NASA's Transition Region and Coronal Explorer (TRACE) spacecraft. Earth has been inserted into this false composite to illustrate the vast scale of this Coronal Loop" (from Astronomy Picture of the Day).

The radiation from the sun travels in an array or band ranging from high frequency gamma and X-rays to low frequency radio waves. Wavelengths sensed by humans include visible light, ultraviolet (burns the skin) and infrared (felt as heat). If a magnetic storm from the sun reaches Earth it can interfere with radios, satellite TV, cell phones, etc., and can induce currents in power lines and pipelines. One visible result can be spectacular auroras in polar areas.

In December 1995 the Solar and Heliospheric Observatory (SOHO) satellite was launched on a mission to specifically study the sun. SOHO was a joint venture of NASA and the European Space Agency. SOHO is presently in position about one million miles from Earth, and after some operational problems, the satellite regained full operational status in mid 2003. Some surprising SOHO findings include

- Deep gas currents speed up and slacken every 16 months. Projections suggest that ultraviolet rays from the sun have become 3 percent stronger over the last 300 years.

- A continual rearrangement of tangled magnetic fields causes a non-stop succession of explosions in the sun's atmosphere, which thereby becomes far hotter.

- A fast solar wind emanates mainly from polar regions.

- Strong magnetic waves seem to accelerate the solar wind. After solar flares, SOHO sees waves rushing across the surface of the sun. Tornadoes as wide as Africa are seen. Typical wind speeds are 31,000 mph, gusting to ten times faster.

Just as all other stars, our sun will eventually die (six billion years from now). As that happens, the sun will swell, reaching up to 100 times its current radius. In that phase, stars are known as red giants. As the sun loses mass it will shrink to its compact dense core and become a white dwarf about the size of Earth. At the same time, the sun will lose its gravitational influence on the planets and they will drift away. Only Mercury, the planet closest to the sun, will continue in its orbit.

As the early solar system formed, angular momentum was key to distributing material in a thin disk orbiting the sun. The material in the disk consolidated into planets, and moons may have formed around the larger planets in the same way. All the planets orbit in the same direction and rotate in the same counter-clockwise direction. The only exception is Venus which rotates in a clockwise direction, perhaps because its spin was disrupted by the impact of a large chunk of cosmic rubble. The sun also revolves, making a complete rotation every 25.3 days.

PLANETS

Astronomers generally speak of nine planets in our solar system but Pluto is more like a comet than anything else, being a rather large piece of cosmic rubble. The other eight planets, then, can be divided neatly into two groups of four. One group of four, known as the terrestrial planets (including Earth) are relatively small and rocky; these four orbit close to the sun. The other four are large, gaseous planets (the gas giants) and orbit farther out from the sun.

Mercury

Mercury is the smallest true planet, and the closest to the sun. It is only 1.5 times the size of our moon, and has no significant atmosphere. Scorched by the sun, the surface temperature on Mercury reaches 800°F during the day but plunges to -290°F at night. The spacecraft Mariner 10 flew by Mercury in the 1970s and found a rocky surface scarred by impact craters of all sizes, dating back to the earliest days of the solar system. Huge scarps, or cliffs, up to 10,000 feet high and 100 miles long snake across the surface. These may have been formed when the planet shrank as its core cooled.

Statistics:

- Diameter: 3031 miles
- Distance from sun: 36 million miles (average)
- Distance from Earth: 57 to 136 million miles
- Year: eighty-eight Earth days
- Time of rotation: fifty-nine Earth days
- Surface temperature: 800°F to -290°F
- Atmosphere: sparse oxygen, sodium, hydrogen, helium
- Composition: iron core, mantle of silicate rocks
- Known satellites: none

Venus

Venus is closer to the earth than any other planet and the two were formed at about the same time from similar material. But Venus has a suffocating, poisonous atmosphere quite different than ours. It has no trace of water on its surface; if it ever existed, it evaporated long ago due to the intense surface heat. Enormous volcanoes have formed huge lava plains, with lava flows thousands of miles long. Only massive meteorites have been able to penetrate the heavy atmosphere to form a few large impact craters.

Statistics:

- Diameter: 7521 miles
- Distance from sun: 67 million miles
- Distance from Earth: 26 to 160 million miles
- Year: 225 Earth days
- Time of rotation: 243 Earth days (clockwise)
- Surface temperature: 864°F
- Atmosphere: carbon dioxide, nitrogen, argon, carbon monoxide, neon, sulfur dioxide
- Composition: iron/nickel core and surface of silicate rock
- Known satellites: none

Earth (see chapter 13).

Briefly, the "third rock from the sun" is one of the rocky planets, only slightly larger than Venus. But unlike Venus, the earth is just the right distance from the sun, i.e., not too hot and not too cold. Earth has the only oceans of liquid water in the solar system and hence has the conditions favorable for the life forms we know. Conventionally, water on the young Earth has been explained as originating from deep in the planet and then released by volcanoes over geologic time. In late 1998, however, SWAS (Submillimeter Wave Astronomy Satellite) discovered that abundant water was formed almost instantaneously during star formation when a nebula begins to collapse. Thus, icy comets entering the earth's atmosphere could be a significant source of water.

While Earth was young, for the first few million years, it was subject to intense meteor showers. About 4.5 billion years ago, an object the size of Mars slammed into the earth, blasting out fragments of vaporized hot rock. This material gradually coalesced in orbit to form the Moon, and the impact created enough heat to melt the entire surface of the earth. This scenario is supported by rock samples from the Moon, which show that the earth and Moon are of the same age and have the same composition. [While I was manager of geological research at Mobil's lab in Dallas, one of the scientists working for me had the honor of being chosen to make petrographic analyses of some of the moon rocks brought back by the astronauts]. The earth and its Moon will be described in more detail in the next chapter.

Statistics:

- Diameter: 7926.4 miles at equator
- Circumference: 24,901.6 miles at equator
- Distance from sun: 93 million miles
- Year: 365.2422 days
- Time of rotation: twenty-three hours, fifty-six minutes
- Surface temperature: 57°F average
- Atmosphere: nitrogen 78.08 percent, oxygen 20.94 percent, argon 0.93 percent, carbon dioxide 0.03 percent, water vapor (variable), trace amounts of neon, helium, krypton, xenon, ozone
- Composition: iron, nickel, silicon, aluminum
- Known satellites: one moon

Mars

The fourth planet from the sun and one of Earth's nearest neighbors, Mars is a small rocky planet colder than and just over half the size of Earth. Sunlight reflected off the surface of Mars reaches the earth in only four minutes and its rusty red color is clearly seen, hence the name "Red Planet." The color stems from the minerals hematite and limonite, weathering products of iron which is twice as plentiful on Mars compared to Earth. About two-thirds of the Martian surface is covered with reddish material consisting of dust, sand and rocks. Winds up to 125 mph whip up huge dust storms.

Like the earth, Mars is tilted on its axis and has seasons. Mars has a relatively warm summer reaching 68°F, but a long, cold winter when temperatures can be -284°F. A few billion years ago Mars was covered by huge volcanoes; Olympus Mons rises 90,000 feet above the surface. Another huge physiographic feature is the Valles Marineris canyon that is 3125 miles long and big enough to hold the Rocky Mountains. Asteroid impacts have created many basins; the crater Gale is 125 miles across.

In 1996 a NASA/Stanford team announced that a meteorite from Mars gave evidence of past life there. The rock sample was recovered in Antarctica and related to Mars because of similarity to soil samples analyzed by a 1976 space probe. Dating showed the rock was 4.5 billion years old and the petrographic analyses relied heavily on indirect evidence. Only the electron microscope images showed shapes similar to known bacteria, but much smaller. When the announcement was made, media hype ensued and heated arguments arose in the scientific community. At present, uncertainty prevails.

In recent years there has been a great deal of speculation about water on Mars. Some features resemble fluvial drainage patterns and new findings support the idea that in the past, large volumes of water were created by episodic melting of the polar ice caps. It is likely that this melting was caused by the impacts of large meteors 60–150 miles wide. Good evidence shows that at least twenty-five large meteors struck Mars about 3.5 billion years ago, at the same time that the river channels formed. In 2005 NASA's Opportunity rover found cross-bedded sedimentary rocks of fluvial origin but conditions may not have been conducive to the deposition of carbonate rocks.

Hints of water and possible life make Mars an enticing target for future human exploration, but it will be a project entailing danger, enormous complexity, and cost. The distance involved, about 300 million miles, would take about six months of travel time. Previous unmanned Mars missions include nineteen failures (mostly Russian) and only a few successes such as the Pathfinder/Sojourner landers in 1997 and the Spirit and Opportunity rovers in 2004. The only plans for the next decade are six robotic missions.

Statistics:

- Diameter: 4223 miles

- Circumference: 13,267 miles

- Distance from sun: 142 million miles

- Distance from Earth: thirty-five to 248 million miles

- Year: 687 Earth days

- Time of rotation: 24.62 hours
- Surface temperature: 68° to -284°F
- Atmosphere: carbon carbon dioxide (95.3 percent), nitrogen (2.7 percent), argon, oxygen, carbon monoxide, neon, krypton, xenon, water vapor
- Composition: silicon, iron
- Known satellites: two (likely asteroids caught in Mars' gravity)

Asteroid Belt

Millions of rock fragments orbit the sun in a broad band called the Asteroid, or Main Belt, beyond Mars but inside the orbit of Jupiter. They range from the size of pebbles to massive bodies like Ceres, 584 miles wide. They are composed of rock and iron and are believed to be leftover fragments from the formation of the solar system. The Asteroid Belt includes ninety percent of all asteroids, and orbits have been calculated for seven thousand of them. Individual asteroids rotate, and take three to six years to orbit the sun.

Some asteroids stray into and others orbit within the inner solar system, crossing the paths of Earth and Mars. These can be of real concern to us. It is believed that 65 million years ago a ten-mile wide asteroid crashed into the Gulf of Mexico near the Yucatan Peninsula forming a crater 120 miles across. It caused monstrous tsunamis and set fires that burned whole continents, producing thick clouds of dust and smoke. Lack of sunlight for months or years caused drastic climatic changes, killing off vegetation and interrupting the food chain. It is believed that this event caused the mass extinction of the dinosaurs.

Jupiter

The four outer planets are called the "Jovian" or "gas giants." Jupiter is the innermost of the four and by far the largest planet in the solar system. Its mass equals 70 percent of all the planets combined. Although Jupiter probably has a rocky core its surface is always hidden by icy clouds of liquid hydrogen. A complex weather system generates massive bands of clouds that race across the surface and also includes the Great Red Spot, Jupiter's signature feature.

The Great Red Spot is an enormous, swirling cloud of gases 25,000 miles wide and resembling a hurricane, and has been observed for over 300 years. The gas circulates at the speed of 225 mph and the spot drifts east and west, keeping a steady distance from the equator. The spot is usually shades of red but sometimes gray or white. Its color may be due to small amounts of sulfur and phosphorus in ammonia crystals or possibly a chemical that changes color in the presence of sunlight.

Jupiter has sixty known moons, the four largest of which were discovered in 1610 by the Italian astronomer Galileo. Galileo used a simple telescope to find what came to be called the "Galilean" satellites and concluded that the Copernicus idea had merit, i.e., not all stars are fixed and rotating around a stationary Earth.

Of the four Galilean moons, Io may be the most interesting. It has many active volcanoes which emit sulfurous gases. The yellow-orange color of Io's surface is probably due to solid sulfur deposits. Io is the most volcanically active body in the entire solar system. Ganymede is the largest of the four with a diameter of 3273 miles. Callisto has a diameter of 2986 miles and both of these two appear to consist of ice and rocky material marked by numerous craters. Europa is the smallest of the four moons with a diameter of 1950 miles and has a smooth, cracked, icy surface. Some of the fractures in the surface ice are more than 3000 km long. The ice is almost certainly floating on liquid water at least part of the time. All the remaining moons are much smaller with diameters of 168 miles and less.

Statistics (of Jupiter):

- Diameter: 88,846 miles
- Mean distance from sun: 483,600,000 miles
- Distance from Earth: 390,700,000 to 600,000,000 miles
- Year: twelve Earth years
- Time of rotation: nine hours, fifty-five minutes
- Average temperature: -250°F
- Atmosphere: hydrogen, helium, methane, ammonia, carbon monoxide, acetylene, phosphine, water vapor
- Known satellites: sixty

Saturn

Saturn is the sixth planet from the sun and second to Jupiter in size. Most scientists believe Saturn is a giant ball of gas that has no solid surface, but a hot, solid inner core of iron and rocky material may exist. Ammonia, methane and water are believed to comprise the innermost atmosphere, whereas the outer region is helium and hydrogen. Saturn is most famous for its spectacular rings which make the planet the most beautiful object in the solar system.

Saturn's rings consist of thousands of narrow bands, organized into seven thin, flat rings that surround the planet at its equator. A space of about 2000 miles separates the rings from one another. The outermost ring is about 180,000 miles in diameter but each ring is only 660–9800 feet thick. They are composed of billions of pieces of ice particles orbiting the planet. The other gas giants also have rings, but they are very weakly developed compared to Saturn.

The numerous moons of Saturn are far outside the ring system. Titan, the largest moon, is 3193 miles in diameter and orbits at a distance of 758,000 miles, once every fifteen days. Its thick atmosphere is mostly nitrogen with some methane and ammonia. The moon is shrouded by orange clouds of complex compounds which include carbon. In January 2005 the Huygens probe found that the rugged surface of Titan has erosional features formed by liquid methane. (p. 418?).

Tethys, another of Saturn's moons, is marked by numerous impact craters but in addition shows a broad trench system several hundred miles long. Iapetus, the outermost large moon, orbits every seventy-nine days at a distance of 2.2 million miles. It appears to be made of dirty ice and snow although the leading side is black colored.

Statistics (of Saturn):

- Diameter: 74,898 miles
- Distance from sun: 888,200,000 miles
- Distance from Earth: 763 to 1030 million miles
- Year: 29.5 Earth years
- Time of rotation: ten hours, thirty-nine minutes
- Surface temperature: -288°F
- Atmosphere: hydrogen, helium, methane, ammonia
- Composition: Possibly a small core of iron and rock, encased in ice and topped by a thick layer of liquid nitrogen
- Known satellites: thirty-three

Uranus

The seventh planet from the sun, Uranus is a giant ball of gas with numerous moons. Frozen methane forms the visible clouds giving a blue-green hue. [Liquefied natural gas (LNG)—which I have observed on tankers in Indonesia—had the same appearance.] It is believed that beneath the methane clouds, thick cloud layers of liquid water and ammonia ice exist. Even deeper, 4700 miles below the top of the clouds, an ocean of liquid water containing dissolved ammonia may be present. Of course, for this to be true, a central hot, rocky core would need to be present to furnish the required heat.

Uranus is unique in that its axis of rotation is tipped over to a horizontal position so that first one pole and then the other points toward the sun during its eighty-four-year orbit. All of Uranus's moons and rings follow orbits around the equator of the planet. It is thought that a massive object impacted Uranus long ago, knocking the planet on its side and creating the present array of moons which formed from the resulting debris.

Recent images of Uranus taken by Voyager 2 show faint banding of the methane clouds parallel to the equator. In addition, hurricane-like swirling masses of gas appear on the surface.

To the present time, twenty-one moons have been discovered. Miranda, about 300 miles in diameter, is one of the most interesting. It has a geologically complex surface with several areas showing very different structural styles. A rift valley five miles deep may result from the impact fragmentation of the moon and then rejoining of the pieces in a haphazard orientation.

Statistics (of Uranus):

- Diameter: 31,763 miles
- Mean distance from the sun: 1.8 billion miles
- Distance from Earth: 1.6 to 2.0 billion miles
- Year: eighty-four Earth years
- Time of rotation: seventeen hours, eight minutes
- Temperature: -357°F
- Atmosphere: hydrogen, helium, and methane
- Known satellites: twenty-one

Neptune

The eighth planet was discovered after two young mathematicians independently predicted its position based upon the behavior of Uranus. In 1846 a German astronomer confirmed with telescope observations that the planet really did exist at the predicted location.

Neptune's atmosphere consists chiefly of hydrogen, helium and water. Clouds at the surface grade downward to compressed gas, and then into liquid form A central core of rock may be present and furnish the heat needed to explain the violent storms in the atmosphere.

Voyager 2 found that Neptune has the fastest winds of all the planets, sometimes over 1500 mph. These winds were present in an area called the Great Dark Spot. The swirling masses of gas resemble a hurricane but wind speeds are ten times faster. The Great Dark Spot was seen to travel around Neptune in just over eighteen hours but by 1994 the Hubble Space Telescope found that the Spot had vanished.

The tilt of Neptune's axis causes the northern and southern hemispheres to heat alternately in seasons and the North Pole has an ice cap. Of eight moons, Triton claims the coldest temperature known in the solar system at -391°F.

Statistics (of Neptune):

- Diameter: 30,800 miles

- Distance from sun: 2.8 billion miles

- Distance from Earth: 2.7 to 2.9 billion miles

- Year: 165 Earth years

- Time of rotation: sixteen hours, seven minutes

- Surface temperature: -353°F

- Atmosphere: hydrogen, helium, methane, acetylene

- Known satellites: eight

Kuiper Belt

This belt of rock debris, ice and frozen gas is believed to be material left over from the beginning of the solar system 4.5 billion years ago. These bodies, called planetesimals, failed to coalesce into planets and were pulled away from the inner solar system by the giant outer planets. The inner edge of the Kuiper Belt exists at a distance of about 2.8 billion miles from the sun and extends outward to 93 billion miles but the weighted average distance for all the material is 3 billion miles.

In 1999 the International Astronomical Union officially ruled Pluto to be the ninth planet, rather than just a large body in the Kuiper Belt. It is 1430 miles in diameter and has a satellite named Chiron with a diameter of 740 miles. Some astronomers call the two the solar system's only "double planet." Pluto orbits about 3.7 billion miles from the sun and it is composed of frozen methane, nitrogen and carbon monoxide at -378°F.

Early in 2005 another possible planet was discovered in the Kuiper Belt. It is slightly larger than Pluto but averages a distance of 9 billion miles from the sun. Called Xena, the icy, rocky object orbits the sun once every 560 years. It also has a moon, appropriately named Gabrielle.

Orbits of material in the Kuiper Belt are sometimes altered by the gravitational pull of the outer planets. When this happens, every 200 years or so, the bodies form comets which swing in toward the inner planets. As the comet approaches the sun, the surface ice begins to vaporize into gases, with some rock particles. These, in turn, stream away, forming a comet tail sometimes 100 million miles long, a spectacular sight in the night sky. When dust particles from a comet's tail enter Earth's atmosphere they burn up and glow as meteors, or shooting stars.

Most meteors are no larger than a grain of sand; others can be as large as a pebble or a grape. As they slam into the earth's atmosphere at 35–45 miles/sec, friction causes them to burn up, vaporize and excite surrounding atoms in the atmosphere. Their brilliant light becomes visible between forty and seventy-five miles above Earth and they disintegrate at altitudes of thirty to sixty miles. Because of the curvature of the earth, no meteor can be seen more than 700 miles away. On a typical day our planet is hit by 25 million mostly unseen meteors, and 16,000 tons of meteoric material rain down annually. As a fascinating sidelight, molecules organized as fullerenes (buckyballs) have been found recently in meteorites billions of years old.

Around August 12 each year Earth experiences the Perseid meteor shower which regularly produces sixty to 100 meteors per hour. The Perseid meteors are encountered when the earth passes through the tail of the comet Swift-Tuttle which swings by the sun every 130 years. Chinese observers recorded the Perseid meteors as early as A.D. 36. The Leonid meteor shower occurs every thirty-three years and in 1833 produced the most brilliant meteor shower ever seen over North America.

Oort Cloud

The Oort cloud lies far beyond the Kuiper Belt, at the very limits of the solar system. The cloud may contain as many as 100 billion icy lumps of dark, frozen debris. This halo of icebergs is about 9 trillion miles from the sun but still within its gravitational control. Sometimes comets from the Oort cloud reach the inner part of the solar system and their fiery tails light up the night sky.

Life on other planets?

This, of course, is a subject of keen interest to many scientists. Knowing that there are 400 billion suns in the Milky Way and perhaps 100 billion billion stars (suns) in the universe, the potential for the existence of other planets is staggering. To date, about 160 other planets have been found orbiting other suns. Most of these planets are believed to be gas giants but a few may be rocky and Earth-like, although none possess favorable living conditions. Recently, British astronomers have reported the evidence for one or more planets, possibly Earth-like, orbiting Vega, a star only twenty-five light years away. Vega is only 350 million years old and three times the size of our sun.

Of course the presence of other planets in other solar systems does not guarantee the existence of life. Gonzales *et al* have argued that each galaxy has a "galactic habitable zone" which excludes the dangerous inner regions and the metal-poor outer region. As pointed out in the chapter "Lifeforms" a combination of specific favorable conditions is required to support life on Earth. Some of the twenty amino acids have been found in meteorites, showing that the potential for life as we know it exists outside the earth's environment. It is remotely possible that life elsewhere does not need water, amino acids, or DNA, and that heat is generated by radioactive elements rather than radiation from a star.

Frank Drake and the late Carl Sagan were among those who first speculated on the possibility of life on other planets. Their work led to development of the "Drake Equation" which attempted to calculate "N," the number of civilizations in the Milky Way sufficiently advanced technologically to broadcast radio transmissions. The equation used probability analysis of highly speculative factors to arrive at Sagan's estimate of at least a million other civilizations in the Milky Way. Playing with the Drake equation may be only one step above parlor games, and some scientists have compared it to the old theological argument over how many angels can dance on the head of a pin.

In 1960 Drake took more practical steps to detect other civilizations by using the eighty-five-foot wide radio telescope at Green Bank, WV, to listen for radio signals from space. In 1980 this effort was greatly expanded with the Very Large Array (VLA) of twenty-seven separate radio telescopes near Socorro, New Mexico. Since then, project SETI, or "Search for Extraterrestrial Intelligence" has been established as a privately funded effort. In 1999 SETI created software that can be used on home computers to help analyze the billions of bits of data. Over one million Web users in 226 countries have downloaded the program to participate in SETI@home but to date no transmissions from other planets have been detected.

Recently, a new approach is being planned using the merged radio signals from an array of as many as 15,000 high-gain, simple antennas. Mapping varying frequencies may provide data from ancient radio waves. Projects of this kind may be undertaken in China, Australia and the Netherlands.

13

EARTH

As the solar system formed, beginning 4.6 billion years ago, it is believed that the Earth and the other three inner planets appeared very early in the process. Each of them formed by the process of accretion, that is, they accumulated dust, rock particles, and larger fragments from the cloud of material surrounding the sun. As they grew larger and their gravity fields expanded, ever more rock fragments were swept up and the amount of available rocky material correspondingly diminished. Inclusions in chondrite meteorites provide ages of 4.566 billion years for these early rocks; dating is done by radioactive isotope techniques.

The early growth of the earth was probably a violent process marked by large impacts with other rock bodies. Huge planetary embryos smashed into each other, forming oceans of magma (molten rock) surrounded by atmospheres of white-hot silicate. It is believed that the moon was formed in an episode like this. An object about half the size of Mars struck Earth a glancing blow, then bounced off into orbit around Earth. The impact caused both the earth and the incipient moon to become molten. After they separated, both primitive bodies continued to grow by additional accretionary impacts.

The core of the earth is believed to have a composition of 85 percent iron and 15 percent nickel, at a temperature of at least 7200°F. The core includes a solid, inner zone with a diameter of about 775 miles and an outer zone 1365 miles thick comprised of viscous but liquid molten metal. The metallic core is believed to have formed by the time the earth was 30 to 60 million years old.

Surrounding the core is the mantle, some 1800 miles thick, made up of various iron-magnesium silicate rocks. The mantle comprises the great bulk of the earth's volume.

The outer layer of the earth is called the crust, divided into oceanic crust about six miles thick and continental crust twenty-five to sixty miles thick. Oceanic crust is composed almost entirely of basaltic igneous rocks whereas continental crust includes a wide variety of acidic igneous, metamorphic and sedimentary rocks. Faults and earthquakes are mostly confined to the crust, which is up to forty-five miles thick and relatively rigid. Separating the crust and mantle is the seismic "Moho" or Mohorovicic discontinuity, discovered by and named for the Croatian seismologist/meteorologist of the same name. He found that seismic velocities jump at the discontinuity due to the change in rocks to a dense, heavy layer of peridotite.

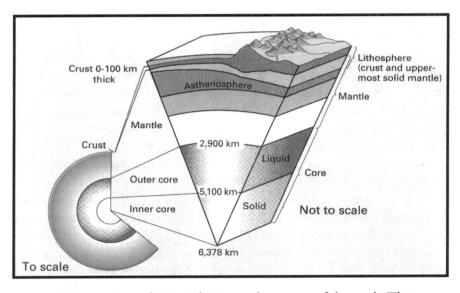

Cutaway views showing the internal structure of the earth. The view drawn to scale shows the crust is literally skin-deep. The cross-section view on right (not to scale) shows the three main layers—crust, mantle and core. From USGS.

The upper mantle is further divided by seismic characteristics into an upper lithosphere and a lower asthenosphere. The base of the lithosphere is from one mile deep at the oceanic ridges to ninety-three miles deep under continents and it is this unit that comprises the continental plates, which ride on the asthenosphere. The latter extends down to a depth of about 430 miles and is so hot that rock becomes plastic and mobile, thereby serving to carry the huge masses of rock involved in plate tectonics.

The earth acts as a huge, weak magnet and has a magnetic field that makes compasses point north. Scientists believe that the earth's magnetic field is caused by internal currents in the outer core. Support for this interpretation came in 1996 when geophysicists found that the earth's core turns slightly faster than the mantle (at the rate of one extra spin every 700–1200 years). The magnetic field extends many hundred miles out into space and has trapped charged particles from the sun, serving to protect the earth.

The solar wind, traveling at one million miles per hour, impacts and distorts the magnetosphere, compacting it on the sun-side of the earth. Some of the charged particles from the sun are channeled toward the north and south (magnetic) poles where they collide violently with gas atoms, giving off spectacular light displays. In the northern hemisphere such light is known as the aurora borealis, or northern lights, at altitudes of about 100 km. In the southern hemisphere the light is called the aurora australis, or southern lights.

The magnetic and geographic poles do not coincide. The difference between the two is called the magnetic declination. At present, the magnetic South Pole is some 13° or 930 miles from the geographic South Pole. The magnetic North Pole is displaced even more from its respective geographic pole. Also, the magnetic poles slowly change their positions which suggest changing currents in the core.

Even more provocative is the knowledge that the earth's magnetic field has "flipped" hundreds of times in the past 150 million years, resulting in the North Pole becoming the South Pole, and vice versa. Scientists have no good explanation for this phenomenon. Polarity reversals have occurred, on average, every 500,000 years. The most recent reversal was 780,000 years ago (the Jaramillo Event) and there are indications that the earth is building toward another.

A reversal may take 4000 years to complete but during that time the earth's protective magnetic shield would be disabled, leading to increased doses of cosmic and solar particles. Genetic effects in living organisms could be expected, but there does not seem to be an obvious correlation of magnetic reversals with major species extinctions.

ROCKS, MINERALS

A mineral is a naturally occurring, crystalline, inorganic compound that has a fairly definite chemical composition and a set of distinctive physical properties. Over 2000 minerals have been identified in the earth's crust but fewer than ten of them comprise 90 percent of the crust by mass. Two elements, oxygen and silicon make up 75 percent of the crust. Abundances of the mineral-forming elements are as follows: oxygen (O) 46.5 percent, silicon (Si) 27.5 percent, aluminum (Al) 8.1 percent, iron (Fe) 5.3 percent, calcium (Ca) 4.0 percent, magnesium (Mg) 2.7 percent, sodium (Na) 2.4 percent, potassium (K) 1.0 percent, and all others 1.6 percent.

Feldspars are the most common minerals in the earth's crust. There are two main types, (1) plagioclase feldspar which contains oxygen, silicon, aluminum and calcium and/or sodium and (2) potassium (or orthoclase) feldspar where potassium substitutes for the calcium/sodium. Some other common minerals are quartz, hornblende, olivine, pyroxene, calcite, dolomite, gypsum and clay.

Minerals can be identified by chemical analysis or X-ray diffraction techniques but both methods are costly. Most definitive of all is the index of refraction, and crystal form, determined from thin sections using a petrographic microscope. More commonly, geologists use distinctive physical properties such as hardness, specific gravity, color, fracture, cleavage, and rarely, fluorescence and phosphorescence.

The earth's crust is made up of rocks formed by various combinations of minerals and processes. Depending on the way they originated, rocks are classified into three general categories, as igneous, metamorphic, and sedimentary.

Igneous rocks are formed by magma or molten rock far beneath the earth's surface. If the magma flows to the surface it is called lava, both in molten and solid form and is an extrusive rock. The most common form of lava is basalt which covers about two-thirds of the earth's surface including almost the entire ocean floor. Basalt is dark colored and low in silica, about 50 percent by weight. Its essential mineral constituents are calcium-rich feldspar and pyroxene. Igneous activity has been so active throughout the history of the earth that igneous rocks are by far the most dominant type, making up 80 percent of the earth's crust.

Much igneous rock does not make its way to the surface but can still cool and solidify to form intrusive rocks. Granite is characteristic of intrusive rocks, often forming batholiths at the core of many mountainous uplifts. The Black Hills has a core of this kind (Harney Peak granite) but vastly larger is the Coast Range batholith of Western Canada. This rock body is some 1000 miles long and up to ninety miles wide. Granite tends to be light colored as it is comprised mainly of coarsely crystalline quartz and orthoclase feldspar. The latter weathers quickly into various clay minerals whereas the quartz contributes huge volumes of quartz grains which may accumulate in various sand bodies.

Most of the earth's extrusive rock occurs as oceanic basalt, supplied from the spreading centers on the ocean floor. This basalt can be several miles thick, accumulated over a period of 200 million years (see Plate Tectonics later in this chapter). Smaller bodies of basalt or lava, when they are onshore, come from fissure eruptions or from volcanoes. Fissure eruptions sometimes supply extremely fluid basaltic lava which can flow many miles over the earth's surface. An example is the Columbia River Plateau basalt which covers an area of 220,000 square miles. Up to 100 separate flows contributed to this body of lava, beginning 17 million years ago. In the Snake River area, the lava is 16,000 feet thick.

Volcanoes are the most spectacular sources of lava and the results of a volcanic eruption can be disastrous. Some volcanoes produce large amounts of very fluid lava which can flow quietly. If much gas is present, however, the event can be explosive. In that case the volcano can spew enormous volumes of rock material ranging in size from fine dust to huge boulders. The expulsion of gas is normal and can include steam (up to 90 percent), HCl, CO_2, SO_2 and other "poisonous gases."

A few of the major volcanic eruptions are described below; they have been selected for historical purposes, for their differing styles, or because of the large number of human casualties. There are more than 500 active volcanoes in the world today, most of them found along the great fault lines where the earth's plates converge and collide. Plate boundaries around the margins of the Pacific Ocean have spawned numerous (330 active) volcanoes, which form the "Ring of Fire." The listed volcanoes can be dated but before recorded history, thousands of equally damaging volcanoes must have occurred.

Thera (now called Santorini), and adjoining small islands, are located in the eastern Mediterranean Sea along the line where the northerly moving African plate collides with the Eurasian plate. Ancient Greek literature indirectly leads to the conclusion that in 1628 B.C. a huge volcanic eruption destroyed the original island and with it the highly developed Minoan civilization. The initial explosion produced clouds of pumice and ash, followed by a salvo of blasts so loud they could be heard from Scandinavia to central Africa and from the Persian Gulf to the Rock of Gibraltar. Superheated gases blasted outward at speeds up to 1200 mph and a pillar of smoke and ash rose to 100,000 feet. The final explosion came when billions of gallons of seawater poured into the white-hot abyss. Thirty cubic kilometers of the island were blown away creating waves 200 to 300 feet high which crashed onto the shores of nearby Crete and beyond. This is the largest recorded volcanic explosion.

Mount Vesuvius stands at 4300 feet and is west of Thera, along the same plate boundary. It has been active for thousands of years and eruptions have occurred on average every twenty-eight years. But on. August 24 and 25, 79 A.D the most destructive one of all wiped out the nearby cities of Pompeii and Herculaneum. Pliny described how the eruption began with a roar like a thunderclap, shooting a cloud of fire, ash and pumice twelve miles into the sky. The ash, pumice and cinders falling over the countryside became so thick that pitch-black darkness ensued. This activity continued all night of the first day. On the morning of the 25th, the first of six ground surges raced down the mountainside. These surges were a deadly mass of pumice and ash mixed with superheated (to 750ºF) steam moving at speeds of sixty to 120 mph. This material killed 2000 fleeing or cowering people. Pompeii was buried beneath several feet of the deadly mix and Herculaneum by sixty feet. As the mixture cooled and hardened, it formed perfect molds around the victims and preserved details of their final moments plus contents of their households. Thus, it created a "marvelously intact museum," revealed by later excavations. On December 16, 1631 another eruption killed about 4000 people.

Mount Etna in Sicily is one of the most active volcanoes in the world, stemming from its location along the same plate boundary as Thera and Vesuvius. On average, it erupts every ten years. One of the most violent explosions occurred in 1169 and killed 15,000 people in the port city of Catania alone. The most lethal eruption came in 1669 when the official death toll was 20,000 but could have been as much as 100,000.

In Indonesia the Tambora volcanic explosion in April 1815 may have been one of the largest, but is not as well documented as Krakatoa, below. Mt. Tambora on the island of Tambora was about 13,000 feet high and approximately thirty-seven miles in diameter at the base. The blast obliterated the uppermost 3,300 feet and formed a caldera of just under four miles in diameter. On the island, 311 miles east of Bali, 117,000 people were killed. Dust circled the globe, causing lower temperatures and contributing to the last years of the "Little Ice Age." In 1816, Europe suffered the "year with no summer," resulting in disastrous harvests, famine and food riots. Ireland saw cold rain for 142 out of 153 days, crops rotted in the fields, and 65,000 people died of starvation or the ensuing typhus epidemic. Typhus and cholera spread around the world in 1816–19.

The island of <u>Krakatoa</u> is in the Sunda Strait between Java and Sumatra in Indonesia. It is near the boundary between the Indian and Eurasian plates. In August 1883 Krakatoa erupted with a thunderous roar, blowing searing ash and pumice as high as seventeen miles. The explosion had the force of one million Hiroshima bombs and the sound traveled over 3000 miles. Chunks of red-hot debris up to eight feet across were blown over an area the size of France.. After some six cubic miles of material was thrown into the sky, the remainder, together with seawater, collapsed into the chasm, which was four miles across and 900 feet deep. This caused a huge explosion and a series of tsunamis, or seismic sea waves, which roared through the Sunda Strait and caused most of the damage. Huge waves up to 130 feet high wiped out 300 villages and 36,000 people were killed. Up to 6500 boats and ships were lost. Great rafts of pumice, volcanic glass so aerated that it floats, drifted as far as 7500 miles across the Indian Ocean. Fine dust circled the globe and temporarily lowered the earth's mean annual temperature. For years, sunsets were multi-colored around the world

<u>Mount Pelée</u> at 4,429 feet dominates the Caribbean island of Martinique, which in 1902 was a French possession. Volcanic activity began modestly in early April but grew more intense during the next month. On May 7, Mount Pelée began roaring and two fiery craters near the summit burned like blast furnaces while emitting black clouds of ash and cinders. Early the next morning, amidst huge explosions, a fissure near the crest opened and a black cloud blew out as from the muzzle of a cannon. This cloud roared down the mountainside and in less than one minute reached the town of St. Pierre, five miles away. In minutes, 30,000 people were dead. Later, scientists named the killer cloud a "nuée ardente" or fiery cloud. Characteristically it is a lethal mixture of superheated steam and other gases mixed with clouds of incandescent ash heated to 1100 to 1300°F, attaining speeds up to 100 mph. As described, the nuée ardente type of volcanic cloud is very similar to the pyroclastic flow at Vesuvius some 1800 years earlier.

<u>Nevado del Ruiz</u> is a 17,457-foot volcanic peak in Colombia. The mountain is capped with snow and is one of the Pacific Rim volcanoes that make up the Ring of Fire. After smaller eruptions in 1595 and 1845, the one in 1985 was the most deadly of all. With very little noise, in the middle

of the night, a mudflow engulfed the town of Armero and 25,000 people were buried in their beds. The mudflows originated high up the slopes of the mountain when superheated magma from the volcano began to melt the massive cap of ice at the summit. Avalanches of mud up to fifty feet thick poured down the slopes at up to 30 mph and joined with floodwaters in the river above Armero. Unfortunately, this deadly combination quickly engulfed the town, and inhabitants were killed in a matter of minutes.

Sedimentary rocks are normally formed by the consolidation of rock material that has been deposited by water. Exceptions include glacial and landslide debris, or sand dunes moved by the wind. Clastic, organic and chemically precipitated rocks are the three main categories. Common clastic sediments include sandstone, gravel and clay or shale. Examples of organic sedimentary rock are coal, oil shale and limestone comprised of fossil material. Chemical precipitates include some limestone and dolomite, gypsum, anhydrite, halite (rock salt), and chert (flint). Most sedimentary rocks show distinct bedding or stratification with younger layers deposited on top of older. This property leads geologists to give formation names to the beds or units in rock sequences.

Sediments and sedimentary rocks make up only 5 percent of the earth's crust but cover 75 percent of the continents. They are very important to our economy because they contain virtually all oil, gas and coal deposits, plus some large metallic accumulations. They are also an important supply of construction materials.

Clastic sedimentary rock incorporates grains, particles or fragments derived from pre-existing rocks. A common example is sand derived as quartz grains from granite. As granite weathers, the feldspar component quickly deteriorates to clay, whereas the quartz is more stable. Quartz fragments accumulate and are transported downhill by streams and rivers. Abrasion occurs during stream transport and the grains tend to become smaller, more rounded and better sorted. Grains are most likely to accumulate in sandbars or in beaches where they eventually become lithified to form sandstone.

Shale is the most common clastic sedimentary rock. It is formed by the lithification of fine-grained mud, clay and silt. When the mud is compacted by the weight of overlying rock material, water is expelled and the clay minerals begin to consolidate.

Limestone is another very important sedimentary rock, composed of calcium carbonate ($CaCO_3$). Its origin may be largely organic, such as compacted or cemented shell fragments or even reef rock built by colonies of corals. Other limestone may be precipitated from saturated carbonate solutions and can be closely associated with anhydrite, gypsum and salt. With the addition of magnesium (Mg), dolomite may form.

Metamorphic rocks are formed by the alteration of pre-existing rocks due to the effects of temperature, pressure, or the gain or loss of chemical components. Metamorphic changes take place in solid rock; if the rocks melt and then harden they are considered igneous rocks. About 15 percent of earth's crust is made up of metamorphic rock.

Metamorphism causes changes in the texture of the rock; for example, foliation is a common characteristic. Foliated rocks tend to split along a smooth plane because of flat, platy or sheet-like minerals such as mica or chlorite, all oriented in the same direction. Foliation develops in response to pressure. Mica schist and chlorite schist are examples of rocks formed from the metamorphism of granitic or basaltic predecessors. Another common transformation is shale to slate.

Metamorphic rocks have the same chemical composition as the original rock but physical characteristics and component minerals may be different because they have been altered to more stable forms in the changed environment. Some examples of changes in sedimentary rocks caused by metamorphic effects are limestone changed to marble; sandstone altered to quartzite; and bituminous coal changed to higher grade anthracite.

FOSSILS AND GEOLOGIC TIME

Fossils are extremely important components when present in sedimentary rocks. Before meeting his end at Vesuvius, Pliny the Elder (the first geologist) had discussed the possible meaning of fossils. But the modern history of paleontology began in the sixteenth century with the scholarly treatise in 1546 by the German physician and mining engineer Georgius Agricola. Then, later in the 1770s, the Swede, Carolus Linnaeus developed the practical system of nomenclature still used today, i.e., phylum-class-order-family-genus-species, with Latin names for genera and species.

Geologists of that time noticed that fossils had a tendency to occur in certain strata and the field of stratigraphy soon developed with geologic maps and stratigraphic sections as important tools. William "Strata" Smith was a British surveyor who gained fame in 1815 for constructing the first geological map. The geologic periods were established on the basis of their fossil assemblages and are shown in the Geologic Time Scale (next page) with a time scale in millions of years. The times are mostly based on radio-metric dating techniques.

Basically, the method measures the radioactive decay of uranium to lead, or other mother-daughter pairs. Uranium-235 has a half-life of 713 million years and decays to lead-207 through seven alpha steps and five beta steps. Uranium-238, the most common isotope of uranium, decays to lead-206 through a series of steps. It has a half-life of 4.5 billion years; therefore about half still exists. These uranium clocks, and other pairs such as potassium-argon and rubidium-strontium, have been used extensively in age-dating rocks. In dating organic material, derived from living organisms, calibrated Carbon-14 is a useful radioactive isotope. It comprises about one part in a million of normal carbon, C-12. C-14 has a half-life of 5730 years; carbon dating therefore is useful on organic material that appeared during the last 50,000 years.

The time scale for the earth on the opposing page shows that the Precambrian era represents more than 4 billion years or over 87 percent of the total time. In this interval very little fossil material is known, probably because (a) there weren't many fossils and (b) the environment at that time, favoring igneous activity, precluded organisms from developing and/or destroyed the remains of any that did. Widespread deposits of unmetamorphosed sedimentary rocks, with abundant fossil remains, first appear in the Cambrian period, 543 million years ago. The Cambrian period was the first time unit of the Paleozoic era lasting some 298 million years. The Cambrian saw the first appearance, and abundance, of trilobites and brachiopods. During this 38-million-year period, most invertebrate phyla were first developed in their earliest forms.

The 67-million-year Ordovician period began 505 million years ago (ma) and is also named for outcrops in Wales and specifically the Ordovices, an ancient Welsh tribe. During this time, brachiopods dominated, together with trilobites and cephalopods. The first true coral reef and jawless fish were present.

The Silurian period lasted for 30 million years, beginning 438 ma. Silurian sediments are mostly marine and during that time luxuriant coral reefs were common. Brachiopods, graptolites and conodonts were very common. The first sharks and boney fishes appeared and the first land plants and ferns began to evolve.

Devonian rocks were first studied in County Devon in southwestern England. The Devonian period included rocks over a time span of

GEOLOGIC TIME SCALE

ERA	PERIOD	EPOCH	
Cenozoic	Quaternary	Holocene	0.01
		Pleistocene	1.6
	Tertiary	Pliocene	5
		Miocene	24
		Oligocene	34
		Eocene	54
		Paleocene	65
Mesozoic	Cretaceous		145
	Jurassic		213
	Triassic		248
Paleozoic	Permian		286
	Carboniferous — Pennsylvanian		325
	Carboniferous — Mississippian		360
	Devonian		408
	Silurian		438
	Ordovician		505
	Cambrian		550
Precambrian	Proterozoic		
		4050	
	Archaean		4600

MILLION YEARS AGO

46 million years beginning 408 ma. During this time desert sandstones were widespread in North America and Europe. On land, the first insects and vegetation flourished. In the seas, corals, sponges and ostracods were abundant but trilobites and graptolites declined. Amphibians evolved from air-breathing fish.

Carboniferous is a British term for coal-bearing strata in Europe beginning 362 ma and lasting for 72 million years. In the U.S. the Carboniferous is divided into lower and upper periods, viz. Mississippian and Pennsylvanian. Shallow-water limestones were common in the Mississippian. The first reptiles, amphibians and spiders appeared, and blastoids reached their climax and then became extinct. The Pennsylvanian period spanned 39 million years and was noted for extensive coal deposits. Fusulinids appeared and, as fossils, became very useful to oil-company geologists for zoning rock units spanning only a few million years.

The 45-million-year Permian period, beginning 290 ma, was named for rock exposures in the Perm area of eastern Russia. During this time, the climate was influenced by extensive accumulations of glacial snow and ice in the Arctic and Antarctic regions. In the latter area, the continents were joined together in a large land body called Pangea. Terrestrial amphibians, mammal-like reptiles and insects flourished in the more temperate areas. But partway through the Permian, a drastic change in climate was caused by enormous volcanic activity in Russia. Clouds of smoke, dust and gases circulated around the earth causing a worldwide black cloud. Photosynthesis was shut down and the entire food chain was disrupted. This last period of the Paleozoic era was marked by a dramatic change in marine life including extinction of all trilobites and fusulinids. Three-fourths of all amphibians vanished and 95 percent of all non-fish species in the oceans became extinct—altogether the greatest mass extinction in geological history (see p. 397).

The Mesozoic era, or middle life, began 248 ma and includes three geologic periods, the Triassic, Jurassic and Cretaceous. At the beginning of the era the continents were joined together in a large land mass called Pangea with a large glaciated area near the South Pole. Then for some reason the continents began to drift apart (continental drift) and by the end of the Cretaceous period, 65 ma, the continents were mostly in their present positions.

During Triassic time of 37 million years, the climate was generally dry, and desert sandstones and red beds are representative rocks. In a few more fertile areas, tree ferns and large conifers thrived together with seed-bearing plants. The first dinosaurs appeared on land, as well as early ammonites in the sea. Near the end of the Triassic, a large meteor struck eastern Canada, disrupting the weather for forty days and causing 95 percent of terrestrial vegetation to become extinct.

Beginning 208 ma, the Jurassic period covered a span of about 63 million years and was named for rocks in the Jura Mountains of France and Switzerland. Polar ice caps had disappeared and the earth had a warm climate. Lush vegetation furnished organic matter that was later altered to coal and oil in several places around the world. The first bird, archaeopteryx appeared, retaining many reptilian features of its predecessors. Many new dinosaur species were present including ferocious predators and the fifty-ton sauropod, *Brachiosaurus*.

The 80-million-year Cretaceous period began 145 ma. It was named from the white cliffs of Dover for their chalk layers or *creta*. Pangea continued its breakup into proto-continents and mid-ocean ridges of basalt filled in along the lines of separation. The new oceanic ridges, formed by molten rocks, furnished a great deal of heat to the oceans. The earth reached a temperature about 27°F hotter, and the CO_2 content of the atmosphere was about six times higher than it is today. Sea level was 660 feet higher than today and the oceans covered four-fifths of the surface of the earth. On land, angiosperm (seed-bearing) plants evolved and plant pollination was aided by insects, attracted to the flowers by color, scent and sweet secretions. Birds developed improved flying skills, and a variety of small mammals evolved, including egg-laying, placental and marsupial types. Herbivorous dinosaurs reached their peak and the eight-ton *Tyrannosaurus rex* ruled, the biggest predator to ever live on Earth.

It is believed that an asteroid impact 65 million years ago ended the Cretaceous period of the Mesozoic era. The ten-mile wide asteroid struck just offshore near the Yucatan Peninsula and created an enormous explosion plus gigantic tsunami waves. At that time, India was passing over a hot spot in the lithosphere as it inched northward toward Tibet. Worldwide reverberations from the asteroid impact may have caused or rejuvenated lava flows in western India. These flows formed the Deccan Traps, 6,600 feet thick over 770,000 square miles. As the Traps built up, clouds of smoke, dust and ash blocked out the sun for months on end and dropped worldwide temperatures 9°F. This created havoc for the ecosystems of the world, and caused massive extinctions of life forms (see pp. 397-398).

Cenozoic (recent life) time began 65 ma and is divided into the Tertiary and Quaternary periods. Mammals became the dominant life form as the continents attained their present positions. Climate and zones of vegetation became established much as at present. The Tertiary period is further divided into five epochs the Paleocene, Eocene, Oligocene, Miocene and Pliocene. Marine microfossils, called foraminifera, are very useful for zoning the Tertiary epochs. Pollen and spores are used for the same purpose in palynology, a specialty using microscopes with even higher magnification. The earliest hominid, or man-like creature, diverged from the chimpanzee line 5 to 6 ma, and the first ancestral human species, *Homo habilis*, appeared 2.6 ma in Africa during the Pliocene epoch. Modern man, *Homo sapiens sapiens* evolved about 195,000 to 150,000 years ago.

Quaternary time began 1.6 ma with the Pleistocene epoch, also called the Great Ice Age. During this time the earth was unusually cold with extensive polar ice caps, and continental glaciers were widespread in North America, Europe, and Asia. Glaciers covered one-third of the earth's surface and 5 percent of the earth's water was locked up as ice. In North America, ice sheets a few miles thick moved southward as far as the mid-continent area of the U.S. and left thick deposits of glacial till (soil), excellent for farming. Glaciations occurred sequentially every 100,000 years, on average, with the cold phases lasting about 80,000 years, separated by inter-glacial times of about 20,000 years.

The Holocene, or Recent epoch began 10,000 years ago and continues into the present. (Because of the scale, Pleistocene and Recent divisions cannot be shown on the time chart).

Glaciers were retreating as the epoch began and are continuing the meltdown today, as part of a trend of global warming. As the climate became warmer, humans made great advances and thirteen of the main civilizations are described on pages 439-456.

PLATE TECTONICS

As early as the nineteenth century, geologists noticed how well the Atlantic coasts of Africa and South America could fit together, like pieces of a jigsaw puzzle. In 1915 Alfred Wegener, a German geophysicist, proposed a theory of continental drift in support of his idea that the continents once were joined together. The fit between west Africa and eastern South America was especially striking.

Wegener pointed out some other scientific evidence that supported his argument. He noted that stratigraphic rock units older than 200 million years were similar near the west coast of Africa and the east coast of South America. He also showed that old mountain ranges in eastern Canada and those in the British Isles and Scandinavia lined up nicely, with similar orientation, structure and rock composition, if the continents were joined together in a super continent called Pangea. If the continents were joined at the edges of their respective continental shelves, the fit was even better. He noted that some 300 million years ago, a glacial ice sheet covered parts of South America, Africa, India and Australia, as shown in (a) below. Figure (b) shows the position of the continents today. Wegener's only problem was that he could not describe an acceptable mechanism for moving the continents and hence most geologists viewed his proposals with skepticism.

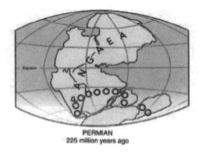 

PERMIAN
225 million years ago

PRESENT DAY

Extent of glaciated rocks (circles). Landmasses by USGS.

In 1944, the British geologist Arthur Holmes suggested the mechanism of convection currents. In the 1960's a remarkable confluence of data and ideas served to confirm the idea of continental drift and the concept of plate tectonics became accepted by almost all geologists. In 1960, Princeton University professor Harry H. Hess suggested the theory of seafloor spreading wherein subterranean molten material rises to the seafloor along mid-oceanic ridges, or spreading centers. The molten material forms new seafloor which moves away at right angles from the ridges. Convection cells in the asthenosphere are believed to drive this process.

The following illustration shows how the Mid-Atlantic Ridge separates the North and South American plates from the Eurasian and African plates. Straight sections of the ridge are offset by transform faults (named by Tuzo Wilson), which serve to accommodate differences in horizontal movement of seafloor away from the ridge.

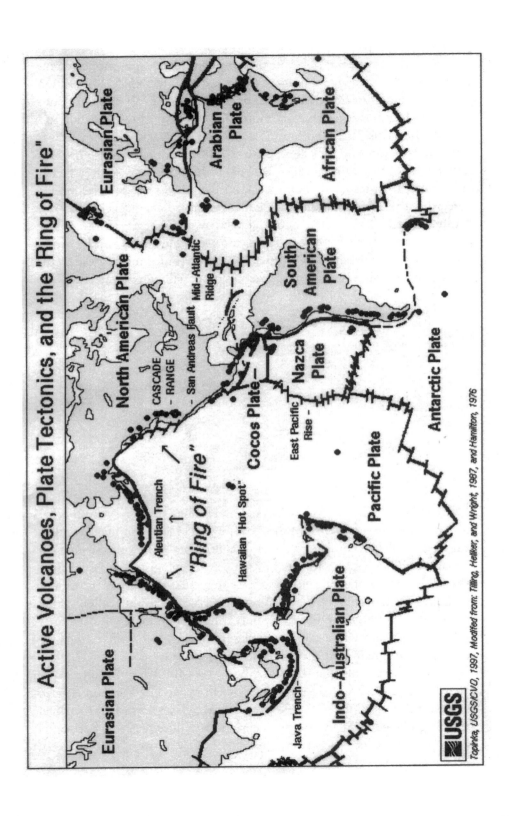

Active Volcanoes, Plate Tectonics, and the "Ring of Fire"

Eurasian Plate

Arabian Plate

African Plate

North American Plate

CASCADE – RANGE –

San Andreas Fault

Mid-Atlantic Ridge

South American Plate

Nazca Plate

Cocos Plate–

East Pacific Rise –

Antarctic Plate

Aleutian Trench

"Ring of Fire"

Hawaiian "Hot Spot"

Pacific Plate

Indo-Australian Plate

Java Trench–

Eurasian Plate

≋USGS

Topinka, USGS/CVO, 1997, Modified from: Tilling, Heliker, and Wright, 1987, and Hamilton, 1976

Due to seafloor spreading, in one year the North American and Europe plates move about 2.5 centimeters apart (about the speed of fingernail growth). Obviously, the youngest parts of the seafloor are along and adjacent to the oceanic ridges and the oldest seafloor is farthest away. No part of the present seafloor is older than about 200 million years, which is when the most recent continental breakup began. When plates converge, one plate tends to plunge below the other along a boundary called a subduction zone. If this belt is in the ocean an oceanic trench may form and some trenches are 36,000 feet deep. Local movements along colliding plates often result in tsunamis, volcanoes, earthquakes, and mountain building. The illustration above, from the USGS, shows the position of some of the twelve major tectonic plates and the Ring of Fire around the Pacific Ocean.

In those places where plates impinge at an angle and tend to slide laterally past each other, long wrench or shear faults develop. Examples are the San Andreas fault in California and the Anatolian fault in Turkey. As stress builds up along such faults the plates eventually overcome frictional resistance and finally break free to relieve the stress. These movements can be sudden and abrupt, causing severe earthquakes. Movement along the San Andreas fault began up to 20 million years ago, at depths up to ten miles. The shift is slow but impressive, and in one million years Los Angeles will have moved twenty-five miles north-northwest of its present location. Plate tectonics began on Earth as long as 4 billion years ago, as Richard Fortey has demonstrated in his recent excellent book *Earth*.

Oceanic exploration has uncovered a puzzling pattern of parallel magnetic stripes in rocks on the ocean floor. On maps, the generally north-south stripes look "zebra-like." In the 1960s the stripes were recognized as representing a long-term history of reversals in the earth's magnetic field. It was found that polarity reversed repeatedly but erratically during geologic time, on average every 500,000 years. As they solidified, igneous rocks retained the polarity they were born with so they held an historical record of the position of the magnetic poles.

During this same time other geologists developed methods to date the ages of the seafloor basalts which showed the magnetic reversals. They used the potassium-argon dating technique that measures the amount of the radioactive isotope potassium-40 and the daughter isotope argon-40. The potassium-40 isotope has a half-life of 1,310 million years and is present in the basalts so it is the most useful marker. Because basaltic rocks of the same age occur on both sides of a spreading center, the pattern of magnetic stripes (reversals) on one side mirrors the pattern on the other. Eventually, scientists were able to date and correlate the magnetic striping patterns for nearly the entire ocean floor. It is quite striking to see that transform faults have offset the stripes in an orderly way. [One of my fellow graduate students at Stanford was Allan Cox, who later earned well-deserved recognition for his work on dating magnetic reversals for the last 4 million years.]

A large number of geologists and geophysicists made important contributions to the concept of plate tectonics. Some of the key scientists included Edward Bullard, John Dewey, Maurice Ewing, Harry Hess, Arthur Holmes, Xavier Le Pichon, Fred Vine and J. Tuzo Wilson. [While chairing the Distinguished Lecture Committee of the American Associatin of Petroleum Geologists, I was able to convince Dr. Wilson to lecture on plate tectonics for our members.]

The understanding of plate tectonics is probably the greatest geological achievement of all time. It explains the geographic position of continents through geologic time and their changing environments. It also provides a logical explanation of how and where mountains are formed. As seen, the collision of tectonic plates is the main cause of earthquakes, and often creates volcanoes.

EARTHQUAKES

Nine out of ten of the largest earthquakes in the last 100 years have occurred along the very active plate boundaries around the Pacific Ocean. However, the list below includes earthquakes that had special historical significance or claimed an unusually large number of victims.

Alexandria, A.D. July 21, 365. A monstrous tsunami (a giant sea wave caused by an earthquake below the sea floor) crashed upon the coast of Greece, Sicily and Egypt. At Alexandria the sea first withdrew, exposing a seafloor with previously unknown giant canyons, then came roaring back in a huge wave that carried ships and debris two miles inland. The sturdy Pharos lighthouse, one of the Seven Wonders of the World, survived, as did the buildings of the world-famous library, but some 50,000 Alexandrians died.

Antioch, May 29, 526. At the time, Antioch was the third largest city in the Roman Empire. It was famous as the home base of the Apostle Paul and where the term Christian was first used. A sudden earthquake collapsed most of the buildings; it was followed by a devastating fire that destroyed anything still standing, killing 250,000–300,000 people. Attempts to rebuild the city failed and in 542 the plague wiped out the remaining populace. Nothing remains to this day.

Shensi Province, China, January 23, 1556. More than 800,000 people died when a massive earthquake collapsed many cliffside caves, excavated by millions of peasants for living quarters.

San Francisco, April 18, 1906. In three minutes, the sixty-year-old city of 450,000 residents was torn up by a shock wave that struck at 5:13 A.M. The wave ripped south at two miles a second from the epicenter ninety miles to the north. After buildings collapsed, more than fifty fires broke out in thirty minutes, burning up 4.7 square miles in the heart of the city. More than 28,000 buildings were destroyed and the smoke could be seen 100 miles out to sea. Characterized as a 100-year quake, it resulted from a sudden and violent shift along the right-lateral San Andreas fault that runs for 800 miles through western California. In the last 15–20 million years, movement along the fault has totaled at least 350 miles. Energy released during the quake surpassed that of all the combined explosives used in World War II. Remarkably, despite the damage, only 500–1000 people died in the Frisco quake.

Messina, Sicily, December 28, 1908. Beginning at 5:20 A.M. three long shocks collapsed more than 90 percent of the city's buildings. Following that, a twenty-six-foot tsunami swept through the rubble and fires fed by ruptured gas mains set the debris ablaze. The earthquake, 7.5 on the Richter scale, originated from the seafloor between Sicily and Italy. It is estimated that 120,000 people were killed in Messina and nearby areas.

Kansu Province, China, December 16, 1920. A quake of magnitude 8.6 killed as many as 200,000 people, mostly from a series of deadly landslides.

Kanto Plain, Japan, September 1, 1923. At its epicenter in Sagami Bay the quake measured 8.3 on the Richter scale. Terrible damage was caused in nearby Tokyo and Yokohama. The initial shock lasted nearly five minutes. Many people were killed outright by collapsing buildings and a following tsunami wave in coastal areas. But fire was the principal cause of destruction and death. In Tokyo, thousands of homes and buildings burned in a fire that could not be put out because the quake had ruptured the water mains. In Tokyo, 300,000 buildings were destroyed including great collections of rare books and priceless art. In Yokohama some 60,000 buildings were lost. Total casualties exceeded 140,000 people with 1.5 million left homeless. The Kanto quake occurred along the Pacific Ocean's tempestuous Ring of Fire which every year produces more than 3000 earthquakes of varying magnitudes.

[Note: In 1935 American seismologist Charles F. Richter developed a scale for comparing the magnitude of earthquakes. As measured by seismographs, each whole number on his scale is ten times the amplitude of the next lower number but each whole-number step represents thirty-one times more energy than the preceding number. No earthquake has ever exceeded 9.5 on the Richter scale.]

Anchorage, March 27, 1964. Alaska's Good Friday quake ranks as the most violent natural cataclysm in the history of North America. Final estimates were 8.3 to 8.6 on the Richter scale, about twice the force of the San Francisco quake in 1906. Beginning at 5:36 P.M. the ground rolled and surged for four minutes, creating havoc in Anchorage and surrounding areas. The epicenter was in Prince William Sound, eighty miles from Anchorage, and tsunami waves traveling 400 mph caused death and destruction thousands of miles away. The shock was felt on the other side of the earth and for two weeks "the entire planet vibrated like a giant tuning fork." Because of fortunate timing only 131 people were killed but 100,000 square miles of terrain were changed and 75 percent of Alaska's commerce and industry was ruined.

Tangshan, China, July 28, 1976. In twenty-three seconds, a quake of magnitude 7.8 to 8.2 almost leveled this city of 1 million people. The epicenter was almost under the city, probably accounting for the high death toll of about 242,000. Immediately preceding the shock there is some evidence of exploding methane gas, probably derived from coal beds in the area. Witnesses described a quick flash of greenish-blue light and vegetation was scorched on one side as if by a giant fireball. The Communist government tried to suppress information at the time so details remain sketchy.

North Sumatra, December 26, 2004. This was the most disastrous tsunami in human history, causing the death of more than 225,000 people with 50,000 missing and 5 million homeless in the coastal areas of eleven countries in Southeast Asia. The dead were listed as 132,000 in Sumatra, 35,000 in Sri Lanka, 12,000 in India, 5000 in Thailand, and others in Somalia, Myanmar and various islands. The epicenter of the earthquake was under the Nias Islands, about seventy-five miles offshore northwest Sumatra, at a depth of about six miles. The magnitude 9 quake was caused by the abrupt slippage, by oblique subduction, of the Australian Plate beneath the Eurasian Plate, raising the Sumatra landmass about twenty-six feet. There may have been lateral movement as well, along a 745 mile section in the Java Trench which reaches depths of 24,000 feet and extends for 1600 miles. The tsunami raced through the ocean at 500 mph, building to a height of 100 feet as it reached the coastal areas. As usual, poor seaside towns suffered the most but some of the plush resorts in Malaysia were hit also, and thousands of vacationing Westerners were victims.

Turkey-Iran-Pakistan-Tibet. A long earthquake belt is formed through these countries where the African plate is driving northward at the rate of about two inches per year. At the eastern end of the trend, India crashed into Tibet beginning about 45 million years ago, eventually forming the Himalayan Mountains. Strong earthquakes occur almost annually somewhere along this earthquake belt, and casualty lists typically run from a few thousand up to 80,000 people. Deaths are numerous because of the mud and brick construction of houses in the villages affected. The heavy walls and ceilings are deadly when they collapse.

ATMOSPHERE AND CLIMATE

At the present time Earth's air is 99 percent nitrogen and oxygen; the full list (by volume) is as follows: nitrogen 78 percent, oxygen 21 percent, water vapor 0–4 percent, argon 0.9 percent, carbon dioxide 0.03 percent, and traces of neon, helium, methane, nitrous oxide, hydrogen, carbon monoxide, ammonia, plus dust, pollen, etc.

About 70 percent of the earth's surface is covered with water and 98 percent of that is in the oceans having an average depth of 12,450 feet and temperature of 39°F. Seawater today has a salt content of 3–4 percent. Most of the fresh water is frozen in the glacial ice sheets of Antarctica and Greenland. Antarctica holds 90 percent of the world's ice, with an average thickness of over 7000 feet. If the Antarctic and Greenland ice caps melted, sea level around the earth would rise by as much as 220 feet.

Summer temperatures in Antarctica seldom exceed 0°F and the coldest reading in the winter of 1983 was -128.6°F at Russia's Vostok station. At the other extreme, a temperature of 136°F was recorded in the Sahara Desert in 1922. But for the most part, Earth's average temperatures are "just right" (for the organisms we know) and in the range of 57–58°F.

When Earth was formed 4.6 billion years ago, the atmosphere and temperatures were far different and inhospitable, however. Molten rocks at the surface, or thin basaltic crust, resulted from constant volcanism, decay of short-lived radioactive elements and accretion compression by infalling rock bodies. Surface temperatures were too high for life as we know it, or for liquid water. The first atmosphere was probably hydrogen and helium but these were soon lost to space because the earth's gravity was not strong enough to hold them. For the first half-billion years primary constituents of the atmosphere were methane, ammonia, carbon dioxide and water vapor. Free oxygen did not appear until halfway through Earth's life. This timing is related to the first appearance of redbeds in the rock record 2.3 billion years ago; the red color results from oxidation of the mineral hematite (Fe_2O_3).

By 4 billion years ago the earth's surface had cooled enough for water to exist in liquid form. The source of the water is believed to be from either outgassing and/or comets. Outgassing involved gases (including water vapor) vented from volcanoes. In the past, most geologists have favored this hypothesis as the main source for the earth's water. In recent years, however, comets have been recognized as another important source. In 1997, NASA's Polar satellite provided evidence of a startling abundance of icy comets entering the earth's atmosphere. These comets hit the upper atmosphere at the rate of 5–30 every minute and break up forming water vapor which eventually turns into rain. Calculations have been made that show this process could raise the level of the oceans by an inch in just 10,000 years, in other words an order of magnitude sufficient to fill the oceans during geologic time.

The earliest oxygen may have originated from photochemical dissociation—the breakup of water molecules by ultraviolet light. This process might account for oxygen levels approximately 1–2 percent of the current. This amount of oxygen could form ozone (O_3), which helps to shield the earth's surface from the sun's UV rays. As mentioned above, 2.3 billion-year-old red beds showed oxygen was available at that time. But the more important process of plant photosynthesis probably accounts for most of the world's oxygen, beginning about 1.9 billion years ago. Blue-green algae (actually cyanobacteria) were important oxygen contributors, and the oxygen content of the atmosphere may have reached 18 percent by the beginning of the Cambrian period, and present levels by 400 ma. The first organisms having advanced, animal-like characteristics appeared 600 ma (see next chapter "Life forms").

MOON

Earth's only moon is nearly spherical with a diameter of 2160 miles, slightly more than one-fourth Earth's diameter. The moon revolves eastward around the earth in a slightly elliptical orbit but the mean distance from Earth is 238,330 miles and is growing at the rate of 12.5 feet per century. The Moon completes one full orbit in about 29.5 solar days, and it rotates at the same rate as it revolves; therefore the same side of the Moon always faces the earth and we never see the other side, which is much less cratered. The human female ovulation time of about 28 days seems to be synchronized to the lunar cycle, a fact that has influenced some ancient and modern religious practices.

Our Moon is the fifth largest in the solar system and is relatively close to Earth so it appears as the second brightest object in the sky. The phases of the Moon we observe are the result of the position of the Moon as seen in reflected light of the sun. When the Moon is on the same meridian as the sun, the new moon occurs (for an instant, no light reflected). For the next seven days a waxing moon appears, with larger crescent areas of the moon lighted each day and the shaded area of the Moon on the left. On the fourteenth day a full moon occurs, then the waning phase begins. During the last quarter a waning crescent appears with the shaded area of the Moon to the right.

As described earlier, the best explanation for the origin of the Moon seems to be that it resulted from the collision of a large rock body with Earth about 4.5 billion years ago. Support for this interpretation has come in large part from hard data collected from the Apollo missions beginning with the first lunar landing on July 20, 1949. We now know the Moon is made of rocky material that has undergone melting, volcanic action and meteor impacts. It has a thick crust (thirty-seven miles), a fairly uniform lithosphere (to 620 miles deep), a partly liquid asthenosphere (460 miles thick) and possibly a small iron core. No magnetic field exists.

Ages of Moon rocks range from about 4.5 billion years in the terrae (light highlands) to 3.2 billion years in the maria (dark basins). The large, dark basins are gigantic impact craters that were later filled with lava flows. Old rocks on the Moon persist whereas those on Earth are eroded and reworked, sometimes through metamorphism. Oxygen isotopic compositions of Moon and Earth rocks show common origins although the Moon has less iron and lacks the volatile elements needed to form water and atmospheric gases. All moon rocks originated through volcanic or other high-temperature processes. Resulting rock types are basalts, anorthosites and breccias. The Moon has no sedimentary rocks such as sandstone, limestone or shale. The surface of the Moon is covered by rubble called the lunar regolith, comprised of rock fragments and dust.

GLACIATION

Continental glaciers appeared on Earth during Proterozoic, Ordovician, Silurian, and Carboniferous times but the Permian, about 250 ma, is better documented. Evidence of Permian glaciers is present in portions of South America, Africa, Australia, Antarctica and the tip of India. Except for Antarctica, all these areas are now far north of the South Pole. But at that time, the five continents were joined together in the huge land mass called Pangea. This major phase of sea-floor spreading began about 200 ma resulting in the separation into the different continental land masses we see today.

The most recent glaciation began with worldwide cooling 2.5 ma in the Pliocene, and continued into the Pleistocene, which began 1.6 ma. Enormous continental glaciers covered areas of northern Asia, the north half of Europe and North America as far south as St. Louis, Kansas City and Pierre, SD. Glaciers up to two miles thick had tremendous weight that once removed, has allowed elastic rebound of up to 1000 feet of the earth's surface. Glaciers in the southern hemisphere grew as well, and 33 percent of the total land area of the world was covered with ice (versus 10 percent now). So much water was locked up as ice that ocean levels were 400–450 feet lower than today. Among other things, this created a land bridge where the Bering Strait is now.

The continental glaciers expanded and retreated many times with each glacial cycle lasting 80,000 years, on average. The relatively warm periods in between, called interglacials, lasted about 20,000 years. Most geologists recognize that Earth at present is in an interglacial time. The most recent glacial period ended about 15,000 years ago but vast areas of permafrost still remain. Overall warming in the last 15,000 years is about 16°F. This is the most logical, factual, and dispassionate way to interpret the meaning of the "global warming" we see today.

Scientists have tried to relate the periodicity of glacial (cold) cycles to other phenomena. For example, solar activity in terms of sunspot cycles (averaging 11 years) had a strong correlation with global temperatures during the period 1880 to 1980. Longer-term changes in climate can be related to changes in Earth's orbit relative to the sun. The earth's axis of rotation "wobbles" with a cycle of 25,748 years, variations of the tilt axis (about three degrees) repeat every 42,000 years and ellipticity of the orbit has a periodicity of about 100,000 years. As early as 1920 the Yugoslavian meteorologist Milutin Milankovitch showed that the amount of heat from the sun varied with the changes in orbit. Superimposed on these cycles may be the Gleissberg cycle of solar activity every eighty-three years, due to oscillations in the motion of the sun itself.

'GLOBAL WARMING'

[This is a subject that has been of particular interest to me since 1968 when I first did some research and began keeping files on relevant information. In 1968 we were trying to evaluate the economics of oil reserves at Prudhoe Bay, and one possibility was to ship crude oil in ice-breaking tankers instead of by pipeline. Although there were some questionable indications of thinning ice in the Arctic Ocean, we concluded that a trans-Alaska pipeline (TAPS) was most feasible. In 1969, the Exxon tanker *Manhattan* did, in fact, make a successful voyage through the Arctic ice pack.]

Global warming needs to be examined in the context of the interglacial warm period we are enjoying at present. Most professional geologists, familiar with Earth's changes over geologic time, would say that warming is an entirely natural and desirable property of the current interglacial time. Geologists would also be comfortable with orbital and solar effects, especially the Milankovitch and Gleissberg cycles. Gerhard argues that science shows solar and orbital variability are the main drivers of Earth's climate and that these effects "cannot be purposefully deflected nor climate modified with current technology."

Ice cores taken from deep holes drilled in the glaciers of Greenland and Antarctica provide some clues about climatic conditions as long ago as 400,000 years. Gases trapped in the ice show that climate has experienced several abrupt changes in temperature and aridity. Some perturbations of the current phase of interglacial warming are as follows:

- 13,000 b.c.—widespread warming/melting of continental glaciers

- 11,000–9700 b.c.—abrupt cooling (Younger Dryas)

- 3000 b.c.—long-term modest cooling trend begins

- 2300 b.c.—worst drought, toppling civilizations in Egypt and India

- a.d. 870–1450—Medieval Warm Event (MWE) with temperatures about 2.0°F above minima, peak in 990. Drought of 500–900 may have destroyed Mayan civilization.

- 1560–1850—Little Ice Age (LIA) had drastic effects in Europe, especially during Maunder Minimum (1645–1715)

- 1910–45—major warming, 1930s drought in U.S. Midwest
- 1945–75—cooling
- 1975–present—warming (about 1.0°F above end of LIA)

There seems to be a modest preponderance of evidence for a world-wide temperature increase of about 1°F in a little over 100 years. Records are hampered by inconsistencies, one of which is surface versus satellite data, and local influences such as the "urban heat island" effect. A more regional effect is seen in the Arctic where warming during the last few decades is almost twice that of other parts of the world.

As early as the nineteenth century, possible global warming caused by a man-made increase in greenhouse gases was first described by J. Fourier, a French mathematician. In 1896, the Swedish chemist S. Arrhenius published a paper calculating how the process could cause a rise in temperature.

The greenhouse effect is an apt comparison of atmospheric gases to the glass in a greenhouse. Most of the visible portion of sunlight is transmitted through the gas as it is through glass. Infrared radiation is returned to the atmosphere where some of it is selectively absorbed by the greenhouse gases which blanket the earth (in trace amounts, except for water vapor). Thus the air near Earth's surface tends to warm up, but not to the same extent as the hot air trapped inside a greenhouse.

In the 1950s Roger Revelle, director of the Scripps Institution of Oceanography began the study of atmospheric CO_2. He was interested in the ocean uptake of CO_2 and noted that about half of the CO_2 from the burning of fossil fuels was remaining in the atmosphere. At a 1975 conference he pointed to the beneficial effects of CO_2 on agriculture. There seems to be little dispute about the rising levels of greenhouse gases. The amount of CO_2 in the atmosphere is about 360 ppm, in line with CO_2 content during several earlier periods of interglacial warming.

During that same time in the 1950s, most of the environmental alarmists, led by Carl Sagan and his "nuclear winter" scare, were concerned about a possible Ice Age. But by the 1980s, many of the same people made a U-turn and began an impassioned campaign against greenhouse gases (specifically CO_2) as a cause of global warming. Political forces in Europe were early participants, with some of the most hysterical language coming from authoritarian Greens.

American environmental groups soon joined the Europeans and it is interesting to analyze the movement. Their strategy has been almost identical to that of the great Alar scare of 1989 (p. 10–11). Recall that in the case of Alar, a little bit of dubious science was distorted by environmentalists, publicized by paid PR groups, and hyped by irresponsible elements of the media. Even scientific journals take sides; in the same issue of *Scientific American* (May, 2004) in which Dr. James Hansen suggested a new direction and different strategy than Kyoto, the editorial page chose to ignore Hansen's rather important ideas, and instead continued to demonize the opposition.

When the environmental alarmists announced their first computer models, they made a number of frightening projections, none of which have come to pass. But some of their most extreme predictions have become embedded in the language and irresponsible people in the media often repeat them. So we keep hearing that temperatures will be from two to ten degrees higher (a huge range of uncertainty) at the end of this century, together with higher sea levels, violent weather, an array of infectious diseases, drought, species extinctions, and so on.

Most outrageous in these cases has been the actions of some politicians who have pushed for ill-conceived and costly governmental action, all based on incomplete and erroneous information.

In his 1992 book *Earth in the Balance* Al Gore propounded the theory that greenhouse gases threaten a catastrophic warming of the earth. With messianic fervor Gore wrote that our "dysfunctional civilization" was "killing the atmosphere with carbon dioxide and other pollutants." His solution? A steep "carbon tax" leading to a "wrenching transformation of society," altering the "very foundation of our civilization." He suggested the goal of completely eliminating the internal combustion engine over a twenty-five-year period.

Gore was one of the chief supporters of the December 1997 Global Treaty on Climate Change, or Kyoto Protocol. This treaty would require the U.S. and other industrially advanced countries—but not China, India, Mexico, Brazil, or others—to reduce carbon emissions to 5 percent below 1990 levels by 2010. Proponents of Kyoto cannot show that it would "make a measurable difference in climate, but they do admit it will create huge increases in the cost of energy" ($43.50/barrel of oil according to Gerhard). In spite of that, they insist that "we take these measures just in case the theory is correct." Fortunately, the Senate in 1997 voted 97–0 against signing the flawed treaty unless developing nations participated. Also, 17,000 American scientists signed a petition opposing the Kyoto Accord.

Some of the more responsible research going on today is trying to come to grips with the effects of clouds and ocean currents. Water vapor accounts for about 60 percent of the greenhouse effect and the "greenhouse gases" for the other 40 percent. Of this 40 percent, CO_2 causes about 50 percent of the greenhouse effect and soot, methane, nitrous oxide, ozone and CFCs (chlorofluorocarbons) together cause the other 50 percent.

Often overlooked is the fact that, except for water vapor, the greenhouse gases are present in trace amounts (.03 percent or less). And of these amounts it is estimated that human activities account for only 5 percent of all carbon dioxide emissions; that is, only nine of the 186 billion tons of CO_2 passing into the atmosphere annually.

Much uncertainty exists concerning the amount of CO_2 taken up by terrestrial and ocean life.In this regard, Sallie Chisholm of M.I.T. and collaborators, have recently explained the importance of certain photoplankton species living in the upper 200 meters of the ocean. By their sheer abundance—up to 20,000 cells per drop of seawater—these cyanobacteria account for about half the total photosynthesis on Earth. In the process they remove nearly as much CO_2 as all land plants, and generate about half the total oxygen supply. Most important is *Prochlorococcus*, with thirty-five species identified so far. In terms of individuals, this may be the most plentiful species on Earth and ancestral forms were the planet's first oxygen producing organisms. Other phytoplankton, especially siliceous single-celled algae called diatoms (used to make diatomaceous earth), process and remove prodigious amounts of CO_2, and return oxygen to the air.

In late 2002 an interesting research project was announced by J. Craig Venter, one of the main players in the Human Genome Project (p. 510-20?). Using funds from his foundation, plus government grants, he will attempt to engineer a new species of super microbe that can scrub CO_2 emissions in power plants. In the process, hydrogen gas would be released. Although the project sounds ambitious and on the outer limits of available technology, Venter's earlier successes demand that his ideas get serious attention.

Ice core data have been very helpful in measuring fluctuations in atmospheric gases during the last few hundred thousand years. Of particular interest is the comparison of the current Holocene interglacial period beginning about 12,000 years ago with the previous Eemian interglacial about 125,000 years ago. The Eemian was warmer than today and the sea level then was sixteen to twenty feet higher.

Recently, several independent investigations have determined that in the last nine glacial cycles of the Pleistocene, atmospheric CO_2 during the interglacials was more than 50 percent higher than during the glaciations. The observed increases can be explained by oceans giving off CO_2 naturally as temperatures rise, due to decreased solubility of CO_2. One other sobering result from ice core data is that CO_2 increases lagged temperature increases by 400–600 years, not vice versa, as the warming theory requires.

James Hansen is director of the NASA Goddard Institute for Space Studies and a researcher at the Columbia University Earth Institute. He has been associated with global warming studies for many years and got in the headlines when he testified before Al Gore's senate committee in 1988. Hansen is considered to have impeccable credentials in this field and his scientific integrity should be admired. In the March 2004 *Scientific American*, Hansen presented some new ideas in his article "Defusing the Global Warming Time Bomb."

In his paper, Hansen points out that the combined effects of soot, methane and ozone are equally important as CO_2 in affecting global warming. He also says the actual, observed trends of CO_2 and methane are far below all IPCC scenarios and that the IPCC projection of 4 percent per year CO_2 increase is implausible. He shows that the growth of total greenhouse gases peaked in the early 1980s and declined thereafter. Methane declined by two-thirds in the last twenty years, CFC's were banned beginning in 1992, and NO_2 has declined as well. As Hansen says, in the last 10–15 years, "the main elements required to halt climate change have come into being with remarkable rapidity."

David Appell has described another factor, called "global dimming," that complicates the modeling of global warming. In this case, clouds, air pollution, and aerosols reduce the amount of solar radiation by about one third the magnitude of warming attributed to CO_2. The aerosols described include micron-size (or less) particles of carbon, dust, sulfates and even sea salt.

A related phenomenon is just beginning to receive the attention it warrants. This concerns the discovery by Indian scientist Veerabhadran Ramanathan, in 1999, of the "Asian Brown Cloud." This huge, deadly body of pollution is caused by the burning of dried animal dung for fuel by 1.5 billion poor villagers throughout Asia. [From personal experience in Turkey, I can confirm that in the villages, when (mostly donkey) dung is burned for heat in the wintertime, it smells just like burning donkey dung!] Dr. Surabit Menon at Columbia University has found that in addition to severe pollution, the brown cloud contributes more to global warming than all industrial CO_2 emissions of the Western world.

In May and again in December 2003, research results added more insights about soot from the "brown cloud." It was shown that this soot, plus that from diesel engines, burning coal, etc. diminished the albedo (reflective property) of ice and snow in the Northern Hemisphere. It was claimed that the soot (carbon from incomplete combustion) caused up to 25 percent of global warming and was twice as potent as CO_2 in changing surface air temperatures. The data were reported in the *Proceedings of the National Academy of Sciences*; the authors, including James Hansen, are respected scientists at the Earth Institute, Columbia University, and at NASA.

This information from top scientists, in a reputable scientific document, was not widely reported by the media. But Hansen's "Time Bomb" article cannot be ignored so easily, and adds considerably more detail to the argument.

Other scientists have criticized erroneous material used by the IPCC, in particular the mathematical technique used to generate the "hockey stick" graph in the "Third Assessment Report" (IPCC 2001) and numerous other publications. The hockey stick graph, published by M. Mann *et al* in 1998, gets its shape by showing an abrupt warming during the last 100 years (to 1980) and flattening out the Medieval Warm Event (A.D. 870–1450) and Little Ice Age (1560–1850) almost to the status of non-events. Mann refused to show his algorithms after McIntyre and McKitrick (2003) used "corrected and updated" data to reshape the curve and stated bluntly that Mann's data set of proxies (including extensive use of tree rings) contains collation errors, unjustifiable truncation or extrapolation of source data, obsolete data, geographical mislocations, incorrect calculation of principal components and other serious defects.

The global warming problem has led to much good research, but more will be needed before the best solution is agreed upon. Many scientists believe that the Kyoto approach will eventually be recognized as ineffective and inappropriate. As proposed, the effect on climate would be trivial; even if every nation on Earth complied with the terms of the Protocol there would be a reduction of only .06°C in projected temperatures in fifty years. Shogren restated Wigley's 1998 prediction that even with Kyoto fully in force, CO_2 concentrations would double in 105 years, instead of 100 years (without Kyoto). As stated by Frederick Seitz "it would be a reckless breach of trust to put in force hasty policies that create real personal and economic hardships for most of the world's population." In fact, early results of the Kyoto approach do not look very good, based on the late 2005 conference in Montreal. Of the thirty-eight industrialized nations, only England and

Germany had complied and then only because of one-time events (England converted from coal to natural gas and Germany phased out the inefficient, polluting industries in East Germany).

In 2001 President Bush took a principled stand and affirmed that the U.S. would not ratify Kyoto, thereby opening him to abuse at home and abroad. In October 2003, Russian President Vladimir Putin seemed to support Bush's position. Countries representing 55 percent of emissions must sign on before the treaty takes effect and only 44 percent had ratified at that point. Mr. Putin said he had learned that "we simply don't know why temperatures are rising, how recent trends relate to long-term temperature variations and, above all, whether or not changing human behavior would matter to any of this." (*Wall Street Journal*, October 28, 2003)

Mr. Putin's chief economic advisor, Andrei Illarionov, said it was necessary to balance costs against benefits, but Russian scientists gave even more meaningful support. Putin's most influential scientific advisor, Yuri Izrael, stated "all the scientific evidence seems to support the same general conclusions, that the Kyoto Protocol is overly expensive, ineffective and based on bad science." But late in 2004, the Russian Parliament approved joining the Kyoto Protocol. Putin's change of heart was partly to curry favor with the World Trade Organization (WTO) and perhaps, more cynically, a belief that Kyoto will never be consummated because of the economic costs.

Dr. Hansen's 2004 report tends to support the stance taken by President Bush in refusing to be pressured into taking unwise and precipitate actions. Hansen put forth specific recommendations for a strategy quite different than the Kyoto approach. He believes that the main danger is rising sea levels due mainly to thermal expansion of ocean water. Global warming has two components and should be controlled as follows: "first, halt or reverse growth in air pollutants, specifically soot, atmospheric ozone and methane; second, keep average fossil-fuel carbon dioxide emissions in the next 50 years about the same as today. The carbon dioxide and non-carbon dioxide portions of the scenario are equally important."

Hansen believes "that the highest prudent level of additional global warming is not more than about one degree C (1.8°F). Control of carbon dioxide emissions will require continued improvements in efficiency, more renewable energy, and new technologies for combustion and sequestration. Hydrogen fuel may become important and next-generation nuclear power likewise.

In summary, it is clear that interglacial warming is indeed underway, to the extent of about 16°F in the past 15,000 years. Cycles of orbital and solar activity have largely controlled this warming, which has seen a number of perturbations—periods of heating and cooling. Another 3° of warming would be the normal expectation, to reach the 19° average of the last nine cycles of the Pleistocene. It is pretentious of some environmentalists to contend that mankind can alter long-term trends of Mother Nature in any significant way. They seem to me to be like the proud little guy on a raft in the recent Sumatra tsunami—and who thinks he is steering the raft. Recall from p. 326 "In one second, the sun gives off more energy than all people have produced during their stay on Earth".

Mankind's small part in the warming is mostly due to the soot effect and greenhouse gases, discussed above. A very interesting project is currently underway in Qatar—Exxon Mobil is investing $7 billion in a gas-to-liquids (GTL) plant, the largest single investment in the company's history. The plant will convert natural gas from the enormous North field to a new, clear form of diesel fuel which causes almost no pollution.

The first goal should be to quantify mankind's relative role in global warming. Nations, in a cooperative effort, no doubt can devise ways to ameliorate some of the adverse effects of both CO_2 and soot. Costs of corrective action should be allocated according to the related causes, feasibility, and commensurate with expected benefits.

With higher fuel costs we are already beginning to see gas-guzzling SUV's being displaced by hybrid cars. Economics of the marketplace may well serve to accomplish much of what the Kyoto crowd wants to do using coercion and punishments. Increasingly, it begins to appear that the Kyoto approach was politicized by environmentalists before the full science was understood, and some people were stampeded into a half-baked scheme that deals with only part of the problem.

In this regard, the Copenhagen Consensus, headed by Danish statistician Bjorn Lomborg, has used a cost-benefit analysis to prioritize the spending on funds for twelve different worldwide projects to help mankind. The Kyoto approach was the least effective of the twelve. At a cost of $94 trillion (1990 dollars), Kyoto would reduce average worldwide warming only 1.2°C in 300 years. Especially troublesome is the fact that costs are immediate whereas the results are far in the future, when the projections and consequences are uncertain (Occam's Razor in reverse!)

The twenty-five-year government effort to promote renewable energy has cost consumers between $30 and $40 billion, but has resulted in only a 1.5 percent market share for wind, solar, geothermal and biomass combined. Intuitively, wind and solar have great appeal but today furnish only

0.1 percent of total U.S. energy use and, of course, both are interruptible and dependent on the whims of the weather (and subject to NIMBY –not in my backyard).

The upcoming Sydney conference to launch the Asia-Pacific Partnership will be a collaborative effort to develop cleaner energy sources. The U.S. will be a member of the Partnership because it will approach the problem using technology, and economics of the market place, rather than the heavy-handed approach of Kyoto.

As a common sense approach to future large-scale energy sources, the stress will likely be on clean coal technology, renewable fuel, natural gas, and atomic (uranium) power. Hydrogen fuel cells may become quite important, especially in vehicular transportation, and hybrid electric-gas cars are already becoming popular. Ethanol will help replace oil as it is phased out as a fuel, and Lomborg has projected the use of crude oil ending in the time frame 2065–2105, as reserves are exhausted.

(Note: In 2004, famous author Michael Crichton wrote a superb book entitled *State of Fear*. It is written as fiction and as such tells an engrossing story concerning environmental extremists. But it is based on solid science, and the Author's Message, Appendix I and II, and Bibliography comprise by far the most important parts of the book. Many of his references are familiar to me and used when I wrote this section on Global Warming. Regrettably, Hansen's 2004 report in *Scientific American* was not published in time for Crichton to use.

In the Author's Message, Crichton emphasizes the need to obtain unbiased research results in order to determine appropriate policy. As he says, "scientists know that continued funding depends on delivering the results the funders desire" and therefore, both environmental and industry-supported research may be biased. He compares some scientists to "Renaissance painters, commissioned to make the portrait the patron wants done" and urges that blinded funding mechanisms be utilized in order to avoid subjectivity, i.e., politicizing science. In Appendix I he quotes Alston Chase "When the search for truth is confused with political advocacy, the pursuit of knowledge is reduced to the quest for power").

14

LIFE FORMS / EVOLUTION

Although there has been a great deal of speculation about life elsewhere in the universe, so far there has been nothing to support the idea. One answer is that life may exist on other planets but we have not found it yet. Another is that it has not evolved as it did on Earth. Or, it may well be that Earth is indeed unique in that existing conditions are "just right" for the development of life, at least as we know it.

In their 1999 book *Rare Earth: Why Complex Life is Rare in the Universe* NASA scientists Brownlee and Ward outlined some of Earth's key "just right" factors as follows:

- Stable orbits of the other planets, all controlled by the right mass of the sun
- Earth's planetary mass large enough to retain its oceans and atmosphere
- Jupiter's presence, serving to sweep up asteroids and comets that otherwise could strike Earth with disastrous results
- Oceans in the right proportions
- Plate tectonics, that helped create the continents and also enhance biodiversity
- The correct tilt of Earth on its axis, creating the seasons

- A large moon, at the correct distance to stabilize Earth's tilt
- Carbon; sufficient to support life but not enough to create a runaway greenhouse effect, as on Venus
- Biological evolution—the pathway to complex plants and animals
- A limited number of asteroid impacts of a magnitude sufficient to cause widespread extinction of pecies
- A magnetosphere serving to protect Earth from charged particles streaming from the sun

The argument for rare life in the universe gets additional support from the statistical analyses made by a number of scientists including Crick, Penrose, Hoyle, Corey and others, summarized in chapters Three and Four. In fact, Sagan's claim of a million other civilizations in the Milky Way galaxy looks increasingly dubious and a second look at the SETI project may be warranted.

AGE OF THE EARTH

For many years the calculations of theologians were widely accepted, but more recently, scientific data have shown that those earlier claims were wildly erroneous.

Genesis described how creation took six days and in 1658 Bishop James Ussher of Ireland calculated that the six days began the night of October 23, 4004 B.C. Ussher deduced this date by counting generations in the Bible, working backward through the Scriptures. In 1833 a respected geologist, George Fairholme, also insisted that God had created the world in six days, each of twenty-four hours duration. Moreover, he held that the Flood was a real, authenticated historical event beginning in 2348 B.C. and lasting one year and ten days. For the next 250 years Ussher's calculations were accepted by much of the Western world. Such famous scientists as Johannes Kepler and Isaac Newton also arrived at dates close to Ussher's, using similar methods.

In opposition to Ussher and the others, however, some of the leading geologists of the time were beginning to recognize that the earth was much older. Even as early as 1766, Antoine-Laurent Lavoisier had wondered about geological processes and the age of rocks in Western Europe. Later he was called the "greatest chemist in human history" but his career was (literally) cut short by the guillotine in 1794. James Hutton, considered the founder of modern geology, by 1785 realized that millions of years would be required for the geologic processes that he observed. Charles Lyell and others realized that fossils they were finding in older rocks were millions of years old. Some calculations of Earth ages, using the thickness of sedimentary rocks, gave results ranging from 17 million to 1 billion years

In 1862, Lord Kelvin made calculations based on heat loss that showed the habitable age of the earth was 200 million years. Bertram Boltwood pioneered in the use of radioactive elements as tools in dating rocks. In 1907, using the uranium-lead technique, he found some Earth rocks to be 2.2 billion years old. More recently, using rocks from a number of sources, the age of the earth has been conclusively determined to be 4.6 billion years.

Fossil evidence has been vital in the tracing of life on Earth, and early geologists classified rock units according to their fossil assemblages. Fossils are the remains of prehistoric organisms, a fact recognized by the ancient Greeks. Fossils can form as original hard parts preserved within enclosing sediments, or as secondary structures formed by impressions (molds or casts) of bones, shells or tracks. The original organic material may also be replaced by percolating minerals such as silica or phosphate, a petrifaction process.

Stephan Jay Gould (recently deceased) was one of the most famous of the modern paleontologists. He wrote several popular books describing some unique and entertaining examples of ancient fossils, and some amusing—and embarrassing—hoaxes to remind us of the need for careful use of data. The lesson is that the confirmation process by peer review should be avidly sought by any reputable scientist.

In his *The Lying Stones of Marrakech*, Gould described one of the earliest victims, Dr. Beringer of Wurzburg. Some of Beringer's own students planted fake fossils for him to find in one of his favorite fossil localities. The fakes were depictions of various organisms, artfully carved in three dimensions on flat stones. Some examples were lizards in their skin, birds with beaks and eyes, bees feeding on flowers, snails next to their eggs, frogs copulating, etc. Also a number of heavenly objects such as comets with tails, the crescent moon and a glowing sun. Still others depicted Hebrew letters. Beringer knew the stones were different than conventional fossils but he did not doubt their authenticity and dismissed claims that they were hand carved. Evidently his students knew him well, a pompous and stubborn ass, because in 1726 he published a wordy scientific volume, complete with twenty-one plates of the remarkable fossils he had found. When he found another "fossil" with his own name written on it he finally realized he had been tricked. Crushed and brokenhearted, Dr Beringer impoverished himself trying to buy up all extant copies of his book and he died soon thereafter.

Gould also described another hoax, that of the phony Piltdown Man. This "fossil" was constructed using the jaw of an orangutan attached to the cranium of a modern human. This fraud was exposed in the early 1950s but only after confusing anthropologists for some forty years.

As recently as 1999, *National Geographic* glowingly described a phony fossil as a missing link between dinosaurs and birds. The fraud was discovered only after a collector paid $80,000 for the stone slab and smuggled it out of China. X-ray analysis showed that the "fossil" was a mosaic of eighty-eight rock fragments glued together. The bird portion was part of the fish-eating *Yanornis martini* and the dinosaur parts came from a *Microraptor zhaoianus*; both living 110 million years ago. Together they were named *Archaeoraptor*, a new fossil name that was later disavowed.

FIRST LIFE

The oldest fossils found so far occur in the Pilbara area of Western Australia and are about 3.5 billion years old. These fossil features, called stromatolites, are curious, cushion-shaped mounds formed by primitive bacteria that deposit layered mats of mineral grains. Modern stromatolites in the process of formation can be observed at Shark Bay, on the coast only 500 miles away. Also at Pilbara, other equally old fossils have been found in the Apex chert at Warrawoona Hills. The fossil material consists of pyritic filaments, the remains of thread-like organisms. If the identification of cyanobacteria is correct it means that processes presaging photosynthesis appeared as long as 3.5 billion years ago. It also means that the Warrawoona microorganisms were already moderately evolved from more primitive precursors.

Isua, in Greenland, shows some indirect evidence of life some 300 million years older than the fossils in Pilbara. The 3.85 billion-year-old banded-iron formations at Isua contain carbon that may indicate an organic origin. Life favors the lighter isotope of carbon, C-12, so the ratio with the heavier isotope, C-13, can be used as an indicator. The C-12 at Isua is about one percent above normal and at Pilbara about three percent. The isotope data at Pilbara is supported by fossil material, whereas that at Isua is not and the evidence is much weaker. Not only are there no fossils, but the isotopic deviation is much less.

Sagan and others believed that life on Earth originated in warm ponds and oceans about four billion years ago. They pictured simple hydrogen-rich molecules of the early atmosphere being broken apart by lightning and ultra-violet light from the sun. Fragments, when recombined and dissolved in the oceans, formed a kind of organic soup of gradually increasing complexity, and it was visualized that "one day, quite by accident, a molecule arose that was able to make copies of itself, using as building blocks other molecules."

In his laboratory at Cornell University, Sagan did some experimental organic chemistry aimed at replicating processes on the early Earth. Hydrogen, water, ammonia, methane and hydrogen sulfide were mixed together in a closed glass vessel and the contents then exposed to electrical sparking, to simulate lightning. After ten minutes, organic material appeared and the interior of the flask was eventually covered with a thick brown tar. The tar turned out to be an extremely rich mix of complex organic molecules, including the constituents of proteins and nucleic acids. These experiments were similar to those done in the early 1950s by one of Harold Urey's students, Stanley Miller. But so far, no one doing these kinds of experiments has achieved a living cell, much less DNA with its genetic code.

The panspermia theory posits that impacting comets, asteroids and meteors brought the first organic matter and water to the earth. When the Giatto spacecraft flew close to Halley's Comet in 1986, it found a black core of material containing carbon, hydrogen, nitrogen and sulfur. Dust grains in the comet's tail contained as much as one-third organic compounds. Benzene, methanol and acetic acid were detected, as well as some of the precursors of nucleic acids. If Halley is typical, comets could easily have supplied enough carbon to Earth for the entire biosphere. Some strange planetesimals, called Centaurs, have recently been found near the Kuiper belt. They are dark red and seemingly rich in hydrocarbons. Organic infusion in this way has some support because of the intense bombardment of Earth by giant comets and asteroids about 3.8 billion years ago, when the first life appeared.

Recently, more attention has been given to a number of "super bugs" having ancient and primitive characteristics. Sometimes called "living fossils," these microbes thrive in extreme conditions similar to those on Earth three to four billion years ago. One group of acid-loving bacteria thrives on a diet of sulfur, extracted from hydrogen-sulfide gas. They produce sulfuric acid and can tolerate fluid with a pH as low as 2.

Other bacteria, called halophiles, live in highly saline water such as in the Dead Sea, the Great Salt Lake in Utah and Lake Magadi in Kenya.

Viable halophiles have been found in salt mines enclosed in ancient salt crystals.

Certain bacteria can tolerate sub-zero temperatures to -320°F, radiation that is lethal to other organisms, pressures to several hundred atmospheres, the absence of oxygen, or extremes of alkalinity. Bacteria have been found in wells at depths down to 10,000 feet.

The 40,000 miles of spreading centers on the seafloor comprise a new focus for investigation. At places along these plate margins, vents release a stream of superheated fluid that can be loaded with minerals and chemicals. Some of these submarine volcanic vents are called black smokers, when dark fluid spews from mineral-coated rock chimneys. At depths of 8000 feet, the seawater at a black smoker can reach 660°F. As the searing fluids encounter the cold seawater, a chemical and thermal pandemonium ensues

These deep-sea vents have been found to be teeming with life. Crabs and giant tubeworms are some of the more exotic animals. But most remarkable of all are some new microbes found in temperatures as high as 230°F. Organisms that can live at these temperatures are known as hyper-thermophiles and at least twenty new genera have been described. These deep-sea organisms live in pitch-black darkness where no sunlight penetrates and plants cannot grow. So the microbes act as the primary producers at the base of the food chain; they obtain their energy directly from the hot chemical stew spewing from the vents.

The "bacteria" that live in these extreme environmental conditions serve to demonstrate the diversity of early life forms. In 1973 Carl Woese showed that over 3 billion years ago, an ancestral organism split into three basic domains, now named Bacteria, Archaea, and Eucarya.

Woese used molecular sequencing techniques that revolutionized the study of microbiology. Although bacteria and archaea are both single-celled microbes that lack a nucleus, the ribosomal proteins in archaea were found to be more similar to those in eukarya than to those in bacteria. Hence, archaea are closer to eukarya. Cells of eukaryotic organisms have nuclei, cytoskeletons and internal membranes and are the predecessors of plants, animals—and humans. Archaea cells have about two million base pairs of DNA whereas a human cell has about three billion base pairs.

The progression from a common ancestor seems to favor bacteria as the earliest but archaea are also quite close to the same ancestor. Together, bacteria and archaea are the most ubiquitous form of life on Earth and make

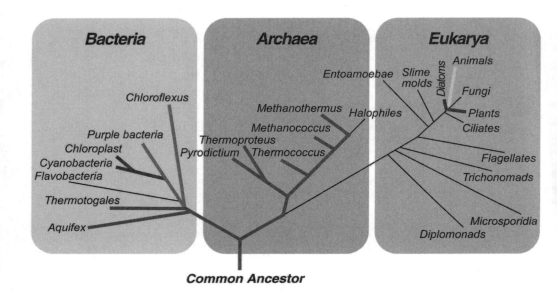

Common Ancestor

From online GSA Today, July 2000. Universal phylogenetic tree showing three domains of life (Bacteria, Archaea, and Eukarya). Evolutionary distances between groups are proportional to line lengths. Observe the requirement for symbiotic transfer of genes for oxygenic photosynthesis between cyanobacteria and plants. Also note position of Methanococcus (p. 411) among the early Archaea.

up 90 percent of the total biomass in the ocean. Eukaryotes probably evolved from the archaean line about 1.6 to 2.1 billion years ago, and acquired their mitochondria and chloroplasts after the split (see p. 407). Another factor is that of "horizontal gene transfer" when the early organisms swapped genes with their neighbors. This process may help explain the transfer of photosynthetic genes from cyanobacteria to oxygen-generating Eukarya plants, in the diagram above

It is believed that by 3.8 billion years ago the surface temperature of the earth was less than 230°F and one-celled microbes appeared. As early as 3 billion years ago, blue-green algae, or cyanobacteria in the oceans were busily generating oxygen through the process of photosynthesis (called the most important single metabolic advance in the history of life on the planet). Plant cells later evolved to contain tiny molecular units called chloroplasts that conduct the process of photosynthesis—the conversion of sunlight, water and carbon dioxide into carbohydrates and oxygen.

Chlorophyll, which makes plants green, is the crucial component in this process. Oxygen became an important constituent of the earth's atmosphere, altering it irreversibly from its original hydrogen-rich character. The nitrogen in today's atmosphere is also a biological product. Thus 99 percent of the earth's atmosphere is of biological origin.

By two billion years ago, according to Sagan, the process of sex arose and this innovation allowed two organisms to exchange whole pages of their genetic instructions producing improved copies for the selection process. Sex itself was a positive attribute and has been pursued enthusiastically ever since—organisms that found it uninteresting quickly became extinct.

Stanford grad Olivia Judson has let her "Dr. Tatiana" amusingly describe how some organisms display their interest in sex. For example, the male paper nautilus octopus gets so enthusiastic while mating that his penis (a modified tentacle) is discharged (explodes) and winds up in the body of his amour. She may carry several of these missiles, from other males, in her body, but Dr. Tatiana did not say if the male could grow a replacement for a repeat performance. Although the male octopus is a literal loser, he is not as bad off as the male praying mantis, which gets his head bitten off by the female after mating. Some of the females prefer biting off the male's head before mating, as it sends the male into a sexual frenzy and he performs his duties anyway. "Females in more than eighty other species have been caught eating their lovers before, during, or after sex." Fortunately, at least in absolute terms, this particular genetic habit was not passed on to humans.

For the first three billion years, life did not evolve much beyond microscopic blue-green algae, or cyanobacteria. Then, 543 million years ago (ma), a huge number of advanced new animal life forms appeared, culminating in an event called the Cambrian explosion. Leading up to this event, during late pre-Cambrian time, some enigmatic creatures called Ediacarans existed. These critters appeared some 580 ma and could be quite large (to a few feet in length). But they had no complex internal organs, nor any recognizable body openings for mouth or anus. They may have been ancestors of such things as jellyfish—or they may have been an early but failed stage in multicellular animal life. The Ediacara fauna died out quickly after 543 ma.

Bottjer (2005) has recently described some fossil specimens found in China which are the oldest animals with a bilateral body style. Named *Vernanimalcula*, they are tiny (the width of a few human hairs), but complex, having a mouth, gut and anus. Having only soft parts, they were fossilized by phosphatization and detected under the microscope by making thousands of thin sections. They seem to indicate that animals developed complexity before large size. Their age, 580–600 ma, suggests that their evolutionary ancestors were even older.

For the first few million years of the Cambrian, fossil remains are a confusing collection of spines, plates, and other fragments. But beginning at 530 ma and lasting for ten million years, the "Cambrian explosion" provided the most astonishing episode in the fossil record.

In 1884, excavations for the railroad being built through the Canadian Rockies of British Columbia uncovered millions of fossils in the Burgess Shale formation. These fossils were from complex animals, the first ones with limbs, segmented bodies, shells, jaws, claws, teeth, and eyes. The fossils discovered included 20–35 new animal phyla, a burst of biological creativity unprecedented in the history of the earth. These were all marine forms but included ancestors of all animals that swim, crawl, fly or walk, including chordates. Although similar fossils have since been found in Cambrian rocks elsewhere, the specimens in the Burgess shale are the best preserved, most numerous, and most diverse.

The explosion was so impressive because it provided the first, startling abundance of animals with hard parts that made good fossils. Certainly the animals must have had predecessors in the pre-Cambrian, represented by tracks and trails, and perhaps phosphatized embryos or larvae of adult forms. Paleontologists recognized that the rapid change in anatomical characteristics was enormously important.

Of all the Cambrian fossils, the trilobites were the most outstanding as they were beautifully designed, rather like large insects, hunting in packs on the sea floor. The first trilobites were fully formed and some had large, well-developed eyes. The earliest species had eyes with many lenses but later types had up to 12,000 lenses, all of them tightly packed and arranged in specific patterns. More than 15,000 species of trilobites have been described, ranging in size from a quarter inch to almost three feet. They were the most persistent forms of marine animal life for 300 million years.

Estimates of the number of all species now living range from three to 100 million and the number of recorded species ranges from 1.4 to 1.8 million, mostly plants and insects. Of all the named species, only about 40,000 are vertebrates. Still to be listed are millions of insects, fungi and microbes. More than 99 percent of all species that have ever lived are now extinct.

DARWIN

Charles Robert Darwin was born in 1809. Both his father and grandfather were eminent physicians in London, and his youth was a privileged one. His academic record at both Edinburgh and Cambridge was undistinguished, but his family connections outweighed that. Thus, a good friend, John Henslow, arranged for Darwin, right out of college, to sail as the unpaid naturalist on HMS *Beagle*. *Beagle* departed from Plymouth in December 1831 on a voyage planned for two years but which lasted five.

During the trip Darwin kept meticulous notes on exploration in South America and the Galapagos Islands, showing skill as a collector, observer and theorist. When Darwin returned to England in 1836, he was widely welcomed by the scientific community. He was soon elected to the Geological Society and to the Royal Society in 1839.

During his time on the *Beagle* and afterward Darwin gave considerable thought to the works of the Scottish geologist James Hutton (1726–97), especially as clarified by Sir Charles Lyell (1797–1875). Hutton emphasized the importance of geologic time (millions of years) and uniformitarianism—i.e., that geological processes are gradual and continuous. Hutton suggested natural selection as an important factor affecting the origin of human races, and Darwin's grandfather had explained how humans—and other species—adapt to their environment. Darwin also was familiar with the argument of Thomas Malthus (1766–1834) concerning the competition for limited resources. And finally, Darwin no doubt was influenced by the knowledge of how artificial selection had been used by mankind to develop the different breeds of dogs, horses, and strains of pigeons.

In 1858, Darwin, with Alfred Wallace, co-authored a paper that discussed evolution by natural selection. The paper got little attention but in 1859 Darwin's landmark *On the Origin of Species by Means of Natural Selection* proved to have a profound influence on scientific thought at the time and ever since. It could have been very helpful to him, but Darwin never got to see the report on genetics, published in 1866, by the Augustinian monk Gregor Mendel. T.H.Huxley strongly supported the theory of evolution and was very articulate in defending Darwin against vehement opposition by prominent theologians of the day.

Darwin's explanation of evolution called upon natural selection of those random changes that were relatively more advantageous to a species. He described a gradual process, utilizing geologic time (thousands of years), wherein species are more successful at reproducing if they are marginally better adapted to their environment. In this process the species that are less well adapted to change gradually disappear, to be replaced by the more adaptable. The "survival of the fittest," over many generations, gives rise to new species. Darwin believed that this "descent with modification" accounted for the huge variety in living things. He believed that all life is related and that today's plants and animals are all descended from earlier ancestors.

In the *Origin of Species* Darwin devoted an entire chapter to "The Imperfection of the Fossil Record." He was concerned that in most cases the fossil record did not show a finely graduated sequence of organic remains. Rather, the organisms seemed to show change by fits and starts. He believed this was due to the geologic record itself, that is, an erratic preservation of fossils full of gaps, or as other authors have said, finding "bony needles in stony haystacks." Gould has added another explanation with the idea of "punctuated equilibria." In this theory, species remain in equilibrium for a long time but then change rapidly in response to some environmental stress. This can be due to climate change, an asteroid impact, a change in sea level, a wobble in the earth's axis of rotation, a magnetic reversal, etc. Those species that can adapt most successfully tend to dominate the gene pool of the surviving population.

Myriad forms have developed and died out during the billions of years that life has existed on Earth—perhaps 5 billion species extinctions in all. More than 99 percent of all species reached a dead-end, almost always by failure to adapt to changing conditions as opposed to some drastic, abrupt, physical disaster.

One very successful but unfortunate example of natural selection is seen in modern hospitals where powerful antibiotics are being defeated by bacterial evolution. Penicillin has become almost useless as an antibiotic. Some would say the bacteria have adapted new traits, rather than a change of species, but minor genetic changes are the first steps leading to major structural ones. In a controlled experiment with *E. coli*, twelve populations of the bacterium rapidly adapted to different conditions in their test tubes. With a new generation every 3½ hours, that is evolution in fast-forward.

In contrast to natural selection, intentional reproduction by artificial selection speeds up the process of developing preferred characteristics in plants and animals. In the case of man's best friend, dogs have been domesticated for about 15,000 years, their likely ancestors being gray wolves perhaps in East Asia. With a few small genetic modifications, different breeds have been developed for desired characteristics such as hunting, herding, racing, beauty, etc. Ten thousand years ago there were no dairy cattle, seedless grapes, or corn that produces 300 bushels/acre. These are all products of evolution by artificial selection, controlled by human intervention.

Many studies have been made of the time required for evolutionary change. Complex anatomical parts such as the eye have been favorite subjects. In the case of the invertebrate eye, at least nine different designs have evolved, independently, in forty to sixty different groups of creatures. Using conservative assumptions it was found that a fish eye could evolve in fewer than 400,000 generations. At one generation per year, less than half a million years would be required.

Recently, the Rosemary and Peter Grant team reported on an extensive study of some of "Darwin's finches" on a small Galapagos island. They caught and banded thousands of finches to trace their lineage through climate change. They found the birds' beaks were modified slightly so as to survive the changing environment. The Grants were able to document corresponding changes in DNA as this occurred. The conclusion was that the power of natural selection was neither slow nor rare and could lead to rapid evolutionary change.

Within a given species, alternative genes or alleles determine the phenotype or form of a species, and any evolutionary change is called microevolution. An example of natural selection is the *E. coli* experiment mentioned above, and one of artificial selection is that of *Brassica oleracea* from which cabbage, cauliflower, broccoli, collards and Brussels sprouts have been derived. One downside to artificial selection is the danger of inbreeding, and possible health problems.

Macroevolution refers to an evolutionary change creating a new species (splitting a species into two), and could lead to a new family, genus or phylum. It is not certain that any new species has ever been developed through artificial selection. In other words, microevolution can be studied directly, but macroevolution cannot be. The "peppered moth" case is a perfect example of natural selection, or survival of the fittest. But it does not demonstrate macroevolution. Although the moths change color to improve their survival rate, they still remain the same species, *Biston betularia*.

Exactly 200 years before Darwin proposed the theory of evolution by natural selection, Bishop Ussher had calculated the date of creation to be 4004 B.C. This date was accepted by most people until it became clear that Darwin's ideas required a time frame of many thousands, if not millions of years for new species to evolve. This difference of opinion set scientists against theologians, and the dispute has raged ever since. In the next chapter, DNA is described as the fundamental control of evolution by passing on genetic information between generations.

Today, almost all scientists, and most theologians, including Catholics, agree that evolution is a valid concept. The agreement breaks down over the cause—scientists invoke natural mutations to explain the millions of species whereas theologians believe that life is controlled (or at least created) by a conscious, rational intelligence, or "Intelligent Design." This is another way of saying God is involved, so the imbroglio intensifies, as science cannot prove—or disprove— the existence of God.

STRANGE CREATURES

Along the way, the fossil record has revealed some astonishing critters. Among the strangest was five-eyed *Opabinia*, with an anterior "nozzle" having claws on the end. With a tail fan and flap-like structures along its trunk, this Cambrian animal was first called a brachiopod, later an arthropod or early crab/lobster. A later, Ordovician scorpion-like arthropod called *Pterygotus* grew to be seven feet long, had eight legs, and a pair of swimming paddles. The males had clasping organs that fit the female sex organs.

An especially repulsive creature is the hagfish, still living but quite similar to its ancestors 340 million years ago. Hagfish are eel-like vertebrates with a skeleton of cartilage. They have a single nostril and degenerated eyes under the skin. They have no jaws or bones but have two pairs of tooth-like rasps on a tongue-like projection. In addition to a normal heart they have three auxiliary hearts; one to pump blood to the liver, one in the head and another tiny one near the tail. Unlike their lamprey cousins, they are scavengers, and can emit gallons of nauseating, toxic slime, thereby their name "slime eels."

[While I was doing fieldwork in Central Montana for my Ph.D. dissertation, I was intrigued by a certain rock unit outcropping in the vicinity of Bear Gulch, in the northeast part of the Big Snowy Mountains. At that time, in 1954–55, I described a bed of limestone about 130 feet thick in the upper part of the Tyler formation. The fossiliferous limestone was dark gray to brown, silicious, hard, platy, and interbedded with softer limestone. From nearby well control, the unit could be delineated as a rock body about twenty-five miles wide and seventy-five miles long, aligned with a pre-existing trend of older rocks. The limestone appeared to be a bay-like appendage of marine conditions to the west and I called it, informally, "lime tongue." George H. Norton, a friend of mine, very properly named it the Bear Gulch member of the Tyler formation. We all realized the Bear Gulch was quite unusual in lithology, stratigraphic position, and age, as it was close to the boundary dividing Mississippian and Pennsylvanian periods.

In the mid 1950s my work was mostly concerned with stratigraphic correlation, nomenclature, lithology, age relationships and environment of deposition. I interpreted the unit to be Late Mississippian and am gratified to note that some fifty years later, petroleum geologists are still using the terminology I helped to introduce. To understand the stratigraphic relationships, information from wells had to be integrated with that from the outcrop exposures, and some of the academic types were handicapped to that extent.]

Beginning in 1968, some outstanding work has been done in recovering and identifying some astonishing fossils from the Bear Gulch limestone. Much of this was done by Richard Lund of Adelphi University in New York, and William G. Melton, Jr. and John R. Horner of the University of Montana in Missoula.

Over a period of ten years or so, they led teams of workers (up to twenty-one at a time) in extensive quarrying operations to find fossils in the Bear Gulch rocks. In this effort they recovered more than 4500 fish specimens representing 113 species. They also found well-preserved cephalopods, sponges, shrimp, brachiopods, pelecypods, starfish and algae. These fossils defined the rocks as Late Mississippian (Namurian) in age, about 320 million years old.

But it was the assemblage of fish fossils that surprised people. Half the specimens could not be identified as to genera or species, and some of the bizarre forms had never been seen before. Over sixty species of sharks and chimaeras were found, plus several coelacanths. Below is a picture of the chondrichthyan shark *Damocles*, the most abundant shark at Bear Gulch. Males had a forward curved dorsal spine, the purpose possibly being to attract females.

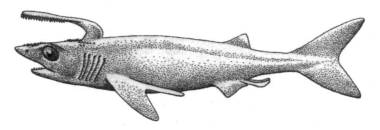

The primitive shark known as Damocles serratus *received its name because its dorsal spine curved forward until its serrated leading edge was underneath and hanging over its head, like the sword that hung over the head of Damocles in ancient Greece, suspended by a single thread to remind him of the uncertainty of life.*

Another fish from the Bear Gulch is shown below. It is one of sixty-nine species of chimaera, the other most numerous fish there. Pincer-shaped grappling hooks on the snout of the males are believed to be sex related.

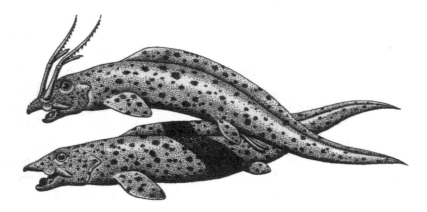

The jaw-breaking Harpagofututor volsellorhinus *was found by Richard Lund in Montana's Bear Gulch Formation. The name comes from the Greek for "grappling hooks," "copulator," and "pincer-snout"; thus it is a copulator with pincer-shaped grappling hooks on its snout.*

Lund has described specimens so well preserved that internal organs are visible, and he has written more than twenty-two publications on the Bear Gulch faunas. One of the wells a few miles to the east of the outcrop had thirty or so feet of chert (a good indicator of high silica content) at the top of the Bear Gulch. It is apparent that a huge number of fish and other animals died simultaneously. Asphyxiation seems the most likely cause, perhaps resulting from drying up of the bay.

Another weird shark fossil has been found in Permo-Carboniferous rocks (280 ma) in Idaho, Russia, Japan, Greenland, and elsewhere. *Helicoprion* is believed to be some kind of tooth, and actually means "circular saw." The saw is coiled in three and a half whorls and is armed with up to 180 sharp teeth. But so far, no convincing case has been presented to explain how this unusual appendage was used.

Helicoprion has a close affinity with Paleozoic sharks but beyond that the mystery is unsolved. The tooth spirals have been identified by scientists as body parts of snails, snakes, ammonites, and even entirely separate animals.

The mysterious fossilized "tooth-whorl" of Helicoprion. *Although there have been some good guesses, no one really knows how this 280-million-year-old shark used its teeth, or for that matter, where on the shark they were located.*

SYMBIOSIS

This process involves microbial invasion of a host body that results in a mutually beneficial relationship. A good example is the gut of humans, which teems with swarms of bacteria that assist in digesting food. The beneficial bacteria themselves thrive in the process, and without them, humans could not survive.

It appears that in the case of animal cells, mitochondria represent the vestiges of early bacterial invaders. The theory is that mitochondria were at one time independent microbes that invaded host cells and took up permanent residence in a process called endosymbiosis. Evolution has made the host cell dominant, but the dependent mitochondria retain some of their original genetic material. In parallel fashion, chloroblasts, which carry out the vital function of photosynthesis in green plants, are believed to be descended from primitive cyanobacteria. So rather than terminating in dead-ends, it appears that some of the critical elements of life survived by melding with other forms.

An interesting type of symbiosis has been observed at subsea hydrothermal vents along plate boundaries, especially as focused at "black smokers," discussed in an earlier section. Volcanic activity can heat the ocean water to 700°F, but the water does not boil because of the intense pressure. Unusual animals live there and instead of oxygen, utilize hydrogen sulfide normally poisonous to living creatures. Animals of this kind include six-foot-long tubeworms, dense schools of two-inch-long *Rimicaris* shrimp, *Calyptogena magnifica* clams, and *Bathymodiolus thermophilus* mussels. It was found that vast numbers of sulfur-oxidizing bacteria lived in the gut of the worms or in the gills of the shellfish. The bacteria were able to oxidize the sulfide and pass on fixed carbon compounds to their host. Each of the host animals was served by its own bacterium species, in a process called endosymbiotic.

Another form of symbiosis provides bioluminescence to certain fish. In this case, luminescent bacteria provide a light source that glows on the host fish while the fish provides a supply of nutrients and oxygen. The fish uses a specialized organ, populated by the light-emitting bacteria, as a lure dangling in front of its mouth. The luminous bacteria *Vibrio* involved in this process must be passed on from generation to generation of fish. Just how this done is still a mystery.

Holloway (2004) has described how bacteria are able to communicate among their own kind and with other species. Millions of *Vibrio* seem to emit light simultaneously, perhaps through some kind of signal called an auto inducer by researchers. Each bacterium can react to its own kind and also other bacteria of a different species. For example, the 600 species of bacteria on your teeth seem to organize themselves in the same order every morning.

FIBONACCI SEQUENCE

The Fibonacci sequence, and ratio, has been called the "blueprint for Mother Nature." This is because some authors claim the numbers show up in relationships throughout nature, including the family trees of cows and bees, the human body, seashells, geometry, art, architecture, music, branching plants, and the spiral patterns seen in pinecones and pineapples. It seems that the Fibonacci ratio, or number, shows up most often in some plants where it appears to be the pattern for most efficient growth.

Evidently a good number of people have Googled this subject, thanks to Dan Brown's *The DaVinci Code*. The Google search showed a wide range of information, some of which, unfortunately, is apparent nonsense. But there is enough intriguing and factual information to warrant a few paragraphs of discussion.

Fibonacci was the nickname of Leonardo of Pisa (1170–1250) who made many contributions to mathematics but is best known for the series of numbers that bear his name. Supposedly the sequence was calculated in order to answer the question "how many pairs of rabbits can be produced in a year beginning with one pair, if each pair begins producing another pair after one month?" The result is the sequence

1,1,2,3,5,8,13,21,34,55,89,144...(a total of 376)

Obviously, each number is the sum of the preceding two and the ratio of each number to its one predecessor (for example 8 to 5 or 89 to 55) is approximately 1.618. This ratio, called the Fibonacci number, is known as the divine proportion or golden ratio, and is called Phi. The famous German astronomer Johannes Kepler considered it to be a treasure of geometry, equally important as the Pythagorean Theorem. The reciprocal phi is 1/Phi or .618.

[Out of curiosity, I investigated the claim that planets in the solar system obey the ratio when comparing their average orbital distances from the sun. My calculations came up with a range of Phi numbers from 1.32 to 2.03, and an average value of 1.71. A number of the Google searchers seem to have over-interpreted the data, however, and I tend to agree with Donald Simanek when he described a "Fibonacci Flim-Flam".]

RETURN TO THE SEA

When vertebrates first emerged from the sea to live on land, it marked one of the major events in the history of animal life. The change from fish to amphibians took millions of years, beginning about 400 million years ago. Just how water-breathing gills were transformed into air-breathing lungs is a process still to be understood. Reptiles and mammals followed, but these changes took place episodically and erratically, generally in the same direction, but with many blind alleys and species extinctions. Some 300 million years later, certain mammals, birds and reptiles returned to the sea, reversing the original transformation. Of all evolutionary events, this was the most surprising and mysterious.

Fossil material shows that whales and dolphins were the first to make the return, beginning about 53 million years ago. Whales appear to have evolved from carnivorous mammals called mesonychids that lived for only about 20 million years. These animals resembled dogs with huge heads and one monster called *Andrewsarchus mongoliensis* grew to be thirteen feet long. Its head was far larger (thirty-five inches long) than an Alaskan brown bear and not far behind *Tyrannosaurus* (fifty-two inches long). However, the skull of a sperm whale, the largest carnivore ever, can be eighteen *feet* long.

Just why the mesonychids took to the sea is unknown. Fossil associations show that they were ecological competitors with ancient crocodiles. The environment was one of tropical vegetation, swamps, coastal fringes and advancing seas. Fossils of ancestral whales have been found in Tertiary rocks of southern Asia and Eocene rocks in northern Egypt. At Whale Valley, at least 406 skeletons have been found, some having hind legs, feet and toes. This area was part of the Tethys Sea, which at that time extended eastward from the Mediterranean to the vicinity of India.

The order Cetacea includes seventy-seven or seventy-eight kinds of whales and dolphins that retain one critical link to their ancestors: they must breathe air. Living whales are further divided into those with teeth and those with baleen, used in feeding. Both types have a long body and a short neck (often with fused cervical vertebrae), paddle-like front limbs, reduced (vestigial) or completely absent hind legs, and a long tail designed to move vertically for propulsion. Nostrils are located on the top of the snout, and complex auditory organs have been developed. All whale species are completely aquatic and perform all their activities in the water, including nursing and giving birth to live young.

The sperm whale is the largest of the odontocetes (toothed whales), can reach sixty feet in length and weigh sixty tons. They live in family groups led by a dominant female. The bulls spend most of the year in Arctic waters and join the family groups only during the mating season. Babies are fourteen feet long when born, weigh two tons and are nursed by their mothers for five years. Moby Dick and his relatives were hunted during three centuries but are now protected and the worldwide population is more than one million.

An adult sperm whale eats 2000 to 3000 pounds of food per day consisting mostly of squid. Beaks of 14,000 squid have been found in the stomach of a feeding sperm whale. They can dive as deep as 10,000 feet to obtain their food and can stay under water up to ninety minutes. There is some indication that they may stun their prey with bursts of ultrasonic sound that they somehow generate using the huge reservoir of clear oil stored in their head.

Sperm whales have a twenty-pound brain, the largest of any animal that has ever lived, but still less than .02 percent of their body weight. They communicate with each other by means of high frequency "clicks." Individual sperm whales seem to have their own signature, consisting of sequences almost sentence-like in their complexity.

They have also developed sophisticated ear bones that allow them to detect the direction of a sound source. The ears are not attached to the skull and each is acoustically isolated by a sac of gas bubbles and oil-mucus emulsion. This allows the whale to hear with each ear separately, and, by the difference in time of arrival in each ear, calculate the position of the source of the sound. This combination of the generation and acquisition of sound permits a kind of echo ranging, an ability unique to the odontocetes.

Two other interesting species are the beluga (Russian for "white") and the narwhal. Belugas are found in the high Arctic and are among the noisiest of whales. These sixteen-foot whales have such a repertory of whistles, squeals, barks and snores that old whalers used to call them "sea canaries." The narwhal is closely related but has only one tooth—the spiraling, ivory tusk of the male. The tusk can grow to be eight feet long and is actually the upper left canine, which has grown through the upper lip of the animal. It possibly is used as a sophisticated sensor.

The baleen whales (mysticetes) split off from the toothed whales about 40 million years ago. The baleen whales do not have the echo sounding ability of the odontocetes and have much different dentition. They feed by straining food-bearing water through baleen sheets that hang from the roof of their mouths. The baleen is "whalebone" a cartilage-like material used in earlier times as corset stays.

The food of the baleen whales primarily is small shrimp and other planktonic crustaceans (krill). The bowhead whale uses its long baleen plates to strain the small organisms from the water as it swims through them with its mouth open. This sieves out the food as the water passes through. Other mysticetes, such as the blue whale, are different in that they take a mouthful of food and water, then force the water out of their mouth through the filter of the baleen, trapping the food in the process.

The feeding technique of baleen whales is obviously successful; the blue whale is the largest animal ever to have lived on Earth. They grow to be over 100 feet long, and weigh 150 tons. In the twentieth century commercial whalers in the Antarctic nearly hunted them to extinction. They have been fully protected since 1966, and the current population of about 5000 blue whales seems to be stabilized.

Fin whales are next in size, reaching eighty feet long and fifty tons in weight. They also were hunted heavily but are now protected throughout the world.

Humpback whales are well known to humans because they breed in coastal waters and were hunted extensively because they are slow swimmers. Their present population is about 15,000. Their feeding behavior has been watched with great interest—a number of whales cooperate in corralling smaller fish underwater and then close in to swallow them in a feeding frenzy at the surface. They also "sing" complex songs that change every year. The eerie, haunting sounds consist of a series of whoops, yawps, moans and gurgles.

Whale watchers also enjoy seeing gray whales during their migration from the Bering Sea to Baja California. This annual 13,000-mile round trip is the longest migration undertaken by any mammal. This population of about 22,000 animals in the eastern Pacific is now protected and is the only one remaining of three original groups. Grays reach forty to fifty feet in length. Their gestation period is one year, so the young are conceived and born in the lagoons of Baja after the mother has made a complete round trip.

The "right" whale got its name because it was the right size and had the right amount of blubber, so they floated when killed. Its baleen plates were up to ten feet long and were commonly used in the manufacture of corset stays, skirt hoops and buggy whips.

Dolphins are closely related and some have developed even more advanced sound ranging capabilities. Under controlled test conditions, they have shown they can differentiate between one-quarter and one-eighth inch spheres, and can locate a swimming fish 300 feet away. The tests of bottlenose dolphins show that this large-brained animal may have a more sophisticated communications system than we do. Other tests found that dolphins sense sound through their lower jaw that transmits it to the inner ear. Sounds that are generated in the blowhole are focused and broadcast from the forehead.

The thirty-six species of dolphins comprise the largest and most diverse family of marine mammals. Included is the misnamed killer whale which hunts in packs and feeds on everything from fish and squid to seals, smaller dolphins and even large whales. It is the most widely distributed of all cetaceans and is found in both hemispheres and the oceans in between.

In addition to whales and dolphins, the sirenians are entirely aquatic. This group includes manatees and dugongs, also called sea cows. Their ancestors appeared about forty million years ago and seem to be most closely related to elephants, and possibly hippos. The living forms are plump, rough-skinned, grayish animals with a broad, paddle-like tail. They are unremarkable in appearance (actually quite ugly), but ancient Greek myths tied them to the sirens of the Odyssey, and later to mermaids.

They prefer warm waters and spend six to eight hours a day feeding, as strict vegetarians on floating plants. They weigh up to a ton and eat 200 to 300 pounds of food every day. They spend the rest of their time resting, either on the bottom or at the water's surface, with only their nostrils exposed. Gestation takes about thirteen months and the young weigh sixty pounds at birth.

The only cold-water sea cow is now extinct and was named for the naturalist on Vitus Bering's expedition in 1741. When the party was wrecked on a remote island at the western end of the Aleutians, the men escaped starvation by finding a herd of the animals. Steller's sea cow was thirty feet long and weighed ten tons, growing a thick layer of fat (up to nine inches) on a diet of kelp. Bering died on the island but his men returned to Russia and reported their find. Within twenty-eight years, Russian sealers had killed all the sea cows on the island and no others were ever found.

Other animals that seem to be in the process of becoming totally aquatic include penguins, sea otters, seals and walruses. The oldest known penguin lived in New Zealand 55 to 60 million years ago. The largest species was from Japan and grew to be over six feet tall. All the known fossil and living species are flightless, aquatic birds that walk upright. They all breed on land and feed at sea, eating fish, squid, and crustaceans. Except for the Galapagos species, all modern species live in cold climates in the southern hemisphere. They are insulated against the cold by tightly packed feathers and a thick layer of fat. Their basic color scheme is black or dark gray and white but some species have a touch of yellow.

Emperor penguins reach a height of four feet and a weight of eighty pounds. The effort they go through to raise their young is remarkable. They travel as much as 150 miles over the pack ice of Antarctica to reach their breeding grounds. Once there, the female lays a single egg on the ice and then leaves for the sea. The male sits on the egg for nine weeks, when the female returns and takes up incubation duties. The male, who has been fasting for fifteen weeks, then heads for the sea. When he returns, both parents take turns feeding the chick and returning to the sea for more food. After the chicks are eight months old, their parents abandon them and the young penguins find their way to the sea. Emperor penguins can dive to depths of 1700 feet and are the only birds in the world that don't make some kind of nest.

King penguins are next in size, reaching three feet and thirty pounds. One million pairs live in the Antarctic. The Adelie penguin nests in large colonies on the coast of Antarctica. Their nests are mounds of stones, hollowed out in the middle. They are strong swimmers and can make prodigious leaps out of the water to escape from their deadly enemies, leopard seals. The penguins have good reason to be terrified—when the seals catch them in their powerful jaws, they shake the penguins out of their skins.

EXTINCTIONS

Perhaps 5 (or 50 according to Mayr) billion species have become extinct, that is, failed to propagate themselves. Most of these were a failure to adjust to changing conditions, usually climatic. But there have been several important mass extinctions where abrupt calamities caused many species to die out simultaneously. The five greatest of these calamities have been listed below (Wade, p. 79).

Chronologically, these were in Late Ordovician, 435 ma, terminating 24 percent of marine families and 45–50 percent of genera, due to sharp changes in sea level; Late Devonian, 357 ma, 22 percent of families and 47–57 percent of genera, due to sea level and climate changes; Permian, 250 ma, more than 50 percent of families, 76–80 percent of genera, and 96 percent of all species, due to great volcanic eruptions and/or asteroid impact; Late Triassic, 198 ma, 24 percent of families and 43–58 percent of genera; End Cretaceous, 65 ma, 16 percent of families, 38–46 percent of genera, and 8 percent of species, including all dinosaurs and ammonites, due to asteroid impact and volcanic eruptions.

Several Permian geologic events about 250 ma had worldwide effects. At that time several continents were joined together in the large land mass Pangea. Widespread glaciers were formed not too far from the South Pole. This fact alone pointed to some severe climatic conditions, with the ice tying up enough water to affect sea level. An enormous contributing factor was a huge flow of volcanic basalt called the Siberian Traps in Russia. Continental lava flows of this kind often have a terraced appearance, hence the term trap derived from the Swedish word for stairs. The lava field, some 870 miles in diameter, was the result of eruptions so large that immense clouds of smoke, dust, and gases in the upper atmosphere probably had worldwide climatic effects, including a drop in temperature. Recently, an old 125-mile-wide crater has been found off the coast of northwestern Australia, suggesting that an asteroid impact may have been a related factor. Over a period of several years, these geologic events wiped out up to 96 percent of all plant and animal species (all trilobites and fusulinids vanished), the worst extinction of life in the history of the earth. It is interesting that the sharpest rise in insect diversity began soon after the Permian disaster.

The most famous mass extinction was the event closing the Cretaceous Period (and Mesozoic Era). Most evidence points to the cause being the impact of a ten-mile-wide asteroid (similar in size to the Permian asteroid) that crashed into Earth 65 million years ago. The resulting explosion triggered monstrous tidal waves or tsunamis, and set fires that burned whole continents, producing thick clouds of smoke and dust. Shock waves traveling through the earth's crust and mantle triggered earthquakes around the globe, and may have caused huge flows of lava from the Deccan Traps in proto-India. These events combined to block sunlight for years, causing temperature changes that killed off vegetation and impacted the food chain. This is believed to be the main reason for killing off the dinosaurs.

Along with the dinosaurs, there was a massive extinction of ammonites. These animals were the dominant invertebrate fauna at that time. In some areas there were hundreds of millions of individuals. All 246 known ammonite genera were wiped out, a result likely caused by the complete loss of their main food, phytoplankton.

Support for the asteroid theory is the 1990 discovery of an impact crater with a diameter of 120 miles, off the coast of the Yucatan Peninsula in Mexico. The crater is called Ciexulub and dated as Cretaceous. Further support comes from the discovery of a worldwide, iridium-enriched layer of sediments at the Cretaceous boundary. Iridium is a precious metal in the platinum group and is a common constituent of asteroids. It is interesting that both the Cretaceous and Permian lava flows seem to be related, in time, to asteroid impacts thousands of miles away.

Over 150 impact craters are present on the earth's surface, and numerous craters are recorded in the geologic rock record. At the present time asteroids are frequently, and sometimes unexpectedly, detected in relatively close proximity to Earth. It is indeed sobering to realize that the impact of an asteroid the size of a football stadium could destroy an area the size of a small state, or produce catastrophic tsunamis in the ocean. Collision with an asteroid only four miles in diameter would mean mass extinction and long-term climate change.

A near miss on March 23, 1989 could have been disastrous. An asteroid one kilometer in diameter was undetected until it whizzed by the earth at 72,000 mph, missing by only six hours, or a little over 400,000 miles. It had the potential energy of twenty thousand one-megaton hydrogen bombs and could have destroyed the life on any continent. In 1994, also undetected, XL1 passed within 65,000 miles. Late in 2003, an asteroid about a mile in diameter passed within 26,000 miles of Earth. Except for a few amateur astronomers, nobody saw it coming. An asteroid named Apophis will pass within 18,640 miles in 2029 and perhaps even closer in 2036.

In early 2001 NASA scientists reported that there were 500 to 1,000 asteroids larger than one kilometer in diameter in the "immediate neighborhood" of Earth. An impacting asteroid of this size could destroy an area the size of a state and an asteroid only seven kilometers in size could cause instantaneous climate change and global mass extinction. Even more sobering is the knowledge that many asteroids are as yet undetected.

NASA recognized the danger and launched the NEAR-Shoemaker spacecraft in 1996 to begin a surveillance of asteroids that might approach

Earth's orbit. The NEAR craft is about nine feet long and enjoyed great success in 2001 when it made a perfect landing on the surface of Eros, 196 million miles away. Eros is a large asteroid, eight miles wide and twenty-one miles long. NEAR transmitted excellent data about the surface characteristics of Eros, augmenting detailed views of the asteroid's appearance gathered while the spacecraft orbited for several months, before landing. So far, NASA has located 3611 near-Earth asteroids of all sizes, with an estimated 100,000 more that are potentially dangerous. They hope to locate 90 percent of the total by 2008, and begin to develop a strategy for countering any on a collision course with Earth.

15

DNA / GENETICS

Modern genetics dates from about 1900 when three plant breeders discovered the long forgotten work of a Bohemian monk named Gregor Mendel. Mendel started his eight-year experiment on peas in 1856, working in the gardens of the monastery where he was an Augustinian friar. He carefully set up a massive and systematic project to determine the statistical relationships of the different generations of peas, as they were crossbred.

Mendel chose seven varieties of peas to cross, using 30,000 plants in all. He crossed round-seeded peas with wrinkled ones, yellow with green, purple with white, tall with short, etc. In every case, the resulting hybrid was just like one of the parents. The other parent's properties seem to have been lost—but they were not. When he planted the hybrids and they were allowed to self-fertilize, the characteristics of the grandparents reappeared intact in one-quarter of the cases. Thus, Mendel established the fundamental rule that inheritance of traits is determined by pairs of factors (later called genes), that are dominant or recessive. Furthermore, the characteristics do not mix but rather, there is a temporary joining together of individual properties. Mendel knew that his results were important and in 1866 published them in a scientific journal of good standing. But recognition came only much later.

At about the same time that Mendel's work was underway, Darwin was beginning to think that evolution is best described by mixing, rather than a true blend of characteristics. Darwin worried about this for many years but evidently never read Mendel's paper. In 1903 the American geneticist,

Walter Sutton, observed that Mendel's rules seemed to apply to chromosomes, i.e., they come in pairs, one from each parent. And, in 1918, Briton Ronald Fisher was able to reconcile the two, stating that "Mendelism supplied the missing parts of the structure erected by Darwin."

By 1902, Archibald Garrod, a doctor and competent biologist, was able to speculate that a gene was a recipe for a single chemical. He based this on his work with a group of patients that seemed to have a hereditary disease, triggered by a Mendelian recessive that showed up when inherited from both parents. The inherited factor (or gene) served to produce a defective enzyme that failed to properly control a needed catalyst. Garrod's book, published in 1909, was prescient in observing that "chemical individuality" must derive from the protein of enzymes.

As stated by Ridley (1999, p. 40), "We now know that the main purpose of genes is to store the recipe for making proteins. It is proteins that do almost every chemical, structural and regulatory thing that is done in the body: they generate energy, fight infection, digest food, form hair, carry oxygen and so on...Every single protein in the body is made from a gene by a translation of the genetic code."

Even after Fisher, a problem remained. Darwin's theory of evolution required that, for change to occur, genes had to mutate. The first artificial mutation won a Nobel Prize for Herman Joe Muller, an unlikely candidate in most respects. A New York Jew, he was difficult and pugnacious, fighting with everyone all his life. He moved to Germany just in time to face the first Nazis and quickly moved on to Russia. He was a fervent Communist (he wanted to see children carefully bred with the character of Marx or Lenin) but had to flee again when he ran into the crackpot theories of Lysenko, who had Stalin's ear. Opponents were shot or imprisoned, so Muller moved on to Spain where he joined the International Brigade during the Spanish Civil War. Eventually he landed at Indiana University and got his Nobel award in 1946. The winning research involved bombarding fruit flies with X-rays, causing their genes to mutate and their offspring to be deformed. The flies had genes after mutation, but not the same genes.

Attracted by Muller's presence at Bloomington, a young, very self-confident graduate student by the name of James Watson arrived there shortly after the end of World War II. Watson developed an obsessive belief that genes were made of DNA, not protein. Evidently he was influenced by the earlier work of Miescher, and Avery.

Dr. Friedrich Miescher isolated "nuclein" or deoxyribonucleic acid (DNA) from the pus-soaked bandages of soldiers in 1869, and with amaz-

ing insight in 1892 predicted that DNA might be able to convey hereditary information. Oswald Avery, an accomplished immunologist, in 1943
described results of a lengthy laboratory experiment in transforming genes.
In careful language his report said the nucleic acids (DNA) possessed the
property of "biological specificity" but in private he was more descriptive,
saying "nucleic acids are not merely structurally important but function-
ally active substances in determining the biochemical activities and specific
characteristics of cells...and it is possible...to induce predictable and hereditary changes in cells."

DOUBLE HELIX

At Indiana University the precocious Watson clashed with Muller, so
Watson moved to Denmark and eventually reached Cambridge in fall,
1951. As fate would have it, Francis Crick was there also and the two soon
began one of the most productive collaborations in the history of science.

The twenty-two-year-old Dr. Watson was a brilliant biologist but tall,
gawky and unkempt. Crick had a background in physics and biology and
was still working on his PhD. He was twelve years older than Watson, and
eloquent and well dressed. Both were convinced about the importance of
DNA and within a few short months they had made what possibly was the
greatest scientific discovery of all time, the structure of DNA. Critical insights came with the help of Rosalind Franklin, a talented crystallographer.
In a lecture she gave in November 1951, she described photographs of the
patterns of X-rays diffracted through DNA crystals.

Sometime later, Watson saw a new X-ray pattern of wet DNA that
Franklin had made and he immediately recognized it as a helical molecule.

Together, Watson and Crick began modeling their famous right-twist-
ing double helix. Their model of DNA shows it to be two parallel strands
of sugar-phosphate "rails" connected by "rungs" of simple molecules called
bases. The four letters used, A, C, G, and T are shorthand for the chemicals, or bases adenine, cytosine, guanine, and thymine. Each letter pairs
with a complementary letter on the opposite strand, i.e., C with G and A
with T to make a full rung and form the double helix. There are four possible bases (see figure on next page).The sequence of bases along a section
of DNA is a molecular message describing the sequence of amino acids the
cell will follow to assemble a protein. As a consequence of this rule, a given
fragment of DNA comprises a gene. In the genetic code,a base sequence of

C-C-A followed by C-A-G is a message saying that in a particular protein, an amino acid called proline is to be followed by one called glutamine.

In the April 25, 1953 issue of *Nature,* Watson and Crick announced their DNA model, shown in a simple sketch of the double helix. The article was only 900 words in length, two scanty pages. The authors decided the order of their names below the title with a coin toss. In the pages following their article, Rosalind Franklin's supporting report included Photograph 51 of the X-ray diffraction pattern indicating a helix structure. Five weeks later Watson and Crick wrote a second, more elaborate paper for *Nature* in which they said, "the precise sequence of the pairs of bases is the code, which carries the genetical information." They also suggested that mutations could result from an alteration in the form or order of the sequences of bases.

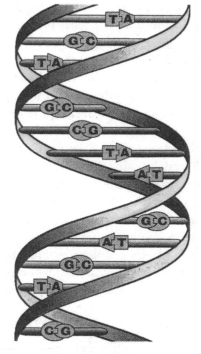

THE DOUBLE HELIX

Sydney Brenner, a young graduate student at Oxford at the same time later collaborated with Crick in some bacterial experiments that proved the genetic code was written in triplets. By the end of 1966 the entire code had been cracked, with only sixty-four possible triplets of a four-letter alphabet. Included were instructions for the twenty amino acids, plus signals to start and stop protein synthesis.

The human body has about 100 trillion cells, including 100 billion brain cells. About 200 cells would fit into the period at the end of this sentence. Each cell nucleus contains its own set of twenty-three pairs of chromosomes, one set passed down by each parent. For convenience, the first twenty-two are numbered 1 through 22 and are called autosomes. The twenty-third pair determines sex; females have two X chromosomes and males have an X and a Y chromosome.

Each chromosome has a protein core with a DNA molecule wound tightly around it. Fully extended, the DNA strands in the nucleus of a single cell would stretch to about six feet, and all DNA in the human body, if placed end to end, could total as much as 8 million miles. The DNA molecule includes 3 billion base pairs of code, and on average, one gene every 40,000 bases.

The body is a complex organism of cells of approximately two hundred distinct types. Like all mammals, humans have muscle cells, bone cells, nerve cells, skin cells, etc. Each organ is comprised of cells whose genes are switched on to perform a certain function. In addition, the genes program cells to coordinate effectively with their neighbors. The genetic code in a human body totals about 3 billion bits of information (all the bases or C, G, A, T). About 98 percent of the human genome is "selfish" or junk DNA, i.e., not involved in the genetic code. Included in the junk, however, are bits of DNA called transposons, which serve to activate or silence genes in an important epigenetic process.

The accomplishment of Watson and Crick has often been compared to that of the brilliant Russian chemist Mendeleev. In 1869, Mendeleev presented his paper describing the periodic table, titled *The Dependence Between the Properties and the Atomic Weights of the Elements*. This table is the most important icon in chemistry and a vital tool of the industrial age. His chart organized the sixty-one elements known at that time in rows and columns based on their atomic weight and other properties. He was so confident that he left gaps in the table where he thought unknown elements belonged. These gaps were later filled by newly-discovered elements, just as he predicted, increasing the total to 115.

Richard Dawkins has observed that 1953, the year of the double helix, will be seen as the year that Darwin's theories went digital. Dawkins points out that genes are pure information that can be encoded and decoded. Except for the rare mutations, genes "can self-copy for ten million generations and scarcely degrade."

The flamboyant Spanish artist Salvador Dali was greatly impressed and said, "this for me is the real proof of the existence of God." In tribute, he created a painting, with subtitle Homage to Crick and Watson, that depicted life, death and the afterlife—represented by DNA, a cubic molecule, and the figure of God reaching down to resurrect the spirit of Christ.

The crucial characteristic of DNA is that it can replicate itself over thousands of generations. But rarely, just like a computer glitch, a copying error or mutation will occur. Usually the mistake is unfavorable but occasionally it has a positive effect, allowing the mutant DNA to out-replicate its competitors and so come to predominate. The impact on evolution theory has been neatly explained by Davies: "This simple process of replication, variation, and elimination is the basis of Darwinian evolution.

Natural selection—the continual sifting of mutants according to their fitness—acts like a ratchet, locking in the advantageous errors and discarding the bad. Starting with the DNA of some primitive ancestor microbe, bit by bit, error by error, the increasingly lengthy instructions for building more complex organisms came to be constructed."

The mutations mentioned by Dawkins and Davies result from any number of sources that can alter DNA. Cosmic rays, gamma waves, ultraviolet radiation, and radioactive decay constantly bombard the double helix. Parental age can be a factor, plus males seem to introduce more errors than females. Cells employ an array of enzymes that protect or repair DNA; an errant base can be replaced, base pairs can be corrected if need be, and a stretch of up to thirty consecutive letters on one strand of the helix can be deleted and replaced. The net result is an error rate of about one mistake in every ten million bases.

As a cell divides, three billion letters of code must be faithfully copied. Fortunately, most transcription errors do no harm, but sometimes, just one mistake can have disastrous results. The following narrative borrows liberally from that described by Ridley concerning Huntington's chorea. This disease stems from just one mutated gene on chromosome 4, but the result is horrible. [It has special meaning to my wife and me because we had a friend who was diagnosed with the disease in 1972.]

The disease was named after George Huntington, a physician's son. Driving on a back road, he suddenly encountered two women, mother and daughter, both tall, thin, almost cadaverous, both bowing, twisting and grimacing as if in agony. Later, when he was a doctor, he investigated further and found that the disease inflicted an inexorable physical and psychiatric decline, often leading to insanity and suicide. A neurologist described it as "the complete ruin of a human being." Without fail, during childhood there were no signs of illness, but the disease struck when the victim was an adult, typically in his/her forties or fifties.

In the late 1970s, a determined young woman named Nancy Wexler set out to find the gene causing Huntington's chorea. The disease had hit four of her relatives so she knew she had a fifty percent chance of getting it too. Her first investigation was in the area of Lake Maracaibo where an eighteenth-century sailor introduced the bad gene. His wife was a fecund ancestor, with 11,000 descendents in eight generations. In 1981, 9000 of them were still alive and at least 371 had full-blown Huntington's. Of the living, 3600 of them had at least one grandparent with the symptoms and therefore had a 25 percent risk factor.

Wexler started drawing blood from over 500 people. She sent the samples to Jim Gusella's lab in Boston and, by 1983, with luck he was able to isolate the problem area to the tip of the short arm of chromosome 4. But the gene laid in a region of text one million letters long. Finally, in 1993, the gene was found and the mutation identified. The repetition of the "word" CAG signaled a long stretch of glutamines in the middle of the protein.

The age of onset of the disease has been calibrated to the number of repetitions. With thirty-nine repetitions of CAG there is a 90 percent probability that dementia will begin by the age of seventy-five, with the first symptoms at age sixty-six; with forty repetitions, the symptoms, on average will commence at age fifty-nine; with forty-one at age fifty-four; with forty-two at age thirty-seven and so on until those who have fifty repetitions will lose their minds at about twenty-seven years of age. Almost everyone has ten to fifteen repeats in their genetic code and with thirty-five or fewer you are fine. This horrifying disease, which takes fifteen to twenty-five years to run its course, bypasses most people by a tiny margin. On a scale where your chromosomes are long enough to reach around the earth, the difference between normality and insanity is less than one inch.

Some mutations affect just one letter of the code but others can affect the entire chromosome. Most cases of Down Syndrome arise from an extra copy of chromosome 21. One in twenty-five people of European descent carry the altered gene that causes cystic fibrosis. In northern Europe an estimated one in ten carry the mutant gene responsible for hemochromatosis, an iron overload disorder, sometimes still treated by the medieval practice of bloodletting. The *p53* gene, the most commonly mutated cancer gene, resides on the short arm of chromosome 17. The age or sex of the parent seems to have a statistical effect on some gene-related problems. Sickle cell anemia is caused by the swap of a single amino acid in one of the protein chains; on the other hand, carriers of the trait have developed a resistance to the parasite *Plasmodium*, which causes malaria. Researchers, to date, have been able to describe more than 5000 distinct genetic disorders, and have identified the genes responsible for 1000.

Scientists read the genetic code in DNA by determining the sequence of amino acids (left twisting, interesting to note) needed to produce a desired protein. Fred Sanger at Cambridge won his first Nobel Prize in 1958 for his early work on this approach. His ten-year project resulted in completely solving the order of the fifty-one amino acid building blocks in the two chains of insulin. Sanger followed up on this work with sequencing of short RNA molecules, leading eventually to the "chain termination" method of DNA sequencing. The latter established the chemical basis for modern automated technology. Sanger's technique of DNA sequencing by chain termination is one of the most referenced scientific papers of all time.

The role of RNA (ribonucleic acid) is as an intermediary in the process of passing on instructions from the DNA to ribosomes, which are mini-factories in the cell. The RNA is a single-stranded molecule, and believed to be the precursor to the twin-stranded DNA. The ribosomes read the RNA message like a laser scanning a bar code, linking amino acids together in a specified sequence to produce the desired protein. When the code on the RNA says "stop," the ribosome separates. Thousands of ribosomes scattered throughout a cell produce tens of thousands of different proteins.

Nucleic acids (DNA and RNA) have been compared to computer software in that they store, and give directions fo,r the formation of proteins. The latter, in turn, have been called the hardware, or building material, of cells and enzymes, that act as chemical catalysts. In the human body, several hundred thousand types of protein, perhaps a million, are involved, and each requires the assembly of thousands of left-twisting amino acids in precise sequences called peptides. As the nucleotides and proteins are interdependent and work together, it seems clear that they must have evolved together, synergetically.

This must have been where life began, including the two crucial factors of metabolism and reproduction. According to Davies (1999, pp. 33–36) the properties required for life include reproduction, metabolism, nutrition, organized complexity, and evolutionary adaptation. The beginning of life on Earth certainly involved very primitive organisms, no doubt even more rudimentary than the modern microbe *Methanococcus jannaschii*, described on p.42, 362 and 526? *M. jannaschii* has a circular chromosome with 1682 genes and is found living in an extremely harsh physical environment. *M. jannaschii* is unique in the respect that it has DNA, and life, but seems to be locked into a primitive evolutionary niche.

So far, the simplest independent, self-replicating cell found is an oceanic bacterium *Pelagibacter ubique*, with only 1354 genes. Also called *SAR11*, it may be the most numerous bacterium on Earth and its combined weight exceeds that of all the fish in the seas.

DNA SEQUENCING

In the mid-1960s, John Craig Venter was a beach bum in California, but matured quickly in Viet Nam in 1967 when faced with death on a large scale. Returning to the States, he immersed himself in his studies and in just six years at UC San Diego earned a PhD in both physiology and pharmacology. By 1990 he was the most influential scientist and leader in sequencing techniques.

His professional career began at SUNY, Buffalo in 1976, and in 1984 he moved to the National Institute of Neurological Disorders and Stroke. At NIH he did work involving purification of proteins, a process so tedious it led to a determined effort to improve the process. In early 1987, Venter's NIH laboratory became one of the first to use the new automated ABI 373A sequencer. The new system, although relying on the established Fred Sanger chemistry, employed fluorescent dyes instead of radioactive compounds to identify each letter of genetic code. The instrument could analyze twenty-four samples simultaneously, yielding about 12,000 letters of DNA per day.

Venter's next move was an ingenious effort to eliminate junk DNA, so time would not be wasted in sequencing long stretches of useless material. He turned to the analysis of "complementary DNA" called cDNA, that is, DNA converted from purified RNA. There was a vast supply readily available in cDNA libraries and the renowned geneticist, Sydney Brenner, in 1986, had argued in favor of a cDNA-sequencing program. Brenner stressed that priority should be given to analyzing the 3 percent of the human genome that contains genes, rather than the 97 percent that was considered junk.

Venter's first project used a library of brain cDNA containing copies of potentially tens of thousands of genes that are active in the brain. In each sample, the ABI machine typically found two to three hundred nucleotides at one end of a gene which were then compared with previously identified genes. Each cDNA sequence was termed an "expressed sequence tag" or "EST." This work revealed the identity of more than 330 novel genes active in the human brain, whereas most other research projects usually dealt with a single gene or two. On June 21, 1991, Venter presented his new EST strategy in a landmark article in *Science*. The article sent shock waves through the scientific community. In only a few months, Venter had almost single-handedly identified more than 10 percent of the world total of 3000 human genes in the public gene databank.

Venter's brash approach ruffled the feathers of some other scientists and he soon became embroiled in a bitter controversy over the issue of gene patents. Before the report in *Science* was published, Reid Adler, one of the brass at NIH, filed a quick patent application covering the first 337 ESTs. And early the next year, Adler added 2421 more ESTs to the list, just ahead of Venter's report in *Nature*. Scientists in the field reacted vociferously with anger and incredulity. As director of the genome center, James Watson labeled the EST program "sheer lunacy," "brainless work," and said it "could be run by monkeys."

In August 1992 the patent office rejected the first round of applications because they were "vague, indefinite, incomplete, (non) descriptive, inaccurate, and incomprehensible." The NIH appealed and, in September, filed on another 4448 ESTs. Director Bernadine Healy argued that the applications should stand and that they were simply a defensive maneuver until the controversy could be resolved.

When the NIH firmly rejected Venter's proposal for a $10 million expansion in his project, he started to talk to other suitors. After some negotiations, he accepted a $70 million offer from Wallace Steinberg, chairman of a venture fund. The ten-year grant, later increased to $85 million, was to set up and operate a nonprofit research center, The Institute for Geonomic Research (TIGR). To profit from his investment, Steinberg incorporated a sister company called Human Genome Sciences (HGS), to market the discoveries made by TIGR.

In mid 1992, Venter set up his new facility in Rockville, MD. Thirty ABI 373A automated DNA sequencers made TIGR the most productive DNA sequencing center in the world, using cDNA samples from 300 different libraries. Tissue came from male and female, old and young, healthy and diseased sources—as many as possible.

Many other scientists disparaged his work, giving him credit only for "scaling up the process." But what most upset his peers was the fact that in just two years, Venter went from an ordinary government scientist to a wealthy entrepreneur in private business. As a founder, he was given a 10 percent share in HGS, worth some $13 million, which provided him the wherewithal to buy a $2 million house and a $4 million racing sailboat.

During this same time, another outstanding individual was making his mark in the field. Francis Collins earned his PhD in physical chemistry at Yale in 1974. During post-doc research at Yale he had the opportunity to work with Sherman Weismann, the "smartest guy" Collins ever met.

In 1985, Collins became interested in the search for the gene responsible for the deadly disease, cystic fibrosis. This is the most common recessively inherited disease among people of European descent. A Canadian geneticist, Lap-Chee Tsui, had mapped the gene to a spot on chromosome 7, but it was in an area of 10 to 20 million bases of unmapped DNA. Finding the offending gene among several hundred could take years unless the process could be expedited.

Collins and Weissman devised a clever scheme to take a stretch of chromosomal DNA, about 100,000 letters in length, and join the ends to form a circle. Then Collins could systematically work from the fused ends toward the gene itself. This technique effectively jumped 100,000 bases and was termed "positional cloning." Collins and Tsui joined forces and in 1989 found the answer: three missing letters of DNA on chromosome 7 in 70 percent of cystic fibrosis patients.

Not long after this, Collins was successful again, this time in finding the gene causing neurofibromatosis, another common inherited disease. In rapid succession, using tools he had helped develop, Collins had identified two genes other researchers had been chasing for years. Collins immediately became a darling of the media, helped enormously by his engaging personality. He had a natural charm plus the ability to communicate effectively with any audience, be it live television, legislators in Washington, large conventions, or bedside counseling. About the time he got his M.D., he became a born-again Christian and has explained that his passion for tracking genes is like "appreciating something...no human had known, but God knew it..."

Thus, in five years, Collins rose from anonymity to the peak of genetic research in government when he was named the second director of the National Center for Human Genome Research. Some have called this organization biology's equivalent of the Manhattan Project. At the press conference in April 1993 Collins effused "My whole career has been spent training for this job—this is more important than putting a man on the moon or splitting the atom."

By 1994, Venter's TIGR had eighty sequencing machines churning out hundreds of thousands of human DNA letters every day, and by the end of the year their database included 150,000 ESTs, or about 35,000 genes. Some of this information was useful to other scientists, and gratifying to Venter. Among the errant genes identified were *p53* on chromosome 17, mutated in 50 percent of all human cancers, and *MSH2* on chromosome 2, altered in 60 percent of colon cancers. Alzheimer's disease was found to be related to *S182* on chromosome 1.

In May, 1995 Venter announced the results of a thirteen-month project to sequence the complete genome of the bacterium *Haemophilus influenzae*. The genome contains 1,830,137 letters of DNA and 1743 genes. The average was about one gene every 1000 bases, meaning almost no junk sequences. More than 1000 genes resembled known genes from other organisms.

For some time, certain scientists bitterly reproached Venter for the perceived delay in releasing his results to the public. So in September 1995 he and his co-authors published in *Nature* the report "The Genome Directory" including nearly 175,000 EST sequences in a 379-page supplement. In conjunction with this, Venter also released other public data in his cDNA database. This release contained more than 345,000 ESTs and led to an early estimate of 60,000 to 80,000 total human genes. These data also allowed Venter to begin to classify genes as to their function. For example, 16 percent have a role in metabolism, 12 percent are used in communicating with other cells, and 4 percent do cell division and DNA replication.

One of the earliest triumphs of the microbial sequencing revolution involved work with the microbe *Methanococcus jannaschii*. The microbe is a curious, methane-producing organism found in the vicinity of thermal vents called white smokers, along deep-sea plate boundaries. The environment at such places is harsh; i.e., temperature 230°F, pressure 3000 psi and no oxygen. This strange microbe seemed to be neither animal nor plant but rather a third, entirely different domain of life. Carl Woese had done work on such a class, which he called Archaea (p. 484?), so Venter initiated a collaborative effort with Woese to determine the sequence of DNA in *M. jannaschii*.

After nearly a year, they had performed over 36,000 reads and had the first complete DNA sequence of Archaea. The circular chromosome encoded 1682 genes that resembled plants and animals more closely than bacteria. By analogy, ancestors of modern life forms could be as old as 3 billion years, i.e., the first cells with a nucleus—the Eukaryotes. So far, however, the oldest DNA actually sequenced goes back only 400,000 years, from plants.

In 1988, management at NIH set a target date of 2005 for completion of the human genome-sequencing project and, toward this end, some foreign organizations made valuable contributions. Among these were the Centre d'Etude du Polymorphisme Humain (CEPH) near Paris, the French Muscular Dystrophy Association, the Science for Peace Foundation in Tunisia, and the Sanger Centre near Cambridge. In February 1996 the Wellcome Trust organized the first international planning session, which culminated in the Bermuda Accord. This accord stated that all human genome sequencing information would be freely available to the public. Organizations agreeing to these terms were Washington University, Stanford, Baylor, TIGR, the Joint Genome Institute, Whitehead Institute, and others in the U.S. as well as laboratories in England, France, Germany and Japan.

Early in 1998, Venter made his next big move in the corporate world. Enticed by powerful new equipment, and a 10 percent share of a new startup company, he resigned from TIGR and signed on with a group soon to be known as Celera Genomics. The new sequencer was called the Prism 3700, was eight times faster than the competition, and could produce up to one million bases of DNA sequence per day.

On May 8, 1998 Venter met face-to-face with the stunned Francis Collins and told him what was about to happen. Venter said he would release his data every three months and would seek patents on only 100 to 300 human genes, less than one percent of the total. Venter also proposed that the new company and the public Human Genome Project share their data. Three days later, Collins and his group reluctantly agreed, no doubt aware that Congress would wonder if, up to that point, the $1.9 billion of public money had been well spent.

By early 1999, Venter and his new company had 230 of the ABI PRISM 3700 sequencers up and running, with an output of 100 million bases per day. This torrent of data was handled by an array of 800 Compaq processors with 80 terabytes of memory (five times the data in the Library of Congress). This computer capacity was second only to that used by the U.S. government to model nuclear explosions. Gene Myers was the key person who designed the computer algorithms used to assemble the millions of random DNA sequences.

At that point the public genome sequencing effort was only 4 percent complete. Apparently in response to the challenge, the Sanger Center at Cambridge announced that $350 million would be added, doubling the program there. This meant that Sanger would be handling about one-third of the consortium's effort. Sadly to say, the level of vitriol coming from the public program leaders during all this bordered on the disgraceful. The academic/governmental approach could not compete with Venter, and their spiteful reaction was to vilify and belittle.

Leaders of the consortium had declared they would not engage in a race with Celera but, race or not, changed their new deadline to spring 2000. Collins vigorously denied they were responding to Celera's timetable, but rather than a finished product, they would produce a "rough draft." Furthermore, the public group began a crash program to acquire PRISM 3700 sequencing machines, and by the end of 1999, Applied Biosystems had shipped 1000 sequencers to 250 different laboratories.

By the end of 1999, Celera was "ripping through 1.2 billion letters of human DNA" per month and the competition was intense, if not declared.

In January 2000 Venter announced that his company had sequenced 90 percent of the human genome and would have nine billion base pairs by summer. In April, Venter testified at a House of Representatives subcommittee meeting, revealing that Celera had sequenced the complete genome of a living human, finding the letters for 30 million fragments an average of three times apiece. He predicted that within a few weeks, all the fragments would be assembled into a complete sequence for all twenty-four chromosomes.

By June, the race was over. According to Collins, the public consortium had sequenced more than 22 billion bases of DNA, with enough repetitions for 99.9 percent accuracy in estimating 3.15 billion bases for the human genome. Celera had sequenced 14.5 billion letters of DNA, to calculate 3.12 billion bases. In 20,000 processing hours on their supercomputer, they made more than 500 million trillion DNA comparisons. No doubt this was the largest computational biology calculation in history. Surprisingly, it found that the human genome includes only about 20–25,000 different genes.

Politicians got in the act and offered their praise of the work by the two groups. At the White House ceremony, James Watson was also honored as the scientist most responsible for instigating the Human Genome Project. In his remarks Collins said "It is humbling to me and awe inspiring to realize that we have caught the first glimpse of our own instruction book, previously known only to God."

But all during this time of mutual congratulations and satisfaction in reaching goals, there was an element of overhanging unease and apprehension. This stemmed from the March 14, 2000 joint announcement by President Clinton and Prime Minister Blair, implying that they opposed the commercial application of gene information. This would be disastrous for Celera, of course, and their stock crashed from a previous high of $290 a share to less than $100. The rest of the biotech sector fell as well, and the panic spread to the whole technology sector of the U.S. stock market. In hindsight, it is clear that this event contributed to the market decline that continued into 2002, and the stock price of Celera (CRA) eventually fell below $7 per share.

All during the late 1990s, the stock market had soared to hugely overvalued levels, powered by tech stocks, dot.com start-ups, etc. The sleaze so prevalent in the Clinton administration carried over into the business world, and Enron, WorldCom, Global Crossing and the like were involved in "creative bookkeeping" and outright fraud. Alan Greenspan had tried to talk down the market with remarks like "irrational exuberance," but it took drastic events to burst the bubble.

Once the sequencing race was over, the biotechnology world turned to more fruitful pursuits. Venter's work on the evolutionary aspects of microbes has been mentioned briefly and equally evocative are the uses of DNA in tracing the movements of prehistoric peoples across the earth. This will be discussed in the next chapter.

USE OF GENETICS

More than 1000 disorders can result from an altered gene, a missing gene, or when the order of letters is changed. A partial list of some genetic diseases includes: hemophilia (poor clotting of blood), Down's Syndrome (mongolism), Huntington's chorea, cystic fibrosis, sickle cell anemia, hemochromatosis (excessive iron), holoprosencephaly (narrowly spaced eyes), Werner's helicase (premature aging), alopecia (loss of hair in clumps), atavism ("throwback" attributes such as excessive hair, webbed digits, three nipples, etc.), Alzheimer's, Parkinson's, adrenoleukodystrophy, achondroplasia (dwarfism), muscular atrophy, polycystic kidney disease, hereditary blindness, hereditary deafness, hypertension, obesity, dyslexia, ALS (Lou Gehrig's disease) and breast cancer.

Some mutated genes provide positive advantages. In the small Italian lakeside village, Limone Sul Garda, about forty residents have lived to be over 100 years old. Their healthy life style and diet, including the daily Chianti, is helpful but a genetic mutation is more important. About one in twenty villagers has a variant form of apolipoprotein A1, which takes cholesterol from the blood and moves it to the liver, where it is broken down.

A small percentage of people have genetic protection against HIV. The *CCR5* receptor on white blood cells sometimes mutates in a way to deny the AIDS virus an opportunity to invade the host cell. In these cases, the *CCR5* gene lacks a stretch of thirty-two letters, preventing production of the receptor.

Without doubt there has been a Pollyannaish acceptance of claims linking various diseases to genetic variants. Recently, Dr. Wacholder at the National Cancer Institute has called attention to this danger, in the case of claims regarding breast cancer. Scientists had concluded that women with mutations in genes named *BRCA1* or *BRCA2* had an 82 percent chance of developing breast cancer by age eighty (versus 12 percent without the mutation). Other studies of *BRCA* found far less risk, and Wacholder pointed out those involved in the study group may have been unrepresentative of the normal population. Other researchers believe that the interaction of multiple genetic variants, the environment, and ethnicity are all important factors that need to be considered. Fifty years after DNA's double helix, and within a decade of the Human Genome Project, there now is less emphasis on single genes. New research will deal more with "systems biology," i.e., the cellular interaction of all genes and proteins.

Physical attributes such as appearance, stature, and perhaps athletic ability are largely affected by heredity. It is obvious that athletes of African ancestry excel, at least in certain sports. Although the genetic difference between races is slight, Troy Duster has shown that three sections of DNA can differentiate Caucasian, Afro-Caribbean, and Asian-Indian.

When it comes to traits or behavior, the subject is more contentious. It has been demonstrated that stress can switch off certain genes temporarily so they do not respond normally. The Whitehead Institute at MIT found that changes in temperature, salinity and sustenance turn on or off fully two-thirds of the genes in yeast—much more than expected.

Concerning homosexuals, 5 percent seems to be the average for estimates made of the total gay and lesbian portion of the human race. This important minority seems to flout Darwin's rules of evolution in that they do not reproduce themselves, yet continue to be born in the same percentage. There seems to be little or no genetic evidence, at least not in DNA. Epigenetic control might exist, however, and the subject was more fully discussed in pp. 85–86?

Mental retardation, resulting from the deletion of certain genes, is well documented, and affects about 3 percent of the population. Any suggestions that genes influence intelligence are sure to stir the passions. Publication of *The Bell Curve* in 1994 caused uproar when it argued that cognitive ability or "general intelligence" was an inherited trait that correlated with race. Several studies have concluded that about half of your IQ is inherited and the rest is due to environment, including family, peers, school, and surroundings. Also, IQ increases with age, together with its heritability. Compared to childhood, in later adolescence innate intelligence becomes more important and outside influences become less so. It is clear that much is yet unknown, and the old argument dealing with the relative effects of nature versus nurture is still alive and well.

In any two people, selected at random, there is about one alteration in every 1000 bases (0.1 percent). Over the entire genome, this means there are about 3 million sequence variations between the two people. These critical differences in individual characteristics are called "single nucleotide polymorphisms" or SNPs, (pronounced "snips"). Everybody carries some flawed genes, and geneticists think that every person has five to ten recessive mutations. If unlucky enough to mate with a person with the same recessive trait, there is a high risk that offspring will have severe problems. A human being has about 750 megabytes of digital information stored as DNA molecules. This same information could be stored on a single CD-ROM, and Craig Venter has predicted that within ten years, every newborn baby will leave the hospital with a personalized DVD disk.

Dr. George M. Church has described the Personal Genome Project (PGP) he and some colleagues have launched recently (*Scientific American*, January 2006). Church is a professor of genetics at Harvard Medical School and was among those in 1984 who recommended the Human Genome Project. Church explains recent improvements in sequencing techniques over the Sanger method, used for the last thirty years. The goal is to achieve sequencing of a human genome at a cost of only $1000 within ten years. This would allow everyone to have their own genomic and phenomic (traits) file giving genealogy, and a personal health profile, leading to personalized medicine. He also explains how some of this information could be misused—by insurers, employers, criminals, etc.

Forensics gained a powerful new tool when it was realized that the DNA of each person is unique. An individual can be identified from tiny bits of material be it a single hair, a drop of blood, a skin or bone fragment, etc. Already, many people have been tied to a crime—or been exonerated—on the basis of DNA information. In the following paragraphs, four examples of the forensic use of DNA are illustrative of what can be accomplished.

In July 1918, Czar Nicholas II of Russia and his family were executed by the Bolsheviks. This was done without trial but as the Communists said, "in accordance with our new democratic principles." The murdered group included the czar and his wife, three of their five children, three servants and the family doctor. The bodies were doused with sulfuric acid, and then buried in a shallow, unmarked grave. Seventy years later, 1000 bone fragments were assembled into nine skeletons and the DNA analysis subsequently was done in England. Matches made with living and dead relatives provided odds of 100 million to 1 that the remains were authentic. In 1998, the Romanov royal family was given official burial in St. Petersburg, with President Boris Yeltsin in attendance.

In 1976, a military coup in Argentina seized power with perhaps 9000 young "subversives" killed. About 200 young children, left without parents, were given to childless couples in the army. The military junta was overthrown in 1983 and, subsequently, an effort was made to reunite the children with their grandparents and relatives. Mitochondrial DNA samples were critical to the process, and dozens of children were successfully returned to their surviving relatives.

On August 17, 1998 independent counsel Kenneth Starr told President Clinton that an FBI analysis provided a perfect DNA match between Clinton's blood and another sample of his body fluids. He had left the other sample on the front of Monica Lewinsky's size 12, dark blue dress. The odds that the donor of the semen on Ms. Lewinsky's dress could have been any other man than Bill Clinton were 1 in 7.8 trillion.

When Saddam Hussein was pulled out of his hiding place in December 2003, his identity was confirmed within a few hours. Cells, probably from a cheek swab, were matched with samples of Saddam's DNA obtained by military personnel earlier in the year. A DNA technique called polymerase chain reaction utilizes billions of copies of repeating chemical letters, such as ATATAT. Matches of this kind typically compare thirteen regions of DNA. One person, for example, might have fifty repeats of AT while another person would have forty-eight or fifty-two. For six regions giving an exact match, the odds of being a certain person are one in a few million. With thirteen matched sequences, the probabilities are literally astronomical.

Scientists have been surprised to find that the human genome has only 20–25,000 different genes, only slightly more than the 19,500 of a simple roundworm with only 1000 cells. One explanation is that in humans, as many as 75 percent of their genes are capable of using a mechanism called "alternative splicing." This allows a single gene to specify the ordering of two or more distinct proteins, including when, where, and what types of proteins are manufactured.

The development of drugs from natural and modified biological systems has created a $35 billion per year industry with 2000 biotechnology companies in the U.S. alone. One estimate of the cost of developing a new drug through clinical trials with real patients is $800 million, over fourteen years. From its beginnings in 1982, the biotechnology industry has grown dramatically. Completion of the Human Genome Project provided vast amounts of genetic information, stored in the world's largest computer database.

Some of the first work was a process called gene-splicing, or recombinant-DNA technology. Valuable natural proteins such as insulin or interferon were produced in cellular factories by growing genetically altered bacteria in a nutrient broth, where they multiplied rapidly.

About 60 percent of gene therapy is aimed at cancer, but the battle still relies largely upon the three brute-force weapons: surgery, radiation and toxic chemotherapy. Most frequently these methods fail, and sometimes they are actually fatal. Another approach has been to use monoclonal antibodies, genetically engineered to fight a specific cancer. Dr. Ronald Levy at Stanford has had some success with this method and helped develop the drug Rituxan, which is not tumor-specific or unique to individual patients. The FDA approved the drug in 1997 and it has a record of shrinking tumors by more than 50 percent in about half of all patients. Levy's current efforts are to find a vaccine, therapeutic in nature that will target B-cell lymphoma, the most common form of non-Hodgkin's lymphomas. Because of poor economics, only 10 percent of the total effort is directed to rare, single-gene diseases.

Irregular heartbeats are a different kind of problem in some people, and the usual treatment is implantation of a pacemaker. A new approach, developed at Johns Hopkins, is the use of genetically modified cells. When properly functioning, a few thousand cells in two key locations trigger electrical pulses that tell other cells when to contract and make the heart beat. The electrical signal is induced by the potassium in the pacemaker cells.

Mark T. Keating and his colleagues at Harvard Medical School (*Scientific American*, December 2005) have developed another approach to helping the growth of heart muscle cells. They used a drug-based approach, combining the growth factor FGF1 with a drug which inhibits the activity of the enzyme p38 MAP kinase.

Gene therapy tries to manipulate, augment, or replace a person's own genes to treat illness. It has been found that some genes carry "silencers" that determine the inheritability of certain characteristics, or conditions, from either parent. In addition, environmental toxins can have the same effects. Genes of this kind are called "imprinted," and humans may have hundreds of imprinted genes. Such genes are detectable with biochemical tests, and this field of research is fast moving because it has clear promise of success.

Epigenetics looks at the addition or removal of molecular bundles that turn genes on or off. A relatively new technology called "RNA interference" shows promise of becoming a powerful tool in finding "magic bullet" type drugs. The technique would allow scientists to silence mutant or bad genes by preventing messenger RNA from passing on information to the ribosomes. Small snippets of RNA can be custom-designed by arming them with enzymes specifically destructive to the target genes. In like fashion, ribosomes can be unblocked in order to start making specific proteins. The bottom line is that gene therapy is much more complicated than previously thought.

"Synthetic biology" is another approach, using genetic engineering to create new organisms, one molecule at a time. By rearranging DNA's chemical components, the goal is to create more complex material such as new drugs, different viruses, in fact possible new species. A step toward producing a truly artificial cell has been described by Albert Libchaber of Rockefeller University. A cell-like assembly he calls a "vesicle bioreactor" has an artificial membrane enclosing fluid extracted from bacteria. Though lacking DNA, the vesicles are able to metabolize nutrients and have practical applications in research, including the understanding of the first natural cells in nature. Big money and names are being drawn to the effort, and the danger of misuse and national security implications are of concern also.

Dr. Leon Kass, chairman of the President's Council on Bioethics, has raised some powerful ethical questions stemming from present and projected gene technology. The ability to enhance athletic performance by augmenting muscle strength and vigor is well known. Also available are psychoactive drugs that can alter mood, memory, or behavior. Genetic means to extend the human lifespan and choose the sex of children is within reach. These are some troublesome matters, indeed, involving the use of biotechnical tools to attain perfection of body and mind according to our own fantasies. Dr. Kass questions if such enhancements are proper, who will have access to the technology, and what kind of society will be created.

Another recent surprise is that plants have shown the ability to retrieve bits of their genetic code from long-dead ancestors when it is to their advantage. Directly inherited DNA code can be edited if older genes, going back at least four generations, can adjust better to environmental threats. Corn, with 40,000 genes, suggests the biological complexity of plants, and an obvious question is whether animals have an equivalent capability.

Agricultural biotechnology, in some ways, has faced more difficulties than that of developing new genetic drugs. The problem is threefold. In the case of crops, scientists must juggle several genes at a time. Government research support has historically been about 42 percent for human health versus 5 percent for agriculture. And genetically modified (GM) crops have faced severe opposition in Europe, plus poor understanding in the U.S.

Nevertheless, the global market for biotech crops was about $5 billion by 2005. In the ten years since biotech crops appeared, a billion acres of GM corn, soybeans, and other crops have been planted globally. Soybeans now are 90 percent GM, cotton is 80 percent and corn is 50 percent. Up to 80 percent of the processed food in the store is GM.

Testing of genetic modifications in crops is devoted about 40 percent to herbicide resistance, 22 percent to insect resistance, 17 percent to product quality and 16 percent to virus resistance.. Typically, soybeans are given a gene that makes them tolerant to the common herbicide Roundup. When the field is sprayed with this herbicide, the weeds are killed but the soybeans are unharmed. GM corn has been involved in more field tests than any other crop In the case of corn, a specific gene, from a soil bacterium that kills insects, is "shot" into the seed kernel, using a device called a gene gun. The corn plant then produces its own pesticide that protects it from insects. The gene gun approach is quite inefficient and Dr. Mary-Dell Chilton is working on new techniques to place new genes on the corn chromosome at predetermined positions.

Despite the widespread use of GM foods in the U.S. the European Union (EU) has maintained a ban on importing GM produce. This stance remains in the face of support by the most prestigious national academies in North America and Europe for genetically engineered crops. These institutions have been joined by the Vatican in stating the need to improve the quantity and quality of food supplies.

For political reasons, some of the European countries have even threatened to withhold economic aid to African countries if the latter accepted American GM food. It is possible that some African countries will allow their own people to suffer hunger and starvation rather than distribute food that Americans have been eating for years with no ill effects. The European environmental groups Greenpeace and the Greens seem to have an unusually strong influence. Norman Borlaug, the 1970 Nobel Peace laureate, has called this situation "tragic and grossly irresponsible."

CLONING AND STEM CELLS

In early 1997 the whole world was astounded by the announcement that a British scientist, Ian Wilmut, had cloned a sheep named Dolly. The procedure Wilmut used was to take a cell from the udder tissue of a six-year-old sheep, fuse it into an empty ovum, or egg, then implant the egg into the womb of a surrogate ewe. Since that time, a cow, pig, goat, cat, rabbit and mouse have also been cloned.

A grim reality of cloning is that just one in 100 cloned embryos develops normally in the womb, and many of those die immediately after birth (Dolly died in February 2003). The survivors often suffer from obesity, liver failure, or joint problems. Recent work at the University of Pennsylvania has shown that a gene called *Oct4* may be to blame. Working with embryonic mouse clones, it was found that *Oct4* was active in the wrong place, or at the wrong time, in about 90 percent of the embryos. In natural embryos, both copies of *Oct4* are switched on at the same time, but in most cloned embryos are randomly inactive.

Human cloning is certainly possible, but all countries seem to agree that such "reproductive cloning" is scientifically unsafe and ethically unacceptable. Nevertheless, some individuals and groups have taken the first steps in trying to produce a human clone. Although most of this work has been done clandestinely, a few groups have been openly defiant in making claims as to their progress. They have said that the world will see a human clone "whether it is outlawed or sanctioned, hidden or announced, damaged or healthy."

Although clones have been described as being like identical twins, recent work has shown that behavioral and even physical traits of cloned siblings can differ. Clones are not exact replicas, just as identical twins often have strikingly varying personalities. In the case of cattle cloned from the same parent, some cows are bold and others are skittish. One explanation could be that two copies of a given gene can be carried by the parents, with one copy turned off if inherited from the mother, whereas the paternal copy can be silenced in other genes.

A driving force for cloning is the growing demand for assisted reproductive technologies. The U.S. has about 370 in vitro fertilization clinics where egg and sperm are brought together in a dish and then implanted in women clients. In 1999 about 170,000 babies were born as the result of in vitro procedures and a market for human eggs has developed. Absent this technique, cloning of one of the parents could be a last resort.

Early in 2003, research results were reported describing how scientists at the University of Pennsylvania had created mouse egg cells from both male and female cells. It is logically predicted that this technology will apply to humans as well, so that human eggs can be grown in the laboratory, with the potential to facilitate human genetic engineering. Later, in October, 2003, *Scientific American* described how cell material was taken from a mare to form a clone that she—not a surrogate mother—foaled herself. Carried to extremes, it theoretically would be possible for a gay male to contribute fresh eggs to mate with the sperm of his partner. Many people will have severe heartburn over this, as it suggests the specter of grotesque births and "human embryo farms."

In 1998, scientists at the University of Wisconsin successfully isolated stem cells from embryos and licensed the process. The potential value of human stem cells was quickly noted. They can transform themselves into any type of human tissue, and they can keep dividing and multiplying indefinitely in the laboratory. Thus, they can be invaluable in transplant procedures by providing unlimited supplies of replacement tissue.

Stem cells are immature, unspecialized cells that can develop into some or all of the body's 220 cell types. Human and other animal cells can be grown in culture dishes; a stable, self-replicating culture derived from a single cell, or a few cells, is called a "cell line." Cells to be cultured can be obtained from four different points. These are (1) fertilized embryos after five days, hence, "embryonic stem cells" (called ES cells), (2) partly developed reproductive cells from five to ten week embryos "embryonic germ cells" (3) blood from umbilical cord at birth "umbilical blood cells" (4) bone marrow and other cell-producing tissues, i.e., "adult stem cells." The longest-living human stem cell line has survived two years; its cells have doubled in number 450 times.

Early in his presidency, George W. Bush had to make a decision concerning government support for embryonic stem-cell research. Intense pressure on the White House came from abortion foes, the Catholic Church, research scientists and the medical industry. Opponents were concerned that destroying embryos would be tantamount to killing the youngest and most vulnerable members of the human race. At stake was part of the NIH budget of $17 billion in support of research. In Bush's words "At its core, this issue forces us to confront fundamental questions about the beginnings of life and the ends of science. It lies at a difficult moral intersection juxtaposing the need to protect life in all its phases with the prospect of saving and improving life in all its stages."

Faced with the profound ethical issues, and the overheated rhetoric of the two camps, Bush organized an effort to develop an administration policy on the issue. He agonized over the matter for several weeks and wound up with a statement of conditional support. Government funds would be available, but only for research using sixty existing cell lines, derived from embryos left over from fertility treatments, and in existence on August 9,

2001. All embryos would be donated and informed consent obtained. Afterwards, neutral observers commented that Bush's compromise was pretty successful—adversaries on both sides were grouching about it. Since then, California voters have approved a $3 billion research effort by the state. Also, a few large private companies have gingerly began work using stem cells from human embryos, recognizing that the research is controversial and has moral, political, economic and scientific risks.

In 2005, promising new stem-cell research was described at Washington University. A new way to grow embryonic stem cells is called "somatic cell nuclear transfer" or SCNT. The word somatic means all the cells of the body except for sperm and eggs. For example, a skin cell could be used to furnish the nucleus which replaces that in an egg. In other words, a cloned embryo could be formed with no human sperm used. The scientists say SCNT is aimed at curing people, not creating people, and research is aimed at generating specific kinds of cells and learning how and where to supply the cells to sites in the body.

For a short time, it appeared that Korean researcher Woo Suk Hwang was ahead of WU. In May 2005, Hwang and his team announced they had eleven stem cell lines, using the SCNT technique to create cloned early-stage embryos. That is, they slipped the nucleus from skin cells into eggs lacking a nucleus, and then extracted the embryo's stem cells. Remarkably, each stem cell line genetically matched its skin cell donor. Hwang became recognized as the world's leading stem cell expert but by the end of 2005 his fame was destroyed by ethics charges. He was forced to resign from his position when it was learned he had used the eggs from one or more of his female lab assistants, and co-workers accused him of fabricating data. The matter is shaping up as one of history's biggest scientific frauds. In its 2005 ranking of top researchers, In their December issue *Scientific American* had named Dr. Hwang the Research Leader of the Year but later retracted that decision.

16

MANKIND

When I was a graduate student at Washington University in St. Louis I ran across a beautiful poem entitled "EVOLUTION" by Langdon Smith. It is appropriate to the subject, reflects the science discussed in earlier chapters, and the references to British geology are especially interesting. The author, Langdon Smith (1858-1908), was a British naturalist who worked for some thirty years at the Museum of Natural History in New York. I recommend it to anyone interested in human evolution.

"When you were a tadpole and I was a fish in the Paleozoic time..." is well known to many people and Delmonico's was still operating, the last I knew. Smith knew his Darwinian evolution well but of course had no knowledge of DNA which has opened new worlds. Smith's poem started with life forms about 400-450 million years ago whereas the earliest ancestors of animal life that eventually evolved to mankind appeared about three billion years ago. Some of our genes have been inherited from these early ancestors and DNA information has yielded enormous insights as to the origin of different life forms.

EARLY MAN

This chapter is about the unusually successful species known as *Homo sapiens sapiens*, or modern mankind. Our closest primate relatives are the so-called anthropoid apes including chimpanzees and gorillas. Nearly all scientists agree that the cradle of mankind was East Africa because that is where almost all hominid fossils have been found. These early hominids walked upright, and adapted to open country, in contrast to their nearby tree-dwelling relatives.

To date, most of the important finds have been made in Kenya, Ethiopia and Tanzania and the preponderance of evidence points to an age of 5 to 6 million years for the divergence of hominids from the chimpanzee line. But in 2002 a French team found remains of a possible new species of hominid nearly 7 million years old. They named it *Sahelanthropus tchadensis*, from the site in northern Chad. This would be the oldest hominid, if it proves out, but the claim is controversial and the site is some 1500 miles west of the East African localities.

In 1950, Pope Pius XII stated that human evolution was an acceptable doctrine, and some fifty years later, John Paul II clearly referred to the chimpanzee relationship in primate evolution. (p. 33?).

Even so, many people are offended when it is suggested that modern mankind is descended from chimpanzees. After all, the two are quite different physically and in behavior. Although modern humans now have a brain size of about 1350 cubic centimeters, the first hominids were comparable with chimpanzees at about 400 cc. The dramatic increase in human brain size came quite recently and is an important difference setting apart modern humans from most other creatures. Some scientists have argued that upright posture and two-legged walking—bipedality—was the crucial adaptation of the human lineage. Paleontologist Richard E. Leakey has said "The fundamental distinction between us...is that we stand upright, with our lower limbs for support and locomotion and our upper limbs free from those functions." Other physical differences are that humans have opposable thumbs and have lost a thick mat of body hair. Female chimpanzees develop breasts only when nursing and the males have penis bones.

Genetically, the most obvious difference is that humans have twenty-three pairs of chromosomes whereas chimps have twenty-four. Human chromosome 2 evidently is equivalent to two chimp chromosomes that fused end to end. When Pope John-Paul II decreed that an "ontological discontinuity" during primate evolution led to humankind, author Matt Ridley irreverently remarked that this chromosomal fusion marked the location of the "soul gene." Other differences occur in chromosomes 4, 9, and 12, and chimps may be less susceptible to leukemia because the position of gene *AF4* is different. Modern chimps are largely immune to the AIDS virus, even though scientists think that the HIV virus was transferred from apes to humans about fifty years ago.

A number of studies have been made showing that the DNA of humans and chimps is more than 98.5 percent identical. By contrast, the DNA of chimps and gorillas is only 97 percent identical.

In 1924, anatomist Raymond Dart announced that an ancestor of modern humans had been found in South Africa. Although derided, he described the find as "southern ape-man," and gave it the name *Australopithecus africanus*. Following that, other specimens of the small, graceful creature were found in South African caves. In addition, a more robust species, with a crested skull, was found in the same places and named *A. robustus*. These South African specimens could be only poorly dated at about 3 million years.

Far more specimens of early hominids have been found further north in Tanzania, Kenya, and Ethiopia. Some of the oldest were uncovered by anthropologists Tim White and Don Johanson in the Hadar area of Ethiopia. *Ardipithecus ramidus*, found in 1997, is dated at 4.4 million years and is believed to be bipedal, but more primitive and ape-like than other hominids. Another small primate, nicknamed "Lucy," has a potassium-argon date of 3.2 million years. The specimen found was between 3½ and four feet tall and nineteen to twenty-one years old. She was lightly built and fully bipedal, with arms slightly longer than the arms of modern humans. Lucy was considered to be a specimen of *Australopithecus afarensis*, based on bones representing 20 percent of a full 206-bone skeleton.

Louis and Mary Leakey caused great excitement in 1959 when they announced they had found hominid fossils at Olduvai Gorge in the Serengeti Plain of northern Tanzania. The Olduvai is a steep-sided ravine about thirty miles long, cutting into a few hundred feet of ancient lakebeds which overlay Pliocene volcanic rocks. It was Mary, an English-born archaeologist, who found the first specimen. The skull was potassium-argon dated to about 1.75 ma and had huge molars, indicative of a vegetarian diet. Because of this it was called "nutcracker man" and was classified as *Australopithecus boisei*. Later, the Leakeys identified another species as *Homo habilis* (handy person) so named because of the associated flaked-stone artifacts and animal bones. *Habilis* tools from the Gona area in Ethiopia have been dated at 2.6 million years.

H. habilis was a graceful, fairly human-looking creature, standing a little over four feet tall and weighing about eighty pounds. These hominids walked upright but their arms and hands showed that they spent time in the trees as well. Their face and skull were less ape-like, and their brain size was larger (600 cc). The tools were quite simple—sharp-edged flakes of lava chipped off a larger piece when needed to cut hide or hack meat off of an animal carcass. Other specimens of *H. habilis* from East Turkana have been K-A dated at 2.6 million years.

Evidently, the Olduvai site was a favorite with ancient man. In the younger rock layers there, remains assigned to *Homo erectus* have been found, and even an *H. sapiens*, dated at 17,000 years. These finds, together with others from the vicinity of the Rift Valley, show a great diversity of hominid populations during the time four to 1½ million years ago (ma).

Researchers believe that *H. erectus* was probably the first hominid to use fire in cooking his food. This step led to a better diet, including more meat, and the evolution of smaller teeth. With the improved diet came larger brains (900 cc). *H. erectus* may have been the first human to migrate out of Africa. Several specimens of a close relative, *Homo ergaster*, have been excavated along with thousands of simple stone tools, in the Republic of Georgia. The remains were dated at 1.75 million years, similar to other finds in Indonesia (where the dating is less certain). *H. erectus*, or a creature slightly more primitive, dated at 1.9 ma has been found in China, near the Three Gorges area on the Yangtze River. None of these populations survived, however, possibly because of the ice age that began 1.6 ma. By 1.0 ma, hominids had been reduced to one lineage, *Homo erectus*, and nowhere outside of Africa.

[The Great Rift Valley of East Africa is the focus for the majority of fossil hominids found so far. I was fascinated by the geology when I visited there, and also by the fact that northern extensions of the Rift Valley served as the main migration path out of Africa. These northern localities in the Middle East later became the birthplace of three of the world's main religions.]

The extended Rift Valley runs 4000 miles from Jordan to Mozambique. With offsets, it represents pull-apart forces that tend to separate the African and Arabian plates and split off East Africa from the rest of the continent. This results in tensional features, including faults and half grabens. Escarpments on both sides of the rift valley average 2000 to 3000 feet high and up to 9000 feet in some places. In Kenya, the rift is thirty to forty miles wide and many large lakes have formed, some with no external drainage. In other places the valley is below sea level. Another characteristic of the trend is the presence of volcanic rocks, mainly lava. Tensional weakness allows basaltic lava flows to reach the surface in several places and build up substantial thicknesses. Mt. Kenya and Kilimanjaro, two of the continent's highest mountains, are of volcanic origin, on the east side of the rift valley. Underlying the rift system is a left-lateral, strike-slip fault that has sixty-six

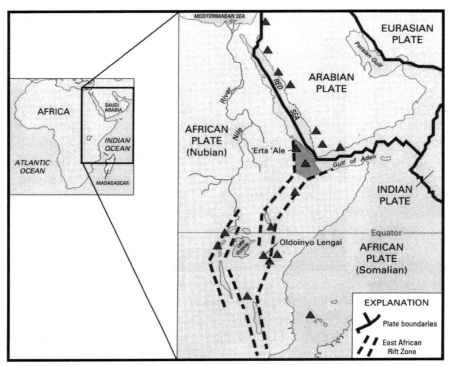

miles of offset. Although movement began in the Eocene, forty ma, most of the lateral motion occurred two to seven ma.

In Jordan, the Dead Sea is below sea level and is near the north end of the rift system. From there the rift passes south through the Gulf of Aqaba, down the Red Sea, then enters Africa through the Afar Triangle in Ethiopia. The rift continues in a southwesterly direction into Kenya with Lakes Shala, Abaya, Stefanie, Turkana (Rudolf), Naivasha, Nakuru, and Natron marking the trend.

At Turkana, the trend jumps 300 miles to the west where Lake Albert is at the northern end of the Western Rift. Lake Victoria is the second largest lake in the world, after Lake Superior, and offset some 100 miles to the east. From Albert, the rift system extends in a huge arcuate trend to the south, marked by Lakes Edward, Kivu, Tanganyika and Nyasa. To date, no fossil hominids have been reported from the Western Rift.

The Afar (Danakil) Triangle is highlighted in the USGS sketch below, together with the historically active volcanoes (black triangles). Geologists recognize it as a triple junction, where three pull-apart plate boundaries meet. The first two legs are formed by rifts down the Red Sea and the Gulf of Aden, and the third leg by the East African Rift. The Afar Triangle is about 350 miles N-S and fifty to 250 miles wide. As the plates pull apart, tensional fractures have released enormous amounts of basaltic rocks, with oceanic lavas forming in the Red Sea and Gulf of Aden. Onshore, upwelling lava flows began early, piling up a thickness of nearly 7000 feet in the Eocene (Trap series), and nearly 14,000 feet in the Plio-Miocene. Intermittent lava flows have continued to the present time. Most of the Danakil Depression is below sea level, has a desert climate, and is known as the "hell hole of creation." It is surprising that in this area, called "one of the most hostile environments in the world," Lucy and other early hominids evolved (admittedly, 3 million years ago, the climate no doubt was quite different).

MODERN MAN

The most important steps in the evolution of modern man unfolded during a time of worldwide, sometimes harsh, climatic changes. For most of geological time, the world's climate was warmer and more uniform than it is today. Major cooling began about 16 million years ago (ma) in the Miocene epoch, and by 3.2 ma, glaciers began to form in northern latitudes.

The Pleistocene epoch (also called the Great Ice Age) began 1.6 ma. This began a long stretch of time when much of the northern and southern hemispheres were covered with great ice sheets. Because so much of the world's surface water was tied up as ice and snow, sea levels fell as much as 450 feet. This in turn caused land bridges to form between Britain and the continent, Siberia and Alaska, and exposed vast areas of continental shelves in coastal areas.

Beginning about 800,000 years ago (ya), there have been at least nine cold periods, or glacial cycles, separated by warm or interglacial periods. Each of them was marked by cooling over tens of thousands of years, followed by a rapid warming and rise in sea levels. The last glacial cycle began about 115,000 ya, and is called the Würm glaciation in Europe, and the Wisconsin continental glacial stage in North America. Glacial conditions were especially intense in Europe about 75,000 ya just when the Neanderthal people were flourishing. There was another intense cold period about 18,000 ya; then beginning 15,000 ya, the earth entered an interglacial period, bringing the warmer climate we enjoy today. The interglacial 128,000 ya was warmer than the one we are in now, at least to this time.

Midway through the Pleistocene ice age, another *Homo* species began a second migration out of Africa, and gradually moved into Europe, China and Indonesia. The oldest specimens, reported in 1995, are the remains of six individuals from a cave in Spain. They have been dated at 800,000 ya and Spanish scientists assigned the name *H. antecessor*, or "one who goes before." This name conflicts with the more widely recognized term *H. heidelbergensis* for a species that shares features with both *H. erectus* and modern *Homo sapiens*. The type locality is near Heidelberg, Germany and was found in 1907. Several other specimens have been found in France and others in Greece, Indonesia (Java man) and China (Peking man). The latter three have age estimates ranging from 250,000 to 700,000 years, and classifications are uncertain. Recently, footprints have been found in southern Italy and a burial site for twenty-seven humans was found in a Spanish cavern, both finds dated at 350,000 years. A stone axe made of rose quartz may signify a tribute to the dead, and hence, the first known funeral ceremony.

There is good agreement that by 195,000 to 150,000 ya, *Homo sapiens* had evolved as a new species, distinct from *H. erectus*. The best-known early population, however, is the Neanderthals, named after Neander Valley near Dusseldorf, Germany, and they eventually spread from Spain to western Asia. They were squat and heavily built, standing about five feet tall. They were tough and well adapted to the arctic cold of the Würm glaciation. A date of 300,000 to 150,000 ya have been given by different authors as the time of the Neanderthal split from the *H. heidelbergensis* line.

The Neanderthals of Europe and Eurasia lived in caves and rock shelters during the winter months and hunted widely during the summer. Their game included large animals including cave bears, their most formidable prey. Their weapons were stone spearheads bound to wooden shafts, which meant confronting their quarry at close range. They made thousands of stone scrapers and blades for shaping wood. They were the first humans to bury their dead, and may have believed in an afterlife, as they left simple items with the body.

Because of their contemporary relationship, the formal species name is *Homo sapiens neanderthalensis* and for some time they lived, side-by-side and apparently peaceably, with *H. sapiens sapiens*. But they could not compete, and the Neanderthals became extinct about 30,000 years ago. *H. neanderthalensis* had a brain size at least as large as *H. sapiens* but for some reason did not make the progress we did. Neanderthals used fire and made clothes, but never developed language, music, art, symbols, use of diverse materials, notation or just sheer cleverness. No doubt the most important

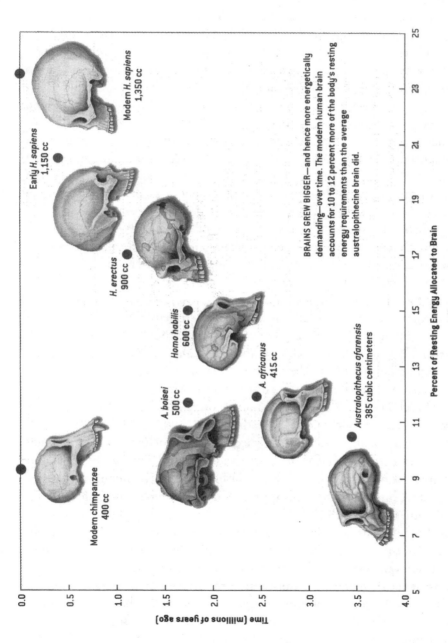

The illustration above shows the trend, over time, of increasing brain size, but is somewhat misleading in that it shows a smooth trend. Actually, there are many branches, leading to extinction of all species except the last. Also, H. neanderthalensis is on another branch (not shown) and had a brain size as large as H. sapiens. (By permission of Scientific American and Cornelia Blik.)

Text within the figure:

Percent of Resting Energy Allocated to Brain

Time (millions of years ago)

Modern H. sapiens 1,350 cc

Early H. sapiens 1,150 cc

H. erectus 900 cc

Homo habilis 600 cc

A. boisei 500 cc

A. africanus 415 cc

Australopithecus afarensis 385 cubic centimeters

Modern chimpanzee 400 cc

BRAINS GREW BIGGER—and hence more energetically demanding—over time. The modern human brain accounts for 10 to 12 percent more of the body's resting energy requirements than the average australopithecine brain did.

of these was speech/language, and without it they were at a terrific disadvantage when competing with *H. sapiens*.

In 2004, a few specimens of pygmy humans were found on Flores Island in Indonesia. Possibly 13,000 to 38,000 years old, they were only three feet tall and weighed fifty-five pounds. They were named *Homo floresiensis*, as a new species, but there have been some who argue they represent only a case of microencephaly, or dwarfism due to insufficient food supply.

DNA has been called the greatest archaeological tool of all time, and for good reason. Complementary information from two unique chromosomes provides data that help reveal the origins and migration patterns of human populations. Among other things, DNA information shows that Neanderthals contributed nothing to the modern human gene pool and that the Neanderthal lineage is four times as old as the modern human lineage.

Drayna has shown how a special class of human DNA with "founder mutations" can be used to trace common ancestors and calculate the approximate date when the mutation first appeared. The entire shared region of DNA including the mutated gene is called a haplotype, which the ancestral founder passes to his descendants. Through time, the haplotype, or "HapMap," will be whittled down in length so that in the case of a short stretch of only 30,000 base pairs of ancestral DNA, the founder mutation may be more than 100,000 years old. In another example, five different haplotypes for the sickle cell mutation show there were five different founders, in malarial regions of Africa and the Middle East.

Mitochondria are membrane-bound organelles in the cell, acting as power centers. Mitochondria have their own DNA and their own ribosomes. Two billion years ago, the ancestors of mitochondria were free-living bacteria. About that time they invaded larger "eukaryotic" cells and became a community of bacteria, multiplying and living entirely within the cell. A human body is comprised of 220 cell types, totaling 100 trillion of these compatible cells and each cell has its millions of mitochondria. Calculations show that if all the mitochondria in the human body were laid end-to-end, they would circle the earth two thousand times.

Their value to anthropologists comes from the fact that mtDNA is confined to a single-ring chromosome that does not take part in sexual mixing. Rather, they reproduce simply by dividing so that each daughter is an exact copy of the mother mtDNA. The mitochondria constitute an independent record of the past, all descended from the female side. Although mtDNA is uncontaminated it is still subject to mutation or errors in copying. Within a species, there will be a few differences in mtDNA, and the number of differences will be a measure of how far back their ancestors diverged.

In 1987, Allan Wilson and co-workers at UC Berkley published one of the first studies of human evolution using mtDNA. They looked at DNA sequences from 147 people representing five modern geographic populations. By comparing differences among them, the sequences fell into two groups: African; and the Asian, Caucasian, Australian and New Guinean populations. The Wilson group came to a dramatic conclusion: "All these mitrochondrial DNAs stem from one woman who is postulated to have lived about 200,000 years ago, probably in Africa." This is how the term "mitochondrial Eve" entered the lexicon. All three billion female humans living today got their mtDNA from their mothers, and all descended from a single woman.

The second, counterpoint tree for men is based on the Y chromosome. Recall that the twenty-third pair consists of an X and a Y chromosome in men and two Xs in women. The X, with 1098 genes and 160 million base pairs of DNA, is a giant compared to the Y, which has only seventy-eight genes and twenty-three million base pairs. A disproportionately high percentage of single-gene inherited human flaws reside in the X chromosome. Variations in susceptibility due to defective genes are unique to women, but their backup copy of the X usually protects them, whereas men are more vulnerable. Men contribute the sex-determining Y chromosome to their sons and all three billion Y-chromosomes that exist today trace back to the Y of a single man who lived sometime in the past. But this "Adam" for the Y chromosome never knew mitochondrial Eve.

According to our DNA, every person alive today is descended from a small group of people living in East Africa about 150,000 years ago. This means about 7500 generations, a mere blink of the eye, in evolutionary terms. The DNA patterns define ten original lineages on the male side and eighteen on the female side.

Most experts agree that *Homo sapiens* evolved in Africa between 195,000 and 150,000 ya, and then spread to other parts of the world. Molecular biologists agree with this model but add that more recent analyses of mtDNA refine the time of separation at around 150,000 years. At the Qafzeh cave in Israel, remains of twenty-one individuals provided ages of 115,000 to 96,000 ya. At the mouth of the Klasies River and the Border cave in South Africa, fossils were found with an age of 120,000 to 100,000 years.

Between 100,000 and 65,000 ya the third migration out of Africa was underway. This one was comprised of the *H. sapiens sapiens* line and some of the earliest groups settled in the Middle East and southwest Asia. From this area, seven of the ten male branches spread through the rest of the world, according to Dr. Luca Cavilli-Sforza at Stanford, using the Y chromosome technique. Dr. Sforza also believes that these Y-chromosome lineages may be associated with the major language groups.

Migrating populations developed the ability to speak, leading eventually to the 6000 or so languages used by the six billion people living today. German scientists recently found that a mutation of the *FOXP2* gene may have triggered the human capacity for speech about 100,000 ya.

In the process of migration, human skin pigmentation was altered in response to the exposure to the sun. The dark brown pigment melanin is synthesized to prevent skin cancer in regions near the equator. Melanin is nature's sunscreen, defending against UV radiation and was a natural component of *H. sapiens'* skin as he evolved. As migrating humans pushed northward, the need for melanin protection diminished, and skin color became lighter in more northerly latitudes. The mutation of a single letter of DNA code (out of 3.1 billion letters in the human genome) led to lighter skin. This had the beneficial effect of enhancing formation of vitamin D in the skin, initiated by shorter-wavelength UVB radiation. The combination of language and skin color has often been used, unscientifically and with some prejudice, to define the races.

About 65,000 ya, the Toba volcanic explosion in north Sumatra created a global catastrophe. An enormous cloud of volcanic ash blotted out the sun, causing summer temperatures to drop 22°F. This six-year drop in temperature, superimposed on the Pleistocene ice age, may have reduced the worldwide population of humans to only 10,000 people, and maybe only 500 women. [While living in Medan, we often visited beautiful Lake Toba, the largest Crater Lake in the world, sixty miles long, with an average depth of 1485 feet.]

The Toba climatic effects may have encouraged the migration of mankind across open water to Australia. These people would have been the early Aborigines. They eventually split into numerous tribal groups with about 260 different languages (160 now extinct) by the time the first Europeans arrived. Although the tribes had some contact with each other, they mostly lived in semi-isolation, which helps account for how backward they were. In New Guinea, tribal isolation is even more pronounced with the result that in a land about the size of Texas, a few million people speak almost 1000 languages.

During this same time, most of the people in the Middle East and North Africa were speaking in languages belonging to the Afro-Asian family. This family includes six subfamilies, the largest of which is the Semitic branch. This includes Hebrew, Aramaic and Arabic—respectively the languages of the Old Testament, New Testament, and Islamic Koran.

For the next 25,000 years after the Toba disaster, a gap exists in the human record. This blow to the human race serves to emphasize the sudden appearance of physiologically modern Cro-Magnon man in Europe about 40,000 ya. They certainly had the power of speech, had jewelry and musical instruments, and skeletons show they were carefully buried. They had a distinctive stone technology based on fine blades. These were long and narrow thin blades that could be made into scrapers, woodworking tools, and the first knives. These enabled the people to make needles from horn material. Needles, in turn, made possible fitted clothing, essential for survival in the long, cold winters in Europe.

By 30,000 ya, the Cro-Magnons had developed elaborate rock paintings and engravings showing remarkable artistic expression. Caves in France such as Lascaux, Altamira and Grotte Chauvet contain art works using techniques such as shading and perspective. Together with a rapid population growth, different authors call this period the "Great Leap Forward" or the "Big Bang" of artistic advances.

At the same time, North Africa enjoyed a favorable climate with good rainfall that supported abundant vegetation and food. Rolling grasslands and trees were common in Egypt and Libya. [I have found petrified wood in the Sahara Desert from this time in history.] One of the advances was the atlatl, a device with a sling-like action that was used to throw spears with more force and accuracy. When the rainfall and climate began to dry up, about 30,000 ya, the people migrated to the Nile Valley. Once there, agriculture and permanent settlements became more prevalent. Grinding stones and sickles were developed and by 15,000 ya, cemeteries were being used. Ritual burial was common and bodies were often decorated with necklaces, pendants, and ornaments of shell and bone.

The world population began to grow rapidly when Cro-Magnon time began. Worldwide human migration, under tough climatic conditions, was underway at the same time. Perhaps this served to ratchet up the process of gaining superior genes, while inferior ones died out. This could have been due to improved diet including more protein, and by the blending of merging populations. During these migrations, the human brain evolved dramatically.

Beginning about 14,000 years ago, or 12,000 B.C., several new civilizations developed around the world and migrations to new regions continued, including East and Northeastern Russia. The first humans (possibly as one tribe of seventy people), probably reached America by way of the land connection between Siberia and Alaska. This land bridge soon disappeared, however, as sea level rose about 450 feet in response to interglacial warming and the melting of the continental glaciers.

Clovis man, dating back to 11,600 B.C., is generally considered by most archaeologists to be the earliest human culture in North America. A site on the Llano Estacado near Clovis, NM is the type locality and at least five other sites are known on the Texas side of the Llano. Flint points for their spears and arrows were mined at the Albites quarries nearby; thousands of pits were dug by the Clovis people to get the distinctively banded flint. They used the atlatl to step up the force of thrown spears, much as the people did in North Africa 30,000 years ago. By 10,000 B.C. Clovis people had spread throughout most of the lower U.S., Mexico and as far south as Patagonia. [From the Llano, it was easy for them to move down the rivers to Central Texas and our little town of Lago Vista on the Colorado River is bracketed by the Levi site, eight miles to the southwest, and by the Wilson-Leonard site, thirteen miles to the northeast.

MAIN CIVILIZATIONS

The following section summarizes some of the civilizations that rose and fell in the last 10,000 years. It appears that organized farming was the critical element. According to Diamond (1999) the earliest known cultivated wheat came from the Fertile Crescent around 8500 B.C. Farming, together with domestication of animals, permitted the growth of urban centers. Writing was almost a necessity to organized government which accompanied the growth of urban centers. The first form of writing consisted of tokens, used to keep track of property and grain supplies. By 4100 B.C. pictographs were in use, and by 3400 B.C. the Sumerians were using a predecessor to cuneiform script. This was recorded by impressions in clay made by a wedge-shaped stylus. Individual characters represented words or syllables, not letters, and thousands of these clay tablets have survived.

The resulting growth in the human population was dramatic. From a worldwide total of maybe 6 million, just prior to organized farming, the number of humans grew to 300 million by A.D. 0. In about 1790 the real exponential rate of growth began and reached one billion in 1860. Today the worldwide population is about six billion and cumulative deaths to this time are about 100 billion.

Mesopotamia

Man's earliest writing appeared in the ancient civilizations of Mesopotamia (modern Iraq) and Egypt at approximately the same time. However, Egypt seemed to lag Mesopotamia somewhat, in both farming and writing. In Mesopotamia, part of the Fertile Crescent, life may have been disrupted in a big way by the Great Flood, described first by Gilgamish (see below) and later in Genesis, 6:1 through 8:22.

In 1998, William Ryan and Walter Pitman, Senior Scientists at Lamont-Doherty described their investigations using modern seismic techniques and geologic methods in the vicinity of the Black Sea. They were able to show that in 5600 B.C., a gigantic flood struck the Black Sea which was a fresh-water lake at that time. The flood came in the form of a tidal wave of seawater from the Mediterranean that burst through the constriction of the Bosporus. The water raced into the lake with enormous force, over the countryside and up rivers, destroying everything in its way. In the wake of the flood, people who survived fled to Turkey, Greece and western Asia, and throughout Europe.

After the flood, normalcy gradually returned, and in Mesopotamia the Tigris and Euphrates Rivers became vital components of the irrigation system that was developed by 4500 B.C. Sumerians moved into the area about 4000 B.C. and soon took control, building better irrigation canals and improving the roads to accommodate wheeled carts. Sumerian writing displays the oldest full texts ever found.

The Sumerians recorded numerical calculations, with their arithmetic based on units of ten. They divided a circle into units of sixty, as precursors to our own system of degrees, minutes and seconds. They wrote poetically, often about their gods and their story of creation, 3000 years before the Old Testament. Their first writing utilized picture representations pressed into wet clay that dried out to form tablets. Over some centuries these were altered into symbols called ideograms, and phonetic letters came to represent spoken sounds.

In the epic of Gilgamish, the narrative of an ancient flood (5600 B.C.?) was described by the hero Gilgamish, who was a great king living in Sumer about 2700 B.C. The flood was ordered by the gods to destroy all of mankind except for one man and his family. The man was instructed to build an ark and load it with the seeds of all living things so life could be preserved. When the flood came with sudden, terrible violence, the man and his family floated for days, while everyone else drowned.

Later conquerors included the Assyrians, Chaldeans, Babylonians, Hittites, Persians, Greeks, Arabs (who brought Islam to Iraq), Mongols, and Ottoman Turks. Britain held a mandate over Iraq from 1919 to 1932, following WWI.

Egypt

In ancient Egypt, permanent settlements were located on the flood-plain of the Nile River by 7000 B.C. A farming culture was in place and the first hieroglyphics appeared about 3000 B.C. It is possible that Sumerian writing had some influence but the two styles are quite different. Also, the hieroglyphics portray typical flora and fauna from the vicinity of the Nile River so most of the system must have been developed in Egypt. Although Mesopotamia and the Nile River were only 900 miles apart, it seems that people in each area independently developed their own system of writing.

Egyptian mythology expressed beliefs distinctive to their own culture, and developed a complex hierarchy of gods and goddesses. Atum was the one and only creator of the universe, and the sun god at the beginning of time. As he was alone, he mated with his shadow and gave birth to a son by spitting him out, and to a daughter by vomiting her up. The son represented rain and principles of order; the daughter represented the air and life. These two then mated and gave birth to children, and then grand-children that became other gods and goddesses. Without going into their names, mythical characters were described for truth, justice and harmony, for the sky, for life, power and stability, for life, wind, storms and deserts, for protection of women during pregnancy and childbirth, etc. All the titles concerned the general theme of life, death and the afterlife. Belief in the afterlife was very important and exemplified in construction of the pyramids.

HISTORY OF MANKIND—TIMELINES

YEARS AGO	MAJOR EVENTS
5–6 million	Hominids diverged from chimpanzees
3.2	Australopithecus afarensis—"Lucy"
2.6	Homo habilis

1.9	Homo erectus—first migration out of Africa
1.6	Pleistocene (Great Ice Age)
780,000	H. antecessor— second migration out of Africa
300,000–150,000	Neanderthals
195,000–150,000	Homo sapiens sapiens
115,000	Würm (Wisconsin) glaciation
100,000–66,000	Third migration out of Africa (H. sapiens)
65,000	Toba eruption
40,000	Cro-Magnon
15,000	Present interglacial warming
13,600	Clovis man
10,500	First organized farming—Fertile Crescent
9000	Egyptian dynasties
8000	Crete/Greece
7600	Black Sea flood
5754	Biblical Adam
5400	Writing
5000	Hinduism
4949	Biblical flood
3780	Abraham
3280	Exodus—fourth migration out of Africa
2568	Buddha born
2013	Christ born
1435	Muhammad born
1135–555	Medieval Warm Event
658	Black Death
550	Printing press
445–155	Little Ice Age
60	Atomic bomb

The end of the Old Kingdom of Egypt was marked by a cooling climate and catastrophic drought between 2300 and 2200 B.C. This was a widespread disaster that adversely affected Crete, Greece, all of the Middle East and as far east as India.

Crete/Greece

The earliest inhabitants of Crete date from about 6000 B.C. They were farmers and craftsmen, making decorated pottery and stone tools. They may have worshipped a female fertility goddess. The Minoan culture on Crete was named after the legendary King Minos, considered a son of Zeus. From their origins about 3000 B.C., the Minoans are considered to be the very beginning of European civilization. This unique culture developed a magnificent social organization with perhaps the single most efficient bureaucracy in antiquity. The emphasis was on commerce and visual culture, all recorded extensively. Their arts and crafts, especially goldsmithing, were outstanding. By 1700 B.C. a sophisticated society had developed with the palace at Knossos as the center of government. There was no evidence of a military presence. Minoans left no written history but had two types of writing, known as Linear A and Linear B. Linear B records on clay tablets have been deciphered, but Linear A has not. In 1628 B.C. the biggest known volcanic eruption (Thera) destroyed most of the Minoan culture and it never recovered fully after that.

About 2000 B.C., invaders from the north moved forcefully into the onshore parts of Greece, but at times settled peacefully with the local inhabitants. The invaders spoke an Indo-European language called Greek. Their society was consumed with warfare and their leaders were war-chiefs. They quickly made advantageous contact with the offshore Minoans who may have had a civilizing influence on the Greeks.

By 1600 B.C., urban centers such as the fortified palace of Mycenae were thriving. The Mycenaeans seem to have adopted much of the religion of the Minoans, namely belief in Zeus and the female goddesses. Cultural creativity blossomed, a system of writing was developed, and the power of the new military city-states began to be felt around the Aegean Sea. Mycenaean invasions (and trade) were recorded in Egypt, Crete, the Middle East and Asia Minor. In 1230 B.C. one of their great military achievements was to destroy Troy, a large commercial center on the shore of Turkey. Shortly after the Trojan War, some catastrophic event in the twelfth century seems to have driven the Mycenaeans into a "Dark Age" when they stopped writing, abandoned some of their cities, and fell into an economic decline.

About 800 B.C., Greek culture revived. Ornamentation on pottery became much more sophisticated and marvelous marble sculptures of the human figure proliferated. The alphabet was invented and Homer wrote his two great epics, the *Iliad* and the *Odyssey*. Greek religion distinguished between the twelve Olympian or sky-gods, and their rank in terms of authority. On Olympus, all the gods formed a society concerned with the three domains of earth, sea and sky. Athens became the cultural center of the Greek world and Athenian drama was widely admired. The classic Greek philosophers, teachers, scientists, doctors, astronomers, mathematicians, etc. have become household words.

Alexander the Great (356–323 B.C.) may be the greatest general of all time. At the age of thirteen he was a student of Aristotle, and at age twenty became king of Macedonia. In his military campaigns he had multiple victories over Persian armies and in thirty or more battles/wars subdued most of the civilized world at that time. Among others, he conquered Afghanistan, Pakistan and India and to maintain good relationships encouraged a strategy of intermarriage between his troops and women of the conquered areas. He founded the city of Alexandria in Egypt, and Greeks came to have a huge influence on the contemporary culture and religions of Jews and Christians.

Stonehenge

Stonehenge is in southern England and its purpose remains an enigma, 5000 years after initial beginnings. It could have been a temple, an astronomical calendar, or a guide to the heavens. Construction involved thousands of people, in three phases, over a time span of 1400 years. The first, fifty-year phase began about 2950 B.C., and involved the construction of 56 pits called "Aubrey Holes." The second phase might have involved erection of great timber posts but this is uncertain. During the third phase, from 2550 to 1600 B.C., most of the stones were put in place. The Sarsen Circle is about 108 feet in diameter, originally comprised of thirty sandstone blocks averaging thirteen feet high. These blocks supported sandstone lintels about ten feet long, forming a continuous circle around the top. Within the circle are ten Trilithons arranged in a horseshoe with the open end facing northeast toward the main entrance. These sandstone blocks weigh up to forty-five tons each and were hauled nineteen miles from their source. The last placement of rocks was an oval of "bluestones" within the large horseshoe, and about sixty other bluestones in a circle inside the outer sandstone circle. The bluestones are igneous rocks weighing about four tons, from the Preseli Mountains about 240 miles away.

Hittite

The Hittite empire controlled most of the Fertile Crescent from 1600 to 1200 B.C. They were a warrior people who invented iron weapons, which gave them an advantage. Their language was from the Indo-European family and they used Akkadian to some extent before developing their own writing. Their capital was located in Anatolia, about 130 miles east of present-day Ankara. The Hittites assimilated much from the Sumerian civilization but the Egyptians considered them as barbarians, especially during a war, about 1300–1200 B.C.

The Hittites used greatly modified and less stringent laws inherited from the Old Babylonians. They adopted many of the gods of the Sumerians and Babylonians, and had considerable tolerance for other religions. This turned out to be of great benefit to the Jews because the Assyrians, who followed the Hittites, exhibited the same tolerance towards other religions, including that of the Hebrews.

Rome

Italians like to tell how their capital city was founded in 753 B.C. by twin boys Romulus and Remus who had been nurtured by a mother wolf. Rome was named after Romulus when he won out in a struggle with his brother.

The Roman Republic was established in 509 B.C., when a coalition of nobles threw out the king, and this form of government lasted for over 400 years. The Senate was the most powerful body of government, controlling finances and foreign policy and could pass legal decrees. The senators were patricians, and served for life. The Assembly was a body of 193 representatives that elected two consuls who shared executive power. The consuls served for only one year and had equal power but could veto a decision made by the other. A representative form of government was never a part of the Roman system.

When it was sacked by the Goths in 390 B.C., Rome was scarcely more than a little state, about twenty miles square. But following that disaster, Rome began a period of strong growth, led by public-spirited free-farmers with military service sometimes considered a privilege. Assimilation of neighboring states was helped by compromise and consensus plus a common language and a growing network of roads. Defeated enemy territories were incorporated equitably, becoming altogether Roman with voting and other rights.

The Romans were noted for their construction skills, leaving a number of great cities, stadia, aqueducts, roads and bridges, often using their signature arches. The concrete they used was sometimes upgraded by using calcined kaolinitic clay or pozzolan volcanic tuff. A great deal of more artistic work remains, in the form of mosaics and a considerable amount of statuary. [When we were living in Turkey we sometimes drove on old Roman roads and over bridges that were at least 2000 years old, and were still in good shape.]

The First Punic War (264–241 B.C.) resulted in the annexation of Sicily but caused some long-term adverse changes. A large number of new slaves upset the free-farmer-soldier economy and the moral fiber of the nation suffered. Slavery was always a component of Roman life—it is estimated that one-third of the total population were slaves. Slaves were often acquired as the spoils of war, were 70–80 percent male, and had an average life span of only twenty years. In later years when wars of conquest were mostly over, slaves were obtained by purchase, as debtors, and by taking charge of abandoned children/foundlings. Reproduction among slaves was always a factor but did not furnish the numbers desired.

The Second Punic War (218–202 B.C.) ended with the defeat of Hannibal and in 146 B.C. the Third War ended with the obliteration of Carthage, situated near the site of modern Tunis. But the Republic was in decline and final subjugation of the North Africans dragged on for years. Finally, a popular leader named Marius refused to give up his consulship at the end of his term and in 106 B.C. took over control of the government, backed by his newly created legions of paid troops. This was the first rule by military commanders.

In 73 B.C. the slave Spartacus led an insurrection of slaves, with trained gladiators among them. They held out for two years in the crater of Vesuvius, a volcano inactive at that time. The uprising was finally put down, and punished with barbaric cruelty. Six thousand captured slaves were crucified along the Appian Way, the great highway running south from Rome.

In 60 B.C., the three great generals Caesar, Crassus and Pompey formed a cabal with the plan to take the government of Rome away from the Senate. Pompey stayed in Rome to protect their position while Caesar was conquering Gaul, which he did in 51 B.C. Meanwhile, Crassus was fighting in Asia Minor and in 53 B.C. suffered the Roman's worst loss ever to the Parthians at Harran, losing 20,000 killed and 10,000 captured. In 49

B.C. Caesar returned to Rome, which led to a showdown with Pompey and the Senate when the latter passed a law ending Caesar's authority. Furthermore, it was illegal for a general to bring his troops past the boundary of his command, which in this case was the Rubicon River. Saying "the die is cast," Caesar crossed the Rubicon and marched upon Pompey and Rome. Pompey was defeated in a series of battles and fled to Egypt, where Caesar had him murdered. After his success, Julius Caesar was named dictator for ten years, and then, for life. Life was not too long, however, and Caesar was stabbed to death in the Senate in 44 B.C.

Octavian, Julius Caesar's nephew, gathered his uncle's forces together and in 31 B.C. defeated Mark Antony at the naval battle of Actium. Octavian Caesar proved to be a good master of the Roman world. He did not entertain foolish thoughts of being god or king, and was not diverted by a queen/lover (like Cleopatra). Instead, he declined to be dictator, and restored freedom to the Senate and people of Rome. In gratitude, the Senate honored him with the title of Augustus Caesar (27 B.C. to A.D. 14), the first of the Roman emperors.

These emperors, with their legions of paid soldiers, continued the campaign of conquest initiated by the military commanders. By about 100 A.D. they had pushed the outer limits of the empire to their maximum extent. Territory under their control included lands in North Africa, Egypt, Syria, Israel, Turkey, Armenia, Iraq, Persia, Spain, France, Belgium, Britain, and Transylvania. Frontiers were protected and civil order was maintained by the Roman legions in a time of peace known as Pax Romana.

Modern Western civilization has been strongly influenced by the culture of ancient Rome. Latin led to the four romance languages of Italian, French, Spanish and Portuguese. Latin forms the root of many English words and is especially common in terms used in the law, medicine, and literature. The system of Roman numerals was developed, and the Julian calendar was introduced by Julius Caesar in 45 B.C.

The first Greek coins were struck about 700 B.C. in western Turkey and the Romans picked up this technology with gusto. Common coins were copper, but the more valuable ones were silver and gold. [When we visited the old Roman ruins at Perge, Aphrodesia, Pergamum, Miletus, Ephesus, etc. we always asked the local kids if they had any "eski para" (old money) for sale and acquired handfuls of Roman coins in that way. Mostly, they were copper, from the period A.D. 260–395 honoring emperors of that time.]

Emperor Justinian (483–565) introduced a code of laws which forms the basis of our system of civil laws. His code dealt with contracts, civil rights, crimes and torts, land and property, marriage, procedures, punishment, voting, etc.

Roman religion adopted many of the Greek gods, built many temples, and filled them with statues. The main gods included Jupiter, Saturn, Venus, Mars, Apollo, Diana, Mercury, Bacchus, etc. Six Vestal Virgins were charged with keeping an eternal flame going in the Temple of Vesta. The girls were selected, as a great honor, from good families, at ages between six and ten. They had to be physically perfect and served for thirty years. In homes, daily worship was conducted by the *pater familias*, as the household priest. Emperor worship came later, with the emperors being deified.

Of course the huge change in religion came when Emperor Constantine (307–337) favored Christianity, beginning in A.D. 313, and was the first Roman emperor to personally convert. In 331 he moved the capital to Byzantium, which then was renamed Constantinople and became the center of the eastern or Orthodox Church. By 380, Christianity had become the state religion of the Roman Empire. The bishop of Rome came to be called the pope and head of the western, or Roman Catholic Church. He was also the actual ruler of the city when it was sacked by the Visigoth Alaric in 410. In 452, when Attila the Hun threatened, the Pope paid a ransom to avoid destruction of the city. In contrast, Constantinople remained viable and endured until 1453, when it fell to the Ottoman Turks.

Olmec

Olmec cities in southern Mexico appeared about 1200 B.C., long after the Clovis people were gone. The cities were built around a central raised mound, used for religious ceremonies. Around 900 B.C., these raised mounds were replaced with pyramidal structures. Houses were made of wooden walls, with clay and palm frond roofs. Basalt from nearby volcanic mountains was used for constructing plazas and pyramids. Nobles were buried with jewels in enclosures with walls of jade.

Farming made use of an extensive irrigation system. By 650 B.C., the Olmecs developed a complex calendar and hieroglyphic system of writing. Their unique art creations showed a strong animal symbolism, in that they believed each person had an animal spirit. Their favorite animals were monkeys, serpents, and especially the jaguar which they believed to be a supernatural creature.

Head art was important, and children of noblemen had their heads deformed at birth. Head sizes were exaggerated in the art forms, modeled after their rulers. Facial features of the large heads had slanted eyes and large lips, leading to arguments over an Asian versus African descent. The Olmec civilization was gone by A.D. 600 but had a strong influence on the Mayas, the best known of the ancient civilizations in southern Mexico/Central America.

Maya

Maya people trace back to the Yucatan around 1600 B.C. but did not reach prominence until about A.D. 250 in southern Mexico and Central America. Borrowing from earlier civilizations such as the Olmecs, Mayas developed or improved knowledge of astronomy, calendars and hieroglyphic writing. Without metal tools, they built elaborate temple-pyramids, palaces and observatories. They were skilled weavers and potters, noted for highly decorated ceremonial appurtenances. As skilled farmers, they cleared large areas of tropical rain forest and built sizable underground reservoirs for storage of rainwater. They constructed terraced gardens and traveled offshore to barter wax, salt, furs, cotton and other products.

Kings and nobles ruled over a system of independent states, each with a rural farming community and large urban areas built around ceremonial centers. A foundation of their culture was a religion that required paying ritual homage to the gods. Their social structure included priests, a privileged class, workers and slaves. Big cities created great wealth, a rich culture and a complex bureaucracy—ultimately an unsustainable society. Overpopulation and too little water led to decline, believed to be triggered by a long drought beginning about A.D. 840, and the civilization died by A.D. 950.

Aztec

In a little more than three hundred years, the Aztecs built an amazing civilization which was ended violently by the Spaniards in 1521.

The Aztecs were a warring people, believed to come to Mexico from the southwestern U.S. beginning about A.D. 1200. They settled in the Central Valley, eventually creating an empire surpassed in size only by the Incas of Peru. The Aztec capitol was founded in 1325 and became a magnificent city called Tenochtitlan, now Mexico City.

The city was built around a shallow lake, which had five islands connected to the mainland by three causeways. Instead of streets there were canals, and people moved about in canoes. Later, the Spanish called it "the Venice of the New World." It was a beautiful, well-run city with a ceremonial plaza paved with stone. Outstanding temples were designed like those of their Mayan predecessors to the south, with terraced steps on the sides of ascending pyramids. More than 200,000 people lived in Tenochtitlan, bigger than any city in Europe at the time.

Advanced farming techniques helped to support the large population. The Aztecs built irrigation systems, terraced the hillsides and enriched the soil with fertilizer. In the southern part of the lake, artificial islands were built by piling soil on rafts that eventually were anchored by the roots of vegetation growing to the lake bottom. Seeds were planted in holes poked in the soft soil by pointed sticks. Corn was the principal crop but the Aztecs planted beans, squash, tomatoes, and peppers as well. They also grew flowers and raised ducks, geese and turkeys.

Gold ornaments, brightly colored woven cloth and salt were products used for trading with peoples to the south. Trading goods were carried by canoe, and on the backs of long caravans of porters. The Aztecs had no wheeled carts or pack animals. Goods received in trade included cotton, rubber, cacao beans (for making chocolate), animal skins and tropical bird feathers.

They developed writing and a counting system based on pictographs, which has been deciphered in part. Counting was based on the number twenty, with one picture representing twenty items, and another twenty × twenty (400).

The Aztecs worshipped gods whom they believed controlled the forces of nature. The god of rain was important, as was the plumed serpent Quetzalcoatl who was the god of wind and resurrection. But the sun god was by far the most important and led to the disturbing habit of human sacrifice. The Aztecs believed that if the sun god was not honored with human hearts and blood, the sun would not rise and the world would end.

Typically, the sacrificial victim would be led up the stairs to the top of the pyramid and then held down on the altar while drums boomed. The Aztec priest would slash open the chest of the victim with a sharp knife, then reach in and pull out the still palpitating heart. The priest would hold the heart aloft for all to see and the body would be kicked down the stairs for butchering. Cannibalism was practiced with many of the bodies.

No human society known in history approached the Aztecs in the number of human sacrifices. A common estimate is 20,000 per year but could have been much more. For example, when the main temple in Tenochtitlan was dedicated in 1487, the reports of human sacrifices range from 20,000 to 80,400.

With hundreds of temples scattered throughout the Aztec empire, many of them needing victims, it appears that the main objective of Aztec war parties was to capture prisoners for sacrifice. Prisoners would then be kept in wooden cages, to be fattened until sacrificed, at temple-pyramids in the capital or local communities. Raids on neighboring peoples to obtain prisoners were continuous, and no doubt engendered extreme fear and hatred.

In November 1519 the Spaniard conquistadors saw the magnificent city of Tenochtitlan for the first time. Buildings were shining white in the sun, in the center of the lake, with long causeways teeming with travelers to and from the citadel. Hernando Cortes led the detachment of less than 400 soldiers, all of who envisioned untold wealth when they saw the metropolis.

Montezuma II, who was the Aztec emperor at the time, made several fatal misjudgments in dealing with the Spaniards. First, he thought they were descendents of the god Quetzalcoatl and deferred accordingly. Then he tried to bribe them into leaving but failed in that approach. When he received them in his splendid court, he was seized by Cortes as a hostage. The Spaniards tried to use the irresolute Montezuma as a proxy ruler but the Aztecs revolted in June 1520 and Montezuma was killed.

In 1521, after a defeat of their forces, the Spaniards were forced to watch the ritual butchery of sixty-two of their companions who had been taken captive. From about a mile away, they saw the captives dragged up the steps of one of the main temple-pyramids. Once on top, the captives were made to dance, accompanied by drums, conches and horns, then have their hearts cut out by the Aztec priests. As described by Bernal Diaz: "Then they kicked the bodies down the steps, and the Indian butchers who were waiting below cut off their arms and legs and flayed their faces, which they afterwards prepared like glove leather, with their beards on, and kept for drunken festivals. Then they ate their flesh with a sauce of peppers and tomatoes."

Later in 1521, Cortes with only 500 men and a few cannons, overthrew the Aztecs and executed their king. This defeat of thousands of mighty Aztec warriors was made possible for two main reasons. First, a plague of smallpox, introduced by the Spaniards, had wiped out up to one-half of the Aztec population, so that they were in a weakened and demoralized condition. Second, the Spaniards had firearms probably more intimidating than effective, and Cortes neutralized the Aztec advantage in numbers by massing 10,000 Indian allies. Over the years, the Aztec raids on their neighbors had made innumerable determined and vengeful enemies, who were more than willing to join the Spaniards. Thus, "a maniacal obsession with blood and torture" eventually led to the downfall of the Aztecs.

Inca

Inca is the title given to each of the thirteen ruling emperors who ruled over the Inca Empire in Peru at about the same time as the Aztecs. The Inca domain included the coastal and mountain regions of Ecuador, Peru, Bolivia, and the northern parts of Chile and Argentina. The Incas knit together mountain and desert areas, economically and socially, in the "greatest political achievement of the American Indians."

Although Peruvian civilization is known from as early as 1500 B.C., Inca history begins about A.D. 1200, with the founding of Cuzco, at 11,207 feet in the Peruvian Andes. Their history ended with the death of the last Inca in 1533 at the hands of the Spaniards. The Incas had no direct contact with the Aztecs or Mayans, and met their demise only ten years after becoming aware of the white man's presence.

Quechua was the language of the Incas and dominant throughout the empire. To this day, it is the language spoken by a large percentage of Peru's inhabitants. Neither the Incas nor any other South American cultures had any form of writing. Rather, folk stories and official records were kept by "rememberers" who used a device called a quipuleaving. This consisted of a main cord with a series of colored strings into which a complex system of knots were tied. This apparatus enabled the keepers of the knots to record taxes, population, soldiers, etc. in a system using decimals, including a symbol for zero.

The population of the Inca Empire was comprised primarily of farmer-soldiers. Agricultural "professionals" guided plant domestication and more than half of the produce that the world eats today was developed in the Andean area of the Incas. Among these are 240 varieties of potatoes, twenty of corn, plus squash, beans, peppers, peanuts, manioc, etc. Water was brought to the crops by superbly engineered canals, and hillsides were terraced to prevent erosion. Seabird guano and llama manure were used as fertilizer (llamas cooperate by leaving their wastes in a localized area).

Incas were superb engineers and architects. The number and size of Inca buildings is overwhelming. Stone was precisely cut to fit a pattern, or rocks were used in massive form, sometimes without mortar. Sun-baked brick was used when stone was unavailable. The huge fortress built to protect Cuzco is an example of their skill. The structure is 1500 feet long and sixty feet high, broken into forty-six salients, angles, and buttresses. 300,000 stones were used, some weighing thirty tons. The stones were beveled and fitted so well structurally that earthquakes have not dislodged them. It took 30,000 workmen over seventy years to complete the fortress.

Over 10,000 miles of all-weather roads were built to connect the empire. The coastal road alone was 2520 miles long and twenty-four feet wide. Rest stations for travelers were placed along the roads every twelve to eighteen miles and the courier system provided rapid communication. The couriers each ran 1½ miles in relay, and could carry a message 1250 miles in five days. The road across the Andes Mountains was narrower but 3250 miles long and had about 100 bridges. The largest bridge built by the Incas was 148 feet long and used suspension techniques.

Goldsmithing was an Inca specialty. Gold and silver mines in the Andes provided huge quantities of the precious metals and have been worked ever since. The best examples of artistry by the goldsmiths were destroyed by the Spaniards, who were dumbfounded by the amount of gold they saw and then stole. They described buildings covered with gold plate, gold fountains, and statuary of gold corn, gold Earth, and twenty life-sized gold llamas grazing on golden grass in a golden enclosure.

The Inca Empire was a totalitarian theocracy, for the ruling Inca was the absolute ruler, the head of the state religion and considered a demigod by the people. Incas believed in a creator god who was the source of power, aided by other, lesser gods. The sun god was the most important of these, and various natural or man-made objects important to everyday life were imbued with a magic or holy spirit. Several ritual platforms have been found at elevations above 17,000 feet, some with evidence of human sacrifices. There was a general belief in an afterlife and the common man, if virtuous, with proper behavior during his lifetime—do not steal, do not lie, do not be lazy—could have a good afterlife. If not, he suffered in a sort of hell where he was cold and starving. Noblemen achieved immortality, no matter what their conduct while living.

The socialistic and bureaucratic structure of the Inca society seemed to work with amazing efficiency. The base of the social pyramid was a commune or clan of families living as a group and sharing land, animals, and crops. No individuals owned land, which was loaned to the members for their annual use. Planting and harvesting were communal, and crops were stored for use as directed by officials. Ten workers had a straw boss, ten of these groups had a foreman and ten foremen were ruled by a headman. For every 10,000 people there were 1331 officials. Another form of work service was directed to road and bridge building, mining, and erection of temples, forts and royal residences. In addition, any worker was subject to military service at any time. While he was absent on military duty, other members of his commune did his work for him.

At the age of twenty, a man was expected to marry—if he did not, a mate was selected for him by the chieftain. For workers, marriage was strictly monogamous but all members of the ruling class had more than one wife. If a woman had special talents or was especially beautiful, she might be chosen to become concubines of the officials or of the Inca himself. The Inca had one real wife but a large ménage of concubines; at the time of the Spanish conquest, the Inca was estimated to have 500 living male descendents. The important administrators were chosen from this group, which also furnished the succeeding Inca who was selected by a council of royal advisors.

It is clear that this arrangement totally benefited the Inca, his family, and top officials. Workers were kept docile by giving them their basic requirements, and intimidated by dictates of the state religion plus layers of bureaucratic controls.

In 1527 Francisco Pizarro appeared briefly on the coast near Ecuador, staying just long enough for his men to infect the populace with a devastating plague of smallpox. Pizarro came back in 1532, with 177 men, of which sixty-seven were cavalry. The Inca at the time, who had won a civil war only two weeks before, was in the mountains at the provincial capital, Cajamarca. Pizarro marched toward the place, through hundreds of narrow defiles where the huge army of the Incas could have annihilated him but failed to do so.

When the Spaniards occupied the city, they invited Atahualpa, the Inca, to a parley, which turned into an ambush. Although the Inca was surrounded by thousands of his men, they came unarmed, as Pizarro wished. After some preliminaries, the Spaniards attacked the unarmed Indians and took the Inca prisoner. Of the Indian contingent, numbering 80,000 altogether, 7000 were killed without the loss of a single Spaniard.

After being held prisoner for eight months, Atahualpa paid a huge ransom, filling the large room in which he was kept twice with silver and once with gold. But it was not enough for the avaricious Spaniards. They kept him in custody and eventually charged him with "crimes against the Spanish state." In 1533 he was executed by strangulation.

After these events, the Inca people were reduced to a strange state of timidity, and the Spaniards advanced easily to Cusco which they captured in November 1533. From there they extended their domination over most of the empire but war with the Incas raged sporadically over the next twenty years and Pizarro himself was murdered in 1541.

A number of reasons have been cited for the amazing success that a handful of Spaniards had in overwhelming hordes of Indians. Among these were the horses, firearms and chain mail armor of the Spanish—in other words, superior and intimidating weapons of war. Too, the Indian rulers totally lacked intelligence as to the Spaniards' intentions, methods and incentives—mainly to acquire wealth and to bring religious salvation to the heathens. Another important factor was that of the diseases that the Europeans introduced into the Indian population, which totally lacked any immunity. Smallpox was especially devastating to both the Aztecs and the Incas; by 1618, only 1.6 million of Mexico's initial population of 20 million had survived. Throughout the Americas, it is estimated that 95 percent of the pre-Columbian native population died from European diseases.

The thirteen civilizations described above came into being during the time 10,000 B.C. to A.D. 1533. Most prevailed for a period of 200 to a few thousand years, the average being 1475 years. Some were terminated by natural disasters such as drought or volcanoes, but most were conquered. Almost all shared the common characteristics of an economy based on farming, a ruler (usually a king), some form of religion with gods and priesthood, writing, a code of laws, and a military organization. Warfare seems to be a never-ending curse and Brassey's Dictionary of Battles lists 7000 battles during the last 3,500 years. Will and Ariel Durant calculated that during that entire time, there were only 268 years without war.

Millions of soldiers and civilians were killed in these battles/wars and in recent years weapons of mass destruction have been developed that are designed specifically to kill large numbers of people. To date, biologic weapons have not been used although they are known to exist. Chemical weapons were used in World War I, and more recently by the Iraqis against Iranians, and on their own Kurdish people. And of course, two atomic bombs were used against Japan to end World War II in 1945.

But during the twentieth century, two murderous political systems were responsible for the worst list of civilian casualties. Ethnic genocide by the Nazis and class genocide by the Communists were both crimes against humanity on a massive scale. Non-combatants killed by the Nazis include 15 million in occupied countries, 6 million Jews, 3.3 million Soviet prisoners of war, 1.1 million deportees, and several hundred thousand gypsies. Altogether about 25 million victims, with the most atrocious killing being the Holocaust—the mass murder of Jews characterized by organized gassing in extermination camps.

In Russia the Bolsheviks employed a system of terror, first against Cossacks and then kulaks (peasant farmers) when they resisted forced collectivization. Certain classes of people were considered to be potential opponents so they were singled out for extermination. Primary suspects were various minority groups, the middle class, teachers, clergy, village leaders, city officials, and professionals such as doctors, police and military officers. Soviet methods of terror included deliberate starvation (6 million in 1932–33), periodic purges (720,000 killed), imprisonment, torture, executions, and forced labor in the gulag concentration camps. The camps took in 1–2 million people every year, and in 1953 held 2,750,000 prisoners. All this brutality was enforced by 366,000 NKVD personnel, compared to 7500 in the German Gestapo (1939 numbers). Terror, such as described above, was standard procedure used by Communists around the world, accounting for about 100 million people killed. A partial list follows (all in millions):

Russia 20, China 65, North Korea 2, Cambodia 2, Vietnam 1, Eastern Europe 1, Africa 1.7, Afghanistan 1.5.

These are terrible examples of inhumane behavior by a few evil men, showing mankind at his worst. The Nazis were finally destroyed militarily in 1945 by a coalition of countries allied against them. The godless Russian Communists, facing resolute opposition during a long Cold War, finally collapsed in the early 1990s. Their economic system essentially was a form of enforced socialism. Managed by a massive, inefficient, and corrupt bureaucracy, it proved no match for the free market system of the West. In addition, the West appealed powerfully to mankind's inherent desire for basic freedom.

THE HUMAN BRAIN

This chapter has been concerned with mankind's origins, evolution, migrations and history. To conclude, the final section deals with the human brain, where the soul resides. The goal, of course, is to investigate the process, and the most likely timing, of the "divine infusion" of man's soul and spirit.

Mankind is clever, capable of intelligent thought, creative, curious, and tenacious in pursuing objectives. The development of fluent speech has been vital to passing on knowledge and ideas through the medium of language. Articulate speech allows expression of emotions, foresight and self-awareness. Writing permits recording what is said plus thoughts, technology, laws, contracts, accounts, personal communications, and music, *ad infinitum*. We have a strong interest in subsistence and technology, plus relationships between the individual, the group and the universe. It is reassuring to recall that *Homo sapiens sapiens* means "wise, wise person," or at least the potential to be wise.

Intelligence can be roughly correlated with brain size. *Homo habilis*, who lived about 2.6 million years ago, had a brain size of about 750 cc. *Homo erectus*, about 1.7 to 1 million years ago, averaged 900 cc in brain size, and modern *Homo sapiens* averages about 1400 cc. The increase in brain size may have been enhanced by more protein (meat) in the diet of humans.

University of Chicago researchers, led by Bruce T. Lahn, have identified seventeen brain-building genes that mutated rapidly to the advantage of early humans. They believe that the human brain evolved through the selection of these genes, which had a multiplying effect in thousands of changes to thousands of genes. Recent work by Lahn's group has shown that humans had a positive selection for the gene *Microcephalin*, possibly contributing to brain enlargement. Based on the average number of mutations between the favored haplotype and its variants, they found that the new clade originated about 37,000 years ago (Cro-Magnon time). Another gene *ASPM*, possibly related to brain enlargement, seems to have originated about 5800 years ago (time of first writing).

In humans, the brain comprises only 2 percent of the total body weight but at least half the human genome is devoted to development of the brain. The brain weight of males is slightly higher—but as a percent of the body weight, that of females is slightly higher.

In complexity, the human brain exceeds even DNA and the three pounds of gray matter is comprised of 100 billion nerve cells or neurons. These neurons are segregated by function in different parts of the brain. They can receive, analyze, coordinate and transmit information. Each neuron has an axon that transmits information across a gap or synapse to a target cell called a dendrite that may have thousands of connections. The information, in the form of an electrical signal, is converted to a chemical message (modulated up to 100 times) across the synapse, then back to an electrical pulse At that point, chemical neurotransmitter molecules activate a response in the dendrite or target cell. Thus there are about 500 trillion connections in the human brain, the "most complicated arrangement of matter known to man." As the brain activates the links or synapses between neurons, the synaptic activity can be staggering—up to 10 quadrillion (10^{16} or 10 to the 16th power) connections a second. This is equivalent to a million Pentium-powered computers running on a few hundred megawatts of electricity. Worded differently, the human brain is much more powerful, millions of times more energy-efficient, and far more compact than a computer.

Both short and long-term memories arise when the synapse or connection between neurons is temporarily sensitized, or "fires." Multiple pathways are involved in translating an electrical pulse into a chemical code that can be understood by the neuron's biochemistry. Variable frequencies of the electric signal control the flow of the required calcium ions through the cell membrane. For long-term memory, a new protein must be synthesized from encoded instructions to messenger RNA (mRNA), received from DNA inside the cell nucleus. Repeated strong neural impulses activate the relevant genes, proteins develop, and the hippocampus remembers the message.

After an egg (ovum) has been fertilized by a sperm, the resulting zygote has a complete set of genes, half from each parent. From the female side, some additional microscopic mitochondria are also included which code for traits on the maternal side only. After a few days, the cells have divided to the thirty-two-cell blastocyst form, which then is implanted on the uterine wall, and the embryonic stage begins.

Concerning ontogeny, certain ancestral features show up as evolutionary relics in the human embryo. At between four and five weeks, the normal human embryo has a rudimentary tail with ten to twelve vertebrae, but by the eighth week the tissue has been mostly ingested by macrophages (white blood cells) that serve the immune system. In adults, all that remains is the coccyx, a small bone, formed by four fused vertebrae, at the base of the spine. Even before that, the human embryo has gill arches, reflecting the fact that mammalian ancestors were once aquatic gill-breathing vertebrates. And even more fundamentally, discs in the human backbone carry traces of the ancestral notochord, which marked the beginning of the vertebrates over 500 million years ago. These stages in human (and other) embryos gave rise to the old observation that "ontogeny recapitulates phylogeny."

Other vestigial features in humans are the appendix, and wisdom teeth or third molars, which hark back to the time early humans had much more plant roughage in their diet. At the molecular level, the pseudogene (present but incapable of functioning) has been identified which formerly was able to synthesize ascorbic acid (vitamin C) to prevent scurvy. Another example of vestigial human genes is the more than ninety-nine genes to detect odors. More than 70 percent of these are now non-operative, and our sense of smell is far less acute than other mammals.

One type of tissue comprises the mesoderm, cells specialized to build muscle and bone. Its first task is to form an elongated structure called the notochord, the progenitor of the backbone. Through chemical influence, the overlying ectoderm layer thickens to form the neural plate. A crease or groove in this body is next enclosed on both sides to form a neural tube, which becomes the nervous system. Normally, this tube will close at both ends, at about twenty-seven days. By this time, precursors of the eyes and ears are evident, a rudimentary heart begins to beat, and a system for blood circulation is formed. The ends of the arms and legs are present and the alimentary canal from mouth to anus is formed.

By the end of the eighth week, the spinal cord is present, cerebral cortex and hemispheres are differentiated, sex is determined, bone building has started and all the organ systems are established. The embryonic stage ends at the end of the second month, and the fetal stage begins. Cell division (mitosis) proceeds at a rapid pace and new neurons are generated at the rate of 250,000 per minute during the nine months of gestation. During this period of rapid growth, a complete cycle of cell development may take only one and a half hours. As the neural cells multiply, they migrate to apparently ordained destinations, in the correct cell layer, where they orient themselves and begin to make appropriate synaptic connections.

The cortex is made up of six cell layers and is the site of higher-level mental activity—perception, reasoning, thought, understanding, etc. The migration of neural cells to the cortex involves a curious mechanism. Temporary or "decoy cells" at the margin of the cortex attract the incoming cells and "enthusiastically establish synaptic connections" with them. After a few weeks, when the great neuro-migrations are over, the decoy cells disappear to be replaced by a permanent set of target cells. During this stage of cell migration, errors in the process may subsequently cause mental problems such as dyslexia, autism, epilepsy, schizophrenia, and perhaps other sociopathic disorders.

By about the twentieth week, the important process of synaptogenesis is well underway. This involves the vast assemblage of neurons and their axons connecting with dendrites through a myriad of connections, called synapses. Each synapse is a point of contiguity (but not continuity) between two neural elements. [It is astonishing to realize that the linking of axons with their target dendrites is structured somewhat similar to the base pairs in a helical coil of DNA.]

Synaptogenesis continues during pregnancy and there is good evidence that the unborn fetus has some awareness of its external environment and will react to some stimuli. At birth, the infant has 100 billion brain cells, but most of the neurons are immature and need to be activated. For the brain to develop properly and reach its full potential, outside stimulation is required: in the case of infants, touch, holding, sound, smell, and vision. From the moment of birth, an infant bonds with its mother through the sense of smell. Without proper stimulation, connections can scramble impulses in the brain and lead to childhood seizures, epilepsy, and language disorders.

Another important factor is that of myelination. Myelin is a fatty substance that serves as insulation around many of the axons. It allows conduction of nerve impulses at speeds ten to 100 times faster. Fibers serving the primary functions of touch, vision, hearing, etc. are myelinated soon after birth but those serving the higher cognitive processes are the latest to myelinate, perhaps in young adulthood. Glial cells form the myelin and have five or six other functions as well. In general, glial cells are considered to be the "glue" in the nervous system, providing support and nutrition to the neurons, which they outnumber by at least 9:1 to as much as 50:1.

Nutritional deficiencies and/or exposure to toxic chemicals are other factors that affect the well-being of the fetus/child. Many studies have shown these have been major causes of malformation and/or learning difficulties. Toxic substances such as tobacco, alcohol, drugs, etc. can have a negative influence on the fetus through the pregnant mother, and through the father various chemical compounds can be damaging up to forty-five days prior to conception.

By the age of eight months, given a secure, stimulating, and loving environment, a normal infant will have sparked 500 trillion synaptic connections. By the age of two, an infant has developed 1000 trillion of these connections. At this time, the highest lifetime density of 15,000 synapses per neuron may have been reached. By the age of three, the root brain architecture is fairly well established and the structure of the brain is almost complete. Repeated experiences become etched into the brain and tend to replace the genetic influence. For the first twelve years of life the brain is at its most receptive, acting like a super-sponge in soaking up new information.

By the age of eighteen, trivial connections have been discarded and the total has been reduced to about 500 trillion. The resulting brain is less able to adapt but is stronger and more powerful. The remaining connections are more stable and give each person's brain a unique structure and chemical balance that determines mind, thought and emotions. It is this pattern—our soul—that influences who we are, and how we think and learn.

Good or bad stimulation, including behavior therapy, can affect the function of brain cells. Stress, and drugs like cocaine, can cause permanent and inappropriate behavior patterns. The best scientific evidence to date indicates that about half the variance between individuals is genetic and the other half results from environmental factors.

In the case of a traumatic experience, stress hormones such as noradrenalin activate the brain's amygdala. Cahill has shown that the right and left hemispheres in men and women respond differently. To help in this field, the use of brain scans, or neuroimaging, has become de rigueur. Positron-emission tomography (PET) and functional magnetic resonance imaging (fMRI) are non-invasive imaging techniques that can reveal anatomical variations in the brain. Some of the gender differences include:

- The frontal and limbic cortex in women is relatively larger, favoring higher cognitive functions and emotional response, whereas the parietal cortex and amygdala in men is larger, favoring physical action.

- The density of neurons seems to follow the same pattern.

- The hippocampus in women is relatively larger, favoring memory storage.

- The production of the neurotransmitter serotonin, which affects emotional behavior, is 52 percent higher in men, perhaps explaining why women are more prone to depression.

- The increased release of dopamine in females may explain why they are more prone to drug addiction.

Because memories are dependent on chemicals, they can be altered by chemicals such as beta blockers. To help in the investigation of complex social and moral behavior, the use of PET and fMRI is likely to be tempting, but not too productive, warns Sharon Begley. The location of responses in the brain is far less important than how or why.

Referring to *H. sapiens sapiens*, Harvard professor Ernst Mayr stated "among millions of lineages or organisms and perhaps 50 billion speciation events, only one led to high intelligence." As shown, modern man has developed speech during the last 100,000 years. The ability to form and express abstract thoughts eventually led to the development of the first primitive written record keeping, by about 7400 B.C. Since that time, more advanced reading and writing could be considered as the main stimulus to the highly complex cognitive abilities of the still-evolving human brain. If this idea has merit, then it could be argued that the major impetus to widespread intellectual development was the invention of Gutenberg's printing press in 1455.

Physiologically, the earliest feasible time during pregnancy for the infusion of man's soul would be after 20 weeks, when elements of the growing brain begin to become organized. But the process continues after birth, to maturity at age 18, and with stimulation, into old age. Thus, it seems possible that infusion of the human soul is a gradual, cumulative process, rather than instantaneous. In like fashion, the soul may have developed during the evolution of mankind. That is, a simple, primitive soul as *Homo sapiens* arose, becoming more complex as man evolved.

17

INDEX

18

BIBLIOGRAPHY

Achenbach, Joel, 2006, The Next Big One: *National Geographic*, April

Adkins, Roy, 2005, Nelson's Trafalgar: Viking

Ahmad, Mubasher, 2002, God & Human Suffering: Interfaith Symposium, Zion City, IL, Dec 8

Ahmed, Akbar S., 2003, Islam Under Siege: Living Dangerously in a Post-honour World: Polity Press

Armstrong, John R., 1989, Seeking Ancient Paths: http://www.asa3.org/ASA/ PSCF/9819/PSCF3-

Bailey, Ronald (editor), 2000, Earth Report 2000: McGraw Hill

Barbour, Ian, 1990, Religion in an Age of Science: HarperSanFrancisco

_____, 1997, Religion and Science: HarperSanFrancisco

Barger, Amy J., 2005, The Midlife Crisis of the Cosmos: *Scientific American,* July

Barrow, John D. and Webb, John K., 2005, Inconstant Constants: *Scientific American*, June

Beckerlegge, Gwilym, 1998, The World Religions Reader: Routledge

Begg, Ean, 1985, The Cult of the Black Virgin: Penquin Books

Begley, Sharon and Rogers, Adam, 1997, War of the Worlds: *Newsweek* Feb 10

Begley, Sharon, 1997, When Galaxies Collide: *Newsweek* Nov 3

_____, 2004, Mellow or Stressed? Mom's Care can Alter DNA of her Offspring: *Wall St. Jour.,* July 16

_____, 2005, Even Scientists Marvel at "Spooky" Behavior of Separated Objects: *Wall St. Jour.*, Oct 13

Behe, Michael J., 1996, Darwin's Black Box: the Biochemical Challenge to Evolution: The Free Press

Berman, Bob, 2002, In the Line of Fire: *Discover*, Aug.

_____, 2002, Our Galactic Carousel: *Discover*, Sep

Bottjer, David J., 2005, The Early Evolution of Animals: *Scientific American*, Aug.

Bousso, Raphael and Polchinski, Joseph, 2004, The String Theory Landscape: *Scientific American*, Sep

Britannica, Encyclopedia, 2002, Muhammad

De Bertodono, Teresa, 2001, Soul Searchers: William B. Eerdmans Publishing Co.

Berversluis, Joel, 2000, Sourcebook of the World's Religions: New World Library

Best, Robert M., 1999, Noah's Ark and the Ziusudra Epic: Enil Press

The Bible as Literature, 1936, Simon & Schuster

The Bible Through the Ages, 1996, *The Reader's Digest*

Bishop, Jerry E., 1994, How it Works, A Biotch Primer: *The Wall Street Journal*, R5

Bloom, Jonathan and Blair, Sheila, 2002, Islam: Yale University Press

Bluemle, John P., 1999, Global Warming: A Geological Perspective: Summary of article in *Environmental Geosciences*, vol 6, no 2

Boyd, Gregory A., 1995, Jesus Under Siege: Victor Books

Boyer, Pascal, 2001, Religion Explained: Basic Books

Bradshaw, Robert I., 1998, Marcion: Portrait of a Heretic: http://www.robibrad. demon.co.uk/Marcion.html

Brands, H.W., 2002, The First American: Anchor Books, Random House

Briffa, Keith R. and Osborn, Timothy J., 2002, Blowing Hot and Cold: *Science*, vol 295, March 22.

Brooke, John and Cantor, Geoffrey, 1998, Reconstructing Nature: the Engagement of Science and Religion: Oxford University Press

Brown, Dan, 2000, Angels & Demons: Simon& Schuster

_____, 2003, The Da Vinci Code: Doubleday

Brown, Paterson, 2000, Metalogos, The Gospels of Thomas & Philip & Truth: www.metalog.org/files/intro.html

Brown, William P., 1999, The Ethos of the Cosmos: William B. Eerdmans Publishing Co.

Bryson, Bill, 2003, A Short History of Nearly Everything: Broadway Books

Caiger, Stephan L., 2003, Bible and Spade: http://www.katapi.org.uk/BAndS/ ChI.htm

Carey, John, 1987, Eyewitness to History: Avon Books

Carr, Bernard J. and Giddings, Steven B., 2005, Quantum Black Holes: *Scientific American*, May

Carson, Rachel, 1962, Silent Spring: Houghton Mifflin, NY

Catechism of the Catholic Church, 1995, Doubleday

Catholic Encyclopedia, 2005, Inquisition: http://www.newadvent.org/cathen/08026a,htm

Chadwick, Owen, 1977, The Reformation: Penguin Books

Chamberlin, E.R., 1969, The Bad Popes: Barnes & Noble Books

de Chardin, Pierre Teilhard, 1969, Christianity and Evolution: Harcourt Brace & Co.

Church, George M., 2006, Genomes for All: *Scientific American*, Jan

Church of Jesus Christ of Latter-Day Saints, 1981, The Book of Mormon: Intellectual Reserve

_____, 1986, The Doctrine and Covenants, Pearl of Great Price: Corp. of the President, Salt Lake City

_____, 1996, Our Heritage, A Brief History of the Church of Jesus Christ of Latter-Day Saints: Intellectual Reserve

Clare, Anthony (host), 1992, Soul of the Universe (3 videotapes): BBC-TV, distrib by Atlas Video, Inc, Bethesda, MD

Cline, David B., 2003, The Search for Dark Matter: *Scientific American*, Mar

Collins, Graham P., 2006, Computing with Quantum Knots: *Scientific American*, April

Colson, Charles, 1999, How Now Shall we Live?: Tyndale House Publ

Colvin, John, 2003, Decisive Battles: Headline Book Publishing

Combes, Françoise, 2005, Ripples in a Galactic Pond: *Scientific American*, Oct.

Connell, Evan S. 2000, Deus lo Volt! Chronicle of the Crusades: Counterpoint

Corey, Michael A., 2001, The God Hypothesis: Rowman and Littlefield Publishers, Inc.

Cornwell, John, 2001, Breaking Faith: Viking Compass

Courtois, Stephane, et al, 1999, The Black Book of Communism: Harvard University Press

Cox, Wade, 2000, Christ's Age at Baptism and the Duration of his Ministry (No. 19), Christian Churches of God, PO Box 369, Woden ACT 2606, Australia: http://www.ccg.org/english/s/p019.html

Cragg, Gerald R., 1970, The Church & the Age of Reason: Penguin Books

Crichton, Michael, 2004, State of Fear: HarperCollins Publishers

Dailey, Timothy J, et al, 1988, Bible Treasury: Publications International

_____, 1998, Prophecies of the Bible

_____, 1998, Secrets of the Bible

Darwin, Charles, 1859, On the Origin of Species: John Murray, London

David M., 1996, Reading the Fractures of Genesis: Westminster John Knox Press

Davies, Paul, 1983, God and the New Physics: Simon & Schuster

_____, 1988, The Cosmic Blueprint: Simon & Schuster

_____, 1992, The Mind of God: Simon & Schuster

_____, 1999, The Fifth Miracle: Simon & Schuster

_____, 2001, Cracking the Genome: The Free Press

Davis, Joyce M., 2003. Martyrs: palgrave, Macmillan

Davis, Kenneth C., 2001, Don't Know Much About the Universe: Harper Collins Publ

Dawkins, Richard, 1987, The Blind Watchmaker: Why the Evidence of Evolution Reveals a Universe without Design: W.W. Norton, NY

_____, 1995, River out of Eden: Basic Books

_____, 2004, The Ancestor's Tale, A Pilgrimage to the Dawn of Evolution: Houghton Mifflin Co.

Deffinbaugh, Bob, 2004, The Transfiguration: http://www.bible.org/page.asp?page_id=597

Dembski, William A., 1999, Intelligent Design: The Bridge Between Science & Theology: InterVarsity Press

Denton, Michael, 1986, Evolution: A Theory in Crisis: Adler And Adler

Dershowitz, Alan M. 2000, The Genesis of Justice: Warner Books

Diamond, Jared, 1999, Guns, Germs, and Steel: W.W. Norton& Co

Dowley, Tim (editor), 1977, Eerdmans' Handbook to the History of Christianity: Wm. B. Eerdmans Publ Co.

Drayna, Dennis, 2005, Founder Mutations: *Scientific American*, Oct.

Dunavan, Claire Panosian, 2005, Tackling Malaria: *Scientific American*, Dec.

Dundes, Alan, 1999, Holy Writ as Oral Lit: Rowman and Littlefield Publ

Ehrlich, Paul, 2000, Human Natures: Genes, Cultures, and Human Prospect: Island Press/Shearwater Books

Ellis, Richard, 2001, Aquagenesis: Viking Penguin

Esper, J., Cook, E.R. and Schweingruber, F. H., 2002, Low-Frequency Signals in Long Tree-Ring Chronologies for Reconstructing Past Temperature Variability: *Science* 295,2250

Esper, Jan and Briffa, Keith, 2002, Tree Rings may Point to Earlier Global Warming: *Science*

Faigman, David L., 1999, Legal Alchemy, the Use and Misuse of Science in the Law: W.H. Freeman

Farah, Caesar E., 2000, Islam: Barron's Educational Series, Hauppauge, NY

Fee, Gordon D., 1994, God's Empowering Presence: Hendrickson Publ.

_____, 1996, Paul, the Spirit, and the People of God: Hendrickson Publ.

Fields, R. Douglas, 2005, Making Memories Stick: *Scientific American*, Feb.

Fortey, Richard, 2005, Earth, an Intimate History: Alfred A. Knopf

Fox, Michael W., 1999, Beyond Evolution: Lyons Press

Franklin, Deborah, 2004, Gas Guzzlers: *Smithsonian*, Feb

Freeland, Stephen J. and Hurst, Laurence D., 2004, Evolution Encoded: *Scientific American*, April

Friedman, Richard Elliott, 1989, Who Wrote the Bible?: Harper

Fuller, J.F.C., 1960, The Generalship of Alexander the Great: Rutgers University Press

Funk, Robert W. (founder), 1995, The Five Gospels (Jesus Seminar): Macmillan Publ. Co.

Gehrels, Neil, Piro, Luigi and Leonard, Peter J.T., 2002, The Brightest Explosions in the Universe: *Scientific American*, Dec.

Genetics Home Reference, 2003, U.S. National Library of Medicine: http://ghr.nlm.nih.gov/

Genetics, Year in Science, 2003, *Discover*, vol 24, no. 1 (Jan)

Gerhard, Lee C. (editor), 2000, Geological Perspectives of Global Climate Change: AAPG Studies in Geology #47, The American Association of Petroleum Geologists, Tulsa, OK

_____, 2004, Climate Change: Conflict of Observational Science, Theory, and Politics: Bull. Amer. Assoc. Petr. Geol., Sep.

_____, 2006, Climate Change: Conflict of Observational Science, theory, and politics: Reply: Bull. Amer. Asoc Petrol. Geol., Mar.

Gerson, Allan and Adler, Jerry, 2001, The Price of Terror: HarperCollinsPubl.

Gibbs, W. Wayt, 2002, Saving Dying Languages: *Scientific American*, Aug

_____, 2003, The Unseen Genome: Genes among Junk: *Scientific American*, Dec

Gollaher, David L., 2000, Circumcision: Basic Books

The Good News (the New Testament), 1956, The American Bible Society

Gonzales, Guillermo, Brownlee, Donald and Ward, Peter D., 2001, Refuges for Life in a Hostile Universe: *Scientific American*, Oct.

Gore, Al, 1992, Earth in the Balance: Ecology and the Human Spirit: Penguin Books

Gould, Stephen J., 1999, Rocks of Ages: Ballantine Publ Group

_____, 2000, The Lying Stones of Marrakech: Harmony Books

Grant, Michael, 1969, The Ancient Mediterranean: History Book Club

_____, 1984, The History of Ancient Israel: History BookClub

Great Disasters, 1989: The Reader's Digest Ass'n

Greene, Brian, 1999, The Elegant Universe: W.W. Norton & Company, NY

Gribbin, John and Goodwin, Simon, 1998, Empire of the Sun: New York University Press

Gribbin, John, and Rees, Martin, 1989, Cosmic Coincidences: Dark Matter, Mankind and Anthropic Cosmology: Bantam Books

Griffith-Jones, Robin, 2000, The Four Witnesses, Harper

Hall, Richard H., 1997 (from 1964 report), The UFO Evidence: Barnes & Noble

Hamilton, Bernard, 1981, The Medieval Inquisition: Holmes & Meier Publishers

Hannity, Sean, 2004, Deliver us from Evil: Regan Books

Hansen, James, 2004, Defusing the Global Warming Time Bomb: *Scientific American*, Mar

Hart, Benjamin, 2004, Faith & Freedom: Jameson Books

Hart, Michael H., 1998, The 100 Most Influential Persons in History: Carol Publ. Group

Hasinger, Günther and Gilli, Roberto, 2002, The Cosmic Reality Check: *Scientific American*, Mar.

Hawking, S.W., 1988, A Brief History of Time: Bantam Press

Hieb, Monte, 2002, Global Warming: A Chilling Perspective: http://www.clearlight.com/-mhieb/WVFossils/ice_ages.html

Hitchcock, Liz (editor), and Project Staff, 2003, The Truth about History: Reader's Digest Assn, London

Holloway, Marguerite, 2004, Talking Bacteria: *Scientific American*, Feb.

Holman, Gordon D., 2006, The Mysterious Origins of Solar Flares: *Scientific American*, April

Holy Bible, 1954, World Publ Co

Holy Bible, 1995, American Bible Society

Hotz, Robert Lee, 2002, Bones of Contention: Scientists Learn from Flying Fossil Forgery: *Austin American Statesman*, Dec. 6

Hoyle, Frederick, 1983, The Intelligent Universe: Holt, Rinehart And Winston

Huxley, Thomas H., 1905, Discourses, Biological and Geological Essays: D. Appleton and Co.

Jablonski, Nina G. and Chaplin, George, 2002 *Scientific American*, Oct

Jacobson, Theodore A. and Parentani, Reynaud, 2005, Black Holes: *Scientific American*, Dec.

Judson, Olivia, 2002, Dr. Tatiana's Sex Advice to all Creation: Metropolitan Books

Kamm, Antony, 1999, The Israelites: Routledge

Kane, Gordon, 2005, The Mysteries of Mass: *Scientific American*, July

Karst, Kitchin, C.R., 1990, Journeys to the ends of the Universe: Adam Hilger

Kauffman, Guinevere and Bosch, Frank van den, 2002, The Life Cycle Of Galaxies: *Scientific American*, June

Kee, Howard Clark, 1983, Understanding the New Testament: Prentice-Hall

Keller, Werner, 1981, The Bible as History: Bantam Books

Kessler, Ronald, 2004, A Matter of Character: Sentinel

Kitcher, Philip, 1994, Abusing Science: The MIT Press

Kotulak, Ronald, 1993, Unlocking the Mysteries of the Brain: *Austin American-Statesman*, June 6

Kuban, Glen J., 1996, A Review of NBC's "The Mysterious Origins of Man": http://members.aol.comPaluxy2/nbc.htm

Kung, Hans, 2003, The Catholic Church: The Modern Library

Laffin, John, 1986, Brassey's Dictionary of Battles: Barnes & Noble

Legates, David R., 2003, Revising 1000 Years of Climate History: National Center for Policy Analysis, No. 450, Aug 8

Lemley, Brad, 2002, Nuclear Planet: *Discover*, Aug

Leonard, William R. 2002, Food for Thought: *Scientific American*, Dec

Louis, David, 1983, 2201 Fascinating Facts: Wing Books

Liderbach, Daniel, 1989, The Numinous Universe: Paulist Press

Loader, William, 2001, Jesus and the Fundamentalism of his Day: William B. Eerdmans Publishing Co.

Lomborg, Bjorn, 2002, The Skeptical Environmentalist: Cambridge University Press

Luhr, James F., 2003, (Smithsonian) Earth: DK Publishing

Lyon, T. Edgar, 1960, Apostasy to Restoration: Deseret Book Co., Salt Lake City

Madden, Thomas F., 1999, A Concise History of the Crusades: Rowman & Littlefield Publ

Maddison, David R. (editor), 2001, The Tree of Life Web Project: http://tolweb.org/tree/phylogeny.html

Maldacena, Juan, 2005, The Illusion of Gravity: *Scientific American*, Nov.

Mann, M.E., Bradley, R.S. & Hughes, M.K., 1988, Global-Scale Temperature Patterns and Climate Forcing Over the Past Six Centuries: *Nature*, No. 392, pp.779-87.

Maricle, Arthur, 2005, The Inquisition: http://www.acts2.com/thebibletruth/The_Inquisition.html

Mayr, E., 1976, Evolution and the Diversity of Life: Harvard U. Press

McCallum, Dennis, 2005, The Waldensian Movement from Waldo to the Reformation: http://www.xenos.org/essays/waldo3.htm

McDowell, Josh,1979, Evidence that Demands a Verdict:Nelsonwood Publ Gp

McIntyre, Stephen, and McKitrick, Ross, 2003, Corrections to the Mann et al (1998) Proxy Data Base and Northern Hemispheric Average Temperature Series: *Energy &Environment*, vol 14, no 6

McKenzie, John L. 1980, The Old Testament Without Illusion: Image Books

_____, 1982, The New Testament Without Illusion: The Crossroad Publishing Co

Metzger, Bruce M., 1987, The Canon of the New Testament: Clarendon Press

Milgrom, Mordehai, 2002, Does Dark Matter Really Exist? : *Scientific American*, Aug

Miller, David, 2001, Brassey's Book of the Crusades: Brassey's, Inc

Miller, Kevin, 2004, What do the Stars Say?: http://www.newcreationism.org/CreationArticle10.html

Mohanty, Subhanjoy and Jayawardhane, Ray, 2006, The Mystery of Brown Dwarf Origins: *Scientific American*, Jan.

Montenat, Christian, Plateaux, Luc, and Roux, Pascal, 1985, How To Read the World: Creation in Evolution: Crossroad Publ.

Montfort, Gregory J. and Boon, Rosemary, 2004, Stages of Brain Development: www.home.iprimus.com.au/rboon

Moreland, J.P., 1989, Cristianity and the Nature of Science: Baker Book House

Morris, H.M., 1974, The Troubled Waters of Evolution: Creation-Life Publishers

Morse, Melvin, 2000, Where God Lives: Cliff Street Books

Morton, Glenn R., 2000, Phylum Level Evolution: http://home.entouch.net/dmd/cambevol.htm

Muller, Richard, 2003, Medieval Global Warming: http://www.techreview.com

Muncaster, Ralph O., 2000, Can Archaeology Prove the Old Testament ?: Harvest House

Mundt, Philip A., 1956, Heath-Amsden Strata, Central Montana: Bull. Amer. Assoc. Petrol. Geol., Vol 40, pp.1915-34.

Murphey, Cecil et al, 1998, The Bible A to Z: Publications International

Musick, John A. and McMillan, Beverly, 2002, The Shark Chronicles: Henry Holt and Co.

Musser, George, 2004, Was Einstein Right?: *Scientific American*, Sep. Mycko, Marcia Jo, 2003, History of Prayer Beads: http://www.beadshows.com/ibs/articles/prayer.html

Nadin, Elvira & Mihai, 2000, Jewish, Does it make a Difference?: Jonathan David Publ

Nee, Watchman, 1968, The Spiritual Man: Christian Fellowship Publishers, Richmond, VA

Neusner, Jacob and Chilton, Bruce, 1997, Christian and Jewish Discourse: Routledge

Pagels, Elaine, 1979, The Gnostic Gospels: Vintage Books

_____, 1989, Adam, Eve and the Serpent: Vintage Books

_____, 1995, Origin of Satan: Vintage Books

_____, 2003, Beyond Belief: The Secret Gospel of Thomas: Random House

Evolution, Origins of Humankind, 2003, PBS

Perakh, Mark, 2004, Not a very big bang about Genesis: www.nctimes.net/~mark/bibl_science/schroeder.html

Plaistad, David A. 2003, Radiometric Dating: Internet www.BIBLE,CA

Polkinghorne, John, 1989, Science and Providence: New Science Library Pope, Kyle, 2000, New Testament Manuscripts from the First Century: http://km-pope.home.att.net/FirstCenturyMSS.html

Porter, J.R., 1995, The Illustrated Guide to the Bible: Oxford University Press

Powell, Corey S., 2002, The Wet Wonder of Starbirth, *Discover*, Sep 16

Pratt, Wallace E., 2000, AAPG EXPLORER, May

Rana, Fazale, et al, 2003, A Scientific and Biblical Response to *Time* Aug 23, 1999 article "Up from the Apes ...:Today's New Reason to Believe, Aug 6

Reader's Digest Bible, 1995: Reader's Digest Assn

Reich, Samuel, 2002, Radio Waves are Useless for Interstellar Communication: Internet

Reynolds, Ronald J., 2002: The Gas between the Stars: *Scientific American*, Jan.

Revelation, 1988, Watch Tower Bible and Tract Society

Ridley, Matt, 1999, Genome: Perennial

Riordan, Michael and Zajc, William A., 2006, The First few Microseconds: *Scientific American*, May

Roberts, Jenny, 1990, Bible Facts: Quantum Books

Ross, Hugh, 1993, The Creator of the Cosmos: NAVPRESS

_____, 1996, Beyond the Cosmos: NAVPRESS

Rowan-Robinson, Michael, 1999, The Nine Numbers of the Cosmos: Oxford University Press

Rubenstein, Richard E., 2003, Aristotle's Children: Harcourt

Ryan, William and Pitman, Walter, 1998, Noah's Flood: The New Scientific Discoveries about the Event that Changed History: Simon & Schuster

Sagan, Carl, 1980, Cosmos: Wings Books

Samples, Kenneth Richard, 2003, Do All Religions Lead to God?: http://www.paoline.com/ahanna/HTML/DARLTG.html

_____, 2003, The Historic Alliance of Christianity and Science: http://www.geocities.com?CapeCanaveral/Hangar/4264/carm

Samuel, Stuart "Spokesman", 1999, The Bible According to Einstein: Jupiter Scientific Publishing Co. N.Y.

Scannapieco, Evan, Petitjean, Patrick and Broadhurst, Tom, 2002, The Emptiest Places: *Scientific American*, Oct.

Scheibel, Arnold B., 2002, Embryological Development of the Human Brain: www.newhorizons.org/neuro/scheibel

Schmidt, Alvin J., 2004, The Great Divide: Regina Orthodox Press, Boston

Schroeder, Gerald, L., 1997, The Science of God: Broadway Books

Schwartz, Stephen, 2002, The Two Faces of Islam: Doubleday

Scott, S.S., 2002, Creation of a Cosmology: Big Bang: Internet

Sheler, Jeffery L., 2001, Days of the Martyrs: U.S. *News World Report*, April 16

Shermer, Michael, 2004, God's Number is Up: *Scientific American*, July

Shestople, Paul, 2002, Big Bang Cosmology Primer: Internet

Shimer, Hervey W. and Schrock, Robert R., 1944, Index Fossils of North America: John Wiley & Sons

Shreeve, James, 2006, The Greatest Journey: *National Geographic*, March

Simanek, Donald E., 2004, Fibonacci Fli-Flam: Internet

Shipman, James T., Wilson, Jerry D., Todd, Aaron W., 1997, An Introduction to Physical Science: Houghton Mifflin

Shogren, Jason F., 2004, Kyoto Protocol: Past, Present and Future: Bull. Amer. Assoc. Petr. Geol. vol. 88, Sep.

Shulman, Sol. 2002, Kings of the Kremlin: Brassey's, London

Singer, S, Fred, 1999, Hot Talk, Cold Science, Global Warming's Unfinished Debate: The Independent Institute

Soon, Willie, and Baliunas, Sallie, 2003, Proxy Climatic and Environmental Changes in the Past 1000 Years: Climate Research CR 23:89-110

Stearns, Peter N. et al, 2001, The Encyclopedia of World History: Houghton Mifflin Co., Boston

Stenger, Victor J., 1988, Not by Design: the Origin of the Universe: Prometheus Books

_____, 1998, Fitting the Bible to the Data: www.infidels.org/library/modern/vic_stenger/schrev.html

Stewart, Don, 2002, Is the Big Bang Theory Compatible with the Bible ?: Internet

Stix, Gary, 2004, The Patent Clerk's Legacy: *Scientific American*, Sep.

_____, 2006, Owning the Stuff of Life: *Scientific American*, Feb.

Stonehill, Paul, 1998, The Soviet UFO Files: CLB International

Strobel, Lee, 1998, The Case for Christ: Zondervan

_____, 2000, The Case for Faith: Zondervan

_____, 2004, The Case for a Creator: Zondervan

Talmage, James E., 1987, Articles of Faith: The Church of Jesus Christ of Latter-Day Saints, Salt Lake City

Templeton, John Marks, 1995, The Humble Approach: CONTINUUM

Thompson, Larry, 2003, More Evidence that Homnosexuality is Genetic: http://www.skeptictank.org/gaygene.htm

Toto, Christian, 2002, What Year is It?: *Washington Times*, Jan 7-13

Toynbee, Arnold, 1958, Christianity among the Religions of the World: Oxford University Press

Twenhofel, William H. and Schrock, Robert R., 1935, Invertebrate Paleontology: McGraw Hill Book Co.

Vidler, Alec R., 1971, The Church in an Age of Revolution: Penguin Books

Wakefield, Julie, 2004, Doom and Gloom by 2100: *Scientific American,* July

Wambsganss,Joachim, 2001, Gravity's Kaleidoscope: *Scientific American*, Nov.

Ward, Peter D. and Brownlee, Donald, 1999, Rare Earth: Why Complex Life is Rare In the Universe: Copernicus, NY

Warren, Rick, 2002, The Purpose Driven Life: Zondervan

_____, 2004, Better Together: Purpose Driven Publ.

Weaver, Kimberly, 2003, The Galactic Odd Couple: *Scientific American*, July

Weichman, Peter B., Square Pegs and Round Holes: www.skeptic.com/review04.html

Weinberg, Steven, 1977, The First Three Minutes: A Modern View of the Origin of the Universe: Basic Books

Wells, Jonathan, 2000, Icons of Evolution: Science or Myth?: Regenery Gateway

Wikipedia the free Encyclopedia, 20005, Medieval Inquisition: http://www.en.wikipedia.org/wiki/Medieval_Inquisition

Wiester, John, 1983, The Genesis Connection: Thomas Nelson Publishers

Wilkins, Michael J. and Moreland, J.P., 1995, Jesus Under Fire: Zondervan Publ House

Wills, Garry, 2002, Saint Augustine's Memory: Penguin Books

Wilson, E.O., 1978, On Human Nature: Harvard U. Press

Wingert, Pat and Brant, Martha, 2005, Reading Your Baby's Mind: *Newsweek*, Aug 15

Witherington III, Ben, 1995: The Jesus Quest: InterVarsity Press

Wilson, Ian, 1999, The Bible is History: Regnery Publ

Wold, Donald J., 1998, Out of Order: Baker Books

Wolfram, Stephan, 2002, A New Kind of Science: Wolfram Media

Wong, Kate, 2003 An Ancestor to Call our Own: *Scientific American*, Jan

Wright, G. Ernest and Fuller, Reginald H., 1960, The Book of the Acts of God: Anchor Books

Wright, Karen, 2002, Celestial Fireworks: *Discover*, Aug

Wright, Robert, 1988, Three Scientists and their Gods: Times Books

Wysong, R.L., 1976, The Creation-Evolution Controversy: Inquiry Press

Yergin, Daniel, 1991, The Prize: Simon & Schuster

Young, Davis A., 1995, The Biblical Flood: Paternoster Press

Young, Edward D. and Carruthers, Margaret, 2001, Trends in Science, Earth Sciences: Helicon Publ Co

Yusuff, Mohammad K., 2003, Zayd ibn Thabit and the Glorious Qur'an: www.irfi.org

Zakaria, Fareed, 2001, Why Do They Hate Us?: *Newsweek*, Oct. 15

Zepf, Stephen E. and Ashman, Keith M., 2003, The Unexpected Youth of Globular Clusters: *Scientific American*, Oct.